The Blackwell Companion
to Political Theology

Nov. 2006

Blackwell Companions to Religion

The Blackwell Companions to Religion series presents a collection of the most recent scholarship and knowledge about world religions. Each volume draws together newly-commissioned essays by distinguished authors in the field, and is presented in a style which is accessible to undergraduate students, as well as scholars and the interested general reader. These volumes approach the subject in a creative and forward-thinking style, providing a forum in which leading scholars in the field can make their views and research available to a wider audience.

Published

The Blackwell Companion to Judaism
Edited by Jacob Neusner and Alan J. Avery-Peck

The Blackwell Companion to Sociology of Religion
Edited by Richard K. Fenn

The Blackwell Companion to the Hebrew Bible
Edited by Leo G. Perdue

The Blackwell Companion to Postmodern Theology
Edited by Graham Ward

The Blackwell Companion to Hinduism
Edited by Gavin Flood

The Blackwell Companion to Political Theology
Edited by Peter Scott and William T. Cavanaugh

The Blackwell Companion to Protestantism
Edited by Alister E. McGrath and Darren C. Marks

The Blackwell Companion to Modern Theology
Edited by Gareth Jones

The Blackwell Companion to Christian Ethics
Edited by Stanley Hauerwas and Samuel Wells

The Blackwell Companion to Religious Ethics
Edited by William Schweiker

The Blackwell Companion to Christian Spirituality
Edited by Arthur Holder

The Blackwell Companion to the Study of Religion
Edited by Robert A. Segal

The Blackwell Companion to the Qur'ān
Edited by Andrew Rippin

The Blackwell Companion to Contemporary Islamic Thought
Edited by Ibrahim M. Abu-Rabi'

The Blackwell Companion to the Bible and Culture
Edited by John F. A. Sawyer

Forthcoming

The Blackwell Companion to Catholicism
Edited by James J. Buckley, Frederick Christian Bauerschmidt, and Trent Pomplun

The Blackwell Companion to Eastern Christianity
Edited by Ken Parry

The Blackwell Companion to Political Theology

Edited by

Peter Scott and William T. Cavanaugh

Blackwell
Publishing

© 2004, 2007 by Blackwell Publishing Ltd
except for editorial material and organization © 2004 by Peter Scott and William T. Cavanaugh

BLACKWELL PUBLISHING
350 Main Street, Malden, MA 02148-5020, USA
9600 Garsington Road, Oxford OX4 2DQ, UK
550 Swanston Street, Carlton, Victoria 3053, Australia

The right of Peter Scott and William T. Cavanaugh to be identified as the Authors of the Editorial Material in this Work has been asserted in accordance with the UK Copyright, Designs, and Patents Act 1988.

First published 2004 by Blackwell Publishing Ltd
First published in paperback 2007 by Blackwell Publishing Ltd

1   2007

Library of Congress Cataloging-in-Publication Data

The Blackwell companion to political theology / edited by Peter Scott and William T. Cavanaugh.
     p. cm. – (Blackwell companions to religion)
Includes bibliographical references and index.
   ISBN 0-631-22342-8 (alk. paper)
   1. Political theology.   I. Scott, Peter, 1961–   II. Cavanaugh, William T.   III. Series.

BR115.P7B634 2003
261.7 – dc21

                                                                                2003008184

ISBN-13: 978-0-631-22342-9 (alk. paper)
ISBN-13: 978-1-4051-5744-5 (paperback)
ISBN-10: 1-4051-5744-5 (paperback)

A catalogue record for this title is available from the British Library.

Set in 10.5 on 12.5 pt Photina
by SNP Best-set Typesetter Ltd, Hong Kong
Printed and bound in the United Kingdom
by TJ International Ltd, Padstow, Cornwall

The publisher's policy is to use permanent paper from mills that operate a sustainable forestry policy, and which has been manufactured from pulp processed using acid-free and elementary chlorine-free practices. Furthermore, the publisher ensures that the text paper and cover board used have met acceptable environmental accreditation standards.

For further information on
Blackwell Publishing, visit our website:
www.blackwellpublishing.com

Contents

Contributors   viii

Introduction to the Paperback Edition   1
William T. Cavanaugh and Peter Scott

Introduction   2
William T. Cavanaugh and Peter Scott

Part I   Traditioned Resources: Scripture, Traditions, Liturgy   5

1   Scripture: Old Testament
    Walter Brueggemann   7

2   Scripture: New Testament
    Christopher Rowland   21

3   Augustine
    Jean Bethke Elshtain   35

4   Aquinas
    Frederick Christian Bauerschmidt   48

5   The Reformation
    Andrew Bradstock   62

6   Liturgy
    Bernd Wannenwetsch   76

Part II   Political Theologies: Survey   91

7   Eastern Orthodox Thought
    Michael Plekon   93

8 Carl Schmitt
Michael Hollerich 107

9 Karl Barth
Haddon Willmer 123

10 Dietrich Bonhoeffer
Stanley Hauerwas 136

11 John Courtney Murray
Michael J. Baxter 150

12 William Temple
Alan M. Suggate 165

13 Reinhold Niebuhr
William Werpehowski 180

14 Feminist Theology, Southern
Kwok Pui-lan 194

15 Feminist Theology, Northern
Elaine Graham 210

16 Jürgen Moltmann
Nicholas Adams 227

17 Johann Baptist Metz
J. Matthew Ashley 241

18 Political Theologies in Asia
Aloysius Pieris 256

19 Black Political Theologies
M. Shawn Copeland 271

20 Gustavo Gutiérrez
Roberto S. Goizueta 288

21 Stanley Hauerwas
R. R. Reno 302

Part III Constructive Political Theology 317

22 Trinity
Kathryn Tanner 319

23 Creation
Peter Scott 333

24 Christology
Raymund Schwager 348

25   Atonement
      Timothy J. Gorringe   363

26   Spirit
      Mark Lewis Taylor   377

27   Church
      William T. Cavanaugh   393

28   Eschatology
      Robert W. Jenson   407

Part IV   Structures and Movements   421

29   State and Civil Society
      Daniel M. Bell, Jr.   423

30   Democracy
      John W. de Gruchy   439

31   Critical Theory
      Marsha Aileen Hewitt   455

32   Postmodernism
      Catherine Pickstock   471

33   Globalization
      Peter Sedgwick   486

Part V   Perspectives   501

34   The Islamic Quest for Sociopolitical Justice
      Bustami Mohamed Khir   503

35   Abrahamic Theo-politics: A Jewish View
      Peter Ochs   519

Index of Names and Subjects   535

Index of Biblical References   563

Contributors

Nicholas Adams is Lecturer in Theology and Ethics, University of Edinburgh, UK.

J. Matthew Ashley is Associate Professor of Theology, University of Notre Dame, Indiana, USA.

Frederick Christian Bauerschmidt is Associate Professor of Theology, Loyola College in Maryland, Baltimore, Maryland, USA.

Michael J. Baxter, CSC, is Assistant Professor of Theology, University of Notre Dame, Indiana, USA.

Daniel M. Bell, Jr., is Assistant Professor, Lutheran Theological Southern Seminary, Columbia, South Carolina, USA.

Andrew Bradstock is Secretary for Church and Society with the United Reformed Church, London, UK and an honorary research fellow at King Alfred's College, Winchester, UK.

Walter Brueggemann is William Marcellus McPheeters Professor of Old Testament, Columbia Theological Seminary, Decatur, Georgia, USA.

William T. Cavanaugh is Associate Professor of Theology, University of St. Thomas, St. Paul, Minnesota, USA.

M. Shawn Copeland is Associate Professor of Systematic Theology, Boston College, Chestnut Hill, Massachusetts, USA.

John W. de Gruchy is Robert Selby Taylor Professor of Christian Studies, University of Cape Town, South Africa.

Jean Bethke Elshtain is Laura Spelman Rockefeller Professor of Social and Political Ethics, University of Chicago Divinity School, Chicago, Illinois, USA.

Roberto S. Goizueta is Professor of Theology, Boston College, Massachusetts, USA.

Timothy J. Gorringe is Professor of Theological Studies, University of Exeter, UK.

Elaine Graham is Samuel Ferguson Professor of Social and Pastoral Theology, University of Manchester, UK.

Stanley Aileen Hauerwas is Gilbert T. Rowe Professor of Christian Ethics, Duke University Divinity School, Durham, North Carolina, USA.

Marsha Aileen Hewitt is Professor of Social Ethics and Contemporary Theology, Trinity College, Toronto, Canada.

Michael J. Hollerich is Associate Professor of Theology, University of St. Thomas, St. Paul, Minnesota, USA.

Robert W. Jenson is Senior Scholar for Research, Center of Theological Inquiry, Princeton, New Jersey, USA.

Bustami Mohamed Khir is a member of the Graduate Institute of Theology and Religion, University of Birmingham, UK.

Kwok Pui-lan is William F. Cole Professor of Christian Theology and Spirituality, Episcopal Divinity School, Cambridge, Massachusetts, USA.

Peter Ochs is Edgar M. Bronfman Professor of Modern Judaic Studies, University of Virginia, USA.

Catherine Pickstock is University Lecturer in the Philosophy of Religion, University of Cambridge, UK.

Aloysius Pieris is Founder-Director, Tulana Research Centre, Kelaniya, Sri Lanka.

Michael Plekon is Professor in the Department of Sociology and Anthropology and the Program in Religion and Culture, Baruch College of the City University of New York, and a priest of the Orthodox Church in America (OCA), serving as associate at St. Gregory the Theologian Church, Wappingers Falls, NY.

R. R. Reno is Associate Professor of Theology, Creighton University, Omaha, Nebraska, USA.

Christopher Rowland is Dean Ireland's Professor of Exegesis of Holy Scripture, Queen's College, University of Oxford, UK.

Raymund Schwager is Professor of Systematic Theology, University of Innsbruck, Austria.

Peter Scott is Senior Lecturer in Christian Social Thought and Director of the Lincoln Theological Institute, University of Manchester, UK.

Peter Sedgwick is the Church of England Policy Advisor on Criminal Justice in the Public Affairs Unit.

Alan M. Suggate was formerly Senior Lecturer in Theology, University of Durham, UK.

Kathryn Tanner is Professor of Theology, The Divinity School, University of Chicago, USA.

Mark Lewis Taylor is Professor of Theology and Culture, Princeton Theological Seminary, USA.

Bernd Wannenwetsch is University Lecturer in Ethics, Oxford University, UK.

William Werpehowski is Professor of Theology, Villanova University, Philadelphia, Pennsylvania, USA.

Haddon Willmer is Emeritus Professor of Theology, University of Leeds, UK, and Research Tutor, Oxford Centre for Mission Studies, UK.

Introduction to the Paperback Edition

Peter M. Scott & William T. Cavanaugh

In the two years since the first publication of this *Companion*, the issues that it seeks to address have – if anything – become more pressing. Every day the newspaper and the internet provide fresh evidence of the political resurgence of faith(s) and the theological nature of so-called "secular" politics.

This paperback edition is therefore very timely and we hope that its publication will allow the important essays contained in this volume to reach an even wider audience. Our aim is to present in a comprehensive way the inherently political nature of theology – its history, constructive engagement, and situatedness – from a variety of perspectives. We are delighted by the positive critical reception that the volume has received and would like to thank the contributors, who are drawn from a variety of traditions and perspectives, for their work. Finally, in the words of the original Introduction, we hope that this collection of essays will continue to bear witness to a better world.

Introduction

William T. Cavanaugh and Peter Scott

Not long after the fall of the Berlin Wall in 1989, Francis Fukuyama declared that we had achieved "the end of history." In 2001, the collapse of other walls, those of the World Trade Center towers, served notice that history was not finished with us yet.

Fukuyama's famous thesis was that, with the ruin of communism, there remained no viable alternative to Western liberalism on the stage of history. We are still sorting through the rude awakening from this fantasy. What seems clear, however, is that the bland, narcotic world that Fukuyama envisioned, the "victory of the VCR" over sectarian strife, has not come to pass. Theological voices have been instrumental in opposing that vision. Theological discourse has refused to stay where liberalism would prefer to put it. Theology is politically important, and those who engage in either theology or politics ignore this fact at a certain peril.

This *Companion* operates with an expansive understanding of what is encompassed by the term "political theology." Theology is broadly understood as discourse about God, and human persons as they relate to God. The political is broadly understood as the use of structural power to organize a society or community of people. Under this spacious rubric, politics may be understood for the purpose of a political theology in terms of the self-governance of communities and individuals; or in terms of Max Weber's more circumscribed definition of politics as seeking state power. Political theology is, then, the analysis and criticism of political arrangements (including cultural–psychological, social and economic aspects) from the perspective of differing interpretations of God's ways with the world.

For the purposes of this volume, political theology is construed primarily as Christian political theology. Not only would the inclusion of other faiths have made an already fat volume unwieldy, but the term "political theology" was coined in a Christian context and has continued to be a significant term primarily within Christian discourse.

Within this general framework, the task of political theology is conceived in different ways by different thinkers. For some, politics is seen as a "given" with its own secular autonomy. Politics and theology are therefore two essentially distinct activities, one to do with public authority, and the other to do in the first place with religious experience and the semiprivate associations of religious believers. The task of political theology might be to relate religious belief to larger societal issues while not confusing the proper autonomy of each.

For others, theology is critical reflection on the political. Theology is related as superstructure to the material politico-economic base. Theology reflects and reinforces just or unjust political arrangements. The task of political theology might then be to expose the ways in which theological discourse reproduces inequalities of class, gender or race, and to reconstruct theology so that it serves the cause of justice.

For still others, theology and politics are essentially similar activities; both are constituted in the production of metaphysical images around which communities are organized. All politics has theology embedded within it, and particular forms of organization are implicit in doctrines of, for example, Trinity, the church and eschatology. There is no essential separation of material base and cultural superstructure. The task then might become one of exposing the false theologies underlying supposedly "secular" politics and promoting the true politics implicit in a true theology.

Political theologies vary in the extent to which social sciences and other secular discourses are employed; the extent to which they are "contextualized" or rooted in a particular people's experience; the extent to which the state is seen as the locus of politics; and the ways in which theological resources – scripture, liturgy, doctrine – are employed. What distinguishes all political theology from other types of theology or political discourse is the explicit attempt to relate discourse about God to the organization of bodies in space and time.

The Blackwell Companion to Political Theology has a dual purpose. On the one hand, it is meant to serve as a reference tool. Each essay is designed to present the reader with an overview of the range of opinion on a given topic, and to guide the reader toward sources representing those views. On the other hand, the *Companion* presents original and constructive essays on the various topics by leading voices in political theology today. Our authors have been instructed to be fair, but not to feign neutrality. The views of the author should and do become clear in the course of each essay, and the authors make many original claims that take the discussion of political theology in new and provocative directions. The result, we trust, is a lively argument within a fascinating and diverse group of scholars.

We editors have tried to do our part by arguing between ourselves as much as possible. We first met when one did an appreciative though critical review of a book by the other, and we have yet to iron out all the theological disagreements between us. Our collaboration has just so been congenial and fruitful. We chose to work together in the hope that our differences would make for a richer volume.

Our choice of topics and authors has followed the same hope. We have tried to give a voice at the table to a great variety of different views that accurately reflect the state of the conversation today. All the same, some readers may be disappointed by the exclusion of some topics and puzzled by the inclusion of others. Here we must lament the limitations of space and confess our own personal limitations. There is no question, for example, that, although the volume contains some voices from the two-thirds world, the volume as a whole is weighted toward the world we know best, and more accurately reflects the state of the conversation in Europe and North America.

The volume is organized into five sections. The first addresses some of the primary resources of the Christian tradition to which theologians appeal in constructing political theologies: scripture, liturgy, Augustine, Aquinas, and some of the great theologians of the Reformation. The second surveys some of the most important figures and movements in political theology. We have included a broad range of methodologies, ecclesial traditions, geographic and social locations, to give a sense for the diversity of political theologies. The third section consists of constructive essays on single theological loci, such as Trinity, atonement, and eschatology. These essays draw out the political implications of select Christian doctrines. The fourth section addresses some important structures and movements (postmodernism, globalization, etc.) from a theological point of view. The fifth section, finally, provides one Islamic response and one Jewish response to the essays in the volume. If Christian political theologians hope to witness to a better world, they must do so in conversation not only with each other, but with those of other faiths, especially the Abrahamic faiths. It is our hope that this volume contributes in some way to that witness.

PART I

Traditioned Resources:
Scripture, Traditions, Liturgy

1 Scripture: Old Testament   7
2 Scripture: New Testament   21
3 Augustine   35
4 Aquinas   48
5 The Reformation   62
6 Liturgy   76

CHAPTER 1
Scripture: Old Testament

Walter Brueggemann

The actual *historical* practice of politics in ancient Israel, the community of the Old Testament, is in dispute among contemporary scholars; to the extent that the practice of politics is recoverable at all, it is unexceptional and replicates common practices of that general context. At the outset one must recognize that scholarship is unsettled and deeply divided over the question of historicity. Some scholars incline to take textual evidence more or less at face value; some find unintended traces of historical matters even in texts that are judged in substance to be historically unreliable; and some believe that the texts are belated ideological constructs almost completely void of historical value. In a brief essay it is not possible to adjudicate such questions in any detail. My own perspective is to accept as roughly reliable the self-presentation of Israel as a clue to its self-discernment, and to realize that even if this self-presentation is not historically reliable, it is in any case the preferred self-presentation with which interpretation must finally deal, albeit with great critical caution (Gottwald 1979: 785 n. 558; 2001).

I

Given such a cautionary acceptance of the data about the political dimension of Israel's life, we may conclude, not surprisingly, that Israel's political life was unexceptional and no doubt much like other political communities that shared its historical environment. Like every political community, ancient Israel had to devise institutions, policies, and practices that apportioned power, goods, and access in a manageable, practicable, sustainable way. And, as in every such community, those ways of managing were endlessly under review and sometimes under criticism and assault. We may identify three characteristic political issues that were subject to dispute and negotiation in that ancient community.

First, there is the long-term tension between centralized political authority – articulated in the Old Testament as monarchy – and local authority, reflecting a segmented social arrangement. This tension is evident in the tricky negotiations over monarchy in 1 Sam. 7–15, in the hard-nosed political dispute of 1 Kgs. 12: 1–19, and in the effective intervention of the "elders of the land" against the power of the state in the trial of Jeremiah in Jer. 26: 16–19.

Second, there is the endlessly problematic question of the distribution of goods between "haves" (now often identified as "urban elites") and "have-nots," the disadvantaged and politically marginalized who likely were agrarian peasants. The monopolizing, marginalizing propensity of monarchy that reached its zenith of power and prestige under Solomon (962–922 BCE) is to be understood as a comprehensive system of production, distribution, and consumption that featured an inordinate standard of extravagance (1 Kgs. 4: 20–8). It was matched by an extravagant temple complex that gave religious legitimation and sanction to economic disproportion (see 1 Kgs. 7: 14–22, 48–51), so that the temple featured a production of images (propaganda) that matched economic exploitation.

There runs through Israel's tradition a counter-theme concerning the advocacy of the excluded (to which we shall return below) that existed in tension with and in dissent from the self-aggrandizement of the urban monopoly with the king at its head (Wilson 1980). This counter-theme is voiced as vigorous advocacy for "widows, orphans, sojourners, and the poor" through economic provisions that seek to curb unfettered accumulation (Deut. 15: 1–18) (Jeffries 1992). That same dissent is articulated by the prophets who, while claiming theological legitimacy, are in fact voices of social advocacy in a political economy that must have resisted such advocacy (see Isa. 5: 8–10; Mic. 2: 1–4; Jer. 5: 27–9). The same accent continues in the exilic and post-exilic periods (see Isa. 61: 1–4; Zech. 7: 9–12; Dan. 4: 27).

Third, the small states of Israel and Judah, and latterly the surviving Judah after the destruction of the Northern Kingdom, had the endless and eventually hopeless task of maintaining state autonomy in the face of imperial pressure and accommodating imperial requirements enough to escape occupation and destruction (Brueggemann 2000). These two small states were located in a particularly vulnerable place in the land bridge between Egypt and the great northern powers. In the Old Testament, this locus concerned especially the Assyrian Empire that first destroyed the Northern Kingdom (721 BCE) and then threatened the Southern Kingdom of Judah (705–701 BCE). In the state of Judah, Ahaz is condemned for having gone too far in appeasement of the Assyrian Tiglath-Pilezer III, so far as to compromise religious symbols (II Kgs. 16: 1–20). Conversely, his own son Hezekiah is championed as one who withstood the heavy pressure of the Assyrian Sennacherib, though in II Kgs. 18: 14–16 Hezekiah is also portrayed as a submissive appeaser of the Assyrians. In the end, the long juggling act failed as the Northern state fell to Assyria in 721 and the Southern state to Babylon in 587. The practical reality of relative impotence in the face of imperial pressure was a defining fact of life for leadership in both states over a long period.

II

On all these counts – (1) centralized authority versus local authority, (2) covenantal relations between haves and have-nots, and (3) autonomous small states in the face of imperial pressure – the text provides evidence of endless critical dispute and negotiation until, at the last, the post-exilic community of Judaism came to terms with a quite localized authority under the relatively benign patronage and tax-collecting apparatus of the Persian Empire after 537 BCE (Weinberg 1992). These seem to be the political realities on the ground.

Such cautious historical discernment and reconstruction situate the ancient community of Israel in the real world of interest, dispute, and negotiation. Because our theme is "political theology," however, we are permitted, indeed required, to go well beyond such seemingly recoverable historical reconstruction as presents ancient Israel as an unexceptional case of politics in the ancient world. When we go beyond such unexceptional historical probability, moreover, we are led to Israel's *theological imagination* (that is, Israel's faith), which is operative everywhere in the text of the Old Testament and everywhere redescribes and resituates what must have been political reality. Thus it is theological imagination of a very particular kind that recasts politics in this community and moves our historical study into a much more complex and demanding interpretive process.

This theological imagination that affirms YHWH, the God of Israel, as the key political player in Israel, is no late "add-on" to an otherwise available historical report. Rather, in the Old Testament and its imaginative presentation of political theology, YHWH stands front and center in the political process and is the defining factor and force around which all other political matters revolve. To attempt, in the interest of "history," to construe what Israel's politics were like apart from or before the theological component of interpretation in ancient Israel is a task endlessly undertaken by scholars; in the end, however, the task is hopeless for discerning Israel's self-understanding. Such a positivistic reconstruction may be to some extent available, but it stands remote from the self-presentation of Israel in the Old Testament wherein there is no politics apart from its defining theological dimension.

Thus the self-presentation of Israel in song and story is inescapably a *theological politics* in which the defining presence of YHWH, the God of Israel, impinges upon every facet of the political; or conversely, Israel's self-presentation is inescapably a *political theology* in which YHWH, the God of Israel, is intensely engaged with questions of power and with policies and practices that variously concern the distribution of goods and access. In Israel's self-presentation, there is no politics not theologically marked, no theology not politically inclined. As a result, this political theology or theological politics is, at the same time, invested with immense gravitas tilted toward absolutism, because things political become "the things of God," but also deabsolutized and made provisional and penultimate by the irascible freedom of YHWH, who does not conform to any stable, containable policy function. The impact of YHWH on the political process in ancient Israel, in ways that absolutize and deabsolutize, is voiced regularly in song and story, in rhetorical practices that remain open, unsettled, and imaginative, always slightly beyond control and closure, but always short of absence.

This peculiar juxtaposition of theology and politics indicates that Israel understood itself as "chosen" and set apart, in its best moments, in order to enact its *theological* peculiarity by the practice of a peculiar *political economy*. This peculiarity, rooted theologically and practiced politically, is the tap root of Israel as a "contrast society." This same peculiarity, moreover, is the ground for thinking of the church as a "contrast society" in the world.

III

When we approach Israel's political theology through Israel's imaginative stories and songs, it is almost inescapable that the Exodus narrative (or its early poetic articulation in the Song of Exodus: Exod. 15: 1–18) should be seen as paradigmatic (Miller 1973: 166–75). In that paradigmatic narrative, YHWH is rendered as the great force and agent who confronts the absolute political power of Pharaoh and, through a series of contests, delegitimates and finally overthrows the imperial power of Egypt that at the outset appeared to be not only intransigent but beyond challenge. Israel's tradition, as it reflects critically upon political questions and processes, endlessly reiterates this "Pharaoh versus YHWH" drama in new contexts, and relentlessly rereads and reinterprets every political question in terms of that defining, paradigmatic narrative.

The question of the historicity of the exodus event is an acute one. Insofar as the Exodus is regarded as historical, it is characteristically placed by scholars in the thirteenth century BCE, wherein the Pharaoh is variously identified as Sethos, Rameses II, or Marniptah (Bright 1959: 107–28). It is clear in any case, however, that Israel's traditionists do not linger long over historical questions, but cast this Exodus memory in a liturgical mode so that it is available for many reuses and is rhetorically open to endlessly reimagined locations and circumstances (Pedersen 1940: 728–37).

The reason for focusing upon the narrative of "Pharaoh versus YHWH" is that YHWH as a political agent in the narrative of Israel is to be understood as the decisive "anti-Pharaoh." Thus we may understand Israel's peculiar and characteristic sense of the political if we reflect on the narrative presentation of Pharaoh as a foil for YHWH (Green 1998). Pharaoh is taken as a historical figure but is quickly transposed into a cipher and metaphor for all threats that Israel opposed on its political horizon:

- Pharaoh is a figure of absolute top-down authority who operates a political-economic system of totalism.

- Pharaoh is characteristically propelled by a nightmare of scarcity, motivated by anxiety about not having enough, and so a determined accumulator and monopolizer (Gen. 41: 14–57).
- Pharaoh brutally enacts his nightmare of anxiety by policies of confiscation and exploitation, and allows no dimension of human awareness or compassion in the implementation of policies grounded in acute anxiety (Gen. 47: 13–26).
- Pharaoh's absolutism is enacted at immense social cost to those upon whom the policies impinge; as Fretheim has noted, moreover, the cost extends beyond its human toll to the savage abuse of the environment (Fretheim 1991).
- Pharaoh's absolutism cannot be sustained, because in his arrogant autonomy he completely miscalculates the limitation imposed on human authority by YHWH's holiness, a limitation embodied and performed by the role and character of YHWH.

In the imagination of Israel, this characterization of Pharaoh lays out the primary lines of Israel's political theology. From that imaginative articulation, it is obvious enough that Israel's positive political commitments, which revolve around YHWH, include the following:

- The political–economic process cannot be a closed, absolute system, but must remain open to serious dialogic transaction, for which the term is "covenant."
- The political economy that prevails is grounded not in a nightmare of scarcity, but in an assumed and affirmed abundance, rooted in God, who is a generous creator (Brueggemann 1999). Thus Exodus 16 functions as a Yahwistic contrast to the scarcity of Pharaoh, a contrast in which "some gathered more, some less. But when they measured it with an omer, those who gathered much had nothing over, and those who gathered little had no shortage; they gathered as much as each of them needed" (Exod. 16: 17–18) (see Brueggemann forthcoming).
- The political enterprise of Israel is not to be a fearful practice of monopoly and acquisitiveness, but is to be a neighborly practice in which communal goods, ordered by a rule of covenantal law, are to be deployed among members of the community – rich and poor – who are all entitled to an adequate share. The curb on accumulation and monopoly is dramatically stated in the provision for the "Year of Release" in Deut. 15: 1–18; (see on Neh. 5 below).
- Israel's political economy is concerned for the practice of compassion for the disenfranchised neighbors (widows, orphans, aliens, the poor; Deut. 24: 17–22), a sharing that is grounded in a lyrical appreciation for the generosity of the earth that is to be celebrated and appropriated, but not exploited or violently used (Deut. 6: 10–12; 8: 7–20). That practice of compassion is motivated, moreover, by the recurring remembrance, "You were slaves in Egypt" (Deut. 10: 19; 15: 15; 24: 22).

- Israel's political economy is to be generously covenantal, so that YHWH, creator of heaven and earth, is acknowledged to be source and ground of all that is, is to be ceded ultimate authority, thanked in gratitude that matches God's primordial generosity, and gladly obeyed, so that social relationships are congruous with YHWH's own generosity. That is, social relationships fully express and embody the reality of YHWH's sovereign practice of generosity.

Israel's political life characteristically is conducted in the tension between a glad embrace of YHWH's covenantal mode of relationship and exploitative practices that disregard covenantal entitlements and restraints. These alternatives are understood in Israel as life-or-death options in the political process. According to Israel's best claim, the choosing of *covenantal relatedness* as a political form of life results in well-being, while the option of *brutalizing totalism* leads to destruction:

> See, I have set before you today life and prosperity, death and adversity. If you obey the commandments of the Lord your God that I am commanding you today, by loving the Lord your God, walking in his ways, and observing his commandments, decrees, and ordinances, then you shall live and become numerous, and the Lord your God will bless you in the land that you are entering to possess. But if your heart turns away and you do not hear, but are led astray to bow down to other gods and serve them, I declare to you today that you shall perish; you shall not live long in the land that you are crossing the Jordan to enter and possess. (Deut. 30: 15–18)

Thus the concrete, practical political issue of the deployment of goods, power, and access is decisively situated in a deep decision of "YHWH versus Pharaoh." Political decisions are understood as proximate subdecisions in the service of a more powerfully defining decision about ultimate governance that is simply the either/or of Pharaoh in absolutizing acquisitiveness or YHWH in covenantal generosity. Every political decision derives from, reflects, and serves this alternative theological decision in favor of covenant with YHWH that Israel is always remaking.

IV

We may dwell more closely on the Exodus narrative as a model for Israel's political theology. At the outset Pharaoh is the defining political reference in the narrative. The emergence of YHWH in the drama of Pharaoh is an immense interruption, so that politics informed by YHWH may be understood as *interruptive politics*, the emergence of a political agent who characteristically disrupts Pharaoh's "politics as usual." Israel always knows about "politics as usual," that is, the deployment of social power without reference to the subversive, detotalizing power of YHWH. But Israel also makes room, characteristically, for the disruptive enactment of YHWH in the midst of "the usual" that keeps the political process endlessly open and capable of fresh, neighborly initiatives.

In the Exodus narrative itself, we may identify six elements that become characteristic of Israel's self-discernment as a peculiar political enterprise.

First, Israel is attentive to *social pain* as a datum of the politics that is evoked in the public process of power. Israel is not so committed to orderly management that it fails to notice and take seriously social pain, because it refuses to regard such pain as a bearable cost of order. Thus already in Exodus 1: 13–14, the pain comes to articulation in the narrative: "The Egyptians became ruthless in imposing tasks on the Israelites, and made their lives bitter with hard service in mortar and bricks and in every kind of field labor. They were ruthless in all the tasks that they imposed on them" (Exod. 1: 13–14).

Second, Israel develops, early on, shrewd *modes of defiance* that were understood as methods that did not invite the wrath of the overlords (see Scott 1985, 1990). Thus the cunning midwives, Shiphrah and Puah, in pretended innocence but in fact in deeply committed piety defy pharaoh's decree in the service of their own community: "But the midwives feared God; they did not do as the king of Egypt commanded them, but they let the boys live . . . The midwives said to Pharaoh, 'Because the Hebrew women are not like the Egyptian women; for they are vigorous and give birth before the midwife comes to them'" (Exod. 1: 17, 19).

Third, while resistance to abusive totalism may take the form of cunning, surreptitious defiance, it can also, however, be enacted as *violence*, as in the case of Moses' murder of an Egyptian. Moses does not quibble about any theoretical right to revolt, but that right is clearly implied in the narrative of Exod. 2: 11–15. Israel's political tradition is developed in the face of oppressive overlords, and Moses embodies the implied obligation of resistance to brutalizing authority.

Fourth, the convergence of pain noticed, defiance practiced, and violence perpetrated occurs in Exod. 2: 23–5, wherein Israel brings its pain to speech and issues *a shrill cry of self-announcement* that refuses the politics of silent submissiveness: "After a long time the king of Egypt died. The Israelites groaned under their slavery, and cried out. Out of the slavery their cry for help rose up to God" (Exod. 2: 23).

These verses are important for the narrative because they include the first reference to YHWH in this account. It is noteworthy that the cry of the Israelites was not addressed to YHWH. This is, rather, a raw political act of giving voice to the irreducible political datum of suffering at the hands of coercive power. The cry cannot in any direct sense be understood as a theological act.

It is equally important, however, that the cry that was raw pain not addressed to anyone "rose up to God." In this peculiar, quite deliberate phrasing Israel's politics of protest is transposed by the magnetism of YHWH into a political theology. In its cry Israel does not know any transcendent assurance or even seek a theological reference. Rather, in Israel's telling, YHWH is simply "there" and draws the cry of pain to YHWH's own self, not because of who Israel is, but because of who YHWH is: an attentive listener to pain from below in a revolutionary mobilization of transformative energy against abusive power.

Fifth, after the evocation of YHWH, the account turns from the wretchedness of Israel in bondage to the odd *hovering of YHWH's holiness* at the edge of the slave camp. Moses, now a political fugitive, summoned and confronted by YHWH, who calls his name (Exod. 3: 4). This enigmatic, theophanic report functions in the larger narrative to intrude YHWH's inscrutable holy purpose and presence into Israel's political vision. This intrusion assures that Israel now has an advocate who more than equalizes Israel's chances against Pharaoh. As a result, Israel can now voice its characteristically distinctive political claim of a theological dimension to its political vision, a convergence that recurs in Israel's life in "turns" that have "abiding astonishment" (Buber 1946: 75–6; Brueggemann 1991). Indeed, Israel's retelling of its public life is a narrative beyond common explanation, surely with abiding astonishment.

Sixth, the political process of Israel, as narrated in the Exodus story, is grounded in YHWH's holy response to pain. In the end, however, that process requires human initiative, so that Moses and his cohorts become "actors in their own history." That is, "salvation history" is not simply YHWH's action, as might be implied by Exod. 14: 13–14; it depends, finally, upon human risk-taking. After YHWH has declared intentionality about the emancipation of the slaves in a series of first-person verbs (Exod. 3: 7–9), the sentence turns to human mandate: "So come, I will send you to Pharaoh to bring my people, the Israelites, out of Egypt" (3: 10).

To be sure, Moses resists and offers a series of excuses (Exod. 3: 11–4: 17). In the end, however, Moses (and Aaron) go to Pharaoh, equipped with a divine commission (5: 1). It is their readiness to confront Pharaoh that sets the narrative in motion and eventuates in the changed circumstances of the slave community.

The rest is "history": there follows the contestation between Pharaoh and the God of Israel (Exod. 7–11), the departure of the slaves from Egypt (Exod. 14), and the peasant dance of freedom (Exod. 15: 20–1). Israel is on its way to Sinai, where it will commit to an alternative form of public power that embraces the holiness of YHWH as a detotalizing reality and the legitimacy of the neighbor as a clue to public practice.

V

I have taken this long with the Exodus narrative and its plot of "YHWH versus Pharaoh" because in this memory (enacted as liturgy) Israel constructs and offers its primal model of the political process that includes acute social analysis, the legitimacy of protest, Holy Presence as a defining factor, human initiative as indispensable, and an alternative (covenantal) mode of public power entertained as a legitimate practical possibility (Buber 1990; Mendenhall 2001:

73–100). On the basis of this model Israel narrates its political life through an intensely committed interpretive process. The narrative accounts in the books of Kings and Chronicles evidence a concern, in the telling of public history, for *continuity* in the flow of public, institutional power; it is clear, however, that the narrative is characteristically focused on certain key episodes of encounter and *disruption* that in a variety of ways replicate the paradigmatic encounter of YHWH and Pharaoh. Thus the primal claims on Israel's political horizon become most clearly visible at the stress points at which Israel's key interpreters and shapers of tradition have the most powerful interpretive say.

The decisive "episode" in this telling is the narrative of Solomon in 1 Kgs. 3–11. Solomon's considerable political–economic achievement is a point of great pride in Israel; he replicated the great empires of his time and is remembered as having brought great wealth and prestige to what had been – only two generations before – a simple hill-country people. Solomon is, in the Old Testament, a metaphor for power politics of the most effective kind: he managed a great trade apparatus, an effective governing bureaucracy, a rational tax-collection plan, a developed military security system, an ambitious building program, and an extensive network of political marriage alliances, all of which were given dramatic legitimacy by his central achievement, the Jerusalem temple (1 Kgs. 6–8).

The narrative report on Solomon, however, claims for the monarchy less than meets the eye. It cannot be mere reportage that Solomon's marriage to "Pharaoh's daughter" pervades the narrative (1 Kgs. 3: 1; 7: 8; 9: 16, 24; 11: 10). This apparently incidental reference may provide a clue to the ironic dimension of the whole of the narrative. Solomon is not only connected to Pharaoh, but replicates Pharaoh and in fact becomes "Israel's Pharaoh," with a highly centralized economy and an ideology of totalism generated by the legitimacy associated with the temple. This totalism inevitably put Israelite peasants back into economic bondage and brought the covenantal practice of public power to a complete shut-down. It is for that reason that the harsh theological judgment on Solomon (1 Kgs. 11: 1–8), the prophetic intrusion against Solomon (11: 26–40), and the political refusal of Northern Israel (1 Kgs. 12: 1–19) altogether stand as a harsh judgment upon Solomon's experiment. The materials of 1 Kgs. 11–12 indicate the reassertion and recovery of covenantal politics that are always vulnerable to exploitative totalism but characteristically find ways of resistance, rearticulation, and re-emergence.

We may mention four other encounters that bespeak the same reassertion of *covenantalism* in the face of *totalism*. In each case it is to be noticed that it is an assumption about YHWH, the guarantor of deabsolutizing of every claim but YHWH's own claim, that becomes the ground for resisting political absolutism.

First, from the perspective of the narrative in 1 Kgs. 16–II Kgs. 10, the Omri dynasty in the north is the greatest challenge to the theological–political claims of Yahwism (876–842 BCE). That theological challenge is most explicit in the contest at Mt. Carmel in 1 Kgs. 18. The political–economic dimension of the dispute, however, is most dramatically voiced in 1 Kgs. 21, in the tale of Naboth's vineyard that features the manipulative royal practices of Jezebel and Ahab, son of Omri. It is clear that the narrative exhibits a dispute between two theories of public power that in turn yield two notions of land possession. Naboth – and eventually Elijah and the narrator – champion an old tribal notion of an inalienable connection between land and landowner in an undeniable entitlement. Conversely, the royal family holds to a notion of royal prerogative in which land is simply a commodity for commercial transaction. The violent termination of the House of Omri indicates the force and the resolve that belonged to the covenantal theory and the readiness of its proponents to resist the conventional alternative, resistance undertaken at great cost (II Kgs. 9–10).

Second, the parallel reigns of Jeroboam II in Northern Israel and Uzziah (Azariah) in Judah constituted a time of immense prosperity in the eighth century (approximately 785–745 BCE). That prosperity was achieved, however, by disregard of the claims of Yahwism, both religious claims and economic claims that were grounded theologically (see II Chron. 26: 16–21). Thus the same social "development" "enjoyed" under Solomon seems to have re-emerged in the midst of the eighth century.

It was in this period that the first of the great "classic prophets," Amos, emerged, though he had Elijah and Elisha as antecedents a century earlier. Amos' remarkable strictures against the economic practices of the dominant society are something of a *novum* in Israel (see 3: 13–15; 4: 1–3; 6: 1–7; 8: 4–6) (Premnath 1988). Perhaps inescapably, such a voice is bound to come face to face with the powers of the dominant regime, an encounter narrated in Amos 7: 10–17. In that encounter, Amaziah, priest at Bethel, speaks for the royal apparatus, rebukes the prophet as a political subversive, and banishes him from the realm. Totalizing systems, of course, by definition must preclude voices of dissent. Before he finishes, however, Amos manages to deliver to the royal–priestly establishment one last poetic utterance that anticipates exile for the royal house, thus foreshadowing the Assyrian termination of the Northern Kingdom in 721 (Amos 7: 16–17). It is, however, not the "prediction" that interests us, but the fact that Israel's political discourse is characteristically a disputatious one between a *covenantalism* that precludes absolutism and advocates a neighborly economic fabric and a *totalism* that absolutizes itself at the expense of God and neighbor.

Third, in Jeremiah 26 the prophet is on trial for his life because he has spoken of the impending destruction of Jerusalem (605 BCE). The religious leaders insist on his execution (v. 11), an insistence that is resisted by the state officials (v. 16). There is more than a little irony in the fact that it is the religious leaders who want Jeremiah silenced, no doubt indicating that they are the ones most deeply inured in the absolute ideology of the temple, thus a parallel to the priest at Bethel in our preceding case.

What particularly interests us, however, is the intervention of "elders of the land" who speak on behalf of Jeremiah by appeal to the words a century earlier (perhaps about 715 BCE) of the prophet Micah, who also had anticipated the destruction of Jerusalem (see Micah 3: 12) (Wolff 1987). This exchange among power factions features a characteristic tension between centralized urban authority and the voice of an outlying village (Seitz 1989). What matters most is that the village elders insist that even Jerusalem is not immune to criticism or, in this interpretation, to the judgment of YHWH and its consequent destruction. This exchange is a dramatic example of the way in which the political process is kept open against the ideological fears that seek to silence all dissent.

The fourth case I cite is the dramatic exchange initiated by Nehemiah in the process of reconstituting post-exilic Judaism (Neh. 5) (perhaps about 444 BCE). It is the premise of the narrative account that the economy is operated by those who practice unrestrained acquisitiveness, even at the expense of their poor neighbors who are fellow Jews. As always, the problem is taxes, mortgages, and interest arrangements through which the acquisitive ones eventually usurp the property of the economically vulnerable ones. Nehemiah's intervention serves to effect an act of solidarity between creditors and debtors in the matter of interest payments: "Let us stop this taking of interest. Restore to them, this very day, their fields, their vineyards, their olive orchards, and their houses, and the interest on money, grain, wine, and oil that you have been exacting from them (vv. 10–11)."

The appeal of Nehemiah may be to old laws precluding the levying of interest in the community (Deut. 23: 19–20). The larger appeal, however, is to the solidarity of all Jews, thus an insistence that normal economic transactions must be curbed and reshaped in the interest of community solidarity and mutual obligation. Thus Nehemiah champions a covenantal economy and takes steps to enact it, a proposal accepted even by those of his own interest-charging class.

VI

This enumeration of dramatic encounters exhibits an interpretive posture in which two perspectives or two practices of public power are characteristically in sharp tension. I believe that this recurring tension is at the center of Israel's self-presentation as a community that practiced an *unexceptional* politics – *except* for its covenantal commitments, which always tilted toward the exceptional. While confrontation seems to be a preferred mode of articulation (and perhaps of practice), confrontation is not in every case a viable strategy. Certainly when Israel lived under the pressures of alien powers that had no sensibility about Israel's peculiar theological tradition, sometimes the political process required patient and careful accommodation.

It is likely that much of the accommodationist literature, ostensibly older, is in fact material generated in the Persian period and placed in the service of emerging Judaism in that period (Smith 1989). In the long period of Persian hegemony, Judaism was granted an important measure of political autonomy, though surely restricted and fundamentally subservient to the needs of the empire. The primary biblical evidence for such an arrangement (which required great accommodation) is the movement led by Ezra and Nehemiah, who did their shared work in fifth-century Jerusalem under commission from the Persians and no doubt with Persian finances. The text provides a peculiar, careful, and intentional balance of Jewish autonomy and deference to imperial requirements. This arrangement was of course not a replica of the confrontation with Pharaoh in the old Exodus narrative, as confrontation in that later environment was impossible.

Lee Humphreys and, in a more critical way, Daniel Smith-Christopher have considered the narratives of Joseph (Gen. 37–50), Esther, and Daniel as examples of "diaspora novellas" that present exilic heroes who resist and accommodate in proper proportion in order to make a statement for faith without foolhardy risk (Humphreys 1973; Smith 1989: 153–78). These narratives are examples of political courage that is matched by a measure of cunning, thus properly classified as narratives of "wisdom," a good judgment about how to survive and what risks to run.

VII

We may conclude with two sorts of observations. First, it is possible to draw up a grid that suggests that certain kinds of literature perform certain political functions for this community, with its acute self-consciousness as the people of YHWH mandated to live its public vision of faith in a world of real power.

The Torah (the five books from Genesis to Deuteronomy) provides the foundational account of faith in history, an account that is to be understood primarily as paradigm and not as "history" (Voegelin 1956; Neusner 1997). This paradigmatic account pivots on the Sinai tradition as the alternative public vision embraced by Israel (Crüsemann 1996: 57). This account accents the distinctiveness of Israel as a theological community grounded in the defining reality of the holy God who is creator of heaven and earth and lord of all the nations. Thus Israel's political vision and self-consciousness are rooted in a theological passion that in the first instant does not make great accommodations to political reality, paradigmatic as the account is.

The prophetic literature – including the "Former Prophets" (Joshua, Judges, Samuel, Kings) – maintains the life and speech of Israel as it seeks to enact its paradigmatic vision in the real world of "haves" and "have-nots," of imperial pressure and centralized authority. The preferred way of acting and telling in this rendering is confrontational; it is to be noticed, however, that this account of faith enacted in the real world of political economy is not romantic. It recognizes the inevitably mixed reality of public power on the ground, such that the culminating event of the entire process of Israel's testimony in the Old Testament is the destruction of Jerusalem and the seeming forfeiture of life with YHWH in the world. Thus the paradigm of Torah has a hard way in the "real world," where the paradigm of absolutism is uncritically taken as "reality." The

Book of Job is the quintessential expression of the "hard way" of this faith in the world (Gutiérrez 1987).

Second, in this traditioning process Israel of course knows full well about this dissonance between faith affirmed and life in the world (Carroll 1979). It is for this reason that we must recognize that politics in ancient Israel is essentially a rhetorical, interpretive process, deeply passionate and open-ended, which, by preference, seeks to legitimate an alternative way in the world in the face of the absolutizing rhetoric of Pharaoh (see Ezek. 28: 3). It is by its rhetoric that Israel keeps the invisible, often silent, YHWH at the center of its political imagination. It is by its rhetoric that Israel insists upon some political realities – the holiness of God and the significance of the neighbor – that have little credence in the imagination of the world. It is by rhetoric that Israel manages to keep the processes of power open when all of "the silencers," in an imagined absolutism, want to stop these poets and storytellers who claim to be uttering a word beyond their own word (Brueggemann 2001: 22–33). Rhetoric of this peculiar kind creates an alternative world of justice, mercy, peace, hope, and fidelity, all so unwelcome in every totalizing project. This "other world" is not privatized, it is not "spiritualized," and it is not magical.

In the end, moreover, these strange constitutive words are not about another world, even if we speak of an "alternative" world. They are rather about this same, already known world – uttered anew. In its daring utterances that reconstitute the world, Israel hopes and waits, obeys and dissents, always defiantly at the edge of the fiery furnaces of totalism, confident, and even when not confident, nonetheless defiant:

> O Nebuchadnezzar, we have no need to present a defense to you in this matter. If our God whom we serve is able to deliver us from the furnace of blazing fire and out of your hand, O king, let him deliver us. But if not, be it known to you, O king, that we will not serve your gods and we will not worship the golden statue that you have set up. (Dan. 3: 16–18)

Israel knows that Nebuchadnezzar (the latter-day counterpart to Pharaoh), in whatever guise, is penultimate.

As the contemporary church ponders and is led by these texts, its own vocation in the world becomes more clear and more radical. These texts empower the church *to imagine* an alternative political economy of covenant, *to practice* that alternative in its own life, and *to testify* to that alternative in the life of the world. Such a church that imagines, practices, and testifies alternatively may be a saving contradiction to the claims so powerful in the world.

References

Bright, J. (1959). *A History of Israel*. Philadelphia: Westminster.

Brueggemann, W. (1991). *Abiding Astonishment: Psalms, Modernity, and the Making of History*. Louisville, Ky: Westminster/John Knox.

Brueggemann, W. (1999). "The Liturgy of Abundance, the Myth of Scarcity." *Christian Century* 116, 342–7.

——(2000). "Always in the Shadow of the Empire." M. L. Budde and R. W. Brimlow (eds), *The Church as Counterculture*, 39–58. Albany, NY: State University of New York Press.

——(2001). "Voice as Counter to Violence." *Calvin Theological Journal* 36, 22–3.

——(forthcoming). "Theme Revisited: Bread Again!" In festschrift in honor of David Clines. Sheffield: Sheffield Academic Press.

Buber, M. (1946). *Moses*. Atlantic Highlands, NJ: Humanities Press International.

——(1990). *The Kingship of God*. Atlantic Highlands, NJ: Humanities Press International.

Carroll, R. P. (1979). *When Prophecy Failed: Reactions and Responses to Failure in the Old Testament Prophetic Traditions*. London: SCM.

Crüsemann, F. (1996). *The Torah: Theology and Social History of Old Testament Law*. Edinburgh: T. & T Clark.

Fretheim, T. E. (1991). "The Plagues as Ecological Signs of Historical Disaster." *Journal of Biblical Literature* 110, 385–96.

Gottwald, N. K. (1979). *The Tribes of Yahweh: A Sociology of the Religion of Liberated Israel, 1250–1050 BC*. Maryknoll, NY: Orbis.

Gutiérrez, Gustavo (1987). *On Job: God-Talk and the Suffering of the Innocent*. Maryknoll, NY: Orbis.

Hamilton, Jeffries M. (1992). *Social Justice and Deuteronomy: The Case of Deuteronomy 15* (SBL Dissertation Series). Atlanta: Scholars Press.

Humphreys, W. Lee (1973). "A Lifestyle for Diaspora: A Study of the Tales of Esther and Daniel." *Journal of Biblical Literature* 92, 211–23.

Mendenhall, George E. (2001). *Ancient Israel's Faith and History: An Introduction to the Bible in Context*, ed. Gary A. Herion. Louisville, Ky.: Westminster John Knox.

Miller, Patrick D., Jr., *The Divine Warrior in Early Israel* (Harvard Semitic Monographs 5). Cambridge, Mass.: Harvard University Press.

Neusner, Jacob (1997). "Paradigmatic versus Historical Thinking: The Case of Rabbinic Judaism." *History and Theory* 36, 353–77.

Premnath, D. N. (1988). "Latfundialization and Isaiah 5: 8–10." *Journal for the Study of the Old Testament* 40, 49–60.

Scott, James C. (1985). *Weapons of the Weak: Everyday Forms of Peasant Resistance*. New Haven: Yale University Press.

——(1990). *Domination and the Arts of Resistance: Hidden Transcripts*. New Haven: Yale University Press.

Seitz, C. R. (1989). *Theology in Conflict: Reactions to the Exile in the Book of Jeremiah*. New York: De Gruyter.

Smith, D. L. (1989). *The Religion of the Landless: The Social Context of the Babylonian Exile*. Indianapolis: Meyer Stone.

Voegelin, E. (1956). *Order and History*, vol. 1: *Israel and Revelation*. Baton Rouge: Louisiana State University Press.

Weinberg, J. (1992). *The Citizen–Temple Community*. Sheffield: JSOT [*Journal for the Study of the Old Testament*] Press.

Wilson, R. R. (1980). *Prophecy and Society in Ancient Israel*. Philadelphia: Fortress.

Wolff, H. W. (1987). "Micah the Moreshite: The Prophet and his Background." In J. Gammie (ed.), *Israelite Wisdom: Theological and Literary Essays in Honor of Samuel Terrien*, 77–84. Missoula: Scholars Press.

CHAPTER 2

Scripture: New Testament

Christopher Rowland

Those who go to the Bible expecting an unambiguous message on the issue of politics need to recall William Blake's witty aphorism: "Both read the Bible day and night / But thou readst black where I read white" (*The Everlasting Gospel*, 1808). That is a salutary reminder to anyone embarking on a consideration of "what the Bible says" on any subject (Barr 1980). In different social and historical contexts, different texts have been used. Thus, with the emergence of Christendom after the conversion of Constantine, an understanding of Christian polity became more tied up with the task of Christianizing society. There was a corresponding diminution of the stark contrast between God and Caesar in history and political arrangements which had applied before the fourth century. Charting these two perspectives would involve describing the complex oscillations between accommodation and separation, between God and Caesar. Different texts have been used to justify these positions. An "accommodationist" position would tend to focus on Romans 13 and read the gospels in the light of that text, as was done, for example in the Alternative Service Book (1980) of the Church of England, in the readings for Pentecost 15. A stark contrast appears between the "accommodationist" and "separatist" positions if one reads the New Testament through the lens of the Apocalypse and gives primacy to the teaching and example of Jesus, who fell foul of the colonial power. Accommodation and separatism are nowhere better seen than in the sixteenth century in the contrasting use of scripture by the magisterial reformers and the early Anabaptists.

Rather than going straight to the biblical texts (cf. O'Donovan 1996), therefore, a context for the interpretation of the contours of an emerging Christian politics in the pages of the New Testament will be suggested here on the basis of early Christian practice, as far as it can be reconstructed from pre-Constantinian sources. The reason for taking this approach is that such early Christian practice is the major witness to the ways in which the scriptures were interpreted. A characteristic strand of that early practice expresses itself in a continuing interplay between "contraries": difference from the surrounding order and living within it; continuity with the Jewish tradition and yet radical departure from it; and the tension between the reality of the continuity of this age and the taste of the age to come.

This will be followed by a much later writer's interpretation of key New Testament texts. The choice of John Milton's treatise on *The Tenure of Kings and Magistrates* is not arbitrary. First, it was written in a situation in which there was the widest divide between the divine and the human kingdoms. As such, it offers an example of biblical interpretation which echoes the sentiments of pre-Constantinian Christianity. Second, Milton offers examples of the interpretation of key Christian texts such as Matt. 22: 15–22 and Rom. 13. 1–10 as part of his argument against those who would claim scriptural authority for a view of human society in which the divine monarch is replicated in human affairs. Milton's text, therefore, offers an opportunity to watch an interpreter at work in a clearly understood context; and a context, moreover, that has a close analogy with the situation of pre-Constantinian Christianity. In the light of the sketch of the interpretive context of earliest Christianity, with its clear prioritization of obedience to God rather than Caesar in private and public life, and a consideration of the scriptures which stresses the critical difference between the divine and human polities, we will consider the Gospel accounts of Jesus' prophetic proclamation of God's kingdom and the ethical challenge it presented to early Christians, and the indications of their engagement with that challenge.

Both pre-Constantinian Christianity and Milton's *Tenure of Kings and Magistrates* exemplify the stark contrast between God's kingdom and the kingdoms of this world which is characteristic of so much of the New Testament. The contrast between this age and the age to come, the present and the future, and between what is and what should be, is a thread which runs through the New Testament and which gives that collection of writings its peculiar theological power. Such a conviction lies at the heart of Christian belief and accentuates the qualitative difference between present and future downplaying the sufficiency of all present political arrangements. This tension, or dialectic, in various forms has been characteristic of Christian political theology down the centuries.

Pre-Constantinian Christianity's Emerging Political Identity

Despite the different strands in scripture, the position taken in this essay is that the main elements of Christian identity, as exemplified in what we can discover about the practice of pre-Constantinian Christianity, and recalled and practiced by minorities within the Christian churches down the centuries, are nonconformist and based on the principle that "we must obey God rather than any human authority" (Acts 5: 29; and see further Bradstock and Rowland 2001). The subversive character of the nascent Christian movement was early recognized by outsiders who, hearing that Christians were proclaiming "another Jesus" and acting against the decrees of Caesar, accused them of "turning the world upside down" (Acts 17: 6; see Hill 1972).

Emerging Christianity before the fourth century CE was characterized by such a counter-cultural, even sectarian, spirit. At the heart of the baptismal experience was the clear message of a transfer from one dominion to another, involving the acceptance of Jesus Christ as king of kings and lord of lords. What is so striking about the New Testament texts is that they were written by people who had little or no political power, with a vision of the world which was at odds with the prevailing ideology. The many indications of impatience with the status quo suggest that they propounded and expected a different kind of understanding of and way of living in the world. Not drawn from one particular race or background, Christians were a different sort of people, committed to a different kind of life and culture, more often than not (until the time of Constantine) at odds with the wisdom and politics of the age. Once it became the religion of the rulers, its inclusive rhetoric could easily be used to serve rather different ends. The radical slogan of Galatians 3: 28, "There is neither Jew nor Greek, slave nor free, male nor female," has a rather different ring when uttered to serve as the "social glue" of an inclusive, cosmopolitan and eventually fragmenting empire.

The emerging pattern of existence in early Christianity, diverse though it undoubtedly was, is characterized by the martyr spirit (in the strict sense of the word). That is not to say that persecution was widespread, but difference and the distinctiveness of lifestyle and practice were. The acts of the Christian martyrs (Musurillo 1972; Lane Fox 1986; Boyarin 1999) are testimony to this distinctiveness, and it was a pattern which was basic to later exemplifications of Christian minorities. Politically, these were people who were not neatly integrated into Greco-Roman society. Because of their allegiance to Jesus, the early Christians were known as members of a superstition, a deviation from the norms of accepted behavior. The New Testament is the collection of documents of a marginal group. Joining the Christian community meant conversion to a position in society which was at odds with its values, nowhere better exemplified than in the conversion accounts in Justin Martyr (First Apology 14) and Cyprian (First Letter to Donatus 3; Kreider 1995). From the position of discomfort, persecution, oppression and minority status throughout history, Christian people have found that biblical texts have resonated with their lives and led them to positions at odds with society. In the face of growing accommodation between the values of God and Caesar, monastic asceticism made its appearance in the desert of Egypt. Originally a hermit-like existence, it evolved into communities of heaven on earth. This way of life threw into the sharpest possible relief the growing worldliness of the churches. There was an emphasis on manual work alternating with prayer and reflection. The solitary voices in the wilderness grew into an integral part of church and society, prompting their own renewal movements in the later Middle Ages pioneered by people like Bernard of Clairvaux and Francis of Assisi, who in their turn sought to recapture the original vision of Jesus and exemplify its political character in communities of perfection (Garnsey and Humfress 2001; Lane Fox 1987; Rousseau Pachomius 1985; Kreider 2001).

The roots of this alternative, counter-cultural, political identity are fundamental for interpreting Christianity's foundation documents as they would have been understood by the Christians of the first centuries. Baptismal liturgies stressed the different character of the citizenship involved in being a member of this new "race." It meant deliverance from the demonic world which controlled the values of the world at large, values which Christians deemed antithetical to human flourishing (Justin First Apology 14). The catechumenate and baptism were part of a process of inculturation into a very different political culture. Paul sketches it in Romans 12, writing of the renewal of the mind and the offering of living sacrifices. For some this was literally true, as the martyr narratives testify. Martyrdom, however, was not extraordinary but at the end of a continuum which saw Christians engaged in a public demonstration of a different political ethos, in which Christ, not Caesar, was Lord (Phil. 2; Rev. 19: 16). That alternative political practice was supported by practical and administrative arrangements manifested in networks of communication and mutual support. The latter in particular embodied an alternative polity which could be seen at the local level (Justin Apology I 65–7) and internationally (Paul's collection for the poor in Jerusalem being the earliest and most remarkable example of this, e.g. Rom. 15: 25; 2 Cor. 8–9).

The Contrast between God and Caesar: John Milton's *The Tenure of Kings and Magistrates* (1649)

In a situation where human monarchy had become so flawed that it had to be resisted and removed in the search for a better kingdom, John Milton (1608–74) explains the extraordinary events of 1649 which saw the execution of the English monarch. Writing at this time of upheaval, Milton rejected the royalists' interpretation of certain biblical passages as a defense of human monarchy and its oppressive consequences. Milton is one of the foremost advocates of an understanding of Christian politics which reflects those radical, nonconformist instincts. He began writing *The Tenure of Kings and Magistrates* (Dzelzainis 1991) during King Charles's trial but completed and published it after his execution. It is a text which is explicitly contextual and, as such, differs in several key respects from the line taken by some of Milton's radical contemporaries like Lilburne and Winstanley. Milton argues the case for the right to execute a tyrant, but also the more radical case for popular sovereignty based on an original social and governmental compact that ensures the people's right to choose and change their governments as they see fit. It is a manifesto of those who value religious liberty and a "free commonwealth" without monarchy or aristocracy. Milton was one of the foremost apologists of nonconformity. In *The Tenure of Kings and Magistrates* we find passages from the Hebrew Bible treated to support the biblical attitude to monarchy, which is then taken further with an examination of famous passages connected with Christianity and royal power (Matt. 22 and Rom. 13: 1 ff.). The work offers a thoroughgoing interaction with major scripture passages which may often be mentioned in passing in other radical or reformist writings, and to which interpreters return again and again down the centuries (Dzelzainis 1991).

In his consideration of Matt. 17: 24–7, Milton points to the fact that if, on the authority of Christ, Peter was a child of God, and therefore free, so also are contemporary Christians and citizens. Turning to Matt. 22: 16–21, he points to Christ's response: To ask for the coin and ask whose image is thereon. The image becomes the basis for a defense of human dignity and the basis of prime responsibility to God:

> if upon beholding the face and countenance of a man, someone would ask whose image is that, would not any one freely reply that it was God's. Since then we belong to God, that is we are truly free, and on that account to be rendered to God alone, surely we cannot, without sin and in fact the greatest sacrilege, hand ourselves over in slavery to Caesar, that is to a man, and especially one who is unjust, wicked and tyrannical?

In similar vein Milton interprets the concluding saying of Jesus as a summons to humanity to recognize the limits of their obligation:

> Render to Caesar the things that are Caesar's, and the things that are God's to God. . . . who does not know that those things which belong to the people should be given back to the people? So not all things are Caesar's. Our liberty is not Caesar's, but is a birthday gift from God. To give back to any Caesar what we did not receive from him would be the most base and unworthy of the origin of man.

Like some modern commentators, Milton demands that we take seriously the context in which the question about the payment of taxes to Caesar was asked (especially Luke 20: 20). Christ wanted not so much to remind us "so obscurely and ambiguously of our duty towards kings or Caesars, as to prove the wickedness and malice of the hypocritical Pharisees."

In contrast to the Israelites who kept – like all the nations – asking for a king, Christ had demanded something different: "you know the princes of the nations are rulers over them" (Matt. 20: 25–7). So that Christian people should not ask for a ruler, like the other nations, Christ warned, "among you it will not be so." There will not be "this proud rule of kings." There is to be none of the "spin" of the "great and the good" who "are called by the plausible title of Benefactors." Milton here draws on the variant version of the saying in Luke, possibly addressed to a community where there was a putative elite: "whoever wishes to become great among you (and who is greater than a prince?) let him be your attendant; and whoever wishes to be first or prince let him be your slave" (Luke 22: 25; Wengst 1985: 103). A Christian king, therefore, is the servant of the people: "But a king will either be no Christian at all, or will be the slave of all. If he clearly wants to be a master, he cannot at the same time be a Christian."

Addressing at 1 Pet. 2: 13–15 the most explicit summons to subordination in the New Testament, Milton stresses the importance of taking the context of the apostle's advice seriously: "Peter wrote this not only for private persons, but also for the strangers [1 Peter 1.1 f.] who were scattered and dispersed throughout most of Asia Minor, who in those places where they were living had no right except that of hospitality." He demands consideration of the root meaning of the verb "be subject." King and governor are appointed by God to punish wrong-doers and praise those who act well, which is the will of God. The basis for this precept is given in 1 Pet. 2: 16: one does this "as free men" – therefore not as slaves. Monarchy and government in their various particulars are said to be human insti-tutions. So if rulers rule with torture and destruction of the good, and praise and reward of wrongdoers, human power should be used to appoint what is good and advantageous for men and women, and remove what is bad and destructive.

Similarly, when he considers Romans 13, Milton refuses to allow that Paul is setting Nero or any other tyrant above all law and punishment. Milton attends to context and points to the difficult situation at the time of writing: "At that time there spread about people's gossip exposing the apostles as rebels and insurrec-tionists, as if they did and said everything to overthrow the common law." The time of writing of Romans reflects a more ordered and just period of governance either under Claudius or the early years of Nero, which were not tyrannical. God prescribes the establishment of magistrates, but the precise form of the gover-nance is a human creation. Such human, political arrangements of God's ordi-nance for order in society will be faulty because they are from men or even the devil. According to Milton, something that is faulty and disorderly cannot be ordained by God. Without magistracy no human life can exist; but if any mag-istracy acts in a fashion contrary to one who supports the good, it cannot be properly ordained by God. In that situation subjection is not demanded, and sen-sible resistance may be contemplated, "for we will not be resisting the power of a magistrate but a robber, a tyrant or an enemy." Subjection is not required in every circumstance, therefore, "but only with the addition of a reason, the reason which is added will be the true rule of our subjection: when we are not subjects under that reason, we are rebels; when we are subjects without that reason, we are slaves and cowards."

In the approaches he takes to the New Testament passages Milton anticipates more recent interpreters (Belo 1981; Clevenot 1985; Wengst 1985), including the authors of the *Kairos Document* (1985), a biblical and theological comment on the political crisis in apartheid South Africa. The authors of the *Kairos Doc-ument* reject the idea that Paul presents an absolute doctrine about the state, and argue that the text must be interpreted in its context, which was a situation in which some Christians believed that they were freed from obeying the state because Christ alone was their king (in other words, they were anarchists). Paul insists on the necessity of some kind of state, but that does not mean that all the state does is approved of by God. When a state does not obey the law of

God and becomes a servant of Satan, it is passages like Rev. 13 to which one should turn instead.

The Four Gospels: Jesus, Prophet and Embodiment of the Kingdom of God

According to Mark's Gospel, Jesus of Nazareth preached the reign of God and thus oriented his heaven to that alternative horizon which Jewish eschatological hopes had kept in view (as is evident from texts like 4Q 521 from the Dead Sea Scrolls; see Vermes 1995: 244). Present political and social arrangements were not the norm, therefore. The imminent arrival of the messianic age heralded new priorities and broadened horizons (Luke 4: 16; Matt. 11: 2 ff.). Political authority in Jerusalem was in fact wielded by the priestly aristocracy and the Judean ruling class. The fact that the challenge is against this group rather than the Romans is merely indicative of the locus of political power. In the Gospel of Mark, Jesus challenges a culture of status and customary practice and institutions. In 10: 42 the disciples want to sit and rule, but are offered only baptism and a cup of suffering.

God's kingdom was the major theme of Jesus' proclamation, exemplified in acts of power and compassion to the disadvantaged and in riddling challenges to hearers through the parables. The frequent designation of him by his followers as Messiah, the anointed and expected king who would bring peace, prosperity, and justice as heralded by the prophecy of Isaiah (Isa. 11), continued that biblical tradition. Despite the attachment to David and the dynasty, exemplified in Psalms 89 and 132, there is throughout the scriptures an ambivalence towards monarchy. On occasion this can take the form of antimonarchical sentiments (1 Sam. 8). In the books of Kings the activities of the Davidic dynasty are a catalogue of misdeeds and iniquity which ultimately puts the whole dynasty in jeopardy. The Torah hardly contemplates monarchy with equanimity (Deut. 17: 14 ff.). Its vision of society is of a community which, if not exactly egalitarian, works according to a vision of social intercourse in which injustice is corrected, whether through the cancellation of debts (Deut. 15) or the Jubilee (Lev. 25, though even here the exigencies of the "real world" demand some kind of dilution of the ideal). Monarchy involved military power and the oppression of the people in the name of expansion, a fact of life in Solomon's reign, ruefully reflected in the law of the king in Deuteronomy 17. It demanded centralization, achieved in the reign of David and Solomon by the creation of a new capital at the Jebusite city of Jerusalem. That center was given ideological justification when the portable ark was sited there and, under Solomon, a temple built to house it and act as a demonstrable sight of God's presence with Israel.

The prophets criticized the distortions of the understanding of divine righteousness. The outsiders Amos and Jeremiah paid the penalty for their contumacious condemnation of false prophecy and of the complacent delusions of grandeur and safety which religion gave to the political establishment in Jerusalem. Israel's reflection on its God and its politics involved recognition that settlement in the land was a mixed blessing. Not only is there nostalgia for the time before arrival in the Promised Land (Hosea) but there is also a frank recognition that settlement meant accommodation with a very different culture, the culture of Canaan, which was an expression of the aspirations of a settled, rather than migrant, people with a severely puritanical culture. The prophets cut isolated figures (e.g. 1 Kgs. 18; Isa. 20), protesting against the dominant thrust of their nation's life, particularly its idolatry and departure from the norms of social justice as set out in the ancestral traditions. The prophets are true radicals, objecting to the modernizing tendencies of their day, the compromises with the lifestyle and values of the surrounding culture, and looking back to the roots of the nation's life (e.g. Hosea 2: 14).

In his words about the kingdom of God or kingdom of heaven, Jesus never offers his hearers a detailed description of it. Instead, he uses stories and sayings to prompt hearers (and also the later readers of his sayings in the Gospels) to think and behave differently, to repent and believe in the good news of the kingdom of God (Mark 1: 15). The Gospels are full of challenges to conventional wisdom about monarchy. Jesus is presented as a humble king (Matt. 21: 5), in contrast with Herod who is no true king of the Jews (2: 2). Herod slaughters the innocents (2: 16ff.), whereas the true king reacts positively to children (18: 2; 19: 14; 20: 31). Those who are pronounced blessed share the characteristics of this humble king (5: 3ff.), who engaged in acts of compassion and healing which affect crowds rather than leaders (9: 36; 14: 14; 15: 32). Final judgement (25: 31 ff.) is based on response to the hidden Son of Man in the destitute lot of his brethren (cf. 7: 21 ff; 10: 42 f.), who will be revealed as in some sense identified with "the least" at the moment of "apocalypse" on the Last Day.

In the Gospel of John, Jesus articulates a redefined understanding of kingship. This king is one who washes his disciples' feet. Jesus' reply to Pilate, "My kingdom is not of this world," is not a statement about the location of God's kingdom but concerns the origin of the inspiration for Jesus' view of the kingdom. Its norms are the result of God's spirit and righteousness. It is otherworldly only in the sense that it is wrong to suppose that the definition of kingship and kingdom is to be found in conventional regal persons and practice.

John the Baptist and Jesus, however, were both hailed as figures in the tradition of the prophets (Matt. 16: 17f., 23: 26ff.). Indeed, John was seen as an embodiment of Elijah's own person (Luke 1: 76; Matt. 11: 13). Like their contemporaries who suffered at the hands of the colonial power (e.g. Josephus, Jewish War vi. 281ff. and 301ff.; Antiquities xviii. 55ff.; xx. 97ff., 167ff., 185ff.; Goodman 1987; Gray 1993), they were thorns in the flesh of those in power. John, according to the Jewish writer Josephus, was suspected of fomenting revolution (Antiquities xviii. 116f.), and that seems to have been the attitude toward Jesus on the part of the hierarchy in Jerusalem, who feared Roman reprisals if Jesus were allowed to go on behaving as he was (John 11: 49). Indeed, in Mark's Gospel Jesus' action in the temple was the last straw which persuaded the authorities to assassinate him. Prophecy is no mere ecclesial office offering occasional admonition or pious platitudes. Like Jeremiah, the prophet must utter prophecies over many "nations, races, languages and kings" (Rev. 10: 11; cf. Jer. 1: 10) and be prepared to pay the price of so doing (Rev. 11: 7; cf. Mark 13: 9 ff.). It is not a specialist vocation, but that to which the church as a whole is called (Bauckham 1993). The continuation of that prophetic task is a central part of the life of the church whose role, like that of Jeremiah and John of Patmos, is to prophesy about many peoples and nations, and to discern the beast and the Babylon in the midst of inhumane actions (whether that be trade or economic life in general) which afflict human lives (Rev. 18: 13; and see further O'Donovan 1996: 11, 62 ff.).

To claim that the New Testament offers complete homogeneity in the way in which God and Caesar interrelate would be to ignore many contradictory strands. These are well represented in Luke–Acts. Familiar passages in Luke's Gospel suggest a different perspective from the conventional: the insignificant Mary and Jesus' birth in obscurity; John's social teaching (3: 10 ff.); the anointing by the prostitute (7: 36 ff.; cf. Mark 14: 3 ff.); the women followers and supporters (8: 2 f.; 13: 10; 23: 27; 23: 49, 55); Samaritans (10: 25 ff.; 17: 11); the concern with the "prodigals" (15: 1 ff.) – all these in different ways "flesh out" the manifesto which Luke's Jesus offers (once again peculiar to this Gospel) in 4: 16. On the other hand, other texts in Luke offer a rather different slant. For example, Luke's version of the Last Supper includes sayings of Jesus at this point, some of which have parallels in other Gospels. One in particular is instructive. In their teaching on discipleship, Mark and Luke respectively have Jesus telling his disciples:

Mark	Luke
You know that among the gentiles the recognized rulers lord it over their subjects, and the great make their authority felt. It shall not be so among you; among you, whoever wants to be great must be your servant, and whoever wants to be first must be the slave of all. For the son of man did not come to be served but to serve, and to give his life a ransom for many.	Among the gentiles kings lord it over their subjects, and those in authority are given the title Benefactor. Not so with you: on the contrary, the greatest among you must bear himself like the youngest, the one who rules like one who serves. For who is greater – the one who sits at table or the servant who waits upon him? Surely the one who sits at table. Yet I am among you like a servant.

A comparison of these two passages reveals that Mark has a general "whoever wants to be first" whereas Luke has "the greatest" and "the one who rules." It has plausibly been suggested that unlike in Mark's community, Luke knew that the Christians he was addressing included persons of relatively high standing in society. No longer does the Christian community consist of the poor Jewish

Christians to whom Paul's churches sent their money and support. As in the church in Corinth there were some, perhaps even a significant number, alongside those who were not powerful or of noble birth, who needed to understand their responsibilities as disciples of one who came to preach good news to the poor.

Elsewhere, there are nods in the direction of accommodation, particularly in Acts. Ananias' and Sapphira's sin is deceiving the Holy Spirit rather than refusal to share their property, perhaps a tacit move away from the practice of the earliest church in Jerusalem. Zacchaeus does not have to sell all his goods. The ambiguity is nowhere more evident than in Luke 16, where the utter repudiation of Mammon and the disparagement of Dives sit uneasily with assertions that one has to use the Mammon of unrighteousness in order to be considered worthy of heaven. According to Acts 10, the account of Cornelius' conversion leaves open the question of the character of life of the newly converted gentile soldier – quite a remarkable omission, given that in the following century there was widespread doubt about whether a Christian should sign up for military service (Hornus 1980). Luke–Acts was probably written to churches that were relatively affluent. They had tasted of the good news of justification by faith and life in the Spirit, and needed to be reminded that there was more to faith than mere religion; and, most important of all, Luke wanted them to take seriously "the option for the poor" (Esler 1986).

"It shall not be so with you": Life in Jerusalem and Babylon

The most uncompromising rejection of the exercise of state power and accommodation with its culture in the New Testament is to be found in the book of Revelation. Its clearly enunciated choice between the Beast and Christ, and Jerusalem and Babylon, represent the character of the early Christian political ethos. The challenge to the complacent, and the word of encouragement to the hard-pressed, stand side by side in a book which unmasks the reality of power and the fallibility of human benevolence. In many ways it offers one of the most penetrating accounts of the church's relationship to the state, and in so doing offers a pungent warning to the kind of cosy accommodation into which churches have allowed themselves to slide. In its stark contrast between the Lamb and the Beast, between the Bride, New Jerusalem, and Babylon, it juxtaposes the choices facing men and women and reminds followers of the Lamb of the dangers of becoming entangled in a political system based on a completely different set of values. What is particularly disturbing is the ruthless questioning of the motives behind the benevolence of the powerful. The deceit that snares practitioners and gullible recipients alike is frightening. The remedy is simple. It involves an exodus and a resistance to joining in life as usual, because that means complicity with the culture of Babylon. One must refuse to join in, choose to contradict, resist, and prophesy against the way the world is ordered. Christian life according to the Apocalypse means embracing the role of the outsider (Wengst 1985; Rowland 1998).

It is in the light of this analysis that we should view the two texts which have become the bedrock of discussions of Christianity and politics: Mark 12: 13–17 (and parallels) and Romans 13. With regard to the former, as Milton correctly pointed out, the context of the saying is one where Jesus is being put to the test by his opponents. This is especially clear in the introduction to Luke's version: "so they watched Jesus and sent spies who pretended to be honest, in order to trap him by what he said, so as to hand him over to the jurisdiction and authority of the governor" (Luke 20: 20; cf. 23: 2). It is no surprise that Jesus gives an ambiguous ruling. In a situation which demanded circumspection, Jesus offered an enigmatic riddle in a situation where he had been put in a tight corner by his opponents. It is a politically acute answer with which those who have found themselves in similar tight corners would readily identify. It exemplifies the kinds of strategy which those in situations of subjugation articulate: the gesture; the coded response; and the witty aphorism which avoids giving offense. Dominated people do not always comply, and even when they mouth the acceptable words favored by the powerful, manage to subvert their apparent compliance with it (Scott 1985; Boyarin 1999: 44–6).

With regard to Romans 13, any interpretation must begin with the preceding chapter, in which Paul offers an outline of Christian polity centering on the renewal of the mind and the demonstration of this change in lives lived sacrificially. This is the norm for what is good and how the good may be achieved. Paul's expectation of Christ's coming and his lordship, expressed throughout the letters, is the necessary context within which the permanence and rightness of any political regime, however enlightened, should be judged. Like Daniel in the court of Nebuchadnezzar, Paul accepts that God has a time and season for every power. The principalities and powers to whom Christians are urged to be subject are part of Christ's triumphal procession (Col. 2: 14). The public demonstration of the way of the Messiah, however, is still to come, "when God will be all in all" (1 Cor. 15: 25). What is offered in Romans 13 is advice for the interim, and a goal for the powers to implement if they would reflect the goodness of God. Insofar as they fail to do this, or interpret the good as what serves their own interests, they undermine the obligation laid upon those in subjection, so carefully enunciated in these verses. Insofar as most political regimes fall short of the goodness of God, subservience and acquiescence are bound to be heavily qualified, as Milton rightly perceived ("an evil and faulty thing, since it is disorderly, cannot possibly be ordained"). Where the early Christian writings part company with Milton, however, is that Daniel, Paul, and the Christian martyrs do not contemplate their witness to the ways of Christ leading them to armed revolt, but instead to the burning fiery furnace or the arena, where the public, political, demonstration of "the better way" would be offered to probably incredulous spectators.

Conclusion

One can look at the pages of the New Testament and find in the synoptic Gospels, the letter of James and the book of Revelation that indomitable, uncompromising spirit which set itself against the values of the present age. Such clear-cut counter-cultural strands are, as has already been suggested, a common feature of early Christian texts. Yet, as the Pauline letters indicate, the new converts, particularly those in the urban environment of the cities of the Empire, had to learn a degree of accommodation with the world as it was, without, somehow, abandoning the stark call to discipleship of the teacher from Nazareth. What is remarkable about the letters of Paul, however, is the way in which this Christian activist maintained the counter-cultural identity of these isolated groups by his traveling and writing. The strange thing about Paul is that the energetic innovator and founder of the gentile church should have been the one who above all sowed the seeds of the accept-ability of the world order as it is and passivity toward it. Nevertheless, as a recent study has reminded us, there is at the heart of this emerging Christian church a distinctive identity in which elite goods and privileges (wealth, power, holiness, and knowledge) ceased merely to be the prerogative of an elite and came to be accessible to all within the common life of the Christian communi-ties (Theissen 1999: 81–118). It comes as no surprise, therefore, that in the history of Christianity many have often looked to the radical Paul as a basis for appeals for change, as the examples of Augustine, Martin Luther, and Karl Barth indicate.

Tensions certainly exist both among the New Testament documents, and, in the case of some writings, within the same document. Such a tension between what was politically and theologically possible and what needed to be held on to, to be heeded whenever possible within the severe constraints posed by historical circumstances, is part of the story of Christian radicalism. Some were more inventive than others in the ways in which they dealt with this conundrum. There were martyrs who brooked no compromise, or found there was no alter-native but to die for their faith. But there were those who sought the freedom within the status quo to pursue their goals. In many ways their ingenuity and their knack for survival bespeaks of that same divine spark that kept the faith alive in the early years of the Christian church. Such were the ways to maintain the commitment to Christ's kingdom in the midst of the political and economic order of an age which demanded compromise.

The picture we have of early Christianity from the sources is a "sectarian" picture which sits uncomfortably with all that we hold dear. From the position of discomfort, persecution, oppression, and minority status, Christian people found that the Bible resonated with their lives. For all their protestations of loyalty to the emperor, they refused to conform to the demands of empire. For them there was another king: Jesus. They looked forward to the time when to him every knee would bow. There could be no compromise between God and

Caesar. Allegiance to the resurrected Christ meant that in any conflict of loyalty the nation-state had to take second place to the pearl of great price which those who confessed Jesus as Lord had discovered.

The eschatological hope of God's kingdom on earth which is such a dominant thread in New Testament theology cannot allow any easy accommodation between the church, the community of those called to bear witness to the reign of God, and political powers. While still living in an age which is passing away, the church is bound to have to make choices about its involvement and participation, based on its assessment of the extent to which, in whole and in part, the kingdoms of this world manifest the way of the Messiah. This is a complicated process in which one might expect significant differences of opinion. But when that wrestling with the issues is carried out in a situation where integration into a political system is a continuing datum, the chances of critical awareness are dramatically diminished and the dangers of being used to baptize social, political and economic systems which are far from reflecting the righteousness of God are increased.

The contrast between Caesar and Christ pervaded early Christian discourse. Thus when Polycarp was brought before the local governor, he refused to swear an oath to the emperor, or burn a pinch of incense to Caesar. In the legends surrounding his death the crowds condemned him as the "destroyer of our gods, who is teaching the whole multitudes to abstain from sacrificing to them or worshipping them" (Martyrdom of Polycarp 10–12). A neutral, apparently secular, action is an event of supreme importance in the eyes of God. The redemptive moment means siding with the Lamb at the moment of testimony, and standing firm in one's convictions and commitment to the horizon of hope symbolized by the Lamb who bears the marks of slaughter. In this respect John's apocalyptic vision is typical of early Christian political understanding. It offers hope to those who stand firm against the insidious blandishments of a decaying culture. The Apocalypse reminds readers of the ultimate character of apparently harmless actions. The odd bit of compromise with the old order is nothing less than being marked by the Beast. All action, however small, is ultimately significant and of infinite value in the divine economy.

In the ordinary situations of life in the present there exist a challenge, a threat, and an opportunity to discover the hidden life of God. The scriptures mix the mundane and the heavenly to convey the deeper character of what it is they seek to communicate. We see this most clearly in Matt. 25: 31 ff., with the subtle relationship between the eschatological judge and his hidden presence in the least of his "brethren" in the midst of the present age: the consequence for final judgment is now being gestated in the womb of history. This is true of the Bible as a whole. All of life is an issue for the religious person, from eating to buying, words and deeds as well as what is narrowly regarded as worship. There is no area of existence which is neutral and unaffected by religious significance. This link between the public and the private, the spiritual and political, which Christianity inherited from Judaism has become a central element of catholic Christianity down the centuries.

Select Bibliography

Barr, J. (1980). "The Bible as a Political Document." In *The Scope and Authority of the Bible: Explorations in Theology 7*, 91–110. London: SCM.

Bauckham, R. (1993). *The Theology of the Book of Revelation*. Cambridge: Cambridge University Press.

Belo, F. (1981). *A Materialist Reading of the Gospel of Mark*. Maryknoll, NY: Orbis.

Bradstock, A., and Rowland, C. (2001). *Radical Christian Writings: A Reader*. Oxford: Blackwell.

Boyarin, D. (1999). *Dying for God: Martyrdom and the Making of Christianity and Judaism*. Stanford: Stanford University Press.

Clevenot, M. (1985). *Materialist Approaches to the Bible*. Maryknoll, NY: Orbis.

Dzelzainis, M. (1991). *John Milton: Political Writings*. Cambridge: Cambridge University Press.

Esler, P. L. (1986). *Community and Gospel in Luke–Acts*. Cambridge: Cambridge University Press.

Garnsey, P., and Humfress, C. (2001). *The Evolution of the Late Antique World*. Cambridge: Orchard.

Goodman, M. (1987). *The Ruling Class of Judaea*. Cambridge: Cambridge University Press.

Gray, R. (1993). *Prophetic Figures in Late Second Temple Jewish Palestine*. Oxford: Clarendon.

Hill, C. (1972). *The World Turned Upside Down*. Harmondsworth: Penguin.

Hornus, M. (1980). *It is Not Lawful for Me To Fight*. Scottdale, Pa.: Herald.

Kairos Document (1985). *Challenge to the Church: A Theological Comment on the Political Crisis in South Africa*. London: Catholic Institute for International Relations.

Kreider, A. (1995). *Worship and Evangelism in Pre-Christendom*. Cambridge: Grove.

—— (2001). *The Origins of Christendom in the West*. Edinburgh: T. & T. Clark.

Lane Fox, R. (1987). *Pagans and Christians*. Harmondsworth: Penguin.

Musurillo, H. (1972). *The Acts of the Christian Martyrs*. Oxford: Clarendon.

O'Donovan, O. (1996). *The Desire of the Nations*. Cambridge: Cambridge University Press.

Rousseau Pachomius, P. R. (1985). *The Making of a Community in Fourth Century Egypt*. Berkeley: University of California Press.

Rensberger, D. (1988). *Overcoming the World*. London: SPCK.

Rowland, C. (1998). *The Book of Revelation: New Interpreter's Bible*, vol. XII. Nashville: Abingdon.

Scott, J. C. (1985). *Domination and the Arts of Resistance: Hidden Transcripts*. New Haven: Yale University Press.

Theissen, G. (1999). *A Theory of Primitive Christian Religion*. London: SCM.

Vermes, G. (1995). *The Dead Sea Scrolls in English*, rev. and ext. 4th edn. Harmondsworth: Penguin.

Wengst, K. (1985). Pax Romana and the Peace of Jesus Christ. London: SCM.

CHAPTER 3

Augustine

Jean Bethke Elshtain

The fate of St. Augustine in the world of political theology has been mixed. He is a thinker of great discursive power who favors powerful narration over deductive systematicity. What is "political" about his theology must, for the most part, be teased out. He never penned a specific treatise on the subject. Despite this, it is fair to say that more words have been spilled on figuring out what an Augustinian political theology is, or might be, than on the tomes of other, more explicit, political theologies. There are particular features to St. Augustine's work that make him a tough nut to crack. From the time of his conversion to Catholic Christianity in 386 to his death as Bishop of Hippo in 430, Augustine wrote some 117 books. He touches on all the central themes of Christian theology and Christian life: the nature of God and human persons, the problem of evil, free will and determinism, war and human aggression, the bases of social life and political order, church doctrine, Christian vocations: the list is nigh endless.

Although a number of his works follow an argumentative line in the manner most often favored by those who write political treatises, especially so given the distinctly juridical or legalistic cast of so much modern political theory and political theology, most often he paints bold strokes on a broad canvas. His enterprise is at once theological, philosophical, historical, cultural, and rhetorical. His works are characterized by an extraordinarily rich surface as well as vast depth, making it difficult to get a handle on if one's own purposes are not so ambitious. He traffics in what we generally call "universals," but he is also a nuanced "particularist" and historicist.

Given this towering enterprise it is, perhaps, unsurprising that attempts have been made to reduce Augustine to manageable size. To that end he has been tagged a political realist and canonized, if you will, as the theological grandfather of a school of thought called "Christian realism" but, as well, of a tradition that includes Machiavelli and Hobbes. For thinkers in the political realism camp, most of whom are not theological thinkers, Augustine, if he is read at all, is read primarily in and through excerpts from his great works that most favorably comport with this "political realism." To this end, his *Confessions* are ignored and book XIX of his 1,091-page masterwork (in the Penguin Classics unabridged version), *The City of God*, is reproduced with certain bits highlighted. Perhaps also a chunk from book I, chapter 1, on "the city of this world, a city which aims at dominion, which holds nations in enslavement, but is itself dominated by that very lust of domination" (Augustine 1972: 5). Book II, chapter 21, is helpful on Augustine's alternative to Cicero's judgment (according to Scipio) on the Roman commonwealth. Book XV, chapter 1, traces lines of descent of the "two cities, speaking allegorically"; Book XIX, chapter 14, as already noted, is mined for a few precepts about the interests government should serve; chapter 15 makes an argument against slavery "by nature" and chapter 21, in which Scipio's definition of a commonwealth as advanced by Cicero makes a second appearance, also seems pertinent. Chapter 7 of Book XIX is culled as the "justification of war" argument. Perhaps – just perhaps – excerpts are drawn from chapters 14, 15, and 16, in order to demonstrate Augustine's insistence that there is a connection between the peace and good of the household in relation to the city. Take all these snippets, plus his scathing comment that what pirates do with one boat, Romans do with a navy, but the one is called brigandage while the other is named Empire, and the student has her quick intake of what I have called "Augustine Lite" (1996). The upshot is a diminished Augustine, numbered among the pessimists and charged with being one of those who stress human cruelty and violence with a concomitant need for order, coercion, punishment, and occasional war as the upshot.

Recognizing the inadequacy of this "normalized" Augustine doesn't mean one has an easy task if one's purpose is to be fair to Augustine's complexity with the enterprise of political theology in mind, in part for the reasons noted above concerning Augustine's way of writing and arguing. But even more pertinent is a political theologian's sense of his or her task. If one construes that task, at least in part, as a way of putting together anthropological presuppositions (what those of us trained as political theorists called "theories of human nature," at least until one dominant contemporary school of thought decided there was no such thing), claims about the political and social order in light of those presuppositions, the role of political theology in relation to these interrelated tasks, and the perils and possibilities inherent in any political activity or order, then Augustine's expansiveness is a welcome thing indeed. If one's aims are narrower or more modest, Augustine's expansiveness is a frustration. I begin from the point of view that his expansiveness is welcome. What follows is a way of highlighting key points of theoretical demarcation in Augustine's work that are rich with implications for political theology. I should make clear – as will be obvious to any reader of Augustine – that I can only scratch the surface of things in a single essay.

Augustine on the Self

In his wonderful biography of St. Augustine, the noted historian of the late antique world, Peter Brown, claims that Augustine has "come as near to us . . .

as the vast gulf that separates a modern man from the culture and religion of the later empire can allow" (1967: 181). *How so?* One reason, surely, lies in Augustine's complex ruminations on the nature of selfhood. This is a theme close to our own preoccupations. Augustine, in fact, anticipates postmodern strategies in dethroning the Cartesian subject even before that subject got erected. For Augustine, the mind can never be transparent to itself; we are never wholly in control of our thoughts; our bodies are essential, not contingent, to who we are and how we think; and we know that we exist not because "I think, therefore I am," but, rather, "I doubt, therefore I know I exist." Only a subject who is a self that can reflect on its-self can doubt. His *Confessions* is a story of a human being who has become a question to himself (Augustine 1961).

Augustine begins the story with an infant – unlike so many who, over the years, begin with adults: in political theory the image of adults signing social contracts pertains, as if human beings sprang full-blown from the head of John Locke! Augustine, however, starts with natality and intimates a developmental account featuring a fragile, dependent creature who is by no means a *tabula rasa*, but, rather, a being at once social and "quarrelsome." Each child enters a world whose Creator declared it good. Each child enters a world as the heir of Adam's foundational sin. Each child, therefore, is in need of God's grace and forgiveness. All human beings are driven by hunger and desire and experience frustration at their inability to express themselves fully and decisively, in a way that prompts others to respond, to be at one's beck and call. Becoming an adult does not mean jettisoning such emotions – these are key ingredients of our natures and our ability to understand – but is, rather, about forming and shaping our passions in light of certain presuppositions about human beings, human willing, and our faltering attempts to will and to act rightly. Augustine's awareness of the sheer messiness of human existence lies at the heart of the withering critical fire he directs at Stoic *apatheia*. For the mind to be in a state "in which the mind cannot be touched by any emotion whatsoever, who would not judge this insensitivity to be the worst of all moral defects?" (Augustine 1972: 565). We begin as, and we remain, beings who love, who yearn, who grieve, who experience frustration. The most important point here is Augustine's insistence that thought can never be purged of the emotions, and that the thinking self expresses complex emotion through thought and in a language that is, hopefully, up to the task.

This leads directly to Augustine on language and the constraints imposed on us by language. As *par excellence* the language users among God's creatures, we bump up all the time against opacity and constraint. In Book XIX, chapter 7, Augustine muses about the ways in which humans are divided by linguistic differences. These differences make it very hard for us to understand one another.

> The diversity of languages separates man from man. For if two men meet and are forced by some compelling reason not to pass on but to stay in company, then if neither knows the other's language, it is easier for dumb animals, even of different kinds, to associate together than these men, although both are human beings. For when men cannot communicate their thoughts to each other, simply because

of difference of language, all the similarity of their common human nature is of
no avail to unite them in fellowship. So true is this that a man would be more cheerful with his dog for company than with a foreigner. I shall be told that the Imperial City has been at pains to impose on conquered peoples not only her yoke but
her language also, as a bond of peace and fellowship, so that there should be no
lack of interpreters but even a profusion of them. True; but think of the cost of this
achievement! Consider the scale of those wars, with all the slaughter of human
beings, all the human blood that was shed. (Augustine 1972: 861)

Here Augustine moves from the murkiness of language, how it divides us
despite our common human nature, to the imposition of a language on diverse
peoples but at a truly terrible price. We find, then, a drawing together of notions
of human nature, language and its centrality in constituting us as living creatures; the complexity of a search for fellowship; and a pithy critique of the
enforced homogeneity of empire. Augustine's powerful theological anthropology compels attention to the ways in which human beings, created in God's
image, communicate. Unsurprisingly, given original sin, language necessarily
reflects our division – the ways in which the self is riven by sin; the ways in which
human societies, too, bear the stain of sin and sinfulness. Human beings can
achieve only what Augustine calls "creature's knowledge." Full knowledge is not
available to human knowers, no matter how brilliant and learned they may be.
We are both limited and enabled by the conventions of language. No one can
jump out of his or her linguistic skin. We are obliged to bow to "normal usage"
if we hope to communicate at all, and we are driven to communicate by our
sociality, a sociality that goes all the way down. This sociality lies at the basis of
Augustine on the nature of human societies.

Augustine on Social Life

Human beings are, I noted above, social all the way down. Created in the image
of God, we are defined by human relationality. The self is not and cannot be free-
standing. Social life is full of ills and yet to be cherished. Thus, civic life, among
those social forms, is not simply what sin has brought into the world but what
emerges, in part, given our capacity for love and our use of reason, as well (alas)
as a pervasive lust for domination attendant upon human affairs. "The philosophers hold the view that the life of the wise man should be social, and in this we
support them heartily." Indeed, the city of God – Augustine's way of characterizing the pilgrim band of Christians during their earthly sojourn in and through
a community of reconciliation and fellowship that presages the heavenly
kingdom – could never have had "its first start . . . if the life of the saints were
not social" (Augustine 1972: 860). All human beings, without exception, are
citizens of the earthly kingdom – the city of Man – and even in this fallen condition there is a kind of "natural likeness" that forges bonds between us. These
"bonds of peace" do not suffice to prevent wars, dissensions, cruelty, and misery

of all kinds, but we are nonetheless called to membership based on a naturalistic sociality and basic morality available to all rational creatures. A kind of unity in plurality pushes toward harmony; but the sin of division – with its origins in pride and willfulness – drives us apart.

Yet it is love of friendship that lies at the root of what might be called Augustine's "practical philosophy": his history, ethics, social and political theology (Burt 1999). Pinioned between alienation and affection, human beings – those "cracked pots" – are caught in the tragedy of alienation but glued by love. Our sociality is given, so for Augustine the question is not "Should we be social?" or "Should we trust enough to love?" but rather "What shall I love and how shall I love it?" (Burt 1999: 5) His complex ethical theory follows; I can only touch on it here, but it must be noted that political life is one form that human social and ethical life assumes. We are always in society and we always seek the consolation of others. Society, for Augustine, is a species of friendship, and friendship is a moral union in and through which human beings strive for a shared good. All of Augustine's central categories, including war and peace, are in the form of a relation of one sort or another. And the more we are united at all levels in a bond of peace, the closer we come to achieving that good at which we aim and which God intends.

For Augustine, neighborliness and reciprocity emerge from ties that bind, beginning with familial bonds and extending from these particular relations outward: the filaments of affection must not stop at the portal to the *domus*. Augustine writes: "The aim was that one man should not combine many relationships in his one self, but that those connections should be separated and spread among individuals, and that in this way they should help to bind social life more effectively by involving in their plurality a plurality of persons" (1972: 623). The social tie is "not confined to a small group" but extends "more widely to a large number with the multiplying links of kinship" (p. 624). The importance of plurality, of the many emerging from a unique one – for God began with the singular – cannot be overestimated in Augustine's work. It is his way of putting into a single frame human uniqueness and individuality with sociality and plurality. Bonds of affection tied human beings from the start. Bonds of kinship and affection bound them further. These relationships got dispersed, finally encompassing the entire globe.

In light of the confusion and confounding of human languages, it is sometimes difficult to repair to this fundamental sociality; but we yearn for it and seek it in and through the social forms we create: thus civic order becomes a primary requisite for human existence. This civic order is a normative good although, *pace* Aristotle, civic order, or what we routinely call "the state," does not fulfill or complete our natures; rather, it expresses them and may do so in ways deadly or ways less cruel. Here it is important to note that, for Augustine, no human being has natural dominion over any other. There is no slavery by nature. We are by nature social, but that doesn't dictate any particular form of social order. Nor does Augustine analogize from the authority of fathers in households to political rule. Classical patriarchal theory holds that rule by fathers is at once natural and political; that a natural right translates into political authority and legitimation. But for Augustine, political authority is different from familial authority. To the extent that one is subject to a ruler, one is subject to him in status only and not by nature.

There are temporal goods that are worthy, peace first and foremost. So human civic life is not simply a remedy for sin – with order and coercion needed to constrain our wickedness – but an expression of our sociality; our desire for fellowship; our capacity for a diffuse *caritas*. It follows that Cicero's definition of a *res publica*, as refracted through the writings of Scipio, is wanting. For Cicero, civic order is an association based on common agreement concerning right and on shared interests. Insufficient, argues Augustine; rather, a people gathered together in a civic order is a gathering or multitude of rational beings united in fellowship by sharing a common love of the same things. Using this definition, we not only define what a society is, we can also assess what it is people hold dear – what *sort* of society is *this*? It is worth noting at this juncture that a debate in current Augustinian scholarship concerns precisely how one should rank the good of political society for Augustine. The traditional, and overly simple, claim that, for Augustine, civic order is simply a remedy for sin has been effectively challenged (Burt 1999). Now the question seems to be just how important to Augustine's thought overall is the good at which civic life tends, and how much this derives from and can be achieved through the exercise of human voluntary activity. The dangers inherent in earthly political life are manifest: the fruits of pride that seeks domination over others and glories only in the self or the "empire." The goods to be attained through civic life are sketchier, but begin with Augustine's basic rule of thumb for human earthly life: namely, that we should do no harm and help whenever we can (a requisite of neighbor love).

If language divides us, then, it can also draw us together insofar as we acknowledge a common humanity. Augustine's critique of the political life of the late Roman Empire was not so much an assault on the edifice of any ordering of corporate life, but based rather on the failure of that public life ever to attain a genuine *res publica*. This, at least, is an argument made by Rowan Williams. A commonwealth is an identifiable social unit. But beyond this obvious fact, how do we distinguish a polity in which the disorder of dominance by the *libido dominandi* pertains from one in which a well-ordered social life pertains – a world in which ordinary peace (*tranquillitas ordinis*) permits the moral formation of citizens in households and in commonwealths to go forward (Williams 1987: 55–72)? A true form of corporate life is "purposive," Williams argues, "existing so as to nurture a particular kind of human life: in both [family and polis], authority is determined in relation to a specific goal" (p. 64).

There are authentic political values, those of civic order, fairness, and the safeguarding of soulcraft: all under God's providence and dauntingly complex for Christians, that pilgrim people, who by definition cannot simply absorb and reflect the norms and understanding of what is worthy that pertain in the surroundings in which they find themselves outside of the body of Christ, the *ecclesia*. Christians are not to hunker down in the church, but to approach the world with a loving worldliness, born out of a recognition of the world's many good-nesses and blessings, and the responsibility of human beings to honor and to sustain those goodnesses as best they can in and through those social institutions they create to sustain human life.

Pace many criticisms of Augustine that charge him with having replaced a public ethic with a "private" and apolitical ethic of *caritas*, Williams insists, correctly, that

> Augustine's condemnation of "public" life in the classical world is, consistently, that it is not public enough, that it is incapable of grounding a stable sense of commonality because of its pervasive implicit elitism, its divisiveness, its lack of a common human *project*; and . . . that the member of the city of God is committed *ex professo* to exercising power when called upon to do so, and, in responding to such a call, does not move from a "church" to a "state" sphere of activity, but continues in the practice of nurturing souls already learned in more limited settings. (1987: 68)

It is the interplay of *caritas* and *cupiditas* that is critical, and whether one or the other prevails at a given point in time, either within the very being of a single person or within the life of a civic order. Augustine would tame the occasions for the reign of *cupiditas* and the activation of the *libido dominandi*, or lust to dominate, and maximize the space within which *caritas* operates. For a lust to dominate taints and perverts all human relations, from family to city. Similarly, a decent love, a concern for the well-being of all in the household or in the city, strengthens the delicate filaments of peace. The sin that mars the earthly city is the story of arbitrary power or the ever-present possibility of such. By contrast, the basis for a more just order is fueled by love. The theme of the two cities is the metaphor that enables Augustine to trace the choreography of human relations. Every human community is plagued by a "poverty stricken kind of power . . . a kind of scramble . . . for lost dominions and . . . honors," but there are simultaneously present the life-forgiving and gentler aspects of loving concern, mutuality, domestic and civic peace (Augustine 1972: 429). There are two fundamentally different attitudes evinced within human social life and enacted by human beings. One attitude is a powerful feeling of the fullness of life. A human being will not be denuded if he or she gives, or makes a gift of, the self to others. One's dependence on others is not a diminution but an enrichment of the self. The other attitude springs from cramped and cribbed selfishness, resentment, a penury of spirit. The way one reaches out or down to others from these different attitudes is strikingly distinct. From a spirit of resentment and contempt, one condescends toward the other; one is hostile to life itself. But from that fellow feeling in our hearts for the misery of others, we come to their help by coming together with them. Authentic compassion (the working-out of *caritas*) eradicates contempt and distance. But this working out can never achieve anything like perfection in the realm of earthly time and history (the *saeculum*).

The Two Cities

In his book *Saeculum* (1970), widely acknowledged as one of the most important attempts to unpack Augustine and to situate him as civic and political theorist, Robert Markus argues that Augustine aimed to achieve a number of
complex things with his characterization of the two cities. One was to sort out
the story of all earthly cities. Augustine, he argues, provides an account of the
earthly city (*civitas terrena*) from Assyria through Rome, and shows the ways in
which even the cherished goal of peace all too often ends in conquest and domination, hence no real peace at all. The fullness of peace is reserved for the heavenly city (*civitas dei*) and its eternal peace. In this way Augustine creates barriers
to the absolutizing and sacralizing of any political arrangement. His repudiation
of the theology underwriting the notion of an *imperium Christianum* lies in part
in his worry that any identification of the city of God with an earthly order
invites sacralization of human arrangements and a dangerous idolatry. At the
same time, earthly institutions have a real claim on us, and our membership in
a polity is not reducible to misery and punishment. Augustine begins with a presumption of the priority of peace over war, and he repudiates all stories of mythical human beginnings that presume disorder and war as our primordial
condition. The earthly city derives from our turning away from love and its
source (God) toward willfullness and a "poverty stricken kind of power." Because
earthly *potestas* is tied to the temptations inherent in that form of power we call
dominion, there can be no such thing as an earthly sacral society or state.

Augustine begins his unpacking of "the origins and ends of the two cities" in
The City of God, part II, book XI. The poverty stricken kind of power is here ref-
erenced and human beings are likened to the fallen angels who have turned
away from God. In book XII Augustine continues the theme of "turning away,"
tying the two cities to ordered or disordered wills and desires. With book XIV we
get the disobedience of the first man leading not to death everlasting, as would
have been the case without God's grace, but to division – within the self, between
self and other, between nations and cultures. Whatever the culture or nation,
none is whole unto himself or itself, complete and perfect; each is marked by the
divisions Augustine here calls "the standard of the flesh" by contrast to "the
standard of the spirit" (1972: 547). This is not a screed against the body but
against the abuse of the body under the rule of the flesh.

With book XV he writes of "two classes" or "two cities, speaking allegorically":
a warning to any who would conflate specific earthly configurations with his
dominant metaphor. It is an allegorical representation of a great mystery. The
clean and the unclean come together within the framework of the church,
within the boundaries of human communities (1972: 648). But the city of God
is turned toward God's will, with which it hopes to be in accord; the city of man
is constructed and run according to man's standards and designs. Given that
there is a "darkness that attends the life of human society," few should sit com-
fortably on "the judge's bench," but sit there the judge must, "for the claims of

human society constrain him and draw him to this duty; and it is unthinkable to him that he should shirk it" (p. 860).

One must not shirk worldly responsibilities, because temporal peace is a good, whether it is the peace of the body, or fellowship with one's own kind, or the provision made for food and clothing and care. Amid the shadows that hover over and among us, there are, as already noted, two rules within our reach and that we should follow: "first, to do no harm to anyone, and, secondly, to help everyone whenever possible" (1972: 873). The most just human civic arrangements are those that afford the widest scope to non-harm-doing and to fellowship and mutuality. If mutuality, even of the earthly imperfect sort, is to be attained, there must be a compromise between human wills and the earthly city must find a way to forge bonds of peace. This she finds very difficult by definition, given the distortions of the lust to dominate.

By contrast, the heavenly city on earthly pilgrimage is better able to forge peace by calling out "citizens from all nations and so collects a society of aliens, speaking all languages." She – the *civitas dei* – does this not by annulling or abolishing earthly differences but even through maintaining them so "long as God can be worshipped" (1972: 878). The life of the saint, the life of the citizen, is a social life. There must be a balance in our attention to earthly affairs; thus a person ought not "to be so leisured as to take no thought in that leisure for the interest of his neighbor, nor so active as to feel no need for the contemplation of God." If we are to "promote the well-being of common people," we must love God and love our neighbor and the one helps to underscore and to animate the other (p. 880). In his reconsideration of book XIX of Augustine's masterwork, Oliver O'Donovan argues that Augustine reformulated

> something like the traditional concept of society and morality in new terms which would give due recognition both to the reality of the moral order which makes social existence possible and to its fundamentally flawed character. Augustine embarks on a radical, but not revolutionary policy of characterising all politics in terms of moral *disorder*, which itself provides an explanation of their political *order*, since, in Augustine's firmly Platonic view, disorder is nothing but a failure in the underlying moral order . . . A vice, in other words, is a perversion of *virtue*; it is a *disorder* which is predatory on some *order*. (O'Donovan 1987: 102)

Refusing to grant a free-standing originary status to disorder or to sin is not only one way Augustine argued against the Manicheans; it remains a radically provocative account that bears profound political implications for our understanding of political evil and evil-doers, a theme I consider in the concluding section below (Elshtain 1995).

Here it is important to note that whatever Augustine's acquiescence in the received social arrangements of his time, he left as a permanent legacy a condemnation of that lust for dominion that distorts the human personality, marriage, the family, and all other human social relations, including civic life and membership. Augustine is scathing in his denunciation of arrogant pridefulness; unstinting in his praise of the works of service, neighborliness, and a love that simultaneously judges and succors (judges because we must distinguish good from evil, selfishness from kindness, and so on). Love and justice are intertwined, on earth and in heaven. Yet the world is filled with horrors, including war. How does Augustine square his regretful justification of a certain sort of war with his call to love and peace? It is to this theme that I now turn.

Augustine on War and Peace

A full treatment of this theme would require an assessment of Augustine's complex theodicy. That is beyond the scope of this essay. But a brief discussion is needed in order to grasp Augustine's theology of war and peace. Augustine acknowledges the seductive allure of evil. He famously tells the story of a youthful prank – stealing pears – that was done not from hunger but from pleasure in the deed itself and in the fellowship with others who took part in the deed. It took Augustine many years, including a sustained detour through Manicheanism, before he rejected decisively metaphysical dualism and repudiated any claim that evil is a self-sustaining, generative principle of opposition to good. The Manicheans had located evil in creation itself as the work of a demonic demiurge; thus the body was tainted by definition. But, for Augustine, creation is good. The body is good, not polluted. It is what we do with the body; what we do to creation, that either marks our bodies with the stain of sin, wickedness, and cruelty or does not, at any given point in time. Augustine's famous articulation of human free will enters at this juncture – a concept Hannah Arendt credits with being an original contribution by Augustine. We can choose to do wrong and we often do, for we are marked from the beginning with the trace of originary disobedience. The choice of evil is in and of itself "an impressive proof that the *nature* is good" (Augustine 1972: 448).

Evil is a falling away from the good, and we are the agents of this falling away – not because the body is corrupt, but because we can defile it. There is no such thing as evil "by nature." Evil is the turning of a limited creature from God to himself and, hence, to an absolutizing of his own flawed will. This turning may become habitual, a kind of second nature. In this way, Augustine gives evil its due without giving it the day. Evil is the name we give to a class of acts and putative motives. The fruits of this turning away include a hatred of finitude and a fateful thirst for what might be called a kind of anticreation: a lust to destroy. War is a species of that destruction; hence, war is always a tragedy even "when just." But if war is first and foremost an example of human sinfullness and a turning from the good, how can it possibly be justified under any circumstances?

It works like this. Augustine begins by deconstructing the Roman peace as a false claim to peace. Instead, Rome conquered and was herself conquered by her own lust to dominate over others. "Think of all the battles fought, all the blood that was poured out, so that almost all the nations of Italy, by whose help the Roman Empire wielded that overwhelming power, should be subjugated as if they were barbarous savages" (Augustine 1972: 127). Rome was driven by a lust for vengeance and cruelty and these impulses triumphed under the cherished name of peace. The Empire became a kingdom without justice, its rulers little more than a criminal gang on a grand scale. Here Augustine famously repeats the story of the rejoinder given by a captured pirate to Alexander the Great when Alexander queried him about his idea in infesting the sea. "And the pirate answered, with uninhibited insolence, 'The same as yours, in infesting the earth! But because I do it with a tiny craft, I'm called a pirate: because you have a mighty navy, you're called an emperor'" (Augustine 1972: 139). Augustine even suggests that the Romans should have erected a monument to the foreign "other" and called her "Aliena" because they made such good use of her by proclaiming that all their wars were defensive; it was, therefore, necessary to conjure up an implacable foreign foe in order to justify these ravages. For Rome, peace became just another name for *dominium*. If war's ravages are, in part, a punishment for sin, human beings sin, often savagely, in enacting that punishment. Primarily, however, Augustine emphasizes the freely chosen nature of war and assigns responsibility to those who engage in it.

If you reflect on the terrible slaughter of war carried out for wicked motives and to unworthy ends, you will determine to wage only limited, justifiable wars even as you lament the fact that they must sometimes be waged, given injustice: so Augustine argues. There are occasional real wars of defense. The wise ruler and polity takes up arms only with great reluctance and penitence. Given Augustine's account of limited justifiability for wars fought only for certain motives, he is frequently lodged as the grandfather of "just war" thinking. (Others, of course, rank him as a forebear of political realism. There is no reason he cannot be both, depending on what one understands by realism and just war respectively.) Augustine appreciates what modern international relations theorists call the "security dilemma." People never possess a kingdom

> so securely as not to fear subjugation by their enemies; in fact, such is the instability of human affairs that no people has ever been allowed such a degree of tranquillity as to remove all dread of hostile attacks on their life in this world. That place which is promised as a dwelling of such peace and security is eternal, and is reserved for eternal beings, in "the mother, the Jerusalem which is free." (Augustine 1972: 743–4)

One must simply live with this shadow, a penumbra of fear and worry, on this earth. But one must not give oneself over to it, not without overweening justification. When one capitulates to this fear, one gets horrible wars of destruction, including social and civic wars. And each war invites another, given the mimetic quality of instantiations of destruction. Each war breeds discontents and resentments that invite a tendency to even the score.

By contrast, the just ruler wages a justifiable war of necessity, whether against unwarranted aggression and attack or to rescue the innocent from certain destruction. The motivation must be neighbor love and a desire for a more authentic peace. This is a grudging endorsement of a lesser evil; war is never named as a normative good, only as a tragic necessity. It must be noted that rescuing the self alone is not a justification for violence: better to suffer wrong than to commit it. But our sociality imbeds certain requirements of neighbor love, most powerfully and poignantly so in the case of the ruler, who bears the responsibility for the well-being of a people. It is, then, through our intrinsic sociality, and under the requirement to do no harm and help whenever one can, that war is occasionally justifiable. Augustine's reasoning here falls within the domain of accounts of comparative justice, and his argument, which is not a fully fleshed out systematic theory of war so much as a theological account of war, involves the occasional violation of a fundamental principle – do not kill unjustly, or murder – in the name of an overriding good.

It is important to observe that a close reading of Augustine's account shows that one must lament even justifiable wars and reflect on them, not with vainglory, but with great sorrow. Not to look back with grief marks one as pitiable and contemptible. There are no victory parades in Augustine's world; for, however just the cause, war stirs up temptations to ravish and to devour, often in order to ensure peace. Just war, for Augustine, is a cautionary tale, not an incautious and reckless call to arms. For peace is a great good, so good that "no word ever falls more gratefully upon the ear, nothing is desired with greater longing, in fact, nothing better can be found." Peace is "delightful" and "dear to the heart of all mankind" (1972: 866).

Augustine Concluded

The vast mountain of Augustinian scholarship keeps growing. It long ago surpassed a book version of Mt. Everest, so much so that no single scholar or group of scholars could master it all. This is true of Augustine's work alone. Peter Brown claims that Isidore of Seville once "wrote that if anyone told you he had read all the works of Augustine, he was a liar" (Brown 1972: 311). One always has the sense with Augustine that one has but scratched the surface. Indeed, his works have not yet been translated entirely into English. That project is now underway, and there are some 17 volumes of his homilies alone that have made their way into translation. Much of the new scholarship on Augustine remarks, often with a sense of critical wonderment, on just how "contemporary" he is given the collapse of political utopianism, by which I mean attempts to order political and social life under an overarching *Weltanschauung* that begins, as any such attempt must, with a flawed anthropology about human malleability and even perfectibility. We recognize, looking back, the mounds of bodies on which so many political projects rest, including the creation of the nation-state system we took for granted for over three centuries and now observe to be fraying around the edges.

The teleology of historic progress is no longer believable, although a version of it is still touted by voluptuaries of techno-progress or genetic engineering that may yet "perfect" the human race. The presumably solid underpinnings of the self gave way in the twentieth century under the onslaught of Nietzsche and Freud. Cultural anthropology taught lessons of cultural contingencies. Contemporary students of rhetoric have rediscovered the importance and vitality of rhetoric and the ways in which all of our political and social life and thought must be cast in available rhetorical forms.

None of this would have surprised Augustine. What would sadden him is the human propensity to substitute one extreme for another: for example, a too thoroughgoing account of disembodied reason gives way to a too thoroughgoing account of reason's demise. Importantly, one must rescue Augustine from those who would appropriate him to a version of political limits or "realism" that downplays his insistence on the great virtue of hope and the call to enact projects of *caritas*. That does not mean he should be called to service on behalf of "markets and democracy." It does mean he can never be enlisted on behalf of the depredators of humankind.

References

Augustine, St. (1961). *The Confessions*. New York: Penguin

——(1963). *De Trinitate*, trans. S. McKenna. Washington DC: Catholic University of America Press.

——(1972). *The City of God*, trans. H. Bettenson. Baltimore: Penguin.

——(1984). *Augustine of Hippo, Selected Writings*, trans. M. T. Clark. New York: Paulist.

Brown, Peter R. L. (1967). *Augustine of Hippo, A Biography*. Berkeley: University of California Press.

——(1972). "Political Society." In R. Markus (ed.), *Augustine: A Collection of Critical Essays*, 311–35. Garden City: Doubleday Anchor.

Burt, Donald X. (1999). *Friendship and Society: An Introduction to Augustine's Practical Philosophy*. Grand Rapids: Eerdmans.

Elshtain, Jean Bethke (1987). *Women and War*. New York: Basic Books.

——(1995). *Augustine and the Limits of Politics*. Notre Dame, Ind.: Notre Dame University Press.

Markus, Robert (1970). *Saeculum: History and Society in the Theology of St. Augustine*. Cambridge: Cambridge University Press.

Milbank, John (1990). *Theology and Social Theory: Beyond Secular Reason*. Oxford: Blackwell.

O'Donovan, Oliver (1987). "Augustine's City of God XIX and Western Political Thought." *Dionysius* 11, 89–110.

Wetzel, James (1992). *Augustine and the Limits of Virtue*. Cambridge: Cambridge University Press.

Williams, Rowan (1987). "Politics and the Soul: A Reading of *The City of God*." *Milltown Studies* 19–20, 55–72.

CHAPTER 4
Aquinas

Frederick Christian Bauerschmidt

In recent years there has been an amazing amount of interest in the ethical and political thought of Thomas Aquinas (c.1224–74). The growth of interest in the "ethics of virtue," both in philosophy (e.g. MacIntyre 1991) and theology (e.g. Porter 1990; Pinckaers 1995), has naturally turned people's attention to Aquinas' subtle and sophisticated analysis of virtue. In other cases, the role of "natural law" in Aquinas' thought has attracted the interest of some legal and political theorists (e.g. Finnis 1998), and even of liberation theologians (Gutiérrez 1993). In what follows, I will argue for the contemporary relevance of Aquinas for political theology, though not primarily on the basis of his appeals to natural law. Rather, by examining some texts from Aquinas that do not appear at first glance to have much at all to do with his moral theology, much less his political theory, I hope to show that the chief importance of Aquinas for political theology is his belief that truth is stronger than kings, and his identification of truth with the God of Israel, incarnate in Jesus Christ.

The Contours of Thomas' Thought: Exegesis of a Text

Let me begin by sketching three formal contours of Thomas' thought.

First, Thomas is concerned with both *logic* and *metaphysics*. His basic approach is to seek clarity of thought and speech by making distinctions that help our thought and speech conform to the order inherent in things. He combines minute analysis of how we use words with deep metaphysical speculation in a way not usually found in modern philosophy. This combination arises from Thomas' overriding concern to find the clearest way in which to convey the content of the Christian tradition, which he does by way of making distinctions and ordering those distinctions in terms of a comprehensive vision of reality.

Second, Thomas' thought is *traditioned*: he thinks as a participant in the give and take of a living tradition (see MacIntyre 1991). While modern thought is distinguished in part by its desire to find an indubitable starting point from which to begin, Thomas approaches thought as a participant in a complex conversation that is already underway. The *quaestio* format, which is at the heart of the *Summa Theologiae* (hereafter *ST*), as well as other texts, presents the living voice of the tradition in the arguments and counter-arguments with which the *quaestio* begins.

Third, Thomas' thought is *scriptural*. The tradition to which Thomas belongs is a conversation initiated by God with humanity, as recorded in the Bible. The fundamental contours of Thomas' thought are not, as sometimes thought, Aristotelian, but biblical. It is true that Thomas freely employs the treasures of philosophy (Platonic as well as Aristotelian) in order to enrich the Christian tradition. But it is the voice of scripture that predominates (see *ST* 1.1.8 *ad* 2), both in posing questions and in answering them. The philosophical tradition is both plundered for its riches and transformed into something that would seem quite odd to either Plato or Aristotle.

In order to see how these formal contours function in practice, let us look at a specific text, since Thomas, as a *magister sacra pagina* (a teacher of the sacred page), was above all an interpreter of texts. This minor text represents one of the random questions (*quaestiones quodlibitales*) with which Thomas dealt on a regular basis in his role as a teacher. In addition to displaying the formal contours of his thought, it can also serve as an introduction to some of the possibilities and problems of Thomas' thought for today. A clear problem raised by this particular text is that, to modern sensibilities, Thomas' treatment of "woman" as an example of "sensual causality" is at best patronizing and at worst overtly sexist. This alerts us to at least one important point in reading Thomas today. Thomas' identification of woman with "sensuality" and man with "intellect" indicates that he, like all of us, is a product of his culture. In this case, he has imbibed certain notions that make "woman" a natural metonym for "sexual attraction." This raises some difficult questions, to which I will return toward the end of this essay, about how social and political power can shape our perception of the natural order of things. A key question, therefore, is whether Thomas' fundamental point that truth is stronger than kings can be used to critique some of his own cultural assumptions.

QUODLIBITAL QUESTION 12.14.1: Whether truth is stronger than wine, a king, or a woman.

Obj. 1: It seems that wine is strongest, since it can change the greatest of men.

Obj. 2: It seems a king is strongest, since he compels a person to that which is most difficult, i.e. to that which exposes him to mortal danger.

Obj. 3: It seems that woman is strongest, since she dominates even a king.

Against this: 3 Esdras 4: 35: "truth is stronger."

I reply: This is a question posed by the youths in Esdras, which they were required to solve. It must be observed, therefore, that if we consider these four (namely, wine, a king, a woman and truth) according to themselves, they are not comparable because they are not of the same genus. However, if they be considered in relation to some effect, they concur in one regard and may thus be compared. Further, this effect in which they concur and according to which they can be compared is the changing of the human heart. Therefore, whichever among them brings about the greatest change in the human heart would seem to be the strongest.

It must be observed that change in human beings sometimes concerns the body and sometimes the soul [*animale*], and this latter change can be in two ways: regarding the senses and regarding the intellect. Furthermore, the intellect is also two-fold: practical and speculative.

Among those things, however, that pertain to natural change according to bodily disposition, the best is wine, which makes people talkative by drunkenness. Among those things that pertain to change in the appetite of the senses, the best is pleasure, especially sexual pleasure, and thus woman is stronger. Likewise in practical matters and human affairs that we can accomplish, the king has the greatest power. In speculative matters the highest and most powerful thing is truth.

Now bodily powers are subordinate to animal powers, animal powers to intellectual powers, and practical intellectual powers to speculative ones. Therefore, simply speaking, truth is most worthy and excellent and strong.

As he begins his reply, Thomas takes four candidates for "strongest" and, with logical rigor, points out the difficulty of comparing them if we simply take them as what they are in themselves. However, he goes on to say that they are all causes of change in the human heart and thus may be compared on that level. Thomas therefore locates them within the context of his understanding of human beings, observing that human beings are both bodily and spiritual (or, as he puts it here, "animal" – from *anima* or "soul"); that our spiritual natures consist in our capacity for sensation, which we share with other animals, and our capacity for thought, which distinguishes us from other animals; and that our capacity for thought can be further divided into thought oriented toward action (practical reason) and thought oriented toward knowledge (speculative reason).

Having made these distinctions, we can see that the human heart can be moved in various ways. Wine can affect us on a physical level, by means of a chemical reaction, turning an otherwise taciturn person into a talkative one. A beautiful woman (or man) affects us not simply on the level of a physical change, but through sensation, specifically pleasurable sensation. Both a king and the truth act on the level of thought, but in distinct ways. A king can command the will to move us to perform some action, but he cannot command the mind to move to assent to something. Only the truth can do that. So there are different kinds of causes of human action and consequently different kinds of human actions: those of the body, those of the senses, those of the will, and those of speculative reason. These distinctions are crucial to the articulation of Thomas' overarching vision of reality (what we might call his "metaphysics"). Thomas claims not only that we can distinguish different kinds of causes of change in the human heart, but that these kinds have a proper ordering, one to another.

This ordering is implicit in his initial description of the different kinds of changes. The most basic (or "lowest") kind of change is that which human beings share in common with all existing things: change though physical or material causes. Change brought about by things that act through the senses is distinctive to sensate beings (i.e. animals), but again is not distinctively human. Thus, the less distinctive causes of action are lower than or "subordinate to" (ordered below) more distinctive causes of action.

But what about the two kinds of causes of action that are equally distinctive of human beings: those that act upon practical reason and those that act upon speculative reason? How are these ordered in relation to each other? The practical intellect and the speculative intellect are not two different powers of reason so much as the application of reason in two different ways: in the former case about the good that is to be pursued (i.e. what we should do) and in the latter case about the truth that is known (i.e. what is the case). And these distinct objects turn out not to be so distinct, since "truth and good include one another; for truth is something good, otherwise it would not be desirable; and good is something true, otherwise it would not be intelligible" (ST 1.79.11 ad 2). Yet a difference remains: practical reason is reasoning about the good that is the cause of *human* action, whereas speculative reason reaches beyond the human to God, the cause of all that is, and thus of all truth (ST 2-2.47.2 ad 1). Therefore causes that operate through the practical intellect are subordinate to those that operate through the speculative intellect. We might say that it is easier to cause behavior than belief. Thus, "truth is stronger" because the hierarchy of causes exemplified by wine, woman, king, and truth corresponds to the ontological hierarchy of inanimate beings, animate beings, intellectual beings, and God, who is the act of existing itself (*esse ipse subsistens*).

So far, so logical and metaphysical. But what about tradition and scripture? Some have taken the question to be a student's joke, posed to baffle the professor, and perhaps it was (though it is not a particularly funny one). More importantly, however, the question is rooted in the text of scripture, specifically the deuterocanonical book of 3 Esdras, in which three young Jewish servants of the Persian King Darius debate this question before their master. Darius' predecessor, Cyrus, had defeated the Babylonians, who had 50 years before destroyed Jerusalem and taken many of its people off into exile. Cyrus had allowed the Jewish exiles to return to their homeland, but many had remained in Babylon, where they had established themselves. At this time the temple in Jerusalem remains in ruins because Darius has yet to fulfill the vow he made to rebuild it.

The first of the three servants argues that wine is strongest, not least because "it makes equal the mind of the king and the orphan, of the slave and the free, of the poor and the rich" (3 Esdras 3: 19). The second young man, more inclined to flattery than wit, argues that the king is stronger, since "all his people and his armies obey him" (4: 10). The third defends the proposition that "women are strongest, but truth is victor over all things" (3: 12). This young man is Zerubbabel, the grandson of King Jehoiachin, who was the last king of Judah before the exile in Babylon. Zerubbabel is not interested in impressing Darius with wit or flattery. He argues that women are stronger than wine, since they give birth to the men who plant the vineyards, and also stronger than kings, pointing to Darius' own fawning behavior with his concubine, Apame, who would "take the crown from the king's head and put it on her own, and slap the king with her left hand" (4: 30).

Then Zerubbabel abruptly shifts gears, announcing that "truth is great, and stronger than all things" (4: 35). What justifies this shift? Zerubbabel's mockery of the king and his concubine points to their pettiness and makes ridiculous their claims to importance. Zerubbabel continues, speaking of truth as a woman (perhaps echoing the figure of "lady wisdom" in the book of Proverbs), a woman who is in striking contrast to Darius' concubine: "with her there is no partiality or preference, but she does what is righteous instead of anything that is unrighteous or wicked" (4: 39). The implicit appeal to Darius is that he pursue the powerful and righteous lady truth, rather than the fickle and untrustworthy Apame. But the punchline to Zerubbabel's encomium to truth comes at the end: "To her belong the strength and the kingship and the power and the majesty of all the ages. Blessed be the God of truth" (4: 40). In this final turn, Zerubbabel makes it clear that to dedicate oneself to the pursuit of truth is to dedicate oneself to the God of Israel.

Darius is won over, smitten by Zerubbabel's portrayal of lady truth. He says, "Ask what you wish," and Zerubbabel replies "I pray therefore that you fulfil the vow whose fulfilment you vowed to the King of heaven with your own lips" (4: 43–6). Darius, confronted with truth, a power greater than his own power as king, agrees to Zerubbabel's request that he rebuild the temple.

Relocating Thomas' discussion in its biblical source helps us see that, though he employs the tools of philosophy, his answer to the question is saturated with biblical understandings of the relationship between power and truth, and the subordination of earthly rulers to God's eternal law. In the story of Zerubbabel we see displayed a fundamental narrative pattern that repeats itself throughout the Old and New Testaments, a pattern that is central to Thomas' thoughts on political order and that is summed up in the verse that Thomas quotes in his quodlibital question: "Truth is stronger."

Speaking Truth to Power

The confrontation between truth and other claimants to the throne of power is expressed perhaps most acutely in the Gospel of John's account of Jesus' appearance before Pilate, the representative of earthly power (John 18: 33–19: 22). Thomas' own commentary on this narrative is instructive. While Thomas casts Pilate in as favorable a light as possible – he is a "just judge" who wishes to know the truth (*Super evangelium S. Ioannis* §2344) – he still sees Pilate as one who cannot understand what Christ says because he is thoroughly bound to "worldly" ways of thinking, unable to imagine a kingdom that is not "physical"

– that is, one of external coercion. Even though Pilate is willing to accept Jesus as a "teacher of the truth" (§2365), he never understands the real relationship between truth and kingship; he never understands that "truth is stronger."

Pilate further misunderstands Jesus' statement that his kingdom is not of this world, in an error that Thomas characterizes as "Manichean," in that the material world is seen as a realm of irredeemable darkness ruled by the forces of brute coercion. Against this, Thomas maintains that while Christ does not reign "in the physical way that those of the earth do" (§2350) – namely, by external coercion – this does not mean that he does not rule this world. Indeed, Christ's kingdom "is here, because it is everywhere" (§2354). While law is often coercive, operating through the threat of punishment (see *ST* 1-2.90.3 *ad* 2), it is not inevitably so. The eternal law by which God guides creation operates from the *interior* of things, not by external coercion; and even in the case of earthly laws, these are coercive to the wicked, because they run contrary to the inclination of their wills, but not to the good, because their wills are in harmony with truth (see *ST* 1-2.96.5). Pilate presumes, in common with the Manichean worldview, that power is always and merely the power of coercion, operating (like wine) on the level of physical force, and that any power that is "not of this world" must not be real power.

Thomas notes Jesus' care in replying to Pilate's questions. When Pilate says, "So you are a king?" Jesus replies, "You say that I am a king." Thomas says, "Our Lord tempered his response about his kingship so that he neither clearly asserted that he was a king – since he was not a king in the sense in which Pilate understood it – nor denied it – since spiritually he was the King of Kings" (§2358). Though Thomas does not use the term here, he is clearly presenting Christ's kingship and worldly kingship as "analogical." The Manichean worldview would have it that if Christ's kingship is "worldly" then it must partake of the darkness of coercion; if it is "unworldly" then it is utterly different from and irrelevant to this realm of darkness. Thomas rejects such an alternative. He denies that Christ is a king according to the mode of physical kingship, but asserts that he is king in another way, the way of righteousness (§2358).

Thomas says that Christ then reveals the "mode and order" (*modum et rationem*) of his kingdom in the statement, "For this I was born and for this I have come into the world, to bear witness to the truth" (§2359). The kingdom of Christ is "unworldly," yet exercised from the very heart of the world. Those he rules, because they have seen the truth manifested by Christ, set their affections not on earthly things but on heavenly ones; yet (as Augustine would put it) they live as pilgrims in this world in order to witness to the truth. Similarly, the authority he receives from the Father is not the shadow power of kings and armies, but is the true power and pattern of the world's creation (see §2351).

Pilate proves a somewhat tragic figure in Thomas' estimation. He asks Jesus in all sincerity, "What is truth?", but he does not wait for the answer (§2364). He is interested in truth, but it is a dilettante's interest; he does not realize that true strength resides in finding the truth. He still trusts in his ability to manipulate the Jews in order to free Christ, whom he has decided is harmless (because powerless). Rather than waiting to hear the truth from Christ, he tries to exploit the Jewish custom of releasing a prisoner at Passover time (§2367). As Thomas continues to describe Pilate's bargaining with those who seek Christ's death, Thomas becomes uncharacteristically passionate in chiding Pilate: "Why then, unrighteous Pilate, was there this shameful bargaining if there was no crime in him?" (§2380). From the human perspective, Pilate has the power to release Jesus, but he continues to pretend that he does not really have the authority to do so, even while boasting of his own power. In engaging in this knot of self-deceit, "he has condemned himself" (§2393).

The final act of this confrontation comes when the Jews threaten Pilate with Caesar's displeasure because "they thought that Pilate would prefer the friendship of Caesar to the friendship of justice" (§2399). They are right; Pilate cannot ignore such a threat because he believes that his power in this matter comes from Caesar. Pilate's capitulation before the threat of Caesar's power shows both his moral failings and his inability to grasp the power of truth. And so truth goes to the cross: "Christ bore his cross as a king does his scepter; his cross is the sign of his glory, which is his universal dominion over all things" (§2414).

Thomas' commentary on the encounter between Pilate and Jesus reveals the precise way in which "truth is stronger." Speaking truth to earthly power is no guarantee that you will not be killed, for the power of "physical" rulers is essentially the power of coercion, which reaches its extreme measure in the death of those who will not comply. But the noncoercive power of truth accomplishes the purposes of truth more inexorably than the purposes of any earthly rule. A martyr for truth can resist an earthly ruler to the point of death, and thus beyond the limits of the ruler's power, but the power of truth has no limits. So, as Aquinas says, Christ's cross becomes the sign of his "universal dominion over all things."

Law, Order, Beauty

To those familiar with the standard account of Aquinas' political thought, what I have written above must seem strange, because I have not mentioned "natural law." This is because I am convinced that the nontheological account of natural law that some claim to find in Aquinas (e.g. Finnis 1998) is simply not there (see Long 2001). While Thomas discusses "natural law" in various places in his writings, one ought not to abstract these discussions from their theological context. Attention to this context yields an account of natural law that is both more theological and more modest than the one often ascribed to Aquinas.

In the *Summa Theologiae*, Thomas' discussion of natural law (1-2.94) occurs in the context of a cluster of questions (1-2.90–108) concerned with law as one of the "external principles" of human action. These questions occur in the larger context of Thomas' discussion of human action in the second part of the *Summa*, which in turn is located in the larger context of the *Summa* as a whole, with its structure of creation coming forth from God and returning to God through

Christ. Of the 512 questions in the *Summa Theologiae*, Aquinas devotes only one, consisting of six articles, to natural law. By way of contrast, he devotes seven questions, a total of 46 articles, to the Torah. While such quantitative information can be misleading, since the notion of natural law crops up throughout the questions on law and in various other places in Aquinas' work, it raises the question of whether the importance of natural law in Aquinas' thought has been overestimated. Our evaluation, however, must ultimately rest on a careful reading, in context, of Thomas' account of natural law.

After a general discussion of "law" (1-2.90–92), Thomas begins not with natural law, but with the basis of all law in the "eternal law," by which "the whole community of the universe is governed by divine reason" (1-2.91.1). This law is a *ratio* (in this sense, an idea or exemplar, but also an "order") existing in God eternally, by which all of the world's actions and movements are directed: the eternal law is both the pattern of divine order within the uncreated being of God, and the pattern of order in which all created things participate and by which they are governed and led to their end. This eternal law is "appropriated" to the divine Word, the second person of the Trinity, by which the Father expresses himself (1-2.93.1, 4).

The natural law is the participation of rational creatures in the eternal law through sharing in divine wisdom (1-2.91.2). While all creatures are guided by the eternal law, rational creatures are guided by God precisely through their intellects. Thomas' initial emphasis is not on natural law as an autonomous human faculty, but on how the human ability to discern good and evil is "nothing else than the imprint on us of the divine light" (1-2.91.2). This participation in divine reason provides rational creatures with "first principles" of moral reasoning. These first principles are not conclusions about particular actions, but rather what one might call the basic "grammar" of such reasoning (see 1-2.94.2). The first precept of moral reasoning – "good is to be done and pursued and evil is to be avoided" – does not tell us whether any particular action is good or evil, but that no action can be simultaneously good (and therefore to be pursued) and evil (and therefore to be avoided) at the same time and in the same way. In other words, all reasoning about action must begin with a recognition of the "grammatical" or logical distinction between good and evil.

However, Thomas thinks that natural law can also yield something more than simply the principle that good is to be pursued and evil is to be avoided. Since all rational creatures participate in divine reason, human beings "naturally" (i.e. by virtue of their rational natures) incline toward those things that they apprehend as good, and therefore our knowledge of what it means to be a human being can yield a skeletal account of those goods we ought to pursue. Thus, we have the goods that we pursue in common with all beings, such as self-preservation; goods that we pursue in common with other living beings, such as nutrition, reproduction, and the nurture of young; and, finally, pursuits peculiar to us as human beings, such as life in community and truth (1-2.94.2).

Thomas follows Aristotle in claiming that the human being is by nature a "social animal" (1-2.61.5; 1-2.95.4) – that is, human society and all it entails is part of what it means to be human. For human beings to flourish as human beings, they need some sort of structured way of living and flourishing *together*. This flourishing together is based on what Thomas calls "the common good." This is neither the aggregate of all individual goods, nor those goods that a given group of individuals happen to have in common. Rather, it is *God* who is the common good of all creatures (1.60.5; 1-2.19.10), both as the source of all created goods, and as the end toward which they are drawn. Beings are drawn to God through what Thomas describes as "the beauty of order" (1.96.3 *ad* 3): the good of ordered diversity reflecting in a finite way the infinite, simple goodness of God. Thus we might say that, on the level of human community, the common good is the good of ordered common life itself, a goodness that is a participation in the goodness of God.

While social life is natural to human beings, this does not mean that untutored human impulse will inevitably lead to the forsaking of individual goods for the common good. Human beings have a "natural aptitude" to pursue good and avoid evil in particular ways, but this aptitude is not sufficient in itself for leading a good life, precisely because those particular goods must be coordinated to reflect the "beauty of order." Thus particular human laws must be instituted in order to train and direct human beings in community to properly order the goods that they pursue by natural inclination (1-2.95.1). Thomas is remarkably undogmatic about which form of government is best suited to this purpose, though he tends to identify pure democracy with mob rule and expresses a preference for a "mixed" form of government incorporating elements of monarchy (one clear head of government), aristocracy (the powers of government distributed among a group), and democracy (those who govern being chosen from the people and by the people) (1-2.105.1). Whatever the polity, however, a government is judged as good or bad according to its ability to properly order human life together.

The presence of the beauty of order in human societies is what we call "justice," and the lack of such order is what we call "tyranny." Aquinas says that "justice, by its nature, implies a certain rightness [*rectitudinem*] of order" (1-2.113.1). A just society is one that is rightly or beautifully ordered by imitating God who, according to his eternal law, "gives to each thing what is due to it by its nature and condition" (1.21.1 *ad* 3). Human communities participate in the beauty of God's order when, for example, they give to children the nurture and education due to them on account of their nature. However, when those entrusted with the leadership of a community fail to render to each what is their due, we have tyranny, which is a kind of perverse imitation of law (1-2.92.1 *ad* 4). Indeed, if justice truthfully mirrors the ordering action of God by caring for each and every one, tyranny is a false representation, because it is an exercise of power that ignores the common good.

The task of justice, understood as our participation in the divine beauty of order, is something to which human beings are called, both as individuals and as communities, but at the same time is a task to which they are in no way adequate. This inadequacy is rooted in human creaturely finitude and exacerbated by human sin. Thus, beyond natural law and human law it was necessary that there be a law given to human beings by God, which Aquinas calls "divine law" (1-2.91.4). This divine law is intended both to strengthen the dictates of natural law and to supplement them by uniting human beings in the right worship of God.

This divine law is first manifested in the Torah of the people Israel, which in the decalogue clearly articulates the natural law for God's people, and in the ceremonial and judicial precepts gives shape to the common life of that people (1-2.99.4). Indeed, Thomas says that "the people of Israel is commended for the beauty of its order" (1-2.105.1 *sed contra*). That beauty lies in part in the relative clarity with which the Torah renders God's eternal law, but above all in its "figurative" quality, by which it points to the new law of Jesus Christ (1-2.104.2). The new law surpasses the old by bringing it to perfection. Whereas the old law directed and ordered human action through external means – promises and punishments – the new law directs and orders human action from within, through the infusion of grace (1-2.107.1 *ad* 2). Indeed, Thomas says that the new law first and foremost simply *is* the grace of the Holy Spirit, ruling (in the sense both of directing and of measuring) our hearts (1-2.106.1). Here we find echoes of Thomas' comments on the distinction in his commentary on John between Christ's kingship and "physical" kingship. However, the new law also commends certain physical action: the sacramental rituals that are a source of grace and the visible acts of human love that are consequences of divinely imparted love (1-2.108.1). Thus the new law, no less than the old, imparts a visible "shape" to the community of God's people, though without recourse to physical coercion.

Attempts to reduce Thomas' discussion of law to the few articles that he devotes to natural law stumble over the fact that his account of law is irreducibly theological. In fact, it is not simply *theological*, but *Christological*. It begins by rooting all law in the eternal law expressed by the Father in the generation of the Son and ends with the new law of Christ, given through the Spirit to his disciples. In between these Christological bookends we do indeed find discussions of natural and human law, and Thomas clearly holds the view that certain particular goods can be realized by societies established on the basis of the natural law written in our hearts. He rejects the position that the seemingly good things that people do apart from grace – such as building houses or having friends (1-2.109.2, 5) – are in actuality sinful. But they do remain incomplete, and radically so, because such natural goodness can only dimly glimpse the eternal law, the divine truth manifested in God's incarnate Word. Though human societies apart from divine law can instantiate particular goods, and even partially order them to the common good, they cannot ultimately attain the truly common good, which is God.

To make this same point from a different angle, let us return to Jesus standing before Pilate. Pilate's human nature has retained sufficient goodness for him to recognize Jesus as a teacher of the truth; it has retained sufficient goodness for him to value the truth enough to want to release Jesus; but because he has not recognized "the gift of God which enables us to believe and love the truth" (§2363), he has not recognized Jesus himself as the truth, the embodiment of the eternal law. Pilate has retained just enough goodness to be morally responsible, and thus, in his condemnation of Christ, "he has condemned himself" (§2393). Like all embodiments of human law and authority left to their own devices, Pilate can be held accountable to justice, but he cannot implement it except in the most ad hoc and ultimately inadequate ways. He cannot enact the beauty of order.

Thomas Today

The reading I have offered of Thomas on politics has argued that what many modern interpreters see as his greatest strength, the autonomy he gives to secular politics through his notion of natural law, is in fact not Thomas' position at all. While Thomas believed that the goodness of human nature was not entirely vitiated by sin, and that just human societies were ordered toward the common good, he also shared the views of his culture that in any rightly ordered society the Gospel would be welcomed and promoted by the laws of that society. He argued that unbelievers should not be allowed to establish their rule over believers (2-2.10.10), that heretics were an illness of the body politic and could under certain circumstances be killed (2-2.11.3), and that an apostate prince could be deprived of his dominion over his subjects (2-2.12.2). He was not, as Lord Acton would have had it, "the first Whig."

Any proposed use of Thomas today must accept the fact that his views are not easily separable from the ecclesial–political situation of his day; and it must equally accept that Thomas' ecclesial–political situation no longer obtains in our day. In order to avoid any facile or distorted applications of what Thomas has to say on politics, we must look carefully at the assumptions of Thomas and his day and at those of our own. Thomas does not share our assumptions. He does not think of the common good as equivalent to the greatest good for the greatest number. He does not think of human societies as primarily instruments by which individuals pursue their private ends. He does not think that questions of ultimate truth must be bracketed in order for societies to function. Indeed, because "truth is stronger," a truly human society can be established only on the basis of eternal truth.

This last point indicates the greatest difference between Thomas' assumptions and contemporary assumptions, which is exemplified by his treatment of Pilate's question, "What is truth?" As noted above, Thomas takes Pilate to be making a serious inquiry. Pilate retains a goodness in his nature that still desires the truth. But contrast Thomas' reading of Pilate with the one given by Nietzsche in *The Antichrist*:

Need I add that in the whole New Testament there is only a *single* figure who commands respect? Pilate, the Roman governor. To take a Jewish affair *seriously* – he does not persuade himself to do that. One Jew more or less – what does it matter? The noble scorn of a Roman, confronted with an impudent abuse of the word "truth," has enriched the New Testament with the only saying *that has value* – one which is its criticism, and even its *annihilation*: "What is truth?" (Nietzsche 1954: 626–7)

Thomas' benign reading of Pilate's question seems to miss the irony in it that is so obvious to us today. It is almost as if Thomas could not imagine that Pilate was *not* genuinely interested in *the* truth, an eternal and universal truth. The question of Nietzsche's Pilate, on the other hand, is redolent of the corrosive irony that relativizes all truth, turning it into, in Nietzsche's phrase, "a mobile army of metaphors, metonyms, and anthropomorphisms – in short, a sum of human relations, which have been enhanced, transposed, and embellished poetically and rhetorically, and which after long use seem firm, canonical, and obligatory to a people" ("On Truth and Lie in an Extra-Moral Sense," §1 in Nietzsche 1954: 46–7). Whatever "truth" Pilate may be concerned with, it is a Roman truth, established by Caesar's rule and the greatness of the Roman people; he is supremely *unconcerned* with the *Jewish* truth of which Jesus speaks.

Pilate's "noble scorn" embodies for Nietzsche the reversal of the hierarchy of power that is at the heart of Thomas' politics. For Aquinas, the truth is more powerful than the king because it is God, eternal truth, who creates the king; for Nietzsche, the king – at least, a "noble" king – is more powerful than truth, because it is he who creates gods for his people. A Roman like Pilate might choose to ignore a Jewish truth, or to destroy it on a cross, but he would never bow before it as being more powerful than Caesar. And indeed, it seems that Nietzsche understood Pilate better than Aquinas did, for it was the reminder of the power of Caesar, the "truth" that Caesar can create, that strengthened the resolve of Pilate.

While few today approach Nietzsche's subtlety with regard to the relationship among politics, truth, and power, his conviction that "truth" is a product of human making and is malleable in the hands of whoever has the most coercive power is widespread, as a practical attitude if not a theoretical position. Liberal societies seek to bracket questions of truth not simply because they seem unresolvable, but because they seem so subject to manipulation by the powerful. And in this they are capable of posing some difficult questions to a thinker like Aquinas, who at times accepts certain cultural assumptions as truths of nature. For example, in the quodlibital question with which we began, Thomas is convinced that he knows the place of "woman" in the order of things. A recognition of the role of human making in our understanding of the truth can lead us to be more critical than Aquinas was in his construal of the "natural" relations of men and women or masters and slaves.

But the corrosive question "What is truth?" can be turned back upon liberal societies themselves. The question that liberal societies must face is whether their bracketing of truth makes them more or less subject to ideological manipulation. Does suspicion of overt truth claims liberate one from the covert claims? Could it be that the forces that shape our lives – forces that shape what we buy, how we earn our living, what we watch and listen to, who and for whom we will kill in war, who we see as "us" and who we see as "them" – are no less absolute in their claims upon us, even if they have abandoned the language of "truth" for the language of "freedom"?

It is perhaps here that Thomas can be genuinely helpful for Christian thinking about politics. The ideal of a Christian prince withers before the Nietzschean understanding of what Pilate is saying when he asks "What is truth?" Particularly when rule – even democratic rule – takes the form of empires, truth must always be subordinate to the rulers. But Thomas' conviction that truth is stronger than kings – or presidents or prime ministers – can still undergird a political vision for Christians. This conviction will not be manifested in laws proscribing heresies or popes deposing princes, nor in claims about the "natural" ordering of relations between slaves and masters or women and men. But it will be manifested by a Christian community that forms people to resist the functional idolatries of the state and the market, that makes its members disobedient subjects of tyrannical regimes, that manifests in its common life the beauty of order. It will be manifested by a church that emulates Zerubbabel before Darius and Jesus before Pilate, a church that speaks truth to kings in the conviction that truth is stronger and that a ruler who does not serve the truth is a tyrant. Such a political vision will have at its heart Thomas' claim that the cross, an instrument of imperial murder, has become the sign of Christ's "universal dominion over all things," a sign of the power of God's truth by which all earthly polities will be judged.

References

Aquinatis, S. Thomae (1996). *Quaestiones de quodlibet.* In *Opera omnia* 25, vol. 2. Paris: Cerf.

——(1948). *Summa Theologiae,* ed. Billuart P. Faucher OP et al. Rome: Marietti. English translation: St. Thomas Aquinas, *Summa Theologica,* trans. the Fathers of the Dominican Province (Westminster, Md: Christian Classics, 1981 [1920]). In a number of places I have modified the translations. References in the text are by part, question, and article.

——(1952). *Super evangelium S. Ioannis, lectura,* ed. P. Raphaelis Cai, OP. Rome: Marietti. English translation: St. Thomas Aquinas, *Commentary on the Gospel of St. John, Part II,* trans. Fabian Larcher OP (Petersham, Mass.: St. Bede's, 1999). In a few places I have modified the translations. References in the text refer to the paragraph numbers from the Marietti edition.

Finnis, John (1998). *Aquinas: Moral, Political, and Legal Theory.* Oxford: Oxford University Press.

Gutiérrez, Gustavo (1993). *Las Casas: In Search of the Poor of Jesus Christ,* trans. Robert R. Barr. Maryknoll, NY: Orbis.

Long, Steven A. (2001). "St. Thomas Aquinas through the Analytic Looking-glass." *The Thomist* 65, 259–300.

MacIntyre, Alasdair (1991). *Three Rival Versions of Moral Enquiry: Encyclopaedia, Genealogy, and Tradition*. Notre Dame, Ind.: University of Notre Dame Press.

Nietzsche, Friedrich (1954). *The Portable Nietzsche*, ed. and trans. Walter Kaufmann. New York: Viking.

Pinckaers, Servais (1995). *The Sources of Christian Ethics*, trans. Mary Thomas Noble. Washington DC: Catholic University of America Press.

Porter, Jean (1990). *The Recovery of Virtue: The Relevance of Aquinas for Christian Ethics*. Louisville, Ky: Westminster/John Knox.

CHAPTER 5
The Reformation

Andrew Bradstock

Reflection on the period we call the Reformation must lead one to doubt whether it is meaningful to categorize ideas as purely "religious" or "political," or to attempt to study them in isolation from one another. Luther's rediscovery of the doctrine of justification through faith may well be understood as a "spiritual experience," yet any appreciation of its impact will be at best partial if it takes no account of its political and ecclesiological repercussions. While preaching salvation as a consequence of God's grace (rather than a financial transaction with the church) may offer spiritual comfort to the individual, it has also enormous implications for the power and stability of the church, and for the status quo of which the church is a part. Little wonder, then, that a recent commentator can claim that Luther "contributed to the dismantling of the edifice of medieval Christendom with a more sweeping stroke than any of his reforming predecessors, Wyclif and Marsilius included" (O'Donovan and O'Donovan 1999: 581).

Martin Luther

Luther's journey toward a recovery of the Pauline and Augustinian understanding of the "justice of God" has been well documented: as he himself recounted, it turned him from hate of a God whose damnation he could not escape, to love for a God whose "grace and sheer mercy . . . justifies us through faith" (Bainton 1978: 65). What his discovery also did was challenge the power, structures, wealth, and influence of the church: for to affirm that the individual is able to relate directly to God is not only to undermine the role of the church as mediator of salvation but to challenge its authority – if not the very concept of authority itself. Hence Luther's explicit attacks on indulgences, the sacramental system of the church, the priesthood, and the powers of the papacy are all profound in their political potential. However, his assertion that all men and women come on equal terms to appropriate God's grace, effecting that appropriation through a direct and individual relationship with God, is in reality much more subversive.

Though politically Luther might be deemed conservative and reactionary, his theological discovery has led to his being hailed as an early figure in the development of modern democracy. His view of salvation as a matter of the individual relating to the divine in a direct, unmediated way, suggests a conception of "church" as the gathering together of people who have shared that experience, not a vast, centralized, hierarchical institution. Whenever believers choose freely to come together to worship, break bread, and hear the Word, there is church – a gathering of all who share the same experience and who have entered into their relationship as equals.

The equality which Luther's theological insights promote leads also to new and democratic notions of authority. The church's traditional view was that divine power filtered down through its own established hierarchy: Luther, however, echoing passages in the epistles such as Gal. 4: 7 – "you are no longer a slave but a child, and if a child then also an heir, through God" – saw authority being shared equally among all believers. Believers enjoying a filial relationship to God not only did not need a priest to mediate their salvation but were themselves "priests," and therefore not under the authority of any claiming that specific title and function within the church. Luther explicitly argues that those holding the office of priest "have no right to rule over us except in so far as we freely concede to it" (Maddox 1996: 112).

It is possible, therefore, to see in Luther's ideas the seeds of the modern idea of individualism, and the more so when the extent of his influence outside the church is considered: for the equality and dissemination of authority for which Luther argued, when translated into a wider political context, have far-reaching consequences indeed. Luther's stress on individuals relating personally to God, being directed by their conscience rather than by authority figures outside of themselves, subverted not only the power of the church but the notion of authority itself. Even though Luther may not have explicitly invited such conclusions to be drawn from his work, his theology could not but become one of the forces undermining the monopoly of political conservatism in his day.

Considering the extent of his output, Luther wrote very little of an explicitly "political" nature: most of what he had to say on the subject can be found in just one work, *Von weltlicher Oberkeit*, published in 1523. Caution needs to be used when assessing this work, however, for the hostile stance toward rulers to be found there is not typical of the views its author held throughout his life. *Von weltlicher Oberkeit* – which might be translated "On Secular [or Temporal] Authority" – was prompted by an action of Duke George of Saxony of which Luther disapproved: the promulgation of an edict prohibiting the sale and possession of his translation of the New Testament. The work's less-than-warm tone toward those in authority is therefore none too surprising; many rulers shared the duke's concern about Luther's ideas, a fact which clearly informed his writing. Yet when faced by what he perceived to be an even greater threat, the "murderous hordes of peasants", just two years later, Luther's tone, as he solicits the support of those in power for his cause, is more conciliatory. There are further complications in trying to connect Luther's ideas in "On Secular Authority" with his theology, for while in places he is clearly working out the political consequences of his religious discovery, elsewhere he would seem to be drawing upon other sources for his ideas.

It could be argued that the central theme of this writing, the dividing off of a separate and limited sphere of operation for the state over against the church, while a logical outworking of his theological position, also reflects Luther's disaffection at the time for the "secular" authorities. Such a separation is entirely consistent with his view of a church as a free, *independent*, and voluntary community, a *Gemeinde* in which every member is king, priest, and prophet. But the sharp separation Luther draws between the "secular" and the "sacred," while maintaining that both are ordained by God, would seem also to be a signal to rulers not to follow Duke George's example in attempting to interfere with the work of the church. The worldly authority has its own sphere of concern, the good ordering of society, and the church *its* own.

Further, God has ordained different means for each of the two "kingdoms" or "governments" to perform their respective functions. The "worldly government," entrusted with the affairs of the world, is effected through rulers, magistrates, and laws backed up by the sword: and it *is* a work of God, for God has ordained that peace and good order should prevail and that sin should be punished. Therefore those enforcing this state of affairs perform a divinely sanctioned role (as Romans 13 makes abundantly clear), whether or not they are themselves true believers. But it operates on different principles from those upon which "spiritual" government rests, for here there is no need of the sword to enforce obedience since the Word is obeyed from a sense of commitment. The believer, unlike the ordinary citizen who needs coercion and the threat of punishment, is indwelt by the Spirit and therefore led to act righteously. It is the believer's nature to do so, Luther argues, just as a tree needs no guidance or force to bear its fruit. As a tree brings forth its fruit naturally, so the believer naturally behaves morally and justly.

This point is worth underlining, for Luther clearly saw two profoundly different moralities at work in the two realms. Christians live by the high principles enshrined in the Sermon on the Mount: they are ruled by the ethic of love and go beyond the law. But one cannot expect *everybody* to be governed by the Sermon's precepts, and therefore a less demanding "human" ethic operates in the public arena which it is necessary to enforce with the threat of punishment. Indeed, if there were no law and government, Luther writes, "then seeing that all the world is evil and that scarcely one human being in a thousand is a true Christian, people would devour each other" (Höpfl 1991: 10). It is as if Luther were admitting that the Sermon on the Mount is a perfect moral guide for the individual Christian but that its moral demands are not necessarily applicable to a wider constituency. Christian ethics, in other words, "is grounded in the doctrine of justification by faith alone, in which the believer gratefully responds to God's grace with good works; public morality is based upon fear and coercion, in which the citizen obeys the law for fear of the consequences of failing to do so" (McGrath 1988: 143).

Hence Luther's argument that the "sacred" and "secular" realms have to be kept separate. In setting up this dichotomy he was, of course, hardly original: Augustine had assumed a distinction between the heavenly and earthly cities in *De Civitate Dei*, and in the fourteenth century William of Ockham also made a clear distinction between spiritual and temporal affairs. Yet neither had gone as far as Luther who, while maintaining the equal status before God of both spheres, asserted that the rule under which each operated must not impinge on the function of the other. Indeed, to confuse the two was the work of the devil himself who, Luther claimed, "never ceases cooking and brewing up the two kingdoms together." It is in the name of the devil that the secular authorities "seek . . . to teach and instruct Christ how he should conduct his Church and his spiritual rule," and the false priests and sectaries are no better when they try to tell people how they should conduct secular rule (Maddox 1996: 107–8). A major culprit for Luther was, of course, the papacy of his day, with its system of canon law. "Where the soul is concerned," Luther writes, "God neither can nor will allow anyone but himself to rule . . . where secular authority takes it upon itself to legislate for the soul, it trespasses on God's government, and merely seduces and ruins souls" (Höpfl 1991: 23).

For Luther, then, just as the human being lives in two worlds, that of reason and that of faith, so there is a distinction between earthly rule, based on reason, and the rule of faith. But what consequences might result from this? At the human level Christians might see themselves being asked to live by two moral standards – in their private life by the Sermon on the Mount, and in the world of public affairs by the standards which govern all people. Thus on the one level they might be guided to forgive one who trespassed against them, but on another – while serving as soldiers in their country's army, for example – to wield the sword.

To a considerable extent Luther's political theology is pragmatic: recognizing that the authorities were better placed than Christian people themselves to further the reformation for which he was calling, he accords them religious dignity by providing a theological underpinning for their position. He also offers constructive advice as to how they might rule more effectively and justly (while acknowledging that they may not take it): they should have the common interest and not their own always uppermost, should always seek wisdom from God, should never wholly trust those with whom they share power, and should not take too legalistic a line on the administration of justice: "a person who can't wink at faults doesn't know how to govern" (Höpfl 1991: 39).

Luther's insistence that rulers be obeyed almost at all costs, and his ferocious condemnation of all who seek to stir up rebellion against them, might also be understood in this light: it is a course likely to admit of good order. Yet by insisting that rulers put the common interest first he is far from giving them license to govern as they will. True, they are not to be denied the perks of the job – dancing, hunting, gaming, and so on – but they are decidedly not to think that "the land and the people are mine; I shall do as I please." A ruler is to protect the people, not lord it over them. But above all rulers should – at least, if they are among the few concerned to act according to Christian principles – follow closely the injunctions of scripture. "God's word will not be guided and twisted to suit princes; rather it is princes who are to be guided by his Word" (Höpfl 1991: 36).

The weaknesses of Luther's political theology have been remarked upon often enough, and there is little to be gained by subjecting it to too detailed a scrutiny. At the level of church responses to the state he has often been blamed for encouraging "quietism" on the part of Christians, even in the face of tyranny and injustice. It is hard not to see this as the logic of his position if all forms of government are understood as instruments of God for the good of society. Unlike Augustine, Luther offers no space for a Christian critique of structural injustice. There is also an inconsistency in Luther's preparedness to advocate support for even the most extreme tyrant (up to the point when conscience dictates otherwise), yet to countenance the killing of those seeking to free the people from this tyranny (Maddox 1996: 116). Luther's reaction to those fomenting rebellion is certainly extreme when compared with his attitude toward unjust rulers, and is evident even from the title of his main writing on the subject, *Against the Murderous and Thieving Hordes of Peasants*. This whole work is nothing less than a diatribe against those who, by "setting themselves against the higher powers, wilfully and with violence . . . have forfeited body and soul, as faithless, perjured, lying disobedient knaves and scoundrels are wont to do" (Rupp and Drewery 1970: 122). Rebellion was not a theoretical issue for Luther, and it clearly exercised him a great deal; as a position it could not have been farther removed from his own, and was utterly indefensible theologically.

Thomas Müntzer

Yet the rebellious spirit against whom much of Luther's ire was directed, the peasant leader Thomas Müntzer, argued with equal passion that in certain circumstances rebellion against the authorities can be warranted from scripture. The groundwork of Müntzer's thinking is a mystical spirituality which demands purgation from the soul of all that hinders the work of God – the "tares" of the parable in Matthew. Müntzer is wedded to the concept of "true" or "authentic" faith which knows and experiences at first hand the sharp edge of the divine plowshare in the soul, uprooting all that is of self and prevents the soul being fully "yielded" to God. It is to be contrasted with the false or "counterfeit" religion of biblical scholars like Luther, which is gleaned only from books and not lived or experienced. Yet Müntzer is also an apocalyptic thinker who understands humankind to be composed of both "wheat" and "tares," the chosen and the lost, growing together until the divine harvester initiates the work of separating them out; and the logic of his thinking demands that there be a concomitant transformation on both the inner and outer levels. Just as the soul needs to be purged of all that hinders God's work, so those who prevent the work of God in the world, the godless false teachers, need to be ruthlessly destroyed.

It is essential for Müntzer that the true faith be preached in the world to counteract the spread of error and false faith, and he assigns responsibility for this task to the secular rulers. In so doing he parts company from a number of his contemporaries, most obviously Luther, who entrusted a rather different mission to those powers. In fact, although both Luther and Müntzer grounded their teaching on government on Romans 13, they drew different conclusions from the text: while Luther placed the emphasis on verse 1, which treats of the duty of the subject *vis-à-vis* the ruler, Müntzer, by focusing particularly on verse 3, draws attention to the duties of governments toward their subjects, arguing that popular support was warranted only in so far as those duties were carried out. And what Müntzer understood as the duties of governments went beyond merely punishing those who stepped out of line: the ruler must actually further the work of God in the world. "[L]et God's true, unwavering purpose be yours," was Müntzer's appeal to the princes; "sweep aside those evil men who obstruct the gospel! Take them out of circulation! Otherwise you will be devils, not the servants of God which Paul calls you in Romans 13" (Matheson 1988: 245–6). For Müntzer the authorities do not exist merely as a necessary evil to maintain peace and order; they have a positive role in the service of God for the protection and propagation of the faith.

The obedience due to rulers under the mandate of Rom. 13: 1 is conditional upon fulfilling the duties laid down for them in verse 3: only in so far as they honor their responsibility to defend the faith are they justified in commanding the obedience of the people. Yet having expounded the passage in this way, Müntzer does not derive from it any legitimation for resistance to governments. His position is rather that, when rulers default in the execution of their duties, their obligations toward the godless will simply devolve to the people: the sword "will be taken from them and will be given to the people who burn with zeal so that the godless can be defeated" (Matheson 1988: 69). Müntzer draws biblical support for this assertion from Daniel chapter 7, one of only a handful of scriptures (including Rom. 13) he uses in discussing questions of government and resistance. The key section in this chapter for Müntzer is verse 27, which speaks, in an apocalyptic context, of all the kingdoms of the world being given over to the saints of the Most High.

It is possible to draw a connection between this verse and the Rom. 13 passage by suggesting that, in Müntzer's mind, Dan. 7: 27 came into play when the requirements of Rom. 13: 3 were not followed, though, again, Müntzer does not establish from this scripture a right of revolt. He does not insist that Daniel 7: 27 be "implemented" immediately on the heels of any dereliction of duty by the rulers; neither does he clarify whether power is to devolve to the people as a result of a (legitimate) use of force by the elect, or through the direct intervention of

God. His position with regard to the latter point appears to be that God and humankind operate "together" to bring about God's judgment on earth. The case of Joshua leading the people of Israel into the Promised Land demonstrates the point: "they did not win the land by the sword, but by the power of God, but the sword was the means used" (Matheson 1988: 250). Almost every time Müntzer refers to this passage he does no more than recognize the inevitability – as with all God-given prophecies – of its fulfillment, albeit after the brief reign of Antichrist.

The dramatic events which he witnessed in the early months of 1525 finally convinced Müntzer of the necessity, indeed the *duty*, both of resistance to the rulers and of action to establish a new sociopolitical order. Not only had the princes of Saxony resisted his admonition to them to take up the sword against God's enemies, they had gone out of their way to show their contempt for just and godly rule by proceeding to oppress the poor in a most violent way. The time for action against them and on behalf of the common people had arrived: indeed, that the people were now rising up against their rulers, provoked by the growing injustice, corruption, and poverty with which they were daily confronted, was a clear sign from God that the Danielic prophecy about the fall of the last worldly kingdom was shortly to be fulfilled. In his "sermon to the princes" on Dan. 2 Müntzer had drawn his hearers' attention to the multilayered statue in Neb-uchadnezzer's dream, explaining that the layers represented the great historic empires and kingdoms of the world which had fallen. Now the only one remain-ing, which represented the present Holy Roman Empire, would shortly be smashed by Jesus himself.

The spread of the peasants' action across Germany in the early part of 1525 would have appeared to Müntzer to have been a decisive phase in the harvest-time of God, a sign that God was "shortening the time," though it is only once he has established a theological justification for revolt that he begins to talk in such terms. He is clear that the corruption of the rulers and their cynicism and violence toward the poor have left the latter no alternative but to rise up to bring them down. "It is the lords themselves who make the poor man their enemy. If they refuse to do away with the causes of insurrection how can trouble be avoided in the long run? If saying that makes me an inciter to insurrection, so be it!" (Matheson 1988: 335). Müntzer thus initially supports violence only as a defensive measure, against violation of common rights by the rulers, and to some extent his transformation from theological dissent to political opposition was forced upon him both by events and by the logic of his own position. The rulers, as a consequence of the violence they had perpetrated upon their sub-jects, had Christian blood on their hands, had forfeited their right to *be* rulers, and had brought down upon themselves the wrath of God. It is only now that Müntzer begins to compare the rulers to Nimrod, common shorthand at the time for tyrannical governors, and to speak approvingly of their downfall.

Convinced, then, that the peasants' uprising was a sign from God that the overthrow of the godless would shortly be accomplished, Müntzer set about forming his Eternal League of God. Whereas his earlier covenants had had a defensive purpose and no restrictions on membership, the Eternal League in Mühlhausen – whose very name was subversive, given that the city's ruling authority called itself the "Eternal Council" – was established with the clear intent of carrying out the final overthrow of the godless. It was more militarist in its structure, and, perhaps to emphasize its role in the fulfillment of Dan. 7: 27, its membership was limited to the saints. If these factors suggest Müntzer envisaged the battle against the godless being close at hand, the apology for his actions he prepared in the days leading up to the final battle at Frankenhausen leaves no room for doubting the apocalyptic significance he attached to the impending scenario. Whatever motives drove the common people to revolt – and they were by no means entirely economic – their struggle became for Müntzer, as he made it his own, the one which would decisively clear the way for the kingdom of God, the reign of the elect.

One final point to be noted about Müntzer's political theology is that, aside from a detailed explanation of how the world will be restored to something like its original prelapsarian state, it pays scant attention to the form society will take in the new age. The most he disclosed – under torture a few days before his execution – was that his aim had been to make all Christians equal and that a common article of faith among those supporting the insurrection was that all things are to be held in common and distribution should be to each according to need. Müntzer also allegedly said under torture that, had events fallen out his way, he would have appropriated land around Mühlhausen and Hesse and, after one warning, put to the sword any nobleman who refused to accept common ownership and distribution according to need. It may also be inferred from Müntzer's confessions under interrogation that he harbored ideas of creating something akin to a "theocratic republic," which, while it would have a communitarian framework, would not wholly discard differences of rank or even private property. That the elect would rule in this new state was set out as early as 1521 in the "Prague Manifesto," echoed later in, for example, Müntzer's letter to the Stolberg community in 1523. Yet it is difficult to avoid the conclusion that Müntzer had no real theory of society, and that his blueprint, such as it was, was clearly intended as a provisional measure to cover an interim period during which the elect would reign before the arrival of the kingdom of God (Scott 1989: 171–2).

The Anabaptists

If Müntzer had only a hazy idea of how a society based on common ownership might develop, many of his contemporaries had both a clearer vision and a commitment to living it out. The Hutterites, who spread from Germany into Moravia in the 1520s, both preached and practiced a radical community of goods (and have maintained it to this day). Like others in the Anabaptist movement, Hutterites picked up the torch of the peasants' cause, arguing that justice for the poor could be ensured only under a communitarian model of living. Even those Anabaptist groups that did not practice total community of goods acknowledged that their so-called possessions were not their own and were to be readily available to help those in need. In this they saw themselves following closely the practice of the first Christians who, in the words of the Congregational Order of 1527, "held all in common, and especially stored up a common fund, from which aid can be given to the poor" (Murray 1997: 13). Private property was seen to be "the greatest enemy of love," as a Hutterite document put it, and the radical pacifism of the movement has led members to withhold the part of their taxes believed to be allocated to military expenditure.

The Anabaptist movement emerged in Switzerland around the time Müntzer was rallying the troops at Frankenhausen, and shared his passion both for social justice and for a wholesale transformation of the church. Anabaptists saw the church as "fallen" and therefore beyond mere reform, and called for its reconstitution along New Testament lines. Crucially, they wanted the church to break the ties it had enjoyed to "the state" since Constantine, and argued, against both the Roman church and the reformer Ulrich Zwingli, that baptism should not be administered to infants but voluntarily entered into by people able to understand its meaning. This was of course a profoundly political stance, undermining the whole concept of a national or "state" church. Unhappy with Zwingli's tardiness in pushing through reforms, and in particular with his concern to obtain the approval of the magistrates at every stage, Anabaptists called for the church to accept as members only those indicating a wish to join it, and to give up its dependence upon tithes imposed by the authorities.

The Anabaptists' concern for "separation" is made explicit in the Schleitheim Confession of Faith drawn up in 1527 by Wilhelm Roubl and Michael Sattler in a small town on the Swiss–German border. The fourth article of this Confession states that the call of the Lord to be separate from evil must mean shunning "all popish and anti-popish works and church services, meetings and church attendance" (Hillerbrand 1968: 133). A document published ten years later, "The Answer of some who are called (Ana)baptists to the Question Why They Do Not Attend the Churches," makes clear that one reason was that Anabaptist meetings operated on fundamentally different principles from those of the more mainstream churches. Rejecting clericalism, Anabaptists encouraged the active participation of all in worship, including in some cases women, basing this practice on the teaching of 1 Cor. 14 (Bradstock and Rowland 2002: 89–90).

Anabaptists were separated not only from the church but from the civil authorities and all their works: here was Luther's separation of powers taken a step or two further. The Schleitheim Confession includes, under the list of things to be shunned, "civic affairs," swearing oaths, military service, and service as a magistrate. While the motives for these positions may well have been fidelity to the teaching of Christ as recorded in scripture, their political implications were not lost on the authorities in both church and state, who hounded Anabaptists mercilessly and even subjected some to the obscenely symbolic punishment of death by drowning. Occasionally Anabaptists would make trouble for themselves, as when a group under Dutch leadership set aside the norms of pacifism and separation and took control of the German town of Münster. Inspired by a belief that the kingdom of God was imminent, and by the Old Testament, they appointed twelve elders, introduced polygamy, and imposed severe penalties for all forms of misconduct. In consequence Anabaptism came to be seen as a violent and dangerous sect, though leaders like Hutter, Menno Simons (from whom the Mennonites take their name), and Dirk Philips did much to rebuild the movement and recover its traditions of pacifism and separation.

John Calvin

If Anabaptists sought to keep the church pure by separating from the world, John Calvin set out to construct a new model of relations between the church and the civil authorities. Calvin is remembered more as a theologian and church reformer than a political theorist, and his political writings hardly extend beyond book IV, chapter 20 (entitled "Civil Government") of his massive *Institutes of the Christian Religion*; yet although his ideas are offered there at a theoretical level, he did attempt to implement them – with a degree of success – in Geneva, the town where he spent the major part of his adult life (and where, interestingly, he never held a position of either civil or religious importance in the city, and was not even granted the status of citizen until he had been resident for nearly 20 years).

It could be claimed that Calvin has exerted an enormous influence in the realms of economics and politics through his famous teaching on "predestination" which he developed from the New Testament letters of Paul and writings of Augustine. This doctrine holds that God has the absolute right to choose whom he will for salvation, which, while ruling out human effort or goodness as a factor in the equation, can lead – as Max Weber famously argued – to concerned individuals seeking from God signs of their having been chosen. These most obviously take the form of economic success, rewards for hard graft and sound investment, and although Calvin himself tended to be wary of commercial activity, holding in high regard the life of poverty, the great economic transformation of much of Europe and the United States in subsequent centuries was led by people claiming allegiance to his ideas.

Calvin's reforming project in Geneva coincided almost exactly with the Council of Trent and reassertion of Catholicism after the blow dealt it by the popularity of Luther's ideas. The reformation movement was now on the defensive, and beginning both to divide up into factions and to score "own goals" (like the debacle at Münster). Thus the need for Calvin and others in the reformed camp not to incur the displeasure of the civil authorities in Europe was even more obvious than it had been in Luther's heyday, and a central strand of Calvin's thought was the necessity of good relations between "church" and "state."

Yet it is unlikely that Calvin was being merely pragmatic, even less cynical, in his espousal of a close relationship between the two institutions; rather – and here he differed substantially from Luther – he held that both institutions were ordained by God to be partners in a common enterprise, the inculcation of godliness among the people. Both must work together, in their differing ways, in the pursuit of this goal. Whereas Luther had been very keen to stress separate areas of concern for the "spiritual" and "secular" authorities, with the latter having no responsibility for the spiritual dimension of life or the affairs of the church, Calvin saw the two as equal partners in a complementary work, namely good government according to the teaching of the Bible, the word of God.

It might be possible to sum up Calvin's views on the relationship between church and state by saying that both share a common task but differ in the powers God has granted them to bring it about. They are "quite distinct," as Calvin puts it, but "in no way incompatible with each other" (Höpfl 1991: 49). The church has a duty to contribute to good and peaceable order by teaching and preaching true doctrine and administering the sacraments, but it has no powers to punish wrongdoers – though it might choose to discipline its own members by, say, excommunication. The magistrates *do* have the God-given right to coerce the people into obeying the law through the threat of punishment, and they can also complement the work of the church by creating and maintaining a climate in which God's word can be taught and heard. Magistrates can also uphold disciplinary measures taken by the church and approve the appointment of officers and ministers of the church.

Calvin was not suggesting that the secular rulers could tell the church what its doctrines should be, or how it should best organize itself, but that they did have a duty to facilitate the promulgation of right religion and prevent its being hindered. And Calvin also thought, in contradistinction to many of his more radical contemporaries, that how the church organized its affairs, and whom it appointed as its leaders, was a matter of public concern and interest. Magistrates and ministers must therefore work closely together, not only because both are appointed by God to pursue the same overall goal, but because their collaboration also makes good common sense since they share responsibility for the same body of people. Many citizens are also Christians, and all Christians are citizens.

The absolute authority in the universe is, for Calvin, God alone, and the purpose of humanity is to build up God's kingdom on earth: hence all government, all politics, is to be ordered to that end (Maddox 1996: 123). But whereas Calvin was clear that a model for the church could be discerned from scripture, that is, one that is largely "collegial" in form, he was less sure that the Bible lent its support to any one particular type of government: God appoints different forms of government in different places. That being so, Calvin found himself, like Luther, urging citizens to be obedient to any and every form of government under which they found themselves, with the exception that any ruler commanding anything contrary to the law of God may be resisted on the grounds that he or she had thereby usurped the authority that is God's alone.

Even if no one form of government seemed to commend itself more than any other in the pages of scripture, Calvin himself was clear that rule by the few was to be preferred to rule by the one. The best form of government, in other words, was one which mirrored that laid down in scripture for the church. Unlike Aquinas, Calvin distrusted monarchy or any individual being granted the power to rule singlehandedly; rather, just as in the church the elders and ministers work in partnership and operate a system of mutual restraint and discipline, so magistrates should put themselves under the subjection of one another. Rule by the one would be more likely to lead to tyranny than to good government, Calvin thought, as examples in the Old Testament and in his own day proved. It was very difficult for any person put in a sole position of authority to avoid seeking his or her own ends. Rule by the few – what Aristotle and Aquinas termed "aristocracy" – was more likely to succeed in fulfilling God's aims for government.

For Calvin, then, unlike many in the Christian tradition, politics was important, and not secondary in God's pecking order to so-called purely spiritual matters. Secular government is divinely instituted, and rulers have a responsibility, to God and to those whom they serve, to carry out vitally important tasks and duties – upholding godly standards in society, combating the spread of heresy, maintaining law and order, relieving the poor, freeing the oppressed, providing for common peace, and executing justice. Hence a calling to political activity or governmental service is not a lesser one for the Christian than, say, the priesthood. On the contrary, magistracy is the highest and most sacred of all vocations: rulers have a commission from God and since (according to Rom. 13) governments are appointed and empowered by God, they are endowed with divine authority and are not to be despised. To despise a ruler is to despise God (Höpfl 1991: 51–5).

As well as rights, rulers also have the responsibility, as Paul's letter to the Roman Christians points out, to protect those in their charge, and this may involve punishing those who act unjustly. This need to punish the wicked raises the question of capital punishment: Is this permitted in the light of the commandment "Thou shalt not kill"? For Calvin it is permitted, because, when the magistrate inflicts punishment on a condemned person, he is not acting on his own behalf but executing God's own judgment. There is a difference, Calvin argues, between "afflicting and harming" another, and avenging, at God's command, those who themselves inflict harm on others (Höpfl 1991: 60f). Romans 13: 4 makes it clear that the magistrate is entitled to use the sword, and any ruler who keeps it sheathed while the wicked are free to massacre and slaughter is guilty of the greatest possible injustice and of dishonoring God who appointed him to his office. It is bad to live under a ruler who permits nothing, Calvin argues, but much worse to live under one who permits everything. This notwithstanding, Calvin also stressed that equitable verdicts cannot be possible unless clemency is also considered, though critics might well point to a discrepancy between his views on paper and his actions in the case of the theologian Servetus, who was burned for heresy in Geneva in 1553 largely as a consequence of a campaign against him led by Calvin.

Calvin argued that magistrates may also need to use the sword to defend their territories, both from outside aggression and from the seditious intent of their own people; and, contrary to many of his more radical contemporaries who argued that the only consistently Christian position was a pacifist one, Calvin argued that Christ, rather than encouraging the soldiers he came across to throw away their weapons, seemed content to confirm them in their occupation. Calvin is clearly a thinker in the just war tradition, arguing that war is not to be entered into lightly, that it should always be a last resort, and that magistrates should never lose sight of their calling to pursue the common good. As with the punishment of wrongdoers, they must never abuse their position by allowing themselves to be carried away by private passion.

In addition to discerning from scripture the rights and responsibilities of rulers, Calvin sets out at some length the duties of their subjects, the first of which is to hold their rulers in high esteem and not see them as a "necessary evil." Rulers are to be obeyed as God is to obeyed, not on account of their own individual personalities but on account of their rank and position. Subjects have a duty to comply with the laws which their rulers pass, to pay their taxes, to share a responsibility for the defense of the realm, and to prove their sincerity in these matters by praying for those in authority over them (as exhorted by Paul in his first letter to Timothy).

But what of rulers who act unjustly, who pursue only their own interests and even use taxes taken from the poor to finance these interests? Here Calvin does not deviate from his claim that all leaders, however good or bad, derive their authority from God, and are therefore to be accorded the same reverence by their subjects. Echoing Aquinas, Calvin makes the point that an ungodly ruler may be raised up in the wisdom of God to execute God's judgment against a people: he or she may be a sign of God's curse on that people, and should not therefore be restrained by the people. Yet while arguing forcibly for obedience to all rulers, even the worst of all possible tyrants, Calvin does concede that God does occasionally raise up "avengers" from among the people as a means of punishing tyrants and freeing the people from their grip (Höpfl 1991: 81). He also acknowledges that those in the middle tiers of government have a responsibility to attempt to restrain the ungodly tendencies of those over them, and that the subject's ultimate obedience is to the God who puts rulers there in the first place and to whom they themselves are answerable (Höpfl 1991: 83).

Curiously, despite Calvin's extreme reluctance to give the common people license to resist or remove their rulers, it is this aspect of his teaching that has been received most enthusiastically by many claiming to be his followers in subsequent centuries. Calvin's dislike of absolute monarchs was clear enough, and where those monarchs were perceived to be behaving unjustly their downfall could be justified on the scriptural grounds Calvin prescribed. Thus, for example, the struggle against the entrenchment of royalty in France in the latter half of the sixteenth century – the so-called Wars of Religion – was spearheaded by a Calvinist movement; Calvinists (most famously John Knox) were behind the attempt to bring the Reformation to Scotland in the face of opposition from a

Catholic queen; and the forces led by Cromwell which brought Charles I to trial in England in 1649 were also decidedly of a Calvinist hue (Maddox 1996: 126–34).

Both Calvin's emphasis on "collegiality" rather than singularity – within the church and in civil affairs – and his stress on the duties of middle-ranking elected officials to check individual tyranny can be seen to have informed and stimulated the growth of popular resistance movements building on his ideas. Yet Calvin's more positive ideas, not least his espousal of the possibility of what he called a "Christian polity" involving both magistrates and ministers working in pursuit of a common goal, also inspired his followers, not least those who set sail for America in the 1620s to establish a new society. Although Calvin's attempts to work out his ideas in his own adopted city of Geneva were thwarted by constant tension between the spiritual and political authorities, that does not detract from the overall value of those ideas, which, perhaps not entirely to his satisfaction, may be seen to have played a significant part in the development of the concept we call political liberalism.

References

Bainton, Roland (1978). *Here I Stand*. Tring: Lion.

Baylor, Michael G. (1991). *The Radical Reformation*. Cambridge: Cambridge University Press.

Bradstock, Andrew (1997). *Faith in the Revolution: The Political Theologies of Müntzer and Winstanley*. London: SPCK.

——, ——, and Rowland, Christopher, eds. (2002). *Radical Christian Writings: A Reader*. Oxford: Blackwell.

Goertz, Hans-Jürgen (1993). *Thomas Müntzer: Apocalyptic Mystic and Revolutionary* (Eng. trans.). Edinburgh: T. & T. Clark.

Hillerbrand, Hans J., ed. (1968). *The Protestant Reformation*. London: Macmillan.

Höpfl, Harro (1991). *Luther and Calvin on Secular Authority*. Cambridge: Cambridge University Press.

McGrath, Alister E. (1988). *Reformation Thought: An Introduction*. Oxford: Blackwell.

Maddox, Graham (1996). *Religion and the Rise of Democracy*. London: Routledge.

Matheson, Peter, ed. (1988). *The Collected Works of Thomas Müntzer*. Edinburgh: T. & T. Clark.

Murray, Stuart (1997). "Introducing the Anabaptists." *Anabaptism Today* 14, 4–18.

O'Donovan, Oliver, and O'Donovan, Joan Lockwood (1999). *From Irenaeus to Grotius: A Sourcebook in Christian Political Thought 1000–1625*. Cambridge: Eerdmans.

Reardon, Bernard M. G. (1981). *Religious Thought in the Reformation*. Harlow: Longman.

Rupp, E. G. and Drewery, Benjamin (1970). *Martin Luther*. London: Edward Arnold.

Scott, Tom (1989). *Thomas Müntzer: Theology and Revolution in the German Reformation*. London: Macmillan.

CHAPTER 6
Liturgy

Bernd Wannenwetsch

In contrast to the prevailing modern tendency to identify the political meaning of the church primarily or exclusively in respect of its relationship to the state or the influence it seeks to bring to bear on civil society, this essay explores the political nature of the church as a *politeia* in its own right (Wannenwetsch 2003). The church as a political entity finds its constitutive and restitutive act in worship, which is the central praxis of the "fellow citizens of the saints" (Eph. 2: 19). Though the political relevance of worship has oftentimes been over-shadowed by other accounts of both worship and politics, it was an essential feature of the original self-understanding of the church from the New Testament on and has re-emerged throughout the history of Christian theology.

Historically and conceptually, the revolutionary novelty that the political worship of the church as *politeia* in its own right has brought about in the world of politics can be seen in its challenge to the reign of political antinomies such as public/private, freedom/necessity, and *vita activa/vita contemplativa*. To the extent those antinomies prevail in various guises, the critical capacity of the Christian political experience of worship will always remain relevant.

In order to understand the conceptual implications of "political worship," a twofold rediscovery is needed: on the one hand of the political dimension in liturgy, and on the other of the liturgical dimension of politics. The first section of this essay describes the historical and conceptual novelty of the Christian understanding of politics, as it was inherent in its liturgy. The second and third sections seek to provide a narrative account of the main threats to the political character of the worshipping church, of the struggle to formulate and refor-mulate this character in changing historical circumstances, and of exemplars of its rediscovery. Concluding remarks address the inherent liturgical character of politics where, according to Rom. 13, those in authority are known as God's "deacons," ordained to serve the people *eis to agathon*: toward the common good.

The Political Nature of Worship

Christ as political deity

The political nature of Christian worship has been recognized from the first, not least by those who opposed it (Horsley 1997). This recognition lies at the heart of the charge of "atheism" that was leveled at the primitive Christian communities. While the Romans knew Christianity to be a religious movement, they still regarded Christians as atheists because they did not partake in the public cult of the state gods, thereby undermining the unity and stability of the *res publica*. Hence Christian "atheism" was seen as not a religious but a political vice. Though Christians typically refuted the charge of being a politically destabilizing community by pointing to their own custom of praying for the welfare of the city and its rulers, they could hardly deny that the Romans were right on one essential point: The Christ whom they worshipped could never be like one of the many household gods (*penates*) of private religious devotion.

As Christians worshipped Christ as *cosmokrator*, ruler of the whole universe, they could not count on the tolerance which the Romans generally offered in matters of private religiosity. Thus a conflict would inevitably arise over the public claim of competing *political* deities. The Christians' refusal to participate in the emperor cult was not merely the result of their abhorrence at treating any human being as a god, but sprang from their worship of their own God on whom they knew depended not only their own salvation but also the welfare of the city.

The new language of the household-polis of God

By refusing to shelter in the protection of private devotion, Christian worship could not but challenge and finally overcome this separation of political life and private existence (Wannenwetsch 1997). This overcoming of separation would become true for both forms in which that separation was inherited from antiquity: its exclusivist separation of free male and wealthy citizens from the debased and unpolitical members of the household; and its inclusivist separation of the life of the citizen into two distinct spheres or "lives," the political life (*bios politikos*) and the theoretical or contemplative life (*bios theoretikos*). If Paul admonishes the congregation to live their present lives as citizens worthy of the Gospel (Phil 1: 27), the verb *politeuomai* suggests one overriding existence or *bios* for the Christian which interlocks the political and contemplative lives, citizenship and worship. As it is expressed in Eph. 2: 19: "You are no longer strangers, but members of God's household and co-citizens of the saints."

In strong contrast to the radical distinction by which the Greco-Roman world had separated these spheres, the "new humanity" (Eph. 4: 13) of the church of Jews and gentiles significantly employs both the language of the household and that of the *polis*, establishing a kind of "political household" or "household *polis*."

For the ancient world it was taken for granted that man received "besides his private life a sort of second life, his *bios politikos*. Therefore every citizen belonged to two orders of existence marked by a sharp distinction in his life between what is his own (*idion*) and what is communal (*koinon*)" (Arendt 1958: 24). It was precisely these two Greek keywords, representing the contrast between two orders of being, that we find being taken up in the New Testament in a completely different way: "The company of those who believed were of one heart and soul, and no one said that any of the things which he possessed was his own [*idion*], but they had everything in common [*koina*]" (Acts 4: 32).

As a corporate action, worship includes in full participation all the representatives of the debased household: women, slaves, children, artisans, and so on – a reconciliation of hitherto unreconciled groups and realms of social life. In Gal. 3: 26ff. Paul lists in pairs the deepest antagonisms of the religious, civil, and sexual life that are to be overcome in the new community of the church. Yet Paul is not implying the negation of all differences (women do not cease being women, nor men being men), except one crucial difference: the political division. These differences, each in its own right representing the public/private antinomy, do not count any more when it comes to the citizenship of God's city.

In this way a new concept of political identity crystallized – an identity maintained and safeguarded not through exclusivity and exclusion but through full participation of all those who were once "noncitizens," strangers and resident aliens (*paroikoi*). Yet this Christian concept of citizenship was not based on the idea of "rights," defining or widening the boundaries of a social entity by expanding access; rather, it is focused on actual participation in political action: Each citizen is conceived as having a ministry in the church's central public event. "When you come together," Paul declares with the Christian worship assembly in view, "*each one* has something: a psalm, a teaching, a tongue, an interpretation. Let all things be done for edification" (1 Cor. 14: 26). The New Testament *ekklesia* certainly had its special office-holders, but their ministries, even over against the congregation, are always viewed as serving the ministries of "the multitude of believers," and do not marginalize these ministries, let alone replace them.

As Aristotle had emphasized, there cannot be a political animal, a *zoon politikon*, without office holding. In this way the practice of *leitourgia* as the work of all the people (the church preferring this term for their worship activity rather than *orgia*, another Greek term for religious activity that was used in a more private sense and especially for mystery cults) can be said to have marked the establishment of a new form of public sphere.

The public character of worship

The historical roots of Christian worship are found in two different sources: the public worship of the Jewish synagogue, and the celebration in private homes of the Lord's Supper. While these two forms of liturgical celebration – the *synaxis* (following the model of the synagogue, comprising reading, sermon, and prayer) and the Eucharist – first existed independently of each other, from the fourth century onward they are regularly linked together in a single service. In order to understand the public character of Christian worship, we must note that it did not draw its character only from public synagogual worship. Though the Eucharist was certainly seen as the "intimate" encounter of baptized believers with their Lord, it was not understood to be a private matter that would have to acquire a public form. This must be said in refutation of the influential idea of a development "From a Private to a Public Worship" put forward by Dom Gregory Dix in his seminal study *The Shape of the Liturgy* (1945: 304ff.). *Contra* Dix, the public character of Christian worship is evident upon examination of several aspects of the primitive Christian communities.

First, certain functions of state sovereignty were claimed for the church's own public life. In 1 Cor. 6: 1–7 Paul demands that civil disputes, if they cannot be avoided, should not be settled by pagan courts but should be laid before internal congregational tribunals. This arbitration was entrusted to a Christian *synhedrin* composed of presbyters and chaired by the bishop. In the light of the admonition in the Sermon on the Mount to be reconciled with one's adversary before offering a sacrifice (Matt. 5: 23) – an injunction already taken up in the instructions about the eucharistic celebration in the *Didache* (14: 2) – the Syrian *Didascalia of the Apostles* required these arbitration tribunals to be held at the beginning of the week, in order to allow enough time for matters to be settled before the Sunday Eucharist (Dix 1945: 106).

Second, the public character of worship is further indicated by the distinction made between different forms of assembly in the Christian congregations themselves. *Ekklesia* means the formal assembly of the (whole) congregation, its *synaxis* or *eucharistia*. Beside this formal assembly, there was another kind of meeting, the *syneleusis*, for the purpose of instruction, for mutual edification, or for the celebration of the *agape*, as love meal (Dix 1945: 20f.). This form of assembly, which was geared rather to private peer groups in the congregation, had a religious character but not a liturgical one, since the *public* exercise of the ministry (including specifically ordained persons) was absent. These different levels were strictly differentiated, at latest from the time of Justin; and in Ignatius we find urgent admonitions not to misunderstand these private meetings for edification as a substitute for participation in public worship (Ignatius, *Epistle to Magnesius* 7, 1).

Third, the church's gathering in households of wealthier members (which continued until the fourth century, when the basilica would accommodate Christian worship) could provoke significant misunderstandings in regard to the public character of Christian worship (Wannenwetsch 1997: 160ff.). There are already echoes of such misunderstanding among the primitive Christian communities, especially when the patrons who hosted the assembly in their houses were tempted to conflate the authority they held as patrons with genuine ecclesial authority. Paul's charges against the Corinthians that they were spoiling the Lord's Supper by treating some members of the congregation according to their (low) worldly status by withholding (more expensive) food from them which was reserved for the higher-status "clients" of the patron (1 Cor. 11: 22) reflects the temptation of patrons to overturn the new public dimension of the Christian worship in favor of standards arising from the logic of the household. Considering this early tension in which the public character of worship was threatened by tendencies to subsume it under private paradigms, scholarly misunderstandings such as Dix's should occasion little surprise. Yet they overlook the theological originality of the public claim in Christian liturgy.

Threats, Losses, Struggles

Ironically – and in contrast to the modern reading of the development – it was exactly Christianity's rise to political power which partially but not completely obscured this nascent theological clarity about the inherent political nature of the church as a worshipping community. We must, of course, avoid the pitfall of presenting a narrative of decline from relatively healthy primitive Christian communities to the compromised church of the Christendom era. In each era, there were *genuine* threats and losses as well as struggle and reforming spirit. Any analysis will have to identify the *shifting* temptations and *diverging* threats as they came about for the church in different situations and times.

If the public nature of the liturgy was first threatened by the power of the private paradigm, it now had to face the threat of being absorbed by the claim of another public, the public of the state, which was becoming increasingly aware of the blessings of the church. Whereas the political character of the church was first confused with a household religion, now it was its role as a civil religion that was prone to causing confusion. This development (which was, in fact, a struggle) must be examined first internally and then externally.

Threats from within: The loss of the offertory

Internally, the political form of the church was eclipsed as the multifold ministry that had characterized the Christian assembly during the first four centuries was increasingly absorbed by the rise of the monarchical episcopate. This was modeled on secular hierarchical authority and gradually took over most of the hitherto indispensable liturgy of the people, such as the offertory or the prayers of intercession. As the distinction between clergy and laity emerged, based on the differentiation between the active ("saying mass") and passive ("attending mass"), the political form of the church underwent a serious eclipse.

This unfortunate tendency was expressed and accelerated by the withering of the offertory – a liturgical event in which the political nature of the congregation was especially visible, as it comprised a subtle interaction of the whole body with a particular stress on the participation of the laity. Dix summarizes its theological significance:

Each communicant from the bishop to the newly confirmed gave *himself* under the forms of bread and wine to God, as God gives Himself to them under the same forms. In the united oblations of all her members the Body of Christ, the church, gave herself to *become* the Body of Christ, the sacrament, in order that receiving again the symbol of herself now transformed and hallowed, she might be truly that which by nature she is, the Body of Christ, and each of her members members of Christ. In this self-giving the order of laity no less than that of the deacons or the high-priestly celebrant had its own indispensable function in the vital act of the Body. The layman brought the sacrifice of himself, of which he is the priest. The deacon, the "servant" of the whole body, "presented" all together in the Person of Christ . . . The high-priest, the bishop "offered" all together, for he alone can speak for the whole Body. In Christ, as His Body, the church is "accepted" by God "in the Beloved". Its sacrifice of itself is taken up into His sacrifice of Himself. (Dix 1945: 117)

The political point of the offertory lies in the strange way in which emphases on individual contribution and communal offering interlock. On the one hand, it was all-important that every individual believer would bring forward his or her own oblation (offering). This implied a certain eucharistic "egalitarianism" which was not only the result of the equality of reception (all share in the same gift) but was already indicated by a particular equality of action: so, for example, the have-nots of the papal school of orphans in Rome were not hidden away but brought the water that was to be mingled with the wine, while the bishop would not only offer all oblations on behalf of the whole body but also had to bring his own personal offering.

All these oblations were seen as representing the lives of the believers in their material complexity, presented to God in order to be taken up by him, to be connected to Christ's sacrifice and transformed into the new life of his body. "There you are on the altar," says St. Augustine in his Sermons on the Eucharist, "there you are in the chalice" (Sermon 229). This "you" was meant to represent the congregation both individually and communally. Everyone needed to be literally present in the elements though his or her own participation in the "offering" of the very goods on the altar. This emphasis on individual presence and participation is particularly obvious in such rites as the "naming" of all communicants between the bringing of the oblations and the offertory prayer, as it was held in the Spanish church, or in the prayer "post nomina" (Dix 1945: 496f.).

It was precisely this stress on individual representation which was to be drawn into the dramatic experience of the offertory and transformed. When the offerings were consecrated, the elements were no longer a series of individual contributions but had been mingled to become an indissoluble *corpus permixtum*. The small portions of wine that the individuals had brought forward would be poured together in the big silver pots whence the eucharistic element was taken to the chalice. Thus the eucharistic elements, consisting of an irreducible composite of expensive and cheap wine (and bread), given by poor and wealthy parishioners, represented the congregation as a whole. The purity of taste is sacrificed for the sake of the theological point of a communal representation of the congregation, with all its members and all aspects of their lives: success and failure, conflict and reconciliation, exclusion and inclusion, and so on. "To the Eucharist we bring not raw materials, nor even the cultivated wheat and grape, but bread and wine, manufactures, bearing upon them all the processes, and the sin, of commercial production" (Robinson 1963: 35).

These pointers may suffice to indicate the nature of the loss when, in the course of most liturgical developments, in both East and West, beginning in the fourth century, the practice of the offertory either faded away or shrunk down to a pale gesture, thereby not only impoverishing the rich eucharistic practice of the ancient church but also eclipsing the implicit political theology inherent in it.

Threats from outside: Civil religion and the idea of two powers

Corresponding to this threat from within was the pressure on the genuine political character of the liturgy from outside. The second threat arose when the alleged "wider" public of the state sought increasingly to absorb the church's liturgy into a civil liturgy by employing the liturgical action of the church to celebrate political events or figures.

The early position in which two distinguished publics, church and state, each had its respective claim shifted within the Christianized state toward the presumption that there was "one coherent public sphere." Any remaining sense of duality coalesced into the concept of two "powers." From the Constantinian era on, theological accounts of politics would typically focus on how authority must be divided between the powers, church and state, implicitly validating the notion that politics is essentially about proper power distribution. This practical anticipation of a view that was theoretically formulated much later (most prominently by Max Weber) resulted, in turn, in concepts of power that would render worship – apart from its civil-religious function – politically irrelevant.

The church might on one side be seen as a purely (and merely) spiritual power, which was located from the outset beyond the political; this view is often associated with Augustine's great apology *De Civitate Dei*. Yet Augustine attributed a crucial role to worship in that he understood devotional love as socially generative: "two loves make two cities" (*De Civitate Dei* 14. 28). Furthermore, his analysis of the political catastrophe of the Empire started from the diagnosis that the claim of the Empire was undermined by its false worship. If the one and true God does not receive his due, the core principle of Roman law *suum cuique* is not done justice (19. 20); therefore the very notion of a *res publica* – where each receives his fair due – is not warranted, and the pretentious nature of the *pax Romana* is exposed as being upheld only by its very opposite: force.

As clearly as Augustine stressed worship as a test case for the political pretentiousness of the Empire, he did not, however, draw out this same logic for the positive conjunction between true worship and true politics. While he saw the possibility for the heavenly city to make use of the relative peace that the earthly city provides, he did not, apart from envisaging some pastoral corrections, systematically explore the ways in which "seeking the best of the city" (Jer. 29) might mean allowing the genuine peace that the heavenly city enjoys to fertilize secular polities.

Emphasizing the categorical difference of the two powers as they operate in the heavenly and earthly city, in correspondence to the two loves (of self or God) or modes of worship in which these entities are engaged, Augustine and the Augustinian tradition of political theology assumed that the duality of the two societies could not be overcome this side of eternity. In turn, other traditions, especially associated with the Germanic kingdoms that replaced the Empire in the West, stressed the oneness of the "Christian society" and located the different powers as operating within this unitive framework. As Pope Gelasius I famously remarked at the beginning of the sixth century, "Two there are by which the world is ruled as princes" (see for this section O'Donovan 1996: 193ff).

While the two powers could be assumed to be mutually supportive, the oneness of a Christian society comprised of state and church would offer plenty of opportunities for the *agon* of both powers seeking to domesticate one another. One way of evading the unfortunate sight of a sheer power play between spiritual and worldly authority was the search for a careful equilibrium of both. This could be approached by claiming the two powers to be so utterly different that the one could hardly get in the other's way, drawing, as Gelasius and numerous others did, on the Old Testament duality of king and priest.

Yet the very emphasis on difference, increasingly understood as difference not in task but in structure – the one relying on force and conquest, the other on the power of the word alone – could give rise to another competition. While Gregory VII concluded from the superiority of justice as a "spiritual thing" papal supremacy over the worldly authority, which was to be enforced by ecclesiastical administrative and jurisdictional authority in its own right, the imperialist theologians of the fourteenth century such as Marsilius of Padua inferred from the same basic insight that the church must completely abstain from all associations with nonspiritual power and leave even its own administration to the worldly authority. Whichever interpretation one is inclined to follow, both converge in the assumption that the political power of the church as the capacity to domesticate or at least influence worldly authority is to be seen to be resting outside the worship of the church.

To be sure, there was in all these models a way in which worship could assume a politically relevant role, as for example in the infamous incident when, at the end of the fourth century, Bishop Ambrose of Milan used the excommunication of the Christian Emperor Theodosius I to urge public repentance of his excessively cruel retaliatory action against the city of Thessalonica. Yet it remains less than clear what caused the emperor's repentance. Was it the experience of worship itself, with its imprint of moderation and mercy, which drew out his action? Or was it the pedagogical function of the excommunication within the power-play between "The Two"?

Even if we hesitate to buy the radical alternative that is suggested by this question, it seems fair to say that as a result of the shifting focus from two publics or societies to two powers or modes of authority, political ethics was by and large reserved for those in power. Rulers could be challenged not to contradict the thrust of the Gospel in their exercise of authority, but the masses would hardly come in as addressees of a political ethics. Their political role tended to be reduced to that of mere subjects rather than citizens.

Rediscoveries

Having characterized the history of the political worship as a complex story of threats, struggles, and losses, we turn now to recount several rediscoveries. As representatives of these hopeful moments in the Christian political tradition, I present two somewhat detailed examples, one from the Reformation period, the other from our own time.

Luther's political theology revisited: The eucharistic restitution of the political animal

Among other things, the Reformation offered an occasion for the rediscovery of the political thrust of the practices and teaching of the primitive and patristic church. It is often overlooked that the emphasis on the universal priesthood of believers also entailed the rediscovery of their universal citizenship. This can be demonstrated in Luther's contribution, though this requires us to approach his political theology at an angle not usually taken. Instead of focusing directly on his doctrine of the Two Kingdoms or his account of the political use of the law, we may more fruitfully come at his political thought via the notion of vocation as associated with his doctrine of the three estates and his early eucharistic teaching (Wannenwetsch 2002).

The idea of political vocation had traditionally been reserved for rulers, not only in the legitimating sense of divine investiture, but also in the sense, typified by Charlemagne and Charles the Bold, that rulers understood their authority as a calling to mirror the merciful way of divine rule and to prepare the way for God's kingdom. But in Reformation thought, and especially in Luther's theology, political vocation was to embrace a greater circle than emperor and princes. His doctrine of three estates implied, strictly speaking, that *every* Christian has a vocation not only for religion, but also for economics and politics. For Luther, man is not only *animal sociale* as in Aquinas, but in fact a *zoon politikon*, a political animal, and this for theological reasons.

"Firstly, the Bible speaks of and teaches about the works of God without any doubt; these are divided into three hierarchies: economics, politics and church" (*oeconomia, politia, ecclesia*: WA TR 5, 218, 14ff.). In conceiving these estates as "fellow-creatures" of humankind ("*concreatae sint*", WA 40 III, 222, 35f.), Luther made clear that they were elementary and paradigmatic forms of social life appropriate to creaturely existence from the beginning.

Neither did Luther conceive of *politia, oeconomia* and *ecclesia* as "pure forms" existing *prior* to humankind, into which men and women must be squeezed to fit, nor as mere functions of cultural history *subsequent* to the creation of man, as arbitrary developments at man's disposal. Although not *media salutis* or means of salvation, for the Reformer, *politia, oeconomia* and *ecclesia* are "holy" in that they are instituted by God and sanctified through his word. *They are like the elements as they are understood in sacramental theology:* "natural material" created by God and entrusted to humankind, yet after the fall constantly in danger of being misread (Bayer 1998). Therefore the word has to fill them (*"accedit verbum ad elementum . . ."*) and explicitly qualify them as "holy" (" . . . *et fit sacramentum"*). Thus, as Luther held out against various forms of religiously motivated "desertion" of those orders: Political and economic life is a divine vocation, a matter of *faith that is exercised in love within these divinely assigned spheres of social life* (Augsburg Confession 16: *"in talibus ordinationibus exercere caritatem"*).

As his notion of vocation is rooted in the account of elementary forms of life as sanctifying powers in accordance with the logic of sacramental "elements," we should not be surprised to find Luther outlining a *eucharistic political theology*. In his treatise on the Eucharist from 1519, "Concerning the Blessed Sacrament of the Holy and True Body of Christ and the Brotherhoods" (WA 2, 742–58), Luther makes clear that celebrating the Eucharist is nothing less than a political act in which the communicants actualize and suffer the citizenship that has been bestowed on them by baptism.

> The significance or purpose of this sacrament is the fellowship of all saints . . . because Christ and all the saints are one holy body, just as the inhabitants of a city are one community and body, each citizen being a member of the other and a member of the entire city. All the saints, therefore, are members of Christ and of the Church, which is a spiritual and eternal city of God.

Luther proceeds to explain the inner logic of this citizenship by the means of a communication of goods:

> This fellowship is of such a nature that all the spiritual possessions of Christ and his saints are imparted and communicated to him who receives this sacrament. Again, all his sufferings and sins are communicated to them . . . like in a city where every citizen shares with all the others the name, honour, freedom, trade, customs, usages, help, support, protection and the like, of that city, and on the other hand shares all the danger of fire and flood, enemies and death, losses, imposts and the like. (Luther 1943: 10f.)

In order to capture the political character of relationships among Christians as a sacramental body, Luther employs the Christological logic of the *communicatio idiomatum*, which originally expresses the intimate relation of the two natures of Christ. In a similarly intimate way, political worship *simultaneously* relates the believers to God and to their fellow citizens.

Though interpreters have often missed this complexity of Luther's political theology, it is noteworthy that the one contemporary theologian who has given perhaps the most powerful stimulus for a rediscovery of the political nature of the church based in its practice of worship implicitly draws on Luther's sacramental theology.

John H. Yoder: Ecclesial model practices for the world

John Howard Yoder (1994: 365ff.) distinguishes three fundamental ways in which the worship of the church can relate to ethics and politics: a sacramentalist account (typical for Roman Catholicism), a symbolist approach (as represented by Zwingli), and a sacramental logic (as Luther developed it).

These possibilities mirror the positions formulated during the controversies in sacramental theology in the Reformation period. The symbolist logic assumes the concrete material practice of worship to be a mere pointer toward the higher reality of the unification between human soul and Christ, which happens in heaven. Hence it typically lends itself to an idealist view of ethics, which interprets the worship practice in terms of an "imperative" to put into practice what is ideally signified there. Accordingly, the community of believers is primarily in view as the addressee of a moral appeal.

The Catholic alternative of sacramentalism assumes, on the contrary, that the liturgical ritual will constitute the new reality by virtue of its right exercise alone (*ex opere operato*); the participation and reception of the community is not seen as an essential feature for this reality to come into being. Hence the inclination to a "realist position" that does not need to employ a political ethics. In contrast to these alternatives, sacramental logic, as Yoder sees it, takes the reality of the *communio* in personal terms as the thing itself. The ethical or political reality is not envisioned as being detached from the material conditions and social fabric of the worshipping community. Rather, the eucharistic communion "is" a social ethics; it forms a political society.

Operating within this (albeit unacknowledged) Lutheran framework, Yoder wants to go a step further and address the question which the Augustinian tradition has largely left unanswered: How does the church as primal political entity impact on other political societies and the state? How can the renewal of politics be fertilized through the renewal of the political self-awareness of the church? Yet the best way to approach these questions seems to be via another question: Which language and metaphorical imagination is best equipped to express this relation most adequately?

Modes of Relating Worship and Politics

Among those who are aware of the political dimension of the worshipping church, we can discern three main models: Those who stress the church as political antitype or counter-society (from Augustine to John Milbank), those who characterize it as an ideal type providing the state with social principles (William Temple and the mainstream liberal Protestant tradition), and those who see it as a paradigm (Karl Barth, Stanley Hauerwas) or model (John H. Yoder).

While the antitype view is right to insist on the question of the truth of politics instead of its mere functionality, distinguishing between true and false kinds of political action rather than between mere "spheres" of it, it does not seem to be interested in whether "counter-politics" can also become "encounter-politics", that is, to allow for the church's politics to "rub off" on the secular city. While the ideal-type account has positively adopted this latter question, it typically disregards the actual concreteness of the church's own practices in favor of a universalizing strategy offering principles that are derived from abstracts such as "sacramentality" rather than drawing out the conceptual implications of the sacramental practices themselves (Wannenwetsch 1996: 270–8).

Within the paradigm/model approach, there is a recognition that political worship is meant neither to merely mirror existing political structures and procedures nor to provide them with a religious rationale, but rather represents the unique politics of God. In being sensitive to the truth in the antitype approach, the paradigmatic logic envisions worship to have more than a negatively "illuminating" impact on secular politics as a simplified reading of Hauerwas' claim would seem to suggest that the church's worship merely makes the world aware that it is the world (Hauerwas 1995: 250).

As a paradigm, the church's positively illuminating impact is more visible at the conceptual level, in providing the secular polity with *another* way of conceiving "power," "authority," "community," "decision-making," "exclusion/inclusion," etc. It does not tell the secular rulers how to enact those concepts in a methodical way, but it sets alarm bells ringing if a policy falls foul of the limits set by the paradigm.

In this vein, Karl Barth speaks of "analogical capacities and needs" that political organizations have and that the church has to answer by giving "directions" drawn from its own core practices. As the state exists unknowingly as a "correspondence and analogue to the Kingdom" (Barth 1954: 32), the church's central political task is that of "reminding" the state. This task of reminding entails the faithful exercise of those practices that may serve the state as "examples of analogies and corollaries of that Kingdom of God." In presenting an "incomplete" list of ecclesial practices with corresponding political concepts such as "baptism and equality," "diversity of charismata and separation of powers," "body of Christ and responsibility," "serving and ruling," Barth emphasizes the complex ways in which "translations and transitions from the one sphere to the other will always be open to discussion . . . [and] will only be more or less obvious and never subject to absolute proof" (p. 42).

Yoder, following in Barth's footsteps though disregarding the intentional methodological restraint in the paradigmatic approach, wants to take it a step further by speaking of the "model" character that the core practices of the church could and should assume for political structures and procedures. He presents a list of five "civil imperatives" which he draws from the primitive Christian worship: egalitarianism as implied by baptism into one body, socialism as implied in the Eucharist, forgiveness, the open meeting, and the universality of giftedness (Yoder 1997: 33).

Yet one wonders whether Yoder's zeal to claim a higher political relevance for those practices as "models" makes him slip back into the common tendency of functionalizing religious practice as a source for political vision and action. For example, he states in regard to the imperative to sharing he sees as inherent in the Eucharist: "To make such sharing seem natural, it helps to have gone through an exodus or a Pentecost together, but neither the substance nor the pertinence of the vision is dependent on a particular faith" (Yoder 1997: 32).

This seems to overlook a crucial feature of the eucharistic celebration. Though the Eucharist is, of course, in a sense "about sharing," it is as much a critique of our civil ideas of "sharing" as a resource for it. If sharing is to follow the rules that are incorporated in eucharistic communion, then it can no longer be accompanied by or fueled by the rhetoric of sacrifice and the air of generous condescension, for we cannot claim to own what we eat, though it is completely ours. (Christ gives himself as *totus Christus*, but only *in usu*.) So in any case of sharing, we do not bow down to others by granting them access to our property; rather, we share together *in* the goods that God has provided for us.

Likewise: Must baptismal egalitarianism not become a *skandalon* for other forms of egalitarianism, if the differences that are overcome for the "fellow citizens of God's people" are precisely political and economic? In focusing on overcoming differences in political and economic positions, baptismal egalitarianism is free to affirm and celebrate differences which other forms of egalitarianism cannot, such as between male and female, differing cultures, individual charismata, etc.

Yoder seems to want more and ends up with less. Claiming a *model* character for ecclesial practices, the direct line that is drawn from "civil imperatives" backwards to those practices buys too readily into the idea of translatability from one language into another without loss: "What the New Testament believers were doing in these several practices . . . can be spoken of in social process terms easily translated into nonreligious terms" (Yoder 1994: 364). This seems to assume that while we know the content and political necessity of a concept of "equality," all we lack is a more stable fundament to ground this imperative or a more effective motivation to strive for its realization.

Any functional request for a "model" lacks exactly the conceptual curiosity which is all important for the church if it is to closely "listen" to the political meaning which its own liturgical practice bears. My own suggestion of a more appropriate language of marking the impact of worship on secular politics employs the metaphorical imagination in which liturgical experience spills over in a complex and manifold way (Wannenwetsch 1997: 275–338).

Conclusion

When we take seriously Paul's "ministerial" characterization of those in power as "God's liturgists" and "God's deacons (to serve you) towards the good" (Rom. 13: 4, 6), worldly authorities must be reminded of what they actually, yet perhaps unknowingly, are. The church owes this remembrance not only to Christian statesmen but also to every ruler and actually to all who are in a state of power at various levels of social life (such as parents) and therefore bearers of political responsibility.

It is not, however, a marginal question whether these de facto "liturgists" or "deacons" know their "business" from experience. It makes a crucial difference when the actors in their political roles understand themselves in liturgical terms or, to name alternatives to this view, as agents of the general will, or as representing God on earth, or as political jobholders, or as managers, etc. If they want to live up to their calling to be "God's liturgists and deacons," they will be well advised to learn what it means to experience a true liturgy and to be served by a genuine deacon.

In this perspective the worship of the church, which provides a sabbatical interruption of the politics of the world by immersing people over and over again into the panesthetical vision of the politics of God, may well be regarded as something like an elementary school for those who bear political responsibility. This political *diakonia*, as important as this service to the world is, does however *not constitute* either the inner rationale or the core of the church's political worship. Its rationale lies solely in the praised lordship of Christ, who happens to rule not an original horde of individual believers but a body of fellow-citizens.

Yet the rediscovery of the primary political nature of the church as it is rooted in worship (liturgy as politics) calls forth a renewed apprehension of political *diakonia* (politics as liturgy). The latter does not constitute another field or type of action but must be seen a mere extension of the practice of "seeking the welfare of the city" that, as the intercessions among other worship practices show, is already part and parcel of the liturgy.

References and Further Reading

Arendt, Hannah (1958). *The Human Condition*, Chicago: University of Chicago Press.

Augustine, Aurelius (1997). *The City of God*. Vol. II of *The Nicene and Post-Nicene Fathers* (repr.). Grand Rapids, Mich.: Eerdmans; Edinburgh: T. & T. Clark.

Barth, Karl (1954). "The Christian Community and the Civil Community." In *Against the Stream: Shorter Post-War Writings 1946–52*, 15–50. London: SCM.

Bayer, Oswald (1998). "Nature and Institution: Luther's Doctrine of the Three Estates," trans. C. Helmer. *Lutheran Quarterly 7*, 125–59.

Dix, Dom Gregory (1945). *The Shape of the Liturgy*. London: A. & C. Black.

Hauerwas, Stanley (1995). "The Liturgical Shape of the Christian Life: Teaching Christian Ethics as Worship." In *In Good Company. The Church as Polis*, 153–68. Notre Dame, Ind.: Notre Dame University Press.

Horsley, Richard A., ed. (1997). *Paul and Empire: Religion and Power in Roman Imperial Society*. Harrisburg, Pa: Trinity.

Luther, Martin (1883_). *Werke. Kritische Gesamtausgabe*. Weimar: Hermann Böhlau Nachfolger (WA).

——(1943) *Works*, vol. II. Philadelphia: Muhlenberg.

O'Donovan, Oliver (1996). *The Desire of the Nations: Rediscovering the Roots of Political Theology*. Cambridge: Cambridge University Press.

Robinson, John A. T. (1963). *Liturgy Coming to Life*. Philadelphia: Westminster.

Wannenwetsch, Bernd (1996). "The Political Worship of the Church: A Critical and Empowering Practice." *Modern Theology* 12, 269–99.

——(1997). *Gottesdienst als Lebensform. Ethik für Christenbürger*. Stuttgart, Berlin, Köln, Mainz: Kohlhammer. Forthcoming in English as *Political Worship: Ethics for Christian Citizens*, trans. Margaret Kohl. Oxford Studies in Theological Ethics. (Oxford: Oxford University Press, 2003).

——(2002). "Luther's Moral Theology." In *Cambridge Companion to Martin Luther*, ed. D. McKim. Cambridge, New York, Melbourne: Cambridge University Press, 120–135.

——(2003). "The Liturgical Origin of the Christian *Politeia*: Overcoming the Weberian Temptation." In Ch. Stumpf and H. Zaborowski (eds.), *Church as Politeia: The Political Self-Understanding of Christianity*. Berlin, New York: De Gruyter.

Yeago, David (1998). "Martin Luther on Grace, Law and Moral Life: Prolegomena to an Ecumenical Discussion of *Veritatis Splendor*." *The Thomist* 62, 163–91.

Yoder, John Howard (1994). "Sacrament as Social Process: Christ the Transformer of Culture." In M. G. Cartwright (ed.), *The Royal Priesthood: Essays Ecclesiological and Ecumenical*, 359–73.Grand Rapids and Cambridge: Eerdmans.

——(1997). "Firstfruits: The Paradigmatic Public Role of God's People." In *For the Nations: Essays Public and Evangelical*, 15–36. Grand Rapids and Cambridge: Eerdmans.

PART II
Political Theologies: Survey

7   Eastern Orthodox Thought   93
8   Carl Schmitt   107
9   Karl Barth   123
10 Dietrich Bonhoeffer   136
11 John Courtney Murray   150
12 William Temple   165
13 Reinhold Niebuhr   180
14 Feminist Theology, Southern   194
15 Feminist Theology, Northern   210
16 Jürgen Moltmann   227
17 Johann Baptist Metz   241
18 Political Theologies in Asia   256
19 Black Political Theologies   271
20 Gustavo Gutiérrez   288
21 Stanley Hauerwas   302

CHAPTER 7
Eastern Orthodox Thought

Michael Plekon

The images most closely associated with Eastern Orthodox Christianity as well as its history do not immediately suggest either a tradition of social–political criticism and analysis or radical stances toward social justice. If anything, certain aspects of the Orthodox tradition, such as the former unity of church and state and the transcendent orientation of the Orthodox liturgy, among other things, seem to suggest at best an obsession with stability and order. At the worst, the Orthodox past might appear to contain a hyper-conservative bias. This can sometimes manifest itself as a negative vision of society and culture, of things material and human; in Max Weber's terms, an "other-worldly" or ascetic stance.

However, things are seldom what they seem, and such is very much the case for the social and political vision of the Orthodox Church and its thinkers in the modern era. The same holds true, surprisingly, for the earlier periods in which the church appears to have been either an extension of the Byzantine or Russian imperial court or the popular cult of an ethnic group. Even in the patristic era of the fourth to the ninth centuries one finds the striking personalities and radical social justice perspectives of John Chrysostom and Basil the Great, two of the greatest of the Greek fathers. With them we find perhaps the first overriding theme of the social and political thought of the Eastern church. Along with the transcendently beautiful character of liturgy in the Orthodox East, its social and political vision is a most *particular*, *concrete*, and *realist* one, namely an authentic concern for the material realities of this world, of flesh and blood human beings and their life. In the fiery homilies of John Chrysostom as patriarch of the greatest city of the Christian East, the gap between the affluence of Constantinople's elites and the poverty of many of its citizens is provocatively underscored. The rich who neglect their suffering brothers and sisters will experience the pain of the rich man Dives in hell, the one who failed to show mercy to the poor man Lazarus. In perhaps his most riveting words, John Chrysostom also observes that, having received in holy communion the body and blood of Christ from an altar of gold (that of the Hagia Sophia, the "Great Church" of Constantinople), one then must celebrate the "sacrament of the brother and sister," seeing Christ and serving him on the altar always before us, that of the neighbor (Chrysostom 1856, 1994; Evdokimov 2001: 82–7).

Here we find a second feature of social and political thought in the church of the East: the *consistent attention to the human individual, a radical personalism*. One thinks of the Dostoevskian character who loves humanity but cannot stand the wretch in front of him. While profoundly sensitive to the communal and social nature of human life, the vision of the Eastern church cannot mistake an abstraction for the concrete person.

Basil goes as far and further: the ornaments, extra clothes, and shoes sitting in our closets are what we have taken, robbed from the poor. The Basiliade, an institutional complex of social services for widows, orphans, the chronically ill, the dying, and the poor was the result of Basil's preaching and pastoral activity as Bishop of Caesarea in the Asia Minor province of Cappadocia. The greatest teachers of the Eastern church pay close attention to the institutions and processes of society. There is an authentic *structural and material awareness and concern* in their thinking: a third characteristic of their vision.

In these Eastern fathers – who are, of course, teachers of the universal church – we also find the fourth salient feature of the social and political teaching of the Eastern church, namely its *constant eschatological reference*. When asked what was the social position and program of the Orthodox Church, the eccentric yet brilliant Russian philosopher Nicolas Fyodorov replied: "The Holy Trinity" (Nicholl 1997: 67–118). All too often we take "eschatology" to mean just the end, the "last things." For the Eastern church it bears the more ancient Gospel meaning of the kingdom of God being present among us. Thus, Fyodorov meant that the Trinity's communion of love is powerful and present, here and now. The Father, Son and Holy Spirit's communion of love is the image for each person and for the world. Justice in this world must always be measured against that of God and his kingdom. And here too we find the fifth dominant character, implied by the previous four, that our life in history and society, in our families, in learning and science, government and business, must be constantly *transformed* in light of the Gospel.

The thinking – and, moreover, the lives – of the three contemporary Orthodox thinkers we will profile here as examples of the social and political thought of the modern Eastern church resonate with the earlier fathers and express the same qualities just described. Here lies the root of the loyalty to the "truth" of socialistic reform and organization, the significance of social, political and economic changes for flesh and blood individuals, that is the hallmark of the political economist and sociologist-become-theologian Fr. Sergius Bulgakov (1877–1944). Yet from here also stemmed his profound rejection of the inhumanity and impersonalism of ideological Marxism. Dominating his vision is the Incarnation and its implications for human life: a vision of the actions of God who has entered time, space and human flesh, always breathing new life, creating new possibilities for the transformation of the world and the human heart.

We will also find a similar vision in the life and work of the lay theologian Paul Evdokimov (1901–70). After graduate studies in theology and philosophy and raising a family, he spent over a decade in the service of the suffering and outcast of society. He served as administrator of ecumenically funded hostels for the marginalized. In his writing, he underscored the radical, "absurd" love of God for humanity, God's "kenotic" or self-emptying compassion – a central theme in Russian theology and spirituality over the centuries.

Finally, I will highlight the discovery by Mother Maria Skobtsova (1891–1945) of the indivisibility of love of God and of the neighbor, her emphasis on the radicalism of Christ's second commandment of love and its rule or principle for life: love is not diminished by giving to others, it is enhanced. Mother Maria's bishop said that her monastic life would be located in the world, in the desert of the human heart, and she put her radical vision into practice in Paris, where she served in several hostels for feeding and sheltering the poor and suffering.

My selection of these three figures by no means indicates that no others in the Eastern church were interested in the social and political realities of human life. For example, training as a canonist, a historian, and a scriptural and liturgical scholar gave Fr. Nicolas Afanasiev (1963, 1975, 1992; Nichols 1989) a unique perspective on the church's relationship to politics and society. Most frequently he was a perceptive critic of the church's tendencies toward authoritarianism and cooptation by the state. Metropolitan John Zizioulas (1985) has contributed discerning ideas to our understanding of the relationship between the individual and the community, to the theology of personhood within the world, society and the church. Likewise, Frs. Stanley Harakas (1999) and John Breck (1999) have pursued many of the ethical questions of our time, from abortion and capital punishment to cloning and euthanasia and other controversial issues in bioethics. Vigen Guroian (1994, 2001) has also raised the questions of how the Incarnation leaves its imprint on all we do, from our use of the environment, the natural world around us, to the treatment of the chronically ill and the dying. The late Frs. Alexander Schmemann (1973, 1979, 2000) and John Meyendorff (1978, 1987a, 1987b) also provided general perspectives on the encounter of the church and each Christian with the complexities of life in modern society. Yet the focus here on the three mentioned – Sergius Bulgakov, Paul Evdokimov, and Maria Skobtsova – is no disservice to these others, for in fact all are connected both directly and indirectly, and these three offer perhaps the most radical and insightful approaches in the Eastern church tradition to the challenge of life in our age.

Sergius Bulgakov

The son of a priest and a seminarian, like many other intellectuals of his generation Sergius Bulgakov left the church and Christianity to follow the Marxist vision of the transformation of society and the individual. Trained in sociology and political economy, he challenged Plekhanov's ideas about the restructuring of Russian society and economy, particularly agriculture, understanding (like Max Weber) the importance of the family, the village, cultural customs and individual motivation. Eventually, with the tragic experience of the Second Duma and the revolution, Bulgakov returned to the faith and the sacramental life of the church, first as an important lay leader in the Great Council of Moscow in 1917–18, which proposed reforms in the Orthodox Church, and later as an ordained priest and theologian. Almost the last twenty years of his life were spent as Dean of the St. Sergius Theological Institute in Paris, where he finally arrived after expulsion from Russia in the early 1920s. Under conditions of poverty and duress, due to criticism and then official examination of his writings under the charge of heresy, Bulgakov nevertheless produced a prodigious body of writing. Paul Valliere (2000) and Antoine Arjakovsky (2000) have argued in their recent studies that Bulgakov's central concern in writing of divine wisdom was to clarify the relationship of God to creation and of humankind to the divine. This he sought to examine in the light of modern thought and experience and principally through the consequence of the Incarnation, namely the "humanity of God" (*Bogochelovechestvo*) as earlier Russian thinkers such as Soloviev had framed it.

For Bulgakov it was axiomatic that it was necessary, indeed urgent, not only for the Orthodox Church but for Christianity as a whole to engage in conversation with the modern world, its institutions, consciousness, and inhabitants. All of the rapid developments that had produced modernity were diagnosed by Bulgakov not as evil but as the present situation of God's working with and in creation. Like the Greek fathers of the church more than a millennium before him, Bulgakov recognized the human capacity for destruction and evil but – being a kind of theological optimist, in the best, deepest sense – he saw God as stronger, the ultimate victor in Christ's Incarnation, death and Resurrection. Like, among others, Gregory of Nyssa and Origen before him, Bulgakov considered the final restoration of all creation (*apokatastasis*) as at least the object of prayer and hope; and, while not appropriate for dogmatizing, such restoration was nonetheless more consonant with the boundless compassion and forgiveness of God and the desire for the ultimate (re)union of the divine with creation, when God would be "all in all." Much of his vision is summed up in his last book, *The Bride of the Lamb*, the final volume in his great trilogy.

While Bulgakov did not offer a book-length discussion of the events of his era, such as the Russian Revolution, the destructiveness of state socialism, the Great Depression, the rise of the Nazis, the Second World War, and the Holocaust, he nevertheless did touch upon all of these in his writings (Bulgakov 1999: 229–67, 293–303) and presented what might be called a summary of his social and political thinking in presentations he made while on visits to America in 1934 and England in 1939. These were the sermon he was invited to preach at the chapel of Seabury-Northwestern Seminary, "Social Teaching in Modern Russian Theology," and the paper read by another for him at the Fellowship of

SS Alban and Sergius, "The Spirit of Prophecy" (Bulgakov 1999: 269–92). It is not just Eastern church thinking in general but Bulgakov's own creative and radical vision that is offered in these texts.

He notes that in the early church there was no particular concern with the social world and politics other than living peaceably, obeying the law and the rulers, and living according to the Word of God. The sense of the imminent Second Coming of Christ also played a significant role in the early church's perspective. But the adoption of Christianity as the official cult of the Roman Empire under Constantine did not only end persecution: it also introduced all kinds of problems, principally the confusion of imperial political interests with ecclesiastical status in the Empire. Only rarely were bishops and teachers such as John Chrysostom and Basil the Great able, as noted above, to speak against the power of wealth and prestige. The monastic movement did begin to raise a continuous note of protest against the world's penetration of Christian thought and practice; but in the long run, even in its time of flourishing, the monastic movement was marginalized and the radical inversion of cultural values found in the Gospel routinely softened or ignored. Marx and other critics were correct in perceiving the church to be on the side of the wealthy and powerful; the church often supported the state blindly and with destructive consequences for ordinary people. But, rather than the extremes of church–state unity or the opposition of the church to any this-worldly activity, Bulgakov sees a third path, one for him aptly expressed by the figure of Wisdom, from the Book of Proverbs 8: 22–31, who is both the creature of God and his co-worker in the making and sustaining of the world (Bulgakov 1993). The destiny of all creation, particularly of humanity, is to be deified, to be in communion with the Creator, filled with the life of God and radiating the glory of this life. All are to be "prophets," messengers of the Lord, not only in word but in action.

Thus the Pentecost event of the descent of the Holy Spirit is a kind of icon of the mission of the church, not only toward the political realm but also toward the rest of the natural and social world. The church is not an institution of the state or society, but is the body of Christ and temple of the Holy Spirit, thus the presence and door into the kingdom of heaven here and now, in the world (Bulgakov 1988: 1–99). The "churching" of the world is not merely its being made more religious but its transfiguration, its full "humanization" and "divinization." Bulgakov imagines the completion of what all creation was meant to be, united again in love with the Creator. The church, therefore, is not the moral arm of the state (Bulgakov 1988: 156–175). It should not use any fear-provoking tactics to scare souls into goodness. Neither is the church the punishing arm of God. The church is healing, forgiveness, resurrection, new life. The very purpose of the church is creative, revealing the "humanity of God" and the divine possibilities of humanity, bringing humanity and everything else back into union with the Lord. For this relationship Bulgakov employs imagery of the Book of Revelation: "The Spirit and the Bride say 'Come'" (Rev. 22: 17). The church, and through it the world, become the spouse of the Lamb. Time becomes eternity. The antipathy between the city of God and the city of the world is abolished, not all at once but in a cumulative, compassionate process (Bulgakov 2002: 379–526).

This is not a naïve, "rosy" Christianity. Bulgakov in other essays recognized the peculiar power of the modern state to enslave and destroy human beings. He recognized the specific inhumanity of modern totalitarian regimes, not only that of the Bolsheviks but also those of Nazi Germany and Mussolini's Italy. Bulgakov underscored the need in the modern world for the gift and the vocation of biblical prophecy, the fearless, strong proclamation of God's word, and the witness to the kingdom in the midst of the world not just by a few specialists but by all Christians.

Paul Evdokimov

Paul Evdokimov was in the first class to graduate from St. Sergius Institute and had Bulgakov, the institute's first dean and professor of dogmatic theology, as his teacher. Yet Bulgakov was not the only influence on him. The radical philosopher Nicolas Berdiaev was an acknowledged shaper of his thinking, as were friends and colleagues such as Fr. Lev Gillet, Fr. Nicolas Afanasiev, and Olivier Clément, among others. Evdokimov's life experiences also played a decisive role in forming his social and political thinking as a theologian. He arrived as an immigrant in Paris in 1923 and studied at both the Sorbonne and the St. Sergius Institute, earning his first doctorate at the University of Aix-en-Provence in 1942 and a second at St. Sergius in 1958. During the Second World War he was active in the French Resistance. At the war's conclusion and for more than a decade thereafter, he directed ecumenically sponsored hostels for refugees, foreign students, and other people in need. Evdokimov writes with untypical emotion about how he was more than an administrator, acting also as counselor, lay pastor, and friend to the residents, with their complicated, often damaged existences. When he later taught at St. Sergius and other theological schools, the experience of this service was always present. Consistently, Evdokimov sought to bring the suffering God who loves absurdly, but without coercion, into contact with the person of our time, with his questions, her rage, with the range of modern human experience.

In an essay entitled "Church and Society" (Evdokimov 2001: 61–94), he synthesizes a dialogue that extended through virtually all of his writings, from his early studies of the theology of Gogol and Dostoevsky to his discerning look at the history of spirituality. What is truly new in the New Testament, he argues, is the ultimate destiny of humankind in the "humanity of God," in the consequences of the Incarnation, life, death and Resurrection of Christ. Though they did not call it this, even the earliest of the fathers, like the apostles and New Testament authors before them, envisioned a "social ecclesiology." The church, being the body of the Risen Christ, drew all to itself, raising everything into the kingdom. The divisions so often seen between Mary and Martha, between action and contemplation, between the sacred and the profane, are illusions. One cannot really love God without loving and serving the brother and sister always present before us. Evdokimov was especially fond of the saying of the desert fathers: "If you want to see God, look at your brother." This does not exclude numerous other possibilities of encountering God in the world, but emphasizes the singular presence of God in the neighbor in need. He even cites Tertullian and Origen on the unique experience of God in the encounter with the neighbor. Repeatedly in his writings, as in his own life, Evdokimov emphasized the truth of the claim in the first letter of John (4: 20), that if we cannot love the brother whom we can see, we cannot love the God who is invisible – or, better, most visible – in the neighbor.

Like Bulgakov, Evdokimov tracks the history of the church's solidarity with the state, with society and culture. While there are indisputable high points in this history, there are great stretches of tragedy and evil resulting from the union. The desert fathers and, after them, the monastics understood the action of Christ to mandate an "ecclesial evangelism" or an "evangelical ecclesiology." The Lord is the one who stands at the door and knocks, waiting to come in to our table, to share the bread of our suffering and of our joy. Evdokimov repeatedly quotes the thirteenth-century Byzantine statesman and theologian Nicolas Cabasilas, describing God as *Philanthropos*, the one whose love for us is without reason, force or measure (*eros manikos*) (Evdokimov 2001: 175–94). Such a God is the core of the Christian attitude toward the state, toward all the institutions of society, in international relations, even with respect to the natural world. It is far from being distinctively Eastern or Orthodox, but is the shared vision of the undivided church of the first millennium. "Beauty will save the world," wrote Dostoevsky, and this was his credo amid the lowest forms of human degradation, springing from his own imprisonment and near-execution by firing squad. Evdokimov, who did his first doctoral dissertation on Dostoevsky, constantly found the evidence of God's presence and love in the beauty surrounding us: that of the natural order, that of the saints as captured in their icons and words, but particularly that of men and women, bearers of the image and likeness of God (Evdokimov 1990). So Evdokimov urged a reclaiming of the radical spirituality of the mothers and fathers of the desert, but in the hidden ordinary, everyday lives of "ecclesial beings" today. "One does not just say prayers, one becomes prayer" (Evdokimov 1998). The appeal is straightforward. If human beings have brought suffering and destruction, then it is also through human action, transformed by the beauty and love of God, that God will accomplish the overturning of this evil. God will be acting through them, as the Bible recounts.

In his own life in the hostels at Bièvres and Sèvres and Massy, and as remembered by those for whom he cared, Paul Evdokimov's vision, like that of the church fathers and the desert fathers and mothers, was always realistic and personal. The distance between the developed and undeveloped nations, he wrote in 1967, could come down to this: an electric toothbrush in the North should not deny a container of milk to a child in the South. He has the patristic quotes at hand too. "Money and all other goods are the common property of all just as the light and air we breathe." This bit of Christian socialism came from Simeon the New Theologian (949–1022). "Women who embroider biblical scenes on their clothing would do better to live out these stories," wrote John Chrysostom, whose "golden mouth" earned him a death march at the end of his life. Basil the Great argued, "You are a thief if you transform into your possessions what you had received only as a steward." It is hard to miss the radical political yet eschatological perspective in the teachings of these fathers and other saints. Evdokimov concludes his meditation on the social and political perspective of the church by arguing for a tax by which the affluence of wealthy nations would be redistributed to reshape the situation of the third world. In an encyclical about the same time, *Progressio populorum*, Pope Paul VI had also called for the setting up of a global fund established by taxes derived from conspicuous consumption, waste, and the buildup of armaments. Only the recent proposal by numerous humanitarian and religious leaders for the Group of Eight leading nations to stop making interest-bearing loans, write off debts, and make outright grants to the poor countries comes close in radicality.

Evdokimov, a man of both the world and the church, understood that no law could affect the interior change of heart that leads to different action. Conversion cannot come through compulsion. Yet traditions of faith can plant the seeds of such personal and then communal transformation. Thus he called for a kind of summit meeting of the leaders of the world's great traditions: the Pope, the Orthodox patriarchs, heads of the churches of the Reformation, rabbis and imams, the entire "family of Abraham." A smaller version of such a gathering has indeed occurred, in 1986 at Assisi, at Pope John Paul II's invitation. Amid outbursts of violence there is still peaceful protest by many groups at meetings of the World Trade Organization, and even celebrities have called for forgiving of debts and gifts of aid to impoverished countries. Evdokimov recognized that, in the words of Paul Eluard, "Everything was not needed to make a world, just love, and nothing else." But he also saw that such change of heart then required action. Affluent nations sharing their wealth was just a beginning; the world community had to go further to cooperate in a plan for a truly global economy, a world society where resources would be managed by all, used by all. Only this would approach the justice of which the Bible speaks.

Maria Skobtsova

A similarly radical view of the Gospel's call to transform the world in love is found first and foremost in the life and writings of Mother Maria Skobtsova (Hackel 1981). One of the most colorful and original figures in the Orthodox Church in the modern era, Elisabeth Pilenko, as she was born, was a gifted poet and part of the circle of the Russian poet Alexander Blok. She was involved in the political turmoil of the Russian Revolution, may have been involved in the plot to assassinate Trotsky, and was herself nearly executed by both the Bolsheviks and the White Army. She was married twice, both marriages ending in divorce, and had three children. After flight to the West, she became deeply involved in providing basic humanitarian aid and counsel to impoverished Russian émigrés, both in the Russian Christian Student Movement and in another service organization, Orthodox Action. The death of her youngest daughter in 1931 from meningitis was a turning point, a moment of conversion. She asked to be admitted to monastic life and, despite some reservations on the part of colleagues, her bishop, Metropolitan Evlogy, did receive her vows, tonsure her and clothe her in the habit on the first Sunday of Lent 1932.

Mother Maria's life was incandescent. She was creative in arguing that monastic life in our time needed to find its modern location and form. If indeed such life was a sign of the presence of God's kingdom in society, then monastics should, as their predecessors did, live the life of the Gospel in the world, serving God by their prayer and by loving the children of God. She had in mind the practical service of suffering people by the desert monastics and the location of many early monastic houses in such urban locations as the Studios monastery in Constantinople and the Basiliade in Caesarea. Incessantly in her writings, Mother Maria stressed the indivisibility of the love of God and the love of the neighbor. Her essays, written in the minutes she could steal from her work, are filled with perceptive observations on the stress of the pace of modern life, and the complex consequences of political upheavals such as the Russian Revolution, then the Great Depression, and finally the Second World War. Before her monastic profession, her life was already committed to service. She traveled around France, visiting and counseling émigrés, raising funds for their assistance, seeking better governmental welfare services, and working to secure retraining and rehabilitation for them. After entering monastic life she rented large residential units both within Paris and in the suburbs, to set up, first at Villa de Saxe, then rue de Lourmel and Noisy-le-Grand, hostels for the homeless and suffering, living centers for the sick and aged. She hoped to attract other women to this monastic life of service, but her colleagues were few and temporary. She had a formidable personality which some could not tolerate. There was a kind of undeclared war between her and her first chaplain, Fr. Kiprian Kern, who could not adapt to her way of life, yet she was also blessed with two very discerning chaplains, Frs. Lev Gillet and Dimitri Klepinine.

Echoing Basil the Great, Mother Maria put her reading of the Gospel's social ethic bluntly. "At the Last Judgment I will not be asked whether I satisfactorily practiced asceticism, nor how many prostrations and bows I have made before the altar. I will be asked whether I fed the hungry, clothed the naked, visited the sick and the prisoners in jail. That is all I will be asked." In her reflections on the "second commandment," that of loving the neighbor as oneself, Mother Maria concluded that, just as one was to love God with one's whole mind, heart, and will, the two commandments were really one (Skobtsova 2003: 45–60). In an essay written in 1937 but never published and located again by Fr. Dimitri's daughter Hélène and her son Antoine, "Types of Religious Lives," Mother Maria conducts not only a theological but also a social–psychological examination of how faith and life are connected, or not, in the social world around her. (Skobtsova 2003: 140–86). She presents ideal types in a probing analysis that is extremely precise in capturing some of the various "styles" of religiosity in the Orthodox Christians she knew. She delineates aesthetic, ritualistic, ascetic, and peculiarly Russian-cultural "types" of religiosity. Of greatest relevance here, though, is her sketch of the simpler, more radical approach one finds in the Gospels and in the lives of many saints. A "peculiar law" seems to be at work, she wrote, quite the opposite of the calculus of everyday life. Rather than being impoverished by every dollar or hour I give away to someone in need, in reality I receive back even more than I give. And what I do not share, what I rather try to hoard, hide, protect, even increase in worth, actually slips away from me, is consumed, as if burned up. The response of so many (in the 1930s) to the people and society around them – to unemployment, homelessness, hunger, the breakup of marriages, families, psyches – namely, to retreat to the movies, the café, was a further tragedy. To want to escape the suffering of others said much about the disappearance of the heart, the loss of community and humanity. One could retreat as well not into jazz or alcohol but into liturgical chant, lives of saints and rituals.

While she painted and embroidered beautiful icons and vestments, Mother Maria nevertheless thought that Christ, entering into the splendor of such worship, would eventually work his way out the church door into the square, the streets outside, where his suffering children were. The Gospel's true force propels Christians out from the eucharistic liturgy and sanctuary into the liturgy of loving and serving the neighbor in everyday life. Mother Maria realized that what she was proposing ran directly counter to ordinary human orientation, counter to our fundamental love of self, then of those closest to us and those most like us. Yet what she read in the Bible about the absolute quality of God's love and his desire that we love in the same manner transcended all these fences of love. The divine form of love will make even the parent see the image of God not only in one's child but also in other children, in other people and their situations. By giving we receive. What we give is not lost but returns many times over, enriching us.

Mother Maria was both loved and reviled in her own Russian community and church. Cutting short her stay at the services to prepare meals, making early morning trips to the meat and produce markets at Les Halles to beg leftovers and day-old items, visiting the cafés to find the lonely and the homeless hanging on to their glasses of cheap wine so as to enjoy the shelter and warmth – her lowering of herself to the level of the unfortunate, in the example of Christ, made her an embarrassment to many of her contemporaries. Reminiscences of her by some notable émigrés contain a mixture of disparaging comments on her nonconformity and passionate nature as well as profound regret at having kept a distance, at looking down on her unusual life of service.

During the Nazi occupation of France, Mother Maria actively assisted many who were targeted by the Gestapo for roundup and the death camps. Fr. Dimitri issued many baptismal certificates to protect Jewish people by incorporation into the community of his parish. Mother Maria fed, hid, and helped other Jewish neighbors to flee. She ministered herself to those held in the Vélodrome d'Hiver during the hot July days of 1942. In the end, she, her remaining son Yuri, and Fr. Dimitri were arrested by the Gestapo and sent on to death camps, where all died. Mother Maria took the place of another woman in a wagon headed to the gas chambers at Ravensbrück, and the camp records note her death on March 31, 1945, Good Friday, just weeks before liberation by the Russian army. She is honored as one of the "righteous among the Gentiles" at Yad Vashem, and many recognize her as a martyr of our time.

Although politically astute and experienced enough in social action to identify the economic and structural causes of dislocation, poverty and war, Mother Maria also understood that the only authentic form of love was that given to an actual person before one. While earlier in life she spoke and worked for reform at all levels of state and society, she eventually formulated what might best be called a personalist social ethic. The Incarnation of God meant, as her confessor Fr. Bulgakov saw it, the "humanity of God." Mother Maria sought to put into action as well as into words the human counterpart of this, namely human care for the other in the manner of God: indulgently, freely, without reservation or demand. Was her work essentially radical philanthropy or charity, with no real political dimension? Quite the contrary, for she was profoundly aware of the reality of the state and its institutions and power. In assisting the suffering, she utilized all the available resources in the French welfare system. During the war, the residents of her hostels were engaged in practical tasks such as preparing clothing for troops and organizing medical supplies; under the occupation the hostel dining rooms fed the neighborhood hungry, using government rations and public funding. She countered the effort to round up the Jews of Paris, and even in the Ravensbrück camp opposed the machinery of death with small but powerful gestures. Her last embroideries were of the Allied invasion of Normandy in the style of the Bayeux tapestry and of the Mother of God holding Jesus not as a child but as the crucified one, the God who makes himself one with all who suffer.

I chose these three remarkable Orthodox Christians of our time solely for the insightful things they wrote about the Christian understanding of social and political life in the modern era. Even more importantly, I present them for the example of their work and existence. Their lives embody the characteristics of the Eastern Orthodox perspective I described earlier. In their lives, each one was politically and socially active. Sergius Bulgakov served in the Second Duma and in the Great Council of Moscow in 1917–18. Mother Maria served as mayor of her hometown of Anapa in the Revolution and was almost executed by both the Bolsheviks and the White Army. Paul Evdokimov participated in the Resistance and then in the providing of service to the suffering, as did Mother Maria. They never denied the need for political change, for government's just and humane treatment of its citizens, and all three recognized the monstrous possibilities of a totalitarian state in our time. Their love for the neighbor and serving of the suffering was, however, direct and personal, not restricted to the dimensions of theory or plans. Despite the power of evil they saw unleashed around them, both in the Russian Revolution and in World War II, they nevertheless could not lose the vision of transformation that they saw in Christ and the Gospel.

Embedded in the vision of these three extraordinary Orthodox Christians is *freedom*, a concept explicitly discussed by their colleague and fellow Orthodox Christian, the philosopher Nicolas Berdiaev. To encounter the other and the world with the mind of Christ, with the heart of God, also means so respecting the neighbor's freedom that there can be no possibility of threat, coercion, or harassment. On the contrary, all three put into practice, in veneration for the freedom of every person, what they absorbed from their prayer and study: the force of the "humanity of God." Though they were born and raised in an authoritarian Russian state and society, though they knew well the excesses of legalism, ritualism, and control in their church, these three – and, as it turns out, many of their fellow émigrés – came to see that love transcends every law and reveals the perfect freedom of the children of God (Plekon 2002). This freedom they recognized to be the material from which a reformed and renewed society and state had to be crafted. Never rejecting the world, the social arena, culture, the arts and sciences, their theological vision saw the raising of all these aspects of human life into the beauty of the kingdom of God. Theirs was at once a perspective fully human, humane, and divine.

There is no single Orthodox social and political theology, given the diverse character of Orthodox Christianity, extending over so many centuries and localized in so many countries, now including western Europe and North America. The lives and work of Fr. Sergius Bulgakov, Paul Evdokimov and Mother Maria Skobtsova nevertheless embody some of the most basic and singular of Eastern Orthodoxy's understandings of the world and life in it. Orthodox Christianity is marked by the vision of the eternal kingdom of heaven and the beauty of God's transcendence. Yet Orthodox Christianity, contrary to assumptions, does not flee the world or condemn it as essentially evil. Rather, intensely aware of God's creation of all things as good and of the entrance of God into creation by the Incarnation of Christ, one should embrace the world as the only place where the drama of salvation occurs. The church, as the outreach of the kingdom of God, seeks to transform the world again into God's good creation. The pitting of the Western Christian passion for social justice and activism against the East's alleged other-worldly passivity is quite false. Many recent examples bear witness to this, the lives of these three and so many others: the efforts of monastics, Patriarch Pavle, the monk Fr. Sava and others to bring peace in the former Yugoslavia; the leadership and intense activism of Archbishop Anastasios of Tirana (2003) and of scores of clergy and lay volunteers in rebuilding Albania; the efforts of the Hosanna Community of lay people, many disciples of Fr. Alexander Men, in introducing social outreach to the young, the homeless, the imprisoned in Moscow and surrounding areas; the recognized effectiveness of the International Orthodox Christian Charities (IOCC) in providing disaster relief worldwide. The examples of Orthodox Christians working "for the life of the world" could be multiplied.

There is no form of government blessed in particular by God. Every form can serve if the rule of love is followed, if human dignity and freedom are respected. Politics and culture are indispensable arenas for Christian discipleship, but all work leads to the kingdom. The human person is a microcosm, at once the glory of God's creating, the object of God's redeeming love, the agent of this transforming compassion for the rest of the world. In sum, Orthodox Christianity treasures the encounter of the divine and the human wherever this occurs.

References

Afanasiev, Nicolas (1975). *L'Eglise du Saint-Esprit*, trans. Marianne Drobot. Paris: Cerf.
——(1963). "Una sancta." *Irénikon*, 36, 436–75.
——(1992). "The Church that Presides in Love." In John Meyendorff (ed.), *The Primacy of Peter*. Crestwood, NY: St. Vladimir's Seminary Press.
Arjakovsky, Antoine (2000). *La revue La Voie (1925–1940): revue de la pensée religieuse russe*. Kiev and Paris: L'Esprit et la Lettre.
Anastasios (Yannoulatos), Archbishop (2003) *Facing the World: Orthodox Christian Essays on Global Concerns*. Crestwood NY: St. Vladimir's Seminary Press.
Breck, John (1999). *The Sacred Gift of Life: Orthodox Christianity and Bioethics*. Crestwood, NY: St. Vladimir's Seminary Press.
Bulgakov, Sergius (1976). *A Bulgakov Anthology*, ed. and trans. James Pain and Nicolas Zernov. Philadelphia: Westminster.
——(1988). *The Orthodox Church*, trans. Lydia Kesich. Crestwood, NY: St. Vladimir's Seminary Press.
——(1993). *Sophia: The Wisdom of God*. Hudson, NY: Lindisfarne.
——(1999). *Sergii Bulgakov: Towards a Russian Political Theology*, ed. and comm. Rowan Williams. Edinburgh: T. & T. Clark.
——(2002). *The Bride of the Lamb*, trans. Boris Jakim. Grand Rapids, Mich.: Eerdmans.
Chrysostom, John (1856). "On Judas' Treachery." Homily 1, 6 in J. P. Migne (ed.), *Patrologia Graeca*, vol. 49, line 381.
——(1994). Homily 50 on Matthew, 4, 5, in *Patrologia Graeca* vol. 58, line 508; and *Nicene and Post-Nicene Fathers*, ser. 1, vol. 10, Hendrickson.
Evdokimov, Paul (1990). *The Art of the Icon: A Theology of Beauty*, trans. Stephen Bigham. Crestwood, NY: St. Vladimir's Seminary Press.
——(1998). *Ages of the Spiritual Life*, trans. and ed. Michael Plekon and Alexis Vinogradov. Crestwood, NY: St. Vladimir's Seminary Press.
——(2001). *In the World, Of the Church: A Paul Evdokimov Reader*, trans. and ed. Michael Plekon and Alexis Vinogradov. Crestwood, NY: St. Vladimir's Seminary Press.
Guroian, Vigen (1994). *Ethics after Christendom: Toward an Ecclesial Ethic*. Grand Rapids, Mich.: Eerdmans.
——(2001). *Incarnate Love: Essays in Orthodox Ethics*, rev. edn. Notre Dame, Ind.: University of Notre Dame Press.
Hackel, Sergei (1981). *Pearl of Great Price: The Life of Mother Maria Skobtsova 1891–1945*. Crestwood, NY: St. Vladimir's Seminary Press.
Harakas, Stanley (1999). *Wholeness of Faith and of Life: Orthodox Christian Ethics*. Brookline, Mass.: Holy Cross Orthodox Press.

Meyendorff, John (1978). *Living Tradition*. Crestwood, NY: St. Vladimir's Seminary Press.

——(1987a). *Witness to the World*. Crestwood, NY: St. Vladimir's Seminary Press.

——(1987b). *Vision of Unity*. Crestwood, NY: St. Vladimir's Seminary Press.

Nicholl, Donald (1997). *Triumphs of the Spirit in Russia*. London: Darton, Longman & Todd.

Nichols, Aidan (1989). *Theology in the Russian Diaspora*, Cambridge: Cambridge University Press.

Plekon, Michael (2002). *Living Icons: Persons of Faith in the Eastern Church*. Notre Dame, Ind.: University of Notre Dame Press.

Schmemann, Alexander (1973). *For the Life of the World*. Crestwood, NY: St. Vladimir's Seminary Press.

——(1979). *Church, World Mission*. Crestwood, NY: St. Vladimir's Seminary Press.

——(2001). *The Journals of Father Alexander Schmemann*. Crestwood, NY: St. Vladimir's Seminary Press.

Skobtsova, Mother Maria (2003). *Mother Maria Skobtsova: Essential Writings*, ed. Hélène Arjakovsky-Klépinine, trans. Richard Pevear and Larissa Volokhonsky. Maryknoll, NY: Orbis.

Valliere, Paul (2000). *Modern Russian Theology: Bukharev, Soloviev, Bulgakov*. Grand Rapids, Mich.: Eerdmans.

Zernov, Nicolas (1966). *The Russian Religious Renaissance of the Twentieth Century*. New York: Macmillan.

Zizioulas, John (1985). *Being as Communion*. Crestwood, NY: St. Vladimir's Seminary Press.

CHAPTER 8
Carl Schmitt

Michael Hollerich

The twentieth-century godfather of political theology is the controversial Catholic jurist and sometime Nazi Carl Schmitt. This "Martin Heidegger of political theory" and "German Hobbes of the twentieth century" (Schmitt 1996b: xii; Meier 1998: 100), as he has been called, is usually credited with reintroducing the concept of political theology into modern discourse. This chapter provides an introduction to Schmitt's life and work, an account of his political theology as he understood it, and a review of the critical reception of his work among his fellow Catholics.

Schmitt scholarship is massive, contentious, and unabating (see Mehring 1993; Gebhardt 1995; Seubert 2002). Reference will be made only to sources used in this presentation.

An "Authentic Case of a Christian Epimetheus"?

Carl Schmitt (1888–1985) was born into a strongly Catholic family in Plettenberg, Westphalia. His modest origins and his religious identity perhaps contributed to his ambition and also to a certain incorrigible insecurity. Trained in legal studies, he rose rapidly from academic obscurity to an appointment at the prestigious Friedrich-Wilhelm University in Berlin in 1933, a position which he lost after World War II because of his complicity with the Third Reich. His advancement was assisted by a prolific outpouring of books and articles on jurisprudence, constitutional and political theory, and broader cultural topics, all written against the backdrop of the Weimar Republic and its fluctuating fortunes. Schmitt's writings reflect his skepticism about the reigning neo-Kantian philosophy of law and about legal positivism, his concern for the viability and legitimacy of Weimar democracy and a fascination with dictatorship, and his hostility to liberalism of all kinds, political, philosophical, economic, and religious. His brilliant style, breadth of interests, and responsiveness to current events won him a reputation well beyond the university world. Catholics hailed him as a promising apologist, though some came to doubt his political and religious loyalties when the Weimar Republic slid into its final crisis and gave way to National Socialism.

Scholars disagree about Schmitt's involvement in the death of democracy. His two biographers, Joseph Bendersky and Paul Noack, have treated him rather deferentially (Bendersky 1983; Noack 1993), whereas Andreas Koenen's *Der Fall Carl Schmitt* makes a perhaps excessive case for the prosecution (Koenen 1995; see Seubert 2002: IIa). Schmitt certainly had serious doubts about parliamentary democracy and the system of party politics. He strongly supported the use of Article 48 of the Weimar constitution, which authorized direct presidential rule in emergencies. By the end of the 1920s he had become an admirer of Mussolini and Italian fascism, an affinity that Piet Tommissen has suggested originated in Schmitt's horror at the revolutionary outbreaks in Germany after World War I (Quaritsch 1988: 91–2). On the other hand, he defended constitutional government, albeit in a presidential and authoritarian form, until the bitter end. He publicly opposed the National Socialists as a lethal threat to the constitution and to sound government. In the fall of 1932 Schmitt was made the Reich government's chief advocate before the Supreme Court to defend the Reich's assumption of direct rule in Prussia, which some regarded as a prelude to dictatorship. He also became an advisor to the ambitious defense minister General Kurt von Schleicher, whose brief tenure as chancellor (December 1932 to January 1933) marked the zenith of Schmitt's influence in public affairs. In January 1933 the chairman of the Catholic Center Party, Prelate Ludwig Kaas, publicly accused him of plotting a Schleicher dictatorship, which reflects the suspicion in which he was now held in the camp of political Catholicism. According to Ernst Huber, then Schmitt's student assistant, that suspicion was not groundless (Huber 1988: 40–50; Lönne 1994: 26–7).

Hitler's chancellorship and the accelerating National Socialist revolution in the spring of 1933 forced Schmitt to reconsider his anti-Nazi views. Perhaps feeling that he needed to prove his loyalty to the new regime, he surprised many of his friends by joining the party on May 1, 1933. His anxieties were intensified a year later on the "Night of the Long Knives," June 30, 1934, when Hitler authorized the murder of more than a hundred party members. Among the victims were also prominent non-Nazi conservatives such as Schmitt's former patron, General Schleicher. From 1933 through 1936 Schmitt held a number of Nazi-approved administrative and editorial appointments, in addition to his university position. During this period he published a series of legal studies that defended and legitimated the regime, including defenses of the 1934 purge and the 1935 Nuremberg racial laws. Such work has stigmatized him ever since as the "crown jurist" of the Third Reich. During this period his writing and his professional activities also reveal a blatant antisemitism. His defenders have argued that he never shared the biological racism of the Nazis, and that his antisemitism was contrived to protect himself against his enemies in the party (Bendersky 1983: 226–36). This position has become much less tenable since the posthumous publication of his diary. Others see his anti-Jewish cultural and religious prejudices as conventional: "Schmitt's anti-Semitism was standard equipment for the educated classes in Weimar, as we see indicated even in one of the few *Vernunft-Republikaner* such as Thomas Mann" (Lauermann 1994: 312). Be that as it may, the war did nothing to diminish those prejudices (Meier 1991: 8–9; 1998: 151–60; see also Gross 2000).

Nazi zealots and academic rivals eventually brought Schmitt down. They were assisted by the efforts of his disillusioned protégé Waldemar Gurian, a prominent Catholic writer who was forced to flee to Switzerland because of his anti-Nazism and his Jewish ancestry. Through a newsletter smuggled into Germany, Gurian campaigned relentlessly to "out" Schmitt as a pseudo-Nazi and cynical servant of whoever held power (Hürten 1972: 12–14, 119–20, 127–8). In 1936 articles in an SS newspaper intimidated Schmitt into resigning most of his posts aside from his university position. From 1937 to the end of the war he kept a low profile and turned his scholarly attention to international law. Even then, however, his publications espoused positions consistent with Hitler's expansionism. After the war he was arrested and spent a year and a half in an American military prison until his release in April 1947. Though he escaped criminal conviction, moral opprobrium clung to Schmitt for the rest of his long life. In the summer of 1945, he inscribed this verdict in his diary: "It is the bad, unworthy and yet authentic case of a *Christian Epimetheus*" (Schmitt 1950: 12): a puzzling statement, though it comes closer to a confession than anything Schmitt published in his lifetime (Meier 1998: 132–4). The mythical Epimetheus (meaning "Afterthought"), brother of Prometheus and husband of Pandora, was guilty of foolishness and fear: frightened by what Zeus had done to his brother, he ignored his brother's advice to take no gifts from Zeus and accepted the woman Pandora as his wife. She, of course, let loose the ills that Prometheus had confined to a jar. But the myth rather underplays Epimetheus' personal responsibility; how did Schmitt see this as a *Christian* story?

After he was forbidden to teach, Schmitt retreated into internal exile in Plettenberg, which he called his "San Casciano," after the place of Machiavelli's forced retirement at the hands of the Medici – another telling self-dramatization, as Heinrich Meier has noted (1991: 2–3). There he eventually resumed writing and eagerly hosted visitors who sought him out for scholarly counsel and discussion. Besides the predictable conservatives, from the late 1960s the political left showed up as well – some leftists, most famously Walter Benjamin, had always found things to admire in Schmitt. Alexander Kojève told Jacob Taubes that Schmitt was the only person in Germany worth talking to (Taubes 1987: 24). Since Schmitt's death in 1985, interest in him has grown rapidly. Today many regard him as one of the most original voices in modern German intellectual history, even though every aspect of his work continues to be contested and argued, not least his services to the Third Reich.

A Political Theologian?

The climate of interpretation

Carl Schmitt frequently denied being a theologian at all (Schmitt 1950: 89; 1970: 30). Being a lay theologian entailed risks he preferred to avoid (1970: 101 n. 1; Wacker 1994a: 286–92). Scholarship took him at his word, reading him primarily as a legal scholar and a political theorist. Even now much of the attention devoted to him comes from a secularist left uninterested in his religious commitments (McCormick 1997; Balakrishnan 2000).

The religious dimension of Schmitt's work did not attract attention until after his death in 1985. First, Schmitt's *Glossarium*, a postwar diary of notes and reflections, appeared in 1991. It contained abundant evidence that he thought of himself explicitly as a Catholic. In an entry for May 23, 1948, he wrote, "For me the Catholic faith is the religion of my fathers. I am Catholic not only by confession but also by historical origin, if I may say so, by race" (Lauermann 1994: 300 n. 16). And a month later: "This is the secret keyword to my entire mental and authorial life: the struggle for the authentically Catholic sharpening . . ." (Wacker 1994b: 7). Second, German Catholic scholarship began to reconsider Carl Schmitt, after trying for 40 years to forget he ever existed. In 1993 the Catholic Academy of Rhabanus Maurus sponsored a symposium on his Catholic identity and his place in German Catholicism past and present (Wacker 1994a: 280–92; 1994b; Lönne 1994; Nichtweiß 1992: 722–830; Dahlheimer 1998). Third, Heinrich Meier's studies of Schmitt and Leo Strauss (Meier 1991, 1995, 1998) argued that political theology was fundamental in Schmitt's thinking (Meier 1998: 27). Meier's reading proposed a deeply religious Schmitt, driven by his Christian faith to wage lifelong war against secular reason, unbelief, and nihilism. Another who took the religious foundations of Schmitt's work seriously was Jacob Taubes, though he approached Schmitt from a left-wing Jewish viewpoint different from Meier's Straussianism. For Taubes, whose interest in political theology was inspired by Schmitt, the Hobbesian decisionist the world knew was really "an apocalypticist of the Counter-Revolution" (Taubes 1987: 16).

The main sources for Schmitt's political theology are a series of short treatises written over half a century, in his trademark polemical and aphoristic style. (Also important, especially for those like Meier who work from the concept of a Schmittian "arcanum," are the two volumes of notes and reflections from the years immediately after World War II, *Ex Captivitate Salus* and the above-mentioned *Glossarium*.) *Political Theology: Four Chapters on the Concept of Sovereignty* (1922; 2nd edn. 1934) and *Roman Catholicism and Political Form* (1923; 2nd edn. 1925) make a complementary set. The first discloses the roots of sovereignty as a secularized theological concept and develops Schmitt's decisionist theory of law: "Sovereign is he who decides on the exception" (Schmitt 1985: 5) The second presents the Roman Catholic Church as a *Machtform*, a bulwark of authority in an unsteady social world. *The Concept of the Political* (1927; 2nd edn. 1932; 3rd edn. 1933), perhaps Schmitt's most influential work, defines the political by the friend–enemy distinction. *The Leviathan in the State Theory of Thomas Hobbes* (1938) is Schmitt's fullest assessment of a political thinker whom he regarded as teacher and intimate friend; it uses Hobbes as a yardstick by which to evaluate the modern deterioration of the state. *Politische Theologie II: Die Legende von der Erledigung jeder Politischen Theologie* (1970), Schmitt's last book, is a hostile response to his late friend Erik Peterson's 1935 monograph *Monotheismus als politisches Problem*. Peterson had ended his book with the sweeping assertion that Nicene trinitarianism and Augustinian eschatology had made a fundamental break with every political theology "which misuses the Christian proclamation for the justification of a political situation" (Peterson 1951: 104–5) a thesis Schmitt believed was directly squarely at him.

Political theology as neutral diagnostic tool

Schmitt called his political theology "a sociology of juristic concepts," a description whose Weberian resonance was meant to stress its purely scholarly and impartial character.

> All significant concepts of the modern theory of the state are secularized theological concepts not only because of their historical development – in which they were transferred from theology to the theory of the state, whereby, for example, the omnipotent God became the omnipotent lawgiver – but also because of their systematic structure, the recognition of which is necessary for a sociological consideration of these concepts. (Schmitt 1985: 36)

Such a sociology was not to be understood as a form of ideology critique to unmask religious and theological constructs as subservient to and derivative from legal and political ones (or of social and economic ones, either). The connection between the two spheres was "consistent and radical," but not directly causal. A "spiritual" philosophy of history was no less plausible than a materialist one. Thus in the nineteenth century, neither the authors of "the political theology of the Restoration" (Juan Donoso Cortés, Joseph de Maistre, Louis de Bonald) nor their revolutionary materialist opponents could prove their cases (Schmitt 1985: 42) Nor did Schmitt's sociology of juristic concepts seek a correlation between ideas and the point of view and activities of a particular social class or professional group. Consciousness was not reducible to a social construction, nor could the representation of social reality in turn be reduced to religious or metaphysical assumptions. What he sought was simply the radical correlation between the two in a given epoch. To take an example from the epoch about which Schmitt himself cared most, the early modern period, it would be false if we were to describe the absolute monarchy of the seventeenth century as the really real of which the Cartesian concept of God was merely a reflection.

[I]t is a sociology of the concept of sovereignty when the historical–political status of the monarchy of that epoch is shown to correspond to the general state of consciousness that was characteristic of western Europeans at that time, and when the juristic construction of a historical–political reality can find a concept whose structure is in accord with the structure of metaphysical concepts. Monarchy thus becomes as self-evident in the consciousness of that period as democracy does in a later epoch . . . The metaphysical image that a definite epoch forges of the world has the same structure as a form of its political organization. (1985: 46)

Political theology and legitimation

But Schmitt's correspondences served purposes beyond the merely diagnostic. Since the correlations were mutually reinforcing, the decline of one meant the inevitable weakening of the other. And in Schmitt's construction of history, that is what has happened, as religious conceptions of the world gave way to philosophical and metaphysical conceptions, and they in turn to the instrumental rationality of technical reason, mathematics, and the natural sciences. For Schmitt it was axiomatic that the political order needed legitimation: "No political system can survive even a generation with only the naked techniques of holding power. *To the political belongs the idea, because there is no politics without authority and no authority without an ethos of belief*" (1996c: 17, emphasis added). "[S]ince Comte we have had many new experiences that affect the ineradicable need for legitimation of every human being" (1970: 101n).

The pairing of *Roman Catholicism and Political Form* with *Political Theology* reflected his conviction that the political and the religious spheres had a unique affinity. This affinity was grounded in their common expression as *law*. The science of the law in Europe was actually descended from canon law on its "maternal" side, though the child eventually had to leave its mother (1950: 69). A political theology was genuinely possible partly because of the peculiar interconnection of the disciplines of the canonist and the jurist (1970: 101).

The political and the religious spheres also shared a common alienation from modern forces such as liberalism, economism, and "technicity" (Schmitt 1988: 32–50; 1996a: 69–79; 1996b: 42–50, 55–62, 68–74). The unhappy effects of these forces were to be seen in such developments as the distinction of public and private in politics and law, the fragmenting of the state by the pluralistic forces of society ("depoliticization"), the pure normativity of law without regard to its roots in personal authority and personal decision, the division of powers in parliamentary democracies and the splintering of sovereignty, the substitution of discussion and debate for decision, the exaltation of private property and *laissez-faire* economics, the reduction of meaning to material production and consumption, and value neutrality in questions of morality and belief. Catholicism, he argued, could accommodate liberal democracy, industrialization, and financial capitalism, but it could never be their ally. "An alliance of the Catholic Church with the present form of industrial capitalism is not possible. The alliance of throne and altar will not be followed by an alliance of office and altar, also not of factory and altar" (1996c: 24). The reason for this incompatibility was the special *representative* role of the church:

> The political power of Catholicism rests neither on economic nor on military means but rather on the absolute realization of authority. The Church also is a "juridical person," though not in the same sense as a joint-stock company. The typical product of the age of production is a method of accounting, whereas the Church is a concrete personal representation of a concrete personality. All knowledgeable witnesses have conceded that the Church is the consummate agency of the juridical spirit and the true heir of Roman jurisprudence. Therein – in its capacity to assume juridical form – lies one of its sociological secrets. But it has the power to assume this or any other form only because it has the power of representation. It represents the *civitas humana*. It represents in every moment the historical connection to the incarnation and crucifixion of Christ. It represents the Person of Christ Himself: God become man in historical reality. Therein lies its superiority over an age of economic thinking. (1996c: 18–19)

The church sought coexistence with the state as a natural partner that, like itself, was also a *societas perfecta*. The state too was based on representation, even if modern parliamentary democracy had obscured that fact. The state too took on "political and juridical forms that are equally immaterial and irritating to the consistency of economic thinking" – immaterial because they took into account other than merely economic values (1996c: 16, 27). Here Schmitt saw no difference between capitalism and Marxism: "The big industrialist has no other ideal than that of Lenin – an 'electrified earth.' They disagree essentially only about the correct method of electrification" (1996c: 13).

Political theology and the question of priority

Did the political trump the theological in Schmitt's political theology? Many of his fellow Catholics believed it did (see next section). On the other hand, Heinrich Meier's influential interpretation argues that Schmitt's thought is deeply determined by a theological agenda. The question of priority is complicated by Schmitt's apparent estrangement from the church in the late 1920s, a development Meier ignored. He shrewdly pointed to what others considered the most nakedly secular and amoral element in Schmitt's thought, the definition of the political as the distinction between friend and enemy, and argued that it was ultimately rooted in Schmitt's political theology (Meier 1998: 27). Hidden behind liberalism's neutralizations is the brutal reality of the modern revolt against God. They are a mask for oppositions and hostilities that are genuinely theological. Atheistic anarchism at least does faith the favor of making its revolt explicit. But bourgeois liberalism discloses the spirit of the age even more meaningfully than does anarchism. Its search for a peaceful, secure, and comfortable existence, free of struggle, challenge, and the need to obey, seeks insidiously to deprive us even of our enemies. But faith knows that the promise of "peace and security" (Meier cites 1 Thess. 5: 3) is an idolatrous delusion that only conceals the final onslaught of the Enemy *par excellence*, the devil himself. "The battle 'for' or 'against' enmity, its affirmation or negation, thereby becomes the political-theological criterion of the first order" (Meier 1998: 24).

It is possible to accept aspects of Meier's central thesis without accepting all of it. He builds his case on the basis of genuine themes in Schmitt's thinking (see Meier 1998: 4–13, 54–65, 66–99). Schmitt certainly believed, for example, that it was impossible to imagine a world without enmity and aggression. The effort to create such a world would itself require intense aggression: a "war to end all wars" would be unusually intense and inhuman (1996a: 36). A world that managed to substitute economic competition for war was merely disguising from itself the coercive force exerted by economic power (1996a: 78–9). That is why an utterly secular world was also an impossibility:

> The core question that in my view arises concerning "the political" concerns the reality of an enemy, whose real possibility I still recognize even in an utterly de-theologized counter-position [he is referring to Hans Blumenberg's 1966 book *Die Legitimität der Neuzeit*]. The careful study of its transformation from the old political theology into one that pretends to a totally new, pure secularity and man-centered humanity [*humane Menschlichkeit*] remains in fact a permanent duty of the scholarly search for knowledge. (Schmitt 1970: 124)

Schmitt's thought as Meier (and Jacob Taubes) presents it has apocalyptic contours that remind us of other nineteenth- and early twentieth-century Christian antimodernists, from Kierkegaard to Dostoevsky and the Russian personalists. Schmitt himself found his forebears among reactionary Catholic thinkers such as the Spanish diplomat Juan Donoso Cortés (Schmitt 1985: 53–66), with whom he shared a belief in human sinfulness and a skepticism that the weakened modern state could provide peace and security. Donoso Cortés and the other "counter-revolutionary philosophers of the state" recognized the ultimately theological nature of the enmity between Christianity and liberalism. They refused to back away from metaphysical principles and truths merely to accommodate liberal commitments to perpetual discussion and negotiation. "Liberalism, with its contradictions and compromises, existed for Donoso Cortés only in that short interim period in which it was possible to answer the question 'Christ or Barabbas?' with a proposal to adjourn or appoint a commission of investigation" (p. 62). They also recognized the deep connection between the eclipse in the early nineteenth century of theistic transcendence (in favor of immanentist metaphysics and pantheism) and legitimist monarchy (in favor of democracy and popular sovereignty). In response they formulated the first political theology (pp. 50–1).

The pessimistic anthropology and antiliberalism of these thinkers figure prominently in Schmitt's *The Concept of the Political*, which defined the specifically political distinction as that between friend and enemy (1996a: 25–37). "The distinction of friend and enemy denotes the utmost degree of intensity of a union or separation, of an association or dissociation." "The political is the most intense and extreme antagonism, and every concrete antagonism becomes that much more political the closer it approaches the most extreme point, that of the friend–enemy grouping" (1996a: 26, 29). The political was thus a criterion and not a domain. It was a judgment about the state of a relationship, not a particular category of human association alongside other associations. Conflict became truly political whenever it became mortal and existential. Until the nineteenth century, the state had been the arbiter of such conflict. But the modern state has been weakened thanks to liberalism, economism, and other forces (1996a: 22–5). As a result, any conflict could assume a genuinely political form, regardless of whether it was originally religious, moral, economic, cultural, etc. (1996a: 37–45).

Schmitt's definition of the political ruled out an optimistic anthropology and rested on the dogma of original sin. "The fundamental theological dogma of the evilness of the world and man leads, just as does the distinction of friend and enemy, to a categorization of men and makes impossible the undifferentiated optimism of a universal conception of man. In a good world among good people, only peace, security, and harmony prevail. Priests and theologians are here just as superfluous as politicians and statesmen" (1996a: 65).

Schmitt's Political Theology and its Catholic Reception

The season of political theology

> Today we are an utterly political species. And our quest for "salvation" comes alive in the political dimension.
>
> Paul Althaus in 1933

In 1922 Schmitt was ahead of his time. With Weimar's final crisis, however, "political theology" became the refrain of a broad and ecumenical chorus, reaching an adulatory crescendo in the months after Hitler came to power (Scholder 1988: I, 99–119, 189–209, 414–40). By then Schmitt's sympathies had shifted away from the political Catholicism of the Center Party, in part perhaps because the church rejected his annulment petition for a marriage that ended in divorce in 1924, thereby making his second marriage noncanonical (Nichtweiß 1992: 727–8). Schmitt increasingly disagreed with the Center Party's commitment to parliamentary democracy, religious confessionalism, tolerance, and pluralism (Lönne 1994: 34–5). A different outlook from the parliamentarism of the Center Party existed among conservative Catholics who looked back nostalgically to the medieval German empire and advocated a Catholic *Reichstheologie* as an antidote to liberal democracy. They favored an organic conception of society, organized as estates or professional groupings, which they believed was reflected in National Socialist rhetoric of a national community, totality claims, and the leadership principle, spelling the welcome end of liberalism, individualism, and the Weimar "party-state." Such ideas were popular among discussion groups like the Catholic Academic Association and the aristocratic fellowship *Kreuz und Adler* ("Cross and Eagle") which met at the Benedictine monastery of Maria Laach, under the benevolent patronage of Abbot Ildefons Herwegen (Böckenförde 1961: 224–51; Nichtweiß 1992: 764–72).

Though he occasionally attended the Maria Laach meetings, Schmitt had scant respect for this *Reichstheologie*. When he made his shaky peace with the Nazis, he preferred a rationale unencumbered by natural law categories or medieval precedents (Böckenförde 1961: 229 n. 45). He probably stood closer to contemporary Protestant political theologians such as Wilhelm Stapel, with whom he was in close contact, and Emmanuel Hirsch, with whose Kierkegaardian decisionism he shared much in common.

In 1934 Schmitt reissued *Political Theology*. In a new preface he noted with satisfaction that Protestant theologians like Friedrich Gogarten, with whom in 1931 he had contemplated co-editing a journal to be called *Der Staat* (Lauermann 1994: 300 n. 17), now recognized that a concept of secularization was essential to understand the course of the past several centuries:

> To be sure, Protestant theology presents a different, supposedly unpolitical doctrine, conceiving of God as the "wholly other," just as in political liberalism the state and politics are conceived of as "the wholly other." We have come to recognize that the political is the total, and as a result we know that any decision about whether something is *unpolitical* is always a *political* decision, irrespective of who decides and what reasons are advanced. This also holds for the question whether a particular theology is a political or an unpolitical theology (Schmitt 1985: 2).

"The political is the total"

This dictum is a revealing corollary to Schmitt's political theology. In *The Concept of the Political* he had defined the political as the measure of existential and even violent conflict. To say it was "the total" meant that when existential conflict broke out, no other criterion for decision-making could claim priority. In his 1938 book on Thomas Hobbes, he would call such competing claims "indirect powers." Schmitt took this term from Catholic doctrine as expounded classically by Robert Bellarmine, according to whom the church exercised a *potestas indirecta* in the sphere of politics, law, and the state, though no longer a direct power as had been the case in the Middle Ages. Schmitt extended its meaning to include any and all social agencies that threatened to destroy the unity of the state: cultural organizations, business corporations, professional associations, and the like (Schmitt 1996b: 71–4). In 1933, to say that the political was the total was to endorse the idea of "the total state." Schmitt himself had popularized the concept of the total state, by which he did not mean precisely what is today thought of as a "totalitarian" state (1996a: 38–9). In *The Concept of the Political* he had said that the total state was a merely polemical concept for describing what had happened to the "neutral state" of the nineteenth century, itself a successor of the "absolute state" of the eighteenth century. The development of the total state was necessitated by nineteenth-century liberalism's neutralizations. The various domains of "society," now split off as separate spheres, had sought to make a claim on the state and its resources. Schmitt strongly disparaged the expropriation of the state by the forces of "society," whose concerns were made into political matters (1996a: 22). The state was thus forced to align itself with society and to close the gap. The total state could not afford to regard anything as nonpolitical (1996a: 23–5). In Schmitt's eyes such a state was more likely to become too *weak* rather than too strong, since it risked overextending itself and becoming dissolved by democratic passions. He originally opposed the National Socialists precisely because he feared that they would cannibalize the state, and his Nazi-era writings, such as *Staat, Bewegung, Volk* ("State, Movement, People") had to turn somersaults to accommodate Nazi populist dynamism. Central to his compromise was the doctrine, enunciated in 1933, that a total state in this weak sense ought to give way to a total state of a strong type, which could exploit modern means of mass communication and enthusiastic mass movements to impose, top-down, the requisite order – in short, fascism.

Regardless of Schmitt's intention, such totalizing language posed obvious dangers, and Catholic critics attacked it head-on (Lönne 1994: 23–33; Dahlheimer 1998: 346–61, 371–81). Gustav Gundlach, a prominent Jesuit moral theologian who had a substantial hand in drafting the 1931 papal encyclical *Quadragesimo Anno*, stood against Schmitt on both political and philosophical grounds. He argued that the experiences of the Weimar period demonstrated the practical wisdom of the parliamentary system for Catholics, whose welfare depended on party discipline and party political action. On natural law grounds he opposed the decisionism and philosophical voluntarism underlying Schmitt's assertion of the total state (Lönne 1994: 32). He showed how natural law argument could be used *against* political theology at the same time that other Catholic thinkers such as Karl Eschweiler were using natural law arguments to validate it (Dahlheimer 1998: 224–8).

The unitary state: Who will decide?

Gundlach had also objected to the way that Schmitt's "friend–enemy" definition of the political reduced the state to a mere question of power and appeared based on an almost Manichean dualism of good and evil, resolvable only by brutal decision and command. The friend–enemy distinction aroused opposition because it collided with traditional Catholic social thinking about the harmony of the orders of society, and because it appeared to contradict so blatantly the evangelical injunction to love the enemy (Lönne 1994: 24–5). To the last charge, Schmitt responded that the love commandment applied only to individual enemies, not to "political" enemies (1996a: 29). As for the basis of the state in power rather than in a moral order, Schmitt never disputed the charge. He often cited Hobbes's tag, *Autoritas non veritas facit legem* (Schmitt 1985: 33, 52; 1996b: 44, 55–6). "For Hobbes God is above all power (*potestas*)" (1996b: 32). Hobbes, he says in *The Concept of the Political*, knew that law was only a human construction. This was true both of positive law ("In this case the rule of law means nothing else than the legitimization of a specific *status quo*") and also of appeals to a higher or better law, "a so-called natural law or law of reason" (1996a: 66–7). In his prison diary he was to call Hobbes "his closest daily company" (1950: 63). He professed to admire Hobbes' resounding rejection of the *potestas indirecta* of Bellarmine and company. Such "distinctions and pseudo-concepts" were deceptive because they laid claim to obedience without having the responsibility for providing protection in return. And it was the state's provision of protection that gave it the right to demand obedience (1950: 67; 1996a: 52–3; 1996b: 71–2, 74, 83, 86). In an age riven with confessional strife, Hobbes restored the power of decision to the state by taking it out of the hands of the warring theologians and the sects (1950: 66–8). As the early modern state took on the tasks and trappings of the spiritual order, it disarmed the theologians by denying them the right, for example, to determine a just war (1950: 69–70).

> *Quis judicabit? Quis interpretabitur?* Who decides *in concreto* for human beings acting in their creaturely independence the question of what is spiritual and what is secular, and how one relates to the *res mixtae*, that, in the interim between the Lord's first and second comings, now determine the entire earthly existence of this spiritual-secular, spiritual-temporal double nature of *humanity?* That is the great Thomas Hobbes question that in my book of 1922, *Political Theology*, I already put into the center of discussion and which led to a theory of decisionism and of the autonomy of action. (1970: 107)

Heinrich Meier has made Schmitt's interpretation of Hobbes a centerpiece of his landmark study (1998: 100–34). In his reading, Schmitt distorted Hobbes to fit his own needs; he was not a "Hobbesian" at all, at least in the conventional sense, but a dedicated if evasive believer. That thesis requires respectful qualification. Too many of Schmitt's contemporaries thought otherwise, including friends such as Erik Peterson, who was particularly disturbed by Schmitt's attack on the church's indirect power: "The polemic against the *potestas indirecta* only has meaning if one has repudiated Christianity and has opted for paganism" (Nichtweiß 1992: 735). Peterson may have been especially disappointed in the defection of someone who had once written compellingly of the church's representative power (Nichtweiß 1994: 57–8). The denial of the indirect power meant a fatal acquiescence in secularization. The unity of the state could not be won at the expense of the church's public (*öffentlich*) character. The church came into being as the eschatological reality of the New Age, which destroyed the closed world of the Old Age. But Schmitt appeared to endorse the *Leviathan*'s lament over the "typically Judeo-Christian splitting of the original political unity" (Schmitt 1996b: 11) – a splitting that Peterson himself thought was rooted in the very words of Jesus (Nichtweiß 1992: 735 n. 118). What Schmitt said of

Hobbes in the *Glossarium* appears to apply to himself as well: Hobbes's displacement of Christianity into marginal domains was accomplished with the intent of "rendering harmless the effect of Christ in the social and political sphere; of de-anarchizing Christianity, while leaving it in the background a certain legitimating function" (Nichtweiß 1994: 46).

Against the instrumentalizing of the church

Much of the criticism of Schmitt's political theology therefore centered on his treatment of the church. Ferocious critics like Waldemar Gurian considered Schmitt no better than a German version of Charles Maurras, the French nationalist and founder of the reactionary movement Action Française. Maurras' atheism had not kept him from enthusiastically supporting the Catholic Church. Already in a 1926 letter to Peterson, Gurian compared the two: "How similar is Maurras to Schmitt; but Maurras is more honorable; he doesn't pretend to look like a Catholic! He is a pagan and the Church a prop for Order! Similar anxiety over theologians as external authority, similar mixture of precisionism, diligence, and bohemianism, similar relation to people. Uncanny!" (Nichtweiß 1992: 729 n. 63). The juridical fixation of Schmitt's conception of the church was a particular problem. The Catholic socialist Ernst Michel objected to treating the church as merely a higher type of politics and ignoring its character as "the sacrament of love" that spoke for the un-represented part of society: "If the Church is as Carl Schmitt renders it, then . . . the Grand Inquisitor is right and Christ is wrong" (Lönne 1994: 28). Seeing the church primarily as "representation" reduced it to being the conservator of the world as it is, either directly as judge or as underwriter of the political form of the state. The church became a last-ditch defense against social chaos and breakdown, "the ark of Noah in a flood of sin," reflecting Schmitt's despair of the church's future in a pluralistic and secularizing world. *The Concept of the Political*'s pessimistic picture of human nature after the Fall was attacked as inconsistent with tridentine orthodoxy (Wacker 1994a: 287–90; 1994c: 137).

Schmitt's instrumentalization of Christianity was the most extreme example of an apologetic strategy quite common among Weimar era Catholics who stressed what the church could do for German society (Ruster 1994: 377–85). All such strategies run the risk of diluting principle for utility, and there is no doubt that Schmitt's political theology crossed the line in this respect. While we should reject Gurian's accusation of dishonesty, there is ample reason for thinking that Schmitt's religious faith was more polemical and "dramaturgical" than substantive in its relationship with the political order; even if that faith revived after the war, it was still "a Lefèbvrism *avant la lettre*" (Faber 1994: 278; Wacker 1994c: 136–7; Lönne 1994: 15; Lauermann 1994: 300). Many of his friends believed that he thought the church of Vatican II had gone mad and had squandered what he most valued in Roman Catholicism (Wacker 1994a: 293).

Political theology and reading the signs of the times

Erik Peterson deserves the last word. Part of Peterson's argument against the possibility of any Christian political theology had rested on St. Augustine's stripping of the sacral patina given to the Roman Empire by Christian apologists such as Eusebius of Caesarea. In *Politische Theologie II* Schmitt objected to this argument because it seemed to deny Christian laypeople the right to see the hand of God in their political well-being: "A church does not consist only of theologians" (Schmitt 1970: 77). With mordant pleasure he pointed to the euphoria of Angelo Roncalli (the future John XXIII!) over the signing of the 1929 Lateran Treaties between the Vatican and Mussolini's government, as a modern example of a Catholic rejoicing at seeing God at work in the world. Schmitt singled out for attack Peterson's invocation of *De Civitate Dei* 3. 30, in which Augustine scorned Cicero for mistakenly placing his bets on Octavian, the future dictator: said Augustine, Cicero was "blind and reckless about what was to come" (*caecus atque improvidus futurorum*) (Peterson 1951: 90). Inappropriate after-the-fact moralizing, sniffed Schmitt. How could Cicero have known, and what choices did he really have, caught between Antony and Caesar's nephew? (Schmitt 1970: 90–1). In a letter to Schmitt written long afterwords, Jacob Taubes defended the justice and the wisdom of Peterson's words from 1935: "That *caecus atque improvidus futurorum* was a coded warning directed at you – but you didn't get it. You had no better friend than Peterson, whom you also brought on the path to the Church. 'True are the wounds that a friend's arrow makes,' says the Psalmist somewhere" (Taubes 1987: 40).

References and Further Reading

Balakrishnan, Gopal (2000). *The Enemy: An Intellectual Portrait of Carl Schmitt*. London and New York: Verso.

Bendersky, Joseph W. (1983). *Carl Schmitt: Theorist for the Reich*. Princeton: Princeton University Press.

Böckenförde, Ernst-Wolfgang (1961). "Der deutsche Katholizismus im Jahre 1933. Eine kritische Betrachtung." *Hochland* 53, 14–39.

Dahlheimer, Manfred (1998). *Carl Schmitt und der deutsche Katholizismus 1888–1936*. Paderborn, Munich, Vienna and Zurich: Ferdinand Schöningh.

Faber, Richard (1994). "Carl Schmitt, der Römer." In Wacker (1994b), 257–78.

Gebhardt, Winfried (1995). "Schmitt, Carl." In *Biographisch-bibliographisches Kirchen-Lexikon*, cols. 486–96. Herzberg: Verlag Traugott Bautz. (Consulted online at http://www.bautz.de/bbkl/s/s1/schmitt_c.shtml.)

Gross, Raphael (2000). *Carl Schmitt und die Juden. Eine deutsche Rechtslehre*. Frankfurt am Main: Suhrkamp.

Huber, Ernst (1988). "Carl Schmitt in der Reichskrise der Weimarer Endzeit." In Quaritsch (1988), 33–50.

Hürten, Heinz (1972). *Waldemar Gurian*. Mainz: Matthias Grünewald.

Koenen, Andreas (1995). *Der Fall Carl Schmitt. Sein Aufstieg zum Kronjuristen des Dritten Reiches*. Darmstadt: Wissenschaftliche Buchgesellschaft.

Lauermann, Manfred (1994). "Carl Schmitt – jenseits biographischer Mode." In Wacker (1994b), 295–319.

Lönne, Karl-Egon (1994). "Carl Schmitt und der Katholizismus der Weimarer Republik." In Wacker (1994b), 11–35.

McCormick, John (1997). *Carl Schmitt's Critique of Liberalism: Against Politics as Technology*. Cambridge: Cambridge University Press.

Mehring, Reinhard (1993). "Vom Umgang mit Carl Schmitt: Zur neueren Literatur." *Geschichte und Gesellschaft* 19, 388–407.

Meier, Heinrich (1991). "Der Philosoph als Feind – zu Carl Schmitts *Glossarium*." Typescript of article published in altered form in *Der Spiegel* 31 (1991), 168–72.

——(1995). *Carl Schmitt and Leo Strauss: The Hidden Dialogue*, trans. J. Harvey Lomax. Chicago and London: University of Chicago Press.

——(1998). *The Lesson of Carl Schmitt: Four Chapters on the Distinction between Political Theology and Political Philosophy*, trans. Marcus Brainard. Chicago and London: University of Chicago Press.

Nichtweiß, Barbara (1992). *Erik Peterson. Neue Sicht auf Leben und Werk*. Freiburg, Basel and Vienna: Herder.

——(1994). "Apokalyptische Verfassungslehren. Carl Schmitt im Horizont der Theologie Erik Petersons." In Wacker (1994b), 37–64.

Noack, Paul (1993). *Carl Schmitt: Eine Biographie*. Berlin: Propyläen.

Peterson, Erik (1951). "Monotheismus als politisches Problem: Ein Beitrag zur Geschichte der politischen Theologie im Imperium Romanum." In *Theologische Traktate*, 45–147. Munich: Kösel.

Quaritsch, Helmut, ed. (1988). *Complexio Oppositorum. Über Carl Schmitt*. Berlin: Duncker & Humblot.

Ruster, Thomas (1994). *Die verlorene Nützlichkeit der Religion. Katholizismus und Moderne in der Weimarer Republik*. Paderborn, Munich, Vienna and Zurich: Ferdinand Schöningh.

Schmitt, Carl (1950). *Ex Captivitate Salus: Erfahrungen der Zeit 1945–47*. Cologne: Greven.

——(1970). *Politische Theologie II: Die Legende von der Erledigung jeder Politischen Theologie*. Berlin: Duncker & Humblot.

——(1985). *Political Theology: Four Chapters on the Concept of Sovereignty*, trans. and intr. George Schwab. Cambridge, Mass., and London: MIT Press.

——(1988). *The Crisis of Parliamentary Democracy*, trans. and intr. Ellen Kennedy. Cambridge, Mass., and London: MIT Press.

——(1991). *Glossarium. Aufzeichnungen der Jahre 1947–1951*, ed. Eberhard Freiherr von Medem. Berlin: Duncker & Humblot.

——(1996a). *The Concept of the Political*, trans. and intr. George Schwab, foreword Tracy B. Strong. Chicago and London: University of Chicago Press.

——(1996b). *The Leviathan in the State Theory of Thomas Hobbes: Meaning and Failure of a Political Symbol*. Foreword and intr. George Schwab, trans. George Schwab and Erna Hilfstein. Westport, Conn., and London: Greenwood.

——(1996c). *Roman Catholicism and Political Form*, trans. and intr. Gary Ulmen. Westport, Conn., and London: Greenwood.

Scholder, Klaus (1988). *The Churches and the Third Reich*, 2 vols., trans. John Bowden. Philadelphia: Fortress.

Schwab, George (1989). *The Challenge of the Exception: An Introduction to the Political Ideas of Carl Schmitt from 1921 to 1936*, 2nd edn. Westport, Conn.: Greenwood.

Seubert, Harald (2002). "Eigene Fragen als Gestalt. Zu neuerer Literatur zu Carl Schmitt." http://www.geocities.com/Athens/Forum/7501/ph/hs/e1.html.

Taubes, Jakob (1987). *Ad Carl Schmitt. Gegenstrebige Fügung*. Berlin: Merve.

Tommissen, Piet (1988). "Bausteine zu einer wissenschaftlichen Biographie (Periode: 1888–1933)." In Quaritsch (1988), 71–100.

Wacker, Bernd (1994a). "Carl Schmitts Katholizismus und die katholische Theologie nach 1945." In Wacker (1994b), 279–94.

——, ed. (1994b). *Die eigentlich katholische Verschärfung . . . : Konfession, Theologie und Politik im Werk Carl Schmitts*. Munich: Wilhelm Fink.

——(1994c). "Die Zweideutigkeit der katholischen Verschärfung – Carl Schmitt und Hugo Ball." In Wacker (1994b), 123–46.

CHAPTER 9

Karl Barth

Haddon Willmer

His Times

Karl Barth (1886–1968) is renowned for his wonder-ful (Barth 1963: 61ff.) commitment to theology. He is less often seen as a theologian *in and for politics*, if not a political theologian, both in his lifetime and now. This essay can be no more than a fragmentary taster to Barth's work. Dealing only with political issues as he talked about them, it will not guess what he might have said on other matters, let alone criticize or defend him where he failed to answer questions which have gained salience in our time (cf. e.g. Katherine Sonderegger, "Barth and Feminism," in Webster 2000: 258–73).

The turbulent half-century between World War I and the Vietnam War, the Prague Spring, and the student revolts of 1968 raised fundamental political issues for anyone like Barth who lived through them with the newspaper in one hand and the Bible in the other. A Swiss, proving himself a friend of Germany where he worked for many years, Barth experienced war and peace, dictatorship and democracy, capitalism and communism, religious politics and political theology. Terrible wars and programs for social welfare intertwined in the massive experimentation of the modern technological state. Order needed somehow to be related to freedom in humanizing practice, freedom to service, duty to rights, pragmatism to imagination, despair to hope. Private interest crossed with public belonging, informed political discussion with media manipulation and extreme coercion. In 1900 Europe, with its intermarried monarchies from Britain to Russia, controlled most of the world; by midcentury, it was broken and divided by the Iron Curtain between the spheres of two superpowers. While, in culture, philosophy, and rhetoric, God was often replaced by Humanity, in practice human beings were disposed of, *en masse*, by evil genocidal powers tricked out with the propagandist languages of progress, racial purity, class justice, and scientific efficiency. The Universal Declaration of Human Rights (1948) was therefore a necessary and considered reaction to "barbarous acts which have outraged the conscience of mankind," a moment of flickering hope in a world where barbarity continues and a consistently effective politically institutional-ized conscience has not been able to eradicate it. Europe descended into hell through its political history, and had to work politically at reconstruction. Because Barth was intensely alive and present to his own time and place, he still speaks usefully to us, for he grappled with basic recurring issues in the cheerful hope and modest realism of faith in God.

What was the state, what was it for, was it necessary, how could its abuses be curbed, what legitimates it? What was the value of human beings? What is the content and foundation of human rights, when power proves human beings to be so easily despised and disposed of? How can we go on being hopeful about humanity, and give some positive meaning to humanism and its values, when humanity repeatedly discredits itself? In Barth's lifetime democracy was a con-tested option, not the respectable consensus. Hitler was popular outside, as well as inside, Germany, for he seemed to order society better than the effete and inde-cisive democracies. Many judged communism, even in Stalin's day, to be worth the loss of freedom and pluralist electoral politics which, even then, was part of its obvious price. For us, who now so easily take democracy as self-evident, although it is still so erratic and unconvincing in its performance, this period is instructive. By retracing Barth's way, we can wrestle with questions to which we give faltering and hazy answers in practice, although we talk as though we had left them behind. Barth helps us because he lived "theologically" through his times, and stimulated genuine political *theology*.

Theology and Politics

Barth was determined to be political only through theology – and he argued that being a theologian gave him something distinctive and useful to offer in politics, though that was not the reason for doing theology (Barth 1939: 82). Theology was true only as obedience to the Word of God. In 1933, urged to respond to Hitler's new Reich by taking a political stance, he declared that, in view of the unclear situation, he would carry on with his students in Bonn, doing "only the-ology *as though nothing had happened*"(Barth 1984: 26; emphasis added). This phrase has often been quoted, to chide him for irresponsible political evasion (Barth 1954: 113) and to confirm the judgment, derived (mistakenly) from his *Epistle to the Romans* and the path he had taken in the 1920s, that his orienta-tion on God as the "totally Other" made him dangerously indifferent to human potential (Barth 1967: 33). Barth, on the contrary, always argued that doing theology seriously, in its integrity, would be a real, decisive, if indirect, contri-bution to politics. He admitted later that he had been too slow in responding to the political situation in the later 1920s, but he did not concede that he should have politicized or given up theology in order to speak to the "situation." When his critics demanded political "realism" Barth reminded them that God in Christ was the source and measure of reality.

From the late 1920s he was clear that dogmatics was not a "free" science (as a university discipline is conventionally thought to be), but one "bound to the sphere of the Church, where and where alone it is possible and sensible" (Barth 1932: ix). Barth valued secular order, and on that basis resisted interference with academic and other freedoms; but his ultimate *theological* opposition to the Nazis' forcible incorporation of all parts of German society into their total project was grounded on theology's total commitment to the true Lord, who was not Hitler or the *Volk* or any similarly human authority. (We do not speak about God by speaking about humanity in a loud voice.) Freedom was not from external restraint, nor even for self-determination, but freedom in the service of the Lord of freedom (Barth 1971: 68). In binding theology to church, Barth was not putting theological scholarship under the control of unlearned church rulers, but requiring theologians to work as members of the community of faithful obedience to God, rather than as freewheeling intellectuals. To take the church more seriously than it took itself implied a commitment to building up the church, thus saving it from religious politics and political religions (Burleigh 2000: 4–14) while fitting it for sober secular politics. He introduced the first of 13 volumes of the *Church Dogmatics* by protesting that for lack of adequate theology many preachers and faithful people were left to find "religious insight in their intoxication of their Nordic blood and their political Führer" (1932: xi).

Barth worked primarily in Switzerland and Germany. Both states traditionally wanted to be "Christian" in some sense and so they recognized churches as public corporations. Theology in public universities was an intellectually lively and popular discipline, with close, if sometimes conflictual, relations with churches. Christendom creaked, but had not yet collapsed. Throughout the period of Barth's life, some were simply at home in the ambiguity of the situation, exploiting what the tradition gave, while it lasted. Others valued it as a social and cultural inheritance under attack and in danger of being lost; so they fought for its restoration. Barth, though historically learned and appreciative of the past, provocatively took another view. The church could not rest on its past, but was the church only in the *present* hearing of the *living* Word of God. In the "church struggle," some made adherence to the sixteenth-century confessions the criterion of the true church, but Barth struggled for a church that was given its true being ever afresh, as a *Bekennende Kirche*, a confessing, rather than a confessional, church. Bonhoeffer's famous question, "Who is Jesus Christ for us today?" was also Barth's. Barth respected inherited confessions of faith and often lectured on them; but quoting a past confession, rather than speaking out of actual faith now, was not merely dead, but deadly.

The political task of the church was not to shore up Christendom. Barth recognized that the historical performance of Christianity was imperfect. Socialists had been quicker and more accurate than most of the church in recognizing, analysing, and attacking the injustice of poverty. The church had held on to privilege in traditionalist hierarchical societies, rather than showing freedom to serve. After 1945, like his Czech colleague J. Hromadka, Barth thought Christians should accept communist expropriations as an historical penitence (West 1958: 73, 252). Renewal was more than progressive improvement; it required repentance and new creation.

The Freedom of God: Let God be God and World be World

Barth's theological strategy was built on God's unqualified freedom to be God in his own chosen way, revealed in his Word, Christ, as witnessed to in scripture. This meant that God was not bound up with, or dependent on, any form of religion, philosophy, culture, or society, however Christian or however powerful. God, as the one Lord of creatures, ensures the radical *secularity* of creation, in the sense that it can never be equated with God, or serve functionally as God, or usurp his authority, or be the focus of human trust and attention and invocation. But Barth never used secularity to condemn or despise the world; he was not an anxious protector of religion in the face of secularism, however "godless." All that is in the world, even humanity at its best, is not more than creature, but it is creature, willed and chosen by God. Why, Barth would ask, should any creature want to get above itself, when it is privileged to be a genuine partner with God? In order to be itself well and truly, the creature must accept and live within limits. The limit we live within is not mere finitude, nor is it the prohibition of idolatry; it is the positive command or permission of God, calling us to be human. Such a theological understanding of the secular prevents the simple rejection or endorsement of secularizing movements in society. Rather, it shows us how to live through their complexity, by working with them insofar as they respect and reflect the true secularity of the creature and resisting them insofar as they share the common Christendom error of a sociopolitical conflation of human and divine.

Distinguish and Relate

A theology of this sort involves a double movement: a *distinction* between God and humanity (along with all creatures) and a *relating*. That is different from a choice between a *separation* by which God and humanity are *opposed* to each other and an *identification* of God and humanity, so that they can be treated as *interchangeable*. It is a mistake to read even the early Barth as though he held to a separation, without a relating.

Distinguishing and relating, and insisting on the two together, was a technique fundamental to Barth's theology. It yielded concepts he could play with and is one of many reasons why reading Barth is fun. The distinction is not drawn from the point of view of the limits of human knowledge, as though the otherness of God consisted in his being unknown, unknowable, or unreachable. Human ignorance does not ground or serve God's transcendence. Barth insisted on the necessity of revelation, by which God simultaneously makes himself known and guards the mystery and freedom of his being. God asserts his transcendence by his presence and activity. The otherness of God is not to be conceded because human knowing or action proves unable to absorb God into itself, which would effect the humanizing of God. God's otherness is rather what God in his freedom speaks and realizes. By being God, God distinguishes himself from all that might be confused with God, whether nature, or powers usurping his place, or the pretensions of human beings. The freedom of God is not his nonhumanity, let alone his antihumanity; it is a freedom which is actualized in God's being for humanity. Thus the distinction can never be detached from the connection, as it would be if God's difference were his nonhumanity.

Barth followed and built on the central Christian dogmas, arguing that God in Christ chose in his freedom to be God with and for human being, as his covenant partner, in the inner history of his whole enterprise in creation. Barth frees Chalcedonian-style Christology from any hint that the unity of divinity and humanity is a natural or necessary reality: it is always the action of the free God, choosing who he will be. Consequently, God in Christ is known only in the immediate reception of the self-giving of God through his own Word. The voice of God is not heard through our sense of the meaning of our moment in history: it could not be the voice of Hitler in the "German hour" of 1933, as E. Hirsch and others said. God always speaks in the one Word, Jesus Christ, the living Lord, who surprises us by doing new things, not being tied to some recorded memory (Barth 1965: 30–2). God is not to be "humanized" in a particular department of history because God is Lord of all (Barth 1933: 79, 378f.).

Two Key Texts

Barth's political theology can be investigated in almost everything he wrote, from the early commentary on the Epistle to the Romans to the posthumously published *The Christian Life*. In some texts, it is more direct or more concretely situational than in others, but through all, a consistent theological understanding is palpable. Here space allows consideration of two major representative texts only.

The Barmen Theological Declaration, 1934

It was thanks to the crisis made and symbolized by Hitler that Barth became a famously influential theologian for politics. He was prepared for the occasion, because, by 1933, his theological learning, skill, and direction were massive and mature. He had extraordinary energy, personal attractiveness and standing as a

well-known church theologian, while not being entangled in church administration. He had come to a clear, neither hasty nor simplistic, political judgment
against Nazism and in favor of social democracy and even moderate nationalism. Barth had a major influence on the Synod of Barmen, May 29–31, 1934,
through months of preparatory work and in writing the final version of its theological declaration (Nicolaisen 1985; Barth 1971: 72). Through the tedious
and self-important intricacies of church politics, he discerned and articulated
theological issues, so that the command and comfort of the Word of God opened
up a way of service and witness and political illumination.

The situation of the church required a *distinction* to be drawn, saying No to
false connections of church and political movement, of faith in God and national
belonging. The No cleared space for a Yes, the making of a *true* connection. The
"German Christians" exalted Hitler as bringing salvation to Germany, like a contemporary living Messiah, the agent of a God alive today; they demanded that
the Protestant churches should cooperate in national renewal under his leadership, not letting separatist ecclesiastical attitudes or theological scruples hold
them back. The German Christians gained control of several regional churches,
often with unconstitutional force, in their drive to assimilate the church, in doctrine and practice, to the Nazi order. In reaction, the Synod of Barmen was the
foundational rallying point of the Confessing Church. The grounds of its resistance, and its positive commitment, were spelt out in its theological declaration.

Although it might anachronistically be wished, Barmen did not offer explicit
political opposition to Hitler, in defense of Weimar's subverted, though imperfect, liberal democracy, of political parties, and of the rights of Jews and other
endangered minorities. Barth later chided himself that he had not seen early
enough the political significance of God's irrevocable election of the Jewish
people and the incompatibility of antisemitism with the confession of Jesus as
Lord. Barth, however, attacked the heresy of the German Christians, not in order
to evade politics, but as the key entry point for responsible action by the church.
If that is so – it is highly debatable – then the criticism of the church's political
action in 1933–4 must turn, not on its failure to work with a nontheological
analysis, but on what it achieved by going through this theological opening. In
Nazi Germany and in communist lands after 1945, Barth consistently dealt with
political issues as a theologian, acting pastorally to help the church to be the
church, so that the church in turn could be the prophetic witness to Jesus Christ.
The church under threat and persecution could easily lose itself in defending its
inheritance. Barth worked to save the church from this loss of identity, not by
protecting its share in the general political right to freedom of religion, but by
calling the church to be faithful to the Word of God. Discerning and doing what
God commanded, singlemindedly and with joy, was more in accord with faith in
God than launching defensive fearful attacks on any enemy. It was thus that
Christians worked in and witnessed to the freedom of God, which was their
freedom and confidence.

According to the first of the declaration's six sharp little paragraphs, the
church has its identity in hearing and obeying the one Word of God, Jesus Christ

– no other voice. The existence of the church, as Barth argued elsewhere, was essentially "theological"; and theology did not belong to marginal cliques of intellectuals, but was a central activity of the church, because it derives from the Word of God. Paragraph II declares that Jesus Christ does not only offer comfort, which in its ultimate form is the assurance of the forgiveness of sins, but makes God's powerful claim upon the whole of our life. Barth's political theology was always a pastoral theology, but his pastoral practice was not so much sympathetic as challenging; it was to call people to responsibility, to the service of God in the world, and so to a humanity which was in analogy to God's reality. God's word "frees us from the godless entanglements in this world, to free, grateful service to his creatures." The claim upon the church, therefore, is for total faithful service to God, and so service throughout God's creation. The church must be church, but not for or in itself in any exclusive way. There may be cultural forms of the world which are godless, but they are not the world which is real because the real is what God wills to create and sustain, and refuses to surrender to any rival. God's world cannot be left in the hands of the devil, or of Hitler, or any other group or system, whatever their power, physical or spiritual. This liberation Barth witnessed to and enjoyed as a thinker and writer – he spoke of the powers of this world as already discredited, discrediting themselves, and being overcome by God in Christ (Barth 1939).

According to paragraph III, since the church is where Jesus Christ acts as the "present Lord," its preaching and organization are not to be aligned with currently ascendant political ideas. And paragraph IV goes on to reject the command-giving Führer as the model or principle of church government; church leaders are not above the church, but members of an organizationally flatter brotherhood, which as a whole is charged with the service of God.

These four paragraphs are the controlling context of, not merely the preamble to, Barmen V, which has famously focused discussion of the political responsibility of the church (Jüngel 1992). State and church exist by divine authority, each with a specific task. The state is to care for justice and peace by the threat and use of force, according to human insight and human capacities in this not yet redeemed world (where the church also stands). Here is no perverse twisting of the doctrine of Two Kingdoms, resigning the political order to the devil of autonomous force, as though he had a kingdom where "might is right," while God in his kingdom practices a gentle spiritual – and ineffectual – order. The Two Kingdoms here are, rather, two complementary means by which the One God rules one human world. Force, according to Barmen V, serves God by requiring and enabling people to work for *peace and justice*. The text's potential for critical opposition to Hitler's policies of *war and injustice* was recognized by some at the time, but to a grievously limited extent, as has been acknowledged often since then, signally in the Stuttgart Declaration of 1945 (Brakelmann 1985; Barnett 1992).

The church is not to aim to dispense with or subvert the state in principle: it is called to give thanks to God for the state, honoring its role in God's order. The church does not use force because, for itself, it trusts the power of the Word, through which God carries all things. It has the specific ministry to the state to *remind* it of God's kingdom (his rule) and so to call rulers and ruled to responsibility. The service of *reminding* the whole political society of the kingdom of God acknowledges the *distinction* God's Word makes between church and state, and even between God's will and the world in its present unredeemed condition. In itself, however, it is an act of *connecting*, of communicating, of argument and appeal. The church will promote peaceful politics by energetically participating in society. It will stir up political discussion, by direct address to political people, and by its witness to the whole Word of God, in its prayer and worship. There is nothing the church cannot talk about publicly, even to the embarrassment of the state, and to its own discomfort: what limits the church is not only that it lacks force, but that all its political contributions must be true witness to God and service to his kingdom. So the relation of church and state is not rightly ordered by policing a separation, to prevent the least trespass from the other side of the fence, but rather requires each to understand and respect the duty of the other, so that there can be a proper partnership, connecting what is distinct, in order that both serve together the one Lord, who has not let the state exempt itself from his service, even when it crucifies the Lord (Barth 1939: 16).

"The Christian Community and the Civil Community"

The influential essay of 1946, "The Christian Community and the Civil Community" (Barth 1954), is the fruit of Barth's intensive thinking about faith and politics through the Nazi period and the war. It reflects a changed situation. After 1945, the focus of concern was less on saving the church from the seduction of political religion, or justifying and fighting a necessary war, and more on building effective humane society out of dehumanized ruins. Barth had not spent the years since 1934 merely insisting that Barmen was the right place to *stand*. Rather, the Word of God had opened up a particular road, and to be faithful meant to be *going forward* along that road. The 1946 essay is a revealing marker on the road being traveled.

The Barmen Declaration could be read in two ways. In one, the twofoldness of church and state was paramount: Barmen V trumped Barmen I. In the other, the one Lordship of Jesus Christ includes both church and state: Barmen I defines the meaning of Barmen V. This second reading may more closely reflect Barth's own intention in 1934, and certainly corresponds to the direction of his thinking thereafter. Church and state, significantly renamed as Christian and civil communities, are still systematically distinguished. The theologically inescapable connection between them is now explained in a way that matches the pluralistic mobility and experimentation of politics, rather than the traditional hierarchical and competitive juxtaposition of church and state as legally defined institutions.

Barth offers a diagrammatic clue to his argument: God is the center of two concentric circles. The Christian community is the inner circle, the civil community the outer. So there is no possibility of the civil community being left outside God's will and care – it has the same center, source, ruler, and goal. The difference between church and state is not that the church belongs to God and the state to itself, or to the devil, but that the church knows God as Lord through his revelation, and so consciously obeys and witnesses, while the state does not know – indeed, as the necessarily pluralist, tolerant, inclusive community, it cannot know God in his Word. The state nevertheless belongs to God, who in his providence brings good even out of evil. Under God, therefore, learning from experience in politics occurs. Though the definitions of "natural law" are at best inconclusive, they repeatedly call people from a worse to a better kind of state (Barth 1954: 28).

Politics as Parable of the Kingdom of God

The church works for a better kind of state, in its own way, from its knowledge of the Word of the God. Barmen V's single word, "reminding," now blossoms into a great tree of political imagination, suggestion, and participation. Between church and state, "a simple and absolute heterogeneity" is as much out of the question as "a simple and absolute equating," so there is only one possibility left: "the existence of the State [is] an allegory, a correspondence and an analogue to the Kingdom of God which the Church preaches and believes in" (Barth 1954: 32; O'Donovan 1996: 213–14).

In his earliest work, the commentary on Romans, Barth had treated politics as parable. Historical action was seen as a gesture toward the reality of the kingdom of God. In relation to God, human action is like playing a game (which, as we know from football, may be very serious though only a game; it is a good game only when played seriously until the whistle goes, when we let it pass away, transcended by the resumption of wider life). Barth was fascinated by Lenin's 1917 revolution, but did not expect it to realize the kingdom of God. God is the great disturber; only his new creation is the complete true revolution. The political revolutionary is truly closer to God than the reactionary who mistakenly expects God to defend existing order; but no change achieved by the revolutionary can be more than a limited analogy of God's revolution. Analogy thus connects while it distinguishes. It maps a space in which human action is called for and is meaningful, as experiment and experience, seeking and learning, obeying and disobeying, witnessing and being blind, having faith and denying.

In 1946, Barth found 12 analogies of the kingdom of God in the "external, relative and provisional existence" of the civil community. Interpreting them required "Christian, spiritual and prophetic knowledge on every side." Some had figured earlier in his work: the relation of divine justification and "a commonly acknowledged law, giving equal protection for all in the State" had been explored in Recht und Rechtfertigung (1937; Eng. trans. Barth 1939). Some foreshadowed expanded exposition in his later theology. The first of the 1946 analogies states that as the one eternal compassionate God proved himself a neighbor to humanity, so in politics, the church is always interested in human beings, and not in abstract causes or ideologies. This theme was taken up in *The Humanity of God* and runs through the *Church Dogmatics*, from volume II on election to volumes III (creation) and IV (reconciliation), written from 1945 to 1959. The priority of concrete persons over causes and generalities, was powerfully argued again in *The Christian Life* (Barth 1981a: 203, 267). When Emil Brunner challenged him in 1948 to denounce communism, as he had opposed Nazism, because they were equally manifestations of the essentially anti-Christian and inhuman evil of totalitarianism, Barth refused for a complex of reasons, including his theologically grounded suspicion of ideological language about social *systems*, which deprived its users of the freedom to respect, respond to, and encourage *persons*. God's proving himself a neighbor, reaching out to all people, was evident in the slogan Barth derived from Paul (Rom. 5), that Christ died for, not against, the ungodly (Barth 1981a: 203, 210, 267; Willmer 1990). Barth could not be a theological Cold Warrior, who beat the Christian faith into a sword for total closed opposition to communism.

The basic, encompassing analogy of God and humanity served as the deep structure of the *Church Dogmatics*. The story of Jesus is the story of humanity, in which the reconciliation of humanity is already accomplished, so that, echoing Barmen I and II, "God in Jesus Christ established and confirmed his original claim to man and hence man's claim against sin and death" (Barth 1954: 35). Jesus Christ is the man who is both elected and rejected by God. Nothing that happens to people in history falls out of the range of what God has already gone through with Jesus, in struggle and in victory, the triumph of God in and for humanity. This is the basis of Barth's humanism, which is not an affirmation of separate individuals, each secluded in his own identity, apart from and against others, but the vindication of Jesus representing all (Sölle 1967). Barth's humanism is a cheerful confidence in God who elects himself to be the God of all, including his enemies and unbelievers – for God's reality transcends human believing and not believing. Barth provoked the suspicion that his theology implied universal salvation. He countered it by inviting people to consider whether the reality of God in Christ does not push us to risk universalism: so it is wise not to brand it a heresy, although it cannot be affirmed as dogma.

Analogy does more than identify significant likeness between God and humanity, revelation and politics. It witnesses to the creative sovereign reality of God, so that analogy moves first *from* God *to* humanity. But it then sets humanity in movement *toward* God, in prayer and action. The Gospel, the Word of God, was not to be read by taking the world as the norm-setting reality. That was the point of Barth's early pungent article on the political realism of Friedrich Naumann (Barth 1919). The core of his opposition to German Christians was that they took Hitler as dominant fact, to which Jesus the Savior was to be adapted as a flexible, subordinate metaphor. The reality of God, however, was never to be diluted, to be regarded as a mere dream, a wished-for unreality. But nor was the reality of God and his new world a visible given: we walk by faith, not by sight.

Analogy does more than identify similarity between two different realities, in a relation of stable distinction. It certainly does not establish a "metaphysic of the state" (Moltmann 1984: 96 n. 10). Analogy generates movement. The coming kingdom of God illumines human life by giving "a direction and a line that must be recognised and adhered to in all circumstances." Prayer represents the faithful knowing response to God: it confesses that the kingdom is God's action, not a human work. Prayer speaks in faith knowing that it is certainly answered already, even when it does not see. It lives confidently on the "already" during the "not yet"; but it is not inhumanly lazy, for it moves in the direction of what it prays for, as much as it is able. In his last major writing, Barth sought one concept to characterize human being as it is shaped within the freedom of the command of God and finally settled on *invocation*: calling on the Father, not talking about God as Father (Barth 1981a: 36, 42f.). Then he developed an intensely spiritual and political reading of the first clauses of the Lord's Prayer. The theologian, in politics and out of it, is not just a theorist, or a teacher, a witness, or a pastor, but one who prays. The one who prays to the Father cannot but look for the kingdom to *come*. Movement, change, expectation beyond what has already been seen, is intrinsic to prayer to the Father of Jesus Christ.

The movement which analogy implies is not a smoothly peaceful spiritual progress toward God. Barth pictures the movement in political and conflictual idiom. God comes to *battle* with a world in rebellion, in denial of its true Lord, where its creatureliness is in disorder. In *Church and State*, looking for "an actual, and therefore inward and vital, connection" between the kingdom of Christ and the kingdoms of this world (Barth 1939: 9), Barth drew upon K. L. Schmidt's lecture on "the conflict of church and state in the New Testament community" to understand the state as angelic power, whose authority belongs to Jesus Christ, so that "in its comparatively independent substance, in its dignity, its function and its purpose, it should serve the Person and the Work of Jesus Christ, and therefore the justification of the sinner" (Barth 1939: 29; Moltmann 1984: 85). This early treatment of the New Testament theology of the powers, which became an influential way of thinking about politics thereafter, seems to have been overlooked in Wink's remarkable study (Wink 1984: 6). In *The Christian Life*, God's "struggle for human righteousness" begins with the "revolt," by which God does not disrupt an existing order, but rather acts "against the disorder" which is produced by various "lordless powers" shaping the human world in contradiction to the kingdom of God (Barth 1981a: 205ff., 232–4). The Blumhardts' affirmation "Jesus is Victor" not merely inspired Barth throughout his life (Barth 1919; 1981a: 256ff.) but was the clue to his relating unabridged faith to the realities of politics.

Conflict and struggle were more than a picture borrowed from politics to explain faith. Barth took his rifle to the mountains in readiness to resist a German invasion of Switzerland. He knew conflicts were inescapable in human experience: "How could the Christian community possibly contract out of such situations?" Barth contracted into them, within the frame of an analogy between God's anger and judgment, which lasts for a moment, whereas his mercy is for eternity. So "violent solutions" to political conflicts have their place, but only "when they are for the moment the ultimate and only possibility available." "May the Church show her inventiveness in the search for other solutions before she joins in the call for violence!" The perfection of the Father in heaven demands "the earthly perfection of a peace policy which really does extend the limits of the humanly possible" (Barth 1954: 41; 1961: 450–70; 1971: 71–85). *Extending* the limits of the *humanly possible*: that is the service of God through the obedience of faith in political practice. It is the political meaning of Christology.

References

Barnett, Victoria (1992). *For the Soul of the People: Protestant Protest against Hitler*. New York and Oxford: Oxford University Press.

Barth, Karl (1919). "Past and Future: Friedrich Naumann and Christoph Blumhardt." In James M. Robinson (ed.), *The Beginnings of Dialectic Theology*, vol. I, 35–45. Richmond, Va.: John Knox, 1968.

——(1928). *The Word of God and the Word of Man*. London: Hodder & Stoughton.

——(1932) *Church Dogmatics* I, 1. Edinburgh: T. & T. Clark.

——(1933). *The Epistle to the Romans*. Oxford: Oxford University Press. (Eng. trans. of 6th German edn., 1928, which was in effect the third edition of 1921 unchanged.)

——(1938). *The Knowledge of God and the Service of God According to the Teaching of the Reformation*. London: Hodder & Stoughton.

——(1939). *Church and State*. London: SCM. (Eng. trans. of *Recht und Rechtfertigung*, 1937.)

——(1945). *The Germans and Ourselves*. London: Nisbet.

——(1946). *Natural Theology*. London: Geoffrey Bles.

——(1954). *Against the Stream: Shorter Post-War Writings 1946–1952*. London: SCM.

——(1961). *Church Dogmatics* III, 4. Edinburgh: T. & T. Clark.

——(1963). *Evangelical Theology: An Introduction*. London: Collins Fontana.

——(1965). *The German Church Conflict*. London: Lutterworth.

——(1967). *The Humanity of God*. London: Collins Fontana.

——(1971). *Fragments Grave and Gay*. London: Collins Fontana.

——(1981a). *The Christian Life: Church Dogmatics* IV, 4. Edinburgh: T. & T. Clark.

——(1981b). *Ethics*. Edinburgh: T. & T. Clark.

——(1984). *Theologische Existenz Heute! (1933)*, ed. Hinrich Stoevesandt. Munich: Chr. Kaiser Verlag.

Biggar, Nigel (1993). *The Hastening that Waits: Karl Barth's Ethics*. Oxford: Clarendon.

Brakelmann, Gunter (1985). "Barmen V. Ein historisch-kritischer Rückblick." *Evangelische Theologie*, Jan.–Feb., 3–20.

Burleigh, Michael (2000). *The Third Reich: A New History*. London: Macmillan.

Jüngel, Eberhard (1992) *Christ, Justice and Peace: Towards a Theology of the State*. Edinburgh: T. & T. Clark.

Marquardt, Friedrich-Wilhelm (1972). *Theologie und Sozialismus: Das Beispiel Karl Barths*. Munich: Chr. Kaiser Verlag.

Moltmann, J. (1984). *On Human Dignity*. London: SCM.

Nicolaisen, Carsten (1985). *Der Weg nach Barmen*. Neukirchen-Vluyn: Neukirchener.

O'Donovan, Oliver (1996). *The Desire of Nations*. Cambridge: Cambridge University Press.

Sölle, D. (1967). *Christ the Representative*. Philadelphia: Fortress.

Stern, J. P. (1975). *Hitler, the Führer and the People*. Glasgow: Collins Fontana.

Ward, W. R. (1979). *Theology, Sociology and Politics: The German Protestant Social Conscience 1890–1933*. Berne: Peter Lang.

Webster, John, ed. (2000). *The Cambridge Companion to Karl Barth*. Cambridge: Cambridge University Press.

West, Charles C. (1958). *Communism and the Theologians*. London: SCM.

Willmer, Haddon (1990). "The Justification of the Godless: Heinrich Vogel and German Guilt." In Keith Robbins (ed.), *Protestant Evangelicalism: Britain, Ireland, Germany and America c.1750–c.1950*, 327–46. Oxford: Blackwell.

Wink, Walter (1984). *Naming the Powers*. Philadelphia: Fortress.

Yoder, John H. (1970). *Karl Barth and the Problem of War*. Nashville: Abingdon.

CHAPTER 10
Dietrich Bonhoeffer

Stanley Hauerwas

The Fragments that were Bonhoeffer's Life and Work

> The primary confession of the Christian before the world is the deed which inter-
> prets itself. If the deed is to have become a force, then the world itself will long to
> confess the Word. This is not the same as loudly shrieking out propaganda. This
> Word must be preserved as the most sacred possession of the community. This is a
> matter between God and the community, not between the community and the
> world. It is the Word of recognition between friends, not a word to use against
> enemies. This attitude was first learned at baptism. The deed alone is our confes-
> sion of faith before the world. (Bonhoeffer 1990: 191)

So wrote Bonhoeffer in 1932, just before the German church's struggle with
Hitler began. This may seem an odd passage with which to begin an essay on
Bonhoeffer's political theology, but it is so only if one assumes a distinction can
be made between Bonhoeffer's theology – at least his early theology found in
Sanctorum Communio (Bonhoeffer 1998) and *Act and Being* (Bonhoeffer 1996a)
– and his later involvement with the *Abwehr* plot against Hitler. Indeed, it will be
the burden of my account of Bonhoeffer's life and theology to show that from
the very beginning Bonhoeffer was attempting to develop a theological politics
from which we still have much to learn (Rasmusson 1995). Bonhoeffer may
have even regarded *Sanctorum Communio* and *Act and Being* as his "academic theology," which no doubt they were, but I will argue that the theological position
Bonhoeffer took in those books made the subsequent politics of his life and work
inevitable.

Anyone who has read Eberhard Bethge's *Dietrich Bonhoeffer: A Biography*
(Bethge 2000) knows it is impossible to distinguish between Bonhoeffer's life and
his work. Indeed, Marilynne Robinson uses the passage with which I began to
challenge those who think the consistency as well as significance of Bonhoef-

fer's theology are given a prominence they might not otherwise have had without his courageous political activity and death (Robinson 1998: 110–11). It is no doubt true that Bonhoeffer's fame as well as his theological significance were attributed to his unfinished *Ethics* (Bonhoeffer 1963) and his *Letters and Papers from Prison* (Bonhoeffer 1971). Many, quite understandably, interpreted some of Bonhoeffer's own remarks in his prison correspondence to suggest his political opposition to the Nazis had occasioned a fundamental shift in his theology (Bonhoeffer 1971: 328, 360). I will try to show, however, that Bonhoeffer's work was from beginning to end the attempt to reclaim the visibility of the church as the necessary condition for the proclamation of the Gospel in a world that no longer privileged Christianity. That he was hanged by the personal order of Himmler on April 9, 1945, at Flossenbürg concentration camp means he has become for those of us who come after him part of God's visibility.

I am aware that some, reading my account of Bonhoeffer and, in particular, my emphasis on his ecclesiology for rightly interpreting his life and work, will suspect my account of Bonhoeffer sounds far too much like positions that have become associated with my own work. I have no reason to deny that may be true, but if it is true it is only because I first learned what I think from reading Bonhoeffer (and Barth). This is the first essay I have ever written on Bonhoeffer, but it is certainly not the first time I have read him. I am sure Bonhoeffer's *Discipleship* (Bonhoeffer 2001), which I read as a student in seminary, was the reason why, some years later, John Howard Yoder's *The Politics of Jesus* (Yoder 1994) had such a profound influence on me. Both books convinced me that Christology cannot be abstracted from accounts of discipleship; or, to put it more systematically, that we must say, as Bonhoeffer does in *Sanctorum Communio*, "the church of Jesus Christ that is actualized by the Holy Spirit is really the church here and now" (Bonhoeffer 1998: 208).

The reason I have not previously written on Bonhoeffer has everything to do with the reception of his work when it was first translated into English. The first book by Bonhoeffer usually read by English readers was *Letters and Papers from Prison* (Bonhoeffer 1971). As a result Bonhoeffer was hailed as champion of the "death of God" movement (Robinson 1963: 22–3, 36–9) and/or one of the first to anticipate the Christian celebration of the "secular city" (Cox 1965: 224–43). On the basis of Bonhoeffer's *Ethics* (Bonhoeffer 1963), Joseph Fletcher went so far as to claim him as an advocate of situation ethics (Fletcher 1966: 28). As a result I simply decided not to claim Bonhoeffer in support of the position I was trying to develop, though in fact he was one of my most important teachers. That I write now about Bonhoeffer is my way of trying to acknowledge a debt long overdue.

Bonhoeffer's decision to participate in the plot to kill Hitler also seemed to make him an unlikely candidate to support a pacifist position. Yet I doubt that Bonhoeffer's involvement with the conspiracy associated with Admiral Canaris and Bonhoeffer's brother-in-law, Hans von Dohnanyi, can ever be understood with certainty. Bonhoeffer gratefully accepted von Dohnanyi's offer to become a member of the *Abwehr* (military counter-intelligence) because it gave him the means to avoid conscription and the dreaded necessity to take the oath of loyalty to Hitler. Yet the secrecy required by the conspiracy means we have no way to determine how Bonhoeffer understood his work with the *Abwehr*. It is by no means clear, for example, that those around Admiral Canaris had a common understanding of whether overthrowing Hitler entailed his assassination (Hoffman 1996: 216–24).[1]

That we cannot know how Bonhoeffer understood his participation in the attempt to kill Hitler, and thus how his whole life "makes sense," is not a peculiarity Bonhoeffer would think unique to his life. The primary confession of the Christian may be the deed which interprets itself, but according to Bonhoeffer our lives cannot be seen as such a deed. Only "Jesus' testimony to himself stands by itself, self-authenticating" (Bonhoeffer 1966: 32). In contrast our lives, no matter how earnestly or faithfully lived, can be no more than fragments. In a letter to Bethge in 1944 Bonhoeffer wrote:

> The important thing today is that we should be able to discern from the fragments of our life how the whole was arranged and planned, and what material it consists of. For really, there are some fragments that are only worth throwing into the dustbin (even a decent "hell" is too good for them), and others whose importance lasts for centuries, because their completion can only be a matter for God, and so they are fragments and must be fragments – I'm thinking, e.g. of the *Art of Fugue*. If our life is but the remotest reflection of such a fragment, if we accumulate, at least for a short time, a wealth of themes and weld them into a harmony in which the great counterpoint is maintained from start to finish, so that at last, when it breaks off abruptly, we can sing no more than the chorale, "I come before thy throne," we will not bemoan the fragmentariness of our life, but rather rejoice in it. I can never get away from Jeremiah 45. Do you still remember that Saturday evening in Finkenwalde when I expounded it? Here, too, is a necessary fragment of life – "but I will give you your life as a prize of war." (Bonhoeffer 1971: 219)

However, thanks to Eberhard Bethge's great biography of Bonhoeffer, we know the main outlines of Bonhoeffer's life, which I can only briefly sketch here. Bonhoeffer was born in 1906, and was raised in an academic and cultured family. His father held the chair of psychology at the University of Berlin. Somewhat inexplicably, early in his life Bonhoeffer decided he wanted to be a pastor and theologian. Accordingly, at the age of 22 he earned his doctorate at Berlin. His dissertation was called *Sanctorum Communio*. He did parish work in Spain for a year as well as study at Union Theological Seminary before returning to Berlin to lecture at the university. One of the early critics of Hitler, he went to London in 1934 to serve as the pastor to two Lutheran churches.

In 1935 he returned to Germany to direct a seminary of the Confessing Church in Finkenwalde. *Discipleship* (Bonhoeffer 2001) as well as *Life Together* (Bonhoeffer 1996c) were written during his time here. The forced closing of the seminary in 1937 occasioned a return to America for Bonhoeffer. Yet he quickly decided he could not stay in America if he was to have a voice in postwar Germany. He returned to Germany to become an envoy for the *Abwehr*, which in effect made him a double agent. He was arrested in 1943 in connection with the assassination attempt on Hitler. He spent the last two years of his life in prison, where he continued to work on his *Ethics* as well as the collection of writings now called *Letters and Papers from Prison*. He was hanged on April 9, 1945, at Flossenbürg.

His was a life that was at once theological and political. It was so, however, not because he died at the hands of the Nazis. Bonhoeffer's life and work would have been political if the Nazis had never existed; for Bonhoeffer saw clearly that the failure of the church when confronted with Hitler began long before the Nazi challenge. Hitler forced a church long accustomed to privileges dependent on its invisibility to become visible. The church in Germany, however, had simply lost the resources to reclaim its space in the world. How that space can be reclaimed, not only in the face of the Nazis but when times seem "normal," is the heart of Bonhoeffer's theological politics.

Bonhoeffer's Recovery of the Political Significance of the Visible Church

In an essay entitled "The Constantinian Sources of Western Social Ethics," John Howard Yoder makes the striking observation that after the Constantinian shift the meaning of the word "Christian" changes. Prior to Constantine it took exceptional conviction to be a Christian. After Constantine it took exceptional courage not to be counted as a Christian. This development, according to Yoder, called forth a new doctrinal development, "namely the doctrine of the invisibility of the church." Before Constantine, one knew as a fact of everyday experience that there was a church, but one had to have faith that God was governing history. After Constantine, people assumed as a fact that God was governing history through the emperor, but one had to take it on faith that within the nominally Christian mass there was a community of true believers. No longer could being a Christian be identified with church membership, since many "Christians" in the church clearly had not chosen to follow Christ. Now to be a Christian is transmuted to "inwardness" (Yoder 1984: 136–7).

Bonhoeffer is a Lutheran, Yoder an Anabaptist, and Lutherans are seldom confused with Anabaptists; but nevertheless Bonhoeffer's account of the challenge facing the church closely parallels Yoder's account above. For example, in notes for lectures at Finkenwalde, Bonhoeffer observes that the consequence of Luther's doctrine of grace is that the church should live in the world and, according to Romans 13, in its ordinances.

> Thus in his own way Luther confirms Constantine's covenant with the church. As a result, a minimal ethic prevailed. Luther of course wanted a complete ethic for everyone, not only for monastic orders. Thus the existence of the Christian became the existence of the citizen. The nature of the church vanished into the invisible realm. But in this way the New Testament message was fundamentally misunderstood, inner-worldliness became a principle. (Bonhoeffer 1965: 324)[2]

Faced with this result, Bonhoeffer argues that the church must define its limits by severing heresy from its body.

> It has to make itself distinct and to be a community which hears the Apocalypse. It has to testify to its alien nature and to resist the false principle of inner-worldliness. Friendship between the church and the world is not normal, but abnormal. The community *must* suffer like Christ, without wonderment. The cross stands *visibly* over the community. (Bonhoeffer 1965: 324)

It is not hard to see how his stress on the necessity of visibility led him to write a book like *Discipleship*. Holiness but names God's way of making his will for his people visible. "To flee into invisibility is to deny the call. Any community of Jesus which wants to be invisible is no longer a community that follows him" (Bonhoeffer 2001: 113).

According to Bonhoeffer, sanctification, properly understood, is the church's politics. For sanctification is possible only within the visible church community.

> That is the "political" character of the church community. A merely personal sanctification which seeks to bypass this openly visible separation of the church-community from the world confuses the pious desires of the religious flesh with the sanctification of the church-community, which has been accomplished in Christ's death and is being actualized by the seal of God . . . Sanctification through the seal of the Holy Spirit always places the church in the midst of struggle. (Bonhoeffer 2001: 261–2)

Bonhoeffer thought that the holiness of the church is necessary for the redemption of the world, which means *Discipleship* – a book often interpreted as an exemplification of his "spirituality" – is the most political of his works.

I am not suggesting that when Bonhoeffer wrote *Sanctorum Communio*, he did so with the clarity that can be found in the lecture he gave at Finkenwalde or in his *Discipleship*. In *Sanctorum Communio* his concerns may be described as more strictly theological, but even that early the "strictly theological" was formulated against the background of Protestant liberal mistakes, and in particular those of Ernst Troeltsch, that made inevitable his unease with the stance of the German churches toward the world. According to Bonhoeffer, "The church is God's new will and purpose for humanity. God's will is always directed toward the concrete, historical human being. But this means that it begins to be implemented *in history*. God's will must become visible and comprehensible at some point in history" (Bonhoeffer 1998: 141).

From the beginning to the end of his work Bonhoeffer relentlessly explores and searches for what it means for the church to faithfully manifest God's visibility. For example, in his *Ethics*, he notes that the church occupies a space in the world through its public worship, its parish life, and its organization. That the church takes up space is but a correlative of God in Jesus Christ occupying space in the world. "And so, too, the Church of Jesus Christ is the place, in other words the space in the world, at which the reign of Jesus Christ over the whole world is evidenced and proclaimed" (Bonhoeffer 1963: 68). Yet this is no new theme in Bonhoeffer, but rather the continued working out of the claim in *Sanctorum Communio* that "the whole church now rests on the unity in Christ, on the fact of Christ existing as church community" (Bonhoeffer 1998: 206–7).

For Bonhoeffer, it is in Jesus Christ that the whole of reality is taken up, that reality has an origin and end.

> For that reason it is only in Him, and with Him as the point of departure, that there can be an action which is in accordance with reality. The origin of action which accords with reality is not the pseudo-Lutheran Christ who exists solely for the purpose of sanctioning the facts as they are, nor the Christ of radical enthusiasm whose function is to bless every revolution, but it is the incarnate God Jesus who has accepted man and who has loved, condemned and reconciled man and with him the world. (Bonhoeffer 1963: 199)

As Christ was in the world, so the church is in the world. These are not pious sentiments, but reality-making claims that challenge the way things are. They are the very heart of Bonhoeffer's theological politics, a politics that requires the church to be the church in order that the world can be the world. Bonhoeffer's call for the world to be the world is but the outworking of his Christology and ecclesiology. For the church to let the world be the world means the church refusing to live by the privileges granted on the world's terms. "Real secularity consists in the church's being able to renounce all privileges and all its property but never Christ's Word and the forgiveness of sins. With Christ and the forgiveness of sins to fall back on, the church is free to give up everything else" (Bonhoeffer 1990: 92). Such freedom, moreover, is the necessary condition for the church to be the zone of truth in a world of mendacity (Bonhoeffer 1965: 160).

Sanctorum Communio was Bonhoeffer's attempt to develop a "specifically Christian sociology" as an alternative to Troeltsch (Bonhoeffer 1998: 277). Bonhoeffer argues that the very categories set out by Troeltsch – church/sect/mysticism, *Gemeinschaft/Gesellschaft* – must be rejected if the visibility of the church is to be reclaimed. Troeltsch confuses questions of origins with essences, with the result that the Gospel is subjected to the world. The very choice between voluntary association and compulsory organization is rendered unacceptable by the "Protestant understanding of the Spirit and the church-community, in the former because it does not take the reality of the Spirit into account at all, and in the latter in that it severs the essential relation between Spirit and church-community, thereby completely losing any sociological interest" (Bonhoeffer 1998: 260).

From Bonhoeffer's perspective, Troeltsch is but one of the most powerful representatives of the Protestant liberal presumption that the Gospel is purely religious, encompassing the outlook of the individual, but indifferent to and unconcerned with worldly institutions (Bonhoeffer 1963: 287). The sociology of Protestant liberalism, therefore, is but the other side of liberal separation of Jesus from the Christ. As a result of such a separation, Protestant liberalism continues the docetic Christological heresy that results in an equally pernicious docetic ecclesiology (Bonhoeffer 1966: 71–85). Protestant liberalism is the theological expression of the sociology of the invisible church that

> conceded to the world the right to determine Christ's place in the world; in the conflict between the church and the world it accepted the comparatively easy terms of peace that the world dictated. Its strength was that it did not try to put the clock back, and that it genuinely accepted the battle (Troeltsch), even though this ended with its defeat. (Bonhoeffer 1971: 327)

Bonhoeffer's work was to provide a complete alternative to the liberal Protestant attempt to make peace with the world. In a lecture at the beginning of his Finkenwalde period concerning the interpretation of scripture, Bonhoeffer asserts that the intention of contemporary Christians "should be not to justify Christianity in this present age, but *to justify the present age before the Christian message*" (Bonhoeffer 1965: 310, emphasis in original). Bonhoeffer's attack in *Letters and Papers from Prison* on the liberal Protestant apologetics that tries to secure "faith" on the edges of life, and on the despair such edges allegedly create, is but a continuation of his attack on Protestant pietism as well as his refusal to let the proclamation of the Gospel be marginalized. For the same reasons he had little regard for existentialist philosophers or psychotherapists, whose practice he regarded as but a secularized Methodism (Bonhoeffer 1971: 326–7).

Unfortunately, Bonhoeffer's suggestion about Barth's "positivism of revelation" and the correlative need for a nonreligious interpretation of theological concepts has led some to think Bonhoeffer wanted Christians to become "secular" (Bonhoeffer 1971: 328). The exact opposite is the case. He is insisting that if reality is redeemed by Christ, Christians must claim the center, refusing to use the "world's" weakness to make the Gospel intelligible. He refuses all strategies that try "to make room for God on the borders," thinking it better to leave problems unsolved. The Gospel is not an answer to questions produced by human anxiety, but a proclamation of a "fact." Thus Bonhoeffer's wonderful remark:

> Belief in the Resurrection is not the solution to the problem of death. God's "beyond" is not the beyond of our cognitive faculties. The transcendence of epistemological theory has nothing to do with the transcendence of God. God is beyond in the midst of life. The church stands, not at the boundaries where human powers give out, but in the middle of the village. (Bonhoeffer 1971: 282)

Bonhoeffer's call for a Christian worldliness, therefore, is not his turning away from the kind of community discipline he so eloquently defended in *Discipleship* and *Life Together*. When he confesses in *Letters and Papers from Prison* that at one time he mistakenly assumed he could acquire faith by living a holy life, he is not rejecting the form of life they lived at Finkenwalde. When he says he now sees some of the dangers of *Discipleship*, though he still stands by the book, he is not returning to the false dualism between sect and church found in Troeltsch. Rather, he is making the Christological point that the Incarnation, the Crucifixion, and the Resurrection must be held in unity if the church's relationship to the world is to be rightly understood. An emphasis on Incarnation too often leads to compromise, an ethic based on cross and Resurrection too often leads to radicalism and enthusiasm (Bonhoeffer 1963: 88–9). The church names that community that lives in radical hope in a world without hope. To so live means the church cannot help but be different from the world; but such a difference is not an end in itself but "the fruits which automatically follow from an authentic proclamation of the gospel" (Bonhoeffer 1973: 160).[3]

The problem Bonhoeffer saw clearly in *Letters and Papers from Prison* was how to respond theologically when the church had been marginalized. He saw that such a marginalization was not a disaster for the church, but rather an opportunity. The challenge was and is the recovery of the significance of the church in a world that knows well it can get along without the church. The challenge before the church is how to go on in a world that offers neither opposition to nor accommodation for the church.

Bonhoeffer's effort to recover the visibility of the church was his "politics" because "it is essential to the revelation of God in Jesus Christ that it occupies space within the world" (Bonhoeffer 1963: 68). Put positively, in Jesus Christ God has occupied space in the world and continues to do so through the work of the Holy Spirit's calling the church to faithfulness. These were the convictions Bonhoeffer brought to his war with the Nazis. These were the convictions that made him the most insightful and powerful force shaping the church's witness against Hitler. In a sense Hitler was exactly the kind of enemy that makes Bonhoeffer's (and Barth's) theological politics so compelling. The question remains, however, whether Bonhoeffer provides an adequate account of how the church must negotiate a world "after Christendom." To explore that question I must attend to what might be called Bonhoeffer's "political ethic." That ethic involves his critique of and attempt to find an alternative to the traditional Lutheran doctrine of the two kingdoms.

Bonhoeffer's Search for a Political Ethic

Bethge reports that at a conference sponsored by the Church Federation Office in 1932, Bonhoeffer (even though he was the youngest speaker at the conference) vigorously attacked the idea of the "orders of creation" introduced by traditional Lutherans. That Bonhoeffer would reject the two-kingdom tradition was inevitable given the direction he had begun in *Sanctorum Communio* and *Act and Being*. Creation simply cannot be self-validating, because Christians have no knowledge of creation separate from redemption. "The creation is a picture of the power and faithfulness of God, demonstrated to us in God's revelation in Jesus Christ. We worship the creator, revealed to us as redeemer" (Bonhoeffer 1996c: 163). Whatever Christians have to say about worldly order, it will have to be said on the presumption that Christ is the reality of all that is.

Bonhoeffer soon returned to the issue of the orders of creation in an address to the Youth Peace Conference in Czechoslovakia in July 1932. Again he attacks those who believe that we must accept that certain orders are present in creation. Such a view entails the presumption that because the nations have been created differently each one is obliged to preserve and develop its own characteristics. He notes that this understanding of the nation is particularly dangerous because "just about everything can be defended by it." Not only is the fallenness of such order ignored, but those who use the orders of creation to justify their commitment to Germany fail to see that "the so-called orders of creation are no longer *per se* revelations of the divine commandment, they are concealed and invisible. Thus the concept of orders of creation must be rejected as a basis for the knowledge of the commandment of God" (Bonhoeffer 1990: 106).

However, if the orders of creation are rejected, then Bonhoeffer must provide some account of how Christians understand the commandment of God for their lives. In *Creation and Fall* Bonhoeffer notes that the Creator does not turn from the fallen world but rather deals with humankind in a distinctive way: "He made them cloaks." Accordingly, the created world becomes the preserved world by which God restrains our distorted passions. Rather than speaking of the orders of creation, Bonhoeffer now describes God's care of our lives as the orders of preservation (Bonhoeffer 1996b: 139). The orders of preservation are not self-validating, but "they all stand under the preservation of God as long as they are still open for Christ; they are *orders of preservation*, not orders of creation. They obtain their value wholly from outside themselves, from Christ, from the new creation" (Bonhoeffer 1965: 166–7, emphasis in original). Any order of the world can, therefore, be dissolved if it prevents our hearing the commandment of Christ.

The question, of course, is what difference changing the name from creation to preservation may make for ethical reflection. Bonhoeffer is obviously struggling to challenge the way the Lutheran "two-order" account fails to be Christological as well as serving as a legitimation of the status quo. In *Christ the Center*, the lectures in Christology Bonhoeffer delivered at Berlin in 1933, he spelled out in more detail some of the implications of his Christological display of the orders of preservation. For example, he observed that since Christ is present in the church after the cross and Resurrection, the church must be understood as the center of history. In fact the state has existed in its proper form only so long as there has been a church, because the state has its proper origin with the cross. Yet the history of which the church is the center is a history made by the state. Accordingly, the visibility of the church does not require that the church must be acknowledged by the state by being made a state church, but rather that the church be the "hidden meaning and promise of the state" (Bonhoeffer 1966: 65).

But if the church is the "hidden meaning" of the state, how can the state know that the church is so if the church is not visible to the state? How is this "hiddenness" of the church for the state consistent with Bonhoeffer's insistence in *Sanctorium Communio* on the church's visibility? Bonhoeffer clearly wants the boundaries of the church to challenge or at least limit the boundaries of the state, but he finds it hard to break Lutheran habits that assume an abstract account of the role of the state is necessary. Thus he will say that the kingdom of God takes form in the state in so far as the state holds itself responsible for stopping the world from flying to pieces through the exercise of its authority; or, that the power of loneliness in the church is destroyed in the confession-occurrence, but "in the state it is restrained through the preservation of community order" (Bonhoeffer 1990: 96–7). Understandably, it does not occur to Bonhoeffer that he does not need to provide an account in principle of what the state is or should be. States exist. They do not need any further legitimization to account for their existence (see Yoder 1998: 78 n. 5).

In his *Ethics* he abandons the language of "orders of preservation" – the German Christians were using similar language – and instead uses the language of the "mandates" (Bonhoeffer 1963: 73–8). According to Bonhoeffer, the scriptures name four mandates: labor, marriage, government, and the church. The mandates receive their intelligibility only as they are created in and directed toward Christ. Accordingly, the authorization to speak on behalf of the church, the family, labor, and government is conferred from above, and then "only so long as they do not encroach upon each other's domains and only so long as they give effect to God's commandment in conjunction and collaboration with one another and each in its own way" (Bonhoeffer 1963: 246). Yet Bonhoeffer does not develop how we would know when one domain has encroached on the other, or what conjunction or collaboration might look like.

It is clear what Bonhoeffer is against, but it is not yet clear what he is for. For example, he is clearly against the distinction between person and office he attributes to the Reformation. He notes this distinction is crucial for justifying the Reformation position on war and on the public use of legal means to repel evil.

> But this distinction between private person and bearer of an office as normative for my behavior is foreign to Jesus. He does not say a word about it. He addresses his disciples as people who have left everything behind to follow him. "Private" and "official" spheres are all completely subject to Jesus' command. The word of Jesus claimed them undividedly. (Bonhoeffer 1963: 134–5)

Yet Bonhoeffer's account of the mandates can invite the distinction between the private and public which results in Christian obedience becoming invisible.

Bonhoeffer's attempt to rethink the Lutheran two-kingdom theology in light of his Christological recovery of the significance of the visible church, I think, failed to escape from the limits of the Lutheran position. However, there is another side to Bonhoeffer's political ethics that is seldom noticed or commented upon. Bethge notes that though Bonhoeffer was shaped by the liberal theological and political tradition, by 1933 he was growing antiliberal not only in his theology but in his politics. Increasingly he thought liberalism – because of either a superciliousness or a weak, *laissez-faire* attitude – was leaving decisions to the tyrant (Bethge 2000: 289).

Nowhere are Bonhoeffer's judgments about political liberalism more clearly stated than in a response he wrote in 1941 to William Paton's *The Church and the New World Order*, a book that explored the church's responsibility for social reconstruction after the war. Bonhoeffer begins by observing that the upheavals of the war have made continental Christians acutely conscious that the future is in God's hands and that no human planning can make men the masters of their fate. Consequently, the churches on the continent have an apocalyptic stance that can lead to other-worldliness, but may also have the more salutary effect of making the church recognize that the life of the church has its own God-given laws which are different from those which govern the life of the world. Accordingly, the church cannot and should not develop detailed plans for reconstruction after the war, but rather remind the nations of the abiding commandments and realities that must be taken seriously if the new order is to be a true order (Bonhoeffer 1965: 109–10).

In particular, Bonhoeffer stresses that in a number of European countries an attempt to return to fully fledged democracy and parliamentarianism would create even more disorder than obtained prior to the era of authoritarianism. Democracy requires a soil that has been prepared by a long spiritual tradition, and most of the nations of Europe, except for some of the smaller ones, do not have the resources for sustaining democracy. This does not mean the only alternative is state absolutism; rather, what should be sought is that each state be limited by the law. This will require a different politics than the politics of liberalism.

In his *Ethics* Bonhoeffer starkly states (and he clearly has in mind the French Revolution) that "the demand for absolute liberty brings men to the depths of slavery" (Bonhoeffer 1963: 38).[4] In his response to Paton, he observes that the Anglo-Saxon freedom is the word that names the struggle against the omnipotence of the state, and the demand for freedom is expressed in the language of "rights and liberties." But "freedom is too negative a word to be used in a situation where *all* order has been destroyed. And liberties are not enough when men seek first of all for some minimum security. These words remind us of the old liberalism which because of its failures is itself largely responsible for the development of State absolutism" (Bonhoeffer 1973: 113).

Bonhoeffer takes up this history again in his *Ethics*, suggesting that these developments cannot help but lead to godlessness and the subsequent deification of man which is the proclamation of nihilism. This godlessness is seldom identified by hostility to the church, but rather this "hopeless godlessness" too often comes in Christian clothing. Such "godlessness" he finds particularly present in the American churches, whose quest to faithfully build the world with Christian principles ends with the total capitulation of the church to the world. Such societies and churches have no confidence in truth, with the result that the place of truth is usurped by sophistic propaganda (Bonhoeffer 1963: 41–3).

The only hope, if Europe is to avoid the plunge into the void after the war, is in the miracle of a new awakening of faith and the institution of God's governance of the world that sets limits to evil. The latter alternative, what Bonhoeffer calls "the restrainer," is the power of the state to establish and maintain order (Bonhoeffer 1963: 44). In his reply to Paton he suggests that such an order limited by law and responsibility, which recognizes commandments that transcend the state, has more "spiritual substance and solidity than the emphasis on the rights of man" (Bonhoeffer 1973: 113). Such an order is entirely different than the order of the church, but they are in close alliance. The church, therefore, cannot fail its responsibility to sustain the restraining work of the state.

Yet the church must never forget that its primary task is to preach the risen Jesus Christ, because in so doing the church

> strikes a mortal blow at the spirit of destruction. The "restrainer," the force of order, sees in the church an ally, and, whatever other elements of order may remain, will seek a place at her side. Justice, truth, science, art, culture, humanity, liberty, patriotism, all at last, after long straying from the path, are once more finding their way back to their fountain-head. The more central the message of the church, the greater now will be her effectiveness. (Bonhoeffer 1963: 45)

Above I suggested that Bonhoeffer's attempt to reclaim the visibility of the church at least put him in the vicinity of trying to imagine a non-Constantinian church. Yet in his *Ethics* he displays habits of mind that clearly seem committed to what we can only call a "Christian civilization." Larry Rasmussen suggests, however, that Bonhoeffer in the last stages of his *Letters and Papers from Prison* began to move away from any Christendom notions (Rasmussen 1972: 85–6). In particular, Rasmussen directs attention to the "Outline for a Book" Bonhoeffer wrote toward the end of his life. Rather than finishing the *Ethics*, which he expressed regret for not having finished, if he had lived I believe, as Rasmussen believes, Bonhoeffer would have first written the book envisaged in his "Outline." For the book hinted at in the "Outline" would have allowed him to extend his reflections about the limits of liberal politics and about the manner in which the church might provide an appropriate alternative.

In his "Outline" Bonhoeffer begins with "a stocktaking of Christianity." In particular he suggests that what it means for humankind to have "come of age" is the dream that humans can be independent of nature. As a result human creations have turned against their creators, enslaving those who sought freedom in their self-created chains. The church, trapped by its invisibility, provides no alternative, unwilling to risk itself on behalf of the world. Such a church is no more than a stop-gap for the embarrassment of our suffering and death (Bonhoeffer 1971: 380–3). In the second chapter of his book Bonhoeffer, in terms reminiscent of *Sanctorum Communio*, suggests he will begin with the question "Who is God?" in order to recover the God who is found only through our "participation in the being of Jesus." Bonhoeffer proposes to end his book with an account of the church that will "have to take the field against the vices of *hubris*, power-worship, envy, and humbug, as the roots of all evil. It will have to speak of moderation, purity, trust, loyalty, constancy, patience, discipline, humility, contentment, and modesty" (Bonhoeffer 1971: 383).

Finally, Bonhoeffer says he intends to explore the importance and power of example, "which has its origin in the humanity of Jesus and is so important in the teachings of Paul," and whose importance has been underestimated (Bonhoeffer 1971: 383). I cannot say that if Bonhoeffer had had the opportunity to write the book suggested in his "Outline," he would have for ever left Constantinianism behind. But I remain convinced Bonhoeffer's attempt to think through what the recovery of the visible church entails – the implication of which I am convinced he was beginning to see in his last proposed book – is an invaluable resource for the challenges that those of us who must live after Bonhoeffer cannot fail to ignore. He is now part of God's exemplification given for our redemption.

Notes

1   Rasmussen (1972) remains one of the best attempts to understand Bonhoeffer's involvement in the plot to kill Hitler. I remain unconvinced, however, that Bonhoeffer thought this aspect of his life could be justified, even if he did, as Rasmussen suggests, think in terms of just war considerations. For quite different accounts see Jones (1995), 3–33; McClendon (1986), 188–211.

2   In *True Patriotism* (Bonhoeffer 1973: 160) Bonhoeffer notes that the defining mark of the Constantinian age was not that Christians began to baptize their children, but "that baptism became a qualification for civic life. The false development lies not in infant baptism but in the secular qualification of baptism. The two should clearly be distinguished."

3   This passage comes from Bonhoeffer's wonderful essay "The Question of Baptism," written in 1942 in response to a controversy in the Confessing Church (Bonhoeffer 1973: 143–64). Bonhoeffer observes that it is very understandable that in a secularized church there is a desire for a pure, authentic, truthful set of believers to exist. Such a desire is understandable, but full of dangers because it is far too easy for a community ideal to take the place of the real community of God, or for such a community to be understood as a contribution made by man.

4   This aspect of Bonhoeffer's work has been attacked in Germany by Klaus-Michael Kodalle (1991). Wolfgang Huber defends Bonhoeffer against Kodalle in his "Bonhoeffer and Modernity," in Floyd and Marsch, eds. (1994), 5–19. I fear I am equally unsympathetic with Kodalle's critique and Huber's defense just to the extent they each remain determined by the categories of liberal political theory. Huber challenges Kodalle's dualism of individual and community, but fails to see that the heart of Bonhoeffer's challenge is ecclesial.

References

Barth, Karl (1961). *Church Dogmatics* III, 4. Edinburgh: T. & T. Clark.

Bethge, Eberhard (2000). *Dietrich Bonhoeffer: A Biography* (rev. edn). Minneapolis: Fortress.

Bonhoeffer, Dietrich (1963). *Ethics*, trans. Neville Horton Smith. New York: Macmillan.

——(1965). *No Rusty Swords*, trans. Edwin Robertson and John Bowden. New York: Harper & Row.

——(1966). *Christ the Center*, trans. John Bowden. New York: Harper & Row.

——(1971). *Letters and Papers from Prison*, trans. Reginald Tuller. New York: Macmillan.

——(1973). *True Patriotism*, trans. Edwin Robertson and John Bowden. New York: Harper & Row.

——(1990). *A Testament to Freedom*, ed. Jeffrey Kellyard and R. Burton Nelson. San Francisco: Harper & Row.

——(1996a). *Act and Being*, trans. Hans-Richard Reuter. Minneapolis: Fortress.

——(1996b). *Creation and Fall*, tr. Martin Rüter and Ilse Tödt. Minneapolis: Fortress.

——(1996c). *Life Together and The Prayerbook of the Bible*, trans. Gerhard Ludwig Müller and Albrecht Schönherr. Minneapolis: Fortress.

——(1998). *Sanctorum Communio*, trans. Reinhard Krauss and Nancy Lukens. Minneapolis: Fortress.

——(2001). *Discipleship*, trans. Martin Kushe and Ilse Tödt. Minneapolis: Fortress.

Cox, Harvey (1965). *The Secular City*. New York: Macmillan.

Feil, Ernst (1985). *The Theology of Dietrich Bonhoeffer*. Philadelphia: Fortress.

Fletcher, Joseph (1966). *Situation Ethics: The New Morality*. Philadelphia: Westminster.

Floyd, Wayne, and Marsh, Charles, eds. (1994). *Theology and the Practice of Responsibility: Essays on Dietrich Bonhoeffer*. Valley Forge, Pa: Trinity International.

Hauerwas, Stanley (ed.), et al. (1999). *The Wisdom of the Cross*. Grand Rapids, Mich.: Eerdmans.

Hoffman, Peter (1996). *The History of the German Resistance, 1933–1945*. Montreal: McGill-Queen's University Press.

Jones, L. Gregory (1995). *Embodying Forgiveness*. Grand Rapids, Mich.: Eerdmans.

Kodalle, Klaus-Michael (1991). *Dietrich Bonhoeffer: Zur Kritik seiner Theologie*. Munich: Gutersloh.

McClendon, James William (1986). *Systematic Theology*, vol. 1. Nashville: Abingdon.

Marsh, Charles (1994). *Reclaiming Dietrich Bonhoeffer: The Promise of his Theology*. New York: Oxford University Press.

Rasmusson, Arne (1995). *The Church as Polis: From Political Theology to Theological Politics as Exemplified by Jürgen Moltmann and Stanley Hauerwas*. Notre Dame, Ind.: University of Notre Dame Press.

Rasmussen, Larry (1972). *Dietrich Bonhoeffer: Reality and Resistance*. Nashville: Abingdon.

Reist, Benjamin (1969). *The Promise of Bonhoeffer*. Philadelphia: Lippincott.

Robinson, John A. T. (1963). *Honest to God*. Philadelphia: Westminster.

Robinson, Marilynne (1998). *The Death of Adam: Essays on Modern Thought*. Boston: Houghton Mifflin.

Yoder, John Howard (1984). *The Priestly Kingdom*. Notre Dame, Ind.: University of Notre Dame Press.

——(1994). *The Politics of Jesus: Nicit Agnus Master*. Grand Rapids: Eerdmans.

——(1998). *The Christian Witness to the State*. Eugene, Oreg.: Wipf & Stock.

CHAPTER 11

John Courtney Murray

Michael J. Baxter

I

> The question is sometimes raised, whether Catholicism is compatible with Ameri-
> can democracy. The question is invalid as well as impertinent; for the manner of
> its position inverts the order of values. It must, of course, be turned round to read,
> whether American democracy is compatible with Catholicism. The question, thus
> turned, is part of the civil question, as put to me. An affirmative answer to it, given
> under something better than curbstone definition of "democracy," is one of the
> truths I hold. (Murray 1960: ix–x)

So wrote John Courtney Murray in the foreword to *We Hold These Truths*. It
was his way of stating the terms of the central question taken up in the book
and announcing his answer to it: the question is whether democracy in the
United States is compatible with Catholicism, and the answer is yes. But more
than this, it was his way of forestalling two criticisms of the argument he would
be advancing in the book.

First, there was the criticism voiced by the Catholic supernaturalists, who
argued that Murray's endorsement of the separation of church and state contradicted the official Catholic teaching that governmental establishment of religion is the ideal and thus marginalized the role of the church in political life.
This criticism was leveled by an energetic and powerful coterie of theologians
who had been attacking Murray's innovative arguments in articles and letters
to the editors of Catholic theological journals ever since the 1940s, and who,
when those efforts failed to deter him, arranged to have his work censored by
the Vatican authorities in 1955. Now, only five years later, owing to a change of
theological climate in Rome, Murray was again able to air his views in print, this
time in a book bringing together ten previously published essays and two new
ones, all dealing with one or another aspect of the relationship between Catholi-

cism and US democracy. But the criticism that he was compromising the church's mission by endorsing the church–state separation had by no means gone away. Hence the assurance, aimed at his traditionalist critics, that the question to be taken up is "whether American democracy is compatible with Catholicism," not the other way around.

This assurance put Murray at odds with a different set of critics who delivered a second formidable criticism of his argument. These were the "secular separationists," as they can be called: those who contended that Murray's call for public discourse based on natural law was an attempt to smuggle a Catholic morality and politics into the operations of government and thus a violation of the establishment clause of the First Amendment. Working from a Protestant, Jewish, or atheist perspective, these critics tapped into deep currents of anti-Catholic sentiment that had become a persistent feature of popular culture in the United States, but they also appealed to a longstanding lineage of legal and political thought that went back to the nation's founding, one that regarded any endeavor to shape national policy according to the standards of a particular moral tradition as an attack on the rights protected by the Constitution, especially an individual's right to religious freedom and freedom of conscience. With scores of his essays published and rebutted in the popular press and two decades' worth of papers delivered and rebutted on the lecture circuit, Murray knew well that this view should be identified and dismissed at the outset. Hence the assurance, directed at the separationists, that he is working with "something better than curbstone definition of 'democracy.'"

In affirming the compatibility of Catholicism and US democracy, then, Murray was at the same time refuting two sets of critics – the Catholic supernaturalists and the secular separationists – each of which described this relationship as one of fundamental conflict, though for very different reasons. Having clearly stated his battle plan in the foreword, Murray attempted with the essays in the rest of the book to prevail at key points along the lines of this two-front war, addressing such topics as (in roughly the order they appear) true and false readings of the First Amendment, the nature of public discourse, higher education, state support of religious schools, censorship, the Incarnation, political freedom, communism, the morality of military force, and the proper understanding of natural law. Taken together, these essays present Murray's alternative description of the relation between Catholicism and US democracy, along with a metanarrative designed to show how such seemingly opposed entities are in fact fundamentally compatible.

If the success of Murray's "compatibility thesis" (as it might be called) were measured by the reception of *We Hold These Truths*, then it would have to be judged as very successful. The book was widely hailed as a milestone in US Catholic thought, so much so that Murray appeared on the cover of *Time* (although his good friend and publisher of the magazine, Henry Luce, certainly had a hand in that). The cover article, a careful summary of the book's argument, gave the compatibility thesis national exposure. The fact that the book was published in the same year Kennedy was elected president added to the sense that Murray had something momentous to say. Moreover, he inspired a generation of Catholics to engage non-Catholics in open, respectful dialogue on matters political and religious, which in turn created a receptive audience for things Catholic among Protestant and Jewish intellectuals. Murray's life and work thus came to represent the aspirations of an entire generation of Catholic intellectuals.

His scholarly career was in many ways typical for a Jesuit priest in the United States – a B.A. from Weston College (1926), an M.A. in Philosophy from Boston College (1927), a three-year stint teaching Latin and English Literature in the Philippines, a master's level theology degree from Woodstock College in Maryland (1933), an advanced degree in theology at the Gregorian University in Rome (1937), then back to Woodstock as professor of theology until his death in 1967 – and his notoriety demonstrated that a classical Catholic education could make a mark on the intellectual life of the nation. This is how he is depicted by most historians of Catholicism in the United States: as an intellectual hero who facilitated Catholicism's coming of age by demonstrating that one can be both fully American and fully Catholic.

Whether or not Murray successfully demonstrated the compatibility between Catholicism and US democracy is a much disputed question. In one respect, he certainly prevailed over his traditionalist critics. Not only did the argument he outlined in *We Hold These Truths* gain the nearly universal endorsement of Catholic intellectuals in the United States, it also made its way into the deliberations of the Second Vatican Council, during which Murray, thanks to the support of Francis Cardinal Spellman, served as a *peritus* (expert consultant). Indeed, he had a shaping hand in writing the final draft of *Dignitatis Humanae*, the Council's Declaration on Religious Liberty which officially affirmed the right of the human person to worship in accord with his or her conscience. In so doing, it granted implicit approval to church–state separation, sending the complaints of Murray's Catholic traditionalist critics into oblivion. The fact that the preponderance of Catholic social ethicists in the United States, both liberal and neoconservative, point to Murray as a mentor or model (e.g. Curran 1982; Neuhaus 1987; Weigel 1987) only goes to show the pervasive and continuing importance of his "compatibility thesis."

In another respect, however, this ostensible compatibility has remained elusive. Indeed, the case can be made that it has become even more elusive in the 35 years since Murray's death, especially with the emergence of the practices of abortion, euthanasia, physician-assisted suicide, divorce, the buying and selling of pornography, and so on, all of which have enjoyed legal protection under the auspices of an increasingly secularized judiciary. Moreover, US society has experience deterioration in civility, public discourse, and a sense of the common good. In response to these developments, Murray would insist that it is therefore all the more urgent to call the nation back to the philosophy on which it was founded, and this is more or less the agenda that his successors continue to take up as their own, in an attempt to finish his project. But as the years go by, and as the nation veers further from that supposed founding philosophy, it must be asked whether or not Murray's compatibility thesis continues to be plausible.

This question is taken up in the concluding section of this essay. As a way of setting the context for that question, I present the broad narrative constituting Murray's compatibility thesis (part II). In the next two sections I sketch out Murray's response to the two criticisms of this thesis, focusing first on the Catholic supernaturalists (part III) and then on the secular separationists (part IV). In the final section (part V), I show that Murray's response to these criticisms reveals intractable tensions in his compatibility thesis.

II

Murray's argument for the compatibility of Catholicism with US democracy rests on the claim that the United States respects the freedom of the church, and in so doing respects the freedom of the Incarnate Son of God, Jesus Christ. He advances this claim by means of narrative of religious freedom through the ages, beginning with the Incarnation. On Murray's account, the Incarnation established a "spiritual order" that transcends the "temporal order," but it was by no means without temporal effects, for the church has traditionally claimed for itself a presence in the temporal order whereby it can live in a manner that is in keeping with its supernatural vocation and with the natural law. This Christian notion of the temporal order providing an *entrée* for the spiritual (*res sacra in temporalibus*) was revolutionary, according to Murray, for two reasons: first, because it destroyed the classical view of society as a single homogeneous structure within which the *ius divinum* becomes subordinated to the *ius civile* under the hand of imperial rule; and second, because it set forth a new political vision in which the freedom of the church would be preserved by means of a limited state (Murray 1960: 202). Thus for Murray, the church and the freedom it claims has an actual, concrete impact on history. As he puts it, in a blunt dismissal of Harnack's ecclesiology: "What appeared within history was not an 'idea' or an 'essence' but an existence, a Thing, a visible institution that occupied ground in this world at the same time that it asserted an astounding new freedom on a title not of this world." The church is a material reality. It occupies space (Murray 1960: 204).

For Murray, then, the Incarnation is no momentary, evanescent event that leaves history and politics intact and untransformed. It is a divinely inaugurated interruption in history which establishes a new "spiritual" order of human existence, and this spiritual order overturns all configurations of political power by confining their field of operation to a temporal order which, in effect, holds their expansive tendencies in check. In this sense, the Incarnation has given birth to a new kind of politics, one in which the power of the state is structured according to the exigencies of the freedom of the church. This new politics was given vivid expression in the celebrated declaration of Pope Gelasius I, "Two there are, august emperor, by which this world is ruled on title of original and sovereign right – the consecrated authority of the priesthood and the royal power"; it is by virtue of this "diarchy" that we can refer to the "revolutionary character of the Christian dispensation" (Murray 1960: 202). The Incarnation of Christ and the establishment of the church thus constitute a political event of world-historical importance. Hence Murray writes of the principle of the freedom of the church: "On any showing, even merely historical, we are here in the presence of a Great Idea, whose entrance into history marked the beginning of a new civilizational era" (Murray 1960: 202).

Much of Murray's scholarship strove to narrate the unfolding of the principle of the freedom of the church in history. In the realm of theory, he traced its development in the writings of Augustine, John of Salisbury, Aquinas, Bellarmine, Leo XIII, Pius XI, Pius XII, and several others, each of whom articulated with varying degrees of clarity the ancient Gelasian diarchy. This has not been, Murray conceded, a linear development. Bellarmine was right to endorse a theory of indirect power of the church, but he misapplied it in light of the political realities of the emerging nation-state (Murray 1948). Also, Leo XIII's vision was limited when it came to assessing modern democracy (Murray 1953). When these thinkers are examined along broad historical lines, there emerges, Murray contends, a definite intellectual tradition centering on a cluster of themes that can be placed under the heading of "Western constitutionalism." This tradition of Western constitutionalism was born in the Middle Ages, as Murray narrates it, but it came of age when the principle of the freedom of the church was codified in written law for the first time in history in the Constitution of the United States, and more specifically in the religion clause of the First Amendment.

On what basis, one might ask, does Murray find continuity between medieval Catholic political theory and the founding principles of the United States? The answer for him is natural law, which was alive and well in the minds of the nation's founders. The claim, in his words, is that "the American political community was organized in an era when the tradition of natural law and natural rights was still vigorous" (Murray 1960: 30). In keeping with this assertion, Murray makes a host of related claims about the continuity of the US foundation with its medieval intellectual inheritance. Take, for example, this: "The American consensus accepted the premise of medieval society, that there is a sense of justice inherent in the people, in virtue of which they are empowered, as the medieval phrase had it, to 'judge, direct, and correct' the process of government. It was this political faith that compelled early American agreement to the institutions of a free speech and a free press" (p. 34). And this: "The philosophy of the Bill of Rights was also tributary to the tradition of natural law, to the idea that man has certain original responsibilities precisely as man, antecedent to his status as citizen" (p. 37). Along the same lines, Murray claims medieval antecedents for the words of one of the nation's most renowned statesmen: "the affirmation in Lincoln's famous phrase, 'this nation under God,' sets the American proposition in fundamental continuity with the central political tradition of the West" (p. 30). In a complementary way, he finds proto-

American impulses in the thought of medieval Christianity's most renowned political theorist, when he claims that the American phrase " '[a] free people under a limited government' would have satisfied the first Whig, St. Thomas Aquinas" (p. 32). Each of these statements is embedded in the sweeping historical assertion that the medieval Catholic tradition of natural law "furnished the basic materials for the American consensus" (p. 30).

For Murray, this "American consensus," at its theoretical core, consists of two principles: the consent of the governed and the limited state. And it is accompanied by a cluster of subsidiary ideas: (1) "government has a moral basis"; (2) "the universal moral law is the foundation of society"; (3) "the legal order of society – that is, the state – is subject to judgment by a law that is not statistical but inherent in the nature of man"; (4) "the eternal reason of God is the ultimate origin of all law"; and (5) "this nation in all its aspects – as a society, a state, an ordered and free relationship between governors and governed – is under God" (Murray 1960: 33–5, 42). Murray does little in the way of arguing the validity of these ideas in the abstract. Instead he concentrates on identifying them with "the American consensus" and thus showing that this consensus belongs in the broad tradition of natural law that he traces back to medieval times – indeed, back further to Gelasius, to the early church, to the Incarnation itself which, as we have seen, established a spiritual order with primacy over all temporal order. Because its founders designed a government that would acknowledge the primacy of the spiritual, the United States is compatible with Catholicism. Indeed, at certain points Murray goes further than mere compatibility, for example, when he describes the foundation of the United States as "providential" (pp. 30, 68).

The message delivered by Murray's narrative, then, is that US democracy is compatible with Catholicism because it is the product of Catholic political theory. But this claim was criticized, as we have seen, by Catholic supernaturalists who argued that Murray's version of Catholic political theory was fundamentally flawed, perhaps even heterodox. It is to this critique and Murray's response to it that we now turn.

III

The Catholic traditionalists criticized Murray because he supported separation of church and state and argued that this was consonant with Catholic teaching. On the face of it, they were right. At the time, the official teaching of the Catholic Church was that Catholic teaching and institutions should be formally and legally supported by the state, and that any political arrangement deviating from this norm is unacceptable in principle and may be tolerated only as a concession for the sake of preserving public peace. The assumption governing this teaching was that legal separation of church and state is detrimental to the life and mission of the church.

Jarring as it may seem, this assumption seems warranted given the bleak situation of the Catholic Church in modern Europe. The French Revolution marked the beginning of a mighty struggle between two opposing political forces: that of monarchy versus that of reform or revolution. The year 1789 ushered in a systematic, often violent persecution of the church in France, carried out by an atheistic state in the name of democracy. Similar threats emerged throughout Europe, as in one country after another reformers or revolutionaries called for the expulsion of the church from political life. In this context, the church's reflexive response was to side with the forces of monarchy. This strategy had its drawbacks: it ignored the extent to which monarchs too were hostile to ecclesial authority, and it earned for the church the reputation of being a reactionary institution. But casting its weight behind monarchy seemed to be the only hope for stemming the revolutionary tide. In particular, it was the only hope for retaining governments that would be amenable to preserving at least some of the church's freedom in the spiritual realm and representing Catholic teaching in laws on certain temporal matters, such as marriage and education. Nevertheless, by the beginning of the twentieth century, it was clear that a new secular order was emerging in Europe, one in which the church's role in temporal affairs was sharply curbed, if not altogether eliminated, and in which its freedom in the spiritual realm was precarious. Church leaders accommodated to this new reality in practice, mainly by signing concordats with various states, but they refused to make any concessions in the realm of theory. In the face of secular political order, this was their way of maintaining that the ills of modern society can be cured only by a return to Christian life and institutions (*Rerum Novarum*, 1891, n. 22). Such factors underlie the insistence in official Catholic teaching that the normative political arrangement is one in which the church receives full legal support of the state.

The challenge for Catholic political theorists was to explain the apparent discrepancy between the insistence in the realm of theory on the normativity of state support for the church and a readiness in practice to settle for less acceptable arrangements. They did so by means of a distinction between "thesis" and "hypothesis," to use the language of the day; or, in more contemporary terms, a distinction between an absolute principle applicable in an ideal situation (the thesis) and a relative principle to be employed in less than ideal circumstances (the hypothesis). Developed by the French Bishop Felix Doupanloup to respond to critics of Pius IX's *Syllabus of Errors* (1864), this thesis/hypothesis distinction allowed the "thesis" of church–state union to be affirmed while the "hypothesis" of church–state separation was accepted in actual fact. This proved to be a useful formulation. It provided Catholic political theorists with the conceptual device needed to account for the church's readiness to negotiate with civil authorities over such matters as education, marital laws, and episcopal appointments, all the while allowing them to uphold the depiction of the Christian (Catholic) state affirmed in the *Syllabus* as the unqualified and unquestionable ideal. From the mid-nineteenth century on, this thesis/hypothesis distinction was a standard feature of Catholic political theory, not only in Europe but also in the United States, where it was used by leading scholars, most famously by John Ryan (Ryan and Millar 1922). It was still in use when Murray began publishing on church and state and when his traditionalist critics published their objections.

In the context of the thesis/hypothesis distinction, the objection of the Catholic supernaturalists was simple: Murray regarded the political arrangement of the United States as fundamentally good, as in effect a "thesis," not merely as an "hypothesis." Two of the most persistent critics of Murray on this score were Joseph Fenton (1906–69) and Francis Connell CSSR (1888–1967), both of Catholic University. As self-appointed upholders of official Catholic teaching on church–state relations, they argued that the constitutional set-up in the United States should be classified as less than ideal, as a hypothesis, and that not to do so would lay the groundwork for "indifferentism." In the Catholic theology of the time, indifferentism was the notion that it does not make any difference which church one belongs to so long as one lives a good life, the assumption being that there is no true church, in the sense of an organized body founded by God for the salvation of humanity (Sheedy 1949: 91–3). In pressing their concern about indifferentism, Fenton and Connell contended that Murray, in not upholding the thesis of the Catholic state, implied that state and society would not benefit from the guidance of the Catholic Church or, more to the point, that the Catholic Church is not the true church.

According to Fenton, a consistent line of papal teaching from Gregory XVI to Leo XIII condemned any attempt to circumscribe the arena of divine sovereignty. "The God of indifferentism is devoid of any real and positive rights over the affairs of human thought, of human expression, or of the civil order," he declared, and to worship such a god would be to worship a limited and therefore false god (Appleby and Haas 1995: 36–7). Connell argued along similar lines. He invoked Pius XI's encyclical *Quas Primas* (1925), which teaches that obedience to Christ is an obligation of all people not only as individuals but also as members of a civil society and state, and noted that while the purpose of civil society is to promote the common temporal good – that is, the good of citizens in this present life – this purpose must be ordered to humanity's supernatural end. "In view of the elevation of all men to the supernatural order," Fenton wrote, "their temporal good embraces the practice of the supernatural virtues, as well as of the natural virtues. Hence, to promote the welfare of its citizens, a government must concern itself with their observance of the supernatural law of Christ as well as of the natural law" (Connell 1948). Both Fenton and Connell insisted that Murray's portrayal of the state as incompetent in matters of religion created a sphere of human activity free from the obligation to obey Christ, a sphere where one's religious beliefs and practices get set aside, a sphere that gives rise to indifferentism. Affirming the thesis or ideal of the Catholic state, they insisted, was the way to check this drift toward indifferentism.

It is important to place this concern with indifferentism in the context of postwar Catholicism in the United States, and more specifically of a growing tendency among Catholics to practice ecumenism or what was then called "intercredal cooperation." The pros and cons of intercredal cooperation were hashed out by Murray, Fenton, Connell, and others in the early 1940s. Murray advocated it. Acknowledging the danger of indifferentism, he argued that there were other dangers associated with the war that should be attended to as well: "the dangers to human life, national and international, involved in the failure of Catholics to co-operate with non-Catholics in the sphere of social reconstruction – dangers so great as to create a necessity for such co-operation" (Murray 1942: 416). Murray held that the basis of such cooperation can be found in the precepts of the natural law, the illuminating light of which "is shared by all men who have not completely lost contact with the Christian tradition that had mediated them. And it is difficult to see why that light cannot be a common source of illumination to all Christians" in such a way that it "brings into focus at least the general lines of the reconstructive task that calls for their common effort" (p. 430).

Fenton and Connell agreed that Catholics should cooperate with non-Catholics in working for peace and social justice, but they saw key dangers too. Connell observed that the wartime mobilization, which had brought together millions of US citizens from various religious backgrounds, was generating a spirit of latitudinarianism, reinforced by the governmental attitude of tolerance of all religion (Appleby and Hass 1995: 28). Fenton detected the same danger, and insisted that Catholics affirm to their non-Catholic compatriots the traditional Catholic teaching that to enjoy the benefits of a life with Christ they must either belong or intend to belong to "the actually existing and visible society founded by our Lord" (Appleby and Haas 1995: 30). Both saw Catholics being swept up into the postwar spirit of liberalism and ecumenism and in the process downplaying the importance of the supernatural life of the church in the temporal order. For this reason they can be properly called Catholic "supernaturalists" (Appleby and Haas 1995: 26–8).

But where they saw mainly problems, Murray saw promise. His assessment was that Catholics in the United States were faring well under church–state separation. After all, the Catholic Church had not been restricted, repressed, or persecuted in any significant way. On the contrary, the church in the United States was flourishing. Why? Because the constitutional separation of church and state had allowed Catholics fully and freely to practice their faith. But if this is the case, Murray asked, of what use is the thesis/hypothesis distinction? His answer was that it is not very useful at all. Indeed, it led to the embarrassing fact that Catholic church–state teaching is entirely irrelevant to Catholics in the United States. As he wrote in a letter to the historian John Tracy Ellis, "Are we to suppose that 30,000,000 Catholics must live perpetually in a state of 'hypothesis'?" (Pellotte 1976: 38). What, then, did Murray do with the traditional teaching on church and state, with the thesis? Because he could not dismiss it or ignore it, he historicized it.

Historicizing the thesis, so to speak, was the task of the series of scholarly articles Murray published in the 1940s and 1950s. They comprised in effect a unified, extended argument that at its theoretical core consists of three steps.

The first step was to posit a key transtemporal principle, as Murray called it, namely, "the primacy of the spiritual," along with three derivative transtemporal principles: the separation of the church from society, the freedom of the church, and the dignity of the human person (Murray 1954). The second step was to show that the thesis of church–state union was forged in an attempt to apply these transtemporal principles within particular historical circumstances. The third step was to argue that those historical circumstances have now changed. Murray used these three steps to reread the writings of several figures, especially those of Leo XIII, who relatively recently had articulated the thesis position in clear terms.

As Murray explained it, the historical circumstances in which Leo wrote about politics were dominated by the French Revolution, which attempted to enclose all institutions within a single framework overseen by the state. In defiance of this political monism, as Murray dubbed it, Leo XIII called for a model of church–state relations in which the church was to exercise paternalistic care in politics. But he did this, Murray contends, because he perceived a danger "in the tragic fact that the once-proud *populus Christianus* had become the Catholic masses, ignorant, apathetic, inert, a prey to the manipulations of erring and unscrupulous leaders" (Murray 1954: 30). Therefore, in the context of the Revolution's omnicompetent state assuming the role of teacher, Leo XIII was compelled to sanction the exercise of paternalistic care in politics, whereby the state intervenes in the order of culture on behalf of the common good. This was necessary, Murray wrote, because European Catholics were an *imperita multitudo*, "the masses," and not a genuine "people." The distinction is crucial. The masses require an external authority to direct them, some form of tutelage, like children do. By contrast, a genuine people is marked by a well-developed community structure and moral identity and is thus capable of self-direction, like adults. The point of the distinction, for Murray, is to show that Leo XIII articulated the thesis of the Catholic state to deal with the European masses but that this thesis is not needed for a genuine people, such as resides in the United States. In other words, the American people are more mature, and in this adult state, are capable on their own of embodying genuine political community (p. 32).

But is it true that the populace in the United States require no external direction? Have the American people reached true political maturity? To shed some light on these questions, we now turn to Murray's response to his secularist separationist critics.

IV

Throughout his work, Murray placed heavy emphasis on the opposition between the continental liberalism associated with the French Revolution and the liberalism of the Western constitutional tradition. And yet, if we return to his grand narrative, we find that the opposition is not so simple. While he sets the

American consensus over against its rival Jacobin laicist tradition of continental Europe, it turns out that this latter tradition has taken root in American soil. Many features of continental liberalism – its endorsement of autonomous human reason, its privatization of religion, its refusal to acknowledge the authority of natural law, its social contract theory of the state, its social atomism (Murray 1960: 28, 29, 38) – were subtly at work at the nation's founding. It can be detected in the minds of those who espoused a voluntarist understanding of law over against an intellectualist one which sees law as an enactment of reason, and also in certain trends in early American legal theory, even Blackstone's (pp. 41–2).

More recently, such features have emerged in the twentieth century as an intellectual force in US universities which, Murray says (paraphrasing Santayana), have "long since bade a quiet good-bye to the whole notion of an American consensus" (Murray 1960: 40). The upshot is that this rival tradition threatens to dissolve the American consensus altogether, a development which, Murray warns us, would pave the way to political chaos: "Perhaps the dissolution, long since begun, may one day be consummated. Perhaps one day the many-storeyed mansion of democracy will be dismantled, levelled to the dimensions of a flat majoritarianism, which is no mansion but a barn, perhaps even a tool shed in which the weapons of tyranny may be forged" (p. 42).

In describing this rival tradition, Murray points to his secular separationist critics, who contend in one way or another that the lack of common standards of reason prevents a public consensus in the United States. In the essay "Two Cases for the Public Consensus: Fact or Need," he reported on his encounters with these critics. While out on the speaking circuit, he would pose the question, "Is there or is there not an American consensus, a public philosophy on which the whole order of the Republic rests?" and then present "the four essential points" that go into making "the affirmative case on the question" (Murray 1960: 82). The four points are (1) that America has a public philosophy; (2) that this public philosophy furnishes the broad purposes, standards, and bases of communication for government; (3) that this public philosophy includes a common understanding of law, of the relation of law to the will and intellect as well as to freedom and morality, of norms of good jurisprudence, of social equality and unity, of the distinction between state and society, of the value of law for moral formation, and of the sacredness of the human person; and (4) that this consensus does not banish dissent but welcomes it as a means of solidifying and further articulating the consensus. Murray reported that after outlining these four essential points, he usually received the following responses from various groups. The individualists would insist that there is no common standard of reason, thus rendering philosophy a private matter. The materialists would say that success in America is defined and measured in material terms, thus rendering public philosophy irrelevant. The positivists would say that there is no truth other than scientific truth, thus rendering public philosophy mythical, poetic, or symbolic, but not permanently truthful. The pragmatists would say that the worth of all philosophies is determined by the free market of ideas, thus rendering public philosophy no longer operative because it is out of fashion. And the contextualists would say that morality in the United States, like all morality, can be reduced down to social mores, customs, fashions, or conventions, thus declaring unfounded any appeal to a moral order in public philosophy. Then, Murray relates, someone would suggest that "the American consensus contains only one tenet – an agreement to disagree." For him this leaves us nowhere: "With this agreement all agreement ends; and this agreement is hardly sufficient to constitute a philosophy" (p. 84).

Murray's report did not end here, however. He explained that he had called for a change in discursive tactics. Instead of arguing that the American consensus is a fact, it should be argued that it is a need. The nation needs a public philosophy because it is in crisis. The starting point for advancing this argument, Murray says, is that the nation is doing badly and that it has no goal other than to survive in the face of the communist threat. It has no conception of world order, or of the principles of this order, or of the forms and modes of organization required. This is because it has no public philosophy or common language. Thus he concludes his report by explaining how a refurbished public philosophy would generate coherent military and economic policies, and so enhance the nation's security in the face of the threat of worldwide communism while at the same time moving the world in the direction of order (Murray 1960: 86–96).

But how effective is this shift from fact to need in the terms of his argument for the American consensus? He assumes that the interlocutors who take issue with his attempt to establish the fact of the American consensus will surely agree on the need for an American consensus. His interlocutors are likely to have a different account of the crisis. What if the individualists, materialists, positivists, pragmatists, and contextualists do not believe that the nation is in crisis? Or, what if they believe it is in crisis, but not the crisis as Murray describes it? Or, what if they believe that a public philosophy will not help to resolve the crisis? These questions Murray does not address, and in not doing so, he fails to face the possibility that these interlocutors may insulate themselves within the confines of their own intellectual, historical, and communal frameworks and refuse to join in the project of developing a public philosophy. Murray's response to this kind of question was that they are being "idiots" – idiots, that is, "in the classical Greek sense of the 'private person' who does not share in the public thought of the City" (Murray 1960: 117). A lot of people in the United States are perfectly content to be idiots in this sense. But if this is the case, where is this American consensus? And if it cannot be located, how can Murray's compatibility thesis hold true?

V

One way to pursue this last question is to recount a crucial passage toward the end of *We Hold These Truths*. After arguing for a foreign policy based on natural law principles, Murray noted that such principles are not found in the nation's policy-making at the present time (1960). Then he addressed a question about these principles posed by Yale professor Julian Hartt ("a friendly critic," as he called him). Hartt's query, as recounted by Murray, was as follows:

> Father Murray has not, I believe, clearly enough come to terms with the question behind every serious consideration of limited war as an option, i.e., where are the ethical principles to fix the appropriate limits? Where, not what: can we make out the lineaments of the community which is the living repository (as it were) of the ethical principles relevant and efficacious to the moral determinations of the limits of warfare? (Murray 1960: 290)

Hartt's question is important because it asks "Where, not what?"; it asks not for principles not to be discussed in the abstract but to be embodied in an actual, specific community. After posing the question, Murray explains, and "after a look around the national lot, Professor Hartt comes to the conclusion that the American community does not qualify; it is not the living repository of what the tradition of reason has said on warfare."

To Hartt's assessment of "the American community," Murray offers the following response: "I am compelled regretfully to agree that he is right. Such is the fact. It may even be that the American community, especially in its 'clerks,' who are the custodians of the public philosophy, is not the repository of the tradition of reason on any moral issue that you would like to name" (Murray 1960: 291). Then Murray goes on say that "this ancient tradition lives, if you will, within the Catholic community; but this community fails to bring it into vital relation with the problems of foreign policy" (Murray 1960: 291). From there, he examines other possible groups in the nation – those who espouse "a sentimental subjectivist scriptural fundamentalism," "the school of the ambiguist," those who favor "the pseudo-morality of secular liberalism," and finally "the ubiquitous pragmatist" – and in each case the finding is the same: they are not a "repository of the tradition of reason". This brings Murray to draw the following conclusion:

> It would seem, therefore, that the moral footing has been eroded from beneath the political principle of consent, which has now come to designate nothing more than the technique of majority opinion as the guide for public action – a technique as apt to produce fatuity in policy and tyranny of rule as to produce wisdom and justice. It was not always so. In the constitutional theory of the West the principle of consent found its moral basis in the belief, which was presumed sufficiently to be the fact, that the people are the living repository of a moral tradition, possessed at least as a heritage of wisdom, that enables them to know what is reasonable in the action of the state – in its laws, its public policies, its uses of force. The people consent because it is reasonable to consent to what, with some evidence, appears as reasonable. Today no such moral tradition lives among the American people. As Professor Hartt suggests, the tradition of reason, which is known as the ethic of natural law, is dead. Those who seek the ironies of history should find one here, in

the fact that the ethic which launched Western constitutionalism and endured long enough as a popular heritage to give essential form to the American system of government has now ceased to sustain the structure and direct the action of this constitutional commonwealth. (Murray 1960: 293–4)

The conclusion Murray draws is that natural law has not been adhered to, the tradition of reason has lost its force, thus "the American consensus" no longer exists.

This conclusion poses a decisive challenge to Murray's overall argument, for the compatibility of US democracy with Catholicism rests on the existence of an American consensus that emerged out of Catholic political thought. If there is no American consensus here and now, then the distinction Murray posited between the European "masses" and the American "people" does not hold. And if this distinction does not hold, the people of the United States will continue to act as "idiots" in Murray's sense. It may be that the Catholic supernaturalists were right to note that politics in the United States was adrift owing to a lack of a supernatural goal. This would explain why Murray's positions on any number of political and legal issues, from nuclear weapons to selective conscientious objection to abortion, have never prevailed in public discourse.

For Murray, this would only increase the sense of responsibility of those formed in the tradition of natural law to articulate the American consensus. Thus the final chapter in *We Hold These Truths* is a clarion call to renew the natural law tradition. But then the question becomes: How long do we wait for the consensus to appear? How long should Christians continue to kill and die for a social order fundamentally at variance with the church's understanding of genuine political community? If Murray was right that the church is the only living repository of the moral tradition, then loyalty to Christ, to the politics of Jesus, must be in fundamental tension with loyalty to the nation-state.

In the years since Murray's death, Catholic social ethicists in the United States have dedicated themselves to pursuing Murray's agenda. But the American consensus remains as elusive as it was in Murray's day; indeed, more elusive. With time, this will no longer point to the plausibility of Murray's compatibility thesis, but rather to its implausibility.

References

Appleby, R. Scott, and Haas, John (1995). "The Last Supernaturalists: Fenton, Connell, and the Threat of Catholic Indifferentism." *US Catholic Historian* 13: 23–48.

Connell, Francis J. (1948). "Christ the King of Civil Rulers," *American Ecclesiastical Review* 119 (October), 244–53.

Curran, Charles (1982). *American Catholic Social Ethics*. Notre Dame, Ind.: University of Notre Dame Press.

Murray, John Courtney (1942). "Christian Co-operation," *Theological Studies* 3 (September), 413–31.

——(1948). "St. Robert Bellarmine on the Indirect Power." *Theological Studies* 9: 491–535.

——(1953). "Leo XIII: Separation of Church and State." *Theological Studies* 14: 145–214.

——(1954). "Leo XIII: Two Concepts of Government. II: Government and the Order of Culture." *Theological Studies* 15: 1–33.

——(1960). *We Hold These Truths.* New York: Sheed & Ward.

Neuhaus, Richard (1987). *The Catholic Moment.* San Francisco: Harper & Row.

Pelotte, Donald E., SSS (1976). *John Courtney Murray: Theologian in Conflict.* Ramsey, NJ: Paulist.

Ryan, John A., and Millar, Moorhouse F. X., SJ, eds. (1922). *The State and the Church.* New York: Macmillan.

Sheedy, Charles E., CSC (1949). *The Christian Virtues.* Notre Dame, Ind.: University of Notre Dame Press.

Weigel, George (1987). *Tranquilitas Ordinis.* Oxford: Oxford University Press.

CHAPTER 12
William Temple

Alan M. Suggate

Temple's Background and Life

The Anglican tradition has several longstanding hallmarks that merit reaffirmation, and in some quarters retrieval, in political theology today: (a) the close relating of the inner life of the church in worship and sacrament to its engagement with the life of the world; (b) attention to scripture and its bearing on the world, with a commitment to mediation over against simplistic deduction; (c) a determination to grasp what is going on in the world in its complexity, and attention to the relevant empirical disciplines; (d) a constructive yet critical sensitivity to movements and institutions in society, including the potentiality of the state for good or ill; (e) an enduring commitment to natural morality and the role of reason in articulating faith and morals and in enabling dialogue with others for a more humane social order; and (f) a belief that there is much wisdom in accumulated historical experience in both church and society.

William Temple was the quintessential Anglican. When he was born in 1881, his father Frederick (1821–1902) was already Bishop of Exeter, and destined to go on to London and Canterbury. Frederick and other leading Anglicans initiated William into the whole Anglican tradition, and especially its liberal catholicism.

At Rugby School William imbibed the ethos instilled by its famous headmaster, Thomas Arnold (1795–1842): intellectual seriousness and social conscience, whereby the privileged were to show leadership in improving social conditions. He accepted Arnold's view that the existence of nations was part of divine providence, and that the kingdoms of the world were to be incorporated into the kingdom of Christ. At Balliol College, Oxford, he was immersed in the dominant British Hegelian tradition, which sought a comprehensive rational understanding of reality, thus reflecting the confidence and optimism of the late Victorian and Edwardian eras. He favored the variant which stressed the centrality of personality. Inspired by Edward Caird, Master of Balliol, in both philosophy and social concern, Temple joined the Christian Social Union, which owed much to the Christian socialist tradition inspired by F. D. Maurice and J. M. Ludlow, and also the Workers' Educational Association. Educational opportunity, political responsibility, and justice in industry and economics remained of vital importance to him to his dying day.

Under these influences, and by natural temperament, Temple developed a Christian philosophy. In *Mens Creatrix* (1917) he declared that the philosophic task was to think clearly and comprehensively about the problems of life. He assumed that the universe was rational, and that by reason the human mind could grasp it whole. He believed the world's principle of unity embraced not only the intellect but imagination and conscience too; the sciences, arts, morality and religion. All these converged toward, but did not meet in, an all-embracing system of truth. Temple then adopted the Christian hypothesis, centrally the Incarnation, to supply the missing unity. Undeterred by World War I, he tried in *Christus Veritas* (1924) to construct a Christocentric metaphysic rooted in the Incarnation. Within it he crystallized a set of principles, centered on the nature of persons, for addressing social questions, and these were deployed at the 1924 Conference on Christian Politics, Economics and Citizenship (COPEC), which Temple convened and chaired. His thinking on Christianity and the state was meanwhile developing in *Church and Nation* (1915), essays he wrote for the quarterly Pilgrim (some were published in *Essays in Christian Politics* in 1927), *Christ in His Church* (1925), and *Christianity and the State* (1928).

The idealism of COPEC was rapidly challenged by the strikes of 1926 and the financial crises from 1929. Temple's Gifford Lectures of 1932–4, *Nature, Man and God*, were the culmination of his quest for a Christian philosophy. Tracing the emergence of mind and spirit from matter, he argued for a sacramental universe, and stressed the explanatory force of the notion of purpose in arguing for theism. He emphasized character and will (defined as the whole personality coordinated for action) in the formation and pursuit of human purpose. He also recognized more frankly the radical nature of human evil.

Temple's thinking from 1934 to his death in 1944 was challenged by the impact of Nazi power and his encounters with European and North American theologians, notably Emil Brunner and Reinhold Niebuhr, especially in connection with the international ecumenical conference on Church, Community, and State at Oxford in 1937. His *Christian Democracy* of that year was consciously an answer to the irrational and godless totalitarianisms of Europe. In the late 1930s Temple was writing that it was no longer possible to aspire to a Christocentric synthesis, for much in this evil world was irrational and unintelligible. Christians were being pressed from a theology of incarnation towards a theology of redemption. The task was not to explain the world but to convert it. This had to be the work of divine grace (DCE 16f.; cf. TWT 94–103).

His change of mind was not simple. He suspended the metaphysical quest, but did not repudiate the role of reason. He expressly rejected the Barthian road. He listened to the Anglo-Catholic Christendom Group and gave it prominence at the

Malvern Conference of 1941. He could see the force of the critique mounted by the young Donald MacKinnon against the smooth syntheses of the older generation of theologians. However, Temple had serious reservations about the Group's project, in the face of totalitarianism and liberalism, of restoring Christendom by defining a Christian social order resting on dogma. He wisely preferred to remain more broadly liberal. His *Citizen and Churchman* (1941) was in continuity with earlier writings on church and state, but it dwelt more on the tensions between the two roles rather than on their complementarity. His *Christianity and Social Order* (1942) carried forward much of his earlier social theology but also reflected his concern with the harsh realities of the world. It gave Christian citizens the impetus and tools to wrestle with the urgent social issues of the day and join in shaping the postwar era. Temple also urged consideration of the catholic natural law tradition, and in 1943 he addressed the Aquinas Society on "Thomism and Modern Needs". In the last year of his life he published "What Christians Stand for in the Secular World" (repr. RE 243–55), by which he wished to be remembered. He agreed with V. A. Demant of the Christendom Group that in the face of powerful ideologies like fascism and communism it was not enough to proclaim ideals and appeal to the will to attain them. Rather, one had to heal the gulf between people's ideals and their ultimate assumptions, for the crisis was not so much moral as cultural. Following Niebuhr, he stressed the need to face up to the egoistic use of power and to pursue justice.

I focus on these later, more mature works, but draw on earlier ones wherever the content appears to remain valid of Temple in later life. I first explore Temple's broad position on church and state, and then his Christian perspectives on politics. Finally, I briefly evaluate his thought and the continuing tradition he represents.

Church and State

Historical relations

Temple concentrates his attention not on the Constantinian settlement but on the experiment of Christendom in the Middle Ages. Church and state were two activities of one international society. The church, as repository and trustee of revelation, attempted to control the state. This was in principle laudable; but the papacy used methods of force appropriate to civil government. The result was an acute secularization of the church and the forfeiture of its spiritual authority. Moreover, in claiming all spiritual activity for itself, it tended to weaken the moral power of the state and reduce it to a mere mechanism for maintaining order (CIC 63; CN 43; cf. CC 9–23).

In protest, the Reformation strongly insisted upon the purely spiritual character of religion, but unfortunately narrowed its range to the individual. This shift was reinforced by Machiavelli, who hastened the emancipation of politics from the control of religion. The state became an end in itself. Christendom was fragmented into rival entities, and most settlements separated church and state (CIC 44, 63–6).

Temple's position

Temple infers from this history a position on establishment. The state must not control religion, nor must the church overstep its own proper function or use the state to coerce in the spiritual sphere. Basically, since the church has a divine commission, establishment is a matter not for the church but for the state. Its real meaning is that the state, by associating itself with the church, proclaims its own recognition that the church has a divine commission and allegiance (CC 38; CIC 73). Actually, Temple increasingly valued establishment for the opportunities it offered the church to guide society, and his own aim was for the voluntary acceptance of a kind of ecumenical Christian commonwealth on a national and international scale. This was all very visionary, scarcely reckoning either with the secularity of society, or with other religions, or with the problematical nature of the church itself. His later thinking tries hard to hold together the vision and social realities.

Temple calls for a new differentiation of functions between church and state. The starting point needs to be the relation of the church to the kingdom of God. The kingdom is neither a purely apocalyptic cataclysm at the end of time, nor an entity built by the personal and civic virtues of human beings. "The Kingdom of God is indeed established by God alone. In part it is here already . . . ; in part it is yet to come through God's action in His own time" (RE 135). For because of human sin the kingdom cannot come in its perfection within human history. "History is not leading us to any form of perfected civilisation which, once established, will abide. It is a process of preparing the way for something outside history all together – the perfected Kingdom of God" (CC 14).

The key instrument of preparation is the church. The church is the creation of God. The supreme service it can render to the world is to be in very deed the church. Its first task is neither missionary extension nor influence upon national life but inward sanctification. The first task of Christians is to worship God and be sanctified. However, Christianity is the most materialistic of all the world's great religions. The Eucharist focuses the sacramentality of all life. Therefore, "The Eucharist divorced from life loses reality; life devoid of worship loses direction and power. It is the worshipping life that can transform the world." The Christian faith is not a system of morals, but a sharing in a new movement of life that has entered into history, and the kingdom of God is a transcendent reality which is continually seeking, and partially achieving, embodiment in the activities and conflicts of the temporal order. Without it, politics and even the ethical struggle might be finally deprived of real significance and we might succumb to a complete secularization of life in which all principles disintegrate in pure relativity, and opportunism is the only wisdom (CC 40, 85–8; TWT 46; RE 254).

In light of this thought, Temple has a complex understanding of the relation between church and state, churchman and citizen. There is bound to be a tension in the soul of the Christian citizen, because on the one hand the church has a revelation which is unique, final, and universal, and on the other hand the state acts for the community with a universal sovereign authority, backed by force. A completely Christian state has never been fulfilled; indeed, it never will or can be. We shall always live in communities with a range of belief and maturity. The problem cannot be solved by making the state absolute in the place of God, as the Nazis did, nor by allocating church and state to entirely separate spheres, as in Lutheran pietism. "No; Church and State . . . have the same sphere – the life of man – but they have different functions in relation to that one sphere; and the Christian citizen has to fulfil his Churchmanship and his citizenship in the whole of his life by responding at all points to the appropriate claims of Church and State" (CC 12f., 65f.). Temple sets out the relation along several avenues, which I summarize (CC 66ff.).

First, the state stands for justice, the church for love. The state is not an end in itself; it is a means to the good life of its citizens. Temple doubts whether the totalitarian claim can be resisted on any humanist basis. The worth of each person and the consequent equality of all are rooted in the reality of God. So is justice, construed as regard for each and every individual. It is particularly concerned with persons or parties having distinct interests which may come into conflict. It therefore appears to apply where love is not supreme. Now, the church calls on all to live by a perfect love which would supersede justice altogether. But even if every individual were rooted in love, justice would not be obsolete. For the chief problems of modern life concern the mutual relations of corporate groups. Love in the hearts of individuals will ease the task of settling those relations, but the church can urge love irrelevantly in public affairs, where it should give primary emphasis to the virtue of justice which is the special concern of the state. Love in such circumstances cannot leave justice behind; rather, the way of love lies through justice, for example through the arbitration of conflicting interests. Christians cannot leave the influence of the Gospel without effect upon this area of human experience until all are devout. In the meantime the Christian citizen should be dedicated to the establishment of justice in the power of the motive of love. "Of course, perfect justice will not be reached; . . . perfect justice is a product of perfect love, not a stage on the way to it." Here one detects the influence of Reinhold Niebuhr's dialectical relating of love and justice.

Second, for the state the material basis of life is primary; for the church the spiritual source and goal is primary. For Temple this distinction is broadly valid, but one cannot say simply that the church is spiritual and the state material. Temple's own sacramental theology forbids it. The state must have some principles to guide its promotion of the good life of its citizens. Moreover, if human beings have an eternal destiny beyond its direct concern, the state should at least not hinder citizens from qualifying for it. The church, for its part, rightly holds property subject to the laws of the state in order to perform its tasks in the world. It has a concern for the basic needs of citizens, and must point out conditions which flout Christian conscience. It cannot advocate specific remedies *qua* church, but it can stimulate those who respect its authority to find and apply a remedy.

Third, the state is the organ of a particular natural community; the church is called to be a universal fellowship of the Spirit. Christians belong to three types of community: the natural communities of family and nation; associations; and the church. Natural communities exist to be themselves, and this entails an egoism. Associations are also capable of egoism, for they involve particular claims to loyalty. Temple believes that there is no hope that sectional loyalties will be checked and set in their right perspective unless there is an overarching loyalty. Christian citizens cannot escape from their citizenship, nor should they try to eliminate narrower loyalties. Rather, they should interpret their citizenship in light of their Christian faith, and check narrower loyalties by reference to wider. Consciousness of belonging to the church will enable this. For the church is in its aim (whatever its failings) an all-inclusive fellowship, the proper object of such an overarching loyalty.

Christianity and Politics

The history of political theory

Temple typically seeks a synthesis of the merits of rival political theories (CS 43–90). He detects two broad types. The first, which he backs, treats political society as a natural growth. As Aristotle saw, human beings are social creatures, and the state arises naturally, first to preserve life and then to promote the good life. The theorists of this type, for example Montesquieu and Vico, tend to avoid abstractions and reflect on the histories of actual societies and states. Temple criticizes Burke for an almost absurd conservatism on some issues, for his mystical view of the state, and indeed for identifying society and state. But Burke did have a vivid sense of history and its continuity, eloquently expressed in his denunciation of revolutionaries who treated society like a machine.

As for the Hegelians, Temple agrees with T. H. Green that law is not only a means whereby I restrain the liberty of others to injure me (as the utilitarians believed), but also a means by which I secure my own liberty to live as a good citizen against my own occasional desires to act otherwise. Green also rightly insisted, following Mazzini, that true social progress had to be founded not on rights but on duties. However, Hegel was wrong to treat the national state as an incarnation of the Absolute. Moreover, Temple refuses to say that society is an "organism"; for its components are persons, independent in judgment and self-directing in purpose.

The other type is social contract theory, referring to the initiation either of society or of government or of both simultaneously. In Plato's *Republic* Glauco gives classic expression to the first. Theories in Christian times were concerned more with government. St. Paul's "The powers that be are ordained of God" committed the church to some form of divine right. The problem was how it was conferred and under what conditions. Both Jesuits and Calvinists developed ideas of popular sovereignty. They did not believe in liberty, but at least they undermined the theory of absolute sovereignty. It is no surprise that Temple rejected Thomas Hobbes.

For Temple, social contract theories do contain partial truths. Glauco's and Hobbes's gloomy view of human nature is grossly defective, but true so far as society is expressed by the police and the penal system. Moreover, social contract theories can well illustrate dissatisfaction with the organization of society: the power of government so easily corrupts those who hold it, and political institutions adapt too slowly to changed circumstances. The importance of contract theory is that sovereignty is an organ of society with its own proper function, which can be transgressed. It can reflect a commendable desire to combine efficient administration, obedience to the law, and freedom. It also bears witness to the belief that the state rests in the last resort on consent and not on force.

Temple declares that the upshot of this survey can be put in terms of the Social Gospel.

> By common consent the two first principles in the Gospel as applied to social order are the Sanctity of Personality and the Fact of Fellowship . . . By God's appointment we are free spirits; by his appointment also we are "members one of another". The whole problem of politics, the whole art of statesmanship, is to do full justice to both those principles without the sacrifice of either in the varying circumstances of successive ages. (CS 89)

Social principles and politics

Temple's social principles are integral to his Christian philosophy and survived the questioning of the late 1930s. They lie at the center of his *Christianity and Social Order*. However, their exposition is preceded by a popular exposition of the doctrine of original sin. "Each of us takes his place in the centre of his own world. But I am not the centre of the world, or the standard of reference as between good and bad; I am not, and God is. In other words, from the beginning I put myself in God's place. This is my original sin." It cannot therefore be the task of the church to sketch a perfect social order and urge people to establish it. Would it be the order that would work best if all were perfect? Or the best order in the world of actual men and women? If the former, it certainly ought not to be attempted; we should wreck it in a fortnight. If the latter, one cannot expect the church to know what it is. Correspondingly, "probably to the end of earthly history statesmen will themselves be men, and will be dealing with men, who abuse freedom and power." A political and economic system is not fundamentally required to express love, though that is desirable, nor justice, though that is the first ethical demand upon it, but to supply some reasonable measure of security against robbery, murder, and starvation. "Its assertion of Original Sin should make the Church intensely realistic, and conspicuously free from Utopianism" (CSO 36–8, cf. 42).

Temple thus speaks not of ideals but of principles. The first two are crucial for our purposes. First, "If each man and woman is a child of God, whom God loves and for whom Christ died, then there is in each a worth absolutely independent of all usefulness to society. The person is primary, not the society; the State exists for the citizen, not the citizen for the State." All distinctly personal qualities should be given the fullest possible scope; the most fundamental is deliberate choice. Freedom is the goal of politics: not simply freedom from compulsion or restraint, but freedom for forming and carrying out a purpose. This implies discipline – at first external, but afterwards a self-discipline. "To train citizens in the capacity for freedom and to give them scope for free action is the supreme end of all true politics" (CSO 44f.).

Second, human beings are naturally and incurably social, and by our mutual influence we actually constitute one another as we are. This influence occurs first in the family, and then in the variegated associations of society intermediate between the family and the state. It is here that liberty is effective; people feel they count for something and that they are mutually dependent. The state should foster all such groupings, giving them freedom to guide their own activities, provided they fall within the general order of the communal life and respect the freedom of other associations (CSO 46–8).

The church can use these principles to make critiques of the existing society (Temple illustrates from long-term unemployment), and then suggest directions in which society should move in order to correspond more closely to the principles. These directions are often called "middle axioms", being intermediate between principles and programs. Temple gives examples in the fields of housing, education, income, industry, and leisure. The church has now reached the limit of its competence, and must hand over to Christian citizens, acting in their civic capacity, the task of working out programs conducive to the well-being of the citizens, in other words the common good, in the circumstances. Here there are questions not only about technique, but also about the social psychology of a mass of citizens (CSO 12, 79, 35f.). In an appendix, rightly distinct from the rest of the book, Temple makes some suggestions for a social program embodying Christian principles, but warns that there can be no program which all Christians ought to support.

Consistently with this method, in *Nature, Man and God* Temple adopted the ethical theory of ideal utilitarianism. His social principles provided the deontological component, but in the estimate of acts he believed that the right thing to do was the best in the circumstances (1934: 192f.).

It was thus no use Christians trying to act as churchpeople in the world, only to find that the world refused to be ordered on principles proper to the church. Nor could they just look out for the secular policy most congenial to them, only to find that their Christianity was merely a dispensable adjunct. They needed to cooperate with all who shared their social aims, but they should also be clear about their distinctive Christian grounds. Temple became increasingly worried, with Demant, about the effectiveness of purely this-worldly philosophies, such as fascism and communism, and saw a sharp difference of thought, and in the long run of practice, between Christians and others (RE 243–6).

Natural order

Alongside the method of principles Temple spoke interchangeably of "natural order" or "natural law." He was rather ambivalent about its basis and relation to the Christian faith. He described it as "the proper function of a human activity as apprehended by a consideration of its own nature," discovered in practice partly by observing the generally accepted standards of judgment. This was a task for human reason. Thus it was a natural, not a supernatural order; but as God was the Creator, this natural order was his order and its law his law (CSO 57). Thus even after 1937 Temple held it possible for people of varying beliefs to agree on certain basic truths about human beings. But he was increasingly aware of the vulnerability of these truths, particularly faced with the phenomenon of Nazism. Indeed, confronted with the attitude which privatized religion, he once went so far as to say that the principles which permeated civilization derived all their validity from faith in God (HNW 10). So he was also very keen that Christians should see those truths as integral to their own faith and crucial to the survival of civilization. He promoted cooperation between Anglicans and Roman Catholics over the concept of natural order. Temple's ambivalence has subsequently been resolved best by the more radical moral theologians of the post-Vatican II Catholic Church, who have spoken of the natural being graced, and have held together theory and historical practice.

Christian democracy

Temple rejected certain exaggerated claims for democracy. The first is that there is an inherent sovereignty in the people. True, all government rests in the last resort on consent. But there are grave difficulties in knowing who "the people" are, and in the French Revolution the resumption of popular sovereignty was marked by cant and fanaticism. "Inherent sovereignty is an attribute of no human person or collection of persons; it is an attribute only of the Moral Law, and of God who is Himself the Moral Law in personal form. Only to God and to Right is an absolute allegiance due." Our earthly contrivances of government are makeshift at best (ECP 70).

Second, *vox populi, vox Dei* is nonsense. The mob were not right in the French Revolution massacres. And the people seldom has a single mind and purpose. Democracy always means in effect the rule of the majority. The majority is not always wise; indeed, the best opinions are mostly held by a small minority. But maybe the majority is more often nearly right than any minority. "And that is as far as it seems safe to go along this road in asserting the claims of democracy" (ECP 70f.; CD 28). Temple has much deeper reasons for espousing democracy.

He argued that a community trained in democratic politics is likely to be more richly developed and more stable than any other. For democracy is a form of constitution which does most justice to the nature of human beings as God made them. In the 1920s Temple had emphasized democracy's roots and inspiration in the concern for individual personality. By 1937, probably under the influence of Reinhold Niebuhr and the crisis in Europe, he extended that basis: democracy "more than any other form of constitution corresponds to the full Christian conception of man – man 'fallen', i.e. selfish, and therefore needing to be governed, and that, too, by force; but man created 'in the image of God,' and therefore capable of responding to moral appeal . . . " (CD 28–30, cf. 40).

Democracy is no panacea. It makes greater demands on the moral resources of a nation than any other form of constitution. It gives a universal outlet for selfishness. A majority may easily become tyrannous; people may succumb to propaganda or the herd instinct; rights may predominate over duties. So far as democracy becomes a mere welter of competing self-interests, it is on the way to perishing and will deserve its doom (CD 29–31; CIC 84f.; ECP 72–80; HNW 22–6). The "most insidious temptation" is the association of democracy with nationalism. Nationalism is a by-product of the democratic movement. "One of the perils . . . is that we shall turn out the Machiavellian Prince to establish a still more dangerous tyrant in the form of a majority acting on Machiavellian principles" (CIC 87f.; CD 13, 23).

There are three tests by which it can be known whether democracy is true to its own root principle: the depth of its concern for justice to individuals; the careful regard which it pays to the rights of minorities; and the scrupulous respect which it offers to individual conscience. The last is the most vital. Respect for the conscientious objector is a hallmark of true democracy (ECP 77).

In the face of these perils and tests, Temple asserts the necessity of a Christian democracy. He believes that democracy is a Christian product in fact, and a necessary result of Christianity in principle, because it was in and through Christianity that the real meaning of personality was revealed. Democracy should therefore recognize its source and allow Christian principles to govern it (CIC 77f., 85).

However, this does not mean that Temple simply deduces democracy from revelation. His pamphlet *Christian Democracy* is not about democracy per se, but illustrates a principle that extends far beyond it. "Democracy with its freedom of thought and speech can be the best and most natural means in the political field of giving full scope to reason . . . The principle with which we are concerned is that of the necessary alliance of Christianity, when true to itself, with reason, and with rational methods." Temple saw himself writing at a time when the Christian tradition was challenged as never since Constantine, and when reason was openly decried. Reason is not synonymous with Christianity; it could never have discovered it, and can never prove it. But there is an intrinsic kinship between the ultimate intuitions of Christian faith and reason. Both communism and fascism are irrational, encouraging a blind faith which violently suppresses any criticism. They appeal to subconscious egoism. Thus they cannot abide the free play of reason, with its universalizing tendency (CD 9–16, 32f., 42). Though the church has by no means always stood for the authority of reason and the free play of critical intelligence, Christian theology has been deeply committed to the appeal to reason.

Christianity is itself a spring of continual progress; for what Christ left the world was not a system of theology or a code of rules for life, but a living fellowship of men and women united in his spirit. That spirit is a permanent ferment of unrest. Because Christianity is the most materialistic of all the great religions, it also affirms the material developments in civilization and the secular knowledge on which they rest, in spite of the temptations they bring. "The social life of man is part of the Divine purpose in Creation, and what is requisite for its maintenance is part of the Divine activity in preserving what Creation has called into being. This is the theological justification of the State and all its apparatus." Law, by its own essential quality of universality, is an expression of reason. The exercise of force for the maintenance of law against lawbreakers is in principle the subjection of force to reason. Determining how best the principles of social life are to be implemented is also a work of reason. It involves reasoning with those who differ from oneself. Reliance upon reason is at once an expression of the spirit of charity and a generating source of it. "When Christianity ceases to regard reason as its chief ally it is false to its own genius"(CD 21, 38–44).

International relations

As the church is to a particular nation, so the world church should be to the international community. And just as the function of the individual state is to promote freedom and fellowship, so the aim must be to create a harmony of independent nations, seeking justice and the common good internationally. Citizenship remains a key concept for Temple.

Confronted twice with world war, Temple was no pacifist. He subscribed to just war theory, and considered pacifism as a universal principle to be heretical in tendency (York Diocesan Leaflet, Nov. 1935). This position was based on three considerations. First, the Gospel fulfills the law and the prophets, and does not supersede them. The kingdoms of the world have their place by God's appointment, with powers and rights to be exercised in obedience to God's laws. If necessary, we must check the aggressor and set free the oppressed (RE 176). Second, we are willy-nilly members of societies and citizens, and need to engage in the civic enterprise of justice, not stand aside from it (KG 86f., 91; TWT 28f.). Force is an indispensable element in the ordering of life, to be used according to that law which expresses the highest welfare of humanity. Temple's sacramental sense led him (rather unwisely) to use here the phrase "the consecration of force" (Church Assembly Report, 4 Feb. 1932; "Education for Peace", Birkbeck College, 18 June 1941). Third, human beings are incapable of living by love unless converted and sanctified by the grace of God. Nations fall radically short. All are therefore entangled in sin, and for that condition one needs not only a theology of the church but a theology of the state, involving obligations for Christian citizens. Temple declared that the universal pacifists he knew lacked such a theology of the state (*York Diocesan Leaflet*, Nov. 1935; CW 10–13; SLL 138).

Temple respected individual universal pacifists and conscientious objectors as witnesses to important but partial truth. He was also aware of some of the tensions in his position. He knew the perils of the use of force, and urged Britons to remember the purpose for which they were fighting: the cause of international law and civilization. They must, therefore, not use methods incompatible with that purpose (TWT 9; RE 178). "We have to do the best we can, being what we are, in the circumstances where we are – and then God be merciful to us sinners!" (Iremonger 1948: 542f.).

Evaluation

Temple's position was not greatly criticized in his lifetime, as he led a virtual consensus. Stephen Spencer (1990) has shown that the early Temple's historicist tendencies include the idea that history carries its own meaning without reference to an eternal world, that the state brings social fulfillment by coercing us into freedom, and that moral duty consists in following the conventions of society and the state. These reflected British Hegelianism. Spencer argues that Temple checked this drift, largely by introducing ideas of different provenance, so that in a piecemeal fashion his historicism declined. The Hegelian influence was indeed powerful and did decline, but from the start there were other strands at work, including Plato and the Christian socialist tradition. Crucial for Temple was his Christian faith, especially the Incarnation. He used Hegelian and other ideas as ways of exploring its meaning.

Temple responded well to the challenges from Donald MacKinnon and Reinhold Niebuhr. MacKinnon pressed Temple further away from smooth syntheses towards a theology of the cross. It is fashionable now to denigrate Niebuhr as a dogmatic pessimist who capitulated to American liberalism. This is not true of him at the height of his powers around 1940, and Temple rightly came to adopt virtually a Niebuhrian position on love and justice. Temple is superior to Niebuhr in his social principles and method of mediation (ideal utilitarianism), his attitudes to natural order, and his sense of the church and sacraments in working out a position on church, society, and state. Two contemporaries of Temple did not commend themselves. His arch-critic Hensley Henson rightly carried little weight because of his own excessive individualism. As for Karl Barth, Temple agreed with the impassable distinction between Creator and creature, and with the necessity of revelation as altogether other than rational inference from experience. But for Temple revelation had to vindicate its claim at the bar of reason and conscience. Quite how he would have further addressed the tension between revelation and reason in the light of sin is impossible to say, but he would not have sided with Barth.

No tradition worthy of the name stands still, and this Anglican tradition has been deployed and developed in the work of the Church of England Board for Social Responsibility and by theologians such as Ronald H. Preston, who has drawn on many sources, particularly Temple and Niebuhr, in elaborating his social theology. This tradition has striking affinities with post-Vatican II Roman Catholic social ethics in northern Europe and North America.

In recent years there have been many challenges to it. Liberative theologies, including black and feminist theologies, rightly press the perspective of the oppressed and marginalized, and take a more critical view of the political and economic status quo than Temple. They warn against a danger with the Temple approach, particularly in the framing of middle axioms: a comfortable accommodation of Christianity to the powers that be, through the supposition that Christian leaders or experts can easily speak with secular authorities in the interests of all. Ronald Preston is well aware of this danger and has argued that the method is quite consistent with concern for the marginalized. Some criticize Temple's method for being too abstract and deductive, pleading for more flexibility and attention to people's stories. In fact Temple recommended a dialectical movement between one's understanding of the faith and one's experience of living in the world. Principles are guides to action, but are themselves tested, clarified, and, if necessary, revised in the light of experience of living. Liberative theologies, however, have difficulties of their own. There is a tendency to demonize globalization, to despair of the political and economic task nationally and internationally, and to put one's faith in the local. Some, such as the Korean Minjung theologian Kim Yong-Bock, look to a kairotic inbreaking of the kingdom of God in favor of "the people". But it is very doubtful whether "the people" can be so easily identified, what relation they have to faith, and whether one should write off any attempt to ameliorate the current situation. The Temple tradition certainly needs to attend more closely to liberative theologies, and has been learning to be less trustful of state power, but it is better equipped to deal more constructively with the inescapable global complexities confronting us in the interim.

Other theological and philosophical challenges to the tradition represented by Temple have come from Alasdair MacIntyre and Stanley Hauerwas. MacIntyre's account of the collapse of the Enlightenment project into interminable debates between rival and incommensurable ethical positions, and Hauerwas' accent on the church as a community of character which is itself a social ethic, have both inspired versions of ethics which stress Christian distinctiveness. Thus within the Anglican Church itself we find the ethics of Michael Banner (Barthian), Oliver O'Donovan (evangelical, recovering a political theology and ethics from the resources of the Bible and earlier Christian tradition) and John Milbank (catholic, pressing a grand Christian narrative against ideology).

Temple had much to say, particularly in his later years, about the vital importance of the church. Those who stand in that tradition can readily agree on the distinctiveness of the Christian story and the importance of Christian communities of character. However, in Britain at least, church and society have been interwoven for centuries, for better or worse. There are no pure ecclesial communities of character. The church remains ever under judgment and problematical, as does talk of a grand Christian narrative. Nor does a strong ecclesiology render otiose or objectionable dialogue with others concerning our common humanity. MacIntyre himself holds that dialogue, though more difficult, is still possible, and Jeffrey Stout and others have pointed to many areas of collaboration in a pluralistic postmodernist world. Indeed, given today's huge tensions it is all the more necessary to pursue dialogue. The Temple tradition has rightly adhered to the possibility of some form of natural morality, centered on the understanding of persons in society. In the order of being, the natural is not a sphere wholly distinct from Christianity; it is graced. In the order of knowledge, human beings of whatever religious or other persuasion do have the capacity to reflect on their fundamental humanity and find some common ground. Christians, like everyone else, inhabit many communities, and concern with Christian character cannot displace questions about action in the world. In determining that action we shall still need to use mediation, grappling with the complexities and sifting through the deliverances of the social sciences. Accommodation to secular ideologies is a constant danger, but not inevitable. While remaining critical and seeking possible alternatives, it is vital to secure a purchase on social and global movements, and to explore the potential of existing institutions for furthering human well-being. There are good theological grounds for exercising reason in this way in the interim before the final coming of the kingdom.

Select Bibliography

Temple's main writings on social and political theology

CC   *Citizen and Churchman.* London: Eyre and Spottiswoode, 1941.

CD   *Christian Democracy.* London: SCM Press, 1937.

CIC   *Christ in His Church.* London: Macmillan, 1925.

CN   *Church and Nation.* London: Macmillan, 1915.

CS   *Christianity and the State.* London: Macmillan, 1928.

CSO   *Christianity and Social Order,* Harmondsworth: Penguin, 1942.

CW   *Christianity and War.* London: Oxford University Press, 1914.

DCE   Chairman's Introduction. In *Doctrine in the Church of England,* London, SPCK, 1–18, 1938.

ECP   *Essays in Christian Politics and Kindred Subjects.* London: Longmans Green, 1927.

HNW   *The Hope of a New World,* London: SCM Press, 1940.

KG   *The Kingdom of God.* London: Macmillan, 1912.

RE   *Religious Experience and other Essays and Addresses,* ed. A. E. Baker. London: James Clarke, 1958.

SLL   *Some Lambeth Letters, 1942–1944,* ed. F. S. Temple. London: Oxford University Press, 1963.

TWT   *Thoughts in War-Time.* London: Macmillan, 1940.

Temple's main philosophical works

Mens Creatrix. London: Macmillan, 1917.
Christus Veritas. London: Macmillan, 1924.
Nature, Man and God. London: Macmillan, 1934.

Works related to Temple

Bayer, Oswald and Suggate, Alan M., eds. (1996). *Worship and Ethics: Lutherans and Anglicans in Dialogue*. Berlin: Walter de Gruyter. (Suggate's two essays: "The Anglican Tradition of Moral Theology," 2–25; "In Search of a Eucharistic Social Ethic," 164–86.)
Craig, Robert (1963). *Social Concern in the Thought of William Temple*. London: Gollancz.
Fletcher, Joseph (1963). *William Temple, Twentieth-Century Christian*. New York: Seabury.
Hastings, Adrian (1991). *A History of English Christianity 1920–1990*. London: Collins.
Iremonger, F. A. (1948). *William Temple, Archbishop of Canterbury: His Life and Letters*. London: Oxford University Press.
Kent, John (1992). *William Temple: Church, State and Society in Britain 1880–1950*. Cambridge: Cambridge University Press.
Lowry, Charles W. (1982). *William Temple: An Archbishop for All Seasons*. Washington: University Press of America.
MacKinnon, D. M. (1941). "Revelation and Social Justice." In *Malvern 1941*, 81–116. London: Longmans, Green.
Matthews, W. R. et al. (1946). *William Temple: An Estimate and an Appreciation*. London: James Clarke.
Norman, E. R. (1976). *Church and Society in England 1770–1970*. Oxford: Clarendon.
Oliver, John (1968). *The Church and Social Order: Social Thought in the Church of England, 1918–1939*. London: Mowbray.
Padgett, Jack F. (1974). *The Christian Philosophy of William Temple*. The Hague: Nijhoff.
Preston, Ronald H. (1981). "William Temple as a Social Theologian." *Theology* 84 (Sept. 1981), 334–41.
Ramsey, A. M. (1960). *From Gore to Temple: The Development of Anglican Theology between* Lux Mundi *and the Second World War, 1889–1939*. London: Longman.
Spencer, Stephen C. (1990). "The Decline of Historicism in William Temple's Social Thought." D.Phil. thesis, Oxford University.
Suggate, Alan M. (1987). *William Temple and Christian Social Ethics Today*. Edinburgh: T. & T. Clark.

CHAPTER 13
Reinhold Niebuhr

William Werpehowski

I

One way to assess a particular political theology involves attending to its case for human political responsibility, on the one hand, and its claims for critical independence, on the other. Inquiry into the first establishes why and how it is that human creatures ought to be concerned with political communities, and how that concern may be embodied in fitting political activities. Yet if the concern and the actions are, as features of our responsibility *for* political society, finally responsible *to God*, then political theology should acknowledge and make provision for its independence from specific political arrangements or ideals. Otherwise there is a danger that our concerns and activities on behalf of political society issue from a final responsibility *to it*, or to some idealized other, and not to its and our sovereign Lord (H. R. Niebuhr 1946: 123–5).

It is a matter, then, of *free* political responsibility. Karl Barth's reflections on politics, for example, sought to affirm Christian freedom for the "civil community" insofar as it is aligned with the divine summons to establish bonds of "fellow humanity" in human relations. This freedom *for* political life is misconstrued if it does not presuppose freedom in independence *from* any political ideology untested by the one Word of God in Jesus Christ. There is no political correlation between Christian faith and cultural and political perspectives exposed by "natural theology"; and the church "trusts and obeys no political system or reality but the power of the Word by which God upholds all things, including all political things" (Barth 1968: 161).

It seems that Reinhold Niebuhr's political ethics can match Barth's in setting a basis for free political responsibility. Niebuhr stood against forms of perfectionist idealism that either flee the conflicts of history in which work for justice takes place, or speak irrelevantly or dangerously to those conflicts. One must acknowledge the fragmentary, partial, and inevitably self-interested perspectives that characterize all political action. While these perspectives in competition foreclose any perfect realization of harmony among and between peoples, however, it is a fact that the norm of human existence is the law of love, which may still find indirect and imperfect expression in history through regulative principles prescribing social equality, liberty, and the like. A realistic political agency ought never to absorb the norm into the principles, since the former always exists in critical tension with embodiments of them, and because no limits approximating the goal of frictionless harmony can be set in advance. Just as the critical impossibility of the ideal of perfect, mutual self-giving in community protects against irresponsible sentimentality, so its critical relevance to every achievement for justice guards against an irresponsible social despair (R. Niebuhr 1979: 64).

There are dissenting voices. Stanley Hauerwas (2001a: 60–1) argues that Reinhold Niebuhr's ethics takes the subject of Christian ethics to be America, and not prophetic Christian faith, let alone the church in which it is formed. Hence "he never questioned the assumption that democracy was the most appropriate form of society and government for Christians" (p. 466). Hans Frei offers another, not unrelated worry in his comparison of the brothers Reinhold and H. Richard Niebuhr. For all of Reinhold's stress on the limits of human rationality and moral sensibility, Frei wonders whether his theological ethics remained adequately contained or contextualized, and therefore limited, on two fronts.

There is, first, the contrast between the brothers' ideas about political agency and human freedom. Reinhold finally maintained a "modern view of human freedom, where even the knowledge of ourselves as limited and not disinterested is simply a function of our originating exercise of agential freedom." This "uninterrupted moral and self-starting initiative on the part of individual persons and especially of human collectivities" may well be the "very opposite" of H. Richard's attempt to build an ethics "dependent on active, divine governance in history," in which our "independence" is "contingent" and our critical freedom is responsive to what God is doing in the world. The upshot for Frei is that Reinhold's ethics more precariously *pitches* or *swerves* to an absence of moral restraint (and self-restraint) in political agency. It may become less qualified, less limited, and less dependent on other agencies acting upon us (as God acts upon us in and with and through all such agencies along with one's own). Hence it may become more one-sided as an expression of a particular or settled political stance (Frei 1993: 231).

On the second front, Frei says that for H. Richard Niebuhr

the chief created agencies under God's governance are not simply the political collectivities of nations and empires . . . divine action is located in the uneasy, at first sign almost ludicrously ill-balanced "polarity" . . . between the nation, or other associated social collectivities, and the church. [His] "radical monotheism" insisted on this polarity because the universality of one sort of group is always henotheistic (we might as well say idolatrous), including, of course, the church. (1993: 231)

The polarity, which is not clearly developed in Reinhold's thought, affords greater protection against idolatry and defensiveness in political life. Both, needless to say, threaten critical independence before God.

Following an exposition of Niebuhr's political ethics in parts II and III of this essay, I consider these criticisms in the final section and propose that, while Niebuhr possesses an array of resources to answer and rebut them, they remain relevant and valid. His case for Christian political responsibility as it stands tends to undermine claims for critical independence. I suggest in conclusion that such claims in political theology require more careful attention to the significance of, first, the practices of the Christian community; second, the lordship of God in history; and third, our discernment of that lordship in its continuing summons to repentance and conversion.

II

Reinhold Niebuhr (1892–1971) was born in Wright City, Missouri, and raised in the German Evangelical Synod (later the Evangelical and Reformed Church). After two years studying at Yale, his work as a pastor in Detroit from 1915 to 1928 exposed him to the burdens and injustices of urban industrial life. He was forced to face the evident irrelevance of his "simple little moral homilies" to these circumstances (R. Niebuhr 1991: 8). He set off next for Union Theological Seminary in New York City, teaching there until his retirement in 1960. Niebuhr produced a large body of writing on political, social, and theological issues, traveled and consulted widely, and earned great influence among political, cultural, and religious leaders.

In the 1930s Niebuhr criticized the "Social Gospel" vision of Washington Gladden, Walter Rauschenbusch, and others. Recognizing the limits of the individualism of nineteenth-century Protestant ethics for responding to the social brutalities of the industrial revolution, the Social Gospel theologians countered with the ethic of Jesus as normative for personal and institutional life. The key here was a doctrine of the kingdom of God, which was deemed in a fashion to be a historical possibility marked by social unity and the overturning of personal and structural assaults on the dignity of persons created by God. Niebuhr (1976: 25) thought that the Social Gospel courted sentimentality and irrelevance because it presented "the law of love as a simple solution for every social problem"; indeed, it was shortsighted and unhelpful in its quest to overcome "the excessive individualism of Christian faith in America . . . because it also preached the same ethic it intended to criticize. It insisted that Christians should practice the law of love not only in personal relations but in the collective relations of mankind. In these relations love as an ecstatic impulse of self-giving is practically impossible."

In contrast to the moralistic tendency to see the church's ministry "to make selfish people unselfish, at least sufficiently unselfish to permit the creation of justice without conflict" (1976: 41), Niebuhr held that an adequate theology of the kingdom of God cannot be removed from an appreciation of the universality of sin in history and of God's thoroughgoing judgment of human vice and pretension. We may strive for the kingdom, "but we do not expect its full realization . . . The Kingdom of God always remains fragmentary and corrupted in history" (1991: 134), since the latter is characterized by self-interested conflicts over power, and because "self-interest and power must be harnessed and beguiled rather than eliminated. In other words, forces which are morally dangerous must be used despite their peril" (1976: 59). Note the critical dialectic. We take responsibility for political goals that are always patient of criticism in terms of an ever-transcending ideal. Overly "idealistic" efforts corrupt realistic responsibility, and yet that responsibility still aspires to the ideal of the kingdom in (still "realistic") ways that forestall premature closure.

Niebuhr's mature theological ethics is based on an interpretation of human nature and its predicament that is very much indebted to the ideas of Augustine, Pascal, and Kierkegaard. The human subject or creature is, on the one hand, finite, limited. Not evil by reason of their limitations, human creatures remain dependent upon the natural world, other persons, and God. They cannot find their fulfillment in a sovereignty of self that denies their very being. On the other hand, the human creature is free, or "indeterminately self-transcendent" with regard to nature, the temporal process, and one's interpersonal environment. Freedom refers, then, to the capacity to evaluate and transform oneself and the world; but it also features the creature's "inability to construct a world of meaning without finding a source and key to the structure of meaning which transcends the world beyond his own capacity to transcend it" (R. Niebuhr 1964a: 164). The qualities of self-transcendence which designate creation "in the image of God" project the person's search for meaning beyond meanings that merely project oneself or one's ideals, however noble or encompassing. Thus Niebuhr (1964a: 158) says that "human life points beyond itself. But it must not make itself that beyond."

While the coincidence of finitude and freedom is the condition for the possibility of creative achievement in history, it also generates anxiety in the form of creaturely insecurity about the individual's dependence and vulnerability. For example, I am aware that my knowledge of and perspective on the human scene is partial; but I am anxiously tempted to deny these limits. I may pretend "to have achieved a degree of knowledge which is beyond the limit of finite life. This is the 'ideological taint' in which all human knowledge is involved and which is always something more than mere ignorance. It is always an effort to hide that ignorance by pretension" (R. Niebuhr 1964a: 182). Anxiety, "the inevitable concomitant of the paradox of freedom and finiteness," is the internal precondition of sin and the internal description of temptation; human creativity, therefore, is "always corrupted by some effort to overcome contingency by raising precisely what is contingent to absolute and unlimited dimensions." The permanent spiritual condition of anxiety gives rise, inevitably but not necessarily, to either pride or sensuality. The one raises one's own finite being and its possibilities to unconditioned significance; the other seeks to escape possibility and self-determination by utterly immersing and losing oneself in some mutable good (p. 185). Or again, pride is transfixed by freedom's surpassing of limits, and sensuality fixes itself on human limits that somehow would embody human freedom in its very denial (Lovin 1995: 148).

"Inevitably but not necessarily": Anxiety is not sin, nor does it on its own compel it. Niebuhr posits the ideal possibility of perfect trust that overcomes the insecurities that anxiety prompts, and so affirms that the root of all sin is unbelief, the failure to trust in God (R. Niebuhr 1964a: 183, 252). The virulent and pathetic nature of sin is most evident when we consider its collective expression, and especially in nations. "The group is more arrogant, hypocritical, self-centered and more ruthless in the pursuit of its ends than the individual." Group life collects and embodies more power and thereby fosters the tendency to make abundant claims for its own significance as the source and end of existence. In the case of the nation, the pretension may well be godlike in its demand for its individual members' unbounded loyalty; and individuals may play along in ways that manifest both sensuality (or sloth) and pride. "Collective egotism does offer the individual an opportunity to lose himself in a larger whole; but it also offers him possibilities of self-aggrandizement beside which mere individual pretensions are implausible and incredible" (pp. 208, 212–13). This dynamic points to one form of "the equality of sin and the inequality of guilt." All human efforts culpably fall short of the glory of God. Guilt, the consequence of sin in injustice, is variable, however, and "those who hold great economic and political power are more guilty of pride against God and of injustice against the weak than those who lack power and prestige" (p. 225). Niebuhr's critical dialectic keeps moving, driving on to denounce the pride of spiritual and cultural leaders as well as the self-righteousness of the weak. He will not turn the point about economic and political power into a law blinding us to other moral realities. Nevertheless, when the ego, individual or collective, is allowed to expand, history teaches us that it likely will expand, and concerning the poor and weak "the mistakes of a too simple social radicalism must not obscure the fact that in a given historical setting the powerful man or class is actually more guilty of injustice and pride than those who lack power" (pp. 224, 226).

III

So Niebuhr argues that we always come up against the constraints of history in sinful people and collectives asserting themselves inordinately and/or abandoning themselves evasively. The prospects for large-scale political and economic groups to transcend self-interest in loving regard for the welfare of others are severely restricted compared with those for individuals. But history has its possibilities, too, as we mentioned with respect to self-transcendence as the coin of creative achievement. Niebuhr gives this point a Christological focus with an account of Jesus Christ as "the perfect norm of human nature" in his perfection of sacrificial love for God and neighbor. Self-transcendence completes itself in such love, although the very cross that reveals this "also indicates that the perfection of man is not attainable in history."

> Sacrificial love transcends history. . . . It is an act in history; but it cannot justify itself in history. From the standpoint of history mutual love is the highest good. Only in mutual love, in which the concern of one person for the interests of another prompts and elicits a reciprocal affection, are the social demands of historical existence satisfied . . . All claims within the general field of interests must be properly satisfied and related to each other harmoniously. The sacrifice of the self for others is therefore a violation of natural standards of morals, as limited by historical existence. (R. Niebuhr 1964b: 69)

Still, sacrificial love is relevant to all historical ethics inasmuch as the norm of mutual love may not be realized if the fear of nonreciprocation dominates human relationships. The analysis turns again in the claim that a love that seeks not its own simply cannot maintain itself in society since it is vulnerable to the inordinate self-assertion of others, and because it will worst its exemplars by their refusal to participate in the "balance of competing wills and interests" (R. Niebuhr 1964b: 2, 72). The love of Jesus Christ is an "impossible possibility" that can never finally be vindicated in history; its historical consequence is a life that ends tragically.

Nevertheless, *agape* or the sacrificial love of the cross *completes* the incompleteness of mutuality, since there are no limits to the latter given human self-transcendence, and no limits to the former perfecting mutual relations. Niebuhr, as usual, makes the point negatively: "even the purest form of *agape*, the love of the enemy and the forgiveness toward the evildoer, do not stand in contradiction to historical possibilities." There will always be an "admixture" of this love with concerns for order and justice in a world of self-interest, coercion, and violence. Yet short of abandoning outright a sense of historical possibility, there is no limit to love's proportion within the admixture. Now this perfecting love also *clarifies* and *limits* what is possible. As a norm it "perennially refutes the pathetic illusions of those who usually deny the dimension of history which reaches into Eternity in one moment, and in the next dream of achieving an unconditioned perfection in history" (R. Niebuhr 1964b: 85–6, 88). Finally, the perfection of the cross *corrects* or *judges* all arrangements for a tolerable social life. The irremovable admixture of self-assertion and love is, of course, always also a *sinful* admixture. No (forgiving) remedial justice is not also vindictive, no communal fellowship is immune to imperialism, no employment of power for impartial justice is not itself partial.

The last point refers again to the "equality of sin." The next repairs to the "inequality of guilt," and it is that there are real moral differences between different social programs to the extent that they realize, for instance, the secure achievement of equality of conditions of life for human creatures. "Equality as a pinnacle of the ideal of justice implicitly points toward love as the final norm of justice; for equal justice is the approximation of brotherhood under the conditions of sin. A higher justice always means a more equal justice." That claims for and against equality carry an "ideological taint" (in one case, stressing its absolute validity without attending to differences of social need or function; in the other, focusing too much on the impossibility of its attainment) does not overcome this fact (R. Niebuhr 1964b: 254–5). And the mere fact hardly overcomes the aforementioned corruptions, and hence their vulnerability to criticism.

Niebuhr's argument for the "principle of government, or the organization of the whole realm of social vitalities," begins with the familiar dictum that "the domination of one life by another is avoided most successfully by an equilibrium of powers and vitalities, so that weakness does not invite enslavement by the strong." Any such equilibrium, however, contains a condition of tension that always manifests in covert or potential conflict. The threat of overt conflict, along with the inevitable, continuing failures in justice, call for an organizing center that arbitrates and reduces conflict (more impartially), redresses injustice, and commands obedience to law by superior power. Then again, government is liable to be partial to certain classes or groups after all, and on its own may abuse communal goods and freedom for the sake of preserving an "order" that places "all rebels against its authority under the moral disadvantage of revolting against order *per se*." Hence democratic societies' greatest achievement is that they embody the principle of resistance to government within the principle of government itself (R. Niebuhr 1964b: 265–8).

Biblical traditions address the moral ambiguity of government by taking it both as an ordinance of God with authority that reflects the divine majesty, and as always and constantly subject to divine judgment insofar as rulers oppress the poor and defy such majesty. As a principle of order, government's power "prevents anarchy; but its power is not identical with divine power," and any pretensions to that signal tyranny. The recognizable upshot is that governments and political actors generally ought to be alert to possibilities of a higher justice in every social situation as well as to the fact that the perils of anarchy and tyranny are present in every political achievement.

> To understand this is to labor for higher justice in terms of the experience of justification by faith. Justification by faith in the realm of justice means that we will not regard the pressures and counter-pressures, the tensions, the overt and covert conflicts by which justice is achieved and maintained, as normative in the absolute sense; but neither will we ease our conscience by seeking to escape our involvement in them. We will know that we cannot purge ourselves of the sin and guilt in which we are involved in the ambiguities of politics without also disavowing responsibility for the creative possibilities of justice. (R. Niebuhr 1964b: 284)

Niebuhr's treatment of the struggle for justice in the world community sounds the same themes. World government must cope with the inevitable (even if implied) hegemony of stronger powers; but this fact portends the threat of imperialism. Hence all national powers ought to be armed with the capacity to resist domination. If central authority is weakened too much, however, we wind up with an unorganized balance of power threatening anarchy. A new world community "must be built by persons who 'when hope is dead will hope by faith'" (R. Niebuhr 1964b: 285).

The quest for justice requires order, and order threatens justice. Justice seeks a proper measure of freedom that honors how "the unique worth of the individual . . . makes it wrong to fit him into any political program as a mere instrument." Freedom, needless to say, can challenge order. The equality that justice demands is also regularly met with resistance in terms of a reassertion of freedom over against authority's coercive enforcement of equality (Lovin 1995: 225–6). Democracies make their way in the face of these possibilities and tensions, seeking "unity within the conditions of freedom," and maintaining "freedom within the framework of order."

> Man's capacity for justice makes democracy possible; but man's inclination to injustice makes democracy necessary . . . If men are inclined to deal unjustly with their fellows, the possession of power aggravates this inclination. . . . The democratic techniques of a free society place checks upon the power of the ruler and the administrator and thus prevent it from becoming vexatious. (R. Niebuhr 1944: xiii–xiv)

Niebuhr's (1991: 257) preference for democracy is tempered by worries over idolatrous devotion to it, "a sin to which Americans are particularly prone." False worship simply compounds ideological taint and the will to power peculiarly present among the especially powerful.

In conclusion, Reinhold Niebuhr the "Christian realist" attacked unchastened idealism as well as a cynicism that would jettison moral values from politics. We have discovered resources in his thought that seem to allow for unceasing critique of extant social arrangements; but he made much, too, of the need to take on moral responsibilities in history, chiding those who evaded them in a vain and futile quest to maintain moral purity. His criticism of many forms of Christian pacifism followed the antiperfectionist line, which he joined to his standard charges of irrelevant idealism and the failure to take sin seriously. The pacifists whom he targets

> merely assert that if only men loved one another, all the complex, and sometimes horrible realities of the political order could be dispensed with. They do not see that their "if" begs the most basic problem of human history. It is because men are sinners that justice can be achieved only by a certain degree of coercion on the one hand, and by resistance to coercion and tyranny on the other. (R. Niebuhr 1992: 35)

A "non-heretical" pacifism does not reject the Christian notion of original sin and will not endorse "the absurd idea that perfect love is guaranteed a simple victory over the world." Instead, it will commend an individual and collective life of self-giving love that also disavows the political task and frees its adherents of responsibility for social justice. A nonresponsible pacifism is pertinent as critical reminder of a norm that stays critical for history despite its historical impossibility. An irresponsible pacifism pursues a political relevance that is delusory and dangerous.

IV

How can anyone deny that Niebuhr's is the quintessential example of a political ethic of free responsibility? His vision, one might say, never rests in uncritical contentment. Justice may be realized in human societies with no positive limit to it set in advance. Yet all achievements fall short and are judged by the law of love, since they are all tainted by sin . . . and so forth.

Let us reconsider the questioning voices.

Stanley Hauerwas believes that Niebuhr was decisive in developing Christian ethics

> as the attempt to develop those theological, moral, and social insights necessary to sustain the ambiguous task of achieving more relatively just societies . . . he assumed that the task of Christian ethics was to formulate the means for Christians to serve their societies, particularly American society. . . . For Niebuhr and the social gospelers the subject of Christian ethics was America. (Hauerwas 2001a: 59–60)

This point of view questions several aspects of Niebuhr's thought. First, it is a kind of anthropological theology, or even a "natural theology," that validates Christian claims in terms of some seemingly inescapable parts of human experience, for example, the persistence of inordinate self-assertion, anxiety over limits given powers of self-transcendence, and the ineradicable sense that mutual harmony in self-giving is normative for human existence. Though he was "a child of the church" with a "profound faith in the God of Jesus Christ" (Hauerwas 2001b: 122), Niebuhr still offered a theology and ethics for which God becomes an answer to and predicate of our human nature and plight so understood. Political activity that is free for the God sovereignly revealed in Jesus Christ is lost to the degree that it is based on a sort of projection of our own self-understanding, and a rejoinder along the lines of the restlessness of radical self-transcendence is unpersuasive. Second, Niebuhr's reticence about the distinctive practices of the Christian community is correlated with demonstrating how political ethics can proceed independently of an ecclesially shaped Christian theology and form of life. This move well served a religiously diverse American scene, just as a standing caution against self-righteousness fostered a humility that supported practices of "tolerance" which ruled out Christian political experiments conducted in the name of a "holiness" unconformed to the terms of justice, coercion, and the balance of power (Hauerwas 2001b: 115–16, 131, 135–7).

Niebuhr's efforts to give democracy "a more adequate cultural basis" by way of Christian vision fuels Hauerwas's concerns. He thinks Niebuhr simply assumes that "liberal" social orders are normative for Christians, and in particular that the quest for justice is soundly and adequately based on working for an ordered balance of power preserving freedom and equality. Christian life and action effectively become "well policed" by the requirement of sustaining liberal democracy as a universal moral achievement. In this case, Christians in their communities may be rendered defenseless when their democracies go to war to defend and extend democratic values (Hauerwas 1994: 98–106). The problem is exacerbated by Niebuhr's penchant for consequentialist analysis that appears to overlook stringent norms that limit violence and protect human rights, such as the absolute immunity of noncombatants from direct attack in wartime. With regard to the United States' use of atomic weapons against Japanese nonmilitary targets in World War II, for example, Niebuhr found reason to justify the slaughter of innocents in order to gain the enemy's unconditional surrender and save American lives. To be sure, and in keeping with his general political ethics, he also named Americans guilty for their evil and subsequent self-righteousness (Fox 1985: 224–5).

Now, Niebuhr questions the idolatry of democracy, as we have seen. Recall, too, his awareness that ruling powers may be partial to political and economic interests. The awareness can clear a space for extensive political critique. The law of love is meant to afford leverage for challenging all specific historical arrangements, democratic or otherwise. As far as Christian "defenselessness" before democracy's wars go, one can weigh in Niebuhr's ready concession "that a wise statesmanship will seek not only to avoid conflict, but to avoid violence in conflict" (R. Niebuhr 1991: 242). Niebuhr's Christian realism, finally, does appear to be patient of revision along the lines Paul Ramsey pursued, correcting its utilitarian excesses (Ramsey 1968: 260).

Hauerwas would likely find all of this beside the point. The anthropological basis of Niebuhr's theology steers it away from the reality of the God to whom we are above all to remain faithful. The inattention of this theology to the social location of distinctively peaceable, nonviolent Christian witness to the world in and from the church leaves Christians only with the social location of democratic culture and above all the nation-state, and tempts them to see their faith as one among many "worldviews" making sense of the human scene in liberal society. The state's claims to loyalty, expressed above all in the claim upon citizens that they may and indeed must kill in wartime, thus will meet with no concretely countervailing prophetic pressure. Principles that protect the innocent, in the end, will give way to the aspirations of nationalism in the state's use of them and other "just war criteria" for the purpose of easing "our" conscience and vindicating "our" moral decency. Christians, for Hauerwas (1994: 105–6), can authentically claim free political responsibility to God if they give up, and struggle mightily to give up, their pretensions to be rulers, or the sorts of folks whose responsibility for society is presumed to determine society through the exercise of the conventions of merely coercive or violent political power. The pretension turns ever so easily into a responsibility to society disloyal to the God disclosed in Jesus Christ. He cites Luke 22: 24–30 as a challenging paradigm:

> A dispute also arose among them, which of them was to be regarded as the greatest. And he said to them, "The kings of the Gentiles exercise lordship over them; and those in authority over them are called benefactors. But not so with you; rather let the greatest among you become as the youngest, and the leader as one who serves. For which is the greater, one who sits at table, or one who serves? Is it not the one who sits at table? But I am among you as one who serves. You are those who have continued with me in my trials; and I assign to you, as my Father assigned to me, a kingdom, that you may eat and drink in my kingdom, and sit on thrones judging the twelve tribes of Israel.

Here and elsewhere, Hauerwas expresses his indebtedness to the work of John Howard Yoder; but the latter may distinguish himself from the former in clearly specifying the character of a positive Christian witness to the state, a witness not just against the nations but for them first of all. Yoder's analysis of the same text from Luke is subversively Niebuhrian. The fact of the rulers' dominion is assumed. The rulers will count themselves benefactors, appealing, for better and worse, to human and moral value. Jesus denies none of this, but simply asks that the disciples do something else, which at least means *not* to play the game of simply showing how the rulers of the nations help us all out, and on the rulers' own terms. In the passage we find both an acknowledgment of power and coercion and authority, and an appeal to moral value in politics. But for Christians the realism of the first point meets with a realism of the second in that the self-justifying appeals to the value of the "common good" are to be critically employed against those who rule, from a political standpoint and governed by the church's faithful, nonviolent witness to Jesus Christ. From this perspective democracy is not valorized as a governing institution or system that somehow demands our assent in terms of Christian values. Christians will instead engage in an ad hoc operation in loyalty to God that both uses democratic ideology against its ideologically tainted spokespersons and witnesses to new forms of community rooted in the practices of disciples (Yoder 1984: 155–9).

Hence Yoder contends that the standpoint of disciples is nonviolent and "set apart" in ways that are, *pace* Reinhold Niebuhr, neither nonresponsible nor irresponsible. The Christian community will not disavow political responsibility, and it will not sentimentally trumpet the law of love amid historical conflict. It will witness to the state – to the democratic state, let us say – as the "least oppressive oligarchy" (Yoder 1984: 158–9), trying to hold it true to its proper functions of limiting violence, upholding the dignity of dissent, and protecting "those categories of persons . . . excluded from the economic and social privileges of the strong" (Yoder 1964: 41). The church will not see the coercion and violence of the state as anything other than the old aeon in which evil is used against itself by God to clear a space for the work of the Gospel. The work itself, moreover, positively implies a number of civil imperatives for any community, such as egalitarianism (given Christians' baptism into one body), a welcoming of the poor into full fellowship (implied in the Eucharist), and a standing social policy of forgiveness (Yoder 1997: 33, 49). Even with respect to war, nonviolent witness may operate on a "continuum of increasing tolerability" that distinguishes wars, not as just or unjust, but as more or less unjust. All of this may be part of evangelization, of repentance and conversion, little by little, to God (Yoder 1964: 48, 25).

One Niebuhrian rejoinder at this point may be that the nonresisting ethic of Jesus is inevitably compromised by any "pacifism" that seeks to change society for the better through immersion in social conflicts shot through with coercion. Even nonviolent resistance buys into coerciveness, into forcing others to act in your interests against their will; but since the difference between this and violent resistance is only one of the degree of coercion involved, judgments of expediency alone (and not judgments of principle in terms of Jesus' nonresistance to evil, overcoming it with good) determine how to proceed. Nonviolent disciples of Jesus Christ thus find themselves participating in the power struggles of history that they would (and, for Niebuhr, ought to) disavow at the price of nonresponsibility (R. Niebuhr 1932: 252, 263–5). Yoder answers, first, by denying that good work for justice under God always requires immersion in coercion, power struggles, or violence. Second, he freely admits that acts of protest or civil disobedience "will be most appropriate when it is most possible to distinguish between their witness function and a self-seeking participation in the power struggle. The difficulty of making this distinction . . . cannot justify avoiding such channels of witness entirely" (1964: 55). Third, the nonviolent resistance of the civil rights movement in the United States was a telling case in point.

> Its nonviolence is not interchangeable with other methods, for it is an expression of genuine love. The purpose of the sit-in is not to coerce the "adversary" but to communicate to him, to "get through to him," to bring to his attention moral dimensions of his behavior which he had not recognized. In line with this end, care is taken to leave him a respectable way out without loss of face. The boycott is not a weapon but a refusal to cooperate with wrong practices. The "demonstrations" are just that: efforts to *point* people's awareness to moral issues. Only for a good cause could such a method work, since it derives the strength of its protest from the wrongness of those protested against. The transformed institutions are an ultimately certain but not an immediately calculable outcome; the method is justified not by its success but by its integrity. (Yoder 1997: 101)

For Yoder and Hauerwas, Christian nonviolent political responsibility begins with Christian communal practices "such as forgiveness and reconciliation. Only by learning how to live through such practices can we as a people come to see the violence, often present in our lives, that would otherwise go unnoticed" (Hauerwas 1994: 130). The issue with Niebuhr is that he failed to take these practices of the church seriously enough in indicating the shape of political witness, and that he put in their place a theologically christened American democratic faith.

If these criticisms of Niebuhr are sound, they rely upon a theology of God's living presence in history that is sounder than his own. Yoder (1994: 163) bluntly draws the contrast in refusing

> the identification of the church's mission and the meaning of history with the function of the state in organizing sinful society. . . . [I]t is clear in the New Testament that the meaning of history is not what the state will achieve in the way of a progressively more tolerable ordering of society but what the church achieves through evangelism and through the leavening process.

Let us grant that Niebuhr would deny the position ascribed to him, for history cannot complete itself through the good ordering of society and is tragic because sinners seek prematurely to do so. He nonetheless drifts in this direction because, as his brother Richard saw, he tends not to place the resurrection of Jesus Christ in history, even though historical Christian faith presupposes it. Thus history appears "simply as the scene of sin and of the ambiguous powers that rule over men" instead of as "the action in which we are being created, chastised, and forgiven . . . [and] as the place where God now rules and does so with precision" (H. R. Niebuhr 1996: 98, 100). Richard Niebuhr placed God's rule not just in evangelism and the leavening process but also in the church's polar relations with the state and other forms of social life. But for him God's living presence in history crucially includes a new life promised to the world and distinctively confessed in the church (however much he also resisted an ecclesialism that overemphasized Christian difference). What is more, attention to God's governance requires more than assenting to the possibilities and limits of historical action as part of an individual or collective process of moral deliberation; it demands explicit, discerning attention to what God is doing in the world in, with, and over against one's action in other individual, social, and natural forms and forces. These forms and forces may bear a call to repentance and conversion, to a permanent revolution of heart and mind that breaks one out of defensive, self-justifying "henotheistic" loyalties, including "American," "democratic" loyalties.

Hans Frei may have been right to find in Reinhold Niebuhr a "modern view of human freedom" with its "uninterrupted . . . and self-starting initiative" that contrasts with H. Richard Niebuhr's ethics of response to divine governance. If so, then freedom as ethical action for justice will tend to float free of various conditioning and limiting factors. My analysis suggests that without considered attention to concrete practices in a church that witnesses to a new life promised and present in the risen Christ, and without an integrally related attention to what God is doing in the world in calling political agencies to repentance and transformation beyond their narrower faiths, political freedom is bereft (cf. Hauerwas 2001b: 240). It is left with a set of Christian "values" that it would seek to embody in political life; but in the relevant case this appears to risk an all too easy Christian accreditation of American democratic institutions. Hence a lonely political freedom runs counter to the free (because critical) political responsibility that Niebuhr sought in so many other powerful ways. It follows, I think, that the theological factors adduced here regarding ecclesial practice, the living presence of God in history, and the call to discernment of God's universal providential agency (Tanner 1992: 98–107) positively contribute to the case for free political responsibility (to God) for political society across the board.

Acknowledgments

I am grateful to Mark Graham, Eugene McCarraher, Edmund N. Santurri, Darlene Fozard Weaver, and the editors of this volume for their helpful criticisms of earlier versions of this essay.

References

Barth, K. (1968). *Community, State, and Church*. Gloucester, Mass.: Peter Smith.

Fox, R. (1985). *Reinhold Niebuhr: A Biography*. New York: Pantheon.

Frei, H. W. (1993). *Theology and Narrative*, ed. G. Hunsinger and W. C. Placher. New York and Oxford: Oxford University Press.

Hauerwas, S. (1994). *Dispatches from the Front*. Durham, NC, and London: Duke University Press.

——(2001a). *The Hauerwas Reader*, ed. J. Berkman and M. Cartwright. Durham, NC, and London: Duke University Press.

——(2001b). *With the Grain of the Universe*. Grand Rapids, Mich.: Brazos.

Lovin, R. W. (1995). *Reinhold Niebuhr and Christian Realism*. Cambridge: Cambridge University Press.

Niebuhr, H. R. (1946). "The Responsibility of the Church for Society." In K. S. Latourette (ed.), *The Gospel, the Church, and the World*. New York: Harper & Row.

——(1996). *Theology, History, and Culture*, ed. W. S. Johnson. New Haven and London: Yale University Press.

Niebuhr, R. (1932). *Moral Man and Immoral Society*. New York: Scribner's.

——(1944). *The Children of Light and the Children of Darkness*. New York: Scribner's.

——(1964a). *The Nature and Destiny of Man*, Vol. I: *Human Nature*. New York: Scribner's.

——(1964b). *The Nature and Destiny of Man*, Vol. II: *Human Destiny*. New York: Scribner's.

——(1976). *Love and Justice*, ed. D. B. Robertson. Gloucester, Mass.: Peter Smith.

——(1979). *An Interpretation of Christian Ethics*. New York: Seabury.

——(1991). *Reinhold Niebuhr: Theologian of Public Life*, ed. L. Rasmussen. Minneapolis: Fortress.

——(1992). "Why the Christian Church is not Pacifist." In R. B. Miller (ed.), *War in the Twentieth Century*. Louisville, Ky: Westminster.

Ramsey, P. (1968). *The Just War*. New York: Scribner's.

Tanner, K. (1992). *The Politics of God*. Minneapolis: Fortress.

Yoder, J. H. (1964). *The Christian Witness to the State*. Newton, KS: Faith and Life.

——(1984). *The Priestly Kingdom*. Notre Dame, Ind.: University of Notre Dame Press.

——(1994). *The Royal Priesthood*, ed. M. G. Cartwright. Grand Rapids, Mich.: Eerdmans.

——(1997). *For the Nations*. Grand Rapids, Mich.: Eerdmans.

CHAPTER 14
Feminist Theology, Southern

Kwok Pui-lan

Beginning to think in a different way requires us to take different positions on the subject of knowing: to open up spaces for new ways of thinking and to consider our own thinking in terms of how our goals affect our perceptions.
Ivone Gebara

Until women's views are listened to and their participation allowed and ensured, the truth will remain hidden, and the call to live the values of the Reign of God will be unheeded.
Musimbi R. A. Kanyoro and Mercy Amba Oduyoye

Political theology in the South emerged from the struggle for political independence after the Second World War and the critique of neocolonialism and the ideology of development. Southern theologians decried the theological hegemony of Europe and North America and reclaimed the right to speak about God as subjects of their own destiny. They developed different forms of contextual theologies to address concrete social and political concerns and to relate the Christian tradition to the lived experiences of the people. While the male theologians might be adamantly against imperialism and corrupt dictatorial regimes, they have not concomitantly denounced patriarchal privileges and the subjugation of women and children, who are the most vulnerable in society. Feminist theologians have to create an alternative space to articulate the theological vision of the hope and aspiration of women.

Because of the multiple oppressions of gender, race, and class, the struggles of women in the South often operate from positions of extreme marginality, outside the established channels of national politics (Young 2001: 361). Women's movements focus on practical social and political issues affecting women, such as education and reproductive rights, specific localized struggles, coalition building with other oppressed groups, and community efforts to address particular needs. Living in such an environment, feminist theologians understand "politics" in a comprehensive and multifaceted sense not limited to state power, participation in government, and political representation and rights. "Politics," for them, concerns the collective welfare of the whole people in the *polis*. Their political theology aims to promote the survival, health, and well-being of the whole community, taking into account how the social, cultural, and psychological dimensions intersect with gender and the politico-economic base.

Since the 1970s, feminist theological movements have gathered momentum in the South through the establishment of national, regional, and global ecumenical networks. Since "the South" is a mental construct covering a vast territory with many cultures, languages, and peoples, we must not homogenize the diverse regions or generalize feminist theologies from radically different backgrounds. Liberation theologians from the South take seriously the contexts from which theology emerges and begin their theological reflection with social analysis. I shall follow their methodology and present a brief discussion of the differences and commonalities of the regions.

Sociopolitical Contexts of Feminist Theology in the South

In *Feminism and Nationalism in the Third World*, Kumari Jayawardena (1986) documented the history of women's participation in anti-imperialist movements in Asia and the Middle East since the 1880s. The emergence of feminist consciousness in the third world took place in the wider political climate of national struggles, the fight against economic exploitation, and the quest for cultural self-definition. The rapidly changing social and political circumstances and the mobilization of the masses enabled women to step outside their domestic spheres and experiment with new roles traditionally denied them. The nature of feminist politics in the South does not narrowly focus on gender inequality and on the freedom and liberation of women. Instead, feminist struggles are generally seen as a part of the overall liberation of the whole people, but with a distinct focus and distinct strategies. Mary John Mananzan (1989: 105) of the Philippines writes: "There is no total human liberation without the liberation of women in society. And this is not an automatic consequence of either economic development or political revolution. In other words, the women's movement is an essential aspect of the very process of societal liberation."

Because of the divergent historical, cultural, and economic situations of the Southern continents, feminist theologians have different emphases and priorities in their social analyses and theological agendas. As Latin American countries won their independence struggles in the nineteenth century, liberation theologians focused on neocolonialism, the failure of the Western development model, and problems of political and military dictatorship. Informed by Marxist social theory, they stressed the preferential option for the poor, liberation and redemption in history, the integration between theology and praxis, and the church's transformative role in bringing about the kingdom of God. Developed in the late 1970s, feminist theology in Latin America shared these concerns, while highlighting the oppressions of machismo cultures and violence against women. The feminist theological agenda has been gradually broadened to include racism, multiple levels of cultural oppression in a continent with various forms of racial hybridity, and environmental justice.

Asian and African feminist theologians tend to highlight the cultural and religious dimensions of oppression because of the impact of entrenched cultural myths, rituals, and traditions on women's roles in society. They are interested in assessing Christianity's role in supporting colonialism and patriarchy, because political independence for many of them happened only a generation ago. Postcolonial interpretation of the Christian past involves new readings of the missionary enterprise, attention to cultural hybridity and resistance, demystifying racial hierarchy, and critical evaluation of the use of the Bible as a tool of oppression. Cultural studies and postcolonial theories have been employed to assist in building more comprehensive frameworks of analysis.

There are also particular concerns for Asian feminist theologians. The economies of countries on the Pacific Rim have developed at a phenomenal rate in the past thirty years. In fact, the twenty-first century has been hailed as the Pacific Century and the "Asian miracle" was touted a model for other developing countries. While Max Weber has attributed capitalistic development in Europe to Calvinistic ethics, Asian feminists point out that the East Asian miracle has been sustained by a political oligarchy, transnational capital, and the revitalization of elements of patriarchal neo-Confucian ethics (Kwok 1995). While the focus has been on the glistening Pacific Rim, countries in the Asian subcontinent are still suffering from abject poverty, compounded by the caste system and violent ethnic clashes. Sexual exploitation of women, especially in the form of sex tourism in Southeast Asia, domestic violence, dowry, the fast spread of HIV/AIDS, and child prostitution are also significant concerns for Asian feminists.

In a continent where many die from famine, malnutrition, unclean water, diseases, and warfare, African feminists have focused on survival, just distribution of resources, and the quality of life. Much of their theological writing has been devoted to the cultural, ritualistic, and religious customs that disempower women, such as the issue of polygamy, the stigma of the pollution of blood, widowhood and rituals of mourning, and female circumcision. At the same time, apartheid in South Africa, as well as racial and ethnic strife in Rwanda, Zimbabwe, and other African countries, have heightened their concerns for racial oppression and the role of religion in social conflicts. African feminist theologians express the "will to arise" as women in their continent continue their strides to gain collective power and respect in their societies.

Because of globalization, women across the South faced similar socioeconomic challenges: women's subsistence economy crushed by larger-scale industries and multinational corporations, the social and economic consequences of large national debts, and in some cases the constant threats of instability and war. The realignment of world powers according to their geopolitical interests and the economic structural adjustments imposed on poorer countries both lead to less political autonomy and less democratic participation. In the transnational movement of capital and the "race to the bottom" for cheaper resources and labor, countries in the South have to compete with one another to be exploited by corporations in the North. In the age of information technology, many women have found that they are totally left out in the postindustrial and technological restructuring process because of lack of access and training.

Feminism, Colonialism, and Christianity

The encounter between Western colonizing culture and indigenous cultures often involved thorny questions pertaining to women's roles and female sexuality, notably veiling, polygamy, child-marriage, footbinding, and *sati*. As an integral part of the colonialist agenda, saving colonized women from their oppression, ignorance, and heathenism appealed to the compassion of Westerners (Narayan 1997: 17) and garnered support for Christian missions. To challenge the collusion of Christianity with colonialism and the predominantly Eurocentric interpretations of the missionary movement, feminist political theology from the South uses several methodologies: questioning missionary sexual theology, unmasking the impact of a monotheistic and androcentric theology on religiously pluralistic cultures, and ideological critique of Christian symbolism.

While the missionary movement has been credited with bringing about the emancipation of women by introducing female education, health care, and monogamous marriages, Southern feminist theologians charge that the imposition of a colonial system and patriarchal church structures actually reinforced a sexual theology that prescribed a dualistic and hierarchical ordering of the sexes. Mananzan (1991) observes that the Roman Catholic Church, accompanying the arrival of the Spaniards in the Philippines, curtailed women's freedom by confining them to the church, kitchen, and children, and the social status of Filipino women became lower after colonialism. The gender ideology of the church exerted pressure in Filipino communities, where the relations between the sexes had hitherto been more inclusive and egalitarian and where matrilineal heritage predominated. During the nineteenth century, Victorian assumptions of sexual prudence and female domesticity influenced missionary sexual theology and ethics. With its deep-seated fear of women's bodies and sexuality, colonial Christianity limited women's leadership in religious and communal activities. Mercy Amba Oduyoye (1992) of Ghana has observed that while Akan women play significant roles in rituals associated with birth, puberty, marriage, and death, their participation in Christian rituals has been marginalized. Marcella Althaus-Reid (2001) from Argentina further charges that colonial sexual theology was not only sexist but also heterosexist, lending its support to the sexual control of women and the policing of sexualities that were considered outside the established norm. The sexual ideologies of the colonizers were forced upon other peoples through violence or the so-called "civilizing mission."

While Western feminist theologians have challenged this androcentric Christian symbolic structure, their counterparts in the South investigated the impact of the introduction of a monotheistic and male-dominated symbolic order into their cultures which had maintained inclusive representations of the divine. Christian mission undermined the myths and practices associated with female divine power. For instance, Musa Dube (2002) points out that among the Ibgo people in Nigeria, women used to enjoy certain economic and social privileges in terms of ownership of property and inheritance, and their gender construction was supported by a spiritual world that recognized female religious imagery and power. Allusion to these powerful goddesses allowed women to carve out their own social space and sphere of influence. But the Christian church and the mission schools systematically condemned goddess religion, and consequently the symbolic structure that bolstered women's self-esteem was shattered. Among the Asian religious traditions, the worship of goddesses and the feminine images of the divine has a long history, dating back to the prehistoric period. Worshipped by women and men, the prevalent goddesses of Ina, Guanyin, Durga, Kali, and Sita, as mothers, consorts, daughters, and protectors, have not been superseded by the male gods as they were in Mesopotamia and prehistoric Europe. Thus, the propagation of a monotheistic Christian God imaged as a male being, modeled after the father, king, and lord, introduced gender asymmetry into the religious symbolic system and reinforced male domination (Kwok 2000: 72–3).

The most sustained demystification of the colonial misuse of Christianity is the ideological critique of Christian symbolisms, focusing particularly on the figures of Jesus and the Virgin Mary. Teresa M. Hinga (1992: 187) from Kenya explains how the imperialistic images of Christ arrived in Africa:

> During the period of colonial and imperial expansionism, the prevailing image of Christ was that of the conqueror. Jesus was the warrior King, in whose name and banner (the cross) new territories, both physical and spiritual, would be fought for, annexed, and subjugated. An imperial Christianity thus had an imperial Christ to match. The Christ of the missionaries was a conquering Christ.

With little respect for the cultures and religions of the African people, the missionaries created alienation and confusion in the Africans, for their culture and identity were to be erased and supplanted by a foreign religion that belonged to the colonizers.

But Hinga notes that the Christ of the missionary enterprise also contained emancipatory impulses, which attracted African followers. African women were able to perceive more liberating images of Christ when they went back to the biblical sources and discovered empowering and healing images from the New Testament. They asserted their theological agency when they interpreted the Bible through their experiences in the African churches and their own cultural lenses. Hinga offers three popular images of Christ in the African context. Some see Jesus as a personal friend, savior, or healer who does not demand women's subjugation, but accepts them as they are and accompanies them in their suffering. Among the African independent churches where women are more vocal and less inhibited than those in the established churches, the image of Christ as the embodiment of the Spirit, the power of God, is prominent. Christ becomes the voice of the voiceless and the power of the powerless in this pneumatic Christology. Another popular image of Christ is that of the iconoclastic prophet, who subverts existing power relations and challenges the status quo. Hinga opines that, to be relevant for women's emancipation, Christ must be a concrete figure who brings hope and courage to the oppressed and vindicates the marginalized in society.

A further dimension of Christology that has been used to solidify colonial rule was the glorification of the suffering and sacrifice of Jesus. Mananzan (1993) noted that during Spanish colonization, the suffering of Christ was highlighted during the annual Holy Week procession, complete with the re-enactment of the nailing to the cross. The emphasis on the Passion and submission of Christ was meant to inculcate both loyalty to Spain and a passive acceptance of the destiny of this life. While Good Friday was dramatized, there was not a concomitant celebration of Easter Sunday: the Resurrection and the beginning of new life. The depiction of a beaten, scourged, and defeated Christ and the direction of salvation toward another world functioned to pacify the people under the colonial masters. Furthermore, women were exhorted to model themselves after the sacrifice and obedience of Christ and to internalize passive and resigned endurance of their own pain and suffering.

To counteract Christian imperialism, Mananzan (1993) and other feminist theologians in Asia rediscovered the subversive and revolutionary power of the Christ symbol. While the Spaniards used Jesus' suffering as a tool for oppression, the Filipino people combined the Passion narrative with their own millennial beliefs to construct a language of anticolonialism in the nineteenth century. For subjugated women, salvation and the Good News does not imply a life of passive suffering and endless sacrifice and denial. The suffering of Jesus was not to be used to condone state terror or domestic violence. Filipino feminists reinterpret Jesus as a fully liberated human being, who confronts the wrongs of society and stands up for justice to bring about the reign of God, while other Asian feminists experiment with new images of Christ, using their cultural and religious resources, as discussed below.

The image of the Virgin Mary, the dominant feminine symbol in the Christian tradition, has been subjected to careful scrutiny both for its oppressive impact and for its revolutionary significance. The Roman Catholic Church has largely portrayed Mary as a gentle and docile model for women, whose submissiveness was idealized to serve colonial and patriarchal interests. Tracing the development of Mariology in Latin America, Ivone Gebara and María Clare Bingemer (1989) point out that in the colonial period, Mary was worshipped as the great protector of the conquistadors against the Indians whom they regarded as infidels. The largely male-centered, dualistic, and idealistic interpretations of Mary did not help women to develop their self-esteem and assert their power. But alongside such colonial images of Mary are other stories of the Virgin, who appears to peoples in numerous ways and intermingles with the poor. Most noteworthy is Our Lady of Guadalupe, who first appeared in 1531 to the Indian Juan Diego, and has been widely venerated as the patroness of the continent. In that story the dark-skinned Virgin adopted the natives as her children and pledged to hear their prayers and offer her loving favor and compassion. In the continuous struggle against neocolonialism and other oppressions, Gebara and Bingemer suggest reclaiming Mary as the mother of the poor, who denounces injustice, announces the coming of the kingdom, and reveals a God who does not cease to perform wonders on behalf of the poor.

Asian feminist theologians have also reclaimed more liberating images of Mary. Mary has been acknowledged for her historical consciousness and for her prophetic anger against the injustice of the rich and powerful. Instead of being set on a high pedestal, Mary is brought down to earth to be a fully liberated human being. Her virginity signals her autonomy and independence, not subjection to others; her mothering role points to her role as a giver of life to God and new humanity. As one of the founders of early Christianity, Mary is remembered for modeling the true discipleship of discernment, risk, and resistance for liberation. She is also seen as the co-redeemer with Christ for the salvation of humankind, because of her role as a model of liberation and her mediating role for the redemption of humanity (Chung 1990: 74–84).

In the ideological critique of Christian symbols, these theologians pay attention to the rhetorical and political functions of theology. Christianity has never been proclaimed in a vacuum, but is always situated within cultural and political discourses of power and authority, particularly so in a colonial context where power is so lopsided. The aim is the recovery of more positive and emancipatory symbols to mitigate the devastating effects of colonial Christianity and to create a new culture and consciousness for Christian women.

Cultural Politics and Theology

As gender became a contested site in the colonial encounter, male national elites responded by upholding male superiority as a longstanding and sacred tradition. In many parts of the South, feminist struggle has been enmeshed in the uneasy intersection of colonialism, nationalism, and Westernization. In some cases, these elite males hark back to a pristine period before colonization when their cultures were unpolluted, and staunchly resist social changes required by "modernization." The revival of fundamentalism and the concomitant restriction of women's social participation are familiar examples. And even when "modernization" is deemed necessary, some national elites hope only to imitate Western scientific and technological development, while keeping intact the spiritual and familial spheres, where they can still find a sense of belonging.

Feminist theology in the South entered the scene when these vigorous debates on cultural identity took place both in the secular sphere and in theological circles. For when male theologians tried to indigenize or contextualize Christianity into their native soils, many of them subscribed to an anthropological understanding of culture as unitary, holistic, governing the value and behavior of the whole people (Tanner 1997: 25–37). The myths of homogeneous national or cultural identity often benefit those who hold power and exclude women, minorities, and other diasporic communities, as Oduyoye (1995: 35) acidly observes: "Each time I hear 'in our culture' or 'the elders say' I cannot help asking, for whose benefit? Some person or group or structure must be reaping ease and plenty from whatever follows." Southern feminist theologians, on the one hand, have to counteract their male colleagues' assumption that feminism is a Western idea and not important to the theological agenda. On the other hand, they want to differentiate themselves from a Western, middle-class feminism, which tends to essentialize women's experience, as if women everywhere were the same, and focus primarily on the sex/gender system of particular societies.

Theologically, this means paying attention to multiple layers of women's oppression and employing this insight as a critical lens to look at the Bible and tradition. A notable example is Elsa Tamez's (1986) rereading of the figure of Hagar, a woman she says complicates the history of salvation. As a slave, Hagar is probably sold to Sarah as her servant out of extreme poverty. As an Egyptian, she is a member of a minority living among the Hebrews, whose customs and cultures are foreign and discriminate against her as a stranger. As a woman, her reproductive function is used to produce a male heir and her mistress is jealous of her and oppresses her. Yet, God with mercy and compassion appears to her in the wilderness and she not only experiences a theophany but also gives a name for God – the God who sees. Tamez's reading challenges a homogenization of the poor in Latin American theology, because she shows that the poor are always gender differentiated and culturally located. Rather than following a Marxist understanding of the poor in an economic sense, her work demonstrates that sexism must be included in the liberation of the poor from the cycles of oppression.

Another methodological concern is to integrate analyses of race and gender. For some time, Latin American theologians have been accused by other third world colleagues of leaving out racial oppression in their class analysis. Tamez (1996) addresses the issue by focusing on cultural violence among the three different levels of Latin American culture – indigenous, black, and mestizo-white. These different levels are interlocked in a complex web, for while the mestizo-white culture is influenced and dominated by that of the rich nations, it in turn marginalizes the black and indigenous women. Tamez advocates greater intercultural dialogue and solidarity among the racial groups.

Feminist theologians in other continents also urge the adoption of a more multilayered, fluid, and contestable notion of culture in theologizing. Musimbi

Kanyoro (2001) implores African feminists to engage in a "cultural hermeneutics" that utilizes insights from cultural analysis in evaluating which traditions should be kept and which should be abandoned. Oduyoye (1995: 19–76) demonstrates how this cultural hermeneutics works by providing a few principles in her critical evaluation of myths, folktales, and proverbs of Africa. She begins by asking how the corpus of "folktalk" reflects women's lives and what their rhetorical functions are in shaping women's attitudes and behavior. She then asks for whose benefit and interests these proverbs and myths are being told and perpetuated. She says women must be courageous enough to discard some of these myths if they are harmful to women, and begin to weave new patterns of meaning that sustain the mutual dependence and reciprocity of the human community.

Oduyoye's cultural hermeneutics is significant because of the primacy of oral resources in doing theology by African women: songs, storytelling, impromptu lyrics sung to interpret the Bible events and proclaim a call to worship. African male theologians have overlooked this rich layer of cultural resources because they devote more time to the written elitist culture. In a recent collection of essays on African women and the Bible, the contributors propose the methodologies of storytelling, the use of divination as social analysis, interpreting with nonacademic women, and challenging patriarchal and colonizing translations (Dube 2001). Since the majority of African Christian women are oral hearers and readers, the storytelling method is of particular importance. Stories are told and retold to interpret social reality, transmit values, and to pass on wisdom from generation to generation. Musa Dube (1998: 53) has called for a new mode of interpretation, using an oral-spiritual framework: "In the feminist oral-Spiritual space, responsible creativity that involves attentive listening to many oppressed voices and empathy; active prophecy that speaks against oppression and seeks liberation; and intent praying that seeks partnership with the divine, can begin to hear, speak and write new words of life and justice."

African feminist theologians are also concerned about cultural practices around rites of passage for women, and issues such as fertility, dowry, widowhood, sexuality, polygamy, and female circumcision. Western feminists have vehemently condemned the practices of polygamy and female circumcision from the perspective of sexual freedom and control of women, but Oduyoye (1992: 22–23) and Kanyoro (2001: 109–11) caution that these practices must be placed in the wider contexts of religious beliefs in Africa, the socioeconomic structure, and assumptions about human sexuality. While Western feminists advocate women's rights to control their bodies, freedom to seek pleasure, and monogamous companionship between two individuals, African cultures may have different understandings of human sexuality grounded in their own beliefs. Polygamy sometimes arises out of dire economic conditions and cannot be condemned outright without considering the situation. While some African feminist theologians call for an end to female circumcision, they are also mindful that some African women regard the practice as a part of their cultural heritage.

The relation between culture and religion also preoccupies Asian feminist theologians: they, too, need to address the issues of dowry, *sati*, widowhood, arranged marriage, and taboos against women in their continent. Indian theologian Aruna Gnanadason (1989), in particular, has written on how these practices limit women and the long history of Indian women's quest for emancipation. But Asian feminist theologians are also concerned about how Asian cultural elements, symbols, and images can be used in theologizing. The controversial presentation of Korean theologian Chung Hyun Kyung (1991) at the seventh assembly of World Council of Churches, in which she used East Asian philosophy, Buddhism, and Korean shamanism as resources for interpreting the Spirit, brought the issues of diversity and syncretism to the fore of the ecumenical debate.

In the ensuing discussion, in which Western Christians raised the limits of diversity and the boundaries of Christian identity, Asian feminist theologians (Kwok 1991; Chung 1996) have made several points. First, they have insisted that Christianity has never been pure and has continuously from its beginning adopted elements from different cultures. It is only when non-Western churches are doing so that more established churches and theologians label such practices as "syncretism" in a derogatory sense to exercise control and power. In fact, the relation between Gospel and culture has never been simply wholesale borrowing or outright rejection, but full of negotiation and contestation, as well as accommodation. If Asian theology is not to be simply the mimicry of Western theology, Asian theologians must be bold enough to experiment with many different forms of cultural dialogues and negotiations (Kwok 2000: 33–36). Second, Asian religious traditions are not driven by belief systems, nor are they primarily shaped by claims to truth and falsity, and as a result doctrinal purity has never been the concern of the common people, especially women. In religiously pluralistic Asia, where religious identities are less clearly defined and tightly bound than in the West, there has been much fluid adaptation and interplay among the traditions of Confucianism, Buddhism, Daoism, and Shinto. A Chinese person, for example, can adopt Confucian, Buddhist, and Daoist practices at different moments, depending on particular circumstances and religious need. Asian feminist theologians often find themselves embodying several religious traditions at once as they claim multiple spiritual roots. Such religious experience allows room for cultural hybridity and cross-fertilization between religions in theology. Third, while the church has found shamanistic practices troubling, these practices form part of the culture of women in Korea, especially among the lower class. Feminist theology needs to re-examine the liberating potential of marginalized women's cultures. Fourth, the critical norm by which Christian claims are to be judged is defined not by whether they conform to the theological system dictated by the West, but by the concrete Christian praxis of solidarity and liberation according to the demand of the Gospel. Noting that poor women do not care much about orthodoxy and have approached many religious resources for sustenance and empowerment, Chung (1990: 113) has challenged Asian feminist theology to move beyond doctrinal purity to risk survival- and liberation-centered syncretism. Some may not go as far as Chung, but her theological position challenges Asian Christians to go beyond their comfort zone to listen to the cries of people in Asia, the majority of whom (97 percent) are not Christian.

Ecojustice and the Struggle for Life

Colonization does not mean only the domination of people, but also the exploitation of natural resources for the development and benefit of the colonizers. In the 1920s Western powers controlled almost half the world's territory. With neocolonialism and globalization, national boundaries are less significant and the whole earth has become "fair game" for unbridled profiteering. Women in the South witness their subsistence and their role as managers of water and forest eroded and changed by the arrival of multinational corporations. Deforestation, pollution, environmental racism, and other ecological disasters have wrought havoc on the livelihood of poor women who simply dream of sufficient fuel and clean drinking water. When the Amazon forest disappears at an alarming rate and global warming threatens the basic fabric of life, the earth as a living organism has been undermined and its sustainability crippled. These life-and-death concerns necessitate theological reflections that take seriously consideration of ecological, feminist, and liberationist perspectives.

Known for her prophetic voice for poor women's rights, Ivone Gebara of Brazil has written the most poignant and comprehensive ecofeminist theology from a Latin American perspective. Her book *Longing for Running Water* both critiques the epistemological framework of traditional theology and offers resources for constructing new understandings of Trinity, Christology, and anthropology (Gebara 1999). She criticizes the hierarchical, dualistic, and patriarchal worldview that creates the dichotomies of God/creation, mind/body, men/women, and culture/nature. Within such a framework, God is modeled after the male ruling class, is outside of nature and controls the whole universe. Anthropocentrism coupled with monotheism allows Christianity, from its imperialist stance, to destroy other religious expressions that it considers inferior and to marginalize women's claim to sacred power.

Gebara distinguishes her ecofeminism from that being developed by more individualistic, middle-class "new age" movements in the North through her attention to race, globalization, and the claims of the poor. She argues that the images of God as patriarchal father, all-powerful Lord, king of all persons and living things, and as omnipotent and omnipresent, have functioned to keep poor women and men dependent on the church and others. Proposing a God of immanence and relationality, she seeks to overcome the dualism of spirit opposing matter and to speak of the interconnectedness of all beings in the mysterious Body of the universe. Such an understanding of the divine underlines the basic relatedness of human beings and our ethical responsibility toward one another and the planet.

Gebara accuses traditional Christologies, most of them hierarchical and anthropocentric, of separating Jesus from all other human beings and from the natural environment. Jesus has been imaged as the Messiah who comes in the guise of a superman, a heroic figure to save humans from their sins. Such atonement theory sustains the culture of dependence and focuses on human beings alone. Gebara invites us to consider a biocentric understanding of salvation, alluding to Jesus' actions on behalf of the sick, the hungry, the outcast, and the oppressed, and his call for the creation of new relationships between human beings and the earth. Jesus is not the powerful Son of God who dies on the cross and is resurrected as our "king," she opines, but is the symbol of the vulnerability of love and compassion:

> Jesus does not come to us in the name of a "superior will" that sent him; rather, he comes from here: from this earth, this body, this flesh, from the evolutionary process that is present both yesterday and today in this Sacred Body within which love resides. It continues in him beyond that, and it is turned into passion for life, into mercy and justice (Gebara 1999: 190).

Gebara's ecofeminist theology draws from and reconstructs the Christian tradition; Asian and indigenous feminists borrow insights from and welcome the contributions of other religions and traditions. While Chung (1996) has proposed a methodology that gives priority to and begins with Asian peoples' stories and religiosity, I have opted for a reinterpretation of the Bible and traditional resources informed by Asian cosmological insights. My concern is that the Bible has enormous power in the Asian churches and great impact on Asian Christian women. I also believe the Bible has rich insights for addressing our ecological crisis if it is not read in a predominantly anthropocentric way. For example, I have written on the possibility of developing an organic model of Christianity that understands sin and redemption not merely as disobedience or egotism of human beings, but as concepts and actions with significant cosmological consequences (Kwok 1997). Such a model pays attention to the plurality of images of Jesus in the New Testament, including the natural symbols: bread of life, the vine and the branches, and the hen protecting her brood. Jesus often shares table fellowship with the outcast, the tax collector, and the marginalized in society, while the miracles of feeding the hungry thousands testify to his concern for concrete human needs. His messianic banquet is open to all and welcomes people of all races.

An organic model may also revision Jesus as the incarnated Wisdom within the larger cultural and religious matrix of the wisdom tradition in the Asian traditions. Western feminist theologians have highlighted the figure of Jesus as Sophia-God, who embodies creative agency, immanence, and the promise of shalom, justice, and salvation. The Wisdom tradition can be examined and reflected upon from the vantage point of other wisdom figures and sages – such as Prajna, Guanyin, and Isis – in Asian and other religious traditions (Kim 2002). Thus, an organic model allows us to encounter Christ in many ways and many cultures, without being limited to a finite, historically conditioned human figure. The importance of Jesus as one epiphany of God does not exclude other christic images that Christians have constructed because of their diverse religious experiences and cultural contexts.

Feminist theologians in the South also look for cultural and religious principles and resources to overcome a mechanistic, capitalistic, and Darwinian mindset. Such cultural retrieval does not simply recreate a romantic past, but constructs a polemical discourse against the myth of globalization that proclaims no alternative exists. From the Indian background, Gnanadason lifts up the principle of Shakti, the feminine and creative source of the universe, characterized by harmony between humans and nature. Indian feminist ecotheology, she says, must draw from the well of the holistic vision based on their spiritual past, and not rely on the ideological and theological assumptions of Western paradigms. Citing the history of the Chipko movement, in which women protected the trees by hugging them, Gnanadason (1996: 79) says ecofeminist theology must come out of women's lived experience, "not only weeping with nature for deliverance and freedom, but out of years of organized resistance against senseless destruction."

Indigenous peoples have spoken passionately about the importance of the land in their sacred memory, rituals, and communal belonging (Weaver 1996). The conquest and pollution of the land is a sin against Mother Earth and a form of cultural genocide, depriving indigenous peoples not only of their means of survival but also of religious sites for cultural preservation. In their cosmological vision for theology and spirituality, Aboriginal and Pacific feminist theologians, such as Anne Pattel-Gray (1991), have emphasized a profound reverence for nature, communal ownership and stewardship, and women's roles in ceremonies and in providing sustenance for life. Similarly in Africa, religious scholars and theologians draw from the rich heritage of inclusive cosmological worldviews in different ethnic groups as resources for constructing a communal ethic of care, responsibility, and environmental justice. In the past, Westerners often labeled African religions pejoratively as animistic or as "nature worship." Feminist theologians have challenged such biases and recovered the significance of rituals and healing practices that teach about human beings' reliance on and collaboration with nature.

Conclusion

Compared to the feminist movement in the North, feminist struggle in the South has not been defined by the liberal politics of the women's suffrage movement, women's rights, and the demand for equal access to opportunities and privileges enjoyed by men. Feminists in the South do not have the luxury of attending to gender oppression alone, without simultaneously taking into consideration class, racial, colonial, and religious oppression. Their political theology takes many forms, including the option for solidarity with the poor, the critique of cultural alienation and racial repression, the challenge of the globalized economy, and activism for ecojustice and protection of nature. Virginia Fabella and Oduyoye (1988: xi) articulate the nature of such a theology:

> Our theology must speak of our struggles and the faith that empowers us. Our theology goes beyond the personal to encompass the community, and beyond gender to embrace humanity in its integrity. Our theology takes cognizance of academic studies but insists on the wider spectrum of women's experience and reality for its inspirations and insights. Being contextual in the Third World has meant that women's theology has embraced the religio-cultural besides the socio-economic and has engaged it in a living dialogue.

In contrast to the political theology of their male counterparts, feminist political theologies from the South do not lay so much emphasis on God as an actor in and judge of human history. Aware of the limitations of anthropocentric discourse about God, feminist theologians avoid portraying human history as the only arena for God. They also question the wisdom of projecting a God that is all-powerful and controlling, a protector and benefactor of women, modeled after privileged males. While male liberation theologians have exhorted the church to bring about social change, female theologians are more realistic about ecclesial power and their optimism more guarded. The church, steeped in male hierarchy and tradition, has to repent for its sexism before it can be a beacon of hope and an agent for change.

Feminist theologians in the South welcome opportunities for dialogue and seek solidarity with women in the North because feminist struggles are increasingly interconnected and global. They have also engaged in crosscultural conversation with women theologians from racial minorities in North America. With passion and compassion, they continue to articulate a new theological voice full of hope and joy, with reverence for life and respect for all things. Integrating theory and praxis, their political theology is rooted in the local, but connected to the global.

References

Althaus-Reid, M. (2001). *Indecent Theology: Theological Perversions in Sex, Gender, and Politics*. London: Routledge.

Chung, H. K. (1990). *Struggle to Be the Sun Again: Introducing Asian Women's Theology*. Maryknoll, NY: Orbis.

——(1991). "Come, Holy Spirit – Renew the Whole Creation." In M. Kinnamon (ed.), *Signs of the Spirit: Official Report, Seventh Assembly*, 37–47. Geneva: World Council of Churches.

——(1996). "Asian Christologies and People's Religions." *Voices from the Third World* 19: 1, 214–27.

Dube, M. (1998). "Scripture, Feminism, and Post-Colonial Contexts." *Concilium* 3, 45–54.

——(2001). "Introduction." In M. Dube (ed.), *Other Ways of Reading: African Women and the Bible*, 1–19. Geneva: World Council of Churches.

——(2002). "Postcoloniality, Feminist Spaces, and Religion." In L. E. Donaldson and P. L. Kwok (eds.), *Postcolonialism, Feminism, and Religious Discourse*, 100–20. New York: Routledge.

Fabella, V., and Oduyoye, M. A., eds. (1988). *With Passion and Compassion: Third World Women Doing Theology*. Maryknoll, NY: Orbis.

Gebara, I. (1999). *Longing for Running Water: Ecofeminism and Liberation*. Minneapolis: Fortress.

Gebara, I., and Bingemer, M. C. (1989). *Mary: Mother of God, Mother of the Poor*. Maryknoll, NY: Orbis.

Gnanadason, A. (1989). "Towards an Indian Feminist Theology." In V. Fabella and S. A. Lee Park (eds.), *We Dare to Dream: Doing Theology as Asian Women*, 117–26. Maryknoll, NY: Orbis.

——(1996). "Toward a Feminist Eco-Theology for India." In R. R. Ruether (ed.), *Women Healing Earth: Third World Women on Ecology, Feminism, and Religion*, 74–81. Maryknoll, NY: Orbis.

Hinga, T. M. (1992). "Jesus Christ and the Liberation of Women in Africa." In M. A. Oduyoye and M. R. A. Kanyoro (eds.), *The Will to Arise: Women, Tradition, and the Church in Africa*, 183–94. Maryknoll, NY: Orbis.

Jayawardena, K. (1986). *Feminism and Nationalism in the Third World*. London: Zed.

Kanyoro, M. R. A. (2001). "Cultural Hermeneutics: An African Contribution." In M. Dube (ed.), *Other Ways of Reading: African Women and the Bible*, 101–13. Geneva: World Council of Churches.

Kim, G. J. S. (2002). *The Grace of Sophia: A Korean North American Women's Christology*. Cleveland, Ohio: Pilgrim.

Kwok, P. L. (1991). "Gospel and Culture." *Christianity and Crisis* 51: 10–11, 223–4.

——(1995). "Business Ethics in the Economic Development of Asia: A Feminist Analysis." *Asia Journal of Theology* 9: 1, 133–45.

——(1997). "Ecology and Christology." *Feminist Theology* 15, 113–25.

——(2000). *Introducing Asian Feminist Theology*. Cleveland, Ohio: Pilgrim.

Mananzan, M. J. (1989). "Redefining Religious Commitment in the Philippine Context." In V. Fabella and S. A. Lee Park (eds.), *We Dare to Dream: Doing Theology as Asian Women*, 101–14. Maryknoll, NY: Orbis.

——(1991). "The Filipino Woman: Before and After the Spanish Conquest of the Philippines." In M. J. Mananzan (ed.), *Essays on Women*, 6–35. Manila: Institute of Women's Studies.

——(1993). "Paschal Mystery from a Philippine Perspective." *Concilium* 2, 86–94.

Narayan, U. (1997). *Dislocating Cultures: Identities, Traditions, and Third World Feminism*. New York: Routledge.

Oduyoye, M. A. (1992). "Women and Ritual in Africa." In M. A. Oduyoye and M. R. A. Musumbi (eds.), *The Will to Arise: Women, Tradition, and the Church in Africa*, 9–24. Maryknoll, NY: Orbis.

——(1995). *Daughters of Anowa: African Women and Patriarchy*. Maryknoll, NY: Orbis.

Pattel-Gray, A. (1991). *Through Aboriginal Eyes: The Cry from the Wilderness*. Geneva: World Council of Churches.

Tamez, E. (1986). "The Woman Who Complicated the History of Salvation." In J. S. Phobee and B. von Wartenberg-Potter (eds.), *New Eyes for Reading: Biblical and Theological Reflections by Women from the Third World*, 5–17. Oak Park, Ill.: Meyer Stone.
——(1996). "Cultural Violence against Women in Latin America." In M. J. Mananzan et al. (eds.), *Women Resisting Violence: Spirituality for Life*, 11–19. Maryknoll, NY: Orbis.
Tanner, K. (1997). *Theories of Culture: A New Agenda for Theology*. Minneapolis: Fortress.
Weaver, J. (1996). *Defending Mother Earth: Native American Perspectives on Environmental Justice*. Maryknoll, NY: Orbis.
Young, R. J. C. (2001). *Postcolonialism: A Historical Introduction*. London: Routledge.

CHAPTER 15
Feminist Theology, Northern

Elaine Graham

Feminist theology has shown that our societal oppression and ecclesial exclusion is not women's "fault", it is not the result of Eve's sin nor is it the will of God or the intention of Jesus Christ. Rather it is engendered by societal and ecclesiastical patriarchy and legitimized by androcentric world-construction in language and symbol systems. Insofar as religious language and symbol system function to legitimate the societal oppression and cultural marginality of women, the struggle against ecclesiastical silencing and ecclesial invisibility is at the heart of women's struggle for justice, liberation, and wholeness.

Elisabeth Schüssler Fiorenza, *"Breaking the Silence – Becoming Visible"*

Introduction

Feminist theology begins with a call for justice. The demand for women's full participation in ecclesial and cultural life underpins the entire feminist theological enterprise. Feminist theology may therefore be characterized as *political theology* in multiple ways: first, in its protest at women's subordination within church and society and second – in common with other twentieth-century theologies of liberation – in its vision of a renewed ecclesial and social order.

Feminist theology thus not only crystallizes questions about the impact of religious institutions and theological systems of belief and practice on the wider social and cultural domain; it also seeks to expose the ways in which the issue of power is embedded in the very formulation of theology itself, tracing and making visible "the political alignments of theological discourse" (Tanner 1997: 187) themselves. Whether it is the androcentric (male-centered) nature of received tradition, the role played by constructions of gender difference in what counts as religion, or the links between hierarchies of power and language used to name the divine, feminist theology identifies the systematic exclusion and suppression of women as a *theological* as well as a cultural/political problem.

"Feminism" is itself a contested term, normally held to refer to that body of theory and practice emerging out of the movements for women's emancipation in the United States and Europe during the twentieth century. It reflects both a sophisticated body of theoretical perspectives and a range of political campaigns: for women's suffrage, for sexual freedom, for equal pay, and for access to contraception, abortion, and medical care, as well as greater cultural, literary, and artistic expression (Tong 1998).

While the politics of gender provides a shared framework for woman-centered politics and theorizing, the common bonds of "women's experience" are complicated by other indices of power and difference, such as class, sexual orientation, race, and nationality. Hence, although the origins and earliest organized manifestations of the twentieth-century women's movement were in the United States and Europe, the diversity of feminist contexts and strategies has always engendered a sensitivity to the plurality and heterogeneity of the phenomenon, even within the societies of the first world. Although they have tended to dominate, both in theological and "secular" scholarship, it is important not to assume white, Anglo American perspectives to be the definitive norm to which other, derivative, forms must correspond. Rather, the proliferation of womanist (African American), *mujerista* (Latin American), Asian, African, Latina (Hispanic American) and feminist voices reflect a global patchwork of related but diverse contexts (Ortega 1995). This essay will concentrate on these core themes of unity and diversity within European American women's theological scholarship – feminist, womanist and Latina – and evaluate their position within the broader pantheon of political theologies.

Historical Overview

Historically, the emergence of the women's movement in Europe and North America may be traced to the social, political, and religious ferment of the seventeenth century. The theological convictions of radical dissenters, such as the Baptists, Society of Friends, Levellers, and other Puritan sects, had clear political implications. A strongly egalitarian theological anthropology, of all created equal in the sight of God, combined with an understanding of revelation in which anyone, regardless of temporal station, could be open to the promptings of the Spirit, plus an emphasis on the primacy of the Word of God in scripture freely available to all believers, helped to create the conditions under which women preachers and prophets could break the mould of male leadership (Mack 1992). During the eighteenth and nineteenth centuries, the same fusion of nonconformist theology and social reform provided vital opportunities for women to gain important skills in political leadership and strategic organization. Women like Elizabeth Cady Stanton, Sojourner Truth, Lucretia Mott, Susan B. Anthony, Elizabeth Fry, Florence Nightingale, Hannah Seacole, and Sara Grimke are remembered today not only as leading figures in campaigns for the abolition of slavery, universal suffrage, and social reform, but as early forerunners of religious feminism (Ruether 1998: 160–77).

Indeed, many contemporary feminist and womanist theologians regard it as part of their scholarly project to recover the contribution of radical Christianity to wider political and social movements and in particular to highlight the role of women. This is an important aspect of the construction of an alternative genealogy of political Christianity, in which progressive gender politics are seen as the forerunners of a contemporary "feminist liberationist Christianity" (Chopp 1995: 55). For example, the Roman Catholic North American Rosemary Radford Ruether, a historian by training, insists on the radical, dissenting traditions of Puritanism, Montanism, and Quakerism as the intellectual and political precursors of contemporary feminist theologies, discredited by those with a vested interest in suppressing their iconoclasm, but now restored as essential resources for a renewed feminist theology of liberation (Ruether 1983, 1998).

The emergence of feminist theology in the latter half of the twentieth century must, similarly, be placed within the context of wider social change. The position of women in the industrial societies of the United States and Europe began to change radically after 1945, due to an expansion of economic and educational opportunity and to technological innovations such as more effective contraception and labor-saving devices in the home. Nevertheless, the mismatch experienced by many women by the middle of the twentieth century between their widening horizons in the face of such improvements, and the persistence of what Betty Friedan termed "the feminine mystique" at the heart of white middle-class domestic gender relations, generated a wave of consciousness-raising and theorizing throughout the 1960s and 1970s.

Developments within the Christian churches themselves also assisted the cause of women. The admission of women to theological seminaries, and the expansion of higher education in general throughout the twentieth century in the United States and Europe, enabled a generation of Roman Catholic and Protestant women to pursue careers in theological teaching and research. The *aggiornamento* of the Second Vatican Council gave permission to a generation of Roman Catholics to explore issues of lay vocation, openness to secular thought, democratization of church structures and involvement in struggles for social justice. The insights of secular political theories, such as Marxism and feminism, thus became legitimate resources for theological analysis that consciously opened itself to the signs of the times, and allied itself with progressive struggles for justice.

Hence, the first generation of feminist theologians began to emerge. In the United States, Valerie Saiving's "The Human Situation: A Feminine View", first published in the *Journal of Religion* in 1960, is often regarded as the first published work of feminist theology. Mary Daly's *The Church and the Second Sex* (1968) is perhaps the first major text of North American feminist theology, although *Women and Religion* (1964), by Margaret Brackenbury Crook, a Unitarian minister and theologian, also broke new ground in its exposure of women's exclusion from the practices and canons of Christianity.

In Europe, the work of such early pioneers was eagerly appropriated. Scholars such as Catharina Halkes, Elisabeth Gossmann, and Kari Elisabeth Børreson began to develop critiques of Christian doctrine and ecclesiology from their particular academic and denominational contexts, although it was not until the mid-1980s that opportunities for university study in feminist theology were freed from church patronage, which often acted as a barrier to the advancement of women. From the emergent tradition of German political theology after 1945, Dorothee Sölle synthesized feminist analysis with radical spirituality, materialist readings of scripture, political activism and a critique of liberal Protestant existentialism to produce one of the most broadly based reconstructions of traditional theology, and remains one of the best-known and influential of contemporary political theologians (Sölle 1990, 2001).

Another factor in consolidating the academic and ecclesial positions of early feminist, womanist and Latina theologians was the encouragement of the World Council of Churches, which from its inception had championed the role of women and the laity within the ecumenical movement. As well as connecting academic and ecclesial theology with matters of practical policy – such as the feminization of poverty, gender roles, and violence against women – WCC influence has done much to bring feminist theologies of the two-thirds world to global prominence (Ortega 1995).

Feminist Theology as Theology of Liberation

Many of the first generation of Anglo American feminist theologians of the 1960s and 1970s were inspired by Latin American liberation theologies, largely by virtue of their shared links to progressive Roman Catholicism. An early example of dialogue between political theologians from North and South America was already by the mid-1970s giving prominence to structures of gender as well as class, race, and ethnicity (Eagleson and Torres 1976). The axiom adopted by Latin American liberation theologians, of "God's preferential option for the poor," was therefore taken to be especially relevant for a critique of women's status; not only were they most frequently among the poorest of the poor economically, but they were endemically and drastically absent from the history, doctrine, and structures of the Christian church itself. Through the work of writers such as Rosemary Ruether, Letty Russell, Ada-Maria Isasi-Diaz, and others, feminist, womanist, and Latina theologians continue to display clear affinities to this tradition through their attention to the dynamics of oppression and the identification of a compensatory tradition of prophetic/liberative teaching.

Yet the political dimensions of feminist theologies also have a distinctive flavor, reflecting the influence of wider second-wave feminist theorizing. The latter has always argued, for example, that "the personal is political," intending this as a corrective to the separation of public and private within orthodox liberal political theory. Politics is thus more adequately conceived as ". . . the conflict over the terms of our practical and passionate relations to one another and over all the resources and assumptions that may influence those terms" (Roberto

Unger, quoted in Tanner 1997: 180). Feminist theologians addressing issues such as work and poverty, disability and violence against women argue that attention to such concrete and immediate issues of concern only serves to illuminate the church's failure to incorporate women's experiences and reality into its pastoral, ethical, and ecclesial priorities (Graham 1993; Bons-Storm 1997; Couture 1991). The lack of credence given to the needs of women, the power of religious teaching in shaping gender stereotypes and expectations, and the uses to which theology has been put in rationalizing female subordination and self-abnegation, represent fatal distortions of the Christian Gospel (Miller-McLemore 2000: 239–41).

The Right Question . . .

From its beginnings, feminist theology addressed itself to perceived biases in the construction of core theological doctrines. Valerie Saiving's 1960 article posed the question of whether Christian understandings of sin and virtue were at root, "gendered": whether, far from sharing a common human condition in this respect, women and men inhabited radically different moral universes. In dialogue with the theological ethics of Reinhold Niebuhr, Saiving claims that conventional renderings of sin as "pride" and self-sufficiency, rather than creaturely dependence on God, reflect experiences which may hold true for men, for whom the establishment of autonomous personal identity is ingrained from early childhood with the boy's need to separate himself from the maternal relationship. (Saiving draws on psychoanalytical theory, albeit unattributed; but she was also articulating a critique of the view still current in liberal feminism that "morality has no sex".)

While typically masculine characteristics are "'pride' and 'will-to-power'", the cultural construction of femininity prizes 'triviality, distractibility, and diffuseness; lack of an organizing center or focus; dependence on others for one's own self-definition . . . sentimentality; gossipy sociability, and mistrust of reason – in short, underdevelopment or negation of the self' (Saiving 1979: 37). As a result, Christian moral teaching commends sacrifice and service as a corrective to pride; but for women, these merely serve to reinforce cultural expectations of self-abnegation and servitude. Sin for women is actually a failure to affirm their own independence and uniqueness; and to overcome these barriers requires a degree of self-love and self-assertion – pride, self-esteem, and dignity – which upbringing and culture have previously denied them.

Saiving set a pattern for much subsequent feminist theology, in her exposure of the inherent androcentricism of the tradition; but her perspective has continued within theological ethics too. Womanist theological reflection on evil and suffering, for example, suggests the dual dynamic of racism and sexism under which black women labor. "Sin" is not a matter solely of personal morality, therefore, but is enmeshed in political and economic structures of dehumanization and discrimination (Townes 1993).

Yet the objective of feminist, womanist, or Latina theologies cannot simply be one of being inducted into the extant tradition. While equality of access to ordained ministry, church leadership, and academic study are desirable goals, it is also clear that such activities have themselves been shaped within androcentric conventions, and that the very structures of theological anthropology themselves have radically excluded or misrepresented women's experience. Lasting change thus demands no less than "an intellectual paradigm shift from an androcentric world-view and theology to a feminist conceptualization of the world, human life, and Christian religion" (Fiorenza 1996b: 167).

Feminist theologians see a fundamental connection, therefore, between systems of patriarchal power in church and society and the deep symbolic structures of Western religion itself. An early articulation of this integral link between the symbolic and the material, between representation and reality, comes from the Jewish feminist theologian Judith Plaskow. She has argued strongly for the pervasive influence of religion as a source of cultural symbols. Adopting Simone de Beauvoir's analysis that women have been characterized as "Other" within a male-centered tradition, she observes that to be human has been equated with being *male*. More fundamentally, however, God is also named through that perspective – as privileging and sanctifying the qualities of hegemonic masculinity:

Obvious and innocuous as male God-language has come to seem, metaphors matter – on both an individual and social level. Though long usage may inure us to the implications of our imagery, religious symbols are neither arbitrary nor inert. . . . The male imagery Jews use in speaking to and about God emerges out of and maintain a religious system in which men are normative Jews and women are perceived as Other. (Plaskow 1980: 125)

It is not enough, Plaskow argues, to engage in feminist deconstruction of Jewish legal prohibitions against women. Nor is it adequate to promote a progressive but nonreligious form of Judaism, because these strategies do nothing to address the deep symbolic underpinning of Western culture. At the root is the naming of ultimate reality, which sacralizes a patriarchal worldview and perpetuates the characterization of women as misbegotten, not to mention preventing them from identifying themselves as made in the divine image. In other words, "the right question is theological" (Plaskow 1983) – and the root question is one of tracing the invisibility and exclusion of women from cultural, religious, and political systems back to their effacement from the very language used to name the divine. Language is thus regarded as a vital political device, by virtue of the pervasive influence of symbolic systems to sanction particular regimes of gender.

At its source, this claim draws upon the sociology of knowledge, identifying much of the theological tradition as the product of partial and ideological interests. Most crucial, of course, is the extent to which official tradition has failed to embrace the lives, achievements, and perspectives of women. As Rosemary Ruether has famously argued:

> The use of feminist theology lies not in its use of the criterion of experience but rather in its use of *women's* experience, which has been almost entirely shut out of theological reflection in the past. The use of women's experience in feminist theology, therefore, explodes as a critical force, exposing classical theology, including its codified traditions, as based on *male* experience rather than on universal human experience. (Ruether 1983: 13)

This enables theologians to argue that the tradition as historically and institutionally experienced is but one representation of the truth, not ultimate reality itself. As the product of human agency, a social and historical construction rather than an ontological given, it can also be contested and transformed (Ruether 1983: 19–20). Thus, such woman-centered theologies are not only disciplines of protest; there is acceptance, too, of the imperative to transform as well as to challenge. This is prompted not only by the need to expose the patriarchal biases of Christian tradition, however, but by the conviction that these very same revelations of faith have real potential for human liberation. This dialectic of "critique" and "reconstruction" represents possibly the most significant, creative – and problematic – contribution of feminist theological scholarship.

Critique and Reconstruction

> From the outset, the goal of liberating women had two aspects. First, feminists sought to identify the various forms of oppression that structured women's lives, and second, they imagined and sought to create an alternative future without oppression. What soon became apparent, however, was that oppression is not always easy to name. In fact, because oppression affects the very way one thinks about oneself and one's world, it is often quite difficult to even see, much less name. Oppression makes itself invisible, distorts vision, and twists thought. Similarly, it is hard to envision new ways of living when everything one experiences is rooted in old, oppressive, forms of knowing and acting. (Jones 2000: 3)

The process of protest and transformation is a recurrent thread within feminist theologies, and is characterized in a variety of ways. Sheila Briggs identifies three critical moments for feminist theological critique and reconstruction: the dismantling of patriarchal foundations; the recovery of women's past; and the transformation of present and future religious institutions. On the basis of such augmented tradition, feminist theology develops a revised alternative trajectory (Briggs 1997: 167; see also Miller and Grenz 1998; Chopp 1995). Similarly, Elisabeth Fiorenza argues for a hermeneutics of suspicion, remembrance, and transformation (1996c: 340), in which "suspicion" is directed towards the "silences, inconsistencies, incoherencies, and ideological mechanisms of andro-centric records and scholarship" (Fiorenza 1996b: 172–3); "remembrance" involves the vital commission to insist on women's inclusion as autonomous subjects, even against the grain of their historical absence and invisibility: "Women are Church, and always have been Church, called and elected by God" (p. 172); and transformation rests on the recovery of the historical evidence of the *ekklesia gynaikon*, or "discipleship of equals," which serves to animate a new paradigm for authentic discipleship and *praxis* by standing as the normative pattern for continuing communities of inclusive faith and practice. Fiorenza's criterion for authentic sources and norms thus places less emphasis on corre-spondence with historical events – as *archetype* – so much as fidelity to the testi-mony of the past as a *prototype* upon which contemporary communities should model themselves.

The androcentric bias within "God-talk" has also emerged as another impor-tant theme, another example of the way in which feminist theologians insist on the politically charged nature of religious language. Dorothee Sölle provides a useful example in her protest against the authoritarian ethic implicit in theo-logical metaphors of lordship, power, and fatherhood. Such language sanctifies what she terms a "Culture of Obedience" in which Christians surrender their destiny to an almighty, other-worldly power, a denial of alternative, life-affirm-ing values of human responsibility and self-worth (Sölle 1996: 152–3). Another direct connection between religious language and politics – in its broadest sense – is drawn by Sallie McFague's reconstitution of philosophical theology, in which "metaphor" is used as both deconstructive and reconstructive device. If all lan-guage for God is a human construct –provisional and contingent – then it is inevitable that it will reflect, maybe even reify, particular social relations. Yet that awareness enables communities of faith both to reflect critically and to engage in constructive renewal; even to generate novel images that address contempo-rary issues such as nuclear threat and ecological crisis (McFague 1982).

McFague's model criticizes the idea of a neutral vantage point from which human beings gain an objective understanding of divine reality. In this respect, she is not unique among contemporary theologians: her work is similar to that of David Tracy and Gordon Kaufman, for example. But the political promptings of feminist and ecological sensibilities enable McFague to make compelling con-nections between theological metaphor and structures of power. The reconsti-tution of trinitarian imagery as "Mother, Lover, Friend" enables a shift to "a new imaginative picture of the relationship between God and the world" (McFague 1987: xiv) which is, for McFague, the precondition for transformative action.

Traditional Christologies, similarly, have also been criticized by feminist and womanist theologians for their implicit biases. The maleness of Jesus has been seen by many writers as an insuperable obstacle to the redemption of women (Daly 1973), although others argue that it is the suffering humanity of Jesus that forms the kernel of a liberative Christology, and in particular his identifica-tion within his own ministry with the marginal and excluded (Ruether 1983).

Jacquelyn Grant has challenged representations of Jesus as a white European by synthesizing Ruether's analysis with that of James Cone, to argue that black women "embody" the reality of the crucified and risen Christ by virtue of the multiple effects of racism, economic disadvantage, and sexism (Grant 1989).

Yet any retelling of history or reconstruction of core doctrines already raises questions about the norms by which renewal is to be guided, and in particular how an authentic, as opposed to androcentric, canon is to be defined. In one of the earliest collections of essays on women and religion, the editors posed the following question: "Do feminists need the past – and if so, what past do they need?" (Christ and Plaskow 1979: 9). This represented a recognition that to name women as theological agents, historically and contemporaneously, also necessarily involves adjusting the criteria for what counts as legitimate knowledge. The processes of critique and retrieval have already required womanist, Latina, and feminist scholars to ask fundamental questions about the very nature of theological knowledge – how it is constituted, communicated, and authenticated.

For example, Ursula King argues that what counts as "religion," what counts as historical evidence for religious activity, what textual and documentary sources we have, is thoroughly "gendered" (King 1995). Grace Jantzen contends that successive interpreters have chosen to construe "mysticism" within an androcentric paradigm, a reworking of mysticism as private and personal, via its associations with "the feminine", interiority, and domesticity (Jantzen 1995). Effectively, this constituted a "privatization" of religious experience, thereby restricting its sphere of influence and diminishing its "political" impact. Motifs of gender are therefore deployed to reconstruct categories of religious experience in a way which fundamentally misrepresents the historical evidence.

While such additions to the historical narrative, and to Christian doctrine itself, have proved powerful means of restoring women as actors and agents, and not merely objects, feminist scholars have also felt the need to develop more sophisticated hermeneutical models in order to account for the systematic exclusion of women from history, and in order to construct ways of reading androcentric sources and texts in such a way as to glimpse agency beyond and beneath the absences. But how would anyone judge what elements of formerly hidden and silenced evidence might legitimately be included? What are the criteria by which such a critical-reconstructive position attempts to renew the existing discipline?

Judith Plaskow, once more, crystallizes a hermeneutical principle enshrined by many other feminist, Latina, and womanist theologians – that of the "canon within the canon" that serves simultaneously as critical and transformative principle: "The female images that exist in the Bible and (particularly the mystical) tradition form an *underground stream* that reminds us of the inadequacy of our imagery without, however, transforming its overwhelmingly male nature" (Plaskow 1983: 227, emphasis added).

The motif of the "underground stream," eclipsed by the dominant tradition yet enduring in parallel to the official tradition, is echoed elsewhere. Rosemary

Ruether talks of the "usable tradition" (Ruether 1983: 21), comprising both mainstream and marginalized sources, which enables Christian theology better to realize the values of the full humanity of women. Although liberatory strands within the extant tradition can be extracted by applying certain hermeneutical criteria, these need to be augmented by additional elements, such as non-canonical sources from the past, which have been constructed as marginal or heretical tradition by hegemonic authorities; and by contemporary resources that are consistent with the emancipatory trajectory of authentic faith.

The range of sources upon which feminist, womanist, and Latina theologians draw reveals the extent to which conventional sources and norms are reconfig-ured. Katie Cannon and Delores Williams both emphasize the centrality of black women's authentic voices for the reconstruction of the womanist theological canon, a resource more likely to be accessible through literary and oral sources than enshrined within official tradition. This may be considered to constitute a kind of "theology in the vernacular," articulated in the "voices, actions, opin-ions, experience, and faith" of African American communities, and especially in the lives of black women. A typical example of such a preoccupation with the hiddenness of black women's genius, and the political imperative to work for its restoration, is the rehabilitation of the work of the African American writer Zora Neale Hurston by the novelist Alice Walker and the womanist theologian Katie Cannon. Walker's vivid account of her attempt to find Hurston's final resting-place, an unmarked grave in the small town where she died, provides a com-pelling metaphor for so much of the project to retrieve and re-evaluate those who died in obscurity but who are now considered definitive forerunners to womanist revisioning (Walker 1984). Katie Cannon draws on Hurston's nonconformist approach to moral reasoning and political agency to articulate a distinctive womanist ethical system grounded in what she terms "quiet grace as truth" (Cannon 1988: 125).

The Cuban theologian Ada-Maria Isasi-Diaz, now based in the United States, adopts an ethnographic approach to the problem of accessing "women's experi-ence." The grassroots organizations of *communidades ecclesial de base* find their equivalent in her accounts of Hispanic American women. Once more, the every-day, "vernacular" quality of their narratives emerges as most striking, enabling Isasi-Diaz to argue that in the face of racism and sexism, Latina women draw on indigenous resources of popular religion and Hispanic culture to forge a distinc-tive ethic of self-esteem and moral agency (Isasi-Diaz 1993). Such an acknowl-edgment of the particular and autobiographical as a resource for the remaking of theological tradition is typical of Latina, feminist, and womanist thought, espe-cially in its strong emphasis, once more, on the personal as political: narrative as revelatory of formerly unsung testimonies of oppression and resistance.

Yet to insist, as feminist, womanist, and Latina theologians do, on the endur-ing liberatory trajectory of some parts of the tradition while maintaining an oppositional stance toward much of its legacy, is in many ways an uncomfort-able, even inconsistent, position. Those who continue to inhabit mainstream ecclesiastical institutions tread a fine line between hegemonic/patriarchal and subversive/feminist sources. This is in some respects a debate about the nature of "usable tradition" itself, and how its deployment actually effects positive change. There is a danger, as critics point out, that one will commit the error of *eisegesis* rather than *exegesis*, and remake the evidence according to one's own preferences (Woodhead 1997). Feminists would respond by arguing that no reading of tradition is objective or neutral, and that their central criterion of "usable tradition" enables them to maintain fidelity to the essentials of the past by means of a contemporary revisionist hermeneutic. Yet there is still some contradiction between those feminist theologians who locate real change in the transformation of consciousness via the power of metaphor and language – as in McFague's advocacy of new models of God, for example – and those who endorse what is effectively a form of *orthopraxy*: Christian doctrines and practices are deemed liberative, not by virtue of an inherent, essentialist meaning, but insofar as they are appropriated in pursuit of practical ends (Hogan 1995; Chopp 1995).

Rebecca Chopp argues that the old (patriarchal) distinction between theory (theology, philosophy, texts, doctrines) and practice (ethics, politics, community) must be erased, in favor of an understanding of theology as the critical discipline which articulates the ultimate values by which Christian obedience and transformation are guided (Chopp 1995). The struggle of women for material and social justice forms the fundamental reality for feminist critique and reconstruction. The adequacy of any theology for women is therefore measured by the extent to which it provides the values and visions for the struggle of women against injustice and towards liberation. "Authentic" tradition is understood not in terms of correspondence with propositional truth, but in the power of a text, doctrine, or practice to inspire faithful action and transformation. Rather than seeking the "canon within a canon," therefore, and identifying the authoritative sources and norms as existing in past origins, this approach regards all "tradition" as a system of symbolic resources in constant circulation, available for strategic deployment.

This alleviates the need for a return to origins, admits that no past time may have been entirely egalitarian, but enables elements of received canonical wisdom to be reappropriated. It also restores a necessary fluidity to the notion of tradition and acknowledges, with Michel Foucault, the ubiquity and interrelatedness of hegemony and resistance. Thus, for Kathryn Tanner, the task is less a total deconstruction of inherited patriarchal concepts, resources, and practices than their "realignment." The influence of poststructuralist theories is also evident here, for meanings are understood to be fluid and available for renegotiation. The question of "usable tradition" re-emerges, therefore, as one of political contestation and pragmatism, as cultural resources for the active construction and deployment of resistance. "Feminist theologians are not forced to produce a feminist discourse from the bottom up; they do not have to try to replace patriarchal theological discourse with another form of theological discourse having as little as possible to do with the first. That kind of enterprise would be quite difficult to maintain in its purity" (Tanner 1997: 188).

The question remains, however, where such communities of realignment and *praxis* might actually reside, and where the dominant focus of feminist liberationist Christianity should be. This may be due to the very pluralism and heterogeneity to which womanist, feminist, and Latina theologians point, not to mention their diversity of constituencies, which reflect the threefold loyalties of David Tracy's "three publics" of Christian theology – political, academic, and ecclesial contexts. Yet such multiplicity of focus may not be an advantage in terms of generating incisive debate about the future at a time when many other factors are also calling into question the coherence and future direction of second-wave feminism itself.

Future Prospects

A glance at the current state of feminist theory reveals an intriguing agenda for the theological community, but also exposes a number of weaknesses in feminist theology as it is currently conceived. Despite – perhaps because of – its emphasis on the crucial impact of the category of "women's experience," for example, Latina, womanist, and feminist theologies have tended to be somewhat undertheorized in terms of critical theories of gender. While recent publications have gone some way toward redressing the lack of attention to feminist theory (Chopp and Daveney 1997; Jones 2000), significant omissions remain.

For example, early confidence in the transparency of women's experience has been complicated by a number of new developments. First, the plurality and specificity of feminist, womanist, and *mujerista* communities has reconfirmed the difficulties inherent in claiming a universal subject, "Woman," as the basis of emancipatory knowledge. Second, the so-called "death of the subject" associated with poststructuralism has been perceived by many, including feminists, as depriving formerly excluded and invisible groups of a coherent discourse of identity and self-determination. As Nancy Hartsock put it, "Why is it, exactly at the moment when so many of us who have been silenced begin to demand the right to name ourselves, to act as subjects rather than objects of history, that just then the concept of subjecthood becomes 'problematic'?" (Hartsock 1990: 206). Third, conventional models of "sex" and "gender," in which the former denoted the biological underpinnings of male and female, and the latter the culturally constructed roles and identities imposed by socialization, have been displaced by new approaches. "Queer theory" (Jagose 1997) unpicks the seamless link connecting biological sex, gender identity, and sexual orientation and challenges the traditional dimorphism of sex/gender systems in favor of a proliferation of identities and preferences (Gudorf 2001). Meanwhile, the neopsychoanalytic feminism of writers such as Luce Irigaray unsettles minimalist or anti-essentialist approaches to sexual difference by celebrating women's embodied difference as the source of a new feminine subjectivity and spirituality (Irigaray 1985).

Some feminist theologians have responded to the challenge by recasting women's experience as "complex, textured amalgams of resistance and collusion" (Ronan 1998: 3), and refuting representational or transparent models of language and subjectivity in favor of those informed by poststructuralism (Fulkerson 1994; Chopp 1989; Ronan 1998). However, no feminist theologian has yet to come to terms with the radical complications of agency, subjectivity, and identity represented by feminist scholars such as Donna Haraway and Judith Butler, partly because both writers express versions of antihumanism: Haraway in her ironic invocation of posthuman subjectivity, and Butler in her skepticism toward any kind of foundationalist notion of agency prior to discourse (Haraway 1991; Butler 1999).

Just as the first generation of feminist theologians were provided with early momentum by the wider women's, civil rights, trade union, and peace movements of the 1960s and 1970s, so the future of the discipline will be affected in part by wider political developments. Given the vogue for "postfeminism" – a confusing phenomenon which seems to wish to claim, simultaneously, that feminism is redundant, having achieved its goals, *and* that it has failed because it has fundamentally misjudged the needs and desires of women (Coward 1999) – or talk of "backlash" (Oakley and Mitchell 1997), and even "third-wave" feminism (Stainton Rogers and Rogers 2001), it is not surprising that the achievements and assumptions of an earlier generation of women have come under scrutiny. Inevitably, the theological voices of women coming to prominence at the beginning of the twenty-first century will sound a different note from those 30 or 40 years their senior; but it is difficult at the moment to identify the equivalents of second-wave feminism and liberation theology as the practical contexts upon which such successor generations will draw.

Conclusion

The earliest generation of feminist theologians were concerned to adopt secular feminist perspectives into theological discourse as a means of exposing its androcentrism. In this respect, feminist theologians allied themselves with secular critics of religion in identifying religious institutions and theological systems as cultural sources of political oppression, and this remains one of their most significant contributions for political theology as a whole. The difference rests, of course, in the conviction of some (but not all) scholars of religion that, despite its ideological uses, Christianity can be reformed – indeed restored – into a more equitable and liberative force. Indeed, this dialectic between the historical reality of religion and its utopian promise is the most consistent and unifying theme across the entire feminist-womanist-Latina spectrum.

Yet it may be time for feminist theologians to challenge more vigorously the incipient secularism of much second-wave (Anglo American) feminism. It may be a measure of its intellectual isolation that feminist perspectives in the study of religion and theology are still largely ignored in the academy. Yet such a perspective fails to acknowledge the experience of many women around the world, and obscures the importance of spirituality for political struggle, as Michele Lelwica has argued:

> I believe it is vital for those of us who study women and religion to take more initiative in addressing the antipathies and assumptions that turn religion and feminism into mortal enemies. Such a polarized dynamic obscures what religious consciousness and feminist consciousness share – at least potentially – namely, an alternative way of seeing and acting in a broken world, a way that points beyond, as it struggles to transform, current realities. (Lelwica 1998: 122–3)

At the heart of feminist liberationist Christianity lies an insistence on the reconstruction of religion in the name of a more wholesome spirituality ("the right question is *theological*"). But feminist theologies remain somewhat divided between approaches that concentrate on reinterpreting key sources, texts, and symbols of the tradition, and those that pursue more practical, political endeavors. Perhaps the significance of feminist interventions in political theology rests in the realization that both are necessary: a reminder of the "power of naming" (Fiorenza 1996a) alongside that of acting. This theme has emerged strongly in this overview, and is concerned with the political – at personal and structural levels – significance of affirming women's presence in religious traditions, of rendering them visible within the prevailing symbolic structures of Christian theology, and nominating them as historical agents. It is also, however, about the interconnectedness of metaphor and power, of symbolic and material; and of the need to harness the power of language, doctrine, and symbol to effect new visions and new structures in church and society.

References

Bons-Storm, R. (1997). "Putting the Little Ones into the Dialogue: a feminist practical theology." In D. Ackermann and R. Bons-Storm (eds.), *Liberating Faith: Feminist Practical Theologies in International Context*, 9–26. Kampen, Netherlands: Kok Pharos.

Briggs, S. (1997). "A History of Our Own: What Would a Feminist History of Theology Look Like?" In R. S. Chopp and S. G. Daveney (eds.), *Horizons in Feminist Theology: Identity, Tradition, and Norms*, 165–78. Minneapolis: Fortress.

Butler, J. (1999). *Gender Trouble: Feminism and the Subversion of Identity*, 2nd edn. London: Routledge.

Cannon, K. G. (1988). *Black Womanist Ethics*. Atlanta: Scholars.

——(1989). "Moral Wisdom in the Black Women's Literary Tradition." In C. P. Christ and J. Plaskow (eds.), *Weaving the Visions: New Patterns in Feminist Spirituality*, 281–92. San Francisco: Harper & Row.

——(1995). *Katie's Canon: Womanism and the Soul of the Black Community*. New York: Continuum.

Chopp, R. S. (1989). *The Power to Speak: Feminism, Language, God*. New York: Crossroad.
——(1995). "Feminist Queries and Metaphysical Musings." *Modern Theology* 11: 1, 47–63.
——(1996). "Theological Methodology." In L. M. Russell and S. Clarkson (eds.), *Dictionary of Feminist Theologies*, 180–2. Louisville, Ky.: Westminster/John Knox.
Chopp, R. S., and Daveney, S. G. (eds.) (1997). *Horizons in Feminist Theology: Identity, Tradition, and Norms*, Minneapolis: Fortress.
Christ, C. P., and Plaskow, J. (1979). "Introduction: WomanSpirit Rising." In C. P. Christ and J. Plaskow (eds.), *WomanSpirit Rising*, 17. San Francisco: Harper & Row.
Collins, P. H. (1991). *Black Feminist Thought*. London: Routledge.
Couture, P. D. (1991). *Blessed Are the Poor? Women's Poverty, Family Policy, and Practical Theology*. Nashville: Abingdon.
Coward, R. (1999). *Sacred Cows: Is Feminism Relevant to the New Millennium?* London: HarperCollins.
Daly, M. (1973). *Beyond God the Father*. Boston: Beacon.
Eagleson, J., and Torres, S., eds. (1976). *Theology in the Americas*. Maryknoll, NY: Orbis.
Fiorenza, E. S. (1983). *In Memory of Her: A Feminist Theological Reconstruction of Christian Origins*. London: SCM.
——(1994a). *Searching the Scriptures*, vol. I: *A Feminist Introduction*. London: SCM.
——(1994b). *Searching the Scriptures*, vol. II: *A Feminist Commentary*. London: SCM.
——(1996a). "Feminist Liberation Theology as Critical Sophialogy." In E. S. Fiorenza (ed.), *The Power of Naming*, xiii–xxxix. Maryknoll, NY: Orbis.
——(1996b). "Breaking the Silence – Becoming Visible." In E. S. Fiorenza (ed.), *The Power of Naming*, 161–74. New York: Orbis.
——(1996c). "Justified by All Her Children: Struggle, Memory and Vision." In E. S. Fiorenza (ed.), *The Power of Naming*, 339–58. New York: Orbis.
Fulkerson, M. M. (1994). *Changing the Subject: Women's Discourses and Feminist Theology*. Minneapolis: Fortress.
Graham, E. L. (1993). "The Sexual Politics of Pastoral Care." In E. L. Graham and M. Halsey (eds.), *Life-Cycles: Women and Pastoral Care*, 210–24. London: SPCK.
Grant, J. (1989). *White Women's Christ and Black Women's Jesus: Feminist Christology and Womanist Response*. Atlanta: Scholars.
Gudorf, C. E. (2001). "The Erosion of Sexual Dimorphism: Challenges to Religion and Religious Ethics." *Journal of the American Academy of Religion* 69: 4, 863–91.
Haraway, D. J. (1991). "A Cyborg Manifesto: Science, Technology, and Socialist-Feminism in the Late Twentieth Century." In *Simians, Cyborgs and Women: The Reinvention of Nature*, 149–82. London, Free Association Books.
Hartsock, N. (1990). "Rethinking Modernism: Minority vs. Majority Theories." *Cultural Critique* 6–7, 187–206.
Hogan, L. (1995). *From Women's Experience to Feminist Theology*. Sheffield: Sheffield Academic Press.
Irigaray, L. (1985). *This Sex Which Is Not One*. Trans. C. Porter and C. Burke, Ithaca, NY: Cornell University Press. (First publ. 1978.)
Isasi-Diaz, A. M. (1993). *En la Lucha/In the Struggle: Elaborating a Mujerista Theology*. Minneapolis: Fortress.
Jagose, A. (1997). *Queer Theory: An Introduction*. New York: New York University Press.

Jantzen, G. M. (1995). *Power, Gender and Christian Mysticism.* Cambridge: Cambridge University Press.

Jones, S. (2000). *Feminist Theory and Christian Theology: Cartographies of Grace.* Minneapolis: Fortress.

Kanyoro, M. R. A. (1996). "Naming." In L. M. Russell and S. Clarkson (eds.), *Dictionary of Feminist Theologies* 191. Louisville, Ky.: Westminster/John Knox.

King, U., ed. (1995). *Religion and Gender.* Oxford: Blackwell.

Lelwica, M. (1998). "From Superstition to Enlightenment in the Race for Pure Consciousness: Antireligious Currents in Popular and Academic Feminist Discourse." *Journal of Feminist Studies in Religion* 14: 2, 108–23.

McFague, S. (1982). *Metaphorical Theology: Models of God in Religious Language.* London: SCM.

——(1987). *Models of God: Theology for an Ecological, Nuclear Age.* London: SCM.

Mack, P. (1992). *Visionary Women: Ecstatic Prophecy in Seventeenth-Century England.* Berkeley: University of California Press.

Miller, L., and Grenz, S. J. (1998). *Fortress Introduction to Contemporary Theologies.* Minneapolis: Fortress.

Miller-McLemore, B. J. (2000). "How Sexuality and Relationships have Revolutionized Pastoral Theology." In S. Pattison and J. W. Woodward (eds.), *Blackwell Reader in Pastoral and Practical Theology,* 233–47. Oxford: Blackwell.

Oakley, A., and Mitchell, J., eds. (1997). *Who's Afraid of Feminism? Seeing Through the Backlash.* London: Penguin.

Ortega, O. (1995). *Women's Visions: Theological Reflection, Celebration, Action.* Geneva: World Council of Churches.

Plaskow, J. (1980). *Standing Again at Sinai.* San Francisco: Harper & Row.

——(1983). "The Right Question is Theological." In S. Heschel (ed.), *On Being a Jewish Feminist,* 223–33. New York: Schocken.

Ronan, Marian (1998). "Reclaiming Women's Experience: A Reading of Selected Christian Feminist Theologies." *Cross Currents* 48: 2, 1–15.

Ruether, R. R. (1983). *Sexism and God-Talk.* London: SCM.

——(1985). *Women-church: Theology and Practice of Feminist Liturgical Communities.* New York: Harper & Row.

——(1998). *Women and Redemption: A Theological History.* London: SCM.

Saiving, V. (1979). "The Human Situation: A Feminine View." In C. P. Christ and J. Plaskow (eds.), *WomanSpirit Rising,* 25–42. San Francisco: Harper & Row. (First publ. 1960.)

Sölle, D. (1990). *Thinking About God: An Introduction to Theology.* London: SCM.

——(1996). "Paternalistic Religion." In E. S. Fiorenza (ed.), *The Power of Naming,* 150–60. New York: Orbis.

——(2001). *The Silent Cry: Mysticism and Resistance.* Minneapolis: Fortress.

Stainton Rogers, W., and Rogers, R. (2001). *The Psychology of Gender and Sexuality.* Milton Keynes: Open University Press.

Tanner, K. (1997). "Social Theory Concerning the 'New Social Movements' and the Practice of Feminist Theology." In R. S. Chopp and S. G. Daveney (eds.), *Horizons in Feminist Theology: Identity, Tradition, and Norms,* 179–97. Minneapolis: Fortress.

Tong, R. (1998). *Feminist Thought: A Comprehensive Introduction,* 2nd edn. Brighton: Harvester Wheatsheaf.

Townes, E. M., ed. (1993). *A Troubling in my Soul: Womanist Perspectives on Evil and Suffering.* Maryknoll, NY: Orbis.

Walker, A. (1984). "Looking for Zora." In *In Search of Our Mothers' Gardens*, 93–116. London: Women's Press.

Williams, D. S. (1993). *Sisters in the Wilderness: The Challenge of Womanist God-Talk.* Maryknoll, NY: Orbis.

Woodhead, L. (1997). "Spiritualising the Sacred: A Critique of Feminist Theology." *Modern Theology* 13: 2, 191–212.

CHAPTER 16
Jürgen Moltmann

Nicholas Adams

Moltmann's political theology is a theology of hope, a theology of the cross, a pneumatology, an ecclesiology, a doctrine of creation, a doctrine of the Trinity, and an eschatology. In other words, political theology is not a separate topic, but a dimension and a language which permeates everything. It is, moreover, a recognizably German political theology, which is to say it is best, although not exclusively, interpreted against the backdrop of German philosophy and German politics. The relationship between ideal and concrete is a big theme in Moltmann's political theology, and the failure of the German political establishment to face up adequately to its mid-twentieth-century history is at the heart of Moltmann's account of the relation between memory and hope. This essay will examine Moltmann's political theology under three headings: "Eschatology," "Christology," and "Ecclesiology." These are not separate, however, because for Moltmann these three (and all other areas of doctrine) mutually inform and develop each other. Moltmann, influenced by Johann Baptist Metz, understands political theology as reflection that arises once one perceives that the church has often colluded with forms of society that privilege the rich, the white, or the male (or, as in Europe, all three), and thus stands in need of radical critique and healing. Moltmann attempts to allow these kinds of reflection to permeate his systematic theology; this chapter traces some of the more significant lines of thought.

The parts of Moltmann's work of particular relevance to political theology can be divided up into three main blocks – first the books explicitly on politics: *Religion, Revolution and the Future* (1969), *Hope and Planning* (1971), *On Human Dignity: Political Theology and Ethics* (1984), and *Creating a Just Future: The Politics of Peace and the Ethics of Creation in a Threatened World* (1989); second, the early trilogy *Theology of Hope* (1965), *The Crucified God* (1974), and *The Church in the Power of the Spirit* (1975); and third, the extended systematic theology: *Trinity and the Kingdom of God* (1981), *God in Creation* (1985), *The Way of Jesus Christ* (1989), *The Spirit of Life: A Universal Affirmation* (1992), *The Coming of*

God: Christian Eschatology (1995), and *Experiences in Theology* (2000). This chapter focuses on the second group, the trilogy, as the major themes can be seen here in clear outline. These works show how Moltmann's theology and political sensibilities develop side-by-side, and I indicate how Moltmann's theology is political, and his politics theological. Discussion of other texts is introduced where their arguments contradict or significantly develop those in the early trilogy. The disadvantage of this approach is that Moltmann's engagement with Marxism and other political movements receives no attention here. Those who wish to explore this fascinating area, not least Moltmann's involvement with the *Paulusgesellschaft* (a forum for Christians and Marxists to meet and discuss), should consult the more singlemindedly political writings.[1]

Eschatology

Moltmann's eschatology, profoundly influenced by the work of the Jewish atheist philosopher Ernst Bloch, is an attempt to describe theologically the relationship between the present and the future. More particularly, Moltmann tries to show how the power of the future illuminates and makes possible what Christians are given, through the Holy Spirit, the power to imagine. The central message of Moltmann's *Theology of Hope* (5th edn. 1965) is that eschatology is not merely an appendix to dogmatics but the medium of theological thinking itself (Moltmann, 1967: 41).[2] Its subsidiary thesis is that the dual heritage of Christian thought from Israel's narrative and Greek philosophy has, in Christian eschatology, been biased toward the latter, and stands in need of correction. Moltmann believes that the Greek *logos*, with its "epiphany of the eternal present of being," obscures "the *promise* which has stamped the language, the hope and the experience of Israel" (pp. 40–1).

Moltmann's eschatological project is to renew Israel's sense of promise, through a sustained reflection on what it means to *anticipate* God's future for the world, given and made known in the life, death, and Resurrection of Jesus Christ. The problems which eschatology tackles arise from the lack of fit between experiences of the present and promises of the future. "Our present experience of suffering, evil and death" stands in stark contradiction to the promise of "a new creation of all things in righteousness and peace" (1967: 19, 23). Which is more real: the present experience or the future promise? Moltmann tries to show that this question is misleading because it rests on dubious assumptions about what reality is, and how Christians ought to describe it. The present is certainly dark, and Christians must not deny or suppress this knowledge. Rather, they must add to it. Christians add their knowledge of Jesus Christ, and thus confront the "closed wall of suffering, guilt and death . . . at the point where they have in actual fact been broken through" in Christ's death and Resurrection (p. 19). Without this knowledge, any idea of a different future would be a pipe-dream that distracts people from addressing life's real hardships.

Because Christian imagination is rooted in a memory of Christ's Resurrection it is freed from the twin dangers of presumption and despair. Presumption means celebrating in advance, like the hare in the fable of the Hare and the Tortoise, and thus failing to understand the fragility of our actions and the real possibility of human failure; despair means giving up because the task seems impossible, and thus failing to understand the difference between what is impossible and what is difficult. The way to God's future is difficult, but not impossible. And because that way is Jesus Christ, the difficulty is not ours to bear alone: we are part of that way, and are able to awaken the power of God's future in the present. Moltmann sums up all of this in one word: *hope*. In doing so, Moltmann joins a tradition he inherits from Joseph Pieper that stretches back to Aquinas and Augustine, and their interpretations of the Lord's Prayer: thy kingdom come. And because eschatology awakens a power to transform the present, it is at the same time political theology.

> The raising of Christ is not merely a consolation in a life that is full of distress and doomed to die, but it is also God's contradiction of suffering and death, of humiliation and offence, and of the wickedness of evil. . . . Faith, wherever it develops into hope, causes not rest but unrest, not patience but impatience. It does not calm the unquiet heart, but is itself this unquiet heart in man. Those who hope in Christ can no longer put up with reality as it is, but begin to suffer under it, to contradict it. Peace with God means conflict with the world. (1967: 21)

Moltmann has set himself a formidable task here. He wishes to marry together the Christian tradition of the "theological virtues" (faith, hope, and love), above all the virtue of hope, with a major topic in twentieth-century German philosophy, namely "anticipation." This means different things for different thinkers. In the philosophy of Gadamer (following Heidegger), anticipation is the act that a reader performs when trying to determine the meaning of a text. A reader "anticipates" what the whole text means, even before she has finished reading it, and interprets the particular passages she is reading in the light of this. There is a feedback where such anticipations are challenged and altered in the light of what is read, and what is read is interpreted in the light of such anticipations. Moltmann learns from this that the eschatological horizon of the Christian narrative "is not a closed system, but includes also open questions and anticipations and is therefore open towards the new and the unknown" (1967: 191). In the philosophy of Ernst Bloch (following Schelling), anticipation is the act of the political visionary who discerns the trajectory of history, has a sense of what is possible, and allows this sense to transform his imagination and his practice. Moltmann learns from this that "hope has the chance of a meaningful existence only when reality itself is in a state of historic flux and when historic reality has room for open possibilities ahead. Christian hope is meaningful only when the world can be changed by him in whom this hope hopes" (p. 92).[3]

Neither of these philosophies is sufficient for a *Christian* account, however, because Gadamer's anticipation of the whole is a revisable product of the reader's activity and Bloch's anticipation of real possibilities is a product of nature's inherent tendency. By contrast, the Christian anticipation of the whole in eschatology is a promise given by God, and thus neither a product of human activity nor revisable by us; and the possibilities of history are given by God, rather than belonging to nature. Moltmann thus needs to modify this strand of German philosophy by appealing to scripture rather than hermeneutics in general (Gadamer), and to Christology rather than natural teleology (Bloch). The result is an understanding of Christian eschatology as human anticipation of the horizon of possibility given by God and made known by God in Jesus Christ.

The main thrust of *Theology of Hope* is to insist that when Christians speak of "reality" they are not concerned exclusively or even primarily with what has happened or what is happening. They must also understand that their anticipations of the future – God's future for creation – are part of reality, have an effect on it, and radically change it. Eschatology does not concern an "eternal present" or the "breaking-in of eternity"; it concerns a promised future which changes the present. Put differently: imagination is real. Politics, for Moltmann, is the art of the imagination just as much as the art of the real.

Moltmann revisits this material in *The Coming of God* (1995), which, in a more sustained way, reads Jewish philosophy (Bloch, Rosenzweig, Scholem, Benjamin) to correct the tendency in some German Christian theology (e.g. Barth, Althaus, Bultmann) to equate eschatology with eternity. Whereas *Theology of Hope* was an experimental Christian rethinking of themes in recent German philosophy, the topics covered in *The Coming of God* (death, the kingdom of God, and the new creation) are dictated more directly by the demands of dogmatic theology. The main difference between *Theology of Hope* and *The Coming of God* is that the former tries to cast the whole of theology from the single perspective of eschatology, whereas the latter reinterprets eschatology as part of a broader network of interrelating doctrines.

Christology

"In the Reformation, the theology of the cross was expounded as a criticism of the church; how can it now be realized as a criticism of society?" (Moltmann 1974: 317). Just as in *Theology of Hope*, Moltmann insists that eschatology makes all finite human action questionable, so in his second major book *The Crucified God* (2nd edn. 1973), he insists that the cross stands as a permanent objection to human certainties. It enables people "to criticize and stand back from the partial historical realities and movements which they have idolized and made absolute" (1974: 17). This change of emphasis, from a largely philosophical framework of eschatology to a more troubled meditation on the crucified Christ, is significant. The philosophical and theological arguments of *Theology of Hope* depend on sophisticated rethinking of the concept of reality through a re-engagement with the Aristotelian tradition of describing things as either "potential" or "actual," transformed by the biblical witness to God's "promise." German philosophy helps Moltmann understand that the human imagination of what is possible has a strong influence on what people think is "real." Imagining the future affects life in the present in a fundamental way: this is one of the central themes in twentieth-century German thought including Heidegger, Bloch, Löwith, and Gadamer. Moltmann adapts this philosophy for theology by speaking not of "the future" but of "God's future" and engagement with scripture. This has enormous explanatory power, and is able to show how imagination is not separate from reality, but lies at the heart of how people understand the world and act in it. At the same time, it explains too much. Tragedy can be absorbed in advance by the knowledge that, although suffering is real, it can be interpreted and contradicted in the light of God's promises for humankind. Eschatology, Moltmann says, "must formulate its statements of hope in contradiction to our present experience of suffering, evil and death" (1967: 19). God's promise does not seem to include suffering. Moltmann changed his mind about this. The image of the crucified Christ cannot be absorbed by eschatology. The crucified Christ does not "contradict" suffering, but embodies it. Likewise, the theology of the cross does not lend itself to philosophical concepts like "anticipation," but is terribly resistant to all concepts. The Crucifixion is not thinkable. Suffering is not a concept. Here, philosophical reasoning is not merely questionable: it gets stuck, or should do, if it is done properly.

The Crucifixion of Christ cannot be assimilated into any neat account of history: there can be no easy talk about what the Crucifixion means. This changes the way Moltmann addresses the political tasks of Christians. It is no longer just a question of allowing eschatology to contradict and question the forms of life that perpetuate suffering and pain. There is also a deeper question: "What does it mean to recall the God who was crucified in a society whose official creed is optimism, and which is knee-deep in blood?" (1974: 4). This does not mean abandoning philosophical thinking and retreating into gnomic utterances. Rather, it means finding philosophical languages that are good at getting stuck, so to speak. Moltmann does not abandon Bloch, but corrects him with a different and difficult strand of German philosophy: the dark and sometimes melancholy philosophy found in the Jewish philosophers Franz Rosenzweig, Walter Benjamin, Theodor Adorno, and Max Horkheimer.[4] These figures struggle with the thought of Hegel, in which everything seems already reconciled in philosophy. In very different ways, the Jewish philosophers insist that it is not the task of philosophy to reconcile things, but rather to articulate and enact the difficulty of thinking in a world of suffering. Again, however, there are difficulties for Moltmann. These philosophies are largely atheistic, and their insights, instead of arising from meditations on scripture, often come from aesthetic criticism. In the more melancholy work, especially that of Adorno, the reasonings do not move beyond showing aporias in existing philosophical approaches. The nearest one can get to articulating the good life is to know that the damaged life is damaged and that, by implication, there must be in principle an undamaged life (but where?). How does Moltmann manage to use this philosophy without letting it force his theological hand? In general, Moltmann learns from this philosophy in a rather patchwork way: as with his use of Bloch and "anticipation," he tends to work with Adorno's "negation" without worrying too much about the metaphysics implied by it (e.g. 1974: 171). This leads to difficulties: chains of reasoning are abandoned at the last minute because they are not going where Moltmann knows he ought to go, the concrete political implications (or rather stark lack of them) implied by this thinking are ignored, and sometimes quite incompatible pictures of the world are sewn together with very visible seams. Nonetheless, this philosophy gives Moltmann a powerful language for exploring the ways in which meditating on Christ's suffering spoils the neat and tidy thinking so characteristic of human attempts to ignore or deny suffering.

Moltmann's political theology arises partly from this interplay between the philosophical practice of negativity and an attempt to articulate the significance of Christ's Crucifixion. He questions those periods of Christian history where theology has been used to support the power and policies of the state and serve the interests of the rich and powerful: there is nothing so neat and tidy as the theologies which have done this. Moltmann, learning from the work of Metz, furthermore rejects any identification between theology and the interests of the bourgeois classes in Germany or anywhere else. This does not just mean blatant abuses of power or collusion with authority: it extends to the tendency of religion to be seen by politicians as a useful contributor to social integration. Christians are under constant pressure to serve patriotic festivals, and find themselves caught between socialist "pantheistic materialism" and capitalist "fetishism involving gold and possessions" (1974: 323). Moltmann insists that the theology of the cross forbids Christians to become uncritical servants of the Roman Empire or any of its successors in history. "Christianity did not come into being as a national religion and therefore cannot be one. It does not bind the hearts of citizens to the state, but lures them away from it" (p. 324). This is not an easy matter, for it creates a dilemma for any political theology:

> the more the churches become departments of bourgeois religion, the more strongly they must suppress recollection of the political trial of Christ and lose their identity as Christian churches, for recollection of it endangers their religio-political relevance. However, if they retreat from the social theme of "bourgeois religion," they become irrelevant sects on the boundary of society and abandon their place for others. (p. 324)

Those who seek to be "relevant" run the risk of abandoning their Christian difference and distinctiveness; those who seek a strong Christian "identity" run the risk of being unintelligible and unrelated to those victims of society they are meant to serve. Moltmann rejects this opposition in favor of a theology of the cross learned from Luther's criticism of the church, but adapted for his modern context: the identity of Christianity as a religion is *already* ruined as a secure haven because of its association with Christ crucified, and its relevance for society is not a product of assimilation to bourgeois interests but its opposition to all idols and its criticisms of society on behalf of the poor, the marginalized, and victims of injustice (p. 325).

The *Pax Christi* is far from identical to the *Pax Romana*, and the authority of God is certainly not represented directly by those in high positions. Human institutions and history bear God's presence only when they embody the service of Christ, a service which extends even to death on the cross (Moltmann 1974: 327). "The consequence for Christian theology is that it must adopt a critical attitude towards political religions in society and in the churches. The political theology of the cross must liberate the state from the political service of idols and must liberate people from political alienation and loss of rights" (p. 327). This does not mean an adolescent posture of rebellion: it does mean the rethinking of every institution with which Christianity comes into contact. "Wherever Christianity extends, the idea of the state changes" (p. 328). This is not a statement of historical fact. Rather, it is a criterion for judgment: if a state becomes "Christian" and the idea of the state does not change, this is a sign that Christianity itself has changed, and has assimilated itself to the interests of the ruling class. "The crucified God is in fact a stateless and classless God. But that does not mean that he is an unpolitical God. He is the God of the poor, the oppressed and the humiliated" (p. 329).

What does this mean in practice? Moltmann understands that scriptural interpretation cannot rest content with the general acknowledgment that God is the God of the poor and the oppressed. Christians have to make concrete judgments. Writing in the early 1970s, Moltmann offers five topics for consideration and action: poverty, institutionalized violence, racism, the environment, and people's increasing sense of their life's meaninglessness. In economics, Christians must fight practices of economic exploitation, promote social welfare, and insist that members of society receive a "satisfying and just share in the products they produce." Insofar as socialism serves these goals, Christians should be socialist (1974: 332). In politics, Christians should oppose the hegemony of particular classes and groups, insist on the adoption of the Universal Declaration of Human Rights as a standard for justice, and seek the liberation of all those who are the victims of political oppression. Insofar as democracy serves these goals, Christians should be democratic (p. 333). In cultural life, Christians should regard racial difference as a source of fruitfulness and productive cooperation. "The recognition of racial and cultural and personal differences and the recognition of one's own identity belong together." Insofar as movements for emancipation serve these goals, Christians should join them (pp. 333–4). In environmental life, Christians should oppose the wanton exploitation of nature, should promote partnership with nature, and should seek peace with nature rather than domination of it (p. 334). Lastly, with respect to socialization, Christians need to acknowledge that it is not enough to have economic, political, cultural, and environmental justice. These things have no "meaning" in themselves, although without them people are in bondage. Christians have to understand these things as taking part in God's fullness. "The freedom of the children of God and the liberation of enslaved nature (Rom. 8: 19ff.) are consummated in the arrival of the complete and universal indwelling of God" (1974: 335). Christians have the gift of faith in God to offer the societies in which they live and work. This faith makes sense of and motivates all the other political actions so sorely needed.

The particular political interventions Moltmann suggests are dated, of course, above all in his omissions: of sexism (quotations from his work have been altered in this article to reflect current practices of inclusive language), of the disabled,[5] of the elderly, of the abuses perpetrated by international corporations, and so forth. This is as it should be: unless concrete recommendations run the risk of being dated, perhaps very quickly, political theology remains mired in generalizations. Moltmann's particular choices are obviously open to dispute even without anachronism. What is more striking is the alarming contemporaneity of his concrete judgments: since they were written, not one of them has been adequately addressed. Updating Moltmann's vision means adding new items for discussion, but not crossing off old ones. It is perhaps not surprising that all the ills of the world have not been healed during one man's lifetime. Nonetheless it is surely cause for concern that, 30 years on, Moltmann's call for justice still sounds like a minority voice within Christianity, let alone within society. Given that Moltmann is himself a mainstream theologian of some significance, it is hard to escape the suspicion that theology itself is a minority voice in Christianity. For this reason, if for no other, Moltmann's discussion of the problem of "identity" and "relevance" in Christianity is still pertinent today.

Ecclesiology

The persuasiveness of any political theology is judged on the strength of its account of the church. How does the church embody, practice, and teach God's love in the world? What is its relationship to secular authority? Where is the church to be found? For Moltmann, these questions cannot be answered satisfactorily in purely formal terms: an adequate description of the church requires detailed description of the historical conditions in which Christians find themselves. Even in his earliest work, however, Moltmann is insistent on one thing: there have been periods of history when leaders in the church believed their task was to conserve the allegedly "natural order" of society; that cannot be the case today. "The Christian Church has not to serve humankind in order that this world may remain what it is, or may be preserved in the state in which it is, but in order that it may transform itself and become what it is promised to be" (1967: 327). This is repeated in his larger study *The Church in the Power of the Spirit* (1975), where Moltmann suggests that in times of peace, long ago, "the church could affirm itself by demonstrating the unbroken and unaltered continuance of its tradition and traditions" (Moltmann 1977: 2). This is no longer possible. Ours is a time of crisis, characterized by great suffering in the church. Under current conditions, the dominant themes are messianic, and a longing for the redemption of God's promise. The tradition embodied by the church is one that changes people and causes them to be born again in the Spirit. "Anyone who enters this messianic tradition accepts the adventure of the Spirit, the experience of liberation, the call to repentance, and common work for the coming kingdom" (1977: 3). The time of unrest is not, however, only an effect of a politically unstable world on the church. Unrest is embedded at the heart of the church itself:

> its "unrest" is implicit in itself, in the crucified Christ to whom it appeals and in the Spirit which is its driving power. . . . The social and cultural upheavals of the present draw its attention to that great upheaval which it itself describes as "new creation," as the "new people of God," which it testifies to the world concerning the future of "the new heaven and the new earth." (1977: 3)

Theologies which try to draw out the political dimension of worship risk instrumentalizing the church, making it a vehicle for something else, other than being the church. Theologies which set themselves the task of describing the difference between the kingdom of God and earthly cities run the risk of using up their energies on critique of society without articulating the creative power of God's love to make good lives possible. How, then, does Moltmann show that political action arises *from* worship (rather than being in competition with it) in his account of the church, and how does he handle the balance between critique and creativity in his account of society? The first question is addressed by suggesting that the church serves a particular *interest*, and that this is the interest of Christ. The second question is handled by considering the relationship between God's glory and Christian life. This is worked out principally through the themes of feasting, friendship, and poverty. We now turn to these.

Influenced deeply by German left-wing philosophy of the 1960s and 1970s, Moltmann asks the critical question of this restless, Spirit-filled church: "whom is it intended to benefit, and for whom and in whose interest is it designed?" (1977: 4). For Moltmann, the concepts of benefit and interest are fully theological; that is to say, their task is to assist the description of the relationship between God and God's creation. Accordingly, Moltmann gives a trinitarian, and then a Christological response: "If the church does everything in the name of the triune God, then theological doctrine will see the church in the trinitarian history of God's dealings with the world." At the same time, "Christ is his church's foundation, its power and its hope. . . . Its only where Christ alone rules, and the church listens to his voice only, that the church arrives at its truth and becomes free and a liberating power in the world" (p. 5). Moltmann echoes the Barmen Declaration of 1934: "Acknowledgement of the sole lordship of Christ in his church makes it impossible to recognize any other 'sources of proclamation apart from or in addition to this sole Word of God'" (p. 5). Because of this, there is no separation between theological understandings of the church, and political and social understandings. The sphere of politics and society *is* the sphere of theology and thus of the church. Whose "interest" does the church serve? Christ's. Whom is it intended to benefit? Those to whom Christ came.

Moltmann places great emphasis on the contemporary meaning of mission. There have been periods of its history when the church was the bearer of European or North American Christian cultural life, which it sought to disseminate in Africa and Asia. This has changed. The church now has a mission in Europe, and it is no longer a European church which has this mission. It is a world church: culturally and racially varied. It is no longer a "national church" and, with a few isolated exceptions, it is no longer an "established church." It is an ecumenical church. "The ecumenical movement seeks the visible unity of Christ's church. It serves to liberate the churches from their ties with the middle-class and political religions of their societies; and in this way it also serves to give the churches renewed life as Christ's church" (Moltmann 1977: 12). Moltmann lists a series of conferences to support this: Lund (1952), Mexico City (1968), Uppsala (1968), Second Vatican Council (1962–5), Bangkok (1973) (1977: 7–15). The change in focus from Europe to the world, and the critical questions about whose interests the church serves, are crucial to Moltmann's ecclesiology, and he aligns himself firmly with the modern "political theology" associated with Metz:

> In the age of the restoration in Europe, the churches, consciously or unconsciously, made [a] basic conservative choice which determines their public statements even today. It is the intention of modern political theology to make people conscious of this basic conservative choice made by the European churches, and to put an end to it, so giving back to the church its political liberty. . . . Modern political theology, unlike its earlier equivalent, is not an ideology of political religions, to which the church has often enough surrendered. It is the critical ending of these unholy alliances made by the church. (1977: 16)

Moltmann shows himself willing to learn from Latin America's theology of revolution and theology of liberation (which were relatively new when Moltmann was writing in 1975): he specifically names Gutiérrez, Assmann, and Bonino as thinkers who have a vital lesson about the liberation of the oppressed and the humiliated to teach European theology.

The church is a witness to God's glory. Moltmann is especially interested in the way in which Christian relationships with God elicit feasting, friendship, and poverty. These three themes are closely related for Moltmann, and although not normally juxtaposed in non-Christian thought, they arise quite naturally for a theologian who understands that the church is the church of Jesus Christ. Reacting against over-authoritarian ecclesiologies which describe Jesus predominantly as Lord, Moltmann tries to draw out the significance of Jesus' transfiguration and of Jesus being not only the Lord of the kingdom but the "Lord of Glory" of 1 Cor. 2: 8 (1977: 109). The kingdom of God is itself a marriage feast, and Easter is a "feast of freedom" where the risen Christ sits with his disciples. Discussions of feasting and joy in theological writings can often seem strangely forced and pedestrian when compared with their subject matter. The theme of feasting calls for something more spontaneous and beautiful. Moltmann thus hosts a more informal discussion, and includes meditations on hymns by St. Paul, Paul Gerhardt, and John Wesley in order to show how the church is engaged with "the laughter of the redeemed, the dance of the liberated and the creative play of fantasy" (1977: 110). Feasting is a rearrangement of time and space, laws and spontaneity, memory and liberation. It does not celebrate in order to deny the lack of freedom which people experience in everyday life but in order to anticipate that freedom and insist that even everyday life is potentially a life of laughter, play, and dance.

There are dangers here: feasting can be darkly and skillfully used as compensation for deeper imprisonment or be instrumentalized as a pressure-valve for passions arising from the experience of real social contradictions. Moreover, there is no simple formula to defend the church's feasting against such abuse. Rather, it has to be watchful and alert. Moltmann does not think European churches are yet in danger of feasting too exuberantly. Far from it: they need to relearn this from the exemplary practices of worship in Pentecostal and independent churches in Africa and elsewhere. At the same time, the crucified Christ is not forgotten or repressed in this feasting: more than anything else, the memory of the Crucifixion forbids Christian feasting from becoming a flight from suffering. Feasting enacts the joy of the risen Christ in solidarity with the groaning creation: it points to Jesus, the risen crucified Christ (1977: 109–14). In later work, Moltmann modifies this picture and arguably abandons it: his account of feasting in *The Coming of God* concentrates on the risen, rather than the crucified, Christ and the dominant theme is not solidarity but laughter. Moltmann does not explain why (1996: 336–9).

The kind of complex feasting described in *The Crucified God*, of pain not just transfigured into joy but actually part of it, gives rise to fellowship and friendship, solidarity and participation in the common life of Christ. The traditional account of the "threefold office of Christ," as prophet, priest, and king, has produced a rich tradition of meditations on the life of Christ. Moltmann argues for more emphasis upon the fellowship which Christ brings and embodies in the world: Christ as prophet, priest, king, and friend (1977: 115). Moltmann admits there is something not quite right about thinking of "friend" as another title of office. It is relational more than honorific. What, for Moltmann, does friendship include? Affection, loyalty, reliability, constancy in disaster, openness, freedom, sympathy, and noncompetitiveness. The theme of friendship allows Moltmann to balance his critique of society with a creative image of the good life: "The positive meaning of a classless society free of domination, without repression and without privileges, lies in friendship. Without the power of friendship and without the goal of a friendly world there is no human hope for the class struggles and struggles for dominance" (p. 116).

Jesus' friendship is explicitly described only twice in scripture: he is the "friend of tax collectors and sinners!" (Luke 7: 34) and he says to his disciples: "You are my friends if you do what I command you" (John 15: 14). Interestingly, neither of these passages lends itself easily to Moltmann's theological task of describing Jesus as "friend of the sinful and the sick" (1977: 117): Luke's description is an account of Jesus' response to a reproach; John's passage makes a strong connection between Jesus' authority and his friendship, whereas Moltmann seems to wish to keep them distinct. Scripture should help Moltmann rethink the very idea of Jesus' lordship *as* friendship, rather than trying, as he does, to correct the one with the other. Similarly, Moltmann has a rather free interpretation of John 15: 15, where Jesus tells the disciples that from now on he does not call them servants, but calls them friends. Moltmann suggests that this is because he relates to the disciples out of joy, not out of condescension (1977: 118). The actual passage of scripture says: "I do not call you servants any longer, because the servant does not know what the master is doing; but I have called you friends, because I have made known to you everything that I have heard from my Father" (John 15: 15, NRSV). The friendship between Jesus and the disciples arises here from a relationship of sharing knowledge, and thus friendship with God, rather than any attitude on Jesus' part. John 15: 14 and John 15: 15, taken together, imply a transformed lordship: a friendship rooted in the sharing of knowledge of God the Father. Nonetheless, it is important to Moltmann's theology of God's glory to indicate the importance of friendship between Jesus and the disciples, between Jesus and the Father, and finally between the disciples and the Father by way of prayer through Jesus: "the Father will give you whatever you ask him in my name" (John 15: 16). Moltmann wonderfully draws out the way friendship and prayer arise from each other: "Prayer and the hearing of prayer are the marks of humanity's friendship with God and God's friendship with humanity . . . God's friend prays out of freedom and trusts to the friendship of the free God" (1977: 119).

Moltmann reinterprets the threefold office in the light of this discussion. "In his divine function as prophet, priest and king, Christ lives and acts as a friend and creates friends." Here Moltmann has a worried afterthought. Friendship is a much misunderstood concept. Just as the category of "anticipation" in *Theology of Hope* corrects Greek philosophical notions of the eternal present with an understanding of God's promise, so "friendship with sinners" has to correct Greek philosophical notions of friendship between equals with an understanding of Jesus' friendship with the unrighteous and the despised. The ancient concept of friendship as equality between those of the same rank is not the only thing needing repair. There is also the modern concept of friendship as intimacy reserved for the private sphere. By contrast, Jesus' friendship is public and widely shared. "The friendship of Jesus cannot be lived and its friendliness cannot be disseminated when friendship is limited to people who are like ourselves and when it is narrowed down to private life" (1977: 121). Christians of all denominations can learn a lot from Quakers, Moltmann suggests, because the Society of Friends show what friendship means through their work in slums and in working for the abolition of slavery. Here, Moltmann has already started his next transition: having moved from feasting to friendship, he now moves from friendship to poverty.

Where is the church found? *Ubi Christus – ibi ecclesia*: where Christ is, there the church is. Where is Christ? In many places: the apostolate, the sacraments, the fellowship of Christians, "the least of the members of his family, his parousia" (1977: 123). The church thus has the task of mediating all of these modes of the presence of Christ. Moltmann devotes space to all of these, but most of all to Christ's presence in the poor. It is often difficult to know where Moltmann's particular emphases lie. His discussions have an encyclopaedic character, and he often tries to cram everything in and summarize all points of view in the course of an argument; and because vast areas of theology are traversed in a few pages, the reader sometimes has to work quite hard to discern what Moltmann thinks is centrally important. In this context, things are clear: Moltmann thinks Christ's friendship with the poor is of utmost importance for understanding who and where the church is. Moltmann develops his account here through interpretation of Matthew 25: 31–46: the son of man as judge of the world. To the righteous the king will say, "I was hungry and you gave me food, I was thirsty and you gave me something to drink, I was a stranger and you welcomed me, I was naked and you gave me clothing, I was sick and you took care of me, I was in prison and you visited me." To the unrighteous he will say, "I was hungry and you gave me no food, I was thirsty and you gave me nothing to drink. . . ." The central message of this parable of the kingdom is that the king's hunger, thirst, estrangement, nakedness, sickness, and imprisonment *are* the hunger and imprisonment of the poor, the "least of these who are members of my family" (Matt.25: 40). Moltmann shows the significance of this for ecclesiology: "The way in which the identification between the Judge of the world and the least of people is formulated is remarkably closely parallel to the identification of Christ with the community of believers" (1977: 126). Whoever hears the apostles, hears Christ; and what is done to "the least" is done to Christ. Moltmann develops this juxtaposition so as to suggest that the church is to be identified with the poor and the hungry. Matthew 25: 31ff. is not first and foremost about ethics and the love of one's neighbor (although it is this too). "The hidden presence of the coming Christ in the poor . . . belongs to ecclesiology first of all, and only after that to ethics" (1977: 127).

Moltmann's account of the church is the heart of his political theology. Where is the church found? Where Christ is. But if Christ is both present in Word and sacrament and present as the judge hidden among the poor, how are these two to be related to each other? "We must talk about a fellowship of believers and a fellowship of the least of his family with Christ. 'He who hears you hears me' – 'He who visits them, visits me.' The two have seldom been successfully combined in the church's history" (1977: 128–9). Interestingly, Moltmann offers a division of labor for these two fellowships: "The apostolate says what the church is. The least of Christ's family say where the church belongs" (p. 129). We see here the whole of Moltmann's political theology summed up in an invitation. He calls for the church to understand itself as two fellowships combined: the fellowship of the apostles and the fellowship of the poor. It is for this reason that the church does not minister to the poor: the church *is* the poor. And for the same reasons, the church is not a church *for* the people. It is the church *of* the people (p. 93). And politics, accordingly, is participation in God's life.

Notes

1   See esp. "The Revolution of Freedom," in *Religion, Revolution and the Future* (1969: 63ff.).
2   All emphases are Moltmann's own. I have freely altered translations from the German so that general pronouns are rendered with inclusive language, but have not indicated this in the text.
3   See also Moltmann's essay on Bloch, "Hope and Confidence," in *Religion, Revolution and the Future* (1969: 148ff.); and the brief discussion of Bloch in *God in Creation* (1985: 42–5).
4   The indices of names to *The Crucified God* and *The Coming of God* show the relevant passages.
5   But cf. Moltmann (1977), 187.

Bibliography

Bauckham, Richard (1995). *The Theology of Jürgen Moltmann*. Edinburgh: T. & T. Clark.
——, ed. (1999). *God Will Be All in All: The Eschatology of Jürgen Moltmann*. (Edinburgh: T. & T. Clark.
Moltmann, Jürgen (1967). *Theology of Hope*, 5th edn, trans. J. Leitch. London: SCM. (First pub. in German 1965.)
——(1969). *Religion, Revolution and the Future*, trans. M. D. Meeks. New York: Scribner's.
——(1971). *Hope and Planning*, trans. M Clarkson. London: SCM.
——(1974). *The Crucified God*, trans. R. Wilson and J. Bowden. London: SCM. (First publ. in German 1972.)
——(1977). *The Church in the Power of the Spirit*, trans. M. Kohl. London: SCM. (First publ. in German 1975.)
——(1981). *Trinity and the Kingdom of God*, trans. M. Kohl. London: SCM.
——(1984). *On Human Dignity: Political Theology and Ethics*, trans. D. Meeks. London: SCM.
——(1985). *God in Creation*, trans. M. Kohl. London: SCM.
——(1989a). *The Way of Jesus Christ*, trans. M. Kohl. London: SCM.
——(1989b). *Creating a Just Future: The Politics of Peace and the Ethics of Creation in a Threatened World*, trans. M. Kohl. London: SCM.
——(1992). *The Spirit of Life: A Universal Affirmation*, trans. M. Kohl. London: SCM.
——(1996). *The Coming of God: Christian Eschatology*, trans. M. Kohl. London: SCM. (First publ. in German 1995.)
——(2000). *Experiences of Theology*, trans. M. Kohl. London: SCM.
Rasmusson, Arne (1995). *The Church as Polis: From Political Theology to Theological Politics as Exemplified by Jürgen Moltmann and Stanley Hauerwas*. Notre Dame, Ind.: University of Notre Dame Press.

CHAPTER 17

Johann Baptist Metz

J. Matthew Ashley

Johann Baptist Metz has frequently asserted that his is a theology oriented not by "system concepts," but rather by "subject concepts." "Subject concepts" are to be evaluated not so much by how they cohere into a system as in terms of their capacity to articulate and undergird the ways that specific persons in specific times and places struggle to become and remain subjects: agents of their own histories, persons who recognize the symbols and narratives that make up that history to be *their* symbols and narratives, rather than an alienating imposition (Metz 1984: 363). This methodological choice, as well as his preference for the short essay over the monograph, complicates the task of giving a systematic overview. The approach taken here will center on Metz's claim that his is a "fundamental practical theology." After constructing an interpretive framework whose lattices are Metz's own concerns as a theologian, I attempt an overview of the particular way in which Metz attempts to meet those concerns in a political theology. To do this I first identify the theological genre (fundamental theology), then the fundamental question (theodicy), and finally the doctrinal locus (eschatology) that limn the basic structure of Metz's theology.

Dangerous Memories and Interruptions: A Theological Itinerary

Born in 1928 in Auerbach in northeast Bavaria, Metz describes his small-town origins as follows:

> One comes from far away when one comes from there. It is as if one were born not fifty years ago, but somewhere along the receding edges of the Middle Ages. I had to approach many things slowly at first, to exert great effort to discover things that

others and that society had long ago discovered and had since become common practice. (Metz 1984: 171)

This recollection places Metz, at least initially, in that generation of Catholic scholars who took it as their work to continue the dialogue with modern (viz. post-Enlightenment) culture and thought that was interrupted by the suppression of modernism in the early twentieth century. Above all, it associates him closely with Karl Rahner. Indeed, Metz's close relationship to Rahner for some three decades, as student, collaborator, and friend, provides the justification for one of this essay's principal heuristic strategies: Metz's theology can almost always be illuminated on a particular point by comparison with Rahner's.

Like Rahner, Metz understands his task as that of helping the Catholic Church make the journey from the "far away" arch-Catholic world of an Auerbach into the secularized, multicultural world of modernity. This implies neither a despairing farewell to that integral Bavarian Catholic culture, with its rich fabric of popular customs and its tacit sacred ontology, nor a complete capitulation to the terms on which modernity will accept claims about reality and how we ought to live in it. Describing Rahner's transcendental paradigm, Metz calls this task "the attempt to appropriate the heritage of the classical Patristic and Scholastic traditions precisely by means of a productive and aggressive dialogue with the challenges of the modern European world" (Metz 1998: 32). The underlying conviction is that the life of faith made possible by "Auerbach" can and must survive the storms of modernization, albeit embodied differently, precisely so as to resist those storms where necessary, and to reweave a new fabric appropriate to a new situation. Without such labors, even were the doctrines, customs, and practices of an Auerbach to survive, they would comprise little more than a museum piece, or another "lifestyle option" to embellish the lives of secularized moderns.

Metz appropriated another, often underappreciated, feature of Rahner's thought. However much Rahner wished to articulate and interpret Christian faith and practices on modernity's terrain, he did not feel compelled thereby to sacrifice every feature of Christianity that appeared incongruous on modern grounds. Thus, Rahner wrote extensive and tightly argued essays on devotion to the Sacred Heart, purgatory, the cult of the saints, and the theology of indulgences (to name a few). He was willing to tarry with these allegedly archaic remnants of an earlier age. Metz praises this practice, naming it the "adventure of religious noncontemporaneity," "creative naivete," and "aggressive fidelity" to the church's tradition (Metz 1984: 171; 1998: 108, 92f.). In fact, Metz believes that "coming from Auerbach" offers a distinct advantage for this "adventure," insofar as it opens up a certain critical distance from the slogans and clichés that define modernity. This distance often enables a theologian to see resources and pitfalls invisible to those who have "grown up" taking them for granted. A theologian who cultivates this "productive noncontemporaneity" will pause just a moment longer with images and concepts that "modern consciousness" wants to discard, but precisely for the sake of "freeing" modern consciousness from the

stultifying circle of what "reasonable persons" accept as rational and practical in the public sphere. Metz's insistence on the contemporary relevance
of the apocalyptic sense for time is a prime example of this "productive
noncontemporaneity."

In 1963 Metz took a position in fundamental theology at the University of
Münster and began to diverge from his friend and teacher. On his own account,
he shifted from transcendental Thomism's focus on epistemology and the Kant
of the *Critique of Pure Reason* to the Kant of the second critique and of the philosophy of history, along with the extension of that line of thought in the work
of Karl Marx (Metz 1970: 63; 1980: 53f.; 1998: 33). At this point another
remembrance became increasingly determinative for Metz's theology:

> Toward the end of the Second World War, when I was sixteen years old, I was taken
> out of school and forced into the army. After a brief period of training at a base in
> Würzburg I arrived at the front, which by that time had already crossed the Rhine
> into Germany. There were well over a hundred in my company, all of whom were
> very young. One evening the company commander sent me with a message to bat-
> talion headquarters. I wandered all night long through destroyed, burning villages
> and farms, and when in the morning I returned to my company I found only – the
> dead, nothing but the dead, overrun by a combined bomber and armored assault.
> I could see now only dead and empty faces, where the day before I had shared child-
> hood fears and youthful laughter. I remember nothing but a wordless cry. Thus I
> see myself to this very day, and behind this memory all of my childhood dreams
> crumble away. A fissure had opened in my powerful Bavarian-Catholic socializa-
> tion, with its impregnable confidence. What would happen if one took this sort of
> thing not to the psychologist but into the Church, and if one would not allow
> oneself to be talked out of such unreconciled memories even by theology, but
> rather wanted to have faith with them and with them speak about God . . . ?
> (Metz 1998: 1f.; cf. 1987: 39f.)

This memory discloses a further interruption in Metz's biography. In the early
1960s Metz responded to the impact of secularization on Catholic cultural–
political identity ("Auerbach") by developing a "theology of the world." While
critiquing an unwarranted secularism that absolutized the world's secularity,
Metz argued that faith and theology must "turn to the world," participating in
God's "turn to the world" in the incarnation of the Second Person of the Trinity
(Metz 1969). This development was shaped to some extent by Metz's encounters
with a number of revisionary Marxists: Roger Garaudy, Ernst Bloch, Max
Horkheimer, Theodor Adorno, and Walter Benjamin. A major part of their
agenda had been to identify and evaluate the prospects for a genuinely human
emancipation in the face of a network of mutually reinforcing modern forces –
economic, scientific, technological, and political – which were proving remarkably capable of absorbing and defusing those social contradictions that Marx had
argued would eventually bring capitalism down. On what would the revolutionary impulse nourish itself in a totalizing social system that could appropriate and even make a profit on human beings' utopian imagination, their

suffering, their outrage? This led them to ask whether underappreciated features of the human life-world – music, art, and literature, for Adorno and Benjamin, and even religion for Garaudy and Bloch – might offer a vantage point "outside" the juggernaut of Western capitalist modernity from which it might be critiqued and transformed in a more human direction.

Two points should be noted about the impact of this intellectual current on Metz. First, Metz eschewed those trajectories within it (or in the "postmodern" generation that claimed to follow these thinkers) that led to a rejection of the modern project *tout court*. For him, what was worth retrieving and developing in their thought was the struggle to "enlighten the Enlightenment," to *redeem* modernity from its own self-destructive dynamic. Second, Metz rejected any tendency to "instrumentalize" religion, even for the worthy goal of social progress. To incorporate religion *within* the modern project (even to save it) would only collude with modernity's own drive to domesticate religion, which is to paralyze it. What Metz appreciated in these thinkers were certain emphases that might help contemporary systematic theologians examine their own allegiance to modern ways of thinking more critically, and understand the dilemma of Christian faith in the modern world in a more radical way than his earlier essays on a "theology of the world" allowed (see Metz 1980: 32–48, 119–35). Let us consider two of these emphases in particular.

First, he took over Ernst Bloch's emphasis on the power of suffering to call into question the present and the future that can be extrapolated from this present, opening up a heretofore undreamed-of "utopian" future. Second, he took from Benjamin the conviction of the importance of memories and stories (particularly those "dangerous," unsettling ones that lead to critical questions about the present) to open up perspectives on the present that escape the power of "technical rationality," with its ability to encompass human hope in a strangling net of facts and "scientific" accounts of that future in which alone "reasonable" persons can hope. Metz began to suspect that the same social forces that repressed human suffering and hope, or assigned them to be therapeutically managed (and depoliticized) by the psychologist – all for the sake of maintaining the political and social status quo – were also a deadly threat to the integrity and vitality of Christian belief.

When he began to ask these sorts of questions, it slowly (too slowly, he himself avers) began to dawn on him that there was one dangerous memory, one history, that had above all been suppressed from both German society and Christian faith and theology: Auschwitz.

> Because of the way Auschwitz was or was not present in theology I slowly became aware of the high content of apathy in theological idealism and its inability to confront historical experience in spite of all its prolific talk about historicity. There was no theology in the whole world which talked so much about historicity as German theologies. Yet they only talk about historicity; they did not mention Auschwitz. It is clear that there is no meaning of history one can save with one's back turned to Auschwitz; there is no truth of history which one can defend, and no God in history whom one can worship with one's back turned to Auschwitz. (Metz 1987: 41f.)

This concern for those who have been swallowed up into the dark underside of history and forgotten by Christian faith and theology led Metz into a natural alliance with the theologians of liberation. His specific concern for Auschwitz has made him particularly sensitive to the ways in which Christianity has minimized or betrayed its still-constitutive relationship to Judaism.

These remembrances and the concerns to which they give rise set up a tensive field of desiderata, challenges, and aporias within which Metz has continually labored to find theological language and argument. They cannot all be easily accommodated by any one "system." Indeed, Metz has increasingly come to insist that theology's job is not so much to assimilate these remembrances into a system as it is to provide a language in which they can be articulated and allowed to irritate our "modern" consciousness. In any event, they provide a set of concerns that help one to make sense of his thought. Here I list four: (1) advocacy of an aggressive and creative engagement with modern culture and thought, along with an impatience with those who dismiss their challenges as irrelevant or external to theological discourse; (2) the concomitant willingness to rub modern culture and thought "against the grain" by holding on to counter-intuitive (to modernity) images and ideas from the tradition (Metz and Wiesel 1999: 40); (3) an insistence that theology and faith must be so constituted that remembrances of history's catastrophes are indispensable if theology is not to become trivial and irrelevant, and Christian faith a banalized reflection of the prevailing social consensus; and finally, (4) a concern that theology "always be ready to make [its] defense to anyone who demands from [it] an account for the hope that is in [it]" (1 Pt 3.15). Theology is always for him "a defense of hope"(Metz 1980: 3) – a defense of hope, furthermore, that cannot be carried off unless it includes unconditional solidarity with and action on behalf of those who suffer, those whose hope is most endangered. In short, it is a hope that must be accompanied by the radical action of Christian discipleship.

The Structure of Metz's Fundamental Theology with a Practical Intent

These concerns pull in different directions, a fact that goes a long way to explain the tensions in Metz's thought. Yet there is an underlying coherence that can be disclosed by considering the genre, determinative question, and doctrinal locus of his theology. First the genre. Metz calls his a "practical fundamental theology," or a "fundamental theology with a practical intent"(Metz 1980: ix, 49, *inter alia*). A brief historical detour into the recent history of Roman Catholic theology can help illuminate what he means by this. Fundamental theology took over many of the functions in Roman Catholic theology that philosophical theology and apologetics had carried out in neoscholasticism. In the latter, the purpose of philosophical theology and apologetics was to defend the reasonableness of the assent of faith to those truths of revelation that provide the starting points for the construction of the various dogmatic treatises. They did this by demonstrating the existence of the ultimate object of faith (proofs for the existence of God), and by arguing for the reasonableness of the assent of faith in general, and then to the truths of scripture and tradition in particular. The latter was done in large measure by appeal to New Testament miracles and to the fulfillment of Old Testament prophecies in Jesus and in the church. Thus, the reasonableness of assenting to this content was defended on grounds external to the intelligibility of that content itself, the elaboration of which was left for the subsequent work of dogmatic theology.

Karl Rahner self-consciously violated this stringent division of dogmatic (viz. systematic) from fundamental theology, and Metz carries that transgression of disciplinary borders over into his own work. Rahner argued that contemporary philosophical pluralism, the "knowledge-explosion" in general, and the impact of modern biblical scholarship combine to make the neoscholastic project untenable in fact, regardless of whether it was ever tenable in principle. Consequently, a successful justification of faith (the task of fundamental theology) would have to draw on the contents of faith, rather than leaving them to subsequent elaboration in systematic theology. This does not entail an exhaustive consideration of a given doctrine, but an investigation on a "first level of reflection." The "new fundamental theology" would elaborate doctrinal contents to the extent necessary for showing how they could cohere with, bring to words, and concretize the modern person's experience of his or her identity, especially as it is threatened by guilt and by the final, always imminent, limit-situation of death. Such an approach derives its persuasive power from its ability to illumine and empower the life of everyday Christians by grounding that life in the mystery of God's presence in the world (Rahner 1978: 3–14; 1982: 123–8).

Metz has high praise for this approach, describing Rahner's theology as a narrative theology that attempts to give a "theologically fleshed out account of life in the light of contemporary Christianity" (Metz 1980: 224; *1977: 200*).[1] Yet, whereas Rahner had taken the endangered identity of the subject as an individual to be the arena within which to demonstrate the truth and relevance of Christian faith, Metz argues that the arena must be expanded to include the individual's constitutive social and political embeddedness:

> In the entire approach of a practical fundamental theology it would be necessary to open this [Rahner's] biographical way of conceiving dogmatic theology to that theological biography of Christianity in which the dual mystical–political constitution of Christian faith – that is to say, its socially responsible form – would be taken even more seriously and became the motive force for theological reflection. (Metz 1980: 224; *1977: 200*)

Rahner, then, conceives of the field within which theological discourse can find some purchase as mapped out by the "mystical–existential" character of human being. This presupposes a theology of grace in which the existential riches and challenges of human life are ultimately destined to be illumined by, taken up into, and fulfilled by the divine life, a destiny that entails reinterpreting and reorienting them even *now*. The consequence for theological method is that theological discourse can be grounded and justified by showing how it can make sense of and empower human existence at the level of this mystical–existential *circumincessio*, and thus at a deeper level than straightforward empirical accounts. Metz agrees, but insists that the existential–biographical framing of human existence is too narrow. It needs to be complemented, corrected, or even subsumed by a political account that stresses more radically the ways we are constitutively related to one another, not just in "I–thou" relationships of personal encounter with the other, but in and through ambivalent historical traditions and conflict-ridden social institutions (now on a global scale).

This account of Metz's approach provides an initial indication of what he thinks makes it a *political* theology. In his view, theology should address believers at those points at which their identity as persons is most threatened by the social and political catastrophes of history. "Political" denotes a basic dimension of human existence in which persons are constituted by historical traditions and social structures that connect them to the lives and experiences of other persons, both present and past. The political "problem" which correlates to Metz's understanding of fundamental theology arises when our tacit conviction that this dimension "make sense" is threatened, or the pain and guilt of our own complicity (conscious or anonymous) in structures which have brought about (and continue to bring about) the annihilation of others becomes too intense, causing us to withdraw from this dimension into a privatized existentiality or a *still*-privatized "I–thou." It is at this point that Christianity shows its "political" character: "Christian faith, if I understand it correctly, is just the capacity *to affirm and live an endangered identity*. This is the precise point at which faith and history are bound together" (Metz 1986: 181, emphasis added).

Second, this comparison with Rahner sheds some light on why Metz does not engage in detailed analyses of specific doctrines and develop arguments for specific praxes in particular social settings, a point on which he has been widely criticized (e.g. Browning 1991: 67f.; Chopp 1986: 79–81). Metz's "practical fundamental theology" *will* appeal to specific doctrines, rather than attempting to justify the hope that Christians have purely by means of philosophical argument or a sociological–historical "metatheory." Yet Metz is convinced that Christianity's crisis cannot be met in the first instance by a more sophisticated elaboration of its doctrines or a detailed "plan" for their application (as important as these might be), without a basic defense of their cognitive–transformative trustworthiness for Christian believers in danger of losing the sense that they are "good news" in the modern world. Metz's theology is an attempt "at a first level of reflection" to demonstrate the truth and transformative power of Christian faith, but now within the arena of historical catastrophes and political struggle rather than that of the individual's attempt to make sense of his or her own existence.

Finally, the comparison suggests another way of illuminating Metz's procedure. A fundamental theology of the type described above cannot succeed unless it is able to arouse in its audience that fundamental uneasiness with one's identity that provides the angle of vision from which the truth and relevance of Christian faith is to be displayed. Crudely put, Christian faith cannot be proposed as "the answer," unless a "question" is first aroused and articulated in its hearers. This is not necessarily an easy task. The question can lie deeply buried under everyday concerns, especially in technicized cultures that reserve all important questions to the sciences and drown all others in a tidal wave of information and entertainment. In *Being and Time*, Martin Heidegger discussed the ways that "forgetfulness of being," or the covering over of the question of being in favor of questions about beings, makes it impossible genuinely to do metaphysics, to disclose the meaning of being. Rahner, who attended Heidegger's seminars from 1934 to 1936, took over this awareness of the challenge facing any fundamental discipline (be it fundamental ontology or fundamental theology). The fundamental question for Rahner has to do with the cohesiveness and authenticity of the vast constellation of everyday decisions that over time make up the "answer" that one gives with one's life to the "question" of one's being (Rahner 1978: 90–116). Do these decisions really belong to me, or are they results of the anonymous pressure of "the they"? The point, let it be noted, is not, however, to "answer" the question or to integrate it into a system. Rather, the question is to be continually opened up anew and allowed to irritate human awareness, thus enabling true thinking, rather than the shallow instrumental–technical thinking that characterizes modern society.

Metz too is concerned that a certain crucial question is taboo in modern societies. Its repression makes it impossible creatively to face the issues raised both by the Enlightenment project and, at a deeper level, by Christian faith. We have already encountered this question and its privileged locus. It is a question that, Metz tells us, forced itself on him in the light of the third remembrance cited above: the remembrance of Auschwitz.

> As I became conscious of the situation "after Auschwitz" the God question forced itself on me in its strangest, most ancient, and most controversial version: that is, in the form of the theodicy question, not in its existential but, to a certain degree, its political garb: discourse about God as the cry for the salvation of others, of those who suffer unjustly, of the victims and the vanquished in our history. (Metz 1998: 55)

This question about the salvation of history's vanquished ones "leverages" a genuine justification of Christian faith ("on a first level of reflection") by opening a clearing where the mystery of God can be encountered in the dense and ambiguous forest of our histories and political involvements. It is a *political* issue; it concerns the fate of *others*, and the ways that social–political structures implicate me in what happens to them. Metz applies Kant's well-known claim that a fully worked out answer to the question "For what may I hope?" comprises the philosophy of religion. Metz emends as follows: "A basic form of Christian hope is also determined by this memory. The question 'What dare I hope?' is transformed into the question 'What dare I hope for you and, in the end, also for me?'" (Metz 1987: 40). It is a question of hope, and of a threatened hope, but now worked out in terms of what threatens *the other*. It is a question with a deep social–political tone. Elsewhere he elaborates on this social rendering as the only framework within which Christian faith can provide an "answer" to the human predicament:

> [Jesus'] images and visions of the Reign of God – of a comprehensive peace among men and women and nature in God's presence, of a home and a father, of a kingdom of peace, of justice and of reconciliation, of tears wiped away and of the laughter of the children of God – cannot be hoped for with only oneself in view and for oneself alone . . . In believing that others can rely on them, in communicating them to others and hoping them "for others," they belong to oneself as well. Only then. (Metz 1998: 164f.)

As with the fundamental question in transcendental ontology (Heidegger) or transcendental fundamental theology (Rahner), Metz's question is not posed in search of a conceptual–systematic "answer." Metz's purpose is continually to arouse the question in human subjectivity, so as to initiate the person into a mode of life which is itself an authentic "response" to the question: a Job-like spirituality of lamentation and complaint.

> In taking up once again the theme of theodicy in theology I am not suggesting (as the word and its history might suggest) a belated and somewhat obstinate attempt to justify God in the face of evil, in the face of suffering and wickedness in the world. What is really at stake is the question of how one is to speak about God at all in the face of the abysmal histories of suffering in the world, in "his" world. In my view this is "the" question for theology; theology must not eliminate it or over-respond to it. It is "the" eschatological question, the question before which theology does not develop its answers reconciling everything, but rather directs its questioning incessantly back toward God. (Metz 1998: 55f.)

If this be the "question" that eventually emerges as determinative for Metz's theology, it is evident why his theological itinerary has always included a critique of the ways that theologies privatize the Christian message. Only if the remembrances of historical catastrophe are not conjured away by theology but are "taken into the Church and into theology" to orient our belief and our talk about God can the endangered character of human identity-in-history become the arena in which Christian faith and action prove themselves true, relevant, and trustworthy, and this dimension be saved and reaffirmed as fundamental to human being. It also becomes clear why his concern has increasingly focused on the way that European culture has abandoned Enlightenment aspirations for a world organized according to universal norms of justice, in which individuals take responsibility for themselves and for their histories. He worries that this great utopian vision, ultimately inspired, in his view, by Christian values, is threatened with exhaustion:

> Do we not see in our social context a new and growing privatization, spread through a gentle seduction by our modern culture industry? Is there not a kind of weariness with being a subject; trained to fit in, do we not think in terms of little niches? Is there not a growing spectator mentality with no obligation to perceive critically, a rather voyeuristic way of dealing with social and political crises? Are there not in our secularized and enlightened world signs of a new, to some extent, second immaturity [*Unmündigkeit*] . . . ? (Metz 1998: 105)

Unmündigkeit clearly alludes to Kant's definition of Enlightenment as that state in which humans emerge from immaturity or tutelage, making use of their reason (at least in arguments in the public sphere) to take charge of history and render it more human. In Metz's view, if the concerns and anxieties that accrue to achieving such a demanding – indeed, perhaps unreasonable – ideal can be soothed and anesthetized by late modern culture, it is not only the end of the Enlightenment project, but a disaster for a Christianity whose authentic sense can only be disclosed against the backdrop of those concerns and anxieties. That is why theology must continually raise the "theodicy question," and why the remembrances of history's catastrophes are indispensable to it.

The theodicy question was described above as an "eschatological question, the question before which theology does not develop its answers reconciling everything, but rather directs its questioning incessantly back toward God." This brings us to the doctrinal focus of Metz's theology: eschatology. While Metz has been concerned from early in his career to demonstrate Christianity's constitutive concern for the world and its history, the way he argued this concern theology shifted dramatically in the 1960s. From a focus on incarnation as the proper doctrinal locus in which to work out the autonomy proper to the world, he turned to eschatology as the proper way to understand the openness of the future and Christians' obligation in faith to participate in history's movement into that open horizon. His meeting with Ernst Bloch in June of 1963 gave decisive impetus to this shift. Bloch, who was so formative for Jürgen Moltmann, had a similar impact on Metz. *Eschatology*, that area of theology that emphasizes history's orientation toward a future that can only be glimpsed now "as in a mirror, darkly," became the sphere within which Metz argued for the church's need to respect and foster the legitimate autonomy of the world as it was drawn toward its future eschatological consummation. But, as arguments over what Jesus meant by the imminence of the reign of God have dramatically illustrated, there is more than one way to make a theology "eschatological," and Metz's movement in this regard, seen against an ecclesiological backdrop, is instructive.

Metz's initial appropriation of eschatology had clear ecclesiological implications. He reconfigured the revisionary Marxist deployment of the theory and practice of "ideology critique" to work out an understanding of the church as the "institution of critical freedom." The church is to safeguard the openness of historical processes from the endemic human temptation to freeze them into ideological absolutes that then underwrite the kind of violence so horrifically characteristic of the twentieth century. It does so by means of an insistence on the sovereignty of the God of the future, which relativizes every particular human project in history (Metz 1969: 107–24). While he never disavowed this notion of "the eschatological proviso," it becomes notably absent in his later work. As always, it is his sensitivity to what "endangers" the political dimension of human subjectivity (as defined above) that lies behind this shift.

As the sixties came to a close and gave way to the more placid seventies, Metz began to diagnose modernity's deepest malady not as a susceptibility to ideologically charged paroxysms of violence, but (as we have already seen) a growing apathy, a "weariness with being a subject." Insofar as, for Metz, being a subject means taking responsibility for oneself and for those others with whom one is always already involved in history and society, what this weariness means is an increasing inability and/or unwillingness to intervene actively in social and political processes that determine what it means to be persons – most seriously, to be precise, processes that determine *who* will count as persons. Metz worries that our sense for the endangered character of human becoming in history has been numbed. We are more informed than ever about catastrophes in our world, but less and less moved to act: "Catastrophes are reported on the radio in between pieces of music. The music plays on like the 'passage of time' rendered audible, rolling mercilessly over everything, that nothing can interrupt. 'When atrocities happen it's like when the rain falls. No one shouts "Stop it!" anymore' – Bertolt Brecht" (Metz 1980: 170f. *1977: 150*).

Metz's aphorism is taken from his tribute to Ernst Bloch in a set of 35 theses entitled "Hope as Imminent Expectation, or the Struggle for Lost Time: Untimely Theses on Apocalyptic" (Metz 1980: 169; *1977: 165*). These theses express Metz's continual concern with time and temporality. This concern eventually sent him back to his early engagement with Heidegger – now, however, not as a source for a Christian existential anthropology, but as the twentieth-century thinker who most understood that modernity has covered over the temporality of human existence. However, while Metz highlights Heidegger's prescience in pointing out our exhausted and dysfunctional dealings with temporality, Metz contends that, rather than turning to the pre-Socratics, "he would have done better to look at the apocalyptic traditions" (Metz and Wiesel 1999: 29). Metz shifted to a strongly apocalyptic form of eschatology.

Metz contends that the backdrop to our deadened sense of time's passage is the modern symbol of evolution, a mythical universalization of the empirical concept, according to which everything passes away, and nothing genuinely new can "interrupt" the course of history. It is the dominance of this mythic symbol that paralyzes human hope and action on behalf of the victims of history, and therefore needs critique and "correction" by an *apocalyptic* eschatology. Metz advocates apocalypticism for its capacity to energize a life full of hope in the God who can interrupt history, who sets bounds to history. Such an apocalyptic hope nourishes *political* hope and action on behalf of others:

> A passionate expectation of the "day of the Lord" does not lead to a pseudo-apocalyptic dream-dance in which all the claims made by discipleship would be dissipated or forgotten. Neither does it lead to that unreflective fanaticism that cannot

see in prayers of longing and expectation anything other than transparent forms of evasion or self-deception. Imminent expectation does not allow discipleship to be postponed. It is not the apocalyptic sense for life that makes us apathetic, but the evolutionistic! It is the time symbol of evolution that paralyzes discipleship. Imminent expectation, on the other hand, proffers perspectives on time and expectation to a hope that has been evolutionistically anaesthetized and seduced. . . . Apocalyptic consciousness . . . stands under the challenge of practical solidarity with "the least of your brothers," as it is called in the little apocalypse of Matthew's Gospel. (Metz 1980: 176f.; *1977: 156*)

This appeal to apocalypticism does not, therefore, culminate in an attempt to calculate the time and events of the last day. It is, rather, a rhetorical device to inspire hope and creative political action. It does so by countering the deadened sense of time and history that, in Metz's view, engenders both fatalistic apathy and desperate fanaticism (see Ashley 2000). Since this hopeful orientation toward the future is always a hope *for the other, even for one's enemy*, Metz insists that it does not engender a violent praxis demonizing and seeking the annihilation of the other, but rather a patient, albeit apocalyptically insistent praxis that bears suffering and disappointment, continuing a struggle for the full humanity of all persons no matter what the cost: "Discipleship in imminent expectation: this is an apocalyptic consciousness that does not cause, but rather accepts suffering – resisting both apathy and hatred" (Metz 1980: 176; *1977: 156*). Ecclesiologically rendered, this apocalyptic eschatology leads not to a focus on the church as the "institution of critical freedom," with its indispensable contribution to history of the eschatological proviso, but to an emphasis on those groups (often small, controversial, and marginalized) in the church that keep this unreasonable (on modern terms) apocalyptic hope alive. This emphasis is particularly evident in Metz's reflections on the place of religious life in the church (Metz 1978; 1998: 150–74).

Let us close with the particular spirituality that Metz associates with this apocalyptic eschatology. An apocalyptic hope in a God "for whom not even the past is fixed," which measures its actions accordingly, is sustained by a certain mystical disposition that Metz calls "*Leiden an Gott.*" I have translated this "suffering unto God" in order to draw the connection with that other active disposition that Metz names "*Rückfragen an Gott,*" going back to God with one's questions. *Leiden an Gott* is not a passive acceptance or endurance, as alternative translations such as "suffer from God" or "suffer God" might suggest. It is an active stance whose exemplars are Job and the Jesus of Mark's passion account – crying out to God and calling God to account. This spirituality can endure the remembrance of suffering, and act out of that remembrance no matter how hopeless such action seems, because it hopes for God's promised response, and calls God to make good on that hope. It is "a God-mysticism with an increased readiness to perceive, a mysticism of open eyes that sees more and not less. It is a mysticism that especially makes visible all invisible and inconvenient suffering, and – convenient or not – pays attention to it and takes responsibility for it, for the sake of a God who is a friend to human beings" (Metz 1998:

163). When Metz speaks of the dual mystical–political character of Christian faith, it is this that defines the mystical complement to the political stance that acknowledges the other in his or her alterity, and, above all, acts politically out of compassion for the other's suffering (Metz, forthcoming 2003).

Conclusions

I have not discussed here several crucial particulars of Metz's project, such as his appeal for a recovery of the Jewish roots of Christianity (Metz 1999). Nor have I examined particular critiques of Metz's work. It has been argued, for example, that Metz's relentless focus on theodicy, on the memory of suffering, and on the still radically endangered project of becoming and remaining a human subject reacts so severely to an ahistorical, triumphalistic Christianity (itself a distortion, to be sure) that he cannot do justice in his Christology and soteriology to the genuine victory that Christian faith asserts has happened, "once for all," in Jesus' death and resurrection (Reno 1992; Tück 1999). I judge that these critiques arise in part from a failure adequately to consult those places where Metz does work out at least the outlines of a Christology that would do this (Metz 1998; Metz and Wiesel 1999), in part from a deep disagreement over the severity of the challenge that the twentieth century's "histories of suffering" pose for Christian faith and theology. These problems do show, however, that Metz has not offered the specific elaborations of doctrinal issues (even in essay form) that were the trademark of his teacher Karl Rahner. I suspect that the Christology of Jon Sobrino both "fits" the underlying approach laid out by Metz's work and answers critiques of Metz's Christological lacunae, but this suggestion can here be only offered, not argued.

Finally, Metz's is a *fundamental* theology, and that is where its contribution lies. It intends a justification "at a first level of reflection" of Christian faith's truth and relevance, and particularly of the *hope* that it offers contemporary men and women. This is particularly pressing in a world in which persons are threatened with a "second immaturity," with giving up on the Enlightenment ideals of freedom, the inalienable dignity of every human being, justice, and the obligation to struggle for these ideals no matter what the cost. What Metz's political theology shows so well is that a Christianity that cannot "render an account of its hope" against the backdrop of these ideals is not just politically irrelevant. More seriously, it is unfaithful to the challenge of the *memoria passionis, mortis, et resurrectionis Jesu*, which can and must animate us toward its own distinctive way of hoping for the future out of a remembered common historical past.

Note

1   Because of flaws in the English translation of *Glaube in Geschichte und Gesellschaft*, at times I give my own translations. As an indication that I have emended the

translation I follow the citation to the English with a reference to the German second edition in italics, thus: (Metz 1980: 224; *1977: 200*).

References

Ashley, J. M. (1998). *Interruptions: Mysticism, Politics and Theology in the Work of Johann Baptist Metz*. Notre Dame, Ind.: University of Notre Dame Press.

——(2000). "Apocalypticism in Political and Liberation Theology: Toward an Historical *Docta Ignorantia*." *Horizons: The Journal of the College Theology Society* 27: 1 (Spring), 22–43.

Browning, Don (1991). *A Fundamental Practical Theology: Descriptive and Strategic Proposals*. Minneapolis: Fortress.

Chopp, Rebecca (1986). *The Praxis of Suffering: An Interpretation of Liberation and Political Theologies*. Maryknoll, NY: Orbis.

Metz, J. B. (1969). *Theology of the World*, trans. William Glen-Doepel. New York: Herder & Herder.

——(1970). "Kirchliche Autorität im Anspruch der Freiheitsgeschichte." in J. B. Metz, J. Moltmann and W. Oellmüller, *Kirche im Prozeß der Aufklärung*. Munich: Kaiser-Grünewald.

——(1977). *Glaube in Geschichte und Gesellschaft*. Mainz: Matthias-Grünewald.

——(1978). *Followers of Christ*, trans. Thomas Linton. Mahwah, NJ: Paulist.

——(1980). *Faith in History and Society: Toward a Practical Fundamental Theology*, trans. David Smith. New York: Crossroad.

——(1984). "Productive Noncontemporaneity." In Jürgen Habermas (ed.), trans. and intr. Andrew Buchwalter, *Observations on "The Spiritual Situation of the Age"*. Cambridge, Mass.: MIT Press.

——(1986). "Politische Theologie und die Herausforderung des Marxismus: Ein Gespräch des Herausgebers mit Johann Baptist Metz." In Peter Rottländer (ed.), *Theologie der Befreiung und Marxismus*. München: Edition Liberación.

——(1987). "Communicating a Dangerous Memory." In Fred Lawrence (ed.), *Communicating a Dangerous Memory: Soundings in Political Theology*. Atlanta: Scholars.

——(1989). "Theology in the New Paradigm: Political Theology." In Hans Küng and David Tracy (eds.), *Paradigm Change in Theology: A Symposium for the Future*. Edinburgh: T. & T. Clark.

——(1998). *A Passion for God: The Mystical-Political Dimension of Christianity*, trans. and intr. J. Matthew Ashley. Mahwah, NJ: Paulist.

——(1999). "Christians and Jews after Auschwitz: Being a Meditation Also on the End of Bourgeois Religion." In John K. Downey (ed.), *Love's Strategy: The Political Theology of Johann Baptist Metz*. Harrisburg, Pa.: Trinity.

——(forthcoming 2003): "Toward a Christianity of Political Compassion." In Kevin Burke SJ and Robert Lassalle-Klein (eds.), *The Love that Produces Hope*. Collegeville, Minn.: Liturgical Press

Metz, J. B., and Wiesel, E. (1999). *Hope Against Hope: Johann Baptist Metz and Elie Wiesel Speak Out on the Holocaust*, trans. J. Matthew Ashley. Mahwah, NJ: Paulist.

Rahner, Karl (1978). *Foundations of Christian Faith: An Introduction to the Idea of Christianity*, trans. William Dych. New York: Crossroad.

——(1982). "The Intellectual Formation of Future Priests." In *Theological Investigations*, vol. VI: *Concerning Vatical Council II*, trans. Karl-H. and Boniface Kruger 113–38. New York: Crossroad.

Reno, R. R. (1992). "Christology in Political and Liberation Theology." *The Thomist* 56: 2 (April), 291–322.

Tück, Jan-Heiner (1999). *Christologie und Theodizee bei Johann Baptist Metz*. Paderborn: Schöningh.

CHAPTER 18
Political Theologies in Asia

Aloysius Pieris

Asian Christianity has registered two species of political theologies. In the second half of the second millennium (from the 1500s onwards) the dominant *political* theology in Asia could be, retrospectively, termed "theology of domination," in contrast with the various "theologies of liberation" that made their appearance during the final decades of that same millennium (from the 1970s onwards). The former was implicitly operative in the policy of *Euro-ecclesiastical expansionism* which resulted from the unholy alliance between Christian missions and Western colonialism. Since this theology was not peculiar to the missionary theology in Asia and is a subject that needs to be handled under a common rubric dealing with a particular period of history in the Western church, the present chapter restricts its scope to the second brand of theology mentioned above.

An Asian political theology can be provisionally described as a species of theology which originates, develops, and culminates in a political option made by an Asian Christian community as a biblically inspired response to a social conflict or a social need affecting both the church and the larger (non-Christian) community around it. To describe every shade of theology that meets that definition is not possible within the purview of this chapter, but a broad sketch of the major trend is outlined in part I under the heading "Asian Third world Theology or Asian Theology of Liberation," with a brief mention of some of its variant forms. In part II, this major trend is taken as the point of reference in presenting Korea's Minjung theology as its anticipation, Dalit theology as a counterpoint movement and Asian feminist theology as a movement parallel to both.

Part I: Asian Third World Theology or Asian Theology of Liberation

The two poles: religiousness and poverty

It was in the 1970s that the terms "third world" and "liberation" began to be recognized as cognate concepts in theology. The idea of a "third" world was not understood primarily as No. 3 in the numerical sense, following the first world of the capitalist countries and the second world of the socialist bloc. Rather, in accordance with its original French usage, *tiers monde*, it connotes an *alternative world* to which the decolonized nations of the 1950s and 1960s aspired: a world different from either of the other two, much in the sense in which the Greek fathers of the church applied the same word *triton (genos)* to Christianity in order to emphasize that their religion was neither Judaism nor hellenistic religion but a *tertium quid*, a "third something." Nevertheless, it has been observed that the third world is to be distinguished by its mass poverty and its being exploited by the other two worlds, not to mention its numerical superiority, which has prompted some to refer to it as the "two-thirds world."

The defeat of the United States in Vietnam, as well as self-reliant China's rise to the status of a world power unaided by any superpower, gave the third world consciousness of Asians a boost in the 1970s. The Non-Aligned Movement was the most expressive political symbol of this new awareness. The Christians of the third world who appropriated this political consciousness increasingly rejected the *development* model of the 1960s and supported the *liberation* agenda of third world leaders for whom the two "developed" worlds were centers of domination. It was true, however, that some liberation theologians leaned towards the social-ist bloc as an inevitable consequence of their aversion to capitalism as a form of Mammon-worship (a fundamental axiom of this theology even today), though there certainly were among them many critical voices raised against the denial of civil liberties in communist regimes.

The Peruvian theologian Gustavo Gutiérrez' epoch-making book *A Theology of Liberation* (1971) had a widespread influence on the thinking of third world theologians, culminating in the formation of the Ecumenical Association of Third World Theologians (EATWOT) in Dar es Salaam in 1976. The Asian version of third world theology began to be referred to more frequently as "Asian liberation theology"; for the expression "third world" had by now acquired the status of a *theological* category, invoking the experience of the hungry children of Jacob travelling westward to the rich country of Egypt in search of economic aid, only to fall victims of the latter's cultural and political domination. The exodus from that enslavement as recorded in the memory of Israel, reaching its climax in the Passover of Jesus from death and slavery to life and freedom in the Spirit, became the biblical axis round which this theology revolved. For the exodus was followed by the establishment of an alternative model of a just society, a third way of organizing the human and the ecological community, which Yahweh and Israel as covenanted partners installed in Canaan, the land that defiantly lay between the two major superpowers of that time, Babylon and Egypt. The exodus of the New Israel resulted also in the Jesus Community, a con-trast society. Hence the third world theologians naturally insisted that the locus of their theologizing would be the basic Christian communities, i.e. the nuclear "kingdom communities of the poor," through which the institutional church would, hopefully, be leavened and fermented by the spirit of the Gospel, enabling it to become what it was originally meant to be: a contrast society.

The Asian version of this theology succeeded in articulating its own identity against the backdrop of the Latin American model during and after a stormy controversy at the Asian Theological Consultation (ATC) of EATWOT in 1979. A distinction was made between its "third worldness," consisting of the poverty and exploitation of the Asian masses, and its "Asianness," specified in terms of its multifaceted religiosity. These two ideas, *poverty* and *religiousness*, which began to dominate the theological scene from then onwards, were both rated as soteriologically "ambivalent." For instance, "poverty", when imposed on the masses by the greed of the wealthy and wasteful few, is an anti-evangelical phenomenon, a counter-sign of God's reign; but when voluntarily embraced, it is the beatitudinal state of Christian discipleship that corresponds to the liberative ascesis of all other Asian religions. Similarly, the "religiousness" of Asia began to be seen as either enslaving or liberating accordingly as the different religions sanction or censure the mass poverty and class hierarchies that manifest and maintain an unjust social order. It is not wealth that is evil in itself; like the bread of the Eucharist, it too can be a sacrament of communion when shared by all, but turns into a cult of Mammon (i.e. a "sin against the body of the Lord") when enjoyed *only* by the selfish few.

In theory, all religions see a causal nexus between organized greed and mass poverty, and conversely, between the practice of opted poverty and the reduction of forced poverty. Therefore, the tools of introspection or self-analysis proper to Asian religions which inculcate liberation from personal greed (acquisitive instinct), as well as the tools of social analysis or class analysis which exposes the mechanism of institutionalized greed (unbridled capitalism) are both employed in conjunction with each other as a strategy for a liberative praxis, which, according to this theology, is also the first formulation of a liberative theory.

In this theology, the "cosmic" religions (pejoratively referred to as "animism" or "nature worship" by Western anthropologists, and rejected as "polytheism" and "idolatry" by early representatives of colonial Christianity) have been positively revalued. The word "cosmic" is actually a neologism that gradually entered the vocabulary of these theologians to indicate the tribal and clannic cultures of Asia and Oceania, as well as the popular forms of the major world religions. These latter are known as "metacosmic" soteriologies, as explained below. In the belief–practice cycle which characterizes these popular tribal and clannic cultures, the powers of nature or cosmic forces manifest and maintain the vital needs of humans, who are participant members of this cosmic community rather than its owners or controllers.

These powers of nature, such as fire, wind, and so on, at once awesome and helpful, are not, therefore, "exploited" as in a technocracy, but reverently relied upon and ritually tamed in favor of human welfare. Technology offers itself as a modern way of taming these natural energies and is not necessarily harmful. For instance, rituals calling for rain during droughts are complemented, not contradicted, by the creation of a modern water-storage and irrigation system, as these mechanisms do not necessarily clash with the ecospirituality of a cosmic religion. But *technocracy*, on the other hand, with its desacralizing effects on the ecocommunity, is damaging to cosmic religiosity. Theologians make this distinction between technology and technocracy in their efforts at integrating the ecocosmic religiosity of the poor into their theological praxis.

Humans, on their death, get absorbed into the cosmos as its energizing forces (gods and ancestors, manes, spirits). All forces of nature are invoked and revered as personal divine beings collaborating with humans; they are not impersonal instruments in human hands. The *devas* in the Indic region, the *phis* in Southeast Asia, the *bons* in Tibet are such cosmic powers interacting with humans. The cult of *kamis* in Japanese Shintoism and the ancestor worship in Chinese Confucianism are culturally refined and religiously exquisite forms of cosmic spirituality. Thus, for instance, a metacosmic religion such as Buddhism has had to incorporate these cults in the process of inculturation in various Asian regions, and therefore what is known as "popular Buddhism" is none other than the regionally specified cosmic base of metacosmic Buddhism.

Note the difference between the "cosmic" and the "secular." Though both are a positive affirmation of the present world, the secular defines itself as the nonsacred, whereas the cosmic points to a *sacred this-worldliness*. Now, being sacred, the cosmos inspires an ecospirituality invoking the "sacramental" theory of creation and clashes with technocracy, i.e. technology vitiated by an "instrumental" theory of creation. On the other hand, the this-worldliness accounts for the conspicuous participation of tribal and clannic people in several waves of revolutionary uprisings recorded in Asian history. Hence, as a religious phenomenon with a revolutionary potential, the cosmic has become an indispensable ingredient of an Asian liberation theology.

The "metacosmic" religions, on the other hand, posit a transphenomenal or supranatural horizon as the soteriological goal defined in either (predominantly, not exclusively) gnostic or (predominantly, not exclusively) agapeic terms. In the gnostic religions, the final goal (e.g. Brahman-Atman in Vedantic Hinduism, Nirvana in Buddhism and Jainism, Dao in Daoism) is reached through *gnosis* or salvific knowledge. Here love is subservient to knowledge. In the second species of soteriology, the ultimate reality (e.g. Yahweh in Judaism, Abba, Father of Jesus, in Christianity, and Allah in Islam) is encountered through *agape* or liberative love. Here, knowledge is absorbed into love. These two streams of metacosmic religiosity are blended together in Asian liberation theology in proportion to their demographic representation in each country or region. For, being the religion of a small minority (a mere 3 per cent) in Asia, except in a few concentrated pockets, Christianity has to articulate its theology of liberation in terms of the liberative thrusts of both gnostic and agapeic forms of metacosmic religions which, however, are never found in their 'pure' form because, when they spread in various parts of Asia, they had to sink their roots always in a cosmic culture as the only natural soil available. In other words, the popular forms of these metacosmic religions (known as popular Buddhism, popular Hinduism, and even popular Christianity) are not rejected as deviations but appreciated as a cosmic expression, or, more precisely, the cosmic base, of these metacosmic religions. Thus an Asian liberation theology is neither Asian nor liberative unless it integrates the personal/spiritual, the social/political, and the cosmic/ecological dimensions of Asia's various soteriologies.

Covenant Christology

Now a word must be said about Christology, which remains the *punctum stantis et cadentis* of any theology that calls itself Christian. The suspicion that Asian theology in general compromises the "uniqueness of Christ" becomes a straight-forward accusation when it comes to liberation theology. Since in an Asian politi-cal theology the politics of poverty and the theology of the Christian religion have a greater task in coming to terms with each other than in any other con-tinent, the Asian paradigm of Christology has been dramatically shifting away from the Chalcedonian model. For the Christological councils of the church neglected the *political* dimension of the historically recorded assassination of Jesus under Pontius Pilate and concentrated unduly on the philosophical problem of reconciling humanity with divinity in the mystery of the Incarna-tion, which lies beyond the pale of historical verification.

The Incarnation, a liberation theologian would argue, has to be interpreted in the light of the life, work, words, and especially the victorious death of Jesus, rather than vice versa; victorious, because the cross is not merely the locus of his death but also of his exaltation, that is, of his Resurrection and Ascension and of Pentecost, which the evangelists spread out as post-crucifixional events to give feeble human minds the time needed to experience them in a slow-motion replay through a series of liturgical celebrations. The cross, in the language of liberation, is the political conflict in which God vanquishes Mammon, love defeats power, life rises from death, and the victim turns victor. It is the symbol of the good news of liberation, of which the main addressees and the sole announcers are today's victims of political conflicts.

The Asian Christians who engage in dialogue with other religions without any concern for the politics of the cross (theologians sometimes called incultur-ationists or indigenizers) might at most confirm the Chalcedonian speculation with parallel theories of god–man cults of Asian origin. But a political theology has to hold together the two baptisms of Jesus: first at the "Jordan of Asian reli-giosity" (choosing discipleship under the Deuteronomic prophetic stream of lib-erative religiosity represented by John, later a victim of a political assassination, rather than under the enslaving religiousness of Essenes, Pharisees, Sadducees or Zealots), and second on the "Calvary of Asian poverty" (as a victim of a polit-ical conspiracy between the imperial colonizer and the local exploiters of the reli-gious-minded masses). This picture of Calvary is so true to reality in most Asian countries that Jesus' self-effacingly brave deeds of love, referred to as "baptism" in the Gospels, present Christ as a humble servant–teacher eliciting love rather than as a triumphalist conqueror demanding submission. It is in this picture of Christ ("meek and humble of heart") – Christ, who never asked anyone to change religion but only change his or her ways (*shub*, *metanoia*) in conformity with his meekness and lowliness – that his uniqueness is revealed. Such a Christ does not compete with the founders of other religions but cross-fertilizes Asian religiosity with the politics of poverty as no other teacher has done. Hence it is in neglecting the political aspect of Jesus' life and death that Chalcedon (though correct in what it tried to affirm, namely, that the human and the divine in Jesus admit neither of fission nor of fusion) has left out what is truly unique to him.

The Asian political theologians point out that traditional Christology has indulged in too much speculation about the Incarnation instead of encouraging a commitment to Christ's mission; that it is primarily a theory from which a praxis has to be strained out speculatively. The message of love which requires the two baptisms mentioned above is absent from this Chalcedonian exercise because the preoccupation with the Incarnation has eclipsed the politics of the cross. The fact that Jesus, who recapitulated the whole of revelation and salvation in the two love commands (Matt. 22: 40), went to the extent not only of telescoping the love of God into love of neighbor (Matt. 7: 12) but also of defining the love of neighbor as our involvement with the victim of robbery and violence that we meet on our life's journey (Luke 10: 29–37), confirms not only that in Jesus God has become my neighbor, but that this divine neighbor of mine is pre-eminently the victim of injustice offering me salvation in exchange for my being involved with his or her plight.

This way of seeing Christ as "God become my oppressed neighbor" could be developed into what one might call "covenant Christology". For the Exodus is a liberation process that culminates in the covenant between Yahweh and the runaway slaves of Egypt. The purpose is to present to the world an alternative society based on justice and love, that is to say, a contrast society wherein Yahweh alone, and no other creature, is served as the sovereign. It was Yahweh's nature not to sign any agreement with the imperial powers or a dominant social class. Hence colonial Christianity, which colluded with the Western oppressors of non-Christian nations, had no mandate to preach God's message of liberation, for Christ is the embodiment of both God and the oppressed in one person. Accordingly, their theology of domination has to be replaced by a theology of liberation which is founded on this covenant.

As the new covenant made flesh, Jesus put his disciples in touch with both partners of the covenant. Whereas Chalcedon saw Christ as a union of "divinity and humanity," liberation Christology sees Jesus as the one in whom "God and the victims of injustice" are encountered as one undividedly salvific (i.e. covenanted) reality. The "person" of Jesus, therefore, is not merely "an individual substance" as presupposed in Chalcedon, but a *corporate person* in so far as he incorporates the poor as his own body. For Asian liberation theologians, to confess "Jesus is the Lord" is to proclaim in word and deed that "Jesus is the new covenant." Hence, to raise one's voice and give public testimony to having "experienced the Lord" in worship assemblies is suspect unless that declaration is authenticated by a passionate involvement with God's inseparable covenant partner, not only through "a personal struggle *to be poor*" but also through "a political struggle *for the poor.*" These two kinds of struggle evoke the two baptisms of Jesus mentioned above. Evidently, the evangelicals and liberationists in Asia speak from two different pulpits; they preach two different Christs.

This covenant Christology can be summed up in the two love commands with which the New Testament has recapitulated the whole of revelation and salvation. Since Jesus is the Word that recapitulates the scriptures, it follows that Jesus is the two-fold love command made flesh. In accordance with this line of reasoning, the first command (worship God alone and no other god) and the second command (love your victim neighbor as Jesus loved us) have been converted, respectively, into two pithy maxims (or *sutras*) which unfold themselves as a liberation Christology: (1) *Jesus is the irrevocable antinomy between God and Mammon* (love of God); and (2) *Jesus is the irrevocable defense pact between God and the poor* (love of neighbor). Thus the love of God (struggle to be evangelically poor) and the love of neighbor (struggle for the socially poor) constitute the liberational praxis, which is at once an act of following Jesus as he lived "in the days of his flesh" and an act of serving Christ "as we know him now" in the poor. It is this double action of discipleship and service that proclaims the Jesus of history to be the Christ of our faith.

This way of encountering Christ as the defense pact which God signs with the poor against their common enemy, Mammon (absolutized wealth), has serious political implications for interreligious cooperation in the area of interhuman justice, a mission that a Christian minority cannot ignore in Asia. Since, in Christ, all that is anti-God coincides with all that is anti-poor, any socioeconomic system which enthrones Mammon (the enemy of both God and the poor) has to be resisted as a violation of the covenant. This is the first axiom in the scriptures and in the teaching of Asian liberation theology. Wherever *God alone* reigns (i.e. in "God's reign", the project of Jesus) there will be no oppressive poverty, but only the liberative poverty of the beatitudes, which is the common inheritance of all religions in Asia. We can define it as *non-idolatrous poverty*, for the following reason. As most of the religious systems of Asia are non-theistic soteriologies, the denial of authentic religiosity is not equated with atheism but with idolatry (addiction to creatures, absolutization of the relative, greed for the contingent, slavery to one's acquisitive instinct – these being the equivalents of what we know as Mammon worship). Thus, the personal struggle *to be poor* (the anti-idolatrous spirituality shared by all religions) is the common platform for interreligious dialogue, whereas the political struggle *for the poor* as a condition of personal salvation constitutes a unique Christian contribution to the dialogue.

With this unique message that social liberation and personal salvation constitute together one inseparable commitment of the new covenant, Christianity does not compete with other religions but complements them. Here again the evangelicals' zeal to convert the pagans is substituted by the liberationists' solidarity with the other religionists. For the latter, the enemy is not people of other religions, but the agents and institutions of Mammon worship cutting across the religious and denominational affiliations.

Finally, an important question needs to be answered: who are the authors of Asian liberation theology/Christology? Not, certainly, academics researching in libraries or teaching in universities. These only *explicitate and articulate* the experiences of the basic human communities where men and women from different religions and no religion struggle to be poor as well as struggle for the poor in politically challenging situations. Their activism is punctuated by a periodic sharing of one another's religious experiences and cross-scriptural studies. The result is neither "syncretism" (a cocktail of religions in which the specific flavor of each religion is modified by that of the others) nor "synthesis" (creation of something entirely new out of the component religions which have, in the process, lost their separate identities altogether), but a *symbiosis* of religions. This means that each religion, challenged by the other religions' unique approach to the liberation praxis, discovers and renames itself in its specificity in response to the other approaches. In the basic human communities it is the non-Christians who help Christians to clarify their religious identity and spell out the uniqueness of Christ, in a way which the academic theologian will later explicate as a Christology.

There are variations in this line of thinking, with different countries evolving their own specific brands of this theology. "Theology of struggle" was one of the names by which some Filipino theologians liked to call their version of this theology, while there has emerged an Indonesian model that calls itself "contextual social theology." The theologians of the Patriotic Association and the Three Self Movement in China seem to view "liberation" not as a goal to be achieved but as a given fact among their people, which the church was called to participate in and appropriate judiciously in its indigenous, i.e. Chinese, manifestation. Parallel trends have been observed in Vietnam. The North Korean equivalent of this tendency is noticed in those Christians who collaborate with the Juche philosophers (discussed below, under "Minjung theology"). The Palestinian Christians, too, have striven to evolve an "ecumenical liberation theology movement", which they call *sabeel* (Arabic for "the way", and also "channel", or "spring" of "living water") and which advocates a non-violent struggle for peace and justice, founded on the life and teaching of Jesus Christ, "the Corner Stone" (which is the name of the journal that promotes it).

Part II: Theology of the Minjung, the Dalits, and the Asian Feminists

The Minjung theology of Korea

Korea's Minjung theology (MT) could very well be the first instance of an Asian political theology. Although it emerged in Korea in the 1970s, it had had about a century of incubation. For MT was actually the third phase of a development that can be traced back to what the Minjung theologians refer to as Minjung Christianity (MC), which, in its turn, was a Christian appropriation of the

Minjung Movement (MM) that contested the Japanese dominance in Korea in the nineteenth century. In MT, the word "Minjung" means the conscientized "people" (corresponding to *laos* in the New Testament) as opposed to the "Daejung", the disoriented "masses" (*ochlos* in the New Testament). Thus MC as well as its theological articulation (MT) presupposes a conversion of the oppressed *masses* into a politically awakened *people* who could take their sociopolitical destiny into their own hands.

A key feature of the MM has been the notion and the role of *han*, a Korean expression that defies translation. It is a mixture of many things: a sense of resignation to inevitable oppression, indignation at the oppressor's inhumanity, anger with oneself for having been caught up in that hopeless situation, and a host of other emotions which are all accumulated to form a powerful source of psychological energy possessing a revolutionary potential capable of being released in a socially organized fashion. In day-to-day life, this revolutionary energy is released by individuals in small doses through rite and ritual with the aid of shamans. But the most dramatic release of collective *han* is the mask dance, in which prophetic humor is exercised by the Minjung against the Confucianist elite and the monastics of metacosmic religion (which in Korea was Buddhism), who allegedly have been siding with the oppressive regime. There are also the great community festivals (*dae-dong gut*) in which the collective ecstasy (*shin-myung*) shatters the accepted system of values in view of a new this-worldly life rather than solely of something beyond. The predominantly cosmic character of these community engagements defines their liberative potential.

Now, the genesis of MC from MM is quite understandable. First of all, in Korea Christianity was introduced not directly by Western missionaries associated with colonialist powers, as in other Asian countries, but by lay persons who had encountered indigenous Christian communities in the churches of neighboring countries. Hence the first Korean converts to (mainly Protestant) Christianity learned from the beginning not to see the Bible as the religious manual of an aggressive Westerner; for the aggressor in their case was an Asian colonizer, namely Buddhist Japan. This situation is unique in Asia. Thus Korean Christianity was not alienated from the anticolonialist agitation, unlike in many other colonized countries where the theology of the indigenous Christians evolved in confrontation with the "domination theology" of the Western Christianizers.

Furthermore, since Japanese and Chinese were hailed as the languages of the Korean *literati* during the Japanese occupation, the appearance of the Bible in the Korean language (printed in the *Hangul* script of the Koreans), thanks to certain farsighted missionaries, had an explosive effect. For, here in this sacred book, the Minjung encountered a God who was in solidarity with them and heard that God's Word of liberation in their own "despised" language, written not only in their own script rather than in that of the colonizer, but also in the folk idiom of narrative, drama, and poetry, so different from the abstract jargon used by the God of missionary catechesis elsewhere. Therefore, this sacred book of the Christians appeared to the Koreans as a charter for freedom in a context of political oppression. No wonder the colonial powers banned the books of Exodus and Daniel as potentially subversive!

Almost from its inception, therefore, Korean Christianity was a *politicized faith*. This is the background to the genesis of MT, which in its present form emerged around the 1970s in South Korea under a very oppressive regime of the post-colonial era. The soil in which it sprouted was the words and deeds of imprisoned and/or tortured farmers, workers, students, professors, and journalists who discovered their prophetic role by a return to the ancient (non-Christian) Korean sources of the Minjung Movement, as appropriated by the first Christians.

Today, this theology is struggling to survive in South Korea amid strong tides of fundamentalist evangelism originating especially from the United States. One development that has been noted in this context is that the dialogue between North Korean and South Korean Christians is marked by a valiant (though not altogether successful) effort to bring together the Juche philosophers among the North Korean Marxists and the Minjung theologians, against opposition from the evangelists. Juche is a non-theistic and secular surrogate of a liberationist "religion" which seems to have disowned the Marxist dogma about religion. This dialogue, which has now been going on for some time, seeks to forge an agreement between the political philosophy of Juche and the political theology of Minjung with a view to the reunification of Korea in confrontation with the military and missionary presence of the American "imperialists."

The Dalit theology of India

The 1970s also saw the emergence of this theology from among the Christian Dalits, that is, "those broken, downtrodden, destroyed" by the nefarious system of discrimination between the so-called high, low, and scheduled castes in India. Their weak self-identity as untouchables and outcastes is derived from centuries of cruel segregation religiously sanctioned by the Hindu "canon law" (*dharmaśāstra*). Today all the "backward" castes (the current euphemism for so-called low castes and outcastes), tribal people, and landless laborers who maintain the primary service sector in contemporary India are loosely termed "Dalits." As in the case of Minjung theology, the Dalit movement, too, was on the scene before the Christians thought of appropriating it theologically. The Dalits had rejected Mahatma Gandhi's appellation *harijan* (people of God) as a brahmanic ruse for condescendingly coopting them into the Hindu religious system. They prefer to be what their name indicates: broken ones. This brokenness includes also their own internal divisions into subcastes.

The Dalit theologians who emerged from among the conscientized Christians of Dalit origin insist that it is the Dalitness of the Christians rather than the Christianness of the Dalits that constitutes their identity, and consequently also the basis of their Christianness. Hence, just as the early Dalit literature (*dalit sahitya*) cites among its sources of inspiration Marx, Lenin, Mao Tse Tung, Che

Guevara, Ho Chi Minh, Martin Luther King Jr., and Malcolm X, rather than Mahatma Gandhi or any of the great Indian reformers, so also Dalit theology finds no inspiration in the works of any of the pioneering Indian Christian theologians or reformers. For Dalit theology by its very origin and nature is a many-sided protest not merely against the Hindu caste system, but equally against the Indian church. Their complaint needs to be spelt out in detail.

First, Christianity, said to have arrived in India during apostolic times, and developed under the patronage of the Persian (East Syrian/Nestorian) church, seemed unaware of the Pauline doctrine of "neither slave nor free" (Gal. 3: 28), allegedly because the New Testament had not yet been written down at that time. The East Syrian Christianity which acclimatized to the Hindu religious ethos was itself affected or rather infected by caste consciousness. It was a millennium and a half before Francis Xavier came to India and baptized the Dalits for the first time. But the process of Indianization of Christianity which followed that event, both in the initiative of Roberto de Nobili in the seventeenth century and in the attempts of the indigenizers of the nineteenth century, as well as those of the modern-day inculturationists, is dismissed as a brahmanization of theology involving Christians who hail from the forward castes (the current term for high castes). For the Dalits, these attempts were no more than a substitution for the colonialist theology of domination of an Indian version of the same.

Second, even though the majority of Indian Christians are Dalits (in some places, 60 per cent, in others 90 per cent), the forward-caste minority continues to take the key roles in church leadership and the academic theological industry. Third, even the liberation theologians are said to come mostly from the same "high" castes; it is claimed that their zeal for the poor did not include a concern for Dalits, and that the Marxist tools of social analysis employed by them are blunted by the neglect of the caste dimension of Indian society. This, incidentally, was also the blind spot of Indian Marxists, they complain. For, unlike Marx who, excusably, depended on information derived from Max Müller's study of Sanskrit literature rather than from any field study of rural India, these Indian Marxists (who were also from the higher castes!) culpably ignored the magnitude of personal and structural violence which the caste system inflicted upon the Dalits.

Understandably, therefore, the Exodus text so central to Indian and other third world liberation theologians is reinterpreted by being traced back to the confessional text, Deut. 26: 5–12, which establishes the historical roots of the Exodus people. For the Dalits regard themselves as the *adivasis* ("original inhabitants") of India, whom the invading *Āryans*, with their colour consciousness (the Vedic word for caste is *varna*, colour), treated as a slave class (*dasyus* in Vedic hymns). Their Dalitness, to which Isaiah (53: 2ff.) alludes in the "one without comeliness," "sorrowful person acquainted with grief," "one from whom people hide their faces," one who "was despised," is precisely that attribute which Jesus, the divine man of sorrows and slave God, had reportedly appropriated as proper to his messianic mission. This Jesus of the Dalits, or rather "Jesus, the Dalit," whom the Gospels proclaim so clearly and emphatically, has never been recognized by the Indian church, not even by the allegedly Indianized sections of it. It is this Jesus who is the center of the Dalit world and from whom, therefore, Dalit Christology radiates.

Today, moreover, Dalitness has become a political discourse which the whole world has been summoned to recognize, especially since the Durban Conference on Racism in 2001 and in the face of contemporary India's militant Hinduism or the ideology of *hindutva*; from which we may conclude that its Christian version may very well be India's major political theology in the future.

Asian feminist theology

One of the anomalies of Asian religiousness is that practically all the major (metacosmic) religions in Asia have had their origin and growth in androcratic societies. Since the Dalits and the Minjung suffered discrimination from the hierarchies of such metacosmic religions, Asian women sometimes have referred to themselves as the "Minjung of the Minjung" or the "Dalits among the Dalits." For even the scriptures of these religions are not free from misogyny or gynophobia. Hence it is not a case of religions bringing redemption to women, but women taking upon themselves the messianic task of redeeming religions from sexism. This means that feminism is the most problematic as well as the most promising political theology in this continent.

As with every other form of political theology, feminism too began with a negative critique of the status quo, and only as a second step has it begun to articulate its own specific form and content in more positive terms. Already EATWOT has been forced to acknowledge its antifeminism by the women participants themselves, who therefore developed their own specific agenda within EATWOT, that is to say, within Asian theology of liberation.

While it would seem that non-Christian women, particularly in India, have made a breakthrough in laying the foundation for a distinctively Asian brand of feminism, the Christian pioneers, barring a few, have tended to apply the dominant model of Western feminism to the Asian context. This was understandably the first wave of Asian feminist theology, accompanied and followed by the second wave which was reflective of the feminist theologians' own personal and collective affirmation of their womanhood within the area of theology, profiting from the contribution of non-Christian women to the feminist debate. The third wave, which is now gaining currency, though not sufficiently documented, reflects the acknowledgment of the class–gender link. Hence, as in Asian liberation theology, so also in Asian feminist theology, the most creative contributions have come from those Christian women who have joined the various (Christian and non-Christian) women's grassroots movements, especially among the poor in rural Asia. The women who are oppressed on the basis of both gender and class and are politically involved in collective action have been recognized as the school in which Christian women (and men) *learn* to articulate a theology that is authentically feminist and authentically Asian.

The observation made above about Asian liberation theologies also holds good for feminist theologies of Asia: namely, that the revolutionary potential (*vis-à-vis* patriarchal domination) is to be cultivated more in cosmic religiosity than in the metacosmic religions. It is in the tribal societies of Asia that there lies the best chance of discovering some sparks of feminism which could be assiduously kindled into a conflagration capable of reducing the androcratic bastions to cinders. However, this is far from saying that tribal cultures are paragons of androgyny. The feminist theologian's hope is that these tribal and other cosmic cultures could redeem the metacosmic religions of their traditional patriarchy through a process of conscientization.

The implication of this hope is that even the metacosmic religions are rooted in cosmic subcultures, usually referred to as popular religiosity (popular Buddhism, popular Hinduism, or popular Christianity), where the cult of female deities has a more natural place. Even more importantly, this popular religiosity is also the heritage of the Asian poor, thus linking gender with class. For instance, the oppressed poor in the Hindu cultures of South Asia have recourse to goddesses such as Kali and Pattini whenever justice is violated. Also Ina, the Filipina mother-god, not to mention the Marian cult in popular Catholicism, or even the cult of Chinese Kwan Yin (Japanese Kannon) in popular Buddhism and popular Daoism, represent the feminist aspiration in the spirituality of the poor. Thus it is in the cosmic ("popular") end of the religious spectrum of Asia that the Asian women discover (for themselves and for men) the religious symbols with which to protest directly or indirectly against their servile state and create a space of freedom for themselves within the family, religious communities, and civil society.

This *cosmic* approach to feminism differs from the *secularist* school of feminism, which is not as successful in Asia as in the West. The latter mode reflects the antireligious impulse of feminists reacting against the antifeminism of religion. But the "cosmic" (as the term is meant in Asian liberation theology) is a blend of the earthly and the womanly within the religiousness of the poor. It is, therefore, a typically Asian religious approach to a political theology of feminism.

The secular factor, however, is not altogether absent. The involvement of women from the oppressed classes in ecological movements, for instance, could be regarded as a secularist parallel to the religious cult of goddesses of justice. For the rape of nature, which is part and parcel of male domination both in politics and at home, affects the rural women of Asia most of all. The mobilization of women in ecological movements has been an important feature in Asian feminism. Hence the feminist theologians of the third wave mobilize, participate in, and study both the cosmic (i.e. popular religious) practices as well as the secular (grassroots) movements of women as the "gyne-ecological" text of their political theology.

Finally, it must be noted that the feminism of Asian Christians is not yet as sharply articulated or widely ramified as the feminist theologies in the West, though it is perhaps more politicized than the latter as a result of the socioeconomic structures that create poverty. Western feminists, nevertheless, continue to have an immense impact on their Asian counterparts. The feminist exegesis of the Bible is an example of Western influence, though even here there are signs of fresh attempts at "cross-scriptural reading" in solidarity with our non-Christian sisters, a methodology pioneered by Asian liberation theologians in basic human communities.

As a postscript, one might add that though the historical Jesus' masculinity is not in question, the Christ which he became in and through his liberation praxis seems to resist gender definition. The literal interpretation of the Pauline observation that "there is neither male nor female in Christ" (Gal. 3: 28) does not seem farfetched for Asian feminists, in whose thought *Christus* and *Christa* are both alternately predicated about Jesus. But a full-blown feminist Christology is yet to come.

Bibliography

Part I: Asian third world theology or Asian theology of liberation

Arokyasamy, S. and Gispert-Sauch, S., eds. (1987). *Liberation in Asia: Theological Perspectives*. Delhi: Vidyajyoti.

Banawiratma, J. B. and Muller, J. (1999). "Contextual Social Theology: An Indonesian Model." *East Asian Pastoral Review* 36: 1–2, 1–249.

Chinese Theological Review. S. Anselmo, Calif.

Fabella, V. and Torres, S., eds. (1980). *Asia's Struggle for Full Humanity*. Maryknoll, NY: Orbis.

——(1983). *Irruption of the Third World: Challenge to Theology*. Maryknoll, NY: Orbis.

Pieris, A. (1988). *An Asian Theology of Liberation*. Edinburgh: T. & T. Clark.

——(1999). *God's Reign for God's Poor: A Return to the Jesus Formula*. Kelaniya: Tulana Jubilee Publications.

——(2000). "Christ beyond Dogma: Doing Christology in the Context of the Religions and the Poor." *Logos* 39: 3, 1–69.

Voices from the Third World. The biannual publication of the Ecumenical Association of Third World Theologians.

Part II: theology of the minjung, the dalits and the Asian feminists
THE MINJUNG THEOLOGY OF KOREA

Cho, Eunsik (2000). "Dialogue between North and South Korean Christians." *Dialogue*, n.s., 28, 79–105.

Chung, Hyun Kyung (1989). "'Han-pu-ri': Doing Theology from Korean Woman's Perspective." In V. Fabella and A. L. Park (eds.), *We Dare to Dream*, 141–5. Maryknoll, NY: Orbis.

Commission on Theological Concerns of the Christian Conference of Asia, ed. (1983). *Minjung Theology: People as Subjects of History*. Maryknoll, NY: Orbis.

Kwon, Jin-Kwan (1991). "Minjung Theology and its Future Task for People's Movement." *CTC* [Christian Theological Concerns] *Bulletin* (Christian Conference of Asia, Hong Kong), 10: 2–3, 16–22.

Lee, Chung Hee (1992). "Liberation Spirituality in Dae-dong Gut." In Virginia Fabella, Peter K. H. Lee and David Kwang-sun Suh, (eds.), *Asian Christian Spirituality: Reclaiming Traditions*, 36–43. Maryknoll, NY: Orbis.

THE DALIT THEOLOGY OF INDIA

Nirmal, Arvind P., ed. (1991). *A Reader in Dalit Theology*. Madras.
Prabharkar, M. E., ed. (1981). *Towards a Dalit Theology*. Delhi.
Rasquinha, Dionysius, SJ, "A Brief Historical Analysis of the Emergence of Dalit Theology." *Vidyajyoti Journal of Theological Reflection* 66: 5, May 2002, 353–70.
Sha, Ganshyam (1990). "Dalit Movement and the Search for Identity." *Social Action* 40: 4, 217–35.
Webster, J. (1994). *Dalit Christians: A History*. Delhi: ISPCK.

ASIAN FEMINIST THEOLOGY

Abraham, D. et al., eds. (1989). *Asian Women Doing Theology: Report from Singapore Conference Nov. 20–29, 1987*. Hong Kong: Asian Women's Resource Centre for Culture and Theology.
Chung, Hyun Kyung (1990). *Struggle to be the Sun Again: Introducing Asian Women's Theology*. Maryknoll, NY: Orbis.
Dietrich, Gabriele (1987). *Women's Movement in India: Conceptual and Religious Reflections* (selected essays). Bangalore: Breakthrough.
Fabella. V. and Park, S. A. L. (1989). *We Dare to Dream: Doing Theology as Asian Women*. Maryknoll, NY: Orbis.
In God's Image. Quarterly published by the Asian Women's Resource Centre, Hong Kong.
Kwok Pui-Lan (1995). *Discovering the Bible in the Non-Biblical World*. Maryknoll, NY: Orbis.
Pieris, A. (1996). *Fire and Water: Basic Issues in Asian Buddhism and Christianity*. Maryknoll, NY: Orbis.

CHAPTER 19
Black Political Theologies

M. Shawn Copeland

. . . for ourselves and for humanity, comrades, We must turn over a new leaf,
We must work out new concepts, and try set afoot a new man [sic].

Franz Fanon

From the angry wail of James Cone's polemic that irrupted in the aftermath
of the assassination of Martin Luther King, Jr., and veered ever so close to separatism to J. Deotis Roberts's poignant insistence that black Christians live out
the reconciling love of God in white racist America; from Delores Williams's
incisive protest at the marginalization and reduction of the lives and experiences
of black women to Willa Boesak's unequivocal examination of black rage
in order to expose and pose the need for a new ethics in postapartheid South
Africa; from Bob Marley's lilting and incriminating music that unmasks the violence and misery endured by African peoples, to Robert Beckford's biting analysis of racism in Britain and black expressive culture's response of *rahtid*
or righteous rage, to Musa Dube's unflinching disclosure of the crucial role of
the Bible in facilitating Western imperialism: If we consider black theology as
comprehensive critical reflection on the human condition, how could it not be
political!

Even if this description elides black theology's contextual and theoretical
development, it confirms that politics lies just beneath the skin – one scratch
yields the political philosopher, two bring forth the theologian. Yet the thoroughgoing political character of black theology is grounded in its willingness to
stand shoulder to shoulder with ordinary women and men and join with them
in the exercise of nitty-gritty hermeneutics, that is, the reading and interpretation of the body of practices and assumptions, norms, habits, and expectations
that shape and enclose the cultural and social (that is, the political, economic,
and technological) matrix in which we live. Black political theology goes to
school by listening to the vernacular: It absorbs street smarts as well as critical
theory; it knows funk, reggae, rap, and dread; it does jazz, pop, and blues; it is
"riddim wise and Scripture smart" (Middleton 2000: 257). For black political
theology esteems ordinary people's critical consciousness of their own predicament and, thus, prizes what Michel Foucault has called subjugated knowledges.
In theoretical response to the exigencies of epistemology and method,
black political theology sides with Ngugi Wa Thiong'o (*and* Bernard Lonergan)
in the struggle to decolonize the mind. The best of black political theology
takes self-criticism seriously, and grasps theory as passionate, communal,

collaborative intellectual engagement aimed to understand, interpret, and transform the culture through creative and healing social praxis grounded in the Gospel.

Black political theology interrogates the cultural and social horizons through which women and men seek to achieve and realize their humanity with joy and dignity in history, even in the thick of oppression and massive social suffering. Black theology does this by shining the spotlight on the complex relation between religion and societal expressions of cultural meanings and values. It explains the difference between the political as the legitimate use of authorized power and its vulgar reduction to predatory, acquisitive contrivance. Black political theology delineates the global market's subtle, yet violent, subjugation of body and mind, labor and spirit; it sniffs out covert and pseudo-innocent forms of antisemitism, sexism, racism, homophobia, imperialism, and colonialism. Black political theology lays bare modernity's subordination of politics to an economics that turns its back on any relation to society's common human good and "absolves" itself from any question about its legitimacy (Habermas 1983: 3–4). Further, black political theology clarifies the surrender of this economics to a technology that exalts a positivistic notion of science and so exiles metaphysics to "extravagance and meaninglessness" (Habermas 1971: 67). This judgment discloses the mercenary, restless itch to displace, to repress irreducible incarnate spirit by technical rationality.

Black political theology does more than bemoan technological rule. As a Christian act of interpretation, black theology orients itself before the cross of Jesus of Nazareth. Thus, it is ever alert to the temptation of institutionalized religion – indeed, the temptation of all human institutions – to yield to a status quo that ever so politely can mask repressive patterns in the culture. Black political theology undertakes the responsibility to articulate a wisdom that slakes our thirst for the presence and reign of God. It strives for justice in neighbor-directed praxis and for humble, righteous anger as it nurtures compassion and solidarity in efforts to reverse structural injustices.

Black political theology interrupts the privatizing, individualizing tendencies that intrude upon human being; it coaxes forward and supports personal transformation of life by laying the foundation for new practices and habits out of which to live authentically in passion and compassion. Black political theology apprehends praxis as a way of life, a way of being authentically human and holy in the world. In other words, black political theology strives to incarnate a praxial answer to the question of Guatemalan poet Otto René Castillo: "What did you do when the poor / suffered, when tenderness / and life / burned out in them?" Thus, black political theology never can allow or permit any form of ranking of the social suffering of "other" human "others." The best of black political theology seeks to follow Jesus of Nazareth: to take up the cause of outcast, despised, and marginalized children, women, and men; to live at the disposal of the cross (Mark 8: 34).

Origins and Development

A protean global phenomenon, black political theology manifested itself almost simultaneously in the late 1960s and early 1970s in the United States, South Africa, and the Caribbean; it would appear in Britain in the late 1980s. In each locale, black political theology negotiates distinct emphases and concerns, thus asserting particularization – *theologies*. Yet such distinctions neither jeopardize nor enervate black political theologies' African heritage, historic traditions of resistance, and pan-African orientation. From that religio-cultural soil, black theologies take their *root-work* – the struggle for black emancipation, existential empowerment, and spiritual liberation in light of the Gospel.

These theologies enacted a twofold intellectual praxis: On the one hand, they took up a critical apologetic to discredit the American and European ersatz Christianity which had so debased the message of Jesus; on the other hand, they protested various forms of white racist supremacy and elucidated black power and black cultural consciousness. Even in their first stages, wherever they appeared, black political theologies differed from European political theologies whose programs were shaped by the epistemological concerns of the Enlightenment, liberal-market meanings of freedom, and modernity's "infatuat[ion] with secularization and technology" (Bosch 1991: 434). Although black political theologies grasped the import of these issues, they could not approve of them uncritically; the historical, cultural, and social situation of the masses of black people around the globe required otherwise. In their second stages, black political theologies stood shoulder to shoulder with segregated, banned, striking, marching, beaten, imprisoned, and murdered black women and men and those few whites who turned their backs on the absurdity of white supremacy. Black political theologies were never comfortable in the academy; and the very *Sitz im Leben* of their origins pulled them to the periphery. These theologies found their centers in Birmingham and Watts (USA), in Sharpeville and Dimbaza (South Africa), in Kingston, Jamaica and St. George's, Grenada (Caribbean), in Notting Hill and Brixton (Britain); their praxial agitation can be traced in these sites of struggle, building up the moral and spiritual courage of down-pressed black women and men; supplying theological interpretations of black power, freedom, and anti-racism movements; engaging and scrutinizing aspects of black expressive cultures.

The United States

In the United States, black political theology in its earliest stages is associated with James Cone (1970, 1975, 1997), Albert Cleage (1968), and J. Deotis Roberts (1971, 1974). In the cultural and social ferment of the 1960s – the civil rights, black power, and black cultural nationalist movements; the murders of

Malcolm X, Medgar Evers, and Martin Luther King, Jr.; the daring of Stokely Carmichael, Robert Moses, and Bernice Johnson Reagon; the courage of Ella Baker, Rosa Parks, and Fannie Lou Hamer – Cone, Cleage, and Roberts insisted that the Gospel of Jesus provided the theological basis for black liberation. Cleage eschewed formal theological analysis for the sermon and associated himself with social constructions of black power and, through the iconography of Detroit's Church of the Black Madonna, revitalized black cultural and religious esthetics. Cone weighed the meaningfulness of Christian doctrines in relation to "the powerlessness of black [people] whose existence is threatened daily by the insidious tentacles of white power" (Cone 1997: 32). Despite the polemical tone of *Black Theology and Black Power*, Cone's theology remained a black *Christian theology*, taking into account, although not explicitly, the religiosity of the enslaved Africans and the tradition of radical advocacy of the black church. In contrast, Roberts cast that religiosity and tradition in a theological formulation that understood liberation and reconciliation as basic to black political theology (Roberts 1971). He presented a theological critique that synthesized faith and ethics and sought to humanize and change social systems of power (Roberts 1974: 35–6).

But the resistance of those systems to change evoked an impertinent and provocative essay, *Is God a White Racist?* (1973) from philosopher William Jones. This work was (and remains) impertinent because it questioned the efficacy of the Exodus paradigm for black theologies. Jones leveled a critique that set the black social condition in the United States alongside the promises of religious, cultural, and social liberation which the Lord God Adonai made to an enslaved people in the book of Exodus. This work was (and remains) provocative because it insists that believers question the relation of God to the "maldistributed, transgenerational, negative," and genocidal character of black social suffering (Jones 1973: 3–22). Jones's essay prodded Cleage, Cone, and Roberts to put forward a doctrine of a God who would side with despised black humanity, who would work with, in, and through women and men as they threw their shoulders against evil and injustice to create thoroughgoing and human change.

South Africa

Black theology turned political in South Africa on March 21, 1960 with the Sharpeville massacre, when police opened fire at a peaceful demonstration, killing 67 blacks and wounding 186 others. In response, the African National Congress (ANC), for nearly five decades the primary and moderate voice of black resistance to apartheid, and the relatively new and militant Pan Africanist Congress (PAC), along with white South African liberals, initiated public demonstrations that gained worldwide attention. Subsequently, the government banned both the ANC and the PAC, arrested black and white anti-apartheid leaders who had not gone underground or fled the country, and in 1965 tried and imprisoned Nelson Mandela. In this situation of overweening repression, the legendary resistance of black South African peoples was paralyzed; but during the early 1970s the black consciousness movement, under the leadership of Steve Biko, animated a new generation. Biko's analysis laid bare the hypocrisy of white liberal attempts to control and mediate black liberation and denounced white usurpation of land along with the policy of bantustanization or the banishment of blacks to the most unproductive areas.

Manas Buthelezi (1975, 1976), Allan A. Boesak (1976, 1981), Simon Maimela (1981), and Frank Chikane formed a theological front line to grapple with the spurious *saeculum* spawned in the South African church–state nexus. Buthelezi and Boesak focused their reflections around apartheid's violation of agapic or neighbor love, and Maimela argued that apartheid constituted a form of social sin. Black political theology in South Africa called for the restoration and redistribution of political and economic power as a concrete expression of love and justice. As general secretary of the South African Council of Churches, Chikane facilitated black and white Christians in the preparation of the *Kairos Document* (1985), which was written during the period when the apartheid regime had imposed a state of emergency and black townships were under military occupation. In expounding Rom. 13: 1–7 in this context, the document uncovered three conflicting operative theologies: (1) a "state theology" mirrored in the white Dutch Reformed Church's support of the apartheid regime; (2) a "church theology" typified in the option of many Christians for cheap peace – reconciliation without justice, restitution, or social change; and (3) a "prophetic theology" grounded in Christian social praxis for justice and social and personal transformation. Chikane also served as the first general secretary of the Institute for Contextual Theology (ITC), which provided creative intellectual space in which theologians could develop new proposals and conduct dialogues with union activists, social scientists, and educators. Black political theology in South Africa derived its authority from the suffering and anguish of ordinary women and men; took its courage from the exuberant defiance of youth *toyi-toying* – stamping their feet and chanting in unison – in front of police batons and whips; and drew its hope from the crucified Jesus.

The Caribbean and Britain

The Caribbean is the convenient name for the 40 island nations, including two mainland states, stretching in an arc of nearly 4,000 kilometers from Cuba in the northwest Caribbean Sea to Trinidad and Tobago off the Venezuelan coast. With the exceptions of Haiti, Cuba, and Grenada, the region tends to be reduced by most Europeans and North Americans to an exotic tourist site; the history of brutal force which its natural beauty conceals is ignored. Diverse in language, race, culture, religion, and political organization, these island nations have endured intense colonial rule – political subjugation, expropriation of human labor and natural resources, regulation of cultural and educational formation, replication and imitation of graded social and pigmented hierarchies. Myths and symbols of white superiority and black inferiority reinforced this *imperium* in church and society well into the late twentieth century.

The November 1971 meeting of the Caribbean Ecumenical Consultation for Development was a first effort to break with the prevailing Eurocentric missiology. The essays in *Troubling of the Waters* (Hamid 1973) represent an effort to theologize from this new standpoint. Under the rubric of Caribbean theology, Noel Erskine (1998) and Kortright Davis (1982, 1983, 1990) have advanced the complex question of identity in the region, while Lewin Williams (1994) pressed the question in geopolitical terms. These theologians owe a debt to the pioneering work of Leonard E. Barrett, whose *Soul-Force* (1974) argued the persistent and pervasive influence of African religio-cultural heritages in the Caribbean diaspora. But, to date, the most trenchant black political theology in the Caribbean has come from Rastafarian musician Bob Marley.

African-descended people have lived in Britain for centuries, but the 500 passengers on the MV *Empire Windrush*'s 1948 voyage from the Caribbean to Tilbury formed the vanguard of a widespread migration from Asia, Africa, and the Caribbean which has been dubbed "recolonization" (Phillips, 1998). The *Windrush* passengers were seeking educational and economic opportunities; however, post-World War Two Britain did not prove immediately hospitable to His Majesty's 'other children,' and bitter conflicts over housing climaxed in the Notting Hill race riot of 1958 (Gilroy 1991). By the 1970s, Caribbean people were an acknowledged part of the British population and began to redefine British identity and develop black British culture. In this endeavor, Jamaican reggae, Rastafarianism, the British black power movement, and African liberation themes fused in black British dread culture which was hospitable to the migrations of black and womanist theologies in the late 1980s. The best-known proponents of black theology in Britain are Robert Beckford, who seeks to formulate a political–cultural theology that is not disengaged from his pentecostal faith (1999), and Joe Aldred, whose work concentrates on pastoral questions.

Contemporary Terrain

Occupied with the forms and effects of white racist supremacy, the first wave of black political theologies was criticized sharply for failing to attend to the triple oppression of black women and to provide an exacting analysis of capitalism. Although attention to antiblack racism remains necessary, its limitations have been conceded. A second wave of black theologians, philosophers, and cultural critics have problematized race analysis through critical race theory and introduced new categories for understanding gender, class, and sexual orientation. New theoretical interpretations of colonialism's global legacy have generated categories such as hybridity and positionality, and destabilized meanings of community, nation, and difference. To discern new responsibilities for black political theology around the globe, we begin by mapping four rather large areas – the black political subject; the black body, sex, sexuality, and sexual orientation; biblical hermeneutics; and Christology – which shape the contemporary terrain.

The black political subject

The second wave of black political theologians and philosophers press this topic in differing ways. In the United States, the continuing work of James Cone (1999) as well as that of Emmanuel Chukwudi Eze (2001), Lewis Ricardo Gordon (1997, 2000), and bell hooks (1992, 1994) illustrates a critical grasp of Victor Anderson's insistence that "ontological blackness" stifles black *human* flourishing (Anderson 1995: 14). At the same time, these scholars remain adamant that conditions basic to that flourishing constitute a formal element in the concrete realization of black freedom. However, for centuries, the most crucial a priori, that is, the very humanity of black or African or African-descended persons, was contested. Thus, to confuse the protest of black or African or African-descended persons against denials of their humanity – dehumanization – as Enlightenment inspired, liberal self-assertion is to miss the radical and dangerous nature of that protest. For black women and men, living and *being* are risky affairs. To put it bluntly, *being black* is a matter of life and death. Thus, analysis of racism remains characteristic of black political theology even as race stands as a contested category.

South African theologians frame this issue in relation to the *postapartheid* context. Willa Boesak in *God's Wrathful Children* (1995) explores the anger and rage which suffuse black life. He distinguishes the creative and healing potential of righteous anger from hate-filled revenge. Boesak summons all Christian churches to re-evaluate their ownership of land that had been expropriated from the indigenous people during the colonial era. In particular, he calls upon Afrikaner churches to shoulder responsibility to help whites overcome irrational fears of blacks. He exhorts whites not merely to confess guilt but to participate in a process of restorative justice, and urges blacks to examine the tendency to indict all whites. Written prior to the establishment of the Truth and Reconciliation Commission (TRC) headed by former Anglican archbishop Desmond Tutu, *God's Wrathful Children* intimates misgivings about the wide latitude the Commission allowed. Boesak writes: "Many whites seem to expect black people not to succumb to bitterness, anger, or aggression no matter how much they are exploited or traumatized. However, a kind of unnatural 'Christian' patience and reasonableness *vis-à-vis* this history of misery is not Christian at all, but a distorted ethos of submissiveness forced upon oppressed people" (1995: 242).

Julian Kunnie interrogates the current South African situation from the perspective of poor rural peasant and working-class blacks who lack adequate food, health care, shelter, education, and employment. He asks the most blunt and uncompromising question, *Is Apartheid Really Dead?* Wielding razor-sharp hermeneutics of suspicion, Kunnie detects a growing collusion between "capitalism and colonialism" and signals this as an attempt to recreate "a European ruling-class culture, at the cost of humiliating black people and forcing us to serve this oppressive culture" (Kunnie 2000: 252). He is nearly scornful of the TRC and contends that it "does not embody justice and subscribes to a convoluted and perverse sense of justice and truth" (pp. 197–8). Kunnie appeals to South Africans to reject capitalistic notions of progress and to embrace "a qualitatively and radically different value system, one that is spiritually and culturally indigenous in its essence, in that it is pro-worker, anti-individualistic and collectively defined, socialistic in its core, and embracing of female leadership and direction" (p. 194).

Given high global rates of black incarceration, the black political subject is an *incarcerated subject* certainly. Robert Beckford is one of a handful of black theologians to address this issue in any detail and does so as part of an interrogation of the rage that boils up in black people due to living under intense, varied, and complex systems of racialized oppression. Beckford scrutinizes the Bible for a *God of the Rahtid*, a "God who [will side with and make] sense of black rage in response to racialised oppression in Britain," yet who will be compatible with the teachings of Jesus (Beckford 2001: 40). Employing the term *rahtid*, a Jamaican derivative of the biblical word "wrath," Beckford aims to retrieve the notion of redemptive vengeance. Because "the least" have an indisputable claim on black political/liberation theology, Beckford grounds his theologizing in concrete praxis. Taking seriously Jesus' appeal to the ancient Jubilee tradition of "setting captives free," he conducts day-long weekly seminars at Birmingham prison. While the notion of prison as a "mission field" is not new, Beckford exploits its potential to serve as a site for radical self-transformation, as it did for King and Malcolm X (p. 134). The men incarcerated at Birmingham may have been caught in structures that "subjugate and sedate black people" into accepting criminal behavior as the only means to escape oppression, but Beckford observes that they have made bad choices and many are hardened criminals. Still, he seeks to "redeem the hustler," for restitution comes through time in prison and "substantive 'heart' [and life] change" (pp. 145, 136). Using film as a common text, Beckford and the prisoners talk to one another about economics, politics, power, and difference; this opens a path for deeper self-examination through which the men reflect upon their situations, confront and express rage, and grasp the meaning of restitution through cultivating practices that sustain meaningful transformation of life (pp. 133–6, 150).

Caribbean theological discourse about the black subject has been fairly muted, perhaps because of the region's racial, cultural, and ethnic diversity and the homogenizing tendency in black discourse to conflate color, ethnicity, and nationality so that the labels "African" or "Jamaican" immediately evoke the image of a dark-skinned person (Chisolm 1997: 75–6). Arguably, the most important work on the black subject in the Caribbean has come not from theology, but from philosophy. In *Caliban's Reason* (2000), Antiguan Paget Henry foregrounds "the need to rethink the problem of the self" (Henry 2000: 274). He argues that Caribbean philosophy and theology must disengage from the discourse of European philosophical anthropologies and invent something new. Henry's project directs Caribbean theologians to appropriate the discursive heritage that emerges from the historic and protracted struggle of Caribbean people against slavery, colonialism, and racism in order, first, to contribute to the construction of a truly humane political and economic order; second, to critique "othering" practices such as intraracial color discrimination and ethnic polarization; and third, to engage the problem of humanity, indeed, to sublate and "go beyond the recoveries of Husserl and Habermas" (p. 281).

The black body, sex, sexuality, and sexual orientation

The black political subject is an *embodied subject*. Since the days of the transatlantic slave trade, the bodies of African and African-descended women and men have been sites of political, economic, and sexual desire. European and European American representative esthetics further scaled these black bodies as primitive, lascivious, repugnant. This evaluation was at once religious and moral. It reflected white Western Christianity's ambivalence toward the body, sex, and sexuality. Yet Stuart Hall reminds us of the agency and creativity of the black political subject in using the body as a "canvas" on which to counter degrading definition and representation, to express oppositional aesthetics, and to mediate resistance and elegance (Hall 1992: 27).

Womanist theology in the United States presents one way of probing the experience of black embodiment and of contesting the biased ways in which African American women have been and continue to be perceived in African American religious, cultural, and interpersonal contexts (Cannon 1995; Williams 1993; Gilkes 2001). As a critical discursive strategy, womanist analysis proposes an esthetics capable and worthy of reclaiming and caring for black women's (and men's) minds, hearts, bodies, sex, and sexuality (hooks 1992; Townes 1998). Kelly Brown Douglas critiques not only the racism that has led to the "domination and demonization" of black bodies, but black theology's and the black church's avoidance of constructive discourse about sex and sexuality. Douglas also questions the neglect of HIV/AIDS which has placed black bodies at grave risk on a global scale (Douglas 1999: 22, 87–108, 139–41). Without dismissing the gravity of this neglect and the responsibility of theology and church, James Evans connects it to the fear and suspicion generated by the syphilis experiments conducted on black male prisoners in Tuskegee, Alabama, from 1932 to 1972. The Tuskegee experiment "confirmed the historical assumption that black bodies could be sacrificed for the health of others" (Evans 1997: 58).

Caribbean theology, like other black political theologies, has appropriated from Latin American theologies of liberation the methodological assumption of the hermeneutical privilege of the poor and oppressed. Theresa Lowe-Ching, a Jamaican of Chinese ancestry, utilizes this assumption to point out the absence of references to the experience of women in Caribbean theology and the dearth of women theologians in the region. Lowe-Ching and Cuban theologian Ofelia Ortega maintain that feminist analysis cannot be discredited as a foreign import (1999). Lowe-Ching declares that "values emphasized in the feminist perspective, i.e., integrity, inclusion, collaboration and mutuality" cannot be dismissed as "antidotes to crisis-causing problems," but ought to participate fully in "fashioning a total way of regarding and approaching the Caribbean reality" (Lowe-Ching 1995: 30).

Biblical hermeneutics

The Bible is intimately connected to the dispossession and oppression of African-descended people. Consider the following anonymous orally transmitted story:

> When the white man came to Africa he had the Bible and the Africans had the land. The white man asked the Africans to bow their heads and said, "Let us pray." After the prayer, the white man had the land and the Africans had the Bible.

For black political theologians in sub-Saharan Africa, this story captures their peoples' experience of colonial Christianity – the poignant mingling of the "good news" with social oppression and cultural imperialism. Itumeleng Mosala and Musa Dube are two scholars on the continent whose work puts them in the forefront of *postcolonial biblical interpretation*.

In his reading of the story of the "white man, the Bible, and black peoples' land," Mosala focuses on land. Writing from within the South African situation of white expropriation of land and black dispossession, he could not do otherwise. Like Kunnie, Mosala's use of Marxian categories is subordinated to the contours of black experience; so, while emphasizing the material dimension of human liberation, Mosala never does so at the expense of its cultural, moral, or spiritual dimensions. Further, by offering a materialist reading of the Book of Micah, he demonstrates that without critical hermeneutics (that is, without forms of interpretation that question the assumptions behind biblical statements and events) "dominant, traditional theology has found the Bible in general politically and ideologically comfortable, notwithstanding the . . . evidence of a morally distorted material situation" (Mosala 1989: 121–2). The demand for land restoration and redistribution always formed an integral part of the anti-apartheid agenda; but Mosala's treatment of the role of the Bible in black land dispossession makes an important contribution to black political theology and biblical hermeneutics around the globe.

Dube parses the story of the "white man, the Bible, and black peoples' land," culling out issues basic to the matrix of imperialism – land, race, power, gender, wealth, struggle, history (Dube 2000). Using literary–rhetorical method, Dube interrogates the intimate relation between empire-building and patriarchy through an intertextual reading of the Bible along with other ancient and modern imperializing texts. In this way, she uncovers imperialism's manipulation of God, gold, and glory in the justification of seizure and conquest (p. 57). Dube poses a new "decolonising feminist biblical practice" that she calls Rahab's reading prism. This exegetical strategy "resist[s] both patriarchal and imperial oppression in order to cultivate a space of liberating interdependence between nations, genders, races, ethnicities, the environment, and development" (p. 111). Rahab's reading prism, "a postcolonial feminist eye," relies on multiple "angles of seeing, reading, and hearing literary texts" and calls for discursive and practical resistance to "imperial and patriarchal oppressive structures and ideologies" (p. 123).

Biblical hermeneutics in the Caribbean has entailed new attention to the reader of the biblical text. Both Ofelia Ortega and Nathaniel Murrell, who was one of the original members of the Society for Biblical Literature's four-year Consultation on the Bible in Caribbean Culture (1994–7), emphasize the reader. Working from a feminist perspective, Ortega underlines the dynamic, liberating character of divine revelation and states that patriarchal texts in the Bible are circumstantial rather than normative because they violate the spirit of the Gospel. She argues that divine revelation manifests itself in the recreation of the text as a result of the liberating encounter between the bodies of the text and the body of the reader (Ortega 1999: 45).

Murrell correlates "improving the quality of life . . . especially for the oppressed, the marginalised, and the disenfranchised" with a "viable and effective" approach to reading the Bible in the Caribbean (Murrell 2000: 21). He singles out four among several such hermeneutical models that Caribbean theologians have proposed: the Chaguaramas project, the Jesus model, the land acquisition model, and Rastafarai's messianic hope (p. 21). For reasons of space, I consider here only the first. The Chaguaramas project takes its name from the site of the 1971 Ecumenical Conference of the Caribbean Council of Churches in Chaguaramas, Trinidad, West Indies. This approach appeals to the church to break with its custodial role in colonial hermeneutics and to repudiate "the dominant political and cultural 'narratives' that controlled and manipulated" the Bible in Caribbean life (p. 21). But, rather than "discard the Bible with the Eurocentric 'colonial bath water'", Chaguaramas hermeneutics calls political and biblical theologians to "hear . . . the Spirit of prophecy" in the social and religious criticism in the region and to appreciate the familiarity with which ordinary Caribbean women and men meet and speak with "the God of the Bible" (p. 22).

Christology

What kind of Christological reflection is demanded of black political theologies? What can it mean to tell poor and despised, unemployed, diseased, imprisoned black women and men that God in Jesus is also alienated, a stranger, a despised "other"? These are questions for Christological meditation that foreground the black political situation.

Robert Beckford offers a collection of pithy essays, *Jesus is Dread* (1998), which probes several symbols and icons functioning within the black pentecostal church and black expressive cultures in Britain. In articulating a black Christology, Beckford takes as a starting point the black cultural matrix marked by the impress of history, syncretism, hybridity, and differences in class, sexuality, gender, age, ethnicity, economics, and political consciousness (Beckford 1998: 138, 140; 1999: 53). 'Black-talk' derives from, produces, and reinforces this matrix, which has political and ontological consequences. Thus, to call Jesus "dread" is to relocate his story and meaning in a black British context and reconsider what he means for oppressed black Britons in their resistance to white supremacy and their work toward a political structure that could transform their neocolonial situation. The "dread" Christ reigns over and participates in the lives and struggles of black folk (Beckford 1998: 146–7). At the same time, Beckford recognizes the limitations of the notion of "dread": its reified character as well as its masculinist and patriarchal overlay. Nonetheless, he affirms the "dread" Christ as the norm by which to do black theology in the black church in pursuit of freedom in Britain.

In the mid-1980s, Kortright Davis delineated the meaning of Jesus Christ as a "paradigm of liberation for black humanity" on personal, religious, historical, and social levels (Davis 1985: 63). A few years later, Winston Persaud, a Guyanese theologian of Indian ancestry, tackled this issue by working out a theology of the cross in dialogue with Karl Marx's anthropology (Persaud 1991). While Persaud rejects Marx's materialist world view as reductive, he nevertheless confirms the Caribbean region's need for new social and material structures. He argues that structural change must be grounded in an "inner spiritual transformation" that finds its fulfillment in obedience to the paradoxical law of the cross of Christ (p. 262). But Persaud would not have us misunderstand praxis or the "powerlessness" of God: to divorce the proclamation of faith and hope in God from genuine loving action, whether a simple deed of kindness or a radical act that seeks to renovate dehumanizing structures, distorts the Gospel (p. 265).

New Responsibilities for Black Political Theologies

Like all theological formulations, black political theologies remain provisional, tentative, halting, imprecise. In the United States, black political theology must contest the deteriorating political and economic situation – in particular, government encroachment on human and civil rights under the guise of national security. In South Africa, black political theology needs to address directly the brutal economic legacy of apartheid and the ravages of HIV/AIDS. In the Caribbean, black political theology ought to speak more clearly to the gang violence that has commandeered the political process. Black political theology in Britain would do well to avoid the trap of binary analysis and add complexity to its critique by engaging the experience and insights of other racial/ethnic and religious communities. Let me conclude with suggestions of five continuing responsibilities of black political theologies on the global scene.

First, black political theologies need to make a rigorous analysis of imperialism, neocolonialism, capitalism, and the practices of democracy. At the heart of this inquiry are the lives, griefs, joys, and hopes of black urban working-class and rural peasant children, women, and men. The 2000 elections in the United States and the political situations in Zimbabwe and Nigeria insinuate the superfluity of the black political subject as self-governing. The persistent absence of black theological critiques in these nations can only mock the rhetoric of black theology as public theology and further distort the church's ministerial praxis.

Second, the geopolitical realignments that have occurred in the wake of September 11 and the war against Iraq press urgent issues on the agenda of black political theologies wherever they are situated. These include (a) continuing clarification of the interaction and mutual conditioning of racism, sexism, heterosexism, economic exploitation, and imperialism on a global scale; (b) careful distinctions between antisemitism, which can never be permitted, and raw ethnocentrism, which can never be indulged; (c) serious dialogue with Judaism and Islam; (d) evaluation of the Palestinian situation; (e) attention to global infringements of human and civil rights; and (f) critical engagement with cultural and religious diversity.

Nearly a decade ago, Lewin Williams issued a wake-up call to Caribbean theologians. The US invasions of Grenada and Panama in the 1980s, he wrote, offered "proof of the willingness of a major power to use military force to destroy and replace unpopular political structures" (Williams 1994: 136). In the aftermath of the war in Iraq, his remarks seem almost prescient; and, in this new situation, black political theologies, wherever their centers, must assume responsibility to defend human life and dignity, creativity, and spirit.

Third, more than thirty years ago, James Cone declared that blackness was not so much a matter of skin color as of placing one's heart, soul, mind, and body with the dispossessed. Black political theologies must encourage, demand, and welcome collaboration. As Gayraud Wilmore once observed, black theology is far too important to be left only to black theologians. The work of white South African theologian Denise Ackermann on HIV/AIDS (2000) and that of white European American Mark Lewis Taylor on the prison industrial complex (2001) are two serious theological contributions to the well-being of African-descended peoples, indeed that of all humanity. Here, black theologians in the United States can learn a good deal from our colleagues in the Caribbean and South Africa, who are making creative intellectual and existential space to understand racial/cultural/ethnic others and to grapple with common problems across racial/cultural/ethnic lines.

Fourth, from the slave trade to the near-genocidal removal of the Taino and Carib peoples, from the white planter's rape of black women to the KKK's lynching and castration of black men, from the murder of Steve Biko to the murder of Stephen Lawrence, violence has marked global black human living decisively. But African and African-descended peoples are not always the victims of institutionalized or random hate-crime violence; black peoples also perpetrate violence against one another and others. This situation suffers from the absence of full-throated black political theological critique. In the Caribbean, black political theology ought to no longer tolerate the brutal gang violence that wastes the blood and potential of black youth. In the United States, black political theology needs to condemn forthrightly the drugs and guns so glorified by hip-hop artists who imitate thug life. Womanist Cheryl Kirk-Duggan (2001) has made a good start on this analysis, but much more is needed. In South Africa, sexual assaults against women, and young and infant girls, demand denunciation. In Britain, black political theology must contest the negative stereotyping of racial/ethnic/religious groups that has re-emerged in Europe, collaborate in reconstructing the meaning of "Britishness" through affirmation of diversity, and challenge the black middle class to a critical self-examination of its tendency toward assimilation and isolation.

Fifth, the meaning of the Gospel is never exhausted and critical interpretation of the cross has never been more necessary. Black political theologies need to agitate for what Beckford has called a "subversive piety" (Beckford 1998: 171). Subversive piety is a retrieval of the revolutionary genius and spirit of the African ancestors, their radical hope in the God of freedom, their commitment to struggle. Subversive piety refuses any attempt at pseudo-holiness or artificial spirituality. It is committed to the Gospel's message (the abiding presence of Christ in the Spirit) and to authentic practices and disciplines (prayer, fasting, hospitality, solidarity); it embraces and incarnates concretely the prophetic Jubilee traditions taught by Jesus. Yet subversive piety is neither strategically nor theologically innocent: it risks attracting criticism because it does not confuse human freedom and praxis with the grace and power of God of freedom who shall absolutely gift our hope with a reign of peace, healing, and joy. Only such piety can sustain self-less long-term participation in the struggle to bring about justice in church and society for ourselves, for our humanity, for all God's creation.

Acknowledgment

My thanks to Anna Kasafi Perkins, my graduate assistant, whose critical eye and thoughtful ear made an invaluable contribution to this essay.

References and Further Reading

Ackermann, D. (2000). "Lamenting Tragedy from 'the Other Side.'" In J. R. Cochrane and B. Klein (eds.), *Sameness and Difference: Problems and Potentials in South African Civil Society, South African Philosophical Studies*, I, 213–241 (Cultural Heritage and Contemporary Series, vol. VI). Washington DC: Council for Research in Values and Philosophy.

Anderson, Victor (1995). *Beyond Ontological Blackness: An Essay on African American Religious and Cultural Criticism*. New York: Continuum.

Beckford, R. (1998). *Jesus is Dread: Black Theology and Black Culture in Britain*. London: Darton, Longman & Todd.

——(1999). "Black Pentecostals and Black Politics." In A. Anderson and W. Hollenweger (eds.), *Pentecostals after a Century: Global Perspectives on a Movement in Transition*, 48–59. Sheffield: Sheffield Academic Press.

——(2001). *God of the Rahtid: Redeeming Rage*. London: Darton, Longman & Todd.

Biko, Steve (1998). *I Write What I Like*, ed. Aelred Stubbs. New York: Harper & Row (First publ. 1978).

Boesak, A. (1976). "Coming In Out of the Wilderness." In S. Torres and V. Fabella (eds.), *The Emergent Gospel*, 76–95. Maryknoll, NY: Orbis.

——(1981). *Farewell to Innocence*. Maryknoll, NY: Orbis.

Boesak, W. (1995). *God's Wrathful Children: Political Oppression and Christian Ethics*. Grand Rapids, Mich.: Eerdmans.

Bosch, D. J. (1991). *Transforming Mission: Paradigm Shifts in Theology of Mission*. Maryknoll, NY: Orbis.

Buthelezi, M. (1975). "Daring to Live for Christ: By Being Human and Suffering for Others." *Journal of Theology for Southern Africa* 11 (June), 7–10.

——(1976). "Toward Indigenous Theology in South Africa." In S. Torres and V. Fabella (eds.), *The Emergent Gospel*, 56–75. Maryknoll, NY: Orbis.

Cannon, K. (1995). Katie's Canon: Womanism and the Soul of the Black Community. New York: Continuum.

Chisholm, C. A. (1997). *A Matter of Principle*. Spanish Town: Autos.

Cleage, A. (1968). *The Black Messiah*. New York: Sheed & Ward.

Cone, J. (1970). *A Black Theology of Liberation*. Philadelphia: Lippincott.

——(1975). *God of the Oppressed*. New York: Seabury.

——(1997). *Black Theology and Black Power*. Maryknoll, NY: Orbis. (First publ. 1969.)

——(1999). "Looking Back, Going Forward: Black Theology as Public Theology." In D. Hopkins (ed.) *Black Faith and Public Talk: Essays in Honor of James H. Cone's Black Theology and Black Power*, 246–59. Maryknoll, NY: Orbis.

Davis, K. (1982). *Mission for Caribbean Change: Caribbean Development as Theological Enterprise*. Frankfurt am Main and Berne: Peter Lang.

——(1983). *Cross and Crown*. Barbados: Cedar.

——(1985). "Jesus Christ and Black Liberation: Toward a Paradigm of Transcendence." *Journal of Religious Thought* 42: 1, 51–67.

——(1990). *Emancipation Still Comin': Explorations in Caribbean Emancipatory Theology*. Maryknoll, NY: Orbis Books.

Douglas, K. B. (1999). *Sexuality and the Black Church: A Womanist Perspective*. Maryknoll, NY: Orbis.

Dube, M. (2000). *Postcolonial Feminist Interpretation of the Bible*. St. Louis: Chalice.

Erskine, N. (1998). *Decolonizing Theology: A Caribbean Perspective*. Maryknoll, NY: Orbis. (First publ. 1981.)

Evans, J. H. (1997). *We Shall All Be Changed: Social Problems and Theological Renewal*. Minneapolis, Minn.: Fortress.

Eze, E. C. (2001). *Achieving Our Humanity: The Idea of the Postracial Future*. New York: Routledge.

Gilkes, Townsend C. (2001). *"If It Wasn't for the Women . . ." Black Women's Experience and Womanist Culture in Church and Community*. Maryknoll, NY: Orbis.

Gilroy, P. (1991). *"There Ain't No Black in the Union Jack:" The Cultural Politics of Race and Nation*. Chicago: University of Chicago Press. (First publ. 1987.)

Gordon, L. R. (1997). *Her Majesty's Other Children: Sketches of Racism from a Neocolonial Age*. Lanham, Md.: Rowan & Littlefield.

——(2000). *Existentia Africana: Understanding Africana Existential Thought*. New York: Routledge.

Gregory, H., ed. (1995). *Caribbean Theology: Preparing for the Challenges Ahead*. Kingston: Canoe 1995.

Habermas, J. (1971). *Knowledge and Human Interests*. Boston: Beacon.

——(1983). *The Theory of Communicative Action: Reason and the Rationalization of Society*. Boston: Beacon.

Hall, S. (1992). "What is the 'Black' in Black Popular Culture?" In G. Dent (ed.), *Black Popular Culture*, 2–29. Seattle: Bay.

Hamid, I., ed. (1973). *Troubling of the Waters*. San Fernando, Trinidad: Rahaman Printery.

Henry, P. (2000). *Caliban's Reason: Introducing Afro-Caribbean Philosophy*. New York: Routledge.

hooks, b. (1992). *Black Looks: Race and Representation*. Boston: South End.

——(1994). *Outlaw Culture: Resisting Representation*. New York: Routledge.

——(1995). *Killing Rage: Ending Racism*. New York: Henry Holt.

Hopkins, D. (1989). *Black Theology USA and South Africa: Politics, Culture, and Liberation*. Maryknoll, NY: Orbis.

Jones, W. R. (1998). *Is God a White Racist? A Preamble to Black Theology*. Boston: Beacon. (First publ. 1973).

Kirk-Duggan, C. (2001). *Misbegotten Anguish: A Theology of Ethics and Violence*. St. Louis, Mo.: Chalice.

Kunnie, J. (2000). *Is Apartheid Really Dead? Pan-Africanist Working-Class Cultural Critical Perspectives*. Oxford: Westview.

Lowe-Ching, T. (1995). "Method in Caribbean Theology." In H. Gregory (ed), *Caribbean Theology: Preparing for the Challenges Ahead*. Kingston: Canoe.

Maimela, S. (1981). "Man in 'White' Theology." *Journal of Theology for Southern Africa* 36 (September), 64–78.

Middleton, D. J. N. (2000). "Riddim Wise and Scripture Smart: Interview and Interpretation with Ras Benjamin Zephaniah." In H. Gossai and N. S. Murrell (eds.), *Religion, Culture, and Tradition in the Caribbean*, 257–70. New York: St. Martin's.

Mosala, I. (1989). *Biblical Hermeneutics and Black Theology in South Africa*. Grand Rapids, Mich.: Eerdmans.

Murrell, N. S. (2000). "Dangerous Memories, Underdevelopment, and the Bible in Colonial Caribbean Experience." In H. Gossai and N. S. Murrell (eds.), *Religion, Culture, and Tradition in the Caribbean*, 9–35. New York: St. Martin's.

Ortega, O. (1999). "God Has Called Us: Caribbean Women Searching for a Better Future." *Caribbean Journal of Religious Studies* 20: 2, 38–46.

Persaud, W. (1991). *The Theology of the Cross and Marx's Anthropology*. New York: Peter Lang.

Phillips, M. (1998). "Windrush – the Passengers." http://www.bbc.co.uk/history, accessed May 11, 2003.

Roberts, J. D. (1971). *Liberation and Reconciliation: A Black Theology*. Philadelphia: Westminster.

——(1974). *A Black Political Theology*. Philadelphia: Westminster.

Robinson, R. (2000). *The Debt: What America Owes to Blacks*. New York: Penguin.

Taylor, M. L. (2001). *The Executed God: The Way of the Cross in Lockdown America*. Minneapolis: Fortress.

Townes, E. (1998). *Breaking the Fine Rain of Death: African American Health Issues and a Womanist Ethic of Care*. New York: Continuum.

Van Dijk, F. J. (1998). "Chanting Down Babylon Outernational: The Rise of Rastafari in Europe, the Caribbean, and the Pacific." In N. Murrell et al. (eds.), *Chanting Down Babylon: The Rastafarian Reader*, 178–198. Philadelphia: Temple University Press.

Williams, D. S. (1993). *Sisters in the Wilderness: The Challenge of Womanist God-Talk*. Maryknoll, NY: Orbis.

Williams, L. (1994). *Caribbean Theology*. New York: Peter Lang.

CHAPTER 20
Gustavo Gutiérrez

Roberto S. Goizueta

A Theology of Liberation: From Lima to Medellín

Few contemporary theologians have influenced the whole range of theological disciplines as has the Peruvian priest Gustavo Gutiérrez, who is often referred to as the "father" of liberation theology. In his classic work *A Theology of Liberation*, Gutiérrez set forth "not so much a new theme for reflection as a *new way* to do theology" (Gutiérrez 1973: 15). Thus, what is most distinctive about liberation theology – and what has come to influence every area of theological and religious studies, from constructive theology to biblical studies – is the theological method which Gutiérrez articulated systematically in that groundbreaking volume. Gutiérrez' theological method rests upon two foundational theses: (1) God loves all persons equally and gratuitously; (2) God loves the poor preferentially.

These insights derived not only from Gutiérrez' reflection upon the scriptures and Christian tradition but also from his own lived experience, which continues to inform his writing to this day. As a child growing up in Peru, he knew the pain of both poverty and physical illness, having been bedridden by osteomyelitis during his teenage years. It was during these years that he began to read extensively, developing a special interest in the relationship between his Christian faith and social justice. It is thus helpful to bear in mind the influence that these early, deeply personal experiences with human suffering has had in the development of Gutiérrez' unusual ability to empathize with and truly "know" the character of human suffering, from the inside.

Initially, these early experiences with illness generated an interest in medicine and medical studies, which Gutiérrez hoped to pursue further by enrolling at the University of San Marcos in Lima, with the intention of eventually entering the field of psychiatry. Only three years into his studies, however, he decided to leave the university in order to enter seminary studies for the Archdiocese of Lima. He was soon sent to Europe for further studies, receiving a master's degree in philosophy and psychology from the Catholic University of Louvain in Belgium (1955) and a master's degree in theology from the Theological Faculty of Lyon in France (1959). Ironically, Gutiérrez did not receive a doctorate in theology until 1985, when Lyon granted him the degree on the basis of his published work and his work's impact on the field of theology.

In 1959 Gutiérrez was ordained and returned from Europe to a teaching position at the Pontifical Catholic University of Peru. The following decade was a formative period for him. The university context made it possible for him to further develop his interest in the thought of such seminal figures as Camus, Marx, and, especially, José Carlos Mariátegui, José María Arguedas, and Cesar Vallejo. As great Peruvian literary figures these last two, particularly, would continue to inspire Gutiérrez' work for many years to come. In his social analysis, Gutiérrez was influenced by Mariátegui's call for the development of a specifically Latin American socialism. Beyond these intellectual influences, however, Gutiérrez found inspiration and intellectual enrichment in his pastoral work as the advisor to the National Union of Catholic Students. The Union was part of the Catholic Action movement. Basing itself in Catholic social teaching, this lay student movement was extremely influential in creating a social consciousness among young Catholic leaders throughout Latin America. As would be the case throughout his life, therefore, Gutiérrez' theology was intimately bound to his ministry as a priest.

The early 1960s were marked by two events that would also prove crucial for the Peruvian theologian's personal and intellectual development: the Second Vatican Council and the rise of popular social movements throughout Latin America. Together, these events helped forge the historical context which would give rise to liberation theology. At the time, the outlines of a "theology of liberation" were already being adumbrated in a continent-wide conversation involving a number of Latin American theologians, most trained in Europe but recently returned to accompany their people in the growing movements for social justice. In a series of meetings, these intellectuals sought explicitly to relate their Christian faith, especially as this had been articulated at Vatican II, to the struggle for justice in Latin America. In his 1968 *La pastoral en la Iglesia en América Latina*, Gutiérrez addressed this issue directly. In July of that same year, during a speech to fellow priests at the National Office of Social Research in Chimbote, Peru, Gutiérrez called for the development of a "theology of liberation," the first time the term had been used in a public forum.

The changes represented by Vatican II, the Latin American popular movements, and the nascent theology of liberation gained institutional visibility and "official" endorsement at the Second General Conference of the Latin American Bishops, which took place in Medellín, Colombia, in the fall of 1968. Here, the bishops explicitly set for themselves the task of implementing the vision of Vatican II in the specific context of the Latin American church. If the Vatican II had challenged the church to look to the "signs of the times" as the locus of God's self-revelation and, thus, the context in which the church must live out its evangelizing mission, the Latin American bishops would accept the challenge of discerning the signs of the times in Latin America and, on that basis, propose a practical, pastoral agenda for the Latin American church.

As the bishops' official theological consultant, Gutiérrez was intimately involved in the Medellín deliberations. The imprint of his thought and spirit is palpable in the final document issued by the bishops. Though the actual phrase "preferential option for the poor" would not be used by the Latin American bishops until their next general conference, in Puebla, Mexico, 11 years later, the final document of Medellín lays out with unmistakable clarity the necessity of such an option. The church, insisted the bishops, must become not only a church *for* the poor, and not only a church *with* the poor; it must become a church *of* the poor.

A New Way to Do Theology: The Preferential Option for the Poor

The first systematic articulation of a liberation theology, grounded in a preferential option for the poor, was set forth in Gutiérrez' *A Theology of Liberation*, published in 1971 (English translation 1973). Here Gutiérrez argued that all theology should be a "critical reflection on Christian praxis in the light of the Word" (Gutiérrez 1973: 13). Theology must be grounded in the concrete, lived faith of the Christian people – the vast majority of whom are poor, in Latin America and indeed throughout the world. And by definition, as Christian that praxis must be illuminated by the Word of God, which will challenge and transform our historical action. Consequently, the relationship between Christian praxis and theological reflection forms a "hermeneutical circle."

Gutiérrez contends that, when read from the perspective of this Christian praxis, that is, from a solidarity with the struggling poor in Latin America, the scriptures reveal a God whose love is universal and gratuitous, on the one hand, and preferentially in solidarity with the poor, on the other. These twin theses appear to be contradictory. However, when understood within the context of a "critical reflection on Christian praxis in the light of the Word," the two theses will be seen as, in fact, mutually implicit. The universality of God's love *implies* God's preferential love for the poor.

To say that God's love is universal is not to say that it is neutral. Indeed, the universality of God's love precludes an "objective," "neutral" God. If God's love is not an ahistorical abstraction but is made manifest in history, and if, moreover, that history is characterized by persistent social conflict wherein the majority of human beings are systematically exploited and denied their dignity by a powerful minority, a neutral God would be one whose very refusal to "take sides" would, de facto, serve the interests of the powerful minority. If God's love does not actively work to transform the unjust status quo, then God's "neutrality" (disguised as "equal love for all people") can only legitimize the injustice.

At the same time, Gutiérrez has always insisted that the option for the poor is "preferential," not "exclusive." That is, we are called to love the poor first because only by doing so can we truly love *all* people. An authentic love for the oppressor must be one born from the conviction that, in a situation of oppression, both the oppressor and the victim are dehumanized. Gutiérrez, however, is not suggesting that the poor, as individuals, are "better" persons than the powerful. The option for the poor is an option to place ourselves in a particular social location, to view reality from a particular perspective: the perspective of the poor, the outcast, the marginalized. We are called to do so, not because the poor are better or more moral than the powerful, but because the God revealed in the scriptures is a God who chooses to be revealed preferentially among the outcasts of society, a God who chooses the poor to be the bearers of the Good News, a God crucified alongside the crucified victims of history. The preferential option for the poor is, above all, a *theological* option: we must opt for the poor because *God* opts for the poor. The rationale lies not in the poor themselves but in God; not in who the poor are but in who God is.

Consequently, argues Gutiérrez, the poor themselves are called to make a preferential option for the poor. The poor too can be seduced by privilege and power; those without power can come to believe that their liberation will be achieved only when they themselves acquire power and wealth. The poor themselves, then, are called to place themselves on the side of the poor, not to abandon their own communities by "opting" for the values of power, wealth, and violence.

A further question remains, however: just who are "the poor"? What do we mean by the term "poverty"? The Gospels, suggests Gutiérrez, reveal three distinct, though inseparable, notions, or forms of poverty: (1) material poverty, (2) spiritual poverty, and (3) voluntary poverty as protest (Gutiérrez 1973: 287–306). The first understanding of poverty is the most visible: this is economic poverty, the poverty that afflicts the poor to whom Luke's beatitudes are addressed ("Blessed are you poor . . ."; Luke 6: 20–3). The second, spiritual poverty, is what characterizes the "poor in spirit" to whom Matthew's beatitudes are addressed (Matt. 5: 3–12). Gutiérrez understands the poor in spirit as those persons whose lives demonstrate a profound sense of their radical dependence on God. Spiritual poverty is the recognition that our lives, and indeed all creation, is in God's hands; such poverty of spirit thus generates a profound trust and confidence in divine providence.

In his discussion of this second notion of poverty, Gutiérrez warns against a particular *mis*interpretation of "spiritual poverty" that has been propounded by many first world Christians over the years and that has – not surprisingly – served their own material, economic interests. First World exegetes and other Christians in privileged situations have often identified spiritual poverty with psychological or emotional "detachment" from one's material wealth. By thus *separating* the notions of spiritual and material poverty, wealthy Christians have been able to rationalize, or legitimate their wealth: one is allowed to be wealthy as long as one remains emotionally "detached" from one's possessions. What matters, then, is simply one's "attitude" toward one's possessions.

Such a premature "spiritualization" of the biblical texts ignores, however, the intrinsic connection between material and spiritual poverty: it is difficult, if not impossible, to be truly "detached" from one's material wealth as long as one *remains* wealthy in the face of so much poverty. Gutiérrez thus contends that Luke's and Matthew's beatitudes have to be read together; "the poor" cannot be understood apart from "the poor in spirit," and vice versa. A genuine spiritual poverty will necessarily manifest itself in a life of material simplicity. Nevertheless, material poverty in and of itself does not guarantee spiritual poverty; one can be materially poor and yet remain captive to the desire for material security and privilege.

This intrinsic connection between material and spiritual poverty is exemplified, above all, in a third notion of poverty, what Gutiérrez calls "poverty as protest." Here, a person voluntarily becomes poor, divesting him/herself of worldly power and privilege, in order to enter into solidarity with the poor. Out of compassion for the poor, a person thereby accepts the risks and vulnerability of poverty as a protest against the evil of poverty, as a way of witnessing to a radically different way of life. The person who thus becomes one with the poor becomes, like the poor themselves, a mirror that reveals to a society its injustices. And, since most persons and societies do not like to have their worldviews, assumptions, values, and self-image questioned, the person who thus holds up a mirror to society is likely to suffer ostracism and persecution – again, like the poor themselves.

The paradigmatic Christian symbol of this notion of "poverty as protest" is of course the Crucified Christ himself: "Though he was in the form of God, . . . he emptied himself and took the form of a slave" (Phil. 2: 6–7). Material and spiritual poverty are united in the act of divine kenosis: Jesus' perfect obedience to the Father (poverty of spirit) leads him to enter into solidarity with the outcasts of his society (material poverty), thereby incurring the wrath of the political and religious leaders. These then crucify the innocent victim, whose tortured body on the cross reveals to the whole world its own profound sinfulness ("Truly, this was the Son of God!": Matt. 27: 54).

Like his theology as a whole, Gutiérrez' threefold understanding of poverty is rooted in a holistic worldview that refuses to separate the spiritual from the material but, instead, sees these are distinct, though intrinsically interrelated, dimensions of one historical process. That holistic worldview is the linchpin of Gutiérrez' theology, from his method to his theological anthropology. If one cannot understand the preferential option for the poor, the foundation of his method, without appreciating his integral cosmovision, neither can one understand the very notion of "liberation" without such an appreciation.

An Integral Liberation

If the key to Gutiérrez' method is the option for the poor, the content of his theology is centered on the notion of "liberation." (Note, again, that Gutiérrez never claims that the *content* of his "theology of liberation" is dramatically new; on the contrary, the call to liberation has always been at the very heart of the Christian kerygma.) That notion must also be viewed integrally, without separating its various dimensions. According to Gutiérrez, liberation should also be understood as encompassing three distinct though inseparable dimensions: (1) political liberation, (2) psychological, or anthropological liberation, and (3) liberation from sin (Gutiérrez 1973: 21–42). At its first level, liberation involves the transformation of social structures. At a deeper, second level, liberation entails an interior, psychological transformation through which the poor person comes to affirm his/her historical agency. Accustomed to seeing him/herself as merely a passive object of history, acted *upon* by historical forces and serving the interests of the powerful elites, the poor person now becomes an authentic historical agent, capable of exercising his/her rights and responsibilities as an actor, an *authentic subject*. Finally, at the deepest, third level, liberation is identified with salvation itself, that liberation from sin effected through the crucified and risen Christ.

Gutiérrez repeatedly underscores the fact that the three dimensions, while theoretically distinct, are always, in practice, intrinsically connected aspects of one, single liberative process. The third, deepest level remains qualitatively different, however, in that its realization is completely dependent on God's activity; salvation is pure gift. While we can and must work for social and personal transformation, the deepest and fullest realization of these is brought about through God's gratuitous love in the person of Jesus Christ. At the same time, that love is always made concrete in history; so, insofar as we help transform history in accord with God's will, we simultaneously open ourselves to and encounter God's grace in history.

Gutiérrez' understanding of liberation is accompanied by a correspondingly holistic, integral notion of sin. On the one hand, human effort alone can never uproot sin at its deepest level. On the other hand, sin is never merely "spiritual" but always manifests itself concretely in the lives of individual persons and in social structures that facilitate and foster sinful behavior. If sin can be defined as the rupture of communion with other persons and God, that rupture is objectified in and mediated by the entire web of structures, organizations, and institutions within which we live out our relationships with others and with God. Those structures may foster values and behavior that impede communion (for example, by implicitly or explicitly fostering violence, conflict, greed, etc.) or they may foster values and behavior that facilitate communion (for example, by rewarding cooperation, compassion, service, etc.). In other words, the human struggle for communion and against sin always reflects the fact that the person is intrinsically a *social* being who is intrinsically connected to others and to God.

A Spirituality of Liberation

Alongside the demands for action in solidarity with the poor, however, the preferential option for the poor also demands a profound spirituality as an essential aspect of any liberating action. At its core, Gutiérrez' theology of liberation is, in fact, a spirituality. He developed his spirituality more fully and explicitly in the books *We Drink from Our Own Wells* and *On Job*. In the former, Gutiérrez outlined a spirituality grounded in a preferential option for the poor and, therefore, drawing on the rich resources of the lived faith of the poor. Such a spirituality would reject any separation between the life of prayer and sociohistorical action; contemplation and action are two sides of the same coin. If, as we have discussed above, one cannot understand the universality and gratuity of God's love apart from God's preferential love for the poor, neither can one's prayer, or "spiritual life," be understood accurately apart from a social praxis that makes credible in history God's love for all persons.

At the very heart of what Gutiérrez has called the "culture of the poor" one finds the expressly spiritual practices, symbols, and narratives which embody a lived faith: "From gratuitousness also comes the language of symbols. . . . In their religious celebrations, whether at especially important moments or in the circumstances of everyday life, the poor turn to the Lord with the trustfulness and spontaneity of a child who speaks to its father and tells him of its suffering and hopes" (Gutiérrez 1984: 111–12). This fact reveals an important dimension of the preferential option for the poor, one which Gutiérrez himself emphasizes, but one too often missed by critics of liberation theologies: the option for the poor necessarily implies an option for the *lived faith* of the poor, an option for the *spirituality* of the poor. To opt for the poor is necessarily to pray as the poor pray, and to pray to the God to whom the poor pray. If, as Gutiérrez avers, at the center of the worldview of the poor is an unshakeable belief that "God first loved us" and that "everything starts from" that belief, then all human praxis becomes, at bottom, an act of worship, an act of prayer . . . and every act of prayer becomes a sociopolitical act. In the absence of such a practical spirituality, lived in response to God's love for us, any putative option for the poor cannot engender true solidarity or empathy. "It is not possible to do theology in Latin America," writes Gutiérrez, "without taking into account the situation of the most downtrodden of history; this means in turn that at some point the theologian must cry out, as Jesus did, 'My God, my God, why hast thou forsaken me?'" (Gutiérrez 1993: 101).

Sociohistorical praxis, then, must not be understood as merely political action. Contemplation, prayer, and worship are themselves essential aspects of praxis. Indeed, in his later writings Gutiérrez is reluctant to talk about a "relationship" between contemplation and action as if these were two different realities. Rather, contemplation is itself an intrinsic dimension of all truly Christian praxis. When this intrinsic connection between action and contemplation is lived out, the option for the poor will be seen as encompassing not only a political dimension but spiritual and affective dimensions as well. The option for the poor will then be lived out as a *response* to God's gratuitous love, which is the "spiritual" source of that option. Likewise, solidarity with the poor will be seen to encompass not only expressly political action but also all those activities through which communion with each other and God is lived out, for example friendship, celebration, domestic life, liturgy. Indeed, in his later writings Gutiérrez places an ever greater stress on the importance of friendship as central to the struggle for justice; the most fundamental form of solidarity is that friendship with individual, flesh-and-blood human persons without which "the poor" too easily become reduced to a mere abstraction.

This emphasis on the contemplative, affective dimension of praxis and the option for the poor is nowhere more evident in Gutiérrez' writings than in his book *On Job*. The question posed in this extended reflection on the Book of Job is: "How can one speak of a loving God in the midst of innocent suffering?" Job is here a Christ-figure, a prototype and model for the believer committed to doing God's will. Gutiérrez invites us to accompany Job as he struggles with both Satan and God, having his faith challenged at every turn in the face of the calamities that befall him, a good man, and that are thus seemingly so unjust. Can Job continue to believe even when he receives no reward for his faith, indeed, even when he experiences nothing but affliction and humiliation before the God whom he loves? Is a genuinely "disinterested" faith possible? Or, having felt himself abandoned by God, will Job in turn himself abandon the God to whom he had previously been so faithful?

Job's response to these questions, concludes Gutiérrez, emerges only insofar as Job refuses to surrender either his conviction of his own innocence (and, therefore, the injustice of his afflictions) or his faith in God, even when, prefiguring the cries of the crucified Jesus on Golgotha, that very faith compels Job to cry out to a silent God, "My God, my God, why . . . ?" In his "dark night of the soul" Job experiences, first, the utter mystery that is God and, therefore, the foolishness of all human attempts to "make sense" of God's unfathomable love for us; and, second, a solidarity with and compassion for all those other persons who, like Job himself, live daily in the midst of death and affliction. The only (relatively) adequate response to the questions posed at the outset of the story, then, is not to be found in tomes of theology or elegantly spun theodicies, but in *silence*, in the silent praxis of compassion born of the contemplative, worshipful encounter with a God who is mystery. According to Gutiérrez, that mystery is revealed precisely at the point where the prophetic language of justice meets the silence of contemplative worship, at the point where the revolutionary and the mystic become one.

The connection between worship and justice is also central to another of Gutiérrez' key works, *Las Casas: In Search of the Poor of Jesus Christ*. The turning point of this major work of historical and theological scholarship is, again, the conversion that the protagonist undergoes when he experiences in his own life the inseparability of love of God and love of neighbor, that is, the inseparability of contemplation and action as two intrinsically related dimensions of Christian faith. Yet again, we find ourselves confronted here by the same twin themes to which Gutiérrez repeatedly returns throughout the corpus of his writing: the universality and gratuity of God's love (before which we are reduced to silent contemplation), and God's preferential love for the poor (which demands our own solidarity with the poor).

The book *Las Casas* treats, of course, the life and thought of the great Spanish missionary and theologian Bartolomé de Las Casas. This is, in some sense, Gutiérrez' "magnum opus," having occupied him, off and on, over the course of 25 years. Known as the "Defender of the Indians," Las Casas' prophetic criticism of Spanish violence against the indigenous peoples of America was made possible only by his conversion from an *encomendero*, or slaveowner, to one who made his own preferential option for the poor. And his conversion took place precisely at the point where his life of prayer encountered his life in the political realm.

The intrinsic connection between orthodoxy and orthopraxis has never been exemplified as clearly as in Las Casas' conversion, while he was preparing to celebrate the eucharistic liturgy on Pentecost, 1514. Reflecting on the scripture readings for the day, he came upon the following words in the Book of Sirach (34: 18–22):

> Tainted his gifts who offers in sacrifice ill-gotten goods! / Mock presents from the lawless win not God's favor. / The Most High approves not the gifts of the godless. / [Nor for their many sacrifices does he forgive their sin.] / Like the man who slays a son in his father's presence / is he who offers sacrifice from the possessions of the poor. / The bread of charity is life itself for the needy, / he who withholds it is a person of blood. / He slays his neighbor who deprives him of his living; / he sheds blood who denies the laborer his wages. (Gutiérrez 1993: 47)

As he read them, Las Casas saw himself mirrored in and challenged by those words: he was preparing to offer to God bread and wine produced by his own Indian slaves. What was thus ostensibly an act of Christian worship was, in fact, an act of idolatry; he was purporting to worship the God of Jesus Christ while, in reality, worshipping a god of violence and destruction, a god who accepted the fruit of exploited human labor. While condemning the Amerindians for their practice of human sacrifice, he himself – along with the rest of the Spaniards – had been sacrificing human blood, sweat, and tears in the form of bread and wine. As Las Casas insisted repeatedly in the wake of his conversion, that *metanoia* implied not only a different way of living but, in so doing, it also implied belief in and worship of a radically different God from the "god" to whom he had previously been offering the Mass. Conversely, any worship conducted in the absence of a solidarity with the poor can only be idolatry.

As the methodological key to Gutiérrez' theology, the preferential option for the poor becomes not only a privileged criterion of Christian orthopraxis (correct practice), calling us to live our faith; it is, more fundamentally, a privileged criterion of orthodoxy itself (correct worship, or *doxa*), calling us to believe in and worship a God who is revealed on the cross, among the crucified peoples of history. Unless we place ourselves alongside the poor, unless we look at reality through their eyes, we are unable to see, recognize, or worship the God who walks with the poor. Conversely, if we lack such a practical solidarity with the poor, the "god" in whom we believe and whom we worship will necessarily be a false god, an idol of our own making.

At the same time, I think we misread Gutiérrez' understanding of the option for the poor if we interpret it as *reducing* Christian faith to such a practical option. It bears repeating that throughout his writings Gutiérrez insists that the warrants for a preferential option for the poor are, above all, *theocentric*: "the ultimate basis for the privileged position of the poor is not in the poor themselves but in God, in the gratuitousness and universality of God's *agapeic love*" (Gutiérrez 1987: 94, emphasis in original). Our praxis of solidarity with the poor is not *itself* the foundation of Christian faith; rather, that praxis is a *response* to God's own initiative, a response to God's own gratuitous revelation in our world and in our own lives. "'God first loved us' (1 John 4: 19)," writes Gutiérrez, "[e]verything starts from there. The gift of God's love is the source of our being and puts its impress on our lives . . . The other is our way for reaching God, but our relationship with God is a precondition for encounter and true communion with the other" (Gutiérrez 1984: 109–12). Before we can "opt for" God or others, God has already opted for us; we can opt for the poor in a preferential way *because* God has already opted for the poor preferentially. And because the God who has chosen and loved us gratuitously is revealed in scripture, in tradition, and in history as a God who has chosen and loved the poor preferentially, we are compelled and empowered to love the poor preferentially. "The ultimate basis of God's preference for the poor," avers Gutiérrez, "is to be found in God's own goodness and not in any analysis of society or in human compassion, however pertinent these reasons may be" (Gutiérrez 1987: xiii).

Indeed, the Peruvian theologian warns against such distorted interpretations of the option for the poor:

A hasty and simplistic interpretation of the liberationist perspective has led some to affirm that its dominant, if not exclusive, themes are commitment, the social dimension of faith, the denunciation of injustices, and others of a similar nature. It is said that the liberationist impulse leaves little room for grasping the necessity of personal conversion as a condition for Christian life . . . Such an interpretation and criticism are simply caricatures. One need only have contact with the Christians in question to appreciate the complexity of their approach and the depth of their spiritual experience. (Gutiérrez 1984: 96)

The caricatures to which Gutiérrez refers quickly became widespread in the media, despite Gutiérrez' clear and consistent assertions that, in the words that appear on the very first page of *A Theology of Liberation*,

our purpose is not to elaborate an ideology to justify postures already taken, nor to undertake a feverish search for security in the face of the radical challenges which confront the faith, nor to fashion a theology from which political action is "deduced". It is rather to let ourselves be judged by the Word of the Lord, to think through our faith, to strengthen our love, and to give reason for our hope from within a commitment which seeks to become more radical, total, and efficacious. It is to reconsider the great themes of the Christian life within this radically changed perspective and with regard to the new questions posed by this commitment. (Gutiérrez 1973: ix)

What defines and makes Christian faith possible is not praxis as such but praxis *as encountered by God's Word*. And it is precisely a supreme confidence in God's gratuitous love for us, as that love is revealed in our lives and in God's Word, that above all characterizes the faith of the poor themselves. Over the years, Gutiérrez' writings have increasingly focused on the faith of the poor as a rich spiritual resource that has sometimes been overlooked in the struggle for justice; the seeds of liberation, which are fundamentally spiritual ("theocentric") are already present in the lived faith of the poor.

Expanding the Vision: Critique and Dialogue

Much of the criticism of liberation theology in general and of Gutiérrez in particular, therefore, has been based less on a thorough knowledge of the literature than on the stereotypes perpetuated by the media. In the Second Introduction to the revised edition of *A Theology of Liberation*, Gutiérrez nevertheless acknowledged the importance of this criticism in helping him to clarify his ideas and to express them with greater precision. In this lengthy essay subtitled "Expanding the Vision" he questioned, for instance, an earlier liberationist tendency to accept uncritically the claims of certain social analytical models, specifically Marxist and dependency theories. All "sciences," he argued, are based upon presuppositions that themselves must be continually revised in the light of changing historical circumstances. No doubt the horrific violence suffered by the Peruvian poor at the hands of the Marxist Sendero Luminoso, all in the name of "the poor," had a profound impact on Gutiérrez' thinking in this regard. Likewise, he acknowledged that, in the early years, he was not always attentive enough to the connotations and implicit associations of certain terminology. So, for example, at various points the revised edition of *A Theology of Liberation* substitutes the term "social conflict" for the more highly charged "class struggle," a term with a more clearly Marxist etymological history.

By virtue of their provenance, perhaps the most significant criticisms were those offered in the two Vatican documents on liberation theology, *Libertatis Nuntius* (1984) and *Libertatis Conscientia* (1986). Issued by the Vatican's Sacred Congregation for the Doctrine of the Faith and its head, Joseph Cardinal Ratzinger, these documents accused "certain" liberation theologians of reducing salvation to political liberation, and politics to Marxist class struggle. The second document, particularly, then proceeded to articulate what Ratzinger considered an authentically Christian theology of liberation. Here, liberation would be understood as rooted solely in and flowing from the salvific work of the Crucified and Risen Lord, as this has been communicated in the scriptures and Christian tradition.

While one might argue that some Latin American liberation theologians did come perilously close to such reductionism, and while Ratzinger's warning may very well have been appropriate, it should be clear from our foregoing discussion that Gutiérrez himself could not be fairly accused of such reductionism. And, indeed, neither of the documents named specific theologians. In *The Truth Shall Make Your Free* (1990), Gutiérrez responded explicitly to the Vatican documents. He affirmed their Christocentric, integral understanding of human freedom while underscoring their prophetic denunciation of injustice in Latin America and their trenchant critique of modern Western individualism.

It is not surprising that the Vatican chose to engage directly, in official documents, the liberation theology movement. As one looks back upon the last third of the twentieth century, the theological insight that has arguably had the greatest impact on the life of the church is the notion that the God of Jesus Christ is revealed in a privileged, preferential way among the poor and marginalized peoples of our world – a notion at the very heart of the Gospel itself. There is not a single corner of the Christian world today that has not felt the impact of the renewed attention to that claim, whether as an impetus for conversion and transformation or as a challenge to established theological and ecclesial practices. Today, one cannot do Christian theology, or even think theologically, without in some way confronting the claims implicit in the preferential option for the poor. As Christianity evolves from a predominantly European religion to a religion whose adherents are predominantly found in the third world, those claims will only grow in their relevance and impact.

Latin American theologians of liberation have been accompanied in their struggles by theologians who, from within their own distinct contexts of marginalization, have been developing other theologies of liberation. Black theologians in the United States, for example, have emphasized the significance of race as a key factor in oppression and, therefore, as a distinct dimension of poverty. Feminist theologians throughout the world have called attention to the way in which gender interacts with economic class and race as a factor that deepens and intensifies the experience of oppression; among the poor, poor women are "doubly oppressed." Indeed, North American feminist theologian Rosemary Radford Ruether has challenged Gutiérrez to become more explicitly engaged in grassroots women's movements in Peru and to appropriate more systematically the insights of feminist theology (Ruether 1996: 28). In Europe, political theologians have analyzed the role of modern Western "bourgeois religion" in the rationalization of global injustice. Gutiérrez has been deeply involved in continuing conversations with these and other theologians who have invited him to expand his understanding of "liberation" by exposing his own theology to the insights derived from other contexts, such as the specific roles of racism and sexism as forms of oppression. While the preferential option for the poor remains at the methodological heart of all theologies of liberation, the understanding of that option continues to be enriched, deepened, and nuanced.

Gutiérrez has personally had a particularly important influence in the development of a US Latino theology. While US Hispanic theologians have been greatly influenced by Latin American liberation theology, Gutiérrez has encouraged them to remain true to their own particular context; to simply import Latin American liberation theology into the North American context – even if the US

Latino context – would be to commit the methodological error for which Latin American theologians had for so long been criticizing the Europeans. The experience of the US Latino community as a cultural minority, for instance, has revealed the particular salience of cultural forms of marginalization. At the same time, the experience of *mestizaje*, or racial–cultural mixture, and the popular religious practices of the poor have been retrieved methodologically as resources for liberation, mediators of God's self-revelation to the poor.

If liberation theology no longer makes the front pages of our newspapers, then, the reason is not that the issues that movement addresses have either disappeared or decreased in significance. On the contrary, global poverty, injustice, and exploitation remain as intransigent as ever, and their consequences as devastating. If the public visibility of liberation theology has diminished, this is, in large part, because the fundamental questions raised by liberation theologians like Gustavo Gutiérrez – questions once considered novel and controversial – are today unavoidable in any theological conversation that demands to be taken seriously by either the churches or the academy. And foremost among those questions is the one that Gutiérrez locates at the very heart of the theological enterprise:

> Our task here is to find the words with which to talk about God in the midst of the starvation of millions, the humiliation of races regarded as inferior, discrimination against women, especially women who are poor, systematic social injustice, a persistent high rate of infant mortality, those who simply "disappear" or are deprived of their freedom, the sufferings of peoples who are struggling for their right to live, the exiles and the refugees, terrorism of every kind, and the corpse-filled common graves of Ayacucho [a scene of civil strife in Peru]. (Gutiérrez 1996: 318)

In the wake of the bloodiest century in the history of humanity, and given the fact that much of that blood will be found on the hands of self-proclaimed "Christians," the victims of that history are today the theologian's principal interlocutors. And, thus, God's preferential solidarity with those victims is an inescapable challenge – *the* inescapable challenge – for Christian theology at the dawn of the twenty-first century. More specifically, the claim that, in the person of the crucified and risen Christ, God is preferentially identified with the victims of history transforms the preferential option for the poor from an ethical imperative into the privileged *locus theologicus* of *all* Christian theology. After such a claim has been explicitly made, no Christian theology can avoid it.

References and Further Reading

Works by Gustavo Gutiérrez cited in text

A Theology of Liberation: History, Politics and Salvation (1973). Maryknoll, NY: Orbis. Rev. edn. with second intr., 1988.
We Drink from Our Own Wells: The Spiritual Journey of a People (1984). Maryknoll, NY: Orbis.

On Job: God-Talk and the Suffering of the Innocent (1987). Maryknoll, NY: Orbis.
The Truth Shall Make You Free: Confrontations (1990). Maryknoll, NY: Orbis.
Las Casas: In Search of the Poor of Jesus Christ (1993). Maryknoll, NY: Orbis.
Gustavo Gutiérrez: Essential Writings, ed. James B. Nickoloff (1996). Maryknoll, NY: Orbis.

Other works by Gutiérrez

The Power of the Poor in History (1983). Maryknoll, NY: Orbis.
The God of Life (1991). Maryknoll, NY: Orbis.
Sharing the Word (1997). Maryknoll, NY: Orbis.

Secondary works on Gutiérrez

Brown, Robert McAfee (1990). *Gustavo Gutiérrez: An Introduction to Liberation Theology.*
    Maryknoll, NY: Orbis.
Cadorette, Curt (1988). *From the Heart of the People: The Theology of Gustavo Gutiérrez.*
    Oak Park, Ill. Meyer-Stone.
Chopp, Rebecca (1986). *The Praxis of Suffering: An Interpretation of Liberation and
    Political Theologies.* Maryknoll, NY: Orbis.
Ellis, Marc H., and Maduro, Otto (eds.), *The Future of Liberation Theology: Essays in Honor
    of Gustavo Gutiérrez.* Maryknoll, NY: Orbis.
Ruether, Rosemary Radford (1996). "Rift between Gutiérrez and Peru Women:
    Liberation Theology Said to Be Too Narrow." *National Catholic Reporter*, Oct. 18, p. 28.

Other theologies of liberation

Aquino, María Pilar (1993). *Our Cry for Life: Feminist Theology from Latin America.*
    Maryknoll, NY: Orbis.
Cone, James H. (1970). *A Black Theology of Liberation.* Philadelphia: Lippincott.
Elizondo, Virgilio (1983). *Galilean Journey: The Mexican-American Promise.* Maryknoll,
    NY: Orbis.
Ferm, Deane William (1986). *Third World Liberation Theologies.* Maryknoll, NY: Orbis.
Goizueta, Roberto S. (1995). *Caminemos con Jesús: Toward a Hispanic/Latino Theology of
    Accompaniment.* Maryknoll, NY: Orbis.
Hennelly, Alfred T., SJ (1995). *Liberation Theologies: The Global Pursuit of Justice.* Mystic,
    Conn.: Twenty-Third Publications.
Isasi Díaz, Ada María (1996). *Mujerista Theology: A Theology for the Twenty-First Century.*
    Maryknoll, NY: Orbis.
Metz, Johann Baptist (1980). *Faith in History and Society: Toward a Practical Fundamental
    Theology.* New York: Seabury/Crossroad.
Ruether, Rosemary Radford (1983). *Sexism and God-Talk.* Boston: Beacon.

CHAPTER 21
Stanley Hauerwas

R. R. Reno

In the final decades of the twentieth century, Stanley Hauerwas articulated the most coherent and influential political theology in and for the North American context. This is not because he has said anything notable about political parties or policies. On many issues of public concern, he expresses an altogether standard academic distaste for "advanced capitalism" (Hauerwas 2000: 35–46). This makes him ambivalent about traditional morality, since according to the same standard academic viewpoint, it is hopelessly implicated in "bourgeois" forms of life that university professors in North America denounce in public and practice in private (Hauerwas 2000: 47–51). His opposition to abortion and euthanasia certainly puts him at odds with those who make a living criticizing "advanced capitalism," but his approach to such topics rarely fits into current political agendas, because he so vigorously resists the usual vocabulary of public debate (e.g. "right to life" or "freedom to choose"). On the question of warfare, Hauerwas is a clear and consistent pacifist, and the implications of his arguments are obvious and pressing. But here, what is so notable and germane is not influential in practice. Pacifists are often admired but rarely imitated. Thus, Hauerwas is an extraordinarily influential political theologian who has no popular views that might align him with an influential party or movement.

There is no paradox in this remarkable influence without influential political positions. For one important governing insight of Hauerwas' work as a whole is that the application of moral principles to politics no more constitutes political theology than the use of calculus for an engineering project constitutes the discipline of mathematics. Trafficking in moral principles and their application would make him something he detests: an ethicist.[1]

This execrable species is the frequent object of Hauerwas' polemics, and a good place to begin an assessment of his political theology. Hauerwas' criticisms of ethics and ethicists have a common theme. As a theological discipline in the United States, ethics treats the nature and exercise of power in society as a settled matter, and it then sets about to show how the moral content of Christianity must guide and govern our use of that power. For example, the ethicist might observe that American society is structured by a capitalist market economy modestly restrained by a representative democracy, and will then turn to assessing these social arrangements according to a Christian principle. In the same way, the ethicist might use a particular Christian frame of reference to comment upon international affairs. Should Christians put their shoulders to the human rights movement? Or, more generally, the ethicist might consider the needs of "modern man," and then set about weighing the pros and cons of various new developments in morality and social thought. The pressing questions, then, are whether, according to Christian principles, the given forms of power and their interactions are just or unjust, and how they ought to be preserved, modified, or overthrown on the basis of those same principles. Or, stated more simply, for the tradition of ethics that Hauerwas dislikes, power is an extra-Christian reality that needs to be modified and moderated (or perhaps even rejected) in light of Christian truths.

Hauerwas recognizes that this approach to ethics can be fascinating and interesting; but he identifies one problem with it, and it is a big problem. Ideas *do* have consequences, and principled assessment of the uses of power *is* a worthy undertaking. But something very important is missing. It was not surprising that in 1968 the students in Paris threw cobblestones and bricks, not books. Bricks hurt more. They have a palpable and immediate force which ethical principles, however creatively and insightfully applied, lack. Bricks have a density that does damage when thrown, and when laid properly, they are a very durable material of construction. In other words, bricks are not ideals or plans, they are potent objects one might take up to implement an ideal or to execute a plan. They are not principled use of power; they *are* instances of power by virtue of their density and weight.

Hauerwas knows that Christian truth is at least as dense and durable as are bricks. This is his signal insight. "I am convinced," he writes in a characteristic affirmation, "that the intelligibility and truthfulness of Christian convictions reside in their practical force" (Hauerwas 1981a: 1). In other words, the intelligibility and truthfulness of Christian conviction resides in their brick-like quality. Being baptized is more like being hit on the head with a brick than it is like going to a teach-in. Celebrating the Eucharist week after week is more like laying a durable foundation for a house than it is like attending weekly lectures. In both instances, we do not learn principles or ideals by which we might *exercise* power. Quite the contrary: in baptism and Eucharist, we are *subject to* something that has power.

For this reason, ethics as practiced in the United States, and much of what has passed as "political theology" elsewhere, is fundamentally misguided.[2] The point is not to try to control or direct secular power according to moral principles or theological concepts. A genuine political theology must attend to the ways in which Christian truth takes form as a power in its own right. A genuine political theology must identify and explicate the *exousia* of Jesus Christ that gives density and force to the life of discipleship. Thus, as a political theologian, Hauerwas places a singular emphasis on Christian power, the solidity of Christian truth that makes a difference in the world.

This intense focus on power is the key to Hauerwas' political theology and his remarkable influence. Across the heterogeneity of his many essays and books, he is always a theologian of the specifically Christian form of power. His search for the density of Christian truth, the brick-like power of the Gospel, is unwavering, even as the specific vocabulary and focus for expressing his findings varies. That consistency is best displayed in the "three Cs" that recur throughout his publications: character, church and Constantinianism. To them we must turn.

Character and the Durable Self

The initial focus of Hauerwas' work seems rather removed from bricks, brick-throwing, and a concern about Christian power in the world. His first book, *Character and the Christian Life*, attempts to give an account of "the nature of the Christian moral life" (Hauerwas 1985: 229). This is just the sort of conceptual focus that threatens to shift attention away from the worldly weight of the Christian life. Yet, in this early study, Hauerwas thinks himself away from concepts and toward his characteristic preoccupation with the living particularity and density of Christian truth.

Writing in the early 1970s, Hauerwas sees two parallel tendencies in the theological and philosophical approaches that dominated midcentury English-speaking academic life. By his reading, much of Protestant thought has been preoccupied with "the metaphor of command." An anxiety about righteousness through works leads to the presumption that an exaggerated emphasis on sanctification undermines the doctrine of justification.[3] This theological outlook consistently blocks the development of a vocabulary to describe continuing human participation in divine purposes. Without continuing participation, the power of Christianity can easily seem occasional and ephemeral. It has to do with the "vertical" dimension of transcendence, not the "horizontal" dimension of everyday life. Furthermore, modern anxieties about scientific determinism have tempted modern moralists to secure a zone of indeterminate freedom as the realm of "values." Free decisions are seen as the key moments of moral significance in lives otherwise embedded in the context of social and natural forces. As a result, moral philosophy sets about to thoroughly analyze the dynamics of decision. Again, the "vertical" is juxtaposed to the "horizontal." Difficult circumstances are carefully assessed so that we might find our way along the narrow paths of duty and obligation. So-called "quandary ethics" take center stage.

For Hauerwas, concerns about righteousness through works and the desire to secure a narrow zone of freedom have encouraged a disembodied and atomistic view of the self. The slide occurs in many ways. Pietism turns inward; neo-orthodoxy treats divine intervention as a series of explosions that shatter worldly forms. Kantian morality focuses on purity of intention, while utilitarianism endorses dispassionate and detached calculations of harms and benefits.

Hauerwas has a great deal to say about these different trends, but it is the end result that is most important. For much of modern moral thought, and for nearly all of what passes as ethical reflection in modern Protestant theology, a Gnostic sensibility prevails. What *really* matters in our lives – our participation in God's justifying grace, our self-determining moments of moral choice, our calculations of utility – is separated from the vast majority of what defines and shapes our lives, and the result is anything but powerful. Restricted to the "vertical," moral and religious life is so distant and ephemeral that it cannot exercise power in the world.

In *Character and the Christian Life*, Hauerwas urges us to think otherwise. He wants us to use character, rather than command, as the "central metaphor." This requires a detailed study of an array of theological and philosophical issues concerning sanctification, agency, and the nature of the self. Theologically, Hauerwas shows how the radical Augustinianism of Barth (which Bultmann does not so much affirm as exploit) is vulnerable to the perversion of "situation ethics" (Hauerwas 1985: 177–8). If the articulation of continuing and durable forms of Christian life and practice is rejected as an encroachment upon God's prevenient grace, then Christian ethicists seem free to just make it up as they go along. Philosophically, Hauerwas makes the case that human agency is always the agency of someone, and to be a person is to have a history and a personality. As Hauerwas never tires of reminding his readers, the illusion of the "view from nowhere" is a close cousin to the "decision from nowhere." Thus, indeterminacy cannot be the signal note of freedom, at least not the freedom of persons.

Hauerwas' *reductio ad absurdum* of the prevailing theological framework for Protestant ethics, as well as his demonstration of the untenable philosophical assumptions of a decision-oriented ethical theory, are compelling. Yet what is most important about *Character and the Christian Life* is the underlying concern, for it leads toward bricks, and the other solid objects that he so often throws at his readers in his later work. Animating his analysis is a clear theological judgment. The Gospel is good news because God does something for us that involves "real change in our mode of being and existence" (Hauerwas 1985: 228). God, moreover, is faithful. He ensures that this real change is continuing and durable. Here is how Hauerwas puts the matter: "To be in Christ is to be determined by the reality that claims to be able to order and form the rest of reality in a way that our life can achieve genuine 'continuity' and 'integrity'" (p. 226). In short, Christ has the power to shape us as persons.

In view of this affirmation, the central topic of *Character and the Christian Life* has a clear role to play. Character is the basis for the "continuity" and "integrity" of a person subject to a power that effects real and lasting change. Virtue denotes the qualities of character that establish continuity and integrity in lives changing for the better. Vice denotes those qualities in lives changing for the worse (and therefore disintegrating). Hauerwas has a great deal to say about the kinds of virtues that make up a Christian character – truthfulness, peaceableness, patience, hope, and more – and what affections and practices constitute and sustain these virtues is a matter of inquiry and debate. More important, however, is the underlying importance of character. "The virtues," Hauerwas writes, "bind our past with our future by providing us with continuity of self"(Hauerwas 1988: 265). The virtues are the ways in which Christian truth "becomes enduring in our intentionality" (Hauerwas 1981b: 2). In short, character denotes the density of our lives. Everything that Hauerwas writes after *Character and the Christian Life* is an extended inquiry into this density. He wants to understand the particular ways the lives of Christians take on weight and solidity. He is eager to explain how this brick-like quality both collides with and resists the worldly powers that dominate our lives, and just this collision and resistance defines the political reality of Christian character.

The Church as Kiln of the Soul

Character and the Christian Life makes a clear case for the centrality of the virtues, but it is strikingly formal in its conclusions. To be in Christ, Hauerwas concludes at the end of this early work, means being shaped by a power, some x, that gives order and form to our lives, that molds our character. Perhaps if Hauerwas were a Lutheran, he would not have hesitated. He would have said that the x is the Gospel. That is the word that Lutherans use when they want to emphasize the thick and weighty power of God. Perhaps if Hauerwas were a Roman Catholic, he would have said that the x is grace, for Roman Catholics often use that word to denote everything that God does for us and in us. But Hauerwas is a Methodist, and Methodists have tent meetings, but they do not have handy theological words. As a result, convinced as he might be about the central importance of character, Hauerwas must investigate the x that, according to the promise of the Gospel, shapes our lives.

The results of Hauerwas' investigations are his signature preoccupations. Unable to use the word "Gospel" in its Lutheran sense, he appeals to narrative, and in so doing he draws attention to the fundamental role of scripture in the formation of Christian character. At the same time, Hauerwas turns to the church and points to the many institutional practices that Roman Catholics always take for granted when they use the word "grace." In both cases, Hauerwas plunges into the details that constitute the x that forms (or should form) the character of Christians. The upshot is a rather plastic vocabulary – narrative, community, church, practices, sacraments, story – that refers to particular instances of God's formative power, that *concreta Christiana*, that give density to our lives. The x is no longer formal. It takes on material content, and political consequences follow directly.

Density is a function of strong forces that hold together potentially fragmenting elements. What, then, holds our lives together? What gives sharp force and real endurance to our characters? For Hauerwas, the glue of personal life is narrative or story. "The metaphors that determine our vision," Hauerwas writes, "must form a coherent story if our lives are to have duration and unity" (Hauerwas 1981b: 3). Narrative and not principle, story and not duty, allow us to make sense out of the dynamic and developmental reality of moral life. For example, St. Augustine's *Confessions* exercise such a profound influence because he can tell a story about his life. His personal transformation makes sense, not because of the fact that he made some "meaningful" decision, or because he "affirmed" his life, but instead because the narrative as a whole makes sense.[4]

The concentrating power of story is a theme that is central to Hauerwas' escape from the impotence of Protestant liberalism. Although Hauerwas consistently reminds us of the importance of adherents to the "Social Gospel", such as Walter Rauschenbusch, who drew attention to the political dimension of Christian convictions, he sees a fundamental problem in their orientation. "They provided," he writes, "a far too limited account of the nature of those convictions and how they work morally" (Hauwerwas 1981a: 90). Emphasis fell on Christian principles that, once isolated from the fabric of Christian speech and practice, became semantically underdetermined. The content of Christian convictions becomes diffuse. God's "love" and "righteousness" were thus easily absorbed into the therapeutic goals and liberal political framework of twentieth-century American culture.

It is against this gaseous tendency that Hauerwas sets the solidifying importance of narrative. Just as our lives take on density when embedded in a story, so also do theological convictions. For Christian theology, "love" and "righteousness" have a determinative meaning precisely as constituents of a story about what God has, in fact, done in the election of Israel, and in the fulfillment of that election in the life, death, and Resurrection of Jesus Christ. As he says pungently, "The Gospel is not about love, but it is about this man, Jesus of Nazareth" (Hauerwas 1981b: 115). Thus, for Hauerwas, "by calling attention to the narrative character of Christian convictions, the reductionistic assumptions associated with the ethics sponsored by Protestant liberalism can be avoided" (Hauerwas 1981a: 90). The story of Jesus of Nazareth gives content to Christian words such as "love" and "righteousness."

The point is not that Christian convictions are somehow clearer in a narrative context. It can be very difficult to see how the justice of the God of Israel can require the exile of the righteous remnant, a difficulty that prefigures the suffering of the righteous Son. Rather, the point is that narrative creates density. Because we must puzzle out the nature of God's righteousness within the narrative, we must account for layer upon layer of event and episode. Concepts are not "clarified"; they are weighted with exegetical reflection that, however inconclusive and complex, is not easily taken captive by rival, extra-Christian interpretations. It is for this reason, and not on the basis of the philosophical arguments he often uses to show the contextual nature of all concepts, that Hauerwas insists, "There are no doctrines for which one must search out moral implications; rather 'doctrines' and 'morality' gain their intelligibility from narratives" (Hauerwas 1981a: 90) Narratives are engines of density, and Christian doctrines have staying power only if they have a weight born of this density.

Story is central to Hauerwas' quest for the brick-like truth of Christian faith, but when we focus on narrative alone there is the danger of a literary abstraction that parallels conceptual abstraction. "Part of the difficulty with the rediscovery of the significance of narrative for theological reflection," Hauerwas cautions, "has been too [much] concentrated attention on texts qua texts" (Hauerwas 1988: 55). Stories are not uniquely potent simply because of their narrative form. Stories have force when they are told and retold. Indeed, they have force when they are enacted as retold. This requires place, memory, and discipline. We must come together to hear the story. A tradition must keep the story forever contemporary. A community of enactment must endorse disciplines that shape us according to the story. Just as St. Augustine's ability to tell the story of his life does not depend upon a "metaphor" of God as Forgiver, but requires a narrative framework into which he can place his own life, so does the power of that narrative framework depend upon the actual practices of repentance that characterize the Christian community. For Hauerwas, "church" identifies this place, memory, and discipline.

Here, Hauerwas is very clear. "Narrative is unintelligible abstracted from an ecclesial context"; and, once abstracted, it is all too tempting "to develop general hermeneutical theories" in "an attempt to substitute a theory of interpretation for the church" (Hauerwas 1988: 55). This temptation must be resisted, for it leads back into the "reductionism" of liberal Protestantism. The narrative *form* supersedes the *content* of what Christians proclaim, and the emptiness of form produces the same vaporous conclusions that characterize earlier forms of theological liberalism. In fact, as Hauerwas likes to say, the story of liberalism is the story that we have no story. We can adopt narratives that disembody our lives. We can anchor our lives in distorting and destructive stories. Therefore, the material link between narrative and church is crucial. The brick-like quality of the Christian life does not come from an abstract commitment to narrative. It comes from adopting the story of Jesus Christ that is remembered and embodied in the church.

For this reason, for Hauerwas, the church is the fundamental and density-creating form of God's power in the world. If you and I are shaped by the church, then we are sturdy stones in the walls of the heavenly city, or (to take a more aggressive mode characteristic of Hauerwas' rhetoric) we are ready projectiles to be lobbed against the threatening, but ultimately hollow forces arrayed against righteousness. If we understand Hauerwas on this point, then his noted remarks about ethics, truth, the world, and the church make sense.

Consider these claims. "The church is an ontological necessity if we are to know rightly that our world is capable of narrative construal." "Without the church the world would have no history." "The faithfulness of the church is crucial for the destiny of the world" (Hauerwas 1988: 61). Such formulations can be deceiving. Hauerwas does not think that a churchless world has no past, present, or future. Rather, he is offering the following postulate. Without the density-conferring work of God in the identity-forming practices of the church, worldly life is ethereal and weightless. We have political, economic, ethnic, familial commitments, to be sure, but the sum of the whole is less than the parts, and as a consequence, we have little ballast against the storms of violence and fear that sweep across our lives. However, if we are formed by the church, then we have weight and density. We have a place to stand against the supposed "necessities" of life (preservation of one's life, protection of one's property, defense of one's own kind) that give evil its seeming cogency and force.

Given this insight, Hauerwas' polemic against "ethics" becomes clear. To try to meet evil with principle and duty is futile. They lack worldly weight to counteract worldly powers. In contrast, the identity-forming practices of the Christian community (Hauerwas can range very widely in his descriptions of these practices) cement our allegiance and solidify our defenses. For this reason, the church, for Hauerwas, simply *is* the social ethic of Christians. To define the principles of righteousness, to intend the good, to clarify duty, to expound upon the Christian vision of justice – all these efforts are well and good as constituent practices within the life of the church; but alone, they are powerless. The church provides the glue that cements together such practices, and many others, into a whole capable of resisting worldly powers.

Thus, for Hauerwas, the church is the kiln of a brick-like soul: not the featherweight soul defined by "ultimate concerns," but soul weighted by the scriptural stories, moral disciplines, and communal practices that make sharing the Eucharist a real rather than ritual act. Here, Hauerwas' theological concerns are classical, not modern. God's truth transforms persons, not political systems. But such classical concerns are not at all apolitical. After all, when frail human flesh is cemented into the People of God, it can resist evil and give solidity to the cause of righteousness. And surely Hauerwas (and the classical tradition) is right. For falsehood has shown itself able to endure many changes of regime. Fear and violence are ready to serve any political program. Yet, as the witness of the martyrs shows so vividly, neither falsehood, nor fear, nor violence can survive the identity-shaping power of divine love.

Thus, for Hauerwas, the church is the foundational sacrament, the sign of redemptive power that makes real that which it signifies. The church is the body of Christ, the enduring worldly form of his work in the world. For this reason, Hauerwas often says that the truth of Christian faith depends upon the church. As he asserts, "The truthfulness of theological claims entails the work they do for the shaping of holy lives" (Hauerwas 2001: 17). God's truth is the power to resist evil: "By being trained through Jesus' story," Hauerwas writes, "we have the means to name and prevent these powers from claiming our lives as their own" (Hauerwas 1981a: 50). Resistance is but the first step. The Lord intends to bring all things to consummation, and that power is present in the life-forming practices of the People of God.[5] Thus, the world has a "history," or more precisely, a truthful history, only insofar as the church's power waxes and worldly powers wane. Indeed, as Hauerwas sets out to show in the conclusion of his recent Gifford Lectures, *With the Grain of the Universe*, all that *is* finds its full weight and reality in light of the proper weight and reality of the church's witness. The more brick-like the church, and our lives as shaped by the church, the more vain and vacuous are the distorting forces of evil, and the more real and purposeful is the created order.

Against Constantinianism

Christian power meets resistance. Being trained through Jesus' story means adopting the practices and habits of a new city, and this cannot help but create a conflict between the church and the world, for the world seeks to put us to its own malign purposes. A great deal of Hauerwas' work focuses on the particular scenes of this conflict, which are many. Materially, this diversity of conflict is unified under a general scheme of violence and peace. Worldly powers, for Hauerwas, are not most visible and potent in injustice or oppression. Instead, worldly powers show their true face in the presumptive necessity of violence. Secular power must threaten in order to be effective. In contrast, the defining practice of the church is peace-making, and precisely because of this, the density of the church necessarily collides with the social "realities" that require menace in order to maintain power.

Hauerwas consistently describes this conflict between the church and worldly power as "Constantinianism." This is a protean term in the Hauerwasian lexicon, and he uses it in diverse ways. At times, he seems to advance an (unconvincing) historical thesis about the "fall" of the primitive church into a captivity to worldly vanity and illusions of social significance. At other times, his use of "Constantinianism" is a rhetorical device for sharpening contrasts. Conflict between the church and world galvanizes, and Hauerwas sees any diminishment of that conflict as "Constantinian." But most often, Hauerwas uses the term "Constantinianism" to denote the ways in which Christian truth becomes innocuous and weightless. It is, as he puts the matter, an approach of "spiritualization," and as he writes, "by 'spiritualization' I mean simply the attempt to make Christianity intelligible without that set of habits called the church" (Hauerwas 1988: 159). Thus, a "Constantinian" is anyone who would make the church invisible and weightless. Assumptions and practices are "Constantinian" if they disembody rather than solidify Christian identity.

Hauerwas is clearest when describing the American situation. By his analysis, the churches configure themselves in light of prevailing political, economic, and cultural arrangements. America *needs* Christianity, and churches clamor to satisfy that need, either in conservative support or in progressive critique. The upshot is a blending and blurring that make Christian character and practice invisible. What is the difference between a generic law-and-order, family-values conservative, and a spokesman for the "Christian Right"? What is the difference between a generic, inclusive progressivist, and a spokesman for liberal Protestantism? Hauerwas wishes a pox upon both houses, for each defines the witness of the Christian in terms of the needs of American society, and the more successfully the church meets these needs, the more invisible it becomes, because the more it blends into the prevailing culture.

Hauerwas' rejection of Constantinianism seems clear. It represents everything that assaults the density-forming reality of Christian life and practice. Yet his formulations can seem contradictory. Consider the following claim. "All our categories have been set by the church's establishment as a necessary part of Western civilization" (Hauerwas 1991: 10). The church becomes a constituent of "civilization," and this role prevents stark and defining contrast. Yet, as we have seen, in his positive articulations of the role of the church – its "necessity" for world destiny, its crucial role for our ability to see the truth of all things – he seems to be establishing Christianity even more forcefully than the so-called Constantinians. This confusion is reinforced by essays with titles such as "In Defense of Cultural Christianity: Reflections on Going to Church" (Hauerwas 1998: 157–73). Still further, Hauerwas consistently and vigorously rejects the radical Augustinianism of many Reformation thinkers, a theological disposition that attacks just those forms of worldly pretension that would seem to animate the Constantinian project. Against this Protestant tradition, he allies himself with the Catholic theological tradition that has been congenial to religious establishment and close involvement with culture.

What seems contradictory need not be so. The church can become invisible and weightless in many different ways, and Hauerwas' apparent contradictions are simply manifestations of his due diligence. On the one hand, Hauerwas attacks the patrons of relevance and responsibility. When prince and bishop blur together, it becomes hard to see the power of God at work in the world. When bourgeois virtues blend with Christian character, it is difficult to identify the specific gravity that the Gospel should take in our lives. In both cases, Christian faith lacks an identifiable form, and the church fails to mark out a distinctive culture and politics of her own. However, the cry for relevance and responsibility is not the only danger. Patrons of radical transcendence and prophets of the "vertical" also contribute to the invisibility of faith. As Hauerwas recognized in his first book, *Character and the Christian Life*, the dominant theological moves that Protestant neo-orthodoxy used to reassert the autonomy of revelation and the sovereignty of God block all forms of Christian embodiment. The "Protestant Principle" makes the church as invisible, perhaps more invisible, than the most Erastian of circumstances.[6]

So, Hauerwas rages against a mistaken view that the church gains weight through alliances to "real" forces (regnant regimes of political, cultural, and intellectual power), and at the same time he attacks modern theological attempts to make Christian invisibility into a spiritual virtue. Against the patrons of relevance and responsibility, he insists that Christianity is not of this world. The church cannot normalize relations with worldly powers in order to take up a regular role in managing secular politics and maintaining culture. Against the patrons of radical transcendence, he insists that Christianity is sacred politics that is very much in the world, if not of it.

This two-front war against "Constantinianism" is, I think, best understood through a story of the conversion of the great pagan apologist, Victorinus, told by St. Augustine. "After examining [the scriptures]," St. Augustine reports, Victorinus "said to Simplicanus, not openly but in the privacy of friendship, 'Did you not know that I am already a Christian?' Simplicanus replied, 'I shall not believe that or count you among the Christians unless I see you in the Church of Christ.' Victorinus laughed and said: 'Then do walls make Christians?'" (Augustine 1991: 136). For St. Augustine, the answer is clear. Walls *do* make Christians. Victorinus is not a Christian until he enters into the public life of the church, submitting himself to instruction in the mysteries and giving his name for baptism.

For Hauerwas, the answer is just as clear. Walls make Christians. The task of political theology is to prepare the bricks for the walls of the church by identifying and displaying the many ways in which the truth of God in Jesus Christ takes on solidity, substance, and continuity in the affairs of men and women. And those walls separate just as much as they encircle. To enter this heavenly city, one leaves behind, often in painful turns of repentance, the earthly city we thought our only possible home. Thus, Hauerwas' polemics against Constantinianism should be understood as ad hoc criticisms of the many ways in which the church has tried to demolish the walls of separation and moderate the wrenching turn of repentance, whether by so distancing faith from practical affairs that "spiritual" becomes a synonym for "impotent," or by so intertwining faith with the habits and practices of the wider culture that the Christian life becomes invisible.

Liberal or Conservative?

Is Hauerwas a liberal or conservative? This is not an easy question to answer, in large part because his political theology systematically undercuts the conceptual assumptions that give rise to such polar options in modernity. Nonetheless, the attempt is worth the effort, if only to clarify the ambition of Hauerwas' political theology.

For Hauerwas, the term "liberal" is best understood as a moral discipline and habit rather than a political program or philosophical agenda. To be a liberal entails adopting practices of critical detachment. Liberalism urges us to cultivate the "capacity to 'step back' from particular judgments and regard them from anyone's point of view" (Hauerwas 1983: 17). Instead of thinking and acting under the compelling influences of inherited and particular forms of life, as a liberal one thinks and acts objectively and impartially, always at a distance from the particular powers of tradition.

Hauerwas' intense polemics against the "step back" clearly make him an enemy of liberalism. Hauerwas might well commend trial by jury or the rights of private property, but in so doing, he would no doubt insist that such social goods must be nurtured by drawing ever closer to the narratives and practices that give them life and urgency in our culture rather than trying to justify them from a universal perspective. For Hauerwas, the problem with liberalism is not what it proposes, concretely, for the organization of society. Instead, the failure of liberalism rests in its antagonism toward all powers other than those supposedly universally resident in the human person (reason, will, feeling – take your pick). The upshot, for Hauerwas, is disastrous. We are given density and potency only insofar as we are initiated into formative traditions and practices. If we want to liberate ourselves from them, as liberalism endorses, then we are condemning ourselves to a weightless impotence; and, seeking a universality we cannot attain, we become victims of whatever formative powers happen to prevail in our society.

Does this, then, make Hauerwas a conservative? When he speaks about our general need for narrative and community in order to have particularized weight and gravity, then he can certainly sound like a defender of the properly superordinate role of tradition. In the American context, the Southern Agrarians, like Hauerwas, criticized modern, abstract humanism. Even more poignantly, the Agrarians decried the deracination caused by modern industrialization. To their collective mind, this detachment from land and tradition produces "fragmentation, division, chaos" (Twelve Southerners 1962: xiv). The rootless person lacks ballast, and the "liberated soul" is easily pressed into the service of the inhumane mass phenomena of modernity.

Not only did the Agrarians share Hauerwas' concern about weightlessness, they also shared his insights into the indispensable role of tradition and narrative. By their accounting, "Humanism, properly speaking, is not an abstract system, but a culture . . . lived out in a definite social tradition." That tradition, in turn, must be particularized "in its tables, chairs, portraits, festivals, laws, marriage customs" (Twelve Southerners 1962: xxvi). Therefore, in order to live a humane life, to cultivate a genuine humanism, we must "look backward rather than forward" (p. 1). We must work to re-establish contact with the particularized forms of life that give life density. Thus did the Agrarians understand our predicament, and no American reader has ever hesitated to call it conservative.

Is this Hauerwas' approach? It is, at least in part. For example, in his discovery of Iris Murdoch early in his career, Hauerwas highlighted her emphasis on the submissive basis for moral vision. We do not decide about the good; rather, we are ravished by its radiance. Or, as he states the point in his own idiom, "By letting the story live through us we come to be transformed, to be as the story is" (Hauerwas 1981b: 115). Here, a vigorous Augustininianism mixes with philosophical insight. God's grace, like the radiance of the good, is the real source of human empowerment, and our roles are given rather than fashioned, received rather than chosen. Thus, the task of the moral and religious life is to "step forward" into ever greater obedience, rather than to "step back" in order to critically assess. The "step forward" involves closer attachment to and closer immersion in the particular forms (the tables, chairs, portraits, festivals, laws, and marriage customs) that shape us into specific and dense persons.

In spite of this conservative pattern of submission, Hauerwas diverges. He wishes us to nurture the identity-forming powers of the church. This means drawing closer to the particularized disciplines and forces that shape persons into church members, and this is a conservative move. But this emphasis upon increased loyalty to the church is not a general principle for the maintenance and enforcement of culture. Instead, even as Hauerwas endorses the identity-forming power of the church, his anti-Constantinian polemics always remind us that the church, and only the church, can and should demand such loyalty. We should distance ourselves – "step back" – from the many other, non-Christian traditions and loyalties that clamor for priority. We must detach ourselves from the secular traditions that shape our lives, especially, thinks Hauerwas, the traditions that motivate our loyalty to the nation-state, and this is very much a liberal move. Thus, we should say that Hauerwas' conservatism with respect to the church – one cannot become too deeply enmeshed in the church – produces a liberalism with respect to all other forms of power. Formed by the church, one can never be more capable of the "step back."

For this reason, Hauerwas' political theology is best understood as a thoroughgoing Christian liberalism. Without doubt, he rejects the liberal ideal of critical detachment. We can never begin by distancing ourselves from that which gives life. We must seek the density of a properly Christian life; otherwise, our claims to freedom and reason are fantasies. Only as we fall under the power of another – God – do we participate in practices that will empower us as agents with sufficient ballast and force to act rather than react. But for just this reason, Hauerwas can consistently adopt the vigorously critical tropes of modern, liberal thought. The "step forward" into a life of discipleship allows us to "step back" from economic, political, military, and cultural forces that dominate contemporary life, because the church has given us a place to stand. In this way, Hauerwas vindicates the liberal desire to escape the debilitation and diminishment of powers presumed and imposed. We can say "no" to the world's rules, if we will but say "yes" to God's law.

So we can say that, for Hauerwas, the Christian who submits to the shaping power of the church is more successfully "liberal" than any secular liberal, or any theological liberal who keeps the identity-forming practices of the church at a distance. It is, perhaps, a great irony that this ardent critic of liberalism should draw such a conclusion. But the irony is fruitful. For Hauerwas may well succeed in doing exactly that which his *bête noire*, liberal Protestantism in America, has failed to do – articulate a theological vision for men and women who wish so to serve the kingdom of God that they will be citizens of the world rather than representatives of an imperial nation and a liberal culture.

Notes

1 Hauerwas' denunciations of the practice of ethics in America are legion. For a particularly witty illustration, see Hauerwas (2000), 55–69.
2 Arne Rasmusson's perceptive and helpful study (Rasmusson 1995) provides a detailed brief against the European tradition of political theology, clearly taking his cues from Hauerwas.
3 Hauerwas later backtracks from such broad characterizations (see Hauerwas 1985: xxvi); nonetheless, he has continued to dismiss the notion that sanctification and justification are rivals in a zero-sum game.
4 See his comments on St. Augustine: Hauerwas (1977), 33–5.
5 For an insightful examination of the future-oriented structure of Hauerwas' use of notions such as truth, see Robert W. Jenson's assessment: Jenson (1992), 285–95.
6 See e.g. his analysis of H. Richard Niebuhr's use of "transcendence" to deracinate Christianity. On its face, Niebuhr's strategy would seem utterly congenial to Hauerwas' attack upon "Constantinianism," and yet he rejects it outright (Hauerwas 1998: 158–60).

References

Augustine (1991). *Confessions*, trans. Henry Chadwick. Oxford: Oxford University Press.
Grant, George Parkin (1985). *English-Speaking Justice*, Notre Dame, Ind.: University of Notre Dame Press.
Gustafson, James (1985). "The Sectarian Temptation: Reflections on Theology, the Church and the University." *CTSA* [Catholic Theological Society of America] *Proceedings* 40, 83–94.
Hauerwas, Stanley (1977). *Truthfulness and Tragedy: Further Investigations in Christian Ethics*, with Richard Bondi and David B. Burrell. Notre Dame, Ind.: University of Notre Dame Press.
——(1981a). *A Community of Character: Toward a Constructive Christian Social Ethic.* Notre Dame, Ind.: University of Notre Dame Press.
——(1981b). *Vision and Virtue: Essays in Christian Ethical Reflection.* Notre Dame, Ind.: University of Notre Dame Press.
——(1983). *The Peaceable Kingdom: A Primer in Christian Ethics.* Notre Dame, Ind.: University of Notre Dame Press.
——(1985). *Character and the Christian Life: A Study in Theological Ethics*, 2nd edn. with new int. San Antonio: Trinity University Press. (First publ. 1975.)
——(1988). *Christian Existence Today: Essays on Church, World, and Living in Between.* Durham, NC: Labyrinth.
——(1991). *After Christendom: How the Church is to Behave if Freedom, Justice, and a Christian Nation Are Bad Ideas.* Nashville: Abingdon.
——(1997). *Wilderness Wanderings: Probing Twentieth-Century Theology and Philosophy.* Boulder, Col.: Westview.
——(1998). *Sanctify Them in the Truth: Holiness Exemplified.* Nashville: Abingdon.
——(2000). *A Better Hope: Resources for a Church Confronting Capitalism, Democracy, and Postmodernity.* Grand Rapids, Mich.: Brazos.

——(2001). *With the Grain of the Universe: The Church's Witness and Natural Theology.* Grand Rapids, Mich.: Brazos.

Jenson, Robert W. (1992). "The Hauerwas Project." *Modern Theology* 8: 3, 285–95.

Rasmusson, Arne (1995). *The Church as Polis: From Political Theology to Theological Ethics as Exemplified by Jürgen Moltmann and Stanley Hauerwas.* Notre Dame, Ind.: University of Notre Dame Press.

Twelve Southerners (1962). *I'll Take My Stand: The South and the Agrarian Tradition.* New York: Harper Torchbooks.

PART III
Constructive Political Theology

22	Trinity	319
23	Creation	333
24	Christology	348
25	Atonement	363
26	Spirit	377
27	Church	393
28	Eschatology	407

CHAPTER 22
Trinity

Kathryn Tanner

Theologians have license to talk about everything in relation to God, their proper subject matter – including politics. Most theologians therefore comment at some point on sociopolitical issues: for example, the propriety of empire, or usury, or established social norms in relations between men and women, free men and slaves. But theology does not wait for such topics to become political theology. All theology is political – it concerns how social relations should be ordered – for two reasons.

The first reason stems from the fact that Christianity is not just a body of beliefs, suitable for abstract intellectual discussion, but a way of living in which beliefs are embedded (see Tanner 1992: 9, 19; 1997: 70, 97). Those beliefs help make that way of living seem meaningful and motivated. Thus, love-filled relations with others make sense if one believes the world is created by, and destined to show the influence of, a loving God. And such relations are well motivated should one believe they are a sign of, or condition for, attaining the highest good imaginable – salvation. Argument over Christian beliefs, for example, over their meanings, associations, and connections, has therefore everything to do with the social relations that seem right – the Christian way to behave. For this reason, political controversies among Christians tend to be fought out over cultural matters – that is, in and through arguments over the meaning of those beliefs with which Christians most identify and in which they are, accordingly, most heavily invested (Tanner 1992: 20; 1997: 56, 74–5, 121, 135). The familiar way in which struggles today over the direction of the national will bring with them fights over the connotations of national values and founding commitments – for instance, in the United States, fights over the meaning of family, fairness, freedom, and equality – finds its Christian analogue: Theology amounts to the cultural politics of Christian communities. Thus, Christians make charitable works the mission of their churches because of what they think Jesus is all about, in much the way Americans give their nation's military exploits unquestioned support because of what they think patriotism is all about. Efforts to undermine popular support for either policy have therefore to be as concerned about the meaning of Jesus or patriotism, respectively, as about the wisdom of such policies in and of themselves.

The second reason theology is political is that, no matter how far the topic seems to stray from it, theology is always making a commentary on the political whenever it incorporates social and political imagery for theological purposes (see Tanner 1997: 93–110, 120–1). The most basic theological claims, of a seemingly strictly theological sort – for example, about who Jesus is, the character of God's grace, etc. – are commonly given sense through the employment of such imagery. Thus, Jesus is often said to be "Lord," to have worked for God's "kingdom," and to have gone to his death to restore "justice" by "paying a debt" or suffering the "punishment fit for the crime" of our sin. The sense of theological claims trades on the associations of their social and political imagery in the historical context of the times. Those associations say something about these theological matters – in the above example, about the way we are to address Jesus in prayer, about the character of God's plan for the world, and about the means by which Jesus saves. But the reverse is true as well: the theological employment of such categories says something about them. The simple fact of use in discussion of divine matters, for example, may give the stamp of approval to the social and political practices to which reference is made: thus, talking of God's status in terms of kingship may be a way of making kings into gods. Or, as in the antimonarchy strains of the Hebrew Bible, it may be a way of deflating the very notion of human kingship by reserving legitimate kingship to God alone. The manner, moreover, in which the associations of such terms are altered in theological use provides a critical commentary on what is problematic about the social and political practices of the times. If Jesus is Lord but, unlike human lords, he humbly serves others at dire cost to himself, that says something about the true character of lordship and about why we should be disappointed with every human lord we know.

Contemporary theologies of the Trinity exhibit both these general reasons why all theology tends to be political theology. Theologians are enlisting support for particular kinds of community – say, egalitarian, inclusive communities, in which differences are respected – through arguments over the Trinity. They are enjoining a political fight on cultural grounds: the meaning of the Trinity is where political disagreements over the shape of church life, and over the social and governmental policies Christians should endorse, are engaged. The Trinity seems an apt site for such engagement not simply because a Christian way of life is highly invested in how this belief is understood. (Indeed, many theologians think they first have to demonstrate, against the likes of Kant and Schleiermacher, that the Trinity *is* a matter for such practical investment.) The Trinity is an especially apt site because of the ease with which its meaning might be developed by incorporating the terms of present political debate. These debates (e.g. between liberals and communitarians, between egalitarians and those favoring a more hierarchical diversity of roles in social organization, and between advocates of economic democracy and those of free market policy) have at their root questions about the relationship between a community and its members, and about the sort of relationships among members that make for community. The unity and diversity of the Trinity might be explicated in such terms – especially when the meaning of "person" in traditional trinitarian discussion is pushed in the direction of modern senses of person – such as a conscious subject oriented to others (Boff 1988: 89, 112–13; O'Donnell 1988: 10–15). The relation between one substance and three persons in the Trinity can be unpacked in terms of a relation between a community and its members; relations among the three trinitarian persons, in terms of the internal constitution of community; etc. As a result of these efforts of interpretation, the Trinity becomes, in turn, a way of commenting on common, very basic political questions of the day. Does community emerge from relations among all its members, rather than from top-down imposition? Are such relations, ideally, among equals? How are communal and personal identities reconciled? Is the individual nothing more than its relations with others in community? Can genuine community be formed out of self-enclosed, atomistic individuals? Or does community, at the other extreme, require a monolithic, closely guarded cultural identity and the suppression of differences among its members?

What the Trinity says about all this is not entirely clear. Although theological judgments here seem quite simple – for example, egalitarian relations among the triune persons suggest the propriety of egalitarian human relations – figuring out the sociopolitical lessons conveyed by the Trinity is a task fraught with complexities and perils. The rest of this chapter systematically discusses these complexities and perils, and suggests how best to meet their challenges, in hopes that here, too, the case of the Trinity might be exemplary, to the benefit of political theologies generally.

Inflated Claims for the Trinity

Many contemporary theologies overestimate the progressive political potential of the Trinity. Monotheism, it is alleged, supports monolithic identities and authoritarian forms of government in which power is held exclusively by a single leader or group; while an internally diverse triune God, whose persons share equally with one another, avoids these dangers (Peterson 1935; Moltmann 1991: 192–202; Boff 1988: 20–4). Overlooked in such a simple contrast are the complexities of theological claims, their fluidity of sense, and complications in their application for political purposes. Thus, contrary to the charges against it, monotheism (particularly when understood to deny that divinity is a general category of things differing from one another in degree) can suggest that no one shares in divinity and that no one can therefore stand in as God's representative. Or, where representatives are permitted, these might be identified with the whole of a people and not simply with their leadership. Moves like these were probably historically instantiated among some ancient Israelites (Assmann 1992: 75–6). Trinitarianism, moreover, is not often – to say the least – historically associated with an egalitarian politics and respect for diversity within community. Among the many possible reasons for this is surely the ambiguous political potential of many aspects of trinitarian theology.

Thus, the Trinity easily suggests the appropriateness of rule by three absolute co-rulers, or (more likely, given the historical paucity of triumvirates) the propriety of a single absolute ruler identified with the Word, the person of the Trinity associated with cosmic order and stability. Both ideas occurred, for example, to Eusebius in his "Oration in Praise of the Emperor Constantine" (1890). While Eusebius subordinated the Word to the Father, these particular political inferences do not depend on that idea and would only be exacerbated by a more "orthodox" doctrine. In the more "orthodox" case the emperor would simply be identified, not with a subordinate principle executing the Father's will, but with a Word equal to the Father himself.

Moreover, many aspects of orthodox trinitarianism apart from those emphasized by political progressives seem politically awkward on their face. Thus, contrary to respect for difference, divine persons are equal to one another because in some very strong sense they are the same: "The Son is everything that the Father is except that the Son is not the Father" – that is, all the predicates assigned to the Father in virtue of the Father's divinity can also be assigned to the Son, just not those like "Father" that specify a distinction of person. (The oneness or unity of the Trinity is often given the same sort of basis – i.e. identity of substance, concretely rather than generically understood – although there are other ways of making that point – e.g. perichoresis, indivisibility, and the priority of the Father in the generation of the other two persons.) Short of tritheism, it is difficult to argue that divine persons are as different from one another as human persons are. Moreover, the various biblical and liturgical *taxes* or orders among divine persons, no matter how complex they are – the classic order of generation and mission (Father–Son–Spirit), along with return to the Father (Son–Spirit–Father), now commonly joined in contemporary theology by Father–Spirit–Son – still differentiate persons by their place within the order. They are therefore ripe for justification of hierarchy: for example, they easily support claims that people are equal despite the disparity of their assigned social roles. The traditional ideas that divine persons are constituted by their relations, and are indivisible in being and act, are also hard to square with a politics fostering the agency of persons effaced in relations with dominant members of society.

While all the views just mentioned are associated with the so-called immanent Trinity, the turn by most contemporary political theologians to the Trinity in its workings with respect to the world as biblically recounted – that is, a turn to the economic Trinity – has its own downsides. Thus, New Testament accounts of Jesus' relations with his Father are much more subordinationalist in flavor than accounts of the immanent Trinity usually are (see e.g. John 14: 28; Mark 13: 32, 10: 18; Luke 18: 18; Matt. 19: 16): Jesus prays to the Father, subordinates his will to the Father, defers to the Father, seems ignorant on occasion of what only the Father knows, etc. This sort of hierarchical relation between Son and Father very obviously suggests the propriety of human hierarchy (as it did, infamously, in Karl Barth's treatment of relations between men and women in the *Church Dogmatics* III, 4 [1961]). Moreover (in contrast to the immanent Trinity), the biblical account of the economic Trinity easily promotes a politically problematic characterization of the nature of the relation between Son and Father: as one of obedience (to the Father's mission, under orders from the Spirit) and of self-sacrifice (death on the cross), if not outright self-evacuation (see von Balthasar 1992: 183–91; Ratzinger 1969: 132–5).

Finally, in both the immanent and the economic Trinity, gendered imagery has enormously problematic political ramifications. Even in perhaps the best-case scenario, where absolutely equal trinitarian persons of unassigned gender are the basis for political conclusions, the essential relatedness of those persons can lead to heterosexism. The importance of differences between male and female for the identity of human persons is presumed and simply substituted within a trinitarian account of the essential relatedness of persons to suggest that the identity of woman is essentially constituted in relation to a male counterpart (Volf 1996: 187).

Clearly, then, trinitarianism can be every bit as dangerous as monotheism; everything depends on how that trinitarianism (or monotheism) is developed and applied. Insisting on the inherent privilege of trinitarianism inclines one to overlook the progressive political potential of Judaism and Islam, and promotes an oddly sharp distinction between Christian trinitarianism and monotheism. It also prompts a highly restrictive sense of what trinitarianism is: trinitarian positions that are not associated with a progressive politics must not really be trinitarian, or their trinitarianism has somehow been severely vitiated. (Moltmann, I think, drifts in all three directions [1991]; LaCugna in the last [1991].)

Ignoring the point that trinitarianism can be every bit as dangerous as monotheism lulls politically progressive trinitarian theologians into lazy platitudes and a false sense of complacency. The point is not that a politically progressive trinitarianism is impossible (or even inadvisable relative to non-trinitarian alternatives), but that such a theology is hard work to produce and must be vigilantly maintained against the ineradicable possibility of non-progressive uses. The only trinitarianism that is clearly more politically progressive than (some forms of) monotheism is trinitarianism within a very specific range of interpretations and modes of application. Indeed, those lauding the political merits of trinitarianism over strict monotheism eventually make clear that this holds only for trinitarianism when *properly* understood and employed – in other words, for the sort of trinitarianism they are actively trying to construct. These theologians systematically try to modify as many as possible of the politically problematic aspects of trinitarianism I have identified. Thus, Moltmann and Volf argue that the persons of the Trinity are not simply constituted by their relations without remainder. Following Moltmann, politically progressive trinitarian theologians tend to downplay the *taxes* among the trinitarian persons by highlighting the perfectly reciprocal perichoretic relations among the persons: the Father is in the Son just as the Son is in the Father, etc. And these perichoretic relations, instead of identity of substance, are made the basis of the Trinity's unity.

The theological merits of these political theologies therefore hinge on the strength of the arguments for such theological moves, a challenge which I think, so far at least, progressive trinitarian theologians have not often adequately met. Inflated confidence in the progressive potential of trinitarianism per se might be doing some damage here, too. Claims for the inherent progressive potential of trinitarianism can amount to a kind of a priori protective strategy, deflecting attention from the fact that progressive theologians are required to assume such a burden of proof for the specific accounts of the Trinity they offer.

These moves in trinitarian theology cannot be primarily based, moreover, on the fact that their espousal would favor a progressive politics, without incurring the complaint of ideological pandering. Indeed, the more arguments for a trinitarian position have such political grounds, the more trinitarian commentary on political matters becomes uninformative as well: that is, what the Trinity tells one about politics is no more than what one already believes about politics (see Kilby 2000: 442–3). While few trinitarian theologians would admit as much, the political advantages of certain views of the Trinity still seem to make up for weaknesses of argument more than they should. Inexplicably to my mind, for example, no one has adequately addressed how the heavy load that perfectly reciprocal perichoresis carries in these theologies is compatible with their equally strong emphasis on the biblical economy, in which Jesus seems clearly to be acting in a non-mutual relation of subordination to the Father (the Son prays to the Father, but the Father doesn't pray to the Son; the Son does the will of the Father, but the Father doesn't do the will of the Son, etc.).

From God to Humans

The major complication for trinitarian political theologies is to determine how to move from a discussion of God to a discussion of human relations when drawing political implications from the Trinity (see Volf 1998a: 191–200; 1998b: 403–7). How exactly does a description of the Trinity apply to us? Three main problems arise here.

First of all, what the Trinity is saying about human relations is unclear because the meaning of the terms used of the Trinity is unclear. Divine persons are equal to one another; but in what sense? The persons are "in" one another; but what does "in" mean here? Divine persons are distinguished from one another in virtue of the character of their relations; but who understands exactly what that character is? So, Hilary of Poitiers: "Begetting is the secret of the Father and the Son. If anyone is convinced of the weakness of his intelligence through failing to understand this mystery . . . he will undoubtedly be even more downcast to learn that I am in the same state of ignorance" (1899: 55, following more felicitous trans. in Boff 1988: 174). What, indeed, does even the language of "person" suggest, if with Augustine we have to say that "the formula three persons was coined, not in order to give a complete explanation by means of it, but in order that we might not be obliged to remain silent" (1956: 92, following more felicitous trans. in Boff 1988: 143). Because God is not very comprehensible to us, and certainly not fully so, discussion of the Trinity, all by itself, seems unable to offer any very specific directives for human relations.

Some theologians would say that the problem here is too great a focus on the so-called immanent Trinity. One can try, it is true, to give a more definite sense to terms used of the Trinity in light of the Trinity's workings in the economy of salvation. One could say, for example, that the unity of the Trinity means the sort of dialogical fellowship enjoyed by Jesus and the one he calls Father. But unless one purports to know much more about relations among the trinitarian persons than is probably warranted, one is still left with very vague recommendations – about the social goods of equality, a diverse community, and mutual relationships of giving and receiving. All the hard, controversial work of figuring out exactly what any of that might mean – What sort or degree of cultural uniformity is required for community? How far can differences in a unified society go? – seems left up to the ingenuity of the theologian arguing on other grounds. This isn't necessarily a bad thing, to the extent it means that the Trinity cannot give answers to political questions without sociohistorical mediation – that is, without the need for study of the causes and consequences of present political circumstances using the best social, political, and economic theories available. But dangers remain. Should, for example, the theologian try to narrow down the senses of terms used of the Trinity following what he or she thinks those terms mean (or should mean) when used of human persons and societies, the account of the Trinity loses its critical edge on political questions, and seems to have been constructed simply to justify the theologian's prior political views. If one is not to be left with vague generalities, the critical question, again, is how one goes about drawing out the implications of the Trinity for human society.

The second problem is that much of what is said about the Trinity simply does not seem directly applicable to humans; human society could take on the very shape of the Trinity only if people were no longer human. So, for example, it seems bound up with the essential finitude of humans that they can only metaphorically speaking be in one another or have overlapping subjectivities (meaning by that, that when one person acts the other is also acting in virtue of that very fact) as trinitarian persons are said to (Volf 1998a: 209, 211). Human finitude also seems to entail that humans give of themselves so that others may gain, in ways that often bring loss to themselves. In the case of trinitarian persons, to the contrary, their perfect equality is usually thought to involve giving without loss and receiving without increase – the first person of the Trinity does not give all of itself to the second at any cost to itself; and the second does not receive from the first what is not already its own. Finally, human persons cannot be constituted by their relations with others in the strong senses affirmed of trinitarian persons (see Weinandy 2000: 115, 119, 128, 134–5, 140, 207–8). Thus, trinitarian persons do not exist prior to the relations among themselves that make them what they are, as humans do *vis-à-vis* the relations with other humans that shape their characters (so that, for instance, I exist prior to those relationships with duplicitous significant others that make me a distrustful person). Trinitarian persons would not exist were the relations among themselves that make them what they are to end; human beings do – I remain despite the deaths of the people and communities who have most contributed to my character. Trinitarian persons do not become more themselves as their relations with others are extended beyond relations among themselves to the world. When various human beings come into contact with persons of the Trinity they therefore come into contact with all that such trinitarian persons are, with those persons in their fully realized character. Human persons, to the contrary, have characters that are progressively shaped as they relate to different people; any one person to whom one relates therefore sees one only in part. For much the same reason, trinitarian persons relate to one another immediately – without any externality or media that might disguise their true selves. Finitude prevents this in the case of human persons.

Direct translation of the Trinity into a social program is problematic, in the third place, because, unlike the peaceful and perfectly loving mutuality of the Trinity, human society is full of suffering, conflict, and sin. Turned into a recommendation for social relations, the Trinity seems unrealistic, hopelessly naïve, and, for that reason, perhaps even politically dangerous. To a world of violent, corrupt, and selfish people, the Trinity seems to offer only the feeble plaint, "Why can't we all just get along?"

Because of these problems with directly translating the Trinity into a recommendation for human relations, theologians often propose the Trinity as only the "utopian goal" (Boff 1988: 6) or "eschatological destiny" of humans (Volf 1998a: 405). If such a proposal means that human society, short of the eschaton, can only ever approximate the character of the Trinity, that seems right. But this is nevertheless a very odd goal or eschatological destiny if it means, as it still seems to, that we must leave behind what essentially makes us human if we are ever to get there. The proposal also seems to imply that the Trinity as goal or ultimate destiny helps direct transformations of society in the meantime; yet left unanswered is once again the critical question of how the Trinity is to do so given the differences between God and us. How is one to move to bridge the gap? For the same reason, the goal of trinitarian community that we are offered seems almost cruelly quixotic: a treasure is dangled before us with no clue as to how we might get to it from the desperate straits of social relations marked by violent conflict, loss, and suffering.

One strategy for bridging the gap is to supplement the move down from the Trinity, when envisioning human society, with a move from below (Volf 1998a: 200; 1998b: 405–6). That is, using one's understanding of human beings as creatures, one can try to figure out the extent to which human relations can imitate trinitarian ones. The Trinity tells us what human relations should be like ideally; the understanding of humans as creatures tells us what sort of approximation of the ideal we are in fact capable of. Thus, the closest approximation to the perichoretic relations among trinitarian *persons* is the mutual conditioning of personal *characteristics* among humans (Volf 1998a: 211–12). I take on my character as I am influenced by others, just as they take on their character through relations with me. As this example suggests, the danger of such a strategy is that the Trinity fails to do any work. We do not need the Trinity to tell us that human beings condition one another by way of their relationships. We do not even need the Trinity to tell us that persons are catholic in their conditioning by others (Volf 1998a: 212): there is nothing especially trinitarian about the idea that individuals are a microcosm of the whole world's influences. These ideas are platitudes of the philosophical literature and recourse to the Trinity does not seem to be doing anything here to move us beyond them. Presumably, it might, if one asked what *sort* of relations with others should condition personal identity – e.g., loving relations, relations in which the other is concerned for one's own good – but the focus here simply on whether and to what extent human identity is relational deflects attention from that more substantive and less formal question. This oddly formal focus is also a problem for another strategy of bridging the gap between divine and human relations, and has a broader cause, to be addressed in the next section.

This other strategy for bridging the gap is to look at the economic Trinity (Moltmann 1991; LaCugna 1991). The theologian does not have to try to figure out what trinitarian relations would be like with human beings in them by bringing an account of the Trinity together with what he or she knows about the limits of human life. The economic Trinity – how the Trinity acts in saving us – is itself the way that the Trinity is brought closer to what humans are capable of. In other words, in the economy the Trinity appears as a dialogical fellowship of love and mutual service – the kind of Trinity that human beings could imitate. The same goes for sin. The economic Trinity is the Trinity entering a world of sin and death. Apart from any theological speculation, the economic Trinity itself therefore gives a clue to how trinitarian relations should be lived out in a world of sin: those relations have the broken and sorrowful character of a Father losing his own Son by way of a death undergone for the sake of others.

However, because it seeks to close the gap by thinking of trinitarian relations as more like human ones, this strategy has a built-in problem: The closer trinitarian relations seem to human ones, the less the Trinity seems to offer advice about how to move beyond them. We all know what dialogical relations of loving fellowship are like; and that is what the Trinity is too. We all know about the way death severs relationships and about how obedience often comes at the price of sacrifice in troubled times; and now the Trinity also seems intimately familiar with all that. Pushing imaginatively beyond those experiences to something better – something more than a unity of mere will and love, something more than sacrifice – would seem to require the Trinity to be something more too. Without being more, the Trinity's potential for critical, informative commentary is simply deflated. But to the extent the Trinity is more – for example, a perichoretic unity and not one of mere will and love – the usual problem of bridging the gap between human and divine simply reappears unaddressed.

This strategy, curiously, also tends to be insufficiently economic. The focus on relations among trinitarian persons in the economy tends to displace interest in what the Trinity in the economy is trying to do for us. The very point of the economy, in other words, tends to become the character of the relations among the persons of the Trinity as they figure in the economy. So, as Moltmann never tires of emphasizing, one should concentrate on the difference that the economy (e.g. the Incarnation) makes for God. In Moltmann's case this is closely tied up with soteriological concerns: What happens among the trinitarian persons creates a place for the world of suffering and sin to enter the divine life and so be overcome. But this focus on relations among the persons of the Trinity themselves in the economy fuels the temptation to see those relations as the very meaning of salvation. In other words, the idea that human relations should take on their character becomes an end in itself, apart from consideration of what such relations among divine persons are doing – bringing about the end of death, sin, and suffering in human lives.

Do We Model Ourselves on the Trinity or Participate in It?

These problems with the strategy of looking to the economic Trinity seem to be the product of not following through on the basic insight of the strategy: that the economic workings of the Trinity are answering the question of how the Trinity applies to human life. That insight basically means that human beings are not left to their own devices in figuring out what the Trinity means for human relations. The Trinity does not simply offer itself to us as an ideal or model for our imitation and leave it up to us to figure out how divine relations are applicable to humans (for criticisms of the modeling idea see Fiddes 2000; Bauckham 1997: 160–2; McFadyen 1992: 12–14). The Trinity in the economy enters our world, closes the gap itself, to show how human relations are to be reformed in its image.

The usual strategy of looking to the economy fails to keep consistently to this insight whenever it views the economic Trinity as closing the gap by making trinitarian relations more like human ones and thereby providing a more easily imitated model. Rather than thinking about the significance of the economic Trinity for us in that way – as presenting a model we can hope to imitate – one should think of the economic Trinity as closing the gap by incorporating the human within it – first, the humanity of Jesus and then, by way of him, in the power of the Spirit, other humans in all their relatedness (see Tanner 2001: 1–95).

Trinitarian relations need not be like human relations in order for humans to be taken up into them in this way – by being joined with Christ in the Spirit and thereby coming to share in Jesus' own relations with Father and Spirit. Since there is no need to close the gap in that fashion, one avoids the problematic trade-off mentioned earlier: The more trinitarian relations seem close in character to human ones (and therefore relations that human beings could imitate) the less the Trinity tells you anything you did not already know about them. Moreover, it is no longer the fact that the Trinity can be imitated by human beings that offers hope to a world of sin and suffering. Instead, such hope is fueled by the idea that humans will be taken up into trinitarian relations far *different* from anything with which they are familiar as sinful creatures.

Furthermore, the problem of an ideal inaccessible to humans is resolved if human relations come to image trinitarian ones as they are swept up into them, and not as they become like them in and of themselves. Human relations need not somehow become more than human in and of themselves and thereby approximate the Trinity. Human relations, which remain fully human, only image the Trinity as they are joined up with its own life. Humans do not attain the heights of trinitarian relations by reproducing them, but by being incorporated into them as the very creatures they are.

The usual strategy of looking to the economy also lapses into the view that we are to model human relations on the Trinity when it fails to follow the economy of the Trinity's workings for us all the way down. That is, it stops with relations among trinitarian persons in the economy by making them a model for human ones rather than following through on what the economy of the Trinity is itself suggesting about human relations. If one looks at the full economy and avoids isolated attention to the trinitarian persons, Jesus' relations with Father and Spirit do not appear in any obvious way to be the model for relations *among humans*. They are, instead, the sort of relations that humans are to have with Father and Spirit, as human beings come to be united with Christ, through the Spirit, and share in his life. The way the persons of the Trinity relate to one another over the course of Jesus' life, relations among the divine persons in which we are to share by being united with Christ in the Spirit, do bring with them changed relations among human beings. But one has to look at the concrete character of Jesus' way of life to see their shape. Jesus' relations with Father and Spirit make his whole life one of worship, praise, and faithful service to the Father's mission of bringing in the kingdom; that is to be the character of our lives too, both in and out of the church, as we come to share Jesus' life. Such a life of worship, praise, and faithful service to the mission of the Father involves a life for others of the sort that Jesus exhibited in his relations with other people. Jesus' relations with other people, then – the character of the basileia, in short – is the shape of human relations that the economy of the Trinity itself specifies. Jesus' way of life toward other people as we share in it *is* the trinitarian form of human social relations. That way of life is what the trinitarian relations as they show themselves in the economy – Jesus' praying to the Father and serving the will of the Father in the power of the Spirit – amount to in human relational terms.

Since the kingdom to come, as it is inaugurated in Jesus' own life, establishes the shape of human relations that the economic workings of the Trinity itself specifies, gone are the merely formal and abstract preoccupations typical of trini-tarian political theology. One cannot stop with attacks on individualism or on monolithic social identities and not consider the character of society more con-cretely. Even nonindividualistic, internally diverse communities must be subject to further critical scrutiny with reference to the goals to which they are dedicated. Are those communities dedicated to anything like what Jesus was dedicated to in his relations with other people? Are they dedicated to policies ensuring the comprehensive well-being of all their members, especially the dis-empowered, following Jesus' own concern for the physical and spiritual well-being of the poor and suffering? Are they dedicated to breaking all analogues of the purity codes distinguishing the righteous from sinners, which Jesus opposed in their disadvantaging of the most vulnerable? And so on.

This strategy of thinking of the economic Trinity in terms of our sharing in it rather than modeling ourselves on it does nothing as it stands to resolve prob-lems of gendered language. (For a very good effort in that regard, see Johnson 1992.) But it does address the remaining problems mentioned earlier in this chapter. For example, the incomprehensibility that holds especially for the imma-nent Trinity is no problem because the Trinity provides us with direction for our social relations by other means – ultimately, by way of the shape of Jesus' own life. The present strategy of looking to the economy avoids, moreover, both the temptation among politically progressive theologians to undercut Jesus' subor-dination to the Father in the economy and the temptation among less progres-sive ones to play it up. There is no point to either, because Jesus' relations with Father and Spirit are not the model for human relations; they are what our relations to the triune God are to be like – relations of worship and service to the Trinity's economic mission; relations that subordinate humans to God in a perfectly appropriate way.

Finally, because of the differentiated way in which human relations are formed in the image of the Trinity, one need not fear that basing political rec-ommendations on the Trinity will produce either an unrealistic politics or an uncritically complacent one. Human relations do not share in the relations among the persons of the Trinity in an undifferentiated way – as if the Trinity were simply a group of friends expanding their social circle to include new members (Bauckham 1997: 160–1). Humans do not, in other words, have the same sort of relationship with members of the Trinity as the persons of the Trinity do, let alone that kind of relationship with one another.

Jesus himself, in this differentiated view, does not have the kind of relation-ship with Father and Spirit in the economy as the Word considered apart from the Incarnation does. Unlike (for instance) the perfect equality of trinitarian persons considered apart from the economy, Jesus, the Word incarnate, subor-dinates himself to the Father – he obeys the Father at least apparently against his own best interests, seems dependent on Father and Spirit for his Resurrec-tion, etc. – in ways that befit the fact that he is not simply the Word but a human being as well. (This is a very old idea, with origins in early church struggles against Arius; see e.g. Athanasius [1957].) Perichoresis becomes dialogical fellowship in the economy because Jesus is indeed a finite human being and not merely the Word who enjoys perichoretic relations with the other members of the Trinity. Jesus appropriately acts in a not perfectly mutual dependence on Father and Spirit, because, once again, of the real differences that his humanity makes for his relations with them. Human beings, similarly, share in the Trinity as human beings with the differences that human life makes. And, unlike Jesus, they do so as mere humans: They share in it by way of Christ and not in his place, as if they were his equivalent.

All these differences account for the fact that the human relations that image the Trinity do not have exactly the same character as the so-called immanent Trinity (those relations are perichoretic, while our relations with one another are not), or as the economic Trinity (Jesus' whole life from the very beginning is lived in perfect correspondence to the Father's will for the kingdom, while our lives come only secondarily into an imperfect correspondence with it, because of our finitude and our sin), or even as Jesus' relations with others (he has a superior position in relating to other people in that he saves them while we do not). Human relations, in short, image the Trinity in ways appropriate to the finitude and sinfulness of human creatures. Political recommendations on the basis of the Trinity can therefore be realistic when carefully gauged in these ways to the character of humans following a highly differentiated theological account of the economy. Yet uncritical complacency is also overcome by knowledge of the heights of relationships above our own in character, heights of relationships that our relations with one another in themselves can only strive to approximate without ever matching – at the highest, the relations among perfectly equal, perichoretic persons swirling in and out of one another without loss or gain in incomprehensible light. Without ever taking on the character of such perfection in and of themselves, human relations will nevertheless gain that height by being united with the Trinity, by coming within the Trinity's own life, as that Trinity itself graciously comes to us into the world.

References

Assman, Jan (1992). *Politische Theologie zwischen Ägypten und Israel*. Munich: Siemens.

Athanasius (1957). "Four Discourses against the Arians." In Philip Schaff and Henry Wace (eds.), *Nicene and Post-Nicene Fathers*, vol. IV. Grand Rapids, Mich.: Eerdmans.

Augustine (1956). "On the Holy Trinity." In Philip Schaff (ed.), *Nicene and Post-Nicene Fathers*, vol. III, Grand Rapids, Mich.: Eerdmans.

Barth, Karl (1961). *Church Dogmatics* III, 4. Edinburgh: T. & T. Clark.

Bauckham, Richard (1997). "Jürgen Moltmann's *The Trinity and the Kingdom of God* and the Question of Pluralism." In Kevin Vanhoozer (ed.), *The Trinity in a Pluralistic Age*, 155–64. Grand Rapids, Mich.: Eerdmans.

Boff, Leonardo (1988). *Trinity and Society*. Maryknoll, NY: Orbis.

Eusebius of Caesarea (1890). "Oration in Praise of the Emperor Constantine." In Philip Schaff and Henry Wace (eds.), *Nicene and Post-Nicene Fathers*, vol. I. New York: Christian Literature Co.

Fiddes, Paul (2000). *Participating in God*. Louisville, Ky: Westminster/John Knox.

Hilary of Poitiers (1899). "On the Trinity." In W. Sanday (ed.), *Nicene and Post-Nicene Fathers*, vol. IX. New York: Scribners.

Johnson, Elizabeth (1992). *She Who Is*. New York: Crossroad.

Kilby, Karen (2000). "Perichoresis and Projection." *Blackfriars* 81: 956, 432–45.

LaCugna, Catherine (1991). *God for Us*. New York: HarperCollins.

McFadyen, Alistair (1992). "The Trinity and Human Individuality." *Theology* 95, 10–18.

Moltmann, Jürgen (1991). *The Trinity and the Kingdom*. New York: HarperCollins.

O'Donnell, John (1988). The Trinity as Divine Community. *Gregorianum* 69: 1, 5–34.

Peterson, Erik (1935). *Der Monotheismus als politisches Problem*. Leipzig: Jakob Hegner.

Ratzinger, Joseph (1969). *Introduction to Christianity*. London: Burns & Oates.

Tanner, Kathryn (1992). *The Politics of God*. Minneapolis: Fortress.

——(1997). *Theories of Culture: A New Agenda for Theology*. Minneapolis: Fortress.

——(2001). *Jesus, Humanity and the Trinity*. Minneapolis: Fortress.

Volf, Miroslav (1996). *Exclusion and Embrace*. Nashville: Abingdon.

——(1998a). *After our Likeness*. Grand Rapids, Mich.: Eerdmans.

——(1998b). " 'The Trinity is our Social Program': The Doctrine of the Trinity and the Shape of Social Engagement." *Modern Theology* 14: 3, 403–23.

von Balthasar, Hans Urs (1992). *Theo-Drama III*. San Francisco: Ignatius.

Weinandy, Thomas (2000). *Does God Suffer?* Notre Dame, Ind.: University of Notre Dame Press.

CHAPTER 23

Creation

Peter Scott

We have to say that no society is too poor to afford a right order of life. And no society is so rich that it can afford to dispense with a right order, or hope to get it merely by becoming rich.

Raymond Williams

In its political witness, the church knows well that the doctrine of creation is central to its deliberations to honor the God of Jesus Christ. This is the case because the turn to creation identifies theological issues central to the truth of human life: What is the creaturely context in which humans (and otherkind) are placed? What is human society in Christian perspective and what is its relationship to other ecological communities? Are there normative aspects to be derived from human nature or from human relations to animals? These are some of the central concerns of a doctrine of creation in a political theology. However, despite such importance, creation is one of the least discussed of the doctrinal themes or loci in political theology. Consequently, the practical aspects of the doctrine usually go unnoticed. So what goes wrong when political theology fails to give the doctrine of creation its due?

To fail to speak of creation is to give too great an emphasis to the theme of redemption. "Such a reduction [of theology to soteriology] also thereby cuts the link between redemption and the physical world, society and world history. If theology does not overcome this tendency, it finds it difficult to relate the faith to such issues as ecological concerns, our vocation in society, and the manifestations of God's Spirit in the world's history" (Hefner 1984: 272). In other words, a lack of attention paid to the theme of creation leads to a political theology that is insufficiently *materialist*. Matter matters to Christianity: how bodies, human and nonhuman, exist in relation to each other in a range of technological, economic–ecological, social, political, and cultural realms is – or should be – central to a present-day Christian political theology. These realms include the authority of political governance: the exercise of the legal, administrative, executive and parliamentary, and enforcement powers of the modern nation-state.

Understood in this way as materialist, political theology does not treat redemption as being saved *from* creation. That would be a misunderstanding of Christian mission. Instead, political theology speaks of the fulfillment *of* creation. Christian testimony concerning creation thereby speaks of the assumption of (human) nature in Christ; of the securing of the unity and diversity of (human and nonhuman) creatures as a constructive task; of the nature and direction of political orderings; and of the persistent demand for the identification and rejection of idols. However, an opposite temptation must be avoided: creation should not be understood as itself a redemptive process. The Resurrection of Jesus Christ is the vindication of creation, not the leaving of creation to its own devices. That is, in any comprehensive consideration of creation for political theology, the relation between creation and *eschatology* also demands sustained attention.

Although little noticed, the theme of creation is implicitly present in all discourses in political theology. This is the case because creation is, as I have already suggested, a way of speaking theologically about political and social idols, about the unity and diversity of creatures, of the relations between social groups and the human race, and of the relations between humanity, nature, and otherkind (animals). Put differently, creation addresses the issue of the organization of bodies. Such political organization of creatureliness invokes discussion of the character of the *imago dei* (humans beings as made in the image of God), natural law, and the orders of creation. The relation between human creatures and other creatures is also considered here, especially the matter of stewardship. These theological notions have been fashioned by Christian tradition to give some account of the ways in which human beings may be understood as related one to another and to their natural context.

This is complex enough. However, the matter is in truth yet more difficult. The doctrine of creation raises the problem of *order* in Christian perspective: how that order is to be understood, in what sense that order is settled or alterable, and against what norms such order is to be judged and developed. The doctrine of creation is invoked in this double sense – order and its norms of judgment – whenever political matters are raised in or by theology. We may characterize this discussion as the *theological problem of political and natural order in the ordering of creatureliness*.

In sum, from the perspective of the doctrine of creation political theology directs its attention to political orders: their present constitution, normative status, and development. Because of this reference to order, often in actual practice construed conservatively, political theology is suspicious of the notion of creation (Westhelle 1998). The suspicion is well-founded. Yet the proper response must be to face these theological difficulties. Indeed, the doctrine of creation, suitably interpreted, offers pertinent resources to a political theology.

The Orderings of Creation

There are two fundamental issues, then, in the consideration of creation in a political theology. First, with which political orderings are Christian communi-

ties confronted, and how are these to be related to the being, action, and purposes of the Creator God? Second, in that creation is always a normative concept,
how is the goodness of creation to be understood? I develop each of these points
in turn.

To understand a doctrine of creation in relation to a political order is, first, to
grasp that order as a political unity in relation to God. We are dealing here with
"Human existence in its totality, because it [the doctrine of creation] always sees
man [*sic*] as standing in a relationship to God" (Prenter 1967: 250). Second,
such an order is to be understood as applicable universally (Hardy 1996: 190).
It is in the doctrine of creation that order is first grasped theologically as related
to God and as universal. A political order is thereby legitimated in a double sense
by an appeal to creation: as validated by God, and as universal. "The God-
ordained order of things" should thereby be understood as having this double
reference. Fascist appeals for support from Christianity invoke the doctrine of
creation in this way but with a restrictive amendment. For example, for the
regime of National Socialism (Germany, 1933–45) under Hitler, not only was a
racist ordering referred to God in which "the other" (the Jew, the communist,
the Gypsy, the homosexual, the mentally disabled) is excluded; additionally, and
just as problematically, the division of the unity of the human race into separate
and identifiable peoples was affirmed as part of God's ordering as universal. The
unity of the human race is conceived in terms of its divisions and such cutting
is proposed (wrongly) as God's blessing in creation. To oppose such fascism theologically thereby requires a relating of political orderings in their totality to God
which understands worldly divisions between peoples always in terms of that
primary and antecedent theological division between creatures and the Creator.
This, as the unhappy recent history of Christianity in Europe indicates (consider
here also apartheid South Africa), is not easily done.

We now may be at a sufficient distance from the Second World War to offer a
cogent theological appraisal. Now consider a different example: globalization.
How should globalization be thought of in the perspective of a doctrine of creation, as related to the Creator God? A benign reading might argue that trade is
a part of the basic – universal – conversation of humanity and that its extension is likely to benefit all participants, if not equally (Sen 1999; see also chapter
33 on "Globalization" by Peter Sedgwick in this volume). A more cautious
reading would argue that the economic and ecological aspects of such intensification of trade require careful attention, together with an account of whether
people participate in such global processes unequally (or not). I do not plan to
argue the matter out here. What, however, is clearly indicated is that a theological account of the present global order is required that is attentive to universal
and normative aspects: as universalizing, does globalization advance or impede
the goodness of God in and by the world? Is this new world order fundamentally
disordered in relation to the purposes of God?

There are, of course, different sorts of order and different modes of orientation. For the purposes of political theology, we may distinguish the following: the

ecological, the economic, the socioethical, the legal and political, and the cultural. There is a "natural" givenness to the ecological order that marks it as different from the others. However, the contrast should not be drawn too sharply: as Karl Marx noted, human beings make history but not in circumstances of their own choosing. The economic, the socioethical, and the cultural should be understood as social structures in and through which human life is made possible and renewed. It is the legal and political that are perhaps most easily altered. Their alteration, however, results in the least significant changes to a specific society.

We find ourselves already in the second issue of the doctrine of creation, as set out above: the goodness of creation. In theological usage, order is always oriented on God's goodness. Which political orders may be understood as in conformity with the goodness of God's creation?[1]

To answer this question, we must first note that human beings secure their basic needs, reproduce their society, and establish satisfying relationships through a social praxis involving all the orders listed above. Such human activity is always carried through according to a norm. As ordered, human life is oriented on goodness and thereby requires a norm for the (partial, anticipatory) realization of that goodness. In sum, human society is always – at least to some extent – purposive. (A certain sort of political liberalism would – wrongly – deny this.) And a norm for goodness is required to guide such purposiveness. The issue for a political theology is how the notion of God's goodness embedded in the doctrine of creation functions as a political norm. How is this norm established, and by which theological criteria? Does the norm operate in liberatory or oppressive ways? Does the norm invoke a static order, or a dynamic one?

Westhelle is right, therefore: political theology should be suspicious of the doctrine in that by appeal to creation justifications of unjust political orderings are smuggled into theology. Such orderings are then ascribed to the goodness of God. Moreover, the transcription of God's life in the life of the creature, Jesus of Nazareth, may also be understood as affirming unjust orderings rather than – as is properly the case – opposing them.

Creation, History, and Covenant

An agenda emerges: the doctrine of creation provides a theological context for the consideration of political norms of goodness in the determination of what is the case universally, and by which the polity is referred to God. To develop this point, some account of the origins of the doctrine is required, as well as a reading of its political implications, especially in connection with covenant.

How might a Christian doctrine of creation be construed? First, creation is the free, unconstrained act of God. Creation is to be understood not as necessary but as contingent: traditionally, this rule has been glossed as *creatio ex nihilo* [creation out of nothing]. In other words, God creates out of God's freedom and will;

there is no pre-existing material nor any resistance to God's will. Creation in its entirety is the result of God's action. "God's relation to the world is like this: not a struggle with pre-existing disorder that is then moulded into a shape, but a pure summons" (Williams 2000: 68). Creation is the free decision of the social God: a gratuitous action. God has no "need" of creation; creating is rather an action of God's love. Against pantheism, we may conclude, the world is contingent, that is, not necessary; it is thereby truly other to God. When God wills to be not-God, creation comes to be. As such, this is the first "political" act: "God does not want to be everything" (Pohier 1985: 266). In such a "political" act, God makes room by means of a desire not to be everything, which eventuates in a movement outward that we call the world. In making room, creatures come to be in an ordering in time and space. If creation is the first salvific act (Gutiérrez 1988: 86–7), it is founded in the first "political" act: a Godly willing that others be.

Second, the order of creation is dependent on God's act. The act of creation is not to be understood as only concerned with a beginning but also with the middle and the end of the world. Nor is creation to be understood as an immanent, creative process; the notion of *natura naturans* is rejected by mainstream Christianity. In sum, the world is internally related to God: it exists, and continues to exist, on account of God's loving purposes. An account of creation that is externally related to God, as in deism's interpretation of creation as machine, is ruled out.

It is likely that the theme of *creatio ex nihilo* has its source in Israel's understanding of the activity of God in the covenant. For example, Rowan Williams traces the theme of creation out of nothing to Israel's return from Babylonian captivity:

> This deliverance, decisive and unexpected, is like a second Exodus; and the Exodus in turn comes to be seen as a sort of recapitulation of creation. Out of a situation where there is no identity, where there are no names, only the anonymity of slavery or the powerlessness of the ghetto, God makes a human community, calls it by *name* (Is. 40–55), gives it or restores to it a community. But this act is not a *process* by which shape is imposed on chaos; it is a summons, a call which establishes the very possibility of an answer. (Williams 2000: 67–8)

Moreover, in mainstream Christian tradition, there can be no discussion of covenant or deliverance except by reference to Jesus Christ (cf. John 1: 1–18). Thus creation is always understood to be an event related to Incarnation. For the movement of God in Incarnation has to do with the liberation and transformation of creation. In other words, creation is understood to be a trinitarian action: creation is the external action of the triune God.

A tendency to contrast creation with history should, in this perspective, be rejected. It is indeed tempting to see creation as a backdrop to human endeavors. There are many inducements in contemporary Western culture to support such a view. Instead, creation should always be seen as co-present (Hardy 1996:

189), as in-between, in every human endeavor. Creation itself has a history which is profoundly interwoven with the history of humanity. Indeed, such a formulation does not do justice to the matter: there are not two histories – the one of creation, the other of humanity – but instead a single history in which humanity and nature are co-participants (Scott 2003). Moreover, if creation is understood as a static backdrop, a more conservative account of history than is required by Christian theology may result. For a political theology, creation should not be collapsed into protology.

Creation on this view is historical and salvific: ordered and receiving its purposes from the salvific purposes of God. In other words, creation is other to God (created out of nothing), settled and yet open. The ordering proposed here is determinate (it is the gift of God in creation) but not fixed, properly proportioned yet receiving its realization from outside itself. The combination of these aspects requires that creation be understood as stable yet open to reorientation. The relation of these aspects is of decisive importance. Why so? To stress the order at the expense of the openness is to apply to creation for the legitimation of "what is." To overstress the openness is to claim that creaturely structures have their order only by imputation and not in the manner of the receipt of a gift, thereby denying their goodness. The first stresses the time-invariant features of creation, the second the time-variant aspects. This is not a distinction between space and time but between those aspects which enjoy regularity through time and those forms that change more rapidly. In terms of the earlier discussion, in a political order the time-invariant aspects refer us to the ecological and then the economic and the time-variant aspects refer to the political and legal. Getting the relationship right between these two is vital: to overstress the time-invariant aspects can be employed to declare that a social order is poor and fixed and therefore cannot afford justice. Or the time-variant aspects may be overemphasized to claim that change will in and of itself produce justice. As Raymond Williams (1989: 222) notes, both options must be refused.

We now see the reason why political theology tends to be suspicious of the doctrine of creation. To affirm only the time-invariant aspect proposes a static view of the created order: " 'Order' is most often an ideological disguise for domination, repression and persecution. . . . Ideologically, the ultimate appeal to justify order goes back to God's creation" (Westhelle 1998: 149). Or, as Ruether (1983: 85) states, what must be criticized is "the model of hierarchy that starts with non-material spirit (God) as the source of the chain of being and continues down to nonspiritual 'matter' as the bottom of the chain of being and the most inferior, valueless, and dominated point in the chain of command." By contrast, to affirm only the time-variant aspect thrusts the political order into a state of flux in which change is confused with restlessness, goodness with wildness, and in which social agency is denied. What is required is the relating of these two aspects, which anyhow are always mutually implicated.

We have seen already that the origins of the doctrine of creation out of nothing may be traced to the way in which YHWH establishes a community from no-community – in other words, creation indicates "associations of different, interdependent creaturely realms" (Welker 1999: 13) given their purposes by God – and also that the relationship of Creator to creature has determinate content. In Judeo-Christian tradition this relationship is called a covenant. Law, as may be seen in the development of covenant between YHWH and Israel, is central to covenant: the giving of the Mosaic Law at Sinai is the classic case (Exodus 19, 20). Yet such law serves the covenantal promises (and not vice versa): law should then be understood as dynamic, as offering a normative account of order in and through which the responsibilities of the community are shaped and turned outward. In line with such an understanding, Jesus' golden rule makes this shape and movement clear: "So always treat others as you would like them to treat you; that is the Law and the Prophets" (Matt. 7: 12; cf. Luke 6: 31).

What is the relation between creation and covenant in a political theology? In a famous formulation, Barth (1958) argues that the covenant is the internal basis of creation. As such, the covenant is to be understood as the rationale of creation: the "material presupposition" of creation. Creation in turn is interpreted as the external basis of the covenant: creation is not the condition or backdrop of the covenant but indicates that humanity in its nature is destined for the covenant. Goodness is not to be regarded simply as the outcome of a process as if goodness were a property of humanity. Instead, goodness is to be associated with covenant: a promissory agreement which establishes community and engenders trust, and without which social life is profoundly impoverished.

So far I have argued that the doctrine of creation is the theological location for the consideration of social order and of the norm of goodness by which a society must organize itself. Furthermore, the doctrine of *creatio ex nihilo* affirms that the present order is divine gift but should not be considered as fixed. The actuality of covenant reinforces and develops this view: creaturely forms are not denied but rather taken up into the promissory character and ex-centric dynamic of covenantal relations. Now it is time to consider some of the ways in which creation has figured in political theology and to review briefly the animated discussion of ecology in the doctrine of creation.

By Nature

If the creaturely realm has its source in the Creator God, is there sufficient stability in human nature to develop a political ethics? If the doctrine of creation indicates what is the case universally, does the consideration of human nature yield ethical principles for the "universal" organization of bodies in time and space? Enter *natural law* (strictly, natural *moral* law), a tradition of moral inquiry that is especially important within Roman Catholicism. For some of its proponents, this style of moral inquiry is the way in which Christianity engages the secular sphere. Although there are attempts to recover the Christological source of natural law in a trinitarian doctrine of creation (see chapter 4 by Bauerschmidt in this volume) and to stress its scriptural provenance (Porter 1999), one influential tendency seeks instead to stress the independence of natural law thinking from the central soteriological themes in Christianity. The so-called "new natural law," associated with the work of John Finnis and Germain Grisez, eschews a theological metaphysic and prefers to speak of basic human "goods" (for a good introduction, see George 1992) which the human cannot oppose (at least, not without considerable harm).

Natural law speaks of universal human nature in two senses: in terms of reason, and in terms of the "essence" of the human, partly established by certain commonalities that humans share with animals. On the first view, the distinguishing mark of natural law is the use of reason in moral discernment. On such a view, liberation theology's turn to Marxism and feminist theology's turn to gender theory can be seen as operating in the natural law tradition. On the second view, the consideration of what is by nature human goes beyond the use of rationality. It is the nature that human beings share that requires consideration, and that shared nature is not restricted to reason. In other words, humans share certain "natural traits" with animals: self-preservation and securing the basic needs of food and shelter. Furthermore, in its classical formulation in Aquinas (see chapter 4 by Bauerschmidt in this volume), specific human traits are also considered as part of natural law. These include the goods of political community, friendship, and knowing the truth of God. Behind this conviction is a theological point: that natural law is "linked to the image of God, that is, the capacity for moral judgment found in all men and women" (Porter 1999: 17).

For some, to be sure, the use of a particular deductive and physicalist reading of natural law by the magisterium in debates in the ethics of procreation has undermined its appeal. (For a discussion of natural law in the debates on homo/sexuality, see Rogers 1999.) However, its attraction is not far to seek: "the distinction between the natural and the conventional [is used] as a warrant for interpreting human action in the light of the diverse forces that ground and limit it" (Porter 1999: 51). In a period which is focusing on the genetic manipulation of the biological and is concerned to understand and practice ecological relations truly, the concern with biological givens is a helpful emphasis. Indeed, natural law theory has been pressed in ecological directions (Northcott 1996). What is problematic, however, is the discernment and selection required to determine what is by nature human. What is "given," and on whose say-so? The political terrors of the doctrine of creation emerge again: should the order of creation with reference to human nature be interpreted as straightforward, obvious, and static? In other words, the *conservatism* of natural law is deeply worrisome. Moreover, it is not only its conservatism that is problematic: the general level of application at which it operates has tended to deny natural law a critical edge (Hughes 1998: 56) which in turn serves to compound its conservatism.

The problem of natural law's conservatism has been picked up by non-Catholics: for example, Hauerwas (1984: 59) has argued that "too often natural law assumptions function as an ideology for sustaining some Christians' presuppositions that their societies – particularly societies of Western democracies – are intrinsic to God's purposes." Furthermore, Hauerwas argues that natural law thinking falsely poses as universal in ways that encourage violence and obscure the narrative shape and particular source of Christian ethics. Once "the particularity of Jesus, his historicity as God's decisive eschatological actor, has been lost," Hauerwas argues (1984: 56, 61), "violence and coercion become conceptually intelligible from a natural law standpoint." In fairness to natural law, it should be insisted that to articulate a universal standpoint is not to claim, as Hauerwas contends, a position "free from history" but instead to think with the grain of human nature: to ask after the creaturely basis of the unity of humankind and normative principles of right order *from a particular epistemological position*. Moreover, there have been sustained attempts – especially by feminist theologians (Cahill 1996; Parsons 1996) – to articulate a more historical and critical notion of natural law. However, part of Hauerwas' critique abides: whether the notion of nature operative here should not be engaged more fully by the particular identity of the *deus Christianorum* is a matter to which I shall return in the final section.

An analogue of such "natural society" may be found in Protestant theology, in the discussion of *orders of creation*.[2] Of Lutheran provenance (although not exclusively so: see Brunner 1937), the concept of orders of creation specifies those realms of human life in which the Christian and the non-Christian by their common nature as human creatures are placed. Human beings are to be found in specific structures or orders of social existence, established by the Creator God, which are common to all. Although the term itself dates only from the mid-nineteenth century, a Reformation tendency is here properly continued: Luther mentions a range of ordinances or estates, including marriage, politics, and the church. Although there is no settled agreement, the orders are generally thought to include marriage and the family, work, government, and culture (sometimes called community).[3] In some lists, the church is also included, as also the state. Some (Brunner 1937: 212) insist that the state is not a natural form but rather has its source in creation's fallenness, while others (Bonhoeffer 1955: 182) maintain that government is anyway dependent on the prior realities of work and marriage and the family. The orders of creation are profoundly contested, largely on account of their misuse by theologians of the *Deutsche Christen* party during the Nazi period, in which it was argued that "God's order could be discovered in the natural conditions of nation and race, and that his will could be seen in the event of Hitler's seizure of power" (Moltmann 1985: xi).

At issue here is not whether these orders enjoy biblical warrant. Bonhoeffer (1955: 179–84) makes a strong case for their biblical basis, and Prenter (1967: 203) argues that the actualization of the commandment of love to God and neighbor, as presented in Old and New Testaments, takes place "within these definite orders and situations: family, nation, state, vocation, work." Rather, the core issue is the *independence* of these universal structures of human society: are these to be understood theologically as autonomous spheres or as related to the purposes of God in creation and redemption? Are particular structures to be confounded with the will of God and thereby rendered autonomous, or to be construed as open to God's agency? Famously, Bonhoeffer struggled with this issue, finally substituting the term "mandates" for "orders of creation" so as forcefully to indicate that we have to do here with "a divinely imposed task rather than a determination of being" (1955: 179). Earlier, Bonhoeffer argued that from the perspective of the orders almost every circumstance can be defended: "One need only hold out something to be God-willed and God-created for it to be vindicated for ever, the division of man into nations, national struggles, war, class struggle, the exploitation of the weak by the strong, the cut-throat competition of economics" (1970: 161). To overcome such confounding of the will of God with creaturely structures, Bonhoeffer proposed to speak of "orders of preservation": that is, the orders are to be placed within a Christological–eschatological horizon.

Such orders of preservation "exist only as long as they are open for the revelation in Christ"; indeed, any order can be dissolved "for the sake of the one who builds up." Interestingly, in the terms established by this essay, what Bonhoeffer seeks to do – although these two moves are not clearly distinguished – is to insist on the universality of these structures and also to develop a Christological norm of goodness for discerning true and false orderings. Explicitly arguing against the self-sufficiency of any political order, Bonhoeffer implicitly queries the status of the modern nation-state. An alternative theological move – different, that is, from Bonhoeffer's Christological perspective – will be explored in the final section: a trinitarian doctrine of creation indicates both universal scope and a norm of goodness.

Ecology

In that human relations with the nonhuman present aspects of creatureliness, the crisis in the ecological relations between humanity and its environment is an appropriate topic for the doctrine of creation. There is no consensus in ecological theology on how best to engage these concerns theologically: how universality and norms of goodness are established is contested. Of special importance are ecofeminist concerns: "male domination of women and domination of nature are interconnected, both in cultural ideology and in social structures" (Ruether 1993: 2) – how are these reproduced in the cultural ideology of "malestream" (Elisabeth Schüssler Fiorenza) theology, and how are these dominations to be resisted?

Broadly, two tendencies in ecological theology may be discerned (see Scott 2003). The first tendency contends that mainstream or traditional Christianity requires redevelopment in order to engage the crisis in human relations with nonhuman nature. This tendency often depends heavily on extra-Christian resources – process philosophy or the "common creation story" told by the natural sciences, for example – for its constructive effort to overcome Christianity's anthropocentrism (and associated androcentrism). A second tendency is reconstructive: mainstream Christian commitments – usually either Incarnation or the concept of *imago dei* – may with suitable revision be recommended as indicating the scope and normative shape of Christian responsibility in an ecological crisis. *Stewardship* is here an important theme.

An important theological issue emerges: in the history of Christianity, personalistic description has been applied to both God and humanity. Thereby a tendency emerges in which humanity is understood as *other* than nature. God and humanity have moral, volitional capacities (albeit they have these differently) that nature does not share. Thus nature is that which is operated upon by God and humanity. There remains, of course, a crucial ontological distinction between humanity and God. Yet a secondary distinction emerges: between humanity and "nature." "Nature is not conceived primarily as man's proper home and the very source and sustenance of his being," writes Kaufman (1972: 353), "but rather as the context of and material for teleological activity by the (nonnatural) wills working upon and in it."

In addressing this secondary distinction between humanity and nature, a range of theological issues may be identified. First, in any attempt to reconfigure human beings within the universality of ecological laws, is the particularity of Jesus Christ a resource or a difficulty? For McFague (1987, 1993) the answer is clear: the concept of Incarnation is transferred from the doctrine of Christ to the doctrine of God. In the transfer, it is substantially transformed in order to indicate God's pantheist presence in and to the world. What remains unclear, in my view, is whether the theological aspect of this development can be sustained: to propose that the world should be understood as the "body of God" implicitly construes a naturalistic interpretation of nature as the image of God. Should the ubiquity of God be construed in this fashion in terms of a philosophical naturalism? Evidence of the impact of such a construal can be seen in the employment of such terms as "norm" and "paradigm" as descriptions of Jesus Christ. As a direct consequence, creation is no longer determined to be in and through Christ. In sum, the particularity of Jesus is not understood as the content of God's relation to the world but instead as an instance or result of that relation.

Second, how to understand the immanence or presence of God is much debated. The aim of the attempt to reconstrue the relation of God to the world is laudable: to overturn those hierarchies of value in which normative status is given to the (male) human. Caught up in this discussion is the theme of the re-enchantment of nature. Should a sense of our deep feelings of connection with nature be understood as contributing to a revalorization of nature? This discussion fails, in my view, to distinguish between the disenchantment of nature and the disgracing of nature. It is true that the ecological crisis is one outcome of the disgracing of nature in which notions of nature have become separated from grace. Through this separation, Western humanity has tended to consider itself as distinct from nature and has acted as if through its actions it gives a *telos* to the nonhuman. Given this separation, the call for the re-enchantment of nature seems ill-judged. Rather than appeal to some enchanting nature, what is instead required, by reference to the actions of the Creator God, is the overcoming of the false and abstractive "making other" of nature.

Third, all ecological theologies stress the theme of relationality: how human societies are to be understood as placed within ecosystems. However, what is the relationship between relationality and responsibility? The standard Christian response to this question is to refer to stewardship. The notion of the Steward is an attempt to reinterpret the presentation of the role of the human in the first chapter of Genesis:

> Then God said, Let us make humankind in our image, according to our likeness; and let them have dominion over the fish of the sea, and over the birds of the heaven, and over the cattle, and over all the wild animals of the earth, and over every creeping thing that creeps upon the earth. . . . God blessed them, and God said to them, "Be fruitful and multiply, and fill the earth and subdue it; and have dominion over the fish of the sea and over the birds of the air and over every living thing that moves upon the earth." (Gen. 1: 26, 28 NRSV)

The notion of stewardship is, then, an exercise in contextual theology for an ecological age: humanity is not lord of nature, but steward; humanity does not have rights of dominion but the responsibilities of a steward (Hall 1986).

Lack of space precludes detailed discussion here (on all this, see Scott 2003) but there are severe practical and theological difficulties with the concept of stewardship that are probably fatal. Certainly, there does appear to be a managerial aspect to the notion, in a fashion that downplays the sheer wickedness in human relations with nature. Furthermore, stewardship implies that nature is in itself benign, and does not exhibit any tendencies toward futility – a view at odds with the scriptural witness. Moreover, I suggest that stewardship remains a popular option in the ecotheology literature because it operates as an atonement metaphor, with subjectivist and exemplarist tendencies (for an excellent example, see Hall 1990: 240). This in turn means that these subjectivist and exemplarist aspects are required to provide the norm of goodness, yet in an ontological vacuum. The stress in the consideration of stewardship tends toward the voluntarist, and the economic–ecological realm in which the will is exercised is not carefully explicated. In other words, the demand for responsible action is not related carefully to the relational situatedness of the human. To what, then, is the steward responding beyond an abstract imperative to act in and against an ecological crisis?

The Creation of Political Theology

In theological critique of the created order, two issues persist: Is what is posited as universal order truly universal, and by what norm of goodness is such order informed/transformed? As we have seen, both parts of this issue are often mis-understood. In Nazi Germany, for example, what is universal was applied to the separateness of nations, and the will of God toward goodness was confounded with the political apparatus of the National Socialist state. However, we have also seen that natural law and the orders of creation try to take forward the central Christian commitment in the realm of politics: what God created is universal and good, and should be employed generously in the service of God and neighbor. From such a perspective the church may identify the responsibilities of political agencies and its own responsibilities in relation to these. In ecological discussion, the crisis in ecological relations is understood as universal, but it is disputed whether such universality should be established by reference to the triune God. Nor is there any agreement on which norms of goodness might inform the trans-formation of human society in a more ecologically sustainable direction.

How, then, should the universal goodness of creation be explicated? As intimated already through this essay, I recommend the reworking of the *ex nihilo* tradition: the triune God creates only through a free decision. As triune, this God does not create creatures because this God has needs, or in order to manipulate. There is nothing that this social God needs: God has no "interests." Creation is not thereby some awful Frankenstein-like experiment with life. To be a creature is to be dependent on God, who is for creatures. To identify creatures as *God's* creatures in a shared realm is to say that these are dependent on this God. This is not the dependence of enslavement. It is apt for creatures to be dependent, on God and so on one another and on their environment. We have here the fundamental dependence that enables us to be creatures: recognition in asymmetrical mutuality by the triune One who has no needs (Williams 2000: 67–75).

Dependencies of many sorts, oriented on the triune One who is beyond manip-ulation, are thereby established as universal. Creatures are "ex-centric": orien-tated on one another in receiving and giving. The political task is to tell the difference between good and bad dependencies. Do we live in a society where people can trust that social processes are operated for their good? Are our ways of life built upon trust or built upon competition? In an ecological age we must also ask: Can nonhuman animals trust the processes of this society to work for their good? How are the interests of the nonhuman – interests in life and flour-ishing – to be taken into account? How are nature's goods shared out? To explore these questions is the task of a trinitarian doctrine of creation for a political the-ology.

Notes

1   In considering this matter, we touch on the link between creation and eschatologi-cal consummation: the laboring God is always the finishing God.
2   Space restrictions prevent discussion of the related concept of *common grace*.

3   A feminist critique would rightly argue that the social conditions of the human repro-
    duction of nature should include a critique of the order of marriage and family,
    which is in part the mediation of nature to men.

References

Barth, Karl (1958). *Church Dogmatics* III, 1. Edinburgh: T. & T. Clark.
Bonhoeffer, Dietrich (1955). *Ethics*. London: SCM.
——(1970). *No Rusty Swords*. London: Fontana.
Brunner, Emil (1937). *The Divine Imperative: A Study in Christian Ethics*. London and
    Redhill: Lutterworth.
Cahill, Lisa Sowle (1996). *Sex, Gender and Christian Ethics*. Cambridge: Cambridge Uni-
    versity Press.
George, Robert P., ed. (1992). *Natural Law Theory*. Oxford: Clarendon.
Gutiérrez, Gustavo (1988). *A Theology of Liberation*, rev. edn. London: SCM. (First publ.
    in English 1973.)
Hall, Douglas John (1986). *Imaging God: Dominion as Stewardship*. Grand Rapids, Mich.:
    Eerdmans; New York: Friendship.
——(1990). *The Steward: A Biblical Symbol Come of Age*. Grand Rapids, Mich.: Eerdmans;
    New York: Friendship.
Hardy, Daniel W. (1996). "Creation." In P. B. Clarke and A. Linzey (eds.), *Dictionary of
    Ethics, Theology and Society*, 189–96. London: Routledge.
Hauerwas, Stanley (1984). *The Peaceable Kingdom*. London: SCM.
Hefner, Philip J. (1984). "Creation." In C. E. Braaten and R. W. Jenson (eds.), *Christian
    Dogmatics*, 267–357. Philadelphia: Fortress.
Hughes, Gerald J. (1998). "Natural Law." In B. Hoose (ed.), *Christian Ethics: An Introduc-
    tion*, 47–58. London: Cassell.
Kaufman, Gordon (1972). "A Problem for Theology: The Concept of Nature." *Harvard
    Theological Review* 65, 337–66.
McFague, Sallie (1987). *Models of God*. London: SCM.
——(1993). *The Body of God*. London: SCM.
Moltmann, Jürgen (1985). *God in Creation*. London: SCM.
Northcott, Michael (1996). *The Environment and Christian Ethics*. Cambridge: Cambridge
    University Press.
Parsons, Susan Frank (1996). *Feminism and Christian Ethics*. Cambridge: Cambridge Uni-
    versity Press.
Pohier, Jacques (1985). *God in Fragments*. London: SCM.
Porter, Jean (1999). *Natural and Divine Law*. Grand Rapids, Mich., and Cambridge:
    Eerdmans.
Prenter, Regin (1967). *Creation and Redemption*. Philadelphia: Fortress.
Rogers, Eugene F. (1999). *Sexuality and the Christian Body*. Oxford: Blackwell.
Ruether, Rosemary R. (1983). *Sexism and God-talk*. London: SCM.
——(1993). *Gaia and God*. London: SCM.
Scott, Peter (2003). *A Political Theology of Nature*. Cambridge: Cambridge University
    Press.
Sen, Amartya (1999). *Development as Freedom*. Oxford: Oxford University Press.
Welker, Michael (1999). *Creation and Reality*. Minneapolis: Fortress.

Westhelle, Vitor (1998). "Creation Motifs in the Search for Vital Space." In S. B. Thistlethwaite and M. P. Engel (eds.), *Lift Every Voice*, 146–58. Maryknoll, NY: Orbis.

Williams, Raymond (1989). *Resources of Hope*. London: Verso.

Williams, Rowan (2000). *On Christian Theology*. Oxford: Blackwell.

CHAPTER 24
Christology*

Raymund Schwager

The twentieth century produced various forms of political theology. These theological debates always involved, either directly or indirectly, a discussion of the fundamental category of sacrifice, which has played a central role in all traditional religions and societies. It also shaped the history of Christianity, which has interpreted Jesus' death on the cross mainly through this concept and has accordingly developed a deep spirituality of self-sacrifice. But the tradition of sacrifice has been called into question by Enlightenment thought, which, at its "normative core," aims directly at "abolishing the morality of the publicly imposed *sacrificium*," as Jürgen Habermas judges (Habermas 1998: 152). The experience of National Socialism, which persistently demanded the sacrifice of the individual for the service of the people, and modern depth psychology contributed further to rendering the religious idea of sacrifice deeply ambiguous and problematic, even in Christian circles. This was probably one of the reasons why early types of liberation theology appealed mainly to Jesus' basileia message of the impending kingdom of God, speaking hardly at all about his saving death. Eventually, within Christian theology massive criticism of the theme of sacrifice emerged, arguing that the patriarchal understanding of a God who demands the sacrifice of his son encourages atrocities, as it promotes the tendency of human beings to turn other human beings into victims (Strahm, ed., 1991). This new theology made its mark by speaking out for the victims of all kinds of oppression.

In the context of these and similar problems, Innsbruckian *dramatic theology* (Schwager 1999; Niewiadomski and Palaver 1992; Schwager, Niewiadomski, et al. 1996; Palaver, Guggenberger, et al. 1998) seeks to address the new questions without finding itself in opposition to tradition. It is marked by a criticism of sacrifice and violence, but does not reject talk of Christ's death as sacrifice. It rec-

* Translated by Karl Möller.

ognizes the diversity of social situations and the plurality of modern culture, but intends to stand out against tendencies toward an unchecked pluralism and arbitrariness. It finds itself confronted by scientific-instrumental reason, which, in stark contrast to postmodern thought, makes a universal claim, believing, as a third culture (Brockman 1995), to be able to give answers even to the traditional philosophical and religious questions. In this pluriform context, dramatic theology seeks to do justice both to the concern for plurality and to the scientific claim of universality. For this reason, it distinguishes, in an allusion to traditional drama, five acts in Jesus' mission, each of which has its own characteristics but all of which are also clearly interconnected by means of their interaction, all exhibiting one coherent plot. Dramatic theology is interested not in the unity of a system but in the unity within a dramatic event, in which the connections derive not from logical conclusions but from decisions made by actors responding, positively or negatively, to other actors. Dramatic theology, therefore, does not shy away from aligning itself with the tradition of the great stories.

In what follows, I begin by sketching briefly the dramatic model before attending to some implications for a theological politics that stands out against conventional political theology (Rasmusson 1995).

The Salvation Drama of Jesus

Since the biblical statements about Jesus' pre-existence, Incarnation and virgin birth reflect a post-Easter perspective, the dramatic model begins with his public ministry. Yet it does not follow the kind of historical-critical exegesis that a priori precludes divine action. On the contrary, this model considers the Gospels to be more critical than much traditional historical-critical exegesis because they expose the mechanisms of collective deception and violence, thus also implicating the modern world (as will be shown later in this essay). Dramatic theology thus regards as significant even those texts that are often disregarded as nonauthentic (e.g. Jesus' words of judgment).

Act 1: The basileia message

With his message of the impending kingdom of God, Jesus did not just teach a concept of God but proclaimed, first of all, a new and definitively binding act of God on Israel's behalf. This divine action, which began in the ministry of Jesus, is meant to reveal who Israel's God really is: namely, a God who does not require human sacrifice or an antecedent act of reconciliation in order to be merciful. This God, whom Jesus addresses in most personal fashion as "Abba," turns to sinners out of his own initiative, graciously offering them his forgiveness (the divine love of enemies). In this way, human hearts are to be won over and transformed so as to become able to forgive each other and respond to evil with good (love of enemies, nonviolence), thus uniting as a new people. By the conversion of many individuals, Jesus' ministry aimed at the gathering and creation of the new Israel, which is to give light like a city on a hill, thus attracting the nations.

Act 2: The message of judgment

Although Jesus' message was realized in his healings and could be directly experienced by the people, following a brief span of public enthusiasm it was increasingly rejected. As the anticipated fundamental conversion did not happen, a new situation developed to which Jesus responded with his message of judgment. Yet despite some drastic words of warning, which, taken by themselves, suggest the image of a wrathful God, Jesus did not render his own message of a God of grace ambiguous. In his words about judgment, he rather revealed the inner consequences of rejection, the mechanisms in which people inevitably get caught up if they do not surrender unreservedly to that gracious forgiveness, so that, by judging others, they bring judgment upon themselves. To these people who thought they did not need God's new offer, believing themselves to be essentially righteous, or who regarded the offer of a forgiving grace made to "public sinners" as scandalous, Jesus in his judgment speeches held up the mirror of their own hearts, at the same time confronting them with the image of a wrathful God. He also exposed their inner spirit of lies and violence, which ultimately leads to a total hardening of hearts – and into hell. Jesus thus intended to stir up his audience, yet his judgment discourse only intensified the conflict so that verbal rejection gave way to scuffles and violence.

Act 3: The Crucifixion

The culmination of the conflict saw the actions of all persons involved becoming determined, more and more, by the reactions of the other participants. For the interpreting and participating observer, this poses the danger of overlooking these connections or of confusing the intentional and the merely permitted. To avoid serious misinterpretations, the dramatic model therefore suggests that we differentiate clearly among the various groups and individuals acting in the event of the Crucifixion as well as among their diverse intentions.

The acts of the sinful people   For a brief period of time, different groups that normally quarreled with one another (Pharisees, Sadducees, Zealots, Herodians – Jews and Gentiles) conspired against Jesus, effectively forming an alliance against him. What he had revealed about human nature, he was now accused of himself, and the dark forces he had exposed now fell back on him. Through the people's reactions, he indirectly became the victim of his own actions. He had unmasked lies and was untruthfully accused himself. He had exposed the mechanisms of violence and was put to death by violent means himself. He had openly pointed to the demonic spirit and was accused of having a demonic spirit himself (in other words, of being a blasphemer). He had announced judgment and was now judged himself. Thus he became an accursed person and an outcast, a bearer of sin and – in the modern sense of the term – a scapegoat.

Jesus' conduct   Jesus did not respond to violence with further violence. In fact, he did not even resort to spiritual violence, to cursing or imprecatory prayer, as the prophet Jeremiah had done in a similar situation (Jer. 15: 5; 18: 18–32). His enemies' reaction rather drove him to put into practice his message of enemy love and nonviolence in his own life, and to impart a concrete shape to the dawning kingdom of God in this extreme situation. When he was crucified, he prayed for his enemies and interceded before God on their behalf (Luke 23: 34). His dedication even led him to identify with them in their misery, as his final words, spoken at the Last Supper, had already implied. Thus, despite the rejection it suffered, the dawning kingdom of God remained effective in Jesus' own dedication. And yet he died in dereliction.

The conduct of Jesus' "Abba"   God was silent as his son was drawn into the utmost suffering and loneliness. Yet this does not mean that Jesus' victorious earthly opponents now suddenly became "instruments in the hand of God, agents and executors" of his divine will, as Barth and also Moltmann thought (Barth 1956: 239; Moltmann 1993). In the face of increasing resistance and human judgment, Jesus unswervingly maintained his claim that the true will of God comes to full expression only in his own actions. Yet the silence of this God gave rise to the question of whether God really is as Jesus had taught. On this the subsequent events had to pass judgment.

Act 4: The Resurrection

At issue in the Resurrection is not just life after death but, first of all, the question that had remained unanswered at Jesus' death: Who was right? The crucified, who had appealed to his "Abba"; or his opponents, who had also acted in the name of Israel's God? Through the Resurrection, God now clearly acknowledges the one the people had condemned and crucified, thereby proving himself to be the God of Jesus Christ and thus also to be a God of radical nonviolence. Seen retrospectively in the light of this revelation, the silence of the heavenly Father at the Crucifixion makes perfect sense. If God had intervened in order to save his son, he would have had to act powerfully, thus effacing the freedom of his opponents. He would have contradicted the message of nonviolence through his own acts of power. The permission even of innocent suffering, therefore, is the price for the radical nonviolence of a God who seeks to win over the hearts of his creatures by their own free will, never intending to coerce or even oppress them.

The words "peace be with you," with which the risen one greeted his disciples, further confirmed God's boundless willingness to forgive. Jesus had already made this known in his basileia message; but through his judgment speech, the impression could have been given that this was restricted. His disciples were in need of renewed forgiveness. In contrast to the people, they had, during his earthly ministry, gained a deeper insight into their master's mystery and yet, in the decisive hour, they deserted and betrayed him. If anyone had personally and individually become guilty at his downfall, it was his disciples; so that the judgment parable of the wicked tenants could, first of all, have been applied to them. This parable portrays the owner of a vineyard who, at first, stands out because of his incomprehensible forbearance and benevolence and who, upon the killing of his slaves, even risks his son. Yet when he too gets killed, the master's forbearance turns into its opposite, and he orders for the wicked, murdering tenants to be killed (cf. Mark 12: 1–10). This judgment parable points to Jesus' destiny, and in accordance with the action of the owner of the vineyard, Easter should have been an hour of judgment. Yet the exact opposite happened. Precisely those who had become the guiltiest were once again offered peace and forgiveness. The God of Jesus Christ thus proves to be much more forbearing than the master in the parable of the wicked tenants; not even by the killing of his own son is he provoked to wrath. This confirms and deepens the interpretation of the words of judgment sketched in the second act, which is also suggested by the parable's final word: "The very stone which the builders rejected has become the head of the corner; this was the Lord's doing, and it is marvelous in our eyes" (Mark 12: 10–11).

Act 5: The coming of the Holy Spirit

Despite the Easter experience and the Easter peace, the disciples remained under the spell of fear. They met behind closed doors. Only the spirit of Pentecost enabled them to be outspoken and step out into the streets of Jerusalem. Thus a new community was created in the public sphere of this world, which stands out against the usual political and religious societies.

Already in the announcement of the dawning kingdom of God, Jesus aimed at the new gathering of Israel and the creation of a new people. Yet, because his message was rejected, God's kingdom was at first forced back on to himself, and there even emerged an antigathering, an alliance of Jews and Gentiles against him. But through his nonviolence and his love of enemies, which led him even to accept his own death, and through the new initiative of the heavenly Father at Easter, the gathered kingdom of the opponents was overcome from within. The new gathering at Easter and Pentecost, achieved through the spirit of love and truth, was therefore no longer simply an announcement but a reality that had persevered to the end in the confrontation with all the counterforces of lying, discord, and violence. In light of this victory, a clear answer was finally given to the question who this Jesus, who had identified himself completely with the dawning kingdom of God, really was: he was the pre-existent son of God, who has no part in this world of lying and violence.

Implications

The drama of salvation outlined above (cf. Schwager 1999) has many implications which, depending on the leading question, can each be carved out in further detail. In this context, we will expound only certain aspects with regard to theological politics.

The role of the church

All types of liberation theology appeal to Jesus' message of the kingdom of God, but many distance themselves from the church, of which they expect but little, usually criticizing it quite systematically. The emphasis on the kingdom of God is entirely justified; but, from the perspective of dramatic theology, the distancing from the church rests on a misapprehension. The experiences of Israel's prophets, as well as Jesus' downfall, indicate quite clearly that ethical appeals and criticism of the status quo are not sufficient to achieve more justice and peace on earth. Not even Jesus' healing power was capable of overcoming the resistance, which is at home deep in the human heart and is related to the forces of lying and violence (Schwager 1997). Only the spirit of Pentecost, which is also the spirit through which Jesus sacrificed himself at the cross (Heb. 9: 14) and through which he was resurrected at Easter (Rom. 1: 4), can win over hearts from within and overcome evil. Yet this spirit leads to the church, creating a new community in the public sphere of our world. Thus a real alternative is introduced, which builds explicitly on God and nonviolence, and on the basis of which all other social and political structures have to be assessed anew.

Innsbruckian dramatic theology therefore welcomes theological approaches that grant political significance to the church as a public and institutional community (Milbank 1990; Milbank et al. 1999; Hauerwas 1995). Not only ethical efforts but God's work in history is what is ultimately decisive, and this work aims at the creation of a people, which can be concretely experienced in the church (Lohfink 1998). Thus a political theology, at a most fundamental level, needs a theology of the church. Yet, as there is much that is sinful at work in the church (cf. Rom. 7: 14–25), another question arises. This concerns the issue of whether the work of God is represented clearly in at least some activities of the church or whether, in the end, all remains ambiguous. Dramatic theology regards the basic structure of the liturgy and, especially, the Eucharist as the simultaneously real and symbolic representation of Jesus' drama, and thus as an enduring sign of unambiguity (Cavanaugh 1998). The liturgical celebration, time and again, reminds us of the one whom the builders (Jews and Gentiles) had rejected, but who has been made the cornerstone by God (cf. Mark 12: 10–11 par.). Thus the aim of Jesus' ministry and of God's work in him is each time anew made present and realized historically. On the other hand, the liturgy, which by itself is always in danger of succumbing to contemporary interests, is kept from being subverted by its central structure of commemoration.

Theology and the social sciences

The reliance of theological politics on the church may cause some to suspect that a mentality of retreat is being fostered, which overlooks the importance of the human and social sciences. Dramatic theology, however, aims precisely at the opposite, that is, at an intensive dialogue with these sciences. To this effect, it utilizes primarily the work of René Girard, who shows that modern criticism is in many respects not antibiblical. It grew, after all, out of the biblical sources and also returns to the Bible, if it is performed radically, subjecting the presuppositions of the modern world themselves to critical questioning.

History, art, and the experiences of everyday life indicate that human beings are desiring and passionate creatures. At the same time, they prove to be imitators, from earliest childhood instinctively learning language, customs, and general knowledge from others. Girard thus shows that even the fundamental and deepest desires do not originate spontaneously but are informed by models in a process called *mimesis*. This instinctive imitation of the striving of others easily leads to two or more desires being directed at the same object, thus generating rivalries, which in turn can intensify, leading to various kinds of tension and conflict. Passions, therefore, are not harmless but always endanger human social existence. Deep striving becomes a force of peace only if it is inspired by a model that is not itself trapped in a current of imitation but aims wholly at an infinite good, in which many can participate so as to become connected to one another, thus preventing the origin of further rivalries (Girard 1965). Against this background, imitation of Christ, who in his whole being was orientated toward "Abba", his God, and who sought to gather human beings in his name, proves to be not just some random possibility but an offer that corresponds most deeply to human nature and that alone can lead to true freedom and full peace.

Yet this offer is issued to a world governed by a different mechanism. The experience of everyday life not only presents human beings as imitating creatures; it also demonstrates that true and lasting peace is extremely difficult to achieve, and that passions are not channeled into beneficial paths by reason alone. Public life is structured by social mechanisms, which create a certain sphere of order. Girard, having demonstrated how passions, being kept in the wake of imitation (*mimesis*), intensify and even tend toward violence, goes on to reveal the mechanisms that check this dangerous tendency. When mutual rivalries and aggressions tip over into the aggression of many against one, then the many, at the expense of the one, again experience for a short time a superficial (and deceptive) peace – through the scapegoat mechanism. One has to be sacrificed for the others to enjoy a little respite.

Something similar happened to Jesus. His wish to gather Israel in the name of his heavenly father at first led to an antigathering, to an alliance of Pharisees, Sadducees, Zealots, and Herodians, of Jews and Gentiles, against the troublesome prophet from Nazareth. Through him Herod and Pontius Pilate, having previously been enemies, became friends (Luke 23: 12). This did not happen by accident. If Jesus, in the name of his God, intended to bring true peace and true reconciliation among human beings, then what happened to him had to expose the deepest structures of a sinful and antigodly world. These are the structures of the scapegoat mechanism, which shifts on to victims what a human society is unable to come to terms with in order to create, at the expense of these victims, time and again a provisional peace. It is better for one human being to die on behalf of the people than for the whole people to perish, argued the high priest at Jesus' sentencing, and this argument is the usual argument of politics. Its normal strategy consists in uniting one's own followers or one's people through polemics against "enemies". Carl Schmitt even regarded this as the very nature of politics (Schmitt 1996; Palaver 1998).

Girard's theory is controversial. Innsbruckian dramatic theology is convinced, however, that from a biblical perspective its basic theses positively force themselves upon us. If Jesus, intending to bring true peace in the power of God, met with massive collective resistance, then, in this resistance, the powers of this world must reveal themselves. To be sure, it has been objected that one cannot speak of a general rejection of Jesus, since many did actually follow him; therefore, the theory of a collective mechanism did not have any biblical warrant. However, John's Gospel, looking back at Jesus' public ministry, gives a fitting answer to this objection. First, it notes that "though he had done so many signs before them, yet they [the Jews] did not believe in him" (John 12: 37). This is followed by two Old Testament quotes from the prophet Isaiah about the hardening of the people, which demonstrate that the general rejection of Jesus conforms to God's earlier experiences with his people. John's Gospel then adds an important qualification, at the same time providing reasons as to why one has to speak of a general rejection: "Nevertheless even many of the authorities believed in him, but for fear of the Pharisees they did not confess it, lest they should be put out of the synagogue" (John 12: 42). Jesus did appeal to many people, arousing some kind of faith. Yet when, after a time of superficial enthusiasm, resistance made itself felt, he was unable to win over the public. On an individual and subjective level, he had been able to reach many in their private attitudes; but the public has its own laws, and these worked against him. John's Gospel even illustrates why this is so: "for they [the leaders] loved the praise of men more than the praise of God" (John 12: 43). To seek reputation and honor means being guided by leading models, and these were other human beings rather than God. John's Gospel therefore clearly points to the principle of imitation, thereby explaining why the public follows laws and forces that are different from the good subjective will of individual human beings.

The same point can be illustrated also with respect to Jesus' disciples. They responded to his call to discipleship and gradually gained some insight into his message and who he was. Peter led the way, confessing him to be the Messiah (Mark 8: 29) and swearing unceasing loyalty (Mark 14: 29, 31). Yet in the hour of his confession, Jesus had to repudiate him as Satan because he had in mind not God's will (Mark 8: 33) but that of humans. In the hour of trial, he followed, despite his oath, precisely the will of the people: he betrayed his master (Mark 14: 66–72). Even within the innermost circle of Jesus' followers, the inherent laws and forces of the public were ultimately stronger than the power that emanated from Jesus. This changed only when the spirit of Pentecost seized the disciples from within, empowering them to witness publicly to their crucified and risen master. At this point, a community was beginning to form that was structured differently from the usual societies of this world. Thus, from the experience of Pentecost, the mechanisms of rejection, the mechanisms that control the public in a world characterized by original sin, become entirely transparent. The pentecostal church identifies this principle clearly, looking back on Old Testament experiences as well as the downfall of Jesus and at the same time voicing its own experience: "for truly in this city there were gathered together against thy holy servant Jesus, whom thou didst anoint, both Herod and Pontius Pilate, with the Gentiles and the peoples of Israel" (Acts 4: 27). Although at the time of Jesus most of the tribes of Israel no longer existed and only a few Gentiles were involved in his trial, the church talks about a universal alliance. It thereby exposes a basic process, which time and again can be seen in the entire history of revelation as well as in the subsequent history of the church: The public has its own unconscious laws, which create (provisional) structures through collective polarizations at the expense of victims or enemies. Jesus, however, having become a victim of these mechanisms himself, stands on the side of the victims.

As the dawning kingdom of God, in and through Jesus, radically confronted the structures of this world, so true Christian theology needs to confront the structures of the public, drawing up a theological politics. Girard's theory helps us to engage, from out of the center of the Christian message, in a critical debate with all human and social sciences that investigate the human being as a desiring and social creature (Lagarde 1994).

Sacrifice

In all traditional societies sacrifices played a central role, shaping public and private life. For traditional Christianity, too, Christ's sacrificial death was of fundamental importance. But, as noted above, the Enlightenment aimed at "abolishing the morality of the publicly imposed *sacrificium*" (Habermas 1998: 152). Yet even modern states have demanded that their soldiers sacrifice themselves for their homeland, and Nietzsche criticized Christianity not because of its theology of sacrifice but, in contrast to the main current of the Enlightenment, because he saw it as a pseudo-humanitarianism, which sought to enforce the view that nobody would be sacrificed any more: "The individual was taken so seriously by Christianity, indeed, was regarded as so absolute that he could no longer be sacrificed: yet the species only exists because of human sacrifices. Before God all 'souls' are equal: yet precisely that is the most dangerous of all possible views" (Nietzsche 1980: 470–1). The problem of sacrifice is thus a complex one and remains, even today, the unresolved and underlying neuralgic issue of any comprehensive theory of society. Girard helps us understand why this is so, and why the problem of sacrifice will continue to be of relevance as long as there is violence between human beings. The sacrificial mechanisms that stabilize any society (threatened, as all societies constantly are, by chaos) are closely connected to ritual (religious) sacrifices, which is why these remain present in a latent sense (even in times of secularization), continue to live in sub-cultures, and attempt to penetrate into the official culture of a post-Christian world.

A theological politics that seeks to penetrate to the root of the political problem therefore needs to face the problem of sacrifice, paying attention to the criticism of sacrifice as well as to the enduring problem of sacrifice and violence. Dramatic theology attempts to do both. On the one hand, it criticizes, in agreement with the Enlightenment and liberal theology, the traditional theology of sacrifice, which claims that the wrath of God had to be pacified and reconciled through the bloody death of his son. On the other hand, it does not understand Jesus' death as the abolition but rather as a radical transformation of sacrifice. Through the dramatic model, we intend to demonstrate that, while God did not desire the death of his son, he did guide him to follow sinners, even into their misery. As the good shepherd, he had to stay with the lost sheep and intercede on their behalf, even as they turned against their shepherd and killed him. Not God, but the people sentenced and crucified Jesus, thus making him the bearer of sin. Yet the one who had been sentenced "sacrificed" himself, remaining true to his mission and responding to the evil that had been done to him with forgiving love, praying and giving himself up for those who killed him. Thus the term "sacrifice" takes on a completely new meaning. It is no longer the slaughtering priests who sacrifice, as in all pre-Christian religions, since in Jesus' death the ones responsible for his slaughter are part of an immoral humanity. The one who sacrifices is now, in a new sense, the one who, seeking the lost, invests his own life, sharing the loneliness of those entrusted to him in order thus to free and redeem them from their self-imprisonment.

Dramatic theology does not suggest a retreat from the world or a path into a subjective inwardness. Nor does it envisage a lasting improvement of the world or the disappearance of the problem of violence. Instead, it expects the church and the believer to face violence in its manifold expressions and even to expose, little by little, the violence that is concealed or veiled. This happens most profoundly in the celebration of the Eucharist, which time and again reminds us that God has made the stone, which the builders had rejected, the head of the corner, that is, the center and the fount of life of a new community. In light of this celebration, we constantly need to expose the processes that cause human beings to be rejected and expelled and, with believing eyes, discover and articulate those processes in the world whereby a new vitality issues from the ones who have been expelled or killed. Yet all this is possible only where people, in their faith in the crucified and resurrected, attempt to prepare themselves, if necessary, to risk and sacrifice their own lives. Archbishop Romero – shot at the altar of his own cathedral in El Salvador in 1980 – did this, and through the circumstances of his death, the connections between the problem of sacrifice and that of violence and the new understanding of the sacrifice as martyrdom have become clear.

Theology of history

Dramatic theology does not reduce the acts of God to ethics, nor does it suggest a one-sided retreat into the inwardness of the soul. It does not count on a church without sinners, nor does it perceive outside the church nothing but wickedness. The dawning kingdom of God, which Jesus proclaimed and lived out to death, comprises more than the visible harvest of the church after Easter. The spirit of God blows where it chooses, even if the church is the only place where its work is clearly recognizable. The conflict between the community of faith and the world therefore remains a complex one, and the perspective of faith needs to open itself up to a theology of history.

By analogy to drama as a stage play, time condensed in the drama of Jesus' life and death. His announcement of the imminent end was not apocalyptic exuberance and subjective deception but an anticipation of the end of time in faith (cf. Pannenberg 1991–7). During the short span of his public ministry, the fundamental clash between the kingdom of God and the dark forces of this world took place. At stake was, albeit in dramatically condensed fashion, the last battle. To this drama in Jesus' mission corresponds an analogous drama in the time after the coming of Christ, as the Revelation of John indicates. It is not a time of linear progress or of constant apostasy, nor is it a time of cyclical repetitions; rather, it is a time of intensified struggle. Hans Urs von Balthasar, in his *Theo-drama*, metaphorically speaks of a "battle of the Logos" and the "defeated one as victor" (von Balthasar 1980: 399–468). Innsbruckian dramatic theology sympathizes with this view, as it also understands the time after the coming of Christ as a time of intensified struggle.

This can be illustrated with a historical overview. The long cycles of the natural religions, and also of the Hindu world and Egyptian royal theology, have been broken. The Roman imperial cult was directly undermined, and even the Christian world did not find a new equilibrium. Dogmatic debates and criticism of the church in the name of the Gospel prepared the way for schisms. In the struggle between Emperor and Pope, the church's claim gradually dissolved the sacral glamour of political authority while the Empire, for its part, humiliated a church bent on rivaling the political authority in the sphere of power. The Reformation eventually demolished the church's self-perception as a uniform community developing without any ruptures throughout the centuries. The center of the visible church, namely the papacy, could now even be viewed as the Antichrist, and the ensuing conflict was experienced as an eschatological one. In the ambit of these diverse and reciprocal criticisms, modern scientific, historical, and social criticism evolved. The new sciences have been understood by their promoters and advocates as significant progress, indeed as a new way to salvation. Yet in reality these sciences are neither good nor evil, nor are they neutral; rather, they have an intensifying character, as the prominent atomic physicist C. F. von Weizsäcker (1970) stresses. They increase the possibilities of good and evil and thus our responsibility in making choices. Since the construction of atomic weapons, they even demonstrate that the human race is able to destroy itself. The full significance of the problem of violence, which is expressed very clearly in the Old and New Testaments, thus becomes empirically tangible. The human race has begun an experiment on itself, which indicates what self-judgment as global self-destruction might mean.

Girard's thinking, which exposes the problem of violence as the central problem of human society, needs to be understood from within this context. It analyses modern society, which emerged out of a dramatic confrontation with Christianity, and uses the resulting questions in order to arrive, retrospectively, at a clearer and more precise understanding of the biblical texts. It moves within a hermeneutical circle that is very wide and constantly widening. This circle does not just include individual interpreters but, being wholly comprehensive, comprises the entire history since the coming of Christ. Looking back over the complex history of the interaction of Christianity with human societies, a retrospective analysis of the Christian texts enables their messages to appear more clearly. Girard's thinking is therefore particularly critical of a half-modernized theology that regards some postulates of the Enlightenment as new dogmas and seeks to determine on the basis of them which parts of the Bible are acceptable and which are not. Girard's thinking, by contrast, finds in the Jewish–Christian history of revelation, and in particular in the drama of Jesus, a critical power from which even modern criticism draws strength, yet without ever reaching its depth.

Dramatic theology by no means claims that with this comprehensive perspective it has reached a standpoint above the entangled paths of history. It rather stresses that the mechanisms of violence go hand in hand with mechanisms of deception. The greater the possibilities of violence, the subtler the possibilities of deception. History thus time and again confronts theology with new unresolved questions; and today the problem of manipulative violence is particularly pressing. Through the modern interplay of medicine, computer science, and genetic engineering, the distinctions between nature and culture, and between a preset creation and human technology, which up to now have been unmistakable, are undermined. The human race is also embarking on an experiment on itself in another way, namely by intervening in its own heredity, manipulatively interfering in such fundamental processes as reproduction. True, as images of God, human beings do partake in God's creative power. Yet how far does this partaking go and where does pretension begin – a pretension that seeks to play God through perverse imitation of God (Augustine) and his creation?

In the Revelation of John, the antigodly forces appear in the images of two animals from the abyss (Rev. 13: 1–18). The first symbolizes political power and the second, which is in the service of the first, ideological power. Of the second animal, it is said that it confuses the inhabitants of the earth through miraculous signs, commanding them to set up a statue in honor of the first animal. It was even "allowed to give breath to the image of the beast so that the image of the beast should speak" (Rev. 13:15). The biblical statement that the ideological power is even given the ability to breathe the human spirit of life into a dead shape attains a totally novel significance in the modern context. The discussion about the possibility of creating artificial life flared up a long time ago. The Revelation of John, in its metaphorical language, regards this as a real possibility, yet one that is *given* to humanity. But the biblical text at the same time speaks about a massive abuse of this ability: the power is given to a "beast" that causes all to be killed "who would not worship the image of the [first] beast" (Rev. 13: 15). According to this view, the creative power, which was always given to humankind as the image of the creator – the ability to procreate offspring (cf. Gen. 5: 3), as well as the freedom and rationality to create cultures – will increase in the time after the coming of Christ; yet it will also increasingly be abused for idolatrous purposes. The drama intensifies, as indeed today is increasingly noticeable. Medical research more and more uses the weakest form of human life as a store of spares in the service of the richer and more successful part of the human race. Human beings thus in a new way become victims of human beings. The fear of "playing God" is already judged to be a "false fear" by some (Dworkin 1999), and a future begins to emerge in which humans become superfluous because creatures brought forth by human ingenuity aspire to abolish human beings (Joy 2000), or because one believes that a new superhuman being, created by the human race, would be better than present humanity (Extropy Institute; Moravec 1998).

Yet the fact remains that, from a Christian perspective, participation in God's creative power is part of the inalienable dignity of humanity; and so that research may therefore not be "demonized" categorically. But where is the dividing line between research that is in tune with God and that which is an idolatrous pretension? This is particularly difficult to assess because the question does not relate just to individual people but also to systems and tendencies, which are effective precisely for the reason that many people, for many generations, have acted on the basis of a similar attitude and logic (scientific and technological rationality), building upon the work of their predecessors. Thus systems develop, and individual human beings are left with hardly any real possibilities for action outside these systems. Christians are therefore tied to a dramatic history, the middle and long-term consequences of which they can no longer gauge. It is thus all the more important that they are part of a community to which it has been promised that it will not be overcome by the forces from below, nor yet by "beasts" with "superhuman" powers. Though the church itself may be assailed by sin, forming wrong conclusions concerning some specific issues, as the place of the ever-present *memoria* of Jesus' drama of salvation it remains the decisive counterforce in a world intent on "playing God." Even when faced with the successes of the powers opposing it, the church need not tremble, because the dramatic history of revelation has shown that precisely when conflicts and crises multiply and evil increases, God acts in new and surprising ways: "but where sin increased, grace abounded all the more" (Rom. 5: 20). It is in this light that dramatic theology views history.

References

Barth, K. (1956). *Church Dogmatics*, vol. IV, 1, *The Doctrine of Reconciliation, Part One*, ed. G. W. Bromiley and T. F. Torrance, trans. G. W. Bromiley. Edinburgh: T. & T. Clark.

Brockman, J. (1995). *The Third Culture: Scientists on the Edge*. New York: Simon & Schuster.

Cavanaugh, W. T. (1998). *Torture and Eucharist: Theology, Politics, and the Body of Christ*. Oxford: Blackwell.

Dworkin, R. (1999). "Die falsche Angst, Gott zu spielen." *Die Zeit*, 16 Sept., Dossier 15–17.

Extropy Institute. *Incubating Positive Futures*. http://www.extropy.org.

Girard, R. (1965). *Deceit, Desire and the Novel: Self and Other in Literary Structure*. Baltimore: Johns Hopkins University Press.

——(1987). *Things Hidden since the Foundation of the World*, trans. S. Bann and M. Metteer. London: Athlone.

——(1994). *Quand ces choses commenceront*. Paris: Arléa.

——(1995). "Mimetische Theorie und Theologie." In J. Niewiadomski and W. Palaver (eds.), *Vom Fluch und Segen der Sündenböcke*, 15–29. Thaur: Kulturverlag.

Habermas, J. (1998). *Die postnationale Konstellation: Politische Essays*. Frankfurt: Suhrkamp.

Hauerwas, S. (1995). *In Good Company: The Church as Polis*. Notre Dame, Ind.: University of Notre Dame Press.

Joy, B. (2000). "Why the Future Doesn't Need Us: Our most powerful 21st-century technologies – robotics, genetic engineering, and nanotech – are threatening to make humans an endangered species." *Wired*, April, 238–62.

Lagarde, F. (1994). *René Girard ou la christianisation des sciences humaines*. New York: Lang.

Lohfink, G. (1998). *Braucht Gott die Kirche? Zur Theologie des Volkes Gottes*. Freiburg: Herder.

Milbank, J. (1990). *Theology and Social Theory: Beyond Secular Reason*. Cambridge, Mass.: Blackwell.

——(1997). "Postmodern Critical Augustinianism: A Short Summa in Forty-two Responses to Unasked Questions." In G. Ward (ed.), *The Postmodern God: A Theological Reader*, 265–78. Oxford: Blackwell.

Milbank, J., Pickstock, C., and Ward, G. (1999). *Radical Orthodoxy: A New Theology*. London: Routledge.

Moltmann, J. (1993). *The Crucified God: The Cross of Christ as the Foundation and Criticism of Christian Theology*, trans. R. A. Wilson and John Bowden. Augsburg: Fortress.

Moravec, H. (1998). *Robot: Mere Machine to Transcendent Mind*. Oxford: Oxford University Press.

Nietzsche, F. (1980). *Sämtliche Werke. Kritische Studienausgabe*, vol. XIII: *Nachgelassene Fragmente 1887–1889*, ed. G. Colli and M. Montinari. München: Deutscher Taschenbuch.

Niewiadomski, J., and Palaver, W. eds. (1992). *Dramatische Erlösungslehre: Ein Symposion*. Innsbruck: Tyrolia.

Nordhofen, E. (1995). "Beleuchtung des schwarzen Lochs." *Die Zeit*, March 3, 66–7.

Palaver, W. (1998). *Die mythischen Quellen des Politischen: Carl Schmitts Freund-Feind-Theorie*. Stuttgart: Kohlhammer.

Palaver, W., Guggenberger, W., et al. (1998). "Pluralismus – ethische Grundintuition – Kirche." *Zeitschrift für Katholische Theologie* 120, 257–89.

Pannenberg, W. (1991–7). *Systematic Theology*, trans. Geoffrey W. Bromiley. Grand Rapids, Mich.: Eerdmans.

Rasmusson, A. (1995). *The Church as Polis: From Political Theology to Theological Politics as Exemplified by Jürgen Moltmann and Stanley Hauerwas*. Notre Dame, Ind.: University of Notre Dame Press.

Schmitt, C. (1996). *The Concept of the Political*, trans. G. Schwab. Chicago: University of Chicago Press.

Schwager, R. (1997). *Erbsünde und Heilsdrama: Im Kontext von Evolution, Gentechnologie und Apokalyptik*. Münster: Lit.

——(1999). *Jesus in the Drama of Salvation: Toward a Biblical Doctrine of Redemption*, trans. P. Haddon and J. Williams. New York: Crossroad.

Schwager, R., Niewiadomski, J., et al. (1996). "Dramatische Theologie als Forschungsprogramm." *ZKTh* 118, 317–44. (English text available at: http://theol.uibk.ac.at/rgkw/xtext/research-0.html.)

Strahm, D., ed. (1991). *Vom Verlangen nach Heilwerden: Christologie in feministisch-theologischer Sicht*. Fribourg: Edition Exodus.

von Balthasar, H. U. (1980). *Theodramtik*, vol. III: *Die Handlung*. Einsiedeln: Johannes.

von Weizsäcker, C. F. (1970). "Die Aufgabe der Kirche in der kommenden Weltgesellschaft." *Evangelische Kommentare* 11, 641.

CHAPTER 25

Atonement

Timothy J. Gorringe

In one of the most famous pieces of historical writing of the twentieth century E. P. Thompson, son of a Methodist missionary to India, took up Elié Halévy's argument that it was Methodism which saved England from revolution and applied it specifically to the atonement. He was led to do so by looking at Andrew Ure's *Philosophy of Manufactures*, which argues that religion is necessary to create a well-disciplined work force. Some power is needed to turn recalcitrant workers into docile wage slaves:

> Where then shall mankind find this transforming power? – in the cross of Christ. It is the sacrifice which removes the guilt of sin: it is the motive which removes love of sin: it mortifies sin by showing its turpitude to be indelible except by such an awful expiation; it atones for disobedience; it excites to obedience; it purchases strength for obedience; it makes obedience practicable; it makes it acceptable; it makes it in a manner unavoidable, for it constrains to it; it is, finally, not only the motive to obedience, but the pattern of it. (Ure 1835: 423–5)

In commentary Thompson turned to the Methodist hymns he knew from his childhood: "True followers of our bleeding Lamb, Now on Thy daily cross we die." He commented: "Work was the Cross from which the 'transformed' industrial worker hung" (Thompson 1968: 406).[1] With heavy irony he entitled his chapter, "The Transforming Power of the Cross."

It is true that there is no agreement on how exactly ideology, as expressed, for example, in theologies, creeds, hymns, and sermons, bears on social, political, and economic reality. Doubtless the question can never be settled once and for all, but this is quite different from arguing that there is no relationship here to be grasped – an assumption which is unfortunately still standard in histories of Christian doctrine.[2] Did Methodism forestall revolution? Was it, in particular, the doctrine of the atonement, or rather the preaching of the cross, which functioned as opiate? It is probably fair to say that contemporary historians are skeptical (Thompson 1985: 126), but against such skepticism we have to set the extraordinary and continuing power of atonement imagery. No council of the church ever laid down what had to be believed about what we call, in English, the atonement.[3] This early sixteenth-century coinage represents a particular construal of the meaning of the cross which, in the West, provided the symbolic center of the Christian faith. In the Christian East the icon provided a much richer and more varied symbolic center, but in the West it was before the crucifix that the poor prayed. It was a cross which was placed on the altar, and which provided the ground plan for the medieval church. It was the cross which bishops, abbots, and later countless lay people wore around their necks. It was the cross which provided the bulk of the imagery in Protestant hymns. Fatefully, it was the cross which Constantine saw in the sky in 312, which urged him on to the victory which gave him sole emperorship. The reversal of symbolic value was already here complete. From being an image of imperial terror, a sign of what would be done to those who challenged the powers that be, it became an aggressive sign, a sign of battle. When Pope Urban II preached the First Crusade at the Council of Clermont in November 1095, urging Christians to "take the cross," the logic of Constantine's vision was but spelt out. Jesus had told his disciples that they would need to "take up their cross" in order to follow him. This was now interpreted as going on crusade, and Urban told his hearers that death in battle for "the Holy Land" would mean absolution and remission of sins (Runciman 1951: 107–9).

The symbolic centrality of the cross means that, although the doctrine of the atonement was set out from time to time in treatises of great systematic rigor, we need a category which goes beyond ideology if we are to understand its social impact. When we try to understand the political significance of the cross we need to turn, I believe, to Raymond Williams' idea of a "structure of feeling." The structure of feeling is the sum of all those things which tell us what it is like to live in a particular society, its emotional undertow, "a very deep and very wide possession, in all actual communities, precisely because it is on it that communication depends" (Williams 1965: 64–5). Abstract treatises spell out, more or less imperfectly, the implications of this structure of feeling. What Williams never saw, and he was a good Protestant in this regard, was the role ritual played in expressing and maintaining such structures. Rituals "provide a kind of didactic theatre through which the onlooker *is taught what to feel, how to react, which sentiments are called for*" (Garland 1990: 67, emphasis added). Think, then, of the significance of the celebration of the Mass, all over western Europe, throughout the Middle Ages, and think of its recalling at its center the death of Christ. In this and countless other ways the cross constituted a structure of feeling which generated particular cultural and political outcomes;[4] and if it is the case, as Steven Runciman argued, that the Byzantine Empire was less bellicose than the West, it is not ridiculous to look at the way different construals of the symbolic center of Christianity, between East and West, generated different structures of feeling and therefore different outcomes (Runciman 1951: 83–8).

In hoc signo vinces. The cross was, of course, in its inception, a political symbol in the literal sense. Crucifixion was an exemplification of the deterrent theory of punishment (Hengel 1977). You crucify to deter any stirrings of revolt. The practice was widely used throughout the ancient world, but by Rome was reserved for slaves and rebels. After the defeat of Spartacus six thousand slaves were crucified on either side of the Via Appia – as a warning (Hengel 1986: 147). What happens, then, when this symbol of terror becomes a central focus of faith? The first answer, which Paul explores in 1 Corinthians, is that it causes absolute consternation:

> In ancient thought, e.g. among the Stoics, an ethical and symbolic interpretation of the crucifixion was still possible, but to assert that God himself accepted death in the form of a crucified Jewish manual worker from Galilee in order to break the power of death and bring salvation to all men could only seem folly and madness to men of ancient times. (Hengel 1986: 181)

This consternation is theologically important. It is the foundation both of what today we call "counter-culture," and also of Nietzsche's "slave morality." Both of these reactions manifest themselves in political attitudes. Paul, as we know, "gloried in the Cross" (Gal. 6: 14). So strange was this idea that he had to resort to a range of metaphors to help people see the point. Contrary to much popular argument, we have to insist that this range means that no one interpretation of the meaning of the cross is dominant in the New Testament. The implications of the various metaphors are suggested, and left to germinate in the corporate memory and imagination of Christendom. They have each risen and fallen in significance over the centuries, each coloring the structure of feeling in a different way, each in some respect issuing out of a given culture, each in turn generating particular cultural and political outcomes. The history of this rise and fall is at the same time a mapping of how the Christian church has understood its political significance. Paul uses four main metaphors: redemption, justification, sacrifice, and reconciliation. In addition, I shall argue, the so-called "Christ hymn" of Phil. 2: 5ff. suggests the redemptive power of solidarity. I shall explore these various images in turn before concluding with some reflections on forgiveness.

Redemption

I begin with the metaphor of redemption. This has two roots, both political. Needless to say, any Jew would understand it in the light of the Exodus from Egypt, the freeing of slaves from bondage. Equally, we know that in the first century many Christians were literally, and not metaphorically, "bought with a price" (1 Cor. 6: 20), namely, on the slave market. Occasionally it was possible for a slave to accrue enough money to buy himself out of slavery.[5] Redemption, then, is about being freed from bondage, oppression, or slavery. Again, we have to ask: How is this achieved through the cross? What is meant by "redemption through his blood" (Eph. 1: 7)? As is well known, some early theologians speculated that we were in bondage to the devil, and that the cross was a bait through which the devil was deceived. The Swedish theologian Gustav Aulen argued that this metaphor, in its various guises, was the dominant form of patristic atonement theology from Irenaeus in the second century to Gregory the Great in the sixth century (Aulen 1931). Were the case accepted it would be interesting to speculate why this was so, but in fact it is arguable (Kelly 1965: ch. 14).[6] Anselm criticized the immorality of many of these arguments, but such critiques are already found in the fourth century. Writing in the shadow of fascism, Aulen sensed the significance of the metaphor, but was unable to exploit it to the full. Barth, in the final fragments of his *Dogmatics*, and above all Walter Wink, have done this (Barth 1981; Wink 1984, 1986, 1992). Wink speaks of the powers (Eph. 6: 12) as the "interiority" or spirituality of movements, cultures, nations, churches, and institutions. These spiritualities shape our lives profoundly so that we easily find ourselves in bondage to them. Wink identifies violence as the true spirituality of the contemporary West, but he goes on to trace that to our habit of dealing with things by distinguishing sharply between those who are good and those who are evil. He shows how this motif is found all the way from the Babylonian myth of Marduk and Tiamat to contemporary cartoons and crime movies. What emerges from this dualistic way of looking at the world he calls the "domination system" because human affairs are everywhere characterized by the struggle for domination. It is this system by which we are trapped.

Christ frees us from this because the cross unmasks the "delusional assumptions" of the domination system: assumptions such as the sanctity of private property, or the supreme value of money. All such delusional assumptions are defended by force. Jesus broke with the domination system by refusing to return violence for violence. "When he was abused, he did not return abuse; when he suffered, he did not threaten; but he trusted himself to the one who judges justly" (1 Pet. 2: 23). This refusal is taken up into the lives of believers. Wink translates Col. 2: 20: "If with Christ you died to the fundamental assumptions of the Domination system (the customary rules and regulations by which society is governed) why do you let yourselves be dictated to as if your lives were still controlled by that System?" Effectively, Wink finds salvation in a critical process, but this raises the hermeneutic question very acutely. As we have seen in the case of the crusade, the scriptural witness to the cross has been used to legitimate behavior precisely opposite to what Jesus seems to have stood for, and the history of the church makes clear that there is no magic formula to prevent such misuse.

The powers, in our world, are structured according to the norms of patriarchy. No account of the political dimension of atonement theology can fail to mention the critique of traditional Christian theology mounted by feminist theology. Rosemary Radford Ruether raises the question of whether a male savior can save women. Though she does not draw on Wink her answer, once again, is in terms of the liberating potential of critique, this time through Jesus' critique of religious and social hierarchy (Ruether 1983). Jesus announces a new humanity through a nonhierarchical lifestyle. Elisabeth Schüssler Fiorenza has more recently developed this idea in speaking of the human problem in terms of "kyriarchy," rule by a dominant elite, rather than just patriarchy (Schüssler Fiorenza 1993). On this understanding redemption is not "once for all." "Christic personhood" continues in the church, and it is "redemptive personhood" which goes ahead of us, calling us to further dimensions of human liberation. I shall return to this idea in the conclusion.

Justification

A second metaphor is that known in the West, and especially since Luther, as "justification." As used in the Western tradition, for example by Karl Barth, it draws on the image of the law court. Barth speaks of "the Judge judged in our place." I am charged and found guilty, but when it comes to sentencing the Judge takes my place. In a society where the law court plays a fundamental role the image has great power, but it is by no means clear that such a forensic reference corresponds to Paul's meaning. Elsa Tamez has argued that Paul's ideas of justification derive from his prison experience, but his use of *dikaiosune* may equally look to the dense usage of the word in the Psalms and Second Isaiah, where the verb translated "to justify" (*dikaioo*) means that God does what is necessary to vindicate God's purposes and where the noun can mean "deliverance." If any judge is in mind in this imagery it seems most likely to be the Hebrew kind, not operating in a court but vindicating the poor, and dealing with the oppressor. Righteousness here delivers *shalom*, a concrete situation of peace and justice in which the rich are put in their place and the poor lifted up. This Hebrew idea is a vital, though neglected, aspect of the biblical meaning of salvation.

At the same time it is entirely possible that in a passage such as Rom. 5: 18–19, Isa. 53: 11 is in mind: "The righteous one, my servant, shall make many righteous, and he shall bear their iniquities." Righteousness language is here conflated with an image of vicarious suffering, perhaps of expiation, and the law court is probably not in view. Nevertheless, we have to grant that in the history of tradition of the past 400 years, a period corresponding with the gradual emergence of a society where all are "equal under the law," and not at the disposal of the sovereign, as in feudal Europe, the forensic metaphor has been extremely important. Ironically, it has been used in what is almost certainly the opposite of its original sense, to reaffirm rather than deconstruct the power of human law. That Christ suffered the penalty of law seemed to justify the proceedings of the courts. In Britain assizes always began with an assize sermon. In nineteenth-century Russia a cross was prominent in courts and, as Tolstoy remarked in *Resurrection*, "No one seemed to realize that the gilt cross with the enamel medallions at the ends, which the priest held out for the people to kiss, was nothing else but the emblem of the gallows on which Christ had been exe-cuted for denouncing the very things now being performed here in his name."[7]

Luther, who was responsible for making the metaphor of justification central in Protestant thought, does not originally seem to have had forensic ideas in view. He began by contrasting the theology of the cross with a theology of glory. The latter shied away from suffering, the former embraced it. For Luther, "being crucified with Christ" meant incurring the hostility of the world. Martyrdom, in fact, was a mark of the true church (von Loewenwich 1976: 118–27). What is at issue in the theology of the cross is the formation of a counter-culture, in which all forms of "works righteousness" count for nothing. Such "works right-eousness," the Anabaptists realized, included the operations of the law. They pushed the critical implications of justification to their logical conclusion and sought a different kind of polity in which people did not deal with each other in adversarial ways, but rather learned forgiveness. This radical vision was instantiated in Cracow for a short time, but destroyed by armed force later in the seventeenth century. Today we find it again in the Mennonite theology of Howard Zehr, which feeds in to programs of restorative justice, and in the neo-Augustinianism of radical orthodoxy, which performs the unlikely feat of cham-pioning Augustine as a proto-counter-cultural figure seeking an "ontology of peace" (Zehr 1990; Milbank 1990, ch. 19).

Sacrifice

We come now to the third of Paul's metaphors. Paul, and the other writers of the epistolary part of the New Testament, lived in a world where cultic sacrifice was still practiced, and it was a natural move to use this imagery to reflect on Christ's death. Opinions vary on how central it is to the New Testament, but what cannot be denied is the grip it has exercised on the Christian imagination. More than any other metaphor it has spoken to the guilt people feel and makes the point, as emphatically as possible, that forgiveness is costly.

In recent years the theory of sacrifice which has generated most comment is that of René Girard. He reads the cross in terms of the scapegoat ritual which, though it is embedded in the account of sacrificial practices in Lev. 16, is not properly speaking a theory of sacrifice. It shares with animal sacrifice the fact that death is often involved (though not actually in Lev. 16), and that it is recounted in the texts as a divinely instituted way of dealing with sin. Girard, a cultural anthropologist, argues that all human cultures are built on mimesis, and this fact is what lies at the root of violence. We all want the same things, but we cannot all have them, and violence is the result. If we want any evidence that this thesis is no piece of academic trifling we need look no further than Susan George's *The Lugano Report*, a sober and chilling account of what is nec-essary for the preservation of capitalism in the twenty-first century (George 1999).[8]

In Girard's view the scapegoat mechanism arose as a means of dealing with mimetic violence. At regular intervals a victim – originally a human, later an animal – would be selected on whom the aggression of the community was poured out. The entire community would participate in killing this victim, venting all its pent-up aggression, and thus delivering the community from random violence until the next time round. The theory is speculative, but what is not speculative is the way in which scapegoating has in fact operated in communities throughout the world. Scapegoating, psychologists have made clear, is a very common way of dealing with guilt. When we know ourselves to be guilty we deal with it by blaming someone else, and turning aggression upon them. The history of the Jews in Europe between the tenth century and the twentieth can largely be understood in these terms. Girard's claim is that Christ understood this mechanism, and exposed it. When he speaks of revealing "things hidden since the foundation of the world" (Matt. 13: 35), he is talking about the secret of violence, the scapegoat mechanism. Jesus himself dies as a scapegoat, but in doing so exposes it once and for all, thus opening up the possibility of a new order without violence.

Does the New Testament confirm Girard's reading? Martin Hengel has demonstrated the importance of Isa. 53 for understanding Christ's death, and this text seems to use scapegoat imagery in speaking of the Servant as "bearing the sins" of others. Girard's claim, however, is that what we find in the New Testament is a demystification of such imagery, until we reach the Epistle to the Hebrews, when the counter-revolution begins. This counter-revolution made possible the scapegoating practice of Christian communities right up to the twentieth century.

Implausible as some aspects of Girard's reading remain, he provides the incalculable service of highlighting the violence implicit in sacrifice. The rhetoric of sacrifice insists that the moral order is damaged if sin is not "paid for." In this it agrees with visceral responses to crime.[9] Criminals must "pay" for what they do, and, according to the same retributive logic, Christ "paid the price for sinners due" and thus balanced the moral accounts of the universe. It is this logic which lies behind the most famous treatise on the atonement ever written, Anselm's *Cur Deus Homo?*, which appeared within a year or two of the preaching of the First Crusade. Anselm effectively marries sacrificial and forensic imagery. In his world an offender had to make "satisfaction" to the offended party, and the amount of satisfaction depended on the social status of that party. Since God is infinite, the amount of satisfaction needed is infinite. Since the offender is humankind, only a human being can make it: hence the need for a "God–man." Colin Gunton argues that the logic of this is to abolish the need for human satisfaction, since all penance falls short, and the "gift" exceeds every debt (Gunton 1988). Neither Anselm himself, however, nor the judges who listened to assize sermons for a thousand years, ever saw this implication, and in debates on hanging in Britain bishops remained some of the most resolute defenders of the death penalty (Potter 1993).

The nineteenth-century histories of doctrine have given Anselm a place which he scarcely deserves in terms of his traceable influence through the

Middle Ages and Reformation. At the same time, the fusion of forensic and sacrificial images has exercised a unique power on the Western mind. Popular preaching, both Catholic and Protestant, urged guilt upon its hearers and then absolved it, resulting in a tangible sense of freedom or release.[10] By his death Christ pays the cost of my sin. The believer is urged to reflect on this, and in particular upon the part he or she has played in that death. In this way the understanding of salvation has been individualized, and the connection of salvation with the kingdom has been lost.

Independently of Girard, the theologians based at the Departmento Ecumenico de Investigaciones (DEI) in Costa Rica have also followed up the connection between sacrificial views of the atonement and violence.[11] Franz Hinkelammert argues that law, not mimesis, is what lies behind sacrifice. It represents an approach to reality uninterested in reconciliation. What we call "structural sin" represents an insistence on legal process. This is precisely the view which lies behind Anselm. However, in scripture we constantly find the need and possibility of forgiveness emphasized. In the Lord's Prayer the petition to be forgiven debt recognizes, with Anselm, that our debt is unpayable, but instead of insisting that therefore we need the death of Christ, it is met rather by forgiving others their debts (Hinkelammert 1992). Hinkelammert applies this to the debts "owed" by poor countries to Western banks. Anselm's principle establishes the need for them to go on paying. As he points out, what this amounts to is an insistence on human sacrifice. As opposed to this is what he calls the "Abrahamic paradigm" in which human sacrifice is once and for all abjured, and forgiveness put in its place.

Elsa Tamez follows Hinkelammert, but brings his critique into relation with justification (Tamez 1992). She argues that Paul's experience of imprisonment taught him at first hand the immorality of "due process of law." What he has in mind in his use of the language of justice is God's justice, the opening up of a new kind of space in which we proceed otherwise than by legal maneuvers. The God who justifies teaches us reconciliation for the sake of a more just world (p. 113). Christ's death does not endorse law but subverts it.

The Anselmian theology of sacrifice rests on an argument for the costliness of forgiveness. Another way of understanding this, however, is in terms of what it costs not to be consumed by bitterness, resentment, and rage, in the face of injustice. What did it cost Jesus, or better, what life practices enabled Jesus to say, on the cross, while being tortured to death, "Father forgive them, they do not know what they are doing" (Luke 23: 34)? These two construals of the costliness of forgiveness ground two quite different political practices. On the one hand we have the kind of appeal to the sacrifice of Christ which we have seen used, completely cynically, by Andrew Ure, where the cross is turned against itself, and used as part of an oppressive ideology. On the other hand we have a schooling in forgiveness which allowed, for example, the Sandinistas to forgive their former torturers. Such a preparedness takes us on to the last of Paul's metaphors: reconciliation.

Reconciliation

New Testament scholarship since the 1970s has emphasized the importance of the divide in the early community between Jews and gentiles. Division calls for reconciliation. Matthew's Gospel, which reflects this division as markedly as Paul's letters, is framed between the command to reconcile (Matt. 5: 21ff.) and the realities of alienation (Matt. 23). The first text is the essential hermeneutical key to the latter. This particular conflict was an especially sore spot for Paul, as we see from Galatians, but in that letter he broadens the horizon, including slaves and free, and even women and men, within the remit of reconciliation. We have his practical attempts to deal with concrete conflicts in these areas in Philemon and 1 Corinthians. Whoever wrote Ephesians put this reconciling work firmly into the context of the cross, seeing it as "breaking down the dividing wall" between different groups (Eph. 2: 13–16).

What can it mean for Jews and gentiles, and by extension other alienated groups, to be reconciled "through the cross"? Presumably what the writer has in mind is that if you identify salvation as occurring through one cursed by the law (Gal. 3: 13) then this teaches a new way of reading the law which in turn opens the way for a new rapprochement between Jews and gentiles. In the Ephesians text the author speaks of "reconciling both groups to God." The reconciliation between God and human beings is indeed the focus of much New Testament use of the metaphor, but we remember once again, from Matthew's Gospel, that human relationships exemplify the relationship with God (Matt. 25: 31ff.). It was by welcoming the stranger and clothing the naked that those on the right hand welcomed the Son of Man. By the same token, reconciliation between alienated people or groups is the concrete instantiation of the reconciliation of God and human beings.

Another dimension of the cross breaking down barriers is suggested by Karl Barth's reading of Greek *nomos* ("law") as "religion" in his exegesis of Romans. Religion (and theology) can bolt and bar our access to God, he insists, can make us deaf to God's claim, and did in fact demonstrably do so in the war theologies of all countries in World War I (Rumscheidt 1972). When that is the case, a fresh wrestling with the Word bursts open what we understand by religion. Significantly, in both his commentaries, though more emphatically in the first than the second, Barth moves on to a political understanding of the significance of what has happened in Christ in his exegesis of Rom. 12–14. The cross, in these accounts, emerges as the critique of all legitimating ideologies. No one has explored this more profoundly than Kosuke Koyama in his attempt to face up to what happened in Japan in the period from 1880 to 1945. Koyama found faith in the midst of the ruins of Tokyo at the end of World War II. He saw that the devastation around him was the result of a false "center symbolism," the idolatry of Japanese power. The cross, he realized, was a critique of all such idols. Following Luther, he understood a true theology of the cross to imply a necessary brokenness, for him the critical dividing line between theology and ideology. The theologically instructed community is necessarily broken, necessarily contains a moment of sharp self-criticism, as opposed to the community governed by ideology, which knows no such necessity (Koyama 1985: 258). Such brokenness protects me against an idolatrous center symbolism, and in this way makes reconciliation possible.

Forgiveness

Reconciliation, Barth's chosen metaphor for the whole work of Christ, requires forgiveness. Forgiveness, we saw, can be understood as requiring Christ's death, or it can be understood as the result of life practices, being traditioned by God's Word, which make forgiveness possible. Beginning with this second sense we understand the church as a counter-culture based, to use John Milbank's terms, on an ontology of peace rather than an ontology of violence (Milbank 1990). Gregory Jones has argued that forgiveness is not letting someone off the hook but a remorselessly difficult option, a craft that may take a lifetime to learn (Jones 1995). Effectively Jones is talking about discipleship, and here we can introduce the much misunderstood idea of the "exemplary" theory of the atonement. The nineteenth-century historians found the origin of this in Abelard's urging that we were led to love by Jesus' example. It was certainly paradoxical that this view should be championed in 1915 by Hastings Rashdall, in the midst of the slaughter of World War I, and later twentieth-century theologians saw it as feeble, Pelagian, and disastrously shortsighted as to the seriousness of sin. To a large extent, however, these protests attack a straw man.

They miss the point for two reasons. First, and most significant, as R. C. Moberly argued a few years before Rashdall, there can be no atonement without Pentecost (Moberly 1909). An exclusive emphasis on the "once for all" event of the cross is nontrinitarian. Moltmann insists that "Whoever speaks of the Trinity speaks of the cross of Christ and does not speculate in heavenly riddles" (Moltmann 1974: 204). This sentence can be inverted, so that in speaking of the cross we speak of the Trinity, and the continuing work of the Spirit. From the very beginning Christianity was a "way," a disciplined following intended to have concrete results . True, Jesus was not a utopian political theorist; but he did teach his disciples to pray that God's kingdom might come on earth, and in the same prayer urged on them the practice of forgiveness. In this connection we have to insist that an exclusive focus on the symbol of "the cross" leads us to miss the significance of his teaching and healing ministry which is also, of course, salvific. As the early community recognized, out of the new forms of prayer and practice learned from Jesus comes an alternative way of doing things (Mark 10: 43). The history of the church can be written as the history of repeated compromises, challenged by repeated calls to live according to the Gospel. If we require any proof that such calls may have momentous political consequences we have only to look at the contribution Benedictine monasticism has made to Western culture.

Second, attacks on exemplarism miss the sense in which, under the Spirit, the community is shaped by its reading of scripture. Ignatius Loyola's *Spiritual Exercises* are an attempt to structure this reading in a way for which the term "example" is quite inadequate. Through this reading God works God's purpose out, a purpose for the whole human community, and not just for individual Christians – a purpose, in other words, with political dimensions. Perhaps the most interesting example of this in the twentieth century is the way Gandhi's practice of fasting to make atonement for communal violence, and to try to bring it to an end, was understood. The American missionary Stanley Jones felt that Gandhi's insistence that people can joyously take on themselves suffering for the sake of national ends "put the cross into politics" (Jones 1926: 92). It may be objected that such readings turn the cross into a "principle," but perhaps rather they are a recognition, firmly grounded in the Gospel, of the cross as a way on which the disciple has to tread.

Solidarity

Another understanding of the way in which salvation works, linked to this understanding of forgiveness, is suggested to us by the great hymn of Phil. 2: 5ff., which understands the cross as demonstrating the "solidarity of the love of God with the unspeakable suffering of those who were tortured and put to death by human cruelty" (Hengel 1986: 180). Hengel argues this, correctly in my view, on the grounds that bringing slavery and the cross together (Phil. 2: 7–8) would have been understood in only one way in the first century. Paradoxically, this way of reading the cross plays no part whatever in the history of Western atonement theology until the twentieth century (though it is foreshadowed in Negro spirituals). Only since the publication of Moltmann's *The Crucified God* in 1973 has it become mainstream, and even then it is contested. Moltmann is, of course, responding to the Holocaust, and to the ruminations of the Frankfurt School on the darkness of history. Is it not the case, they ask, that the torturers, the administrators of the concentration camps, are effectively the victors of history?[12] No, Moltmann answers, because from the cross we learn that God is alongside the gassed and the murdered. "God in Auschwitz and Auschwitz in the crucified God – that is the basis for a real hope which both embraces and overcomes the world, and the ground for a love which is stronger than death and can sustain death" (Moltmann 1974: 278).

The perception of solidarity as a political factor of the first order is probably traceable to the labor union struggles of the nineteenth century, though we find the reality of such solidarity in the accounts of earlier class struggles, going as far back as Spartacus. It becomes fundamental for liberation theology, especially in light of Paulo Freire's *Pedagogy of the Oppressed*. It implies a quite different understanding of power, a move from the passive – the victims, who are acted upon – to the active, where unity is strength. It licenses a reading of history which is not the history of "great men" (*sic*) but of peoples' movements, constantly put down, constantly arising in another place and another form.

Part and parcel of this is a new reading of church history as a history of the poor and lowly who from the start found strength in the crucified savior. For these people, in one form or another crucified throughout history, a savior who was not crucified would have nothing to say. This leads to a quite different understanding of Constantine's motto. Far from "taking the cross," it harks back rather to the perception of the first centuries that "the blood of the martyrs is the seed of the church." This in turn rests on rituals of remembrance, as martyrs have a significance only when their stories are told. As such, church history is not an academic matter, but a site of ideological contest, in itself deeply political. Thus the cult of saints of the high Middle Ages, with the elevation of spurious saints (St. George!), can be understood as a way of turning the critical power of martyrologies. Some forms of pentecostalism have the same effect today (Berryman 1996). Despite this, as E. P. Thompson and Norman Cohn have demonstrated, alternative memories continue to sustain the struggle of the poor.

It is important to distinguish this account of redemption from the patristic and medieval idea of Christ as a victim. The first stanza of the sixth-century hymn "Sing My Tongue the Glorious Battle" ends:

> Tell how Christ, the world's Redeemer,
> As a Victim won the day.

Victimhood here was Christ's willing assumption of sacrifice. From this starting point a mysticism of suffering developed which understood pain as something positive, an identification with the crucified Christ (Spivey 2001). The Latin American theologians have documented how important this has been in South America, and how it has bred fatalism and political passivity (Sobrino 1978). The theology of the crucified God, by contrast, looks to a future state of *shalom*. It seeks peace and justice now, including the conversion of the persecutor, the godforsaken and dehumanized who operate the systems of terror, but also hopes for the vindication of the victim in the new creation. It offers a hope for the "last days," which acts proleptically here and now. The cross, then, has been taken from the isolation of the sacrificial theory, and understood as lying at the heart of the ongoing life of the triune God, open to history, open to vulnerability, actively seeking the salvation of the godless and godforsaken.

In hoc signo vinces. The cross began as a political symbol and remains one. In a world where the poor are routinely sacrificed on the altars of corporate capital, it speaks of the once-for-all abolition of all sacrifice; in a world where the poor are disproportionately imprisoned and executed, it calls all judicial punishments into question; in a world of manifold alienations, it is a standing proclamation of the possibility of reconciliation; in a world dominated by the powers, it continues to provide, as it did for the first-century communities, a critique of their delusionary assumptions. In this sense it is possible to agree with the ancient tradition of the church: *Ave crux, unica spes.*

Notes

1   Thompson's father lost his faith in India and wrote a play, *Atonement*, which protested the death penalty, racism, and the penal doctrine of the atonement. This must have affected his son's later attack on Methodist understandings of the atonement.

2   This is the view of two of the most sophisticated commentators on the relationship. See Comaroff and Comaroff (1997), xv.

3   The Council of Sens in 1141 condemned Abelard's teaching on the atonement, among other teachings, but was not prescriptive.

4   The claim that religious practices or beliefs generate certain political outcomes is of course unprovable, but for evidence see Spivey (2001), ch. 4.

5   I am not sure if there is any instance of a female slave buying herself out.

6   Kelly argues that the sacrificial idea is dominant, if any one is.

7   I have tried to follow this story through in some detail in *God's Just Vengeance* (Gorringe 1996).

8   George extrapolates from contemporary corporation policy to provide a fictional account of what measures would be needed for the survival of capitalism in the next century, before turning to analysis.

9   In Britain in 1993 two boys, aged ten and eleven, abducted, tortured, and murdered a two-year-old, Jamie Bulger, leaving him on a railway track to be run over by a train. Popular indignation at their release has been high, on the grounds that they have not "paid" for what they did.

10 See the examples in Thompson (1968), ch. 11, and James Joyce, *Portrait of the Artist as a Young Man* (1916).

11 A meeting between these theologians and Girard was, however, held in São Paulo in 1990 and the proceedings published as *Sobre idolos y sacrificios* (San José: DEI, 1991). I am indebted, in the next two paragraphs, to the work of James Grenfell, "The Theme of Justice in Latin American Liberation Theology," unpublished D.Phil. thesis, University of Oxford, 2000.

12 Moltmann refers especially to the first volume of Max Horkheimer's *Critical Theory* (1968).

References

Aulen, G. (1931). *Christus Victor*. London: SPCK.

Barth, K. (1933). *The Epistle to the Romans*. London: Oxford University Press.

Barth, K. (1981). *The Christian Life*. Edinburgh: T. & T. Clark.

Berryman, P. (1996). *Religion in the Megacity*. New York: Orbis.

Comaroff, J., and Comaroff, J. (1997). *Of Revelation and Revolution*, vol. II. Chicago: University of Chicago Press.

Freire, P. (1972). *The Pedagogy of the Oppressed*. Harmondsworth: Penguin.

Garland, D. (1990). *Punishment and Modern Society*. Oxford: Clarendon.

George, S. (1999). *The Lugano Report*. London: Pluto.

Gorringe, T. J. (1996). *God's Just Vengeance: Crime, Violence and the Rhetoric of Salvation*. Cambridge: Cambridge University Press.

Gunton, C. (1988). *The Actuality of Atonement*. Edinburgh: T. & T. Clark.

Hengel, M. (1977). *Crucifixion*. London: SCM.

——(1986). *The Cross of the Son of God*. London: SCM.

Hinkelammert, F. (1992). *Sacrifcios humanos y la sociedad occidental: lucifer y la bestia*. San José, Costa Rica: Departmento Ecumenico de Investigaciones.

Jones, E. Stanley (1926). *The Christ of the Indian Road*. London: Hodder & Stoughton.

Jones, L. Gregory (1995). *Embodying Forgiveness*. Grand Rapids, Mich.: Eerdmans.

Kelly, J. N. D. (1965). *Early Christian Doctrines*, 3rd edn. London: A. & C. Black.

Koyama, K. (1985). *Mount Fuji and Mount Sinai: A Critique of Idols*. New York: Orbis.

Loewenwich, W. von (1976). *Luther's Theology of the Cross*. Belfast: Christian Journals.

Milbank, J. (1990). *Theology and Social Theory*. Oxford: Blackwell.

Moberly, R. C. (1909). *Atonement and Personality*. London: J. Murray.

Moltmann, J. (1974). *The Crucified God*. London: SCM. (First publ. in German 1973.)

Potter, H. (1993). *Hanging in Judgement: Religion and the Death Penalty in England*. London: SCM.

Ruether, R. (1983). *Sexism and God-Talk*. London: SCM.

Runciman, S. (1951). *A History of the Crusades*, vol. I. Cambridge: Cambridge University Press.

Rumscheidt, H. M. (1972). *Revelation and Theology: An Analysis of the Barth–Harnack Correspondence of 1923*. Cambridge: Cambridge University Press.

Schüssler Fiorenza, E. (1993). *Discipleship of Equals*. London: SCM.

Sobrino, J. (1978). *Christology at the Crossroads: A Latin American View*. London: SCM.

Spivey, N. (2001). *Enduring Creation: Art, Pain and Fortitude*. London: Thames & Hudson.

Tamez, E. (1992). *Contra toda condena*. San José, Costa Rica: Departmento Ecumenico de Investigaciones.

Thompson, E. P. (1968). *The Making of the English Working Class*. Harmondsworth: Penguin.

Thompson, K. (1985). "Religion, Class and Control." In R. Bocock and K. Thompson (eds.), *Religion and Ideology*. Manchester: Manchester University Press.

Ure, A. (1835). *Philosophy of Manufactures*. London.

Williams, R. (1965). *The Long Revolution*. Harmondsworth: Penguin.

Wink, W. (1984). *Naming the Powers*. Minneapolis: Fortress.

——(1986). *Unmasking the Powers*. Minneapolis: Fortress.

——(1992). *Engaging the Powers*. Minneapolis: Fortress.

Zehr, H. (1990). *Changing Lenses*. Scottsdale, Ontario: Herald.

CHAPTER 26
Spirit

Mark Lewis Taylor

Some of the most dramatic sites for political theology arise from the interplay between Christian views of the Holy Spirit and African beliefs in spirits and mediumship. This is not just an issue in African Christianity. It is an interplay that has also catalyzed change for many diverse peoples thrown into diaspora along the Atlantic coasts of Europe, Africa, and the Americas. These changes have been as political and revolutionary as they have been religious.

Sites of such change include revolts and revolution in England during the seventeenth century, Atlantic coast riots and the "American revolution" in North America in the eighteenth century, and resistance movements for the abolition of slavery (in the Americas and Europe) throughout the seventeenth to nineteenth centuries (Linebaugh and Rediker 2000: 327–34).

One emblem of this partnership between Christian Holy Spirit and African spirits lies in the history of a saying attributed to John the Baptist about Jesus' coming work of the spirit. It is recorded in the first century's New Testament Gospels, portions of it still sung out by Bob Marley in the twentieth. The Baptist proclaimed that the spirit's work against arrogance and pride would be like what happens when "the axe is laid to the root" (Matt. 3: 10–11). In the English revolution, Levellers and Diggers would use this biblical phrase to rally the poor against the arrogant rich. Evangelicals and secular radicals used the phrase in their movements for social justice in Britain and the Caribbean. Jamaican-born abolitionists published a journal entitled *The Axe Laid to the Root* (Linebaugh and Rediker 2000: 301–18), in which numerous essays against slavery appeared. Bob Marley's song, written with Lee Perry, still resounds (Perry and Marley 1973: #2):

> If you are the big tree, let me tell you that
> We are the small axe, sharp and ready
> Ready to cut you down (well sharp)
> To cut you down.

The song was just one expression of Marley's Rastafarian spirituality, an African/Caribbean movement that interacted with Christian Spirit discourse amid political travail (Murrell et al. 1998: 326ff.; Beckford 1998).

In this chapter, I first seek to explain why and how Christian understandings of the Holy Spirit could be open to this interplay with African traditions that yield a spirit of political and liberating change. Second, I will highlight how the history of this partnership catalyzed a "mystical politics" in the revolutionary Atlantic. Finally, I will conclude by noting how the presence of this partnership and its concrete history might affect a future political theology of liberating spirit.

Holy Spirit: A Mystical Politics of Liberation

While theologians often speak of a doctrine of the Holy Spirit, talk of the "Holy Spirit" has been hard to formalize as doctrine. One of the early church fathers writing on the Holy Spirit, Gregory of Nazianzus, had to confess the problem of elusive subject matter. "To be only slightly in error [about the Holy Spirit] was to be orthodox" (Pelikan 1971: 213).

It will be helpful here to follow just a bit of this error of orthodoxy. Amid the struggle with the elusive discourse of Holy Spirit, we can understand how this complex notion persistently emerges to speak of liberating communal change. This liberating function comes to the fore dramatically in settings of oppression and colonization, and this is what especially opened the doctrine of the Holy Spirit to partnership with the African notions of spirits that were deployed against oppressive structures like slavery (Ventura 1985: 113).

Three major sources of theological discourse about the Holy Spirit have steeped Christian ideas of the Holy Spirit in meanings of liberating practice of one sort or another. These are certain biblical emphases, a doctrinal dilemma in debates about "the person" of the Holy Spirit, and the imperial frame of early Jesus movements.

Biblical emphases

Many still read biblical references to the Holy Spirit as primarily having to do with extraordinary signs. Believers may think of miraculous workings of God, which are thought to involve a number of extra-body or psychic experiences, all defying established Western science's views of how things happen. These can all be grouped together as kinds of "spiritism."

The Bible abounds with many references to such spiritistic phenomena. The miracle stories about Jesus have often been read as miraculous, extraordinary signs. The writer of the Acts of the Apostles pauses to marvel at the signs and wonders performed by early Christians in the power of the Spirit.

These spiritistic phenomena, however, do not capture the meanings distinctive to biblical understandings of the Holy Spirit. Spiritistic phenomena, after all, are hardly unique to the Bible. From the time of Greek dramatists like Euripides or the Greek philosopher Democritus, marvelous powers and miraculous acts were regularly believed and depicted. Similarly, extraordinary spiritistic phenomena are not limited to the past. Glossolalia, for example, is a kind of spiritistic practice known in several religions and cultural contexts (Goodman 1972). To gain understanding of the Holy Spirit, biblical scholars have had to look beyond the sheer fact of extraordinary spiritism.

Biblical texts do not easily yield up a unified position on the meaning of the Holy Spirit, and certainly not all relevant passages can be examined here. Those who survey the whole range of biblical discourse on spirit, however, discern in it what I will term a "mystical communalism," in which "Holy Spirit" refers primarily to the mystery of God as intrinsic to, immanent in, communal life and development.

For the Gospels of Mark and Matthew, for example, there is a remembrance of the Hebrew scriptures' supposition that the Holy Spirit is God's power to perform special acts in history and community. These include acts of deliverance from Egypt (Exod. 3–14), and human acts of craftsmanship and artistic design (Exod. 35: 31–2). Here, the mystery of the spirit of God is not so much *above* as *in* these special and ordinary acts of history and culture.

When the writer of Luke and Acts summarizes diverse spiritistic wonders (healings, speaking in tongues, deliverances from prison, among others), the emphasis falls even then on the Christian *community's* specific power to execute concretely its basic tasks. New Testament scholar G. W. Lampe summarizes this tendency: "The Spirit *links together* and *binds into a single operation* of God, the whole series of events that began in the Jerusalem temple with the annunciation to Zechariah and reached a climax in the free proclamation of the kingdom of God in the capital city of the Gentile world by the leading apostle" (Lampe 1962: 633, emphasis added).

The notion of Holy Spirit as empowerer of community, a community that proclaims Christ, is also stressed in the writings of Paul and John. Paul, even when writing about seemingly individualistic and spiritistic phenomena, takes the Spirit as primarily Christ's presence in and among the faithful. A summary of Paul's logic here was ably given by New Testament theologian Herman Ridderbos:

> The thought is not that the Spirit first shows himself [*sic*] to individual believers, brings them together into one whole, and thus constitutes the body of Christ. . . .
> The sequence is accordingly the reverse: those who by virtue of the *corporate bond* have been united with Christ as the second Adam, have died and been buried with him, may know themselves to be dead to sin and alive to God, may also know themselves to be "in the Spirit." They are, *because included in this new life context*, no longer in the flesh, but in the Spirit. (Ridderbos 1975: 221, emphasis added)

The Johannine literature, although often referring to the Spirit as "from above," nevertheless presents the Spirit as personal presence and comforter, dwelling with and in the community of love. It was the writer in the Johannine epistles who stressed that the one who does not love cannot love God (1 John 4: 20).

These biblical emphases, then, stress a biblical notion of the Holy Spirit that is integrally bound up with the creation and nurture of communities of agapic love (Outka 1972). The effect of this emphasis on community is not to override the mystical meanings of spirit, but to envision them as located in the experience of love in a communal ethos, and hence ethically relevant. It is a mystical practice, where transcending experiences of the sacred, paradoxically, spring up most dynamically in ways immanent to concrete human experiences of agapic community.

This is not a social reductionism, either in the sense of reducing the mystery of God "down to" *only* the social, or in the sense of reducing the mystery of the human individual to *only* social functions. Instead, both God and individual are located in, found in, known in, and come into their own fullest meanings within, humans' relational ethos of agapic love. Thus these biblical emphases have blended the mystical with the social, in a mystical communalism.

A doctrinal dilemma

Centuries of doctrinal development have been devoted to explaining claims that the Holy Spirit is a unique "person" in a divine Trinity. New Testament analysts have routinely pointed out that the term "Holy Spirit" is, in the scriptures, less "a person," and more a "mysterious power of God," "mode of God's activity," "distinctive endowment of God to people," or again, a "mode of God's operation in the church" (Lampe 1962: 626).

What is particularly striking about the attempts to develop the Holy Spirit as person is their arrival at a dilemma, the only way out of which seems to be through a return to some of the biblical emphases summarized in my previous section, thus underscoring a mystical–communal interpretation of the Holy Spirit.

Consider the nature of the dilemma. On the one hand, Christian theologians, in accord with orthodox trinitarian formulas, have long discussed the Holy Spirit as one of three "persons" in a Godhead. On the other hand, most efforts to fill out a view of the person-like quality of this "third person" flounder, providing, mainly, various portrayals of a general, divine force and presence.

Both horns of this dilemma are problematic. If one holds to the claim of the first horn, one fails to give the Holy Spirit a persuasive sense of being a "person." It certainly does not have the symbolic clarity given by terms like "Father" and "Son," the names used for the other two persons in the Trinity. Those theologians who do reason their way to some argument that the Holy Spirit is a person usually display doctrinal argumentation so complex and intricate that it is graspable only in the rarefied atmosphere of a dogmatic elite.

The claim of the other horn of the dilemma, which may seem like a necessity given the failures to clarify the "person" of the Holy Spirit, is also unsatisfactory. This is because the language left over for referring to the Holy Spirit, that of a general divine force and presence, depersonalizes Christian discourse about divine spirit. Talk of the Holy Spirit as "person" at least had a virtue of satisfying people's need for symbols of God and of Spirit, which deployed personal imagery. As anthropologists and scholars of comparative religion have emphasized, there seems to exist, interculturally, a human drive to order social life in accord with some symbol system that relates that social life to an ultimate reality portrayed in terms of personal spirits (Douglas 1970: 45). Some theologians, however, actually prefer impersonal pronouns for the Spirit, to signify the Spirit's work in all creation – as force, power, the movement of the non-human. Paul Tillich's comprehensive correlation of "Spirit" with "Life" is just one well-known example (Tillich 1967: III, 11–294).

Discourse about the Holy Spirit as person did not speak to this need for impersonal metaphors, unless it was articulated in relation to the power of the Creator in the creation. Yet the Holy Spirit as person persisted, in spite of its troubling dilemma and rarefied doctrinal conceptuality, because it was a key place in Christian symbols where the faithful located those aspects of their personal talk about God that could not be adequately included under the personal imagery of Father and Son.

Resulting from this dilemma is a challenge to theologians: how to acknowledge the failure of traditional talk about the Holy Spirit as person, without depriving Christians of a person-like symbolic imagery of spirit. Such a deprivation may seem to be no loss, except that not only does it tend to consign the Holy Spirit to becoming something like what Joseph Haroutunian called an "oblong blur," it also leaves many to reach for repersonalizations of spirit discourse that yield superstitious notions of the Holy Spirit, as "friendly ghost" or personal "guardian angel" (Haroutunian 1975: 319–20). Ghosts and guardian angels may be welcome in some personal mythologies, but they rarely enable a communally shared understanding of the Holy Spirit.

The way forward to meeting the challenge posed by the dilemma is to allow the notion of person, when used for the divine life, to be reconstructed by the mystical communalism of the biblical narratives. That is to say, the "personal" nature of spirit is understood less as discrete ego, and more in the cultural terms of relation. In these latter terms, a person is constituted by the mutual relations to others. To be a person is to be a self within multiple and changing relations, in nature and diverse human contexts (Tillich 1967: I, 168–70; MacMurray 1961). On this model, the Holy Spirit is "inter-person." It is divine personal presence, but a presence that is interpersonal, relational, intersubjective. Perhaps one of the clearest examples of the flourishing of such a view of the self lies in the tendency in Jamaican vernacular to refer to one's self in conversation as "I-an'-I" (Murrell et al. 1998: 107ff.). St. Augustine is exemplary of doctrinal debate already pointing in the direction of this interaction between beings as constituting the "person(s)" of the Holy Spirit. In his *De Trinitate*, he experimented with imagery of the first person (the Father) as the "Lover," the second person (the Son) as the "Beloved," giving to the third person, the role of "Love" between them (Schaff 1956: 215–17).

More recently, other theologians have proposed renderings of the interpersonal meaning of Holy Spirit. One of the most radical formulations of the social character of the mystery of Holy Spirit was given by Schleiermacher who even seemed, at points, to identify the Holy Spirit with the church's life (Schleiermacher 1976: 560–1). In the twentieth century, Tillich is well known for frequently discussing the Holy Spirit as "Spiritual Community," an ideal community realized in history as one of faith and love, under the impact of "the biblical picture of Jesus as the Christ" (Tillich 1967: II, 86–245 *passim*).

Twentieth-century liberation theologians, such as those in Latin America, or contemporary feminist theologians, have also stressed the interpersonal as the locus of the Holy Spirit. For Gustavo Gutiérrez, the Holy Spirit refers primarily to divine presence in the "specific fabric of human relationships, in persons who are in concrete historical situations" (Gutiérrez 1988: 109). Feminist theologian Sallie McFague argues that feminists see the Holy Spirit as "a central, if not primary, 'name' for God," but emphasizes the spirit of God as "basically and radically immanent" and *in relations* of "love and empowerment, of life and liberty, for people and for the natural world" (McFague 1996: 147).

In all these ways, the person-like imagery of divine spirit is preserved but the notion of "Holy Spirit as person" is refocused as *inter*personal. The liberation and feminist readings, however, draw from still another source, one giving to Holy Spirit not just a mystical communal interpersonalism but also a pointed and liberating focus. To this we now turn.

Imperial framing of early Jesus movements

The imperial context of the Jesus movements tends to give their spirit discourse another trait. The biblical narrative's view of the Spirit as an agapic mystical communalism can be seen as related to conflicts of power. Hence, the Spirit's mystical communalism is also a mystical politics.

Consider the imperial frame. Jesus' life and work were played out in Galilee and Judea, under a Roman rule and occupation fusing local Herodian kings and religious elites into a ruling apparatus centered on a temple–state system in Jerusalem (Mack 1995). Jesus' closeness to agrarian life and Galilean peoples gave his work a distinctive spiritual character that put him in tension with this ruling apparatus and its religious supporters (Sawicki 2000).

Galilee was a site that was a crossroads of imperial conflict, and its agrarian peoples were long subordinated to meeting the economic and political needs of empire. They also had generated years of resistance to empire (Horsley 1995: 275–6). Jesus, too, would be seen as marginal to the ruling religious and political elites centered on the temple-state in Jerusalem.

Many official churches have stripped their message of much of its political meaning, but it was intrinsic to the early Jesus movement. The very notion of "Gospel," as applied to Jesus' message, for example, was derived from the Roman imperial discourse, where it was used for the "glad tidings" that conquering generals would announce to the citizens after battle (Myers 1988: 123–4). Its appropriation for Jesus' basic message suggests an overall challenge to the religion and politics of the standing imperial order.

There are many more signs of the anti-imperial character of the Jesus movement than can be treated in this essay. We might list just a few: the Gospel presentations of Jesus as contesting the temple-state; Mark's not-so-veiled suggestion that Jesus was in opposition to Roman occupying soldiers with his story of Jesus' exorcism of a demon named "Legion"; Jesus' death by crucifixion, a mode of execution reserved for the seditious who threatened the religiously backed imperial order; the apostle Paul's centering his message on the imperially distasteful notion that a shamed crucified one could be "Lord" (*kyrios*) or "Savior" (*soter*), terms traditionally used for the Caesars.

Even in the well-known passage about the Holy Spirit descending upon believers on the fifth Sunday after Easter ("Pentecost"), we can note the counterimperial implications of the Spirit's emergence. As narrated in Acts 2, people from many lands are described as hearing the new message about Jesus, and hearing it in their own languages. Most traditional interpreters focus on this event in its "extraordinariness," i.e. the strangeness of many hearing in their own diverse tongues. The real marvel, however, is not the surprising translation of a message into many tongues, but that the multilinguistic understanding among many peoples proceeds *from Galileans* (Acts 2: 7). This suggests also a new polity, one present and emergent from the striking anti-imperial space of tiny resistant Galilee.

When one recalls the content of the message of the Jesus figure, whom the writer of Luke and Acts says was working in the "power of the Spirit" (Luke 4: 14), the Galilean interest in contesting the political reach of empire is strong indeed. Luke's Jesus is dramatically portrayed as one who reaches back to the prophets in order to advance a radically inclusive message of liberation.

> The Spirit of the Lord is upon me,
> because he has anointed me to preach good news to the poor.
> He has sent me to proclaim release to the captives
> and recovery of sight to the blind,
> to set at liberty those who are oppressed,
> to proclaim the acceptable year of the Lord. (Luke 4: 18)

This liberating message etches into the Bible's mystical communalism of agapic practice a strong anti-imperial posture and practice.

The community of spirit in the Jesus movement, therefore, was profoundly anti-imperial in nature, indeed was such almost by definition of context. It tended to develop a communal ethos that rejected the establishment of hierarchical power (Schüssler Fiorenza 1993: 94; cf. Horsley and Silberman 1997:

163–83). It was marked by a restless political contentiousness; a series of large and small daily resistances to oppressive powers, and a building of new community for and among repressed groups (Sawicki 2000: 172–4). This gave the Spirit of God in Christian community a liberationist character, and this means that the mystical communion of agapic praxis had a strong political element.

That the Spirit was liberating or freeing signified also, of course, that the divine life was, in itself (and not just for the world), distinguished by that freedom. Hence the divine life that is believed to act in history, etched deeply into the dynamism and structure of all creation, is a veritable pulsing of freedom, a resource for catalyzing change in the present (to varying degrees) or change in an eschatological or apocalyptic future (Tillich 1967: I, 232–3).

Leveling Spirit: Liberating Struggle in the Revolutionary Atlantic

Because the mystical political strains of Christian spirit discourse cannot be missed, it should not be surprising that restless and repressed groups throughout history should find Christianity's spirit discourse pertinent to their struggles.

In this section, I have two aims. First, I seek to give some examples of how the mystical political dimensions of Christian spirit discourse have actually been present as historical practice, not merely as only a plausible conceptual theology as presented in the first section of the essay. Second, I want to show that the concrete history of a mystical politics can be found within and in close contact to Western Christianity, especially in the spirit discourses that unite African and Christian themes, as I noted at the outset.

Both of these aims can be achieved by looking first to the Levellers and Diggers of the English revolution and then following ways in which they were brought into contact and mutual dialogue with African peoples during the history of "the revolutionary Atlantic" (Linebaugh and Rediker 2000). This is a long and complex, multicultural history, and I cannot do full justice to it here. I highlight just a few features.

We might introduce the mystical politics at work in history through the lament by James Madison, a key architect of the US Constitution and one of the early US presidents. In 1787 he warned of certain groups who had an excessive love of liberty, a "leveling spirit." Who were these folk? According to Linebaugh and Rediker, they were a "motley crew" of secular and religious radicals who had been fomenting revolutionary change all around the Atlantic coasts for nearly two centuries (Linebaugh and Rediker 2000: 211–47). Madison was not the only one nervous about the leveling spirit. British admirals worried about rebels and sailors steeped in revolutionary spirit, "almost Levellers," said one admiral (pp. 215, 236). Let us follow this talk of "leveling spirit" into the contexts of religious radicalism of seventeenth-century England.

The English fight for the commons

In late sixteenth and seventeenth centuries, English merchant classes and landowners took advantage of new national and international market opportunities. To do this, however, they had to forcibly evict masses of people from their homelands and redeploy their labor power for other economic projects at new sites (Linebaugh and Rediker 2000: 17).

In England, this occurred in a most tumultuous way when the more powerful classes began the practice of enclosure, that is, enclosing and claiming possession for their own use of arable lands previously held in common. Enclosure required the eviction of many smallholders, the displacement of rural tenants, and the casting out of thousands from their land. This was a colossal shift: "a quarter of the land in England was enclosed" (Linebaugh and Rediker 2000: 17). The land was cleared of trees, marshes were drained and fields were hedged, resulting in an overall "obliteration of the commoning *habitus*," such that by the end of the seventeenth century "only an eighth of England remained wooded" (p. 43). For those who were not "redeployed" to other locations or sent off across the seas, there was the terror of being abandoned without work, land or credit to a life of vagabondage, becoming subject to "the merciless cruelty of a labor and criminal code as severe and terrifying as any that had yet appeared in modern history" (p. 18).

It was in this setting that the Levellers and Diggers were born, and "the leveling spirit" that Madison warned about took rise. "Levellers" was a name first used in the Midlands Revolt of 1607, when many threatened by the expropriations took direct action to remove the enclosures. Their direct actions often merged with those who became known as "Diggers," so named because their actions as soon-to-be dispossessed people included filling in the ditches newly dug for the enclosing hedges, and working common land after enclosure (Linebaugh and Rediker 2000: 18; Bradstock 1997: 72–5).

The Levellers and Diggers disseminated their ideas in several tracts and manifestoes of the seventeenth century: *A Light Shining in Buckinghamshire: A Discovery of the Main Grounds and Original Causes of All the Slavery In the World, but Chiefly in England* (1648); *The True Leveller's Standard Advanced* ("The Digger Manifesto") of 1649; and, in May 1649, the *Agreement of the Free People of England* (Linebaugh and Rediker 2000: 85, 101, 235).

A key writer during this period, and exemplary of the mix of political radicalism and spirit discourse, is Gerard Winstanley. He is often described as "the most articulate voice of revolution during the late 1640s" in England:

> He opposed slavery, dispossession, the destruction of the commons, poverty, wage labor, private property, and the death penalty. He was not the first person to come up with a rational plan for social reconstruction, but he was, as Christopher Hill has noted, the first to express such a plan in the vernacular and to call on a particular social class – the common people – to put it into action. (Linebaugh and Rediker 2000: 140)

It was Winstanley who, referring to the hedges of the vicious enclosure process, saw that "The teeth of *all nations* have been set on edge by this sour grape, the covetous murdering sword." He linked expropriation *in England* to Gambia's and Barbados' suffering worked *by England* and so "moved toward a planetary consciousness of class" (Linebaugh and Rediker 2000: 141). He preached a future deliverance arising "from among the poor common people" in his texts, for example *A Declaration from the Poor Oppressed People of England* (1649).

The future deliverance Winstanley preached depended on the coming of an "age of Spirit" that he awaited (Knott 1980: 86). This Spirit, for all its radical, transformative potential, was seen as a markedly communal set of events (Bradstock 1997: 89). The Spirit lived in a "glorious liberty," which the Apostle Paul wrote of in Rom. 8, but which was already present in people's "groaning," enabling their moving from the "first fruits" tasted now to a future realization. This passage on the Holy Spirit was crucial to Winstanley's millennialism, and he interlaced quotations of the Spirit passages in Rom. 8 throughout all his writings (Linebaugh and Rediker 2000: 110–11). He closed one of his tracts with these words: "And here I end, having put my Arm as far as my strength will go to advance Righteousness: I have Writ, I have Acted, I have Peace: and now I must wait to see the Spirit do his own work in the hearts of others." (Linebaugh and Rediker 2000: 103).

Winstanley's work and hope were vigorously Spirit-oriented. Other words of his about the Spirit take us to the next section. Elsewhere, he wrote: "Now the Spirit spreading itself from East to West, from North to South in sons and daughters is everlasting, and never dies: but is still everlasting, and rising higher and higher in manifesting himself in and to mankind" (Linebaugh and Rediker 2000: 142).

The Levellers at sea

This religious radicalism was disseminated all around the Atlantic in the late seventeenth century, especially when the English ship attained the notable distinction of being "the engine of commerce, the machine of empire." Ships were floating factories that united several of the major modes of production organized by new capitalist forces for the exploitation of labor (Linebaugh and Rediker 2000: 149).

The ship, however, also became a factory producing interaction between rebels and disenchanted workers from all around the Atlantic. The Levellers and Diggers, displaced from their commons in England, entered this mix of radicals at sea. They were an astonishingly diverse lot, yet shared a fundamental sense of exploitation and rage, especially provoked by the injustice of forced impressments into navies (Linebaugh and Rediker 2000: 228–36). Africans and African Americans, escaped from slavery and/or always vulnerable to it, added additional vigor and determination to maritime resistance.

Sailors' resistance often culminated in the mutinies and organized resistance of piracy. Pirates, much maligned by centuries of European scholars and story-tellers, have been re-presented by recent historians like Linebaugh and Rediker as having some surprising traits. Pirates' ships were democratic spaces in an undemocratic age, making their captains' governance dependent upon majority vote. They were egalitarian in a hierarchical age, dividing their loot and stolen goods in a new equal fashion, "leveling" the wage inequality that existed in almost all other maritime workplaces (Linebaugh and Rediker 2000: 162–7). Many free blacks and runaway slaves found refuge in the pirate ships, "multiracial maroon communities, in which rebels used the high seas as other [runaways] used the mountains and jungles" (p. 167).

In new radical community with the spiritualities and radicalism of the peoples of the sea, the Levellers kept alive the dream of the commons which had been lost not only in England but in other contexts as well.

> the commons were more than a specific English agrarian practice or its American variants; the same concept underlay the clachan [Scottish and Irish hamlet], the sept [branch of a family clan], the rundale [a joint occupation of land, also in early Irish and Scottish contexts], the West African village, and the indigenous tradition of long fallow agriculture of Native Americans – *in other words it encompassed all those parts of the Earth that remained unprivatized, unenclosed, a noncommodity, a support for the manifold human values of mutuality.* (Linebaugh and Rediker 2000: 26, emphasis added)

The valuing of the commons here is no mere romanticization of organic solidarity and communal utopia. On the contrary: for those with leveling spirit at sea and in seaports around the Atlantic, the commons was a way of life adopted for survival. The alternative, which had so cruelly been meted out to them, was displacement, torture, and death.

Thus it was that diverse groups of the Levellers at sea, in tandem with groups from all around the Atlantic, formed a multicultural "motley crew" of the world's displaced peoples, a "hydrarchy" (rule of the waters) from below, which grew up to rival the hydrarchy from above, British maritime and military systems. The leveling motley crew helped mobilize mass resistance to poor wages and unjust working conditions either side of the Atlantic. They led urban mobs in London, fomented many of the riots in seaport towns of the North American colonies, and built the revolutionary climate that informed the less revolutionary sorts like Samuel Adams, Thomas Paine, and Thomas Jefferson.

Indeed, Linebaugh and Rediker describe this motley crew of the world's enspirited slaves, sailors, and commoners as "the driving force of the revolutionary crisis in the 1760s and 1770s" (2000: 212). This "motley crew" of the displaced, English and African, slaves and sailors, were the real architects of American revolution in the late seventeenth century, creating a revolutionary ethos all along North America's Atlantic coast (p. 214). It was among such as these that Madison feared a "leveling spirit."

Historically, the fusion of Christian and African mystical politics, that liberating spirit of the Levellers, is dramatically present in the Jamaican Robert Wedderburn. I have already referred to the journal he edited, *The Axe Laid to the Root*, which "gave life to a transatlantic intellectual dialogue that synthesized African, American, and European voices" (Linebaugh and Rediker 2000: 306). The newspaper's title was found preached from Jamaica to New York, where runaway slaves are said to have heard of the inspiring "small axe." In his writings, not only did Wedderburn remember and record his own slave family's personal terror in Jamaica, he also witnessed the disciplinary terror and horrific punishments meted out to defenders of the commons, whether on the Caribbean plantation or the maritime ship. In England, he joined a number of workers' movements, abolitionist efforts, and mutinies. Coming from Jamaica to England, and journeying back to the Africanized Caribbean (also a site for Asian and indigenous peoples), Wedderburn imbibed the leveling principles and spirit, and enriched them with the spiritual life and vitality of African peoples. In correspondence back to Jamaica from England, he challenged his readers to recall "the purity of the maroons," that is, their intrepid struggle for abolition and freedom.

Wedderburn was a crucial linchpin in an emerging spiritual politics of the revolutionary Atlantic. Through his writings on African spirituality, early Christianity, Caribbean revivalism, and slave religion, Wedderburn

> linked through time the communist Christian in the ancient Near East with the Leveller in England and with the Native Baptist in Jamaica. He linked through space the slave and the maroon with the sailor and the dockworker, with the commoner and the artisan and the factory worker; . . . he linked the slave with the working-class and middle-class opponent of slavery in the metropolis. He was the kind of person for whom "the idea of abolishing the slave trade is connected to the leveling system and the rights of man." (Linebaugh and Rediker 2000: 326)

Wedderburn is a dramatic figure who not only displays the mystical politics of liberating spirit to be very much a historical phenomenon, but who, in his person, also embodies the multicontinental working of Spirit in which Winstanley had put his hopes.

Toward a Political Theology of Liberating Spirit

I conclude by briefly noting four major lines of inquiry that invite further development, given the partnership of Christian, African, and other spirit discourses of liberating struggle in the revolutionary Atlantic.

Liberation theology in the North Atlantic

The political orientation of this legacy of Christian spirit discourse means that there are vital and longstanding traditions of "liberation theology" in the North

Atlantic that need to be explored. This has two consequences. First, it should blur the distinction often made between so-called first world "political theology" and third world "liberation theology." The traditions of the North Atlantic have long had their liberation theologies among communities of the displaced and poor. Many theological educators in North American settings often view liberation theology as having its primary focus "abroad" in developing countries of, say, Latin America. We need to acknowledge not only the black theologies of liberation and feminist liberation theologies, but also the existence of many elements of liberating spirit at work among communities of the poor in the United States and Europe. It is time for theologians to acknowledge that reality, perhaps following the important work of Andrew Bradstock's study of Müntzer and Winstanley in *Faith in the Revolution* (1997).

Second, contemporary political and liberation theology stands to be enriched by the content of these North Atlantic spirit traditions. Following in the spirit discourse of the Levellers and Diggers, for example, theologians today might start thinking anew on theological ideas that were crucial to their spirituality of liberating struggle: (a) the antinomianism they cultivated from scriptures like "All things are lawful for me" (1 Cor. 10: 23), which African slaves and abolitionists read as license to foment change for the enslaved and exploited everywhere (Linebaugh and Rediker 2000: 81, 235); (b) the notion of "the glory of God," a bestowal of Spirit that was interpreted as breaking every yoke of oppression, held dear by Africans throughout the revolutionary Atlantic, such as the so-called "Blackymore Maide named Francis" in Bristol, England (pp. 83–4, 99); (c) the belief that "God is no respecter of persons" in the sending of the Spirit, a notion found in the Digger Manifesto of 1649 and in the denunciations against racism by Marcus Garvey in 1926 (p. 100); and (d) the biblical notion of jubilee, which Christian spirituality established as a panethnic and international discourse (p. 320). The message of jubilee was part of a "discourse of deliverance," flowing through the Leveller/Digger liberation theologies and well "fortified by African-American preachers such as Sambo Scriven, who traveled to the Bahamas, George Liele, who went to Jamaica, and John Marrant, who preached in London and Nova Scotia" (p. 268). Historians have good cause to link the biblical "trumpet of jubilee" to the "shell-blow jubilee" of Jamaica and Haitian slave resistance (p. 326).

Intercontinental and intercultural community

The sites analyzed as "spiritual" communities, inviting the work of political theology, need to become intercontinental and intercultural ones. The spirit that thrives among peoples in resistance is associated with their roles as shifting, often forcibly displaced, moving from place to place, mixing cultural ways from continent to continent. This was certainly the case for the spirit at work among the Levellers, Diggers, slaves, and sailors in Africa and the Americas. There is sometimes a tendency to see liberation and political theology through the lens of a kind of contextualism, which links theological discourses to bounded and landed settings. To follow the spirit of resistance, however, theologians will also need to analyze the culturally and continentally hybrid worlds of peoples on the move across lands and seas. Future political and liberation theologies, perhaps especially in the age of globalized culture and power, will need to work from a much more fluid sense of contextuality.

Charismatic and pentecostal groups

The work of this chapter suggests that political and liberation theologies would also do well to intensify their studies of various charismatic and pentecostal groups, especially in communities of the poor, in order to explore new fusions of spirit with liberating politics. Especially in the United States, there has been a tendency to see pentecostal emphases on the Holy Spirit as fusing with politics only on the political right, but the history explored in this essay suggests otherwise. Indeed, for some time now scholars have had to take note of how pentecostal discourses, usually seen as "other-worldly" actually have political functions, including liberating ones. The groundbreaking work of Robert Beckford in Britain – *Jesus is Dread* (1998) and *Dread and Pentecostal* (2000) – is just one example. Recent actions by neopentecostal indigenous evangelicals in Ecuador, jousting with neoliberal policies of the transnational market, suggests that this Spirit-led radicalism is alive as a mode of resistance elsewhere as well, and deployed by diverse peoples (Ainger 2001; Batista 2000).

The interreligious character of the Spirit

Finally, the interactive and fluid locations toward which I have sent political theology in this essay require that the Spirit be reflected on, even by Christian liberation and political theologians, in its fully interreligious character. Recall that as the "leveling spirit" arose amid English Levellers and Diggers, and then interacted with political and spiritual aspirations of slaves, indentured servants, sailors, soldiers, and the disenfranchised from around the Atlantic, the "Spirit" or "spirits" invoked rarely belonged to any one religious tradition. They certainly were not simply Christian, Yoruban, Quechua, or Vodun, though all of these could feed the spirit discourse of a mystical politics of resistance. As with Marley's "Small Axe," and the centuries of tradition that lie behind that song's idea, the Spirit of resistance fused its vitality and character by crossing the many religious languages, just as cultures and continents were crossed. The revolutionary Atlantic challenges political theology, then, to enter into the full and creative syncretism of religious expression deployed by communities in struggle for liberation.

References

Ainger, Katherine (2001). "Indigenous Peoples Open a Crack in History." *New Internationalist*, Oct. 5, 6.

Batista, Israel (2000). *Comunidades de Jubileo: las iglesias evangélicas en el nuevo milenio*. Quito: Ediciones Consejo Latinoamericano de iglesias.

Beckford, Robert (1998). *Jesus is Dread: Black Theology and Black Culture in Britain*. London: Darton, Longman, & Todd.

—— (2000). *Dread and Pentecostal*. London: SPCK.

Bradstock, Andrew (1997). *Faith in the Revolution: The Political Theology of Müntzer and Winstanley*. London: SPCK.

Douglas, Mary (1970). *Natural Symbols: Explorations in Cosmology*. London: Barrie & Rockliffe/Cresset.

Goodman, Felicitas D. (1972). *Speaking in Tongues: A Cross-Cultural Study of Glossolalia*. Chicago: University of Chicago Press.

Gutiérrez, Gustavo (1988). *A Theology of Liberation: History, Politics and Salvation*, rev. edn. Maryknoll, NY: Orbis.

Haroutunian, Joseph (1975). "Holy Spirit." In *Westminster Dictionary of Christian Theology*. Philadelphia: Westminster.

Horsley, Richard A. (1995). *Galilee: History, Politics, People*. Valley Forge, Pa.: Trinity.

——, ed. (1997). *Paul and Empire: Religion and Power in Roman Imperial Society*. Harrisburg, Pa.: Trinity.

Horsley, Richard A., and Silberman, Neil Asher (1997). *The Message of the Kingdom*. New York: Grosset/Putnam.

Knott, James R. (1980). *The Sword of the Spirit: Puritan Responses to the Bible*. Chicago: University of Chicago Press.

Lampe, G. W. H. (1962). "Holy Spirit." In *The Interpreter's Dictionary of the Bible*, vol. II, 626–39. Nashville: Abingdon.

Linebaugh, Peter, and Rediker, Marcus (2000). *The Many-Headed Hydra: Slaves, Sailors, Commoners and the Hidden History of the Revolutionary Atlantic*. Boston: Beacon.

McFague, Sallie (1996). "Holy Spirit." In *Dictionary of Feminist Theologies*, ed. Letty M. Russell and J. Shannon Clarkson, 146–7. Philadelphia: Westminster/John Knox.

Mack, Burton (1995). *Who Wrote the New Testament? The Making of the Christian Myth*. New York: HarperCollins.

MacMurray, John (1961). *Persons in Relation*. London: Faber.

Murrell, Nathaniel; Spencer, William David; and McFarlane, Adrian A., eds., (1998). *Chanting Down Babylon: A Rastafari Reader*. Philadelphia: Temple University Press.

Myers, Ched (1988). *Binding the Strong Man: A Political Reading of Mark's Story of Jesus*. Maryknoll, NY: Orbis.

Outka, Gene H. (1972). *Agape: An Ethical Analysis*. New Haven: Yale University Press.

Pelikan, Jaroslav (1971). *The Christian Tradition: A History of the Development of Doctrine*, vol. I. Chicago: University of Chicago Press.

Perry, Lee, and Marley, Bob (1973). *African Herbsman*. London: Trojan Records.

Ridderbos, Herman (1975). *Paul: An Outline of his Theology*. Grand Rapids, Mich.: Eerdmans.

Sawicki, Marianne (2000). *Crossing Galilee: Architectures of Contact in the Occupied Land of Jesus*. Harrisburg, Pa.: Trinity.

Schaff, Philip, ed. (1956). *A Select Library of the Nicene and Post-Nicene Fathers of the Christian Church*, vol. III. Grand Rapids, Mich.: Eerdmans.

Schleiermacher, Friedrich (1976). *The Christian Faith*, 2nd edn. Philadelphia: Fortress. (First publ. 1830.)

Schüssler Fiorenza, Elisabeth (1993). *Discipleship of Equals: A Critical Feminist Ekklesialogy of Liberation*. New York: Crossroad.

Tillich, Paul (1967). *Systematic Theology*, 3 vols. Chicago: University of Chicago Press.

Ventura, Michael (1985). *Shadow Dancing in the USA*. New York: St. Martin's.

CHAPTER 27

Church

William T. Cavanaugh

In one way or another, all political theologies at the end of the twentieth century can be read as so many attempts to come to grips with the death of
Christendom without simply acquiescing in the privatization of the church.
Nevertheless, Christian political theology has strangely neglected the topic of the
church. This neglect is strange from the point of view of theology, but perfectly
understandable from the point of view of politics in the modern liberal nation-
state. From the latter point of view, politics has been emancipated and properly
differentiated from theology. Politics takes place in an autonomous, secular
sphere, established on its own foundations. The church may or may not contribute to this process in various ways, but secular history and salvation history
are two distinct processes. Even for most theologians who do not accept the
Enlightenment story of secularization, the end of Christendom is to be accepted
as the proper separation of the church from worldly power. The politics of the
nation-state appears as a universal, encompassing all citizens regardless of their
other affiliations. The church, in contrast, is a particular association, one of
many that inhabit civil society. To base a politics in the church would be to set
politics on a particularist and sectarian footing. The church may therefore make
some contribution to the larger political life, but is not itself a political body.

In this essay I contend that a full theological understanding of the church
requires us to refuse this political marginalization of the church. Any adequate
ecclesiology must acknowledge the political implications of two crucial theological data: first, there is no separate history of politics apart from the history
of salvation; and second, the church is indispensable to the history of salvation.

Israel and the Body of Christ

Unless we anachronistically read a Weberian definition of politics – that is, the
idea that politics is defined as having to do with attaining and maintaining power

over the apparatus of the state – back into the scriptures, then Israel/the church are clearly political entities in the general sense that they give order through law and ritual to the social life and everyday practices of a distinctive community of people. The political significance of the church cannot be told from a merely sociological viewpoint, however, but must begin from its theological significance in the history of salvation. At the heart of the modern reluctance to see the church as itself a type of politics is the inability to see it as more than a gathering of individuals, who are assumed to be the real subject of salvation. In the biblical witness, however, salvation is inherently social. The Jewish and Christian conviction about salvation is remarkable precisely in that *salvation has a history*. Salvation is a fully public event that unfolds in historical time before the watching eyes of the nations. Salvation is not a matter of pulling a few individual survivors from the wreckage of creation after the Fall, but is about the re-creation of a new heaven and a new earth (2 Pet. 3: 13; Rev. 21: 1). The history of salvation is not told separately from the history of politics. In the scriptures the story of salvation takes flesh on a public stage and interacts with pharaohs, kings, and Caesars. Salvation itself is imaged as a coming kingdom and a new city.

Indispensable to the history of salvation are Israel and the church. God calls a community of people to be a foretaste of salvation, one concrete community called to live differently, so that others may taste and see God's peaceful revolution and be blessed too. Even political theologies that try to keep political history and salvation history together tend to neglect the centrality of the people of God to the history of salvation. "How odd of God / To choose the Jews" remains the unspoken refrain, for the idea of a chosen people is an affront to the universalism of modern politics. It is nevertheless a basic theological datum, one that in the recent past was often elided by supersessionism: namely, the argument that the church opens up and universalizes the particularism of Israel. As Gerhard Lohfink's important book *Does God Need the Church?* argues, however, the theologic of the salvation of the *whole world* through *one particular people* (Gen. 12: 3) is implicit in the logic of a creation with freedom:

> [H]ow can anyone change the world and society at its roots without taking away freedom? It can only be that God begins in a small way, at one single place in the world. There must be a place, visible, tangible, where the salvation of the world can begin: that is, where the world becomes what it is supposed to be according to God's plan. Beginning at that place, the new thing can spread abroad, but not through persuasion, not through indoctrination, not through violence. Everyone must have the opportunity to come and see. All must have the chance to behold and test this new thing. Then, if they want to, they can allow themselves to be drawn into the history of salvation that God is creating . . . What drives them to the new thing cannot be force, not even moral pressure, but only the fascination of a world that is changed. (Lohfink 1999: 27)

To avoid supersessionism, some such explanation of the logic of election is necessary, given the basic scriptural datum that Israel and the church are central to the history of salvation and therefore of political history.

The Israelites, of course, most often did not in fact look much different from other communities. The Old Testament tells the history of salvation in a penitential key, highlighting the sin of the Israelites from which salvation is promised. The claim of the Israelites to be the people of God is not a claim of moral superiority for the Israelites, but a claim that the very drama of sin and salvation is being embodied to the world in Israel. Central to this embodiment are covenant, liturgy, and law. As Walter Brueggemann writes, "Deuteronomy offers covenant as a radical and systemic alternative to the politics of autonomy, the economics of exploitation, and the theology of self-indulgence" (Brueggemann 2000: 48). Indeed, theology and politics are inseparable, for the autonomy of royal power – in this context both Israelite and Assyrian – is an autonomy *vis-à-vis* God, and therefore a form of idolatry. Liturgy is never merely "religious" or other-worldly, but is the enacted drama of the different kind of power and the different kind of political order that YHWH wills over against the oppressors of Israel: "This distinctive community is invited to affirm that *the world constructed in liturgy* is more reliable and more credible than the world 'out there'" (p. 43, emphasis in original). The Torah likewise is not "religious" law, but covers every aspect of life, from "civil" and "criminal" law to body hair, from governance to birds' nests.

Nevertheless, Israel in its self-understanding is not a political entity of the same order as other ancient political units. Israel's experience of what we would call "statehood" is relatively brief, from the reign of David to the conquests by the Assyrians and Babylonians, and Israel's experience of statehood is not what gives it identity or continuity. The preceding period of tribal confederacy (1200–1000 BCE) was not merely the "prenational" period, as if it were just a primitive form preliminary to monarchy. Tribal confederacy may have been a deliberate counter-model to the monarchies of the Canaanite city-states (Lohfink 1999: 107–8). When the Deuteronomist tells the story, the shift to kingship is cast in a negative light (1 Sam. 8). The social order codified by the Torah reaches back behind kingship for its norms and avoids any connection with the Davidic "state." Both in the forms of its post-exilic temple community and in the federation of synagogues that follows, the people of Israel is a *tertium quid*. The synagogal community is neither a *polis* nor a *koinon*. A *koinon*, or association, was a subset of the whole *polis*. A *koinon* was a club formed around particular or special interests. The concern of the synagogue, however, was for the whole of life, as mandated by the Torah. Synagogues maintained communication with each other and were concerned to remain connected to the land of Israel. The Roman Empire recognized their peculiar status, and granted them exemption from military service and from the imperial cult (Lohfink 1999: 116–18).

The church adopted this model from the synagogue and began to employ the term *ekklesia* to denote the peculiar political status of the people of God. The *ekklesia* was the "assembly" of all those with citizen rights in a Greek city-state. The church's use of the term *ekklesia* may have its ultimate roots in the Deuteronomic phrase "the day of the assembly" at Sinai (Deut. 9: 10, 10: 4, 18: 16). In adopting the term *ekklesia*, the church was making a claim to being more than a mere *koinon*. The church was not a mere part of a whole but was itself a whole, whose interests were not particular but catholic; they embraced the fate of the entire world. The church saw itself as the eschatological fulfillment of Israel, and therefore as the witness and embodiment of salvation to the world. The church was not *polis*, and yet it used the language of the kingdom of God to describe the very concrete and visible fulfillment of Israel that was "at hand" in the event of Jesus Christ (Mark 1: 15). The church was not *polis*, and yet it used the language of citizenship to describe membership in it (Eph. 2: 19; Phil. 3: 20). In the church, citizenship was available through baptism to those excluded from such status in the *polis*, namely women, children, and slaves.

The scholarly recovery of the Jewishness of Jesus over the last few decades (e.g. Sanders 1985) has important implications for the political significance of the church, because it puts to rest the (often antisemitic) spiritualization and interiorization of the Gospel. Jesus does not come to replace the crudely external Law and make it a matter of personal faith and motivation; he comes not to abolish the Law but to fulfill it (Matt. 5: 17–18). Baptism and Eucharist now become the center of the ritual fulfillment of the Law, enacting a liturgical drama that recalls the confrontation of Christ with the powers and calls the participants into the body of Christ. The eucharistic body and the body of the community are so closely connected that Paul is convinced that divisions in the community along socioeconomic lines threaten to turn the Eucharist into an occasion of condemnation (1 Cor. 11: 17–34). The Body of Christ was not a mystery cult but a new way of living reconciled lives in the world, and this way included all aspects of life. The church was to be the visible eschatological sign of God's plan of salvation for all of creation. That it often was not demanded, as Paul saw, that the story of the church be told penitentially.

It should be no surprise that the Romans treated the church as a political threat whose practices were subversive of good order in the Empire. Pliny, in a letter to the Emperor Trajan (*c.*110 CE), reports that he applied Trajan's ban on political societies to the Christian communities of Asia Minor. In the Roman view, Christian failure to worship the pagan gods and their assumption that allegiance to Caesar conflicted with allegiance to Christ was not simply a religious matter, but concerned imperial political order. As N. T. Wright notes, Christians did not attempt to defend themselves from persecution with the claim that they were merely a "private club" or *collegium* for the advancement of particular interests. They continued to proclaim the kingship of Christ, even if such kingship was not based on the model of Caesar's (Wright 1992: 346–57). That Christ's kingdom is not of (*ek*) the world (John 18: 36) was regarded as a statement of origin; the kingdom is not from the world, but it is in the world and deeply concerned with it.

Christendom and Church

If the history of salvation did not simply begin a long detour in the fourth century, we must be able to account for the continuity of the church before and after Constantine. We are accustomed to viewing the establishment of Christianity as the official creed of the Roman Empire as marking a radical break with the church's past, and it did. But there is a deeper continuity, insofar as the church had always thought of itself as a body with political significance. The Constantinian shift was not from other-worldly to worldly church, from Christ-against-culture to Christ-of-culture, from sect-type to church-type. Rather, the shift was in the way Christians read what God was doing in salvation history. Oliver O'Donovan's work is helpful not merely because it makes a positive account of Christendom possible, but because it makes the Constantinian shift *explicable*. Fourth-century Christians did not simply become drunk with power and move the church off its foundations. Many Christians now imagined that God had finally brought the governmental powers under God's rule, and thus the church's political task had changed – perhaps temporarily – from martyrdom to government (O'Donovan 1996: 215–17). Constantine was not the beginning of political theology, but rather represented a shift in Christian thinking and practice regarding how the kingdom of God was being made manifest in the world.

The long experiment with Christendom that followed Constantine finally and definitively crumbled in the twentieth century. The contemporary ferment of political theology can be understood as an attempt once again to reimagine what God is doing with the principalities and powers in the present age. The separation of the church from the means of violence is – I think rightly – generally accepted as a good. If we are not to build an account of Christendom on the abandonment of the church by the Holy Spirit, however, we need to say more than that Christendom is a diversion in the search for the proper form of the church. Constantine does not represent the mere "fall" of the church from some pristine state of righteousness, nor does Christendom represent an unfortunate intermingling of two essentially distinct things – theology and politics, church and state – that we enlightened people of modernity have finally managed properly to sort out and separate. What is lumped together under the term "Christendom" is in fact a very complex series of attempts to take seriously the inherently political nature of the church and its instrumental role in the integral salvation of the world in Jesus Christ. After the fall of the Roman Empire in the West, the church was left holding the bag, as it were, and people turned to their local bishops as judges and protectors. As kingship developed, occasions for conflict between church and temporal rulers increased, primarily because kingship itself was viewed theologically as a scripturally and liturgically sanctioned office of order within the people of God. Conflicts between civil and ecclesiastical authorities were due not to the confusion of *essentially* distinct responsibilities but, on the contrary, to the inherent inseparability of church and politics (Tierney 1964: 1–11).

Nevertheless, although we cannot simply dismiss Christendom as some terrible mistake of the Holy Spirit, the ambiguities involved in Christian wielding of coercive power eventually brought the experiment of Christendom crashing to earth. In the Augustinian view that dominated the early Middle Ages, coercive government was not natural to human being, but with the Fall became necessary because of human sinfulness. As long as an eschatological focus could be maintained, it was possible to view the use of coercion by the temporal authorities as only temporarily necessary while we await the fullness of the kingdom of God to be realized in a new heaven and a new earth. Thus Augustine taught that the "earthly peace" enforced by coercion could be made use of by the *civitas dei* as something merely borrowed and temporary:

> The heavenly city, or rather the part of it which sojourns on earth and lives by faith, makes use of this peace only because it must, until this mortal condition which necessitates it shall pass away. Consequently, so long as it lives like a captive and a stranger in the earthly city, though it has already received the promise of redemption, and the gift of the Spirit as the earnest of it, it makes no scruple to obey the laws of the earthly city, whereby the things necessary for the maintenance of this mortal life are administered. (Augustine 1950: 695–6 [XIX. 17])

The difference between spiritual and temporal authority is a difference of time, not space; spiritual authority deals with the eternal, temporal authority with the provisional measures necessary between the first and second comings of Jesus Christ. Politics remains projected onto salvation history.

With the waning of the Augustinian view and the rediscovery of Aristotle and Roman law in the eleventh and twelfth centuries, however, there begins the process of turning the temporal into a space, one that will eventually be seen as standing outside the church. Coercive government is endowed with permanence; it is not an unfortunate necessity based on the contingent reality of human sinfulness that awaits the consummation of Christ's kingdom, but rather a natural and inevitable feature of human society based on the intrinsically social nature of human being. According to Aquinas, it is "natural" for human beings to live in the society of many, but such a multitude would disintegrate "unless there were a general ruling force within the body which watches over the common good of all members" (Aquinas 1949: 5–6). This sense of the naturalness and permanence of coercive government is captured by the rise in the later Middle Ages of the terminology and reality of the "state," a static and permanent institution that stands separate from both ruler and ruled (Skinner 1978: 352–8). At the same time that temporal authority was thus losing its eschatological reference and becoming "spatialized," to use Catherine Pickstock's term (Pickstock 1998: 135–66), the temporal was also being redefined as a space essentially separate from the spiritual. In the investiture controversy, kingship was effectively stripped of its liturgical reference in order to safeguard the independence and superiority of the spiritual authority of the church. With the passage of time, however, this would prove to be a Pyrrhic victory for the church, because it set the stage for the rise of a self-sufficient and autonomous civil authority that would be sacralized on its own terms, quite apart from the church (Kantorowicz 1957; Cavanaugh 1998: 212–21).

The ambiguity and tension of the earlier Augustinian view of coercive power as an intra-ecclesial mode of restraining sin thus broke open into a complete split between coercive power and spiritual authority, or between power and love. In the modern era, the national state would arise as the autonomous bearer of lethal power over bodies, and the church would take its place as the caretaker of souls. Temporal and spiritual would come to occupy distinct spaces; the temporal referred to certain things – politics, business, etc. – and the spiritual to others – conscience, sacraments, and so on. Christianity would become interiorized as a "religion," and the modern distinctions between religion and politics, church and state, would become institutionalized in the secular nation-state. This process would be fully completed only in the twentieth century. Not coincidentally, the twentieth century produced a tremendous flourishing of theologies of the political, as Christians attempted to puzzle through the political implications of the Gospel after Christendom. The church has finally been freed from Christendom, from the ambiguities of the wielding of coercive power. We have not, however, been freed from the question of the political nature of the church. Political theologies are built on the recognition that we cannot submit to the privatization of the church. What role they leave for the church, however, varies greatly.

Politically Indirect Ecclesiology

Most post-Christendom theologies of the political do not simply embrace the idea that salvation history has been privatized, but they nevertheless endorse the relative autonomy of politics from theology and make the influence of the church on politics indirect. Christendom saw various kinds of claims of church authority over temporal power, some based on claims that the church possessed direct political authority, others based on the idea that the church's authority in the temporal was *potestas indirecta*. The latter theories were based on the spiritual power – typically possessed by the Pope – to discipline any erring member of his flock, including and especially temporal rulers (Tierney 1964: 2–5). Post-Christendom political theology recognizes that the church cannot simply renounce politics and retreat to private concerns, but it tends to operate at one more remove of indirectness from the medieval conception of indirect power. In Christendom, questions of the direct or indirect power of the church over the temporal had to do with the power of the church to discipline Christian rulers. In modern secular societies, however, political theologies tend to operate at an additional remove from the state, staking a claim to influence the state only through the activities of Christian citizens in civil society. Furthermore, most assume that, when addressing a pluralistic society, theology cannot be directly politicized, but must first be translated into some more publicly accessible form of discourse in order to have an influence in civil society.

For Jacques Maritain, for example, the fall of Christendom has allowed a proper distinction between the temporal and the spiritual, which are spatialized as "planes." This is not merely a concession made by the church, but is the outworking of the Gospel itself. Christ made clear that his kingdom is spiritual, not of this world. In contrast to the pagans, Christ interiorized the sacred, locating it in the human heart, removed from the vicissitudes of time. In a corollary move, Christ liberated us by making a sharp distinction between what is Caesar's and what is God's. The genesis and growth of the modern secular state is therefore not the rejection of the Christian ideal but, on the contrary, offers the opportunity for the full flowering of the Christian spiritual life properly untangled from its confusion with material culture (Maritain 1931: 1).

Though the temporal plane has its own relative autonomy, however, it remains subordinate to the spiritual plane; the merely natural virtues involved in political and social life – running businesses, governments, and wars – are meant to be "elevated" by the supernatural spiritual virtues. The church, nevertheless, unites souls outside of temporal space and time and is not directly involved in the realm of political ethics. The church, therefore, does not act as a body on the temporal plane, but exerts an indirect influence through the individual. The individual Christian acting on the temporal plane of the political and the social is animated by the spiritual plane. On the temporal plane, the Christian acts "as Christian," but not "as a Christian as such" (Maritain, 1968: 294). In this way, a "New Christendom" is possible in which the state remains explicitly secular, but individual Christians bring the inchoate influence of the Gospel to bear on public life, without speaking explicitly Christian language in the public forum.

John Courtney Murray provides another influential example of the indirect political influence of the church. Here the key distinction is between state and civil society. The state is to play a limited role within society, that of protecting public order. The realm of freedom and moral agency is civil society, and the pursuit of the common good is a matter for society as a whole. The church has no access to the coercive power of the state, but contributes to the common good by attempting to "permeate all the institutions of society – economic, social, cultural, political – with the Christian spirit of truth, justice, love, and freedom" (Murray 1993: 183). Here Murray recasts the medieval notion of the "indirect power" of the church so that its subject is not the ruler or the state but the individual conscience of the Christian citizen of the nation-state. For Murray the church itself is meant to be a vibrant and robust association at the service of society, but (as in Maritain) the church is not in view as itself a political institution; the political implications of the Gospel must be translated into a "spirit" that permeates material institutions. Furthermore, there is a bifurcation of the natural and the supernatural, such that, in the pluralistic public realm, the church must not speak theologically, but in the language of the natural law, which is in theory accessible to any reasonable person, Christian or not (Murray 1960: 295–336).

It is this requirement to make the Christian message intelligible within the confines of a post-Christendom political liberalism that makes the church drop out of Reinhold Niebuhr's political theology almost entirely. Niebuhr is no less convinced than Murray that religion is necessary to sustain the ethos of a pluralistic democracy. Niebuhr, however, is much less confident than Murray that the church has privileged access to some truths essential to the common good. For Niebuhr, religion's contribution to the proper functioning of a democratic social order is the recognition that such claims to privileged access are most often due to the sin of pride. Sin pervades the human condition, and conflict of self-interests is inevitable. The genius of democracy is precisely that it balances such interests and refuses to allow any particular claims to achieve universal status. Christianity, with its anthropology of human sinfulness, thus serves a democratic order by relativizing any claim to justice and truth. "Religious faith ought therefore to be a constant fount of humility; for it ought to encourage men to moderate their natural pride and to achieve some decent consciousness of the relativity of their own statement of even the most ultimate truth" (Niebuhr 1944: 135). Such humility, of course, precludes the possibility that the church be given some kind of privileged position for mediating God's will for the ordering of society. Ecclesiology is simply absent from Niebuhr's political theology. He no doubt assumed that the church was sociologically necessary for Christianity to exist in organized form, but any claim that the church was the source of an alternative politics could only be treated as a manifestation of pride, and thus a threat to a democratic political order.

The above political ecclesiologies share an atomizing pathology; the emphasis is on the individual Christian citizen acting in the temporal realm. The church does not act as a body in the temporal. The new political theology of Johann Baptist Metz, on the other hand, sees the church acting as an "institution of social criticism" within modern secular democratic society. Metz's ecclesiology nevertheless still aims at an indirect influence of the church in political matters. Metz begins with the acceptance of the "proper" emancipation of the political from the religious. Indeed, the autonomy of the political in Metz is less encumbered by the kind of explicit subordination to the spiritual that is found in Maritain. For Metz, the Enlightenment signifies the achievement of the maturity of human freedom. The secularized political order is an order of freedom; political realities are no longer given but are subject to free human action. As in Maritain, the outlines of salvation history are seen only in the relative autonomy of the world from the church. Secularization is not the dethroning of Christ in the world, but rather "the decisive point of his dominion in history" (Metz 1969: 19), for it is Christianity that sets the world free to be itself. Metz considers the old versions of political theology – Bonald, Donoso Cortés, Schmitt, and others – to be "precritical" because they do not accept the Enlightenment critique of religion; they believe that theology can be directly politicized. At the same time, however, Metz is concerned that the legitimate separation of the church from the political sphere should not result in the mere privatization of the church, the delivering over of the Gospel to the anemic embrace of bourgeois sentimentality. Metz's solution is that the church take its place in civil society as an "institution of social criticism" whose mission is defined as a service to the history of freedom unfolding since the Enlightenment. On the basis of the memory of Jesus' confrontation with the powers and his preference for the marginalized, the church will criticize all social forms as falling short of the kingdom of God. Even the church itself is put under the "'eschatological proviso,' which makes every historically real status of society appear to be provisional" (Metz 1969: 114). The criticism the church provides is not merely negative, but a challenge to make actual in the present the eschatological promises of the biblical tradition: freedom, peace, justice, and reconciliation. Because theology cannot be directly politicized, however, theology must be translated into "practical public reason" for consumption in the arena of civil society.

Metz's positive evaluation of secularization was taken over by much of liberation theology. The work of Gustavo Gutiérrez has the great merit of emphasizing that there are not two histories, one sacred and one profane, one of salvation and the other of politics: "The history of salvation is the very heart of human history" (Gutiérrez 1988: 86). However, this evaluation has the effect of de-emphasizing ecclesiology. For Gutiérrez, the Maritainian model of political theology that preceded liberation theology in Latin America was still infected by a "certain ecclesiastical narcissism" because of its desire to create "a society inspired by Christian principles" (p. 36). Secularization demands that we recognize the full autonomy of the temporal, an "entirely worldly world" that operates on the assumption that human beings in their freedom are the agents of history. According to Gutiérrez, secularization is not an anti-Christian impulse but simply the outworking of the biblical idea that creation is separate from the Creator, and that "God has proclaimed humankind lord of this creation" (p. 42). The world is autonomous, but it is also permeated by God's grace. Gutiérrez thus wishes to overcome the bourgeois privatization of the church by elevating the spiritual status of the mundane political world and by breaking down the barriers between theology and politics. The church is the explicit witness to the liberation of humanity from sin, including social and political sin of all kinds. The church, however, is not epistemologically privileged in understanding social and political processes, which operate within their own worldly autonomy and are thus best understood by the social sciences:

> rather than define the world in relation to the religious phenomenon, it would seem that religion should be redefined in relation to the profane . . . [I]f formerly the tendency was to see the world in terms of the Church, today almost the reverse is true: the Church is seen in terms of the world. In the past, the Church used the world for its own ends; today many Christians – and non-Christians – ask themselves if they should, for example, use the influence of the Church to accelerate the process of transformation of social structures. (p. 42)

Despite criticisms of liberation theology for politicizing the faith, there is little room here for a directly political ecclesiology. The church contributes to the transformation of political and social structures, but the church plays an instrumental role, and is not itself envisioned as a kind of politics. As an autonomous process, politics is in some sense "outside" the church, and so the application of the church to politics is once again indirect.

Church as Polity

As different as the above approaches are from one another, they share the assumption that the modern separation of theology and politics is proper and that politics resides in a different autonomous space from that marked out by the church. The church must therefore approach politics indirectly, from afar. There is a different approach, however, that seeks to overcome this division by examining the politics embedded in core Christian theological themes, without need of translation from theology to politics or vice versa. Key to this approach is reimagining the political as a direct response to God's activity in the world, a return to the Augustinian conviction that politics is truly politics only when mapped onto salvation history. God's acts and human acts are not to be identified, but both take place, as O'Donovan says, in the "one public history which is the theatre of God's saving purposes and mankind's social undertakings" (O'Donovan 1996: 2). Central to this reimagining is the conviction that the church is at the heart of God's plan of salvation.

Oliver O'Donovan's work is unusual in this respect, because it regards Christendom as the most significant practical instance of the conviction that theology is politics. As O'Donovan sees it, Christendom is simply the unfolding drama of God's rule as manifested in the Old Testament and as fulfilled in the kingship of Christ. If Christology is given its due political weight, then after the Ascension the nations could simply not refuse to acknowledge Christ. If Christ really is the fulfillment of the salvation history begun in Israel, then God must in fact be using the governing authorities for his own purposes in bringing about a new social order. Nevertheless, the government is not the church; the church exists to serve as a distinctive witness, to remind the government of its temporary status. As ruler, the ruler is meant to judge; as member of the church, the ruler is meant to judge with clemency; and the church is there to signal the inherent tension between the two obligations (O'Donovan 1996: 200). The church thus plays a central role in the transformation of the social order. The church itself bears the fullness of God's politics through history. "Does the authority of the Gospel word confer no social structure on the community which bears it? Does that community have no 'social space' determined by the truth?" (p. 208). There can be no question of a disembodied Christianity that serves only, in a Gnostic fashion, to inform the consciences of individual citizens occupying an autonomous political space.

O'Donovan presents a serious challenge to Christian accommodation to liberal social orders. Nevertheless, he locates himself in an established national church and depends upon the state to be the police department of the church. His repositioning of politics within salvation history recovers the eschatological dimension missing from much of contemporary political theology, but his eschatology has a strong accent on the "already" of Christ's victory. As a result, he puts a great deal of emphasis on the biblical images of rule, to the exclusion of images of wandering, pilgrimage, exile, and resident alien status. These themes are taken up by Stanley Hauerwas who, though in fundamental sympathy with O'Donovan's retrieval of eschatological politics, would place the emphasis more decidedly on the "not yet." Hauerwas has no doubt that God's reign will triumph, but he wants to be more reticent than O'Donovan about how in fact God's reign is manifested on the way. The lordship of Jesus, Hauerwas suspects, is nothing like the worldly rule of states, and is most often found in the signs of weakness and contradiction that mark the Christian way of the cross. The political task of the church post-Christendom is to suffer rulers as faithfully as possible, to the point of martyrdom if necessary, to wait upon the Lord and not to presume to rule in his place (Hauerwas 1997: 199–224).

Such a reticence about the reign of God seems to prompt Hauerwas to say more about the church, to identify the church fully as *polis* (as the subtitle of one of his books indicates) – though it is a *polis* without a police department. Unencumbered by the need to rule, the church is called to be "a 'contrast model' for all polities that know not God" (Hauerwas 1981: 84). The church's role in the history of salvation is precisely to bear God's politics through history. The hallmark of God's politics is that authority operates through the power of the truth, and not through violence. In the modern nation-state, the autonomy of politics from God's rule ensures that social order is based only on the arbitrary suppression of will by will. The role of the church is not merely to make policy recommendations to the state, but to embody a different sort of politics, so that the world may be able to see a truthful politics and be transformed. The church does not thereby withdraw from the world but serves it, both by being the sign of God's salvation of the world and by reminding the world of what the world still is not.

Questions

The most common objection to the suggestion that the church itself embodies a politics is that such a politics is sectarian. Such an objection depends on a relatively novel sociological use of the term "sect." In theological parlance, a sect was a group that put itself outside the authority of the church. The difference between the Waldensians and the Franciscans lay not in their attitudes toward "culture" or the "world," but in their relationships to church authority. In the twentieth century, however, "sect" came to indicate a group whose practices put it at odds with the dominant culture and political elites of the nation-state. The underlying assumption is that it is not the church but the nation-state that is "catholic"; the church, insofar as it is a political actor, is a particular association of civil society that is encompassed by the larger universal political sphere of the nation-state. Theologically speaking, this is a grave error. As even O'Donovan recognizes, the church was catholic even in the catacombs (O'Donovan 1996: 216). Salvation history is not a subset of world history, but simply is the history – not yet complete or legible – of human action in a grace-soaked world. As widely as O'Donovan's Christendom differs from Hauerwas' resident aliens, both agree that political theology cannot be done without an account of the directly political nature of the church and its role in salvation history.

If salvation is not of the church but of the world, however, there can be no question of a withdrawal of the church from the world. The church catholic is to live like the Jews of the diaspora, "to seek the welfare of the city where I have sent you into exile" (Jer. 29: 7), even if that city is Babylon (Yoder 1997: 1–5). Without seeking to rule, the church has more to contribute precisely because it is the bearer of God's politics, and because it is catholic, transnational, transcending the parochial borders of the nation-state.

Nevertheless, some difficult issues need attention if a directly political ecclesiology is to be developed. Though "the church" is a crucial theological locus, it is by no means always clear in practice where the boundaries of the church lie. "Church" and "world" are often more prescriptive rather than descriptive terms; in practice, the church is full of the world. This is as it should be; the dialectical drama of sin and salvation implies a dialogical relationship between the church and its others, which include the world and God. Indeed, the Holy Spirit blows where it will, and the activity of the Spirit is not limited to the church. The church is therefore a relational body, and not a closed system. The church is not a *polis*; *ekklesia* names something closer to a universal "culture" that is assembled from out of the particular cultures of the world (Healy 2000: 159–75).

The church is not only crossed by nonchurch elements; it also contains anti-Christ elements. The church is a *corpus permixtum*, full of both saints and sinners. As Nicholas Healy reminds us, ecclesiology must maintain both poles of Paul's dictum in Gal. 6: 14, "far be it from me to glory except in the cross of our Lord Jesus Christ." On the one hand, we must not boast of the church, as if the church were already the answer to all the world's social ills; on the other hand, we must glory in Christ, and regard the church as a key actor in the unfolding of the drama of salvation which Christ's cross has won (Healy 2000: 1–24). The eschatological "not yet" means that the history of the drama so far needs to be told hopefully but penitentially, with room for marginal voices and conflicts. The story is not told in an epic manner, as if the church were made to rule. As the embodiment of God's politics, the church nevertheless muddles through. God is in charge of all of history. The church's job is to try to discern in each concrete circumstance how best to embody the politics of the cross in a suffering world.

References

Aquinas, St. Thomas (1949). *On Kingship*. Toronto: Pontifical Institute of Medieval Studies.

Augustine, St. (1950). *The City of God*. New York: Modern Library.

Brueggemann, Walter (2000). "Always in the Shadow of the Empire." In Michael Budde and Robert Brimlow (eds.), *The Church as Counterculture*. Albany, NY: State University of New York Press.

Cavanaugh, William (1998). *Torture and Eucharist*. Oxford: Blackwell.

Gutiérrez, Gustavo (1988). *A Theology of Liberation*, rev. edn. Maryknoll, NY: Orbis.

Hauerwas, Stanley (1981). *A Community of Character*. Notre Dame, Ind.: University of Notre Dame Press.

——(1997). *Wilderness Wanderings*. Boulder, Col.: Westview.

Healy, Nicholas (2000). *Church, World, and the Christian Life*. Cambridge: Cambridge University Press.

Kantorowicz, Ernst (1957). *The King's Two Bodies*. Princeton: Princeton University Press.

Lohfink, Gerhard (1999). *Does God Need the Church?* Collegeville, Minn.: Liturgical.

Maritain, Jacques (1931). *The Things That Are Not Caesar's*. New York: Charles Scribner's Sons.

——(1968). *Integral Humanism*. New York: Charles Scribner's Sons.

Metz, Johann Baptist (1969). *Theology of the World*. New York: Seabury.

Murray, John Courtney (1960). *We Hold These Truths*. Kansas City: Sheed & Ward.

——(1993). *Religious Liberty*. Louisville, Ky.: Westminster/John Knox.

Niebuhr, Reinhold (1944). *The Children of Light and the Children of Darkness*. New York: Charles Scribner's Sons.

O'Donovan, Oliver (1996). *The Desire of the Nations*. Cambridge: Cambridge University Press.

Pickstock, Catherine (1998). *After Writing*. Oxford: Blackwell.

Sanders, E. P. (1985). *Jesus and Judaism*. London: SCM.

Skinner, Quentin (1978). *The Foundations of Modern Political Thought*, vol. II. Cambridge: Cambridge University Press.

Tierney, Brian (1964). *The Crisis of Church and State 1050–1300*. Englewood Cliffs, NJ: Prentice-Hall.

Wright, N. T. (1992). *The New Testament and the People of God*. Minneapolis: Fortress.

Yoder, John Howard (1997). *For the Nations*. Grand Rapids, Mich.: Eerdmans.

CHAPTER 28
Eschatology

Robert W. Jenson

Eschatology and Politics

"Eschatology" in the title of this chapter refers to Christian discourse about a final outcome and transformation, an "eschaton," of history. The great meta-physical divide is doubtless between those who think a dramatic story can truly be told about reality as a whole and those who think not. Judaism and Christianity present the definitive instance of the first position. Reality, their scriptures promise, is going someplace, and its twists and turns are therefore plotted. If we think that someplace abstractly, we speak of an eschaton; if we think it personally, we speak of God.

It must be said at the beginning that Christianity thus anticipates an event that is so fundamental a transformation of created being that even calling it an "event" stretches language to the breaking point. What sort of "event," after all, has no successor? Unless it be the event of God's own actuality, the event of the triune life?

The scriptures contain many scenarios of the end times; but these are not easily harmonized, are at key points allusive in their diction and in the sequences of their narrative, and are surely best taken – though there is no space to argue that here – as evocations of one single occurrence, that will be at once the con-clusion of history and in its own sheer actuality the reality of "eternal life," of "the kingdom of God."

Perhaps, despite first thought, there is much conceptual analysis and material–poetic construction that can be done to specify this event, and much revisionary metaphysics that grow out of specifying it; but again, any general effort on those lines (Jenson 1999: 309–69) would exhaust the space of this chapter. Perhaps one may in almost unintelligible summary speak of an infinite implosion of love, of a created community pressed and agitated into perfect mutuality by the surrounding life of the triune God. For the rest, readers should take this paragraph and its predecessor as a sort of notice posted, which they should bear in mind through the following.

We are in this chapter to consider how Christian eschatology and political discourse relate under the common rubric "theology." We must begin by noting a fundamental circumstance: that the scriptures' eschatology and the classical eschatology of the Christian church are directly and almost exclusively a discourse about politics, so that no extrapolations are needed to move between eschatology and politics, in either direction. In the promise to Abraham and in the writings of the prophets, the eschaton is the fulfillment of Israel's political structures; in the Gospels it is a "kingdom," which precisely as a kingdom "of heaven" is a political entity also in this age, as the Roman authorities quickly perceived (Wright 1998); elsewhere in the New Testament it is a *polis* (Heb. 13: 14) which, unlike this world's would-be polities, is genuinely a structure of peace and justice; in Augustine's lovely phrase, one of *tranquilitas ordinis*, the lively tranquility enabled by mutually affirmed ordering to one another. Indeed, biblical and classical Christian eschatology can be taken directly as political theory, if we do not allow the modern West's secularized constructs to stand paradigm for what is meant by "theory" (Milbank 1990).

Eschatology is thus the initial form and should be a principal guide for Christian reflection on politics. I will begin with some hasty biblical exegesis, and continue by instancing the relentlessly eschatological classic of Christian political theory, Augustine's *City of God*.

I suspect that every chapter of this work will have its own way of using the word "politics." It will be prudent to lay out this chapter's quite naïve usages at the start.

Notoriously, the word "politics" now has two very different common uses, to which this essay will adhere. In a generally Aristotelian and traditional Christian theological sense, a polity is the arena of a community's moral deliberation, whether this arena is an assembly of all citizens, an absolute ruler's bedchamber, or something in between. "Politics" then consists of the processes of such deliberation: argument and executable decision of such questions as "What shall we teach our children?" or "What would be a just distribution of communal goods?" But the word now carries another and almost opposite sense also: "politics" is precisely what must be kept out of such communal deliberation, lest it lose its moral character. Here "politics" is the manipulation of the community and the struggle to occupy positions from which this may be done, both of which efforts of course suppress politics in the former sense. The relation between these uses poses a rather crude irony: How does it happen that precisely those known as "politicians" regularly exhort each other to "keep politics out of this" when they claim to deal seriously with the community's good, that is, when they claim actually to function as political agents?

We will see that Christian eschatology interprets both phenomena we label "politics," and moreover provides an understanding of the relation between them. We are political creatures in the first sense because righteous discourse in community is the end for which our Creator intends us. That we turn this calling into its own suppression is much of what Christian theology calls "sin," and is what will be judged, that is, put behind us, at the end. And the link between the two is a structure of human being, in Augustine's language, that we *desire*, indeed that we desire eschatologically: we long for a final Good and do so communally.

Israel's Eschatological History

The call to Abraham, which begins the story of Israel,[1] was not to found a new cult or pursue a pattern of piety or become wise, all possibilities well known in the ancient world, but to perform a historical act with political significance: to lead a migration. And the promise in the call was the creation of a new nation with a specific relation to other nations, namely that it would be their "blessing," that is, the possibility of their flourishing. The actual creation of this nation then occurs as a political conflict within history: the "Exodus," the liberation of an oppressed people from imperial domination.

To be sure, all nations in fact begin historically, but in antiquity they did not acknowledge this in their own cases – nor indeed do they now in practice. Rather, a normal ancient nation told the story of its beginning mythically and so apolitically, as the account of an always recurring origin, which is identical with the always recurring origin of the universe. Israel, per contra (Jenson 1997: 63–74), knew that its beginning *followed* the Creation by a significant span of time, and even followed a kind of prenational existence of its own, the period of "the patriarchs," so that there was a time when it was not, so that its origin was itself a temporal, historical event. Indeed, this acknowledgment was an article of its creed: it confessed, "A wandering Aramaean was my father" (Deut. 26: 5), not, for example, "With/from deity I come forth." Israel knew it was *contingent*, that acts of decision were constitutive in its being – what if Abraham had said, "I won't go?" Thus its self-understanding was communally moral, that is, political, from its root.

Scholarship generally agrees that the one Israel of the twelve tribes was first constituted inside Canaan, after the tribes' entries into the land. Much about its initial polity is disputed. Was it for a time an "amphictiony," a cultically united confederation? How much of the story told in the books of Judges and Samuel is historical? For our purposes, one point is knowable and decisive: in the earliest times, legislation and jurisdiction were supposed to belong directly to "the Lord," the specific God of Israel, who spoke through "men of God," "prophets" in the later terminology: persons so taken over by God that their judgments are his judgments. When Israel eventually wanted to have a normal mid-Eastern monarchy, to "be like other nations," the Lord said to the currently judging prophet, "[T]hey have rejected me from being king over them" (1 Sam. 8: 7–20).

Israel cast a paradigmatic picture of this divine government through prophets in the story of the "40 years" between the Exodus and the entry into Canaan, under the leadership of *the* prophet, Moses (Deut. 34: 5–12). In the story of the 40 years, the counterpart to legislation and jurisdiction by a prophet is a community on the move, with no "abiding city," a nation that understands itself from the wilderness and from the goal of its trek through that wilderness. For the Word of the Lord is always what it was for Abraham, a summons to "Go . . ." and a promise, "I will . . ." The constitution of this polity was "the covenant," a compact granted by God to Israel, which was based on God's act to make an oppressed populace into a nation, which gave them a fundamental law – in briefest material formulation, "the ten commandments" (Exod. 20) – and which again contained a universal promise, that among the nations, which all belong in one way or another to the Lord, this one should be the "kingdom of priests" for the others (Exod. 19: 5). Israel's polity was thus intrinsically eschatological from the start, in that the good it was communally to cultivate would, if fully accomplished, unify all nations in worship of the Lord – an event which would of course explode the framework of history as we now live it.

A monarchy was indeed established, under David and Solomon a modest empire. Despite its origin in Israel's desire to be a normal nation, this polity too had its Israelite peculiarities. Even David, the dynastic founder, had to be legitimated in the role by being himself a prophet, whose "last words" began with the announcement of a prophetic seizure: "The Spirit of the Lord is upon me" (2 Sam. 23: 1–2). The kings were subject always to harassment by prophets – sometimes from among their own household shamans – who claimed to overrule human counsels with the word of God. Most vitally, the moral content of the covenant with the monarchy was the same as that of the desert covenant: *righteousness*, the condition in which each member of a community uses his or her position for the benefit of each other member, the solidarity requisite for a people on the move.

Nevertheless, after *c.*1000 BCE there was a more or less normal monarchy, with a capital city and the usual economic and military powers. The desert's portable sanctuary tent was replaced with a proper temple of the region and period, after the pyramids the most *fixed* object in the architectural repertoire of humanity; this one, however, lacked that for which such temples were normally built, the boxed-in and thereby itself fixed image of the god. Like the desert community, this polity understood itself as based on covenant, even though this was a covenant with a dynasty and a place.

A pseudo-Hegelian argument can perhaps be constructed, to trace Providence's intention with this second covenant. That the Lord made Israel a monarchy – even as a concession – comports with description of his intention for them as "political." For a people directed exclusively by immediate prophetic utterance would, strictly speaking, have no politics in *either* of the usages identified at the beginning of this chapter, there being neither a communal forum of decision nor a way to suppress a decision-making that was directly in the hands of God. Thus references above to a prophetical "polity" stretch the word a bit. To be sure, Israel's picture of the desert covenant was at least in part an ideological retrojection – historically, of course, there must have been some sort of clan jurisdiction and assemblies for special purposes – but the point here is the way Israel *saw* its history. Perhaps we may say that the royal covenant established the eschatological drive of the desert covenant within the history of this age, and so made the community of the Lord and his people be what we more properly may call a polity, something more and less than sheerly "the wandering God-folk."

So we must think of a polity that is placed geographically, trades and makes war, and makes its communal decisions by the usual communal debates and efforts to suppress them, but is legitimized by a word direct from God, knows about its own historical fragility, and is disquieted by at least subliminal feeling that it should always be somehow on the move. While the prophets' interventions had various occasions and matter, they in one way or another always had the performative force explicitly formulated by Isaiah II: "Forget the old things; see, I am about to do something new" (Isa. 43: 18–19). Such a polity will obviously be in permanent unease, torn between the – at least apparent – demands of survival in this world and the demands of eschatological righteousness.

The main event of Israel's history after the establishment of the monarchy was its long-drawn-out undoing, caught as it was between the alternately advancing empires of Mesopotamia and the Nile, and weakened by a tribal split into two states. Babylon finished the process in the early sixth century, punishing Judea's acceptance of Egyptian suzerainty by razing Jerusalem and the temple and deporting the Jewish elites to Babylon. Contrary to what might have been expected, the decades of "the exile" became the occasion of a final radicalizing of prophecy. The "something new" now promised by the exilic and post-exilic prophets is a fulfillment of Israel's mission that is plainly and often explicitly beyond the possibilities of history in its present terms (Jenson 1997: 69–71); in exilic and post-exilic prophecy Israel's political hopes are openly eschatological. "Nation shall not take up the sword against nation, neither shall they learn war anymore" (Mic. 4: 3), which demands nothing less than that God "will destroy the shroud that is cast over all peoples . . . , he will swallow up death forever" (Isa. 25: 7). Finally, in the "apocalyptic" schemes cast in the last time of Israel's prophecy, the difference between "this age" and "the age to come" is explicit and indeed ontological. The age to come is nonetheless – or rather, all the more – envisioned as a polity (Jenson 1997: 70–1).

Jesus then came preaching, "The Kingdom of heaven has come near" (Mark 1: 15): so near, indeed, that to follow him was to enter into it and to turn away from him was to balk at the gate (Mark 10: 21–7). With that, the eschaton-polity, the universal polity of peace, appeared as a possibility for present citizenship. And when the God of Israel raised this Jesus from the death to which his radicalism had brought him, following him became a continuing possibility within this world, open to Jews and gentiles, and a mission began to bring all into this citizenship. Thus we arrive at the end of the history we have been following: of the eschatological promise that is about politics, and the history of whose making is itself canonical Israel's political history. And thus we arrive also with Augustine, the founding political theorist of at least the Western church.

Augustine

As Augustine (Jenson 1999: 76–85) read the scriptures, it seemed right to adopt a term of Greek and Roman political discourse for what God eternally intends for his creatures. God's eternal intent is that there shall be a perfect created *civitas*, a perfect polity.[2] That is, continuing in the language of Roman theory, God intends a *res publica*, a "public thing," with sovereignty and citizenship and mutual duties, that is perfect in that it fully achieves – or rather is given – the blessing which a polity is supposed to bring its citizens, the *tranquilitas ordinis*. This polity must coexist with creation, since God's will is always done, but it is eschatological in that protologically its only members are angels, and in that so soon as it has human members it appears as a pilgrim community struggling through this age, implicated with this age's evils, and animated by longing for its own final fulfillment.

Augustine does not so much borrow from Roman political theory as subvert it, to make a weapon against any ultimate claims by a polity of this age. He cites Cicero citing Scipio: a *res publica* in the proper sense is a community united by agreed law, and there can be agreed law only where there is prior community in virtue, that is, prior mutual devotion to a common good. This is exactly right, says Augustine; but no polity of the fallen world can meet this standard, since the only good we could have fully in common is the one God, and the fallen world is constituted precisely by refusal to turn to him. Therefore political arrangements in this age can be called *res publicae* only by generous analogy. They are at best approximations of true polity, united by love of diachronically and synchronically *partial* goods, and are ordained by God to preserve his fallen creatures from the total destruction that would follow a mere war of all against all.

An inner contradiction thus destabilizes every polity of this age. The one triune God can only be "enjoyed" and so is immune to exploitation by our love of self; there is nothing we can "use" this God for. But partial goods can indeed be used for our antecedent purposes, in fact they invite such use, and so they can be manipulated by self-love. Therefore the very same partial goods that draw a polity of this age together simultaneously tempt each of its members to aggrandize him- or herself at the others' expense. The self-destructive inner dynamic of every polity of this age is self-love in its political form, the passion to dominate: *libido dominandi*, as Augustine calls it.

In the midst of the polities of this age stands God's polity, in its form for this age. The church is a struggling, tempted, and ambiguous presence of God's polity – we do not even know who finally belongs to it. But it is nothing less than that. Its unity is constituted in worship of the one God, that is, in jointly enacted desire for the one possible common good. Therefore so long as the church does not utterly cease to be church by ceasing to worship the true God, its gravest defections and strifes cannot undo its *tranquilitas*, for God is indeed but one for all – lest this be thought romantic, we should remember that Augustine was a bishop during one of the most strife-filled periods of church history. What must always be in our vision when thinking of Augustine's City of God is the Eucharist, a public space where the one God gives himself to his community, and where in consequence all sorts and conditions of humanity drink from one cup and eat of one loaf, and whose parliament of common and mutual prayer is a perfect participatory democracy.)

The loves which unite this world's polities are mere negatives of the love of God which unites the church. If we will not worship the one God, we must worship something that is *not* one, the polytheistic pantheon of usual religion; thus another name for what holds a polity of this age together is idolatry. Yet even so, such loves formally imitate the love of God, and even the imitation can sustain a little shared law for a little while. Indeed, the *libido dominandi* itself can and does harbor real if fragile virtues; in Augustine's eyes, Roman love of glory was itself once glorious. Perhaps, recalling Augustine's neo-Platonism, we can interpret him to say that earthly polities are brought into being and endure for a time by *memory* of what real polity would be.

So the famous maxim: "Two loves make the two polities, love of self (in its political form, the *libido dominandi*) the earthly polity . . . , love of God the heavenly" (Augustine 1972: xiv. 28). The distinction is eschatological. Every created self will pass away; indeed, love of self is the very principle of historical decay: "He that seeks his life will lose it." Love of God will not pass away, for he is what all things pass on to. Thus the gates of hell will sooner or later prevail against every polity of this age. They will not prevail against the church, which will be fulfilled precisely by the judgment that burns away its accommodations to this age.

Modernity

If the purpose of this chapter were historical, we would barely have begun. Since it is not, the enormous leap about to be made is perhaps justifiable. Leaping over most of theological history, and so over persons as vital for eschatological reflection as Thomas Aquinas or Jonathan Edwards, and leaving out counterexamples to the point of caricature, we next note that the church's tendency in modernity has been to depoliticize eschatology and de-eschatologize politics.

The "church father of the nineteenth century" may perhaps serve as a paradigm. According to Friedrich Schleiermacher, although communication of Christ's blessedness takes place in the diachronic community of the church, the salvation which is the content of this relation is an individual experience, which indeed seeks to share itself but is not shaped by the success or failure of the sharing. The great promises of the prophets, with their political and generally communal content, must be regarded as "visionary" speech that cannot "yield knowledge" (Schleiermacher 1976: II, 163). They cannot describe something we may expect actually to happen, since a fundamental transformation of history's ways is impossible (II, 157).

Or we may turn to a "church father" of the twentieth century, to Rudolf Bultmann (Jenson 1969: 158–75). The eschaton for Bultmann is not a future event at all, but what happens in the moment of authentic decision, when the word of the cross calls me out of security in the circumstances of this world. To strip the Bible's message to such fighting trim, it must, said Bultmann, be "demythologized." But what does he mean by "myth?" The common content of his various definitions is that a myth is any story that depicts God as involved in a temporal succession of events. The "word-event" of the speaking and hearing of the word of the cross is an event that stops time, which is why it is the eschaton. We might very well paraphrase "demythologizing the Gospel" as "depoliticizing eschatology."

Neo-Protestantism, which now must include Roman Catholic replayings of it, was modernity's form of Christianity, and we should no more reject it in every aspect than we would generally wish simply to do without the achievements of modernity. But in the present matter, faithfulness to scripture and the tradition surely impose a task, which we may perhaps dub the "repoliticizing of eschatology."

To achieve this, to cast a political eschatology, will require something more than simply going back behind modernity to more traditional eschatology. Augustine may provide a model and an inspiration, but merely affirming him will not quite turn the theological corner. We are required to go back to fundamentals. Indeed, in my judgment, we are required to go all the way back to the doctrine of God. Readers should recall the merely modal difference between speaking of the eschaton and of God the eschatos: between speaking of the final event and of the final person.

The Polity in God

In the scriptures, the eschatological fulfillment of Augustine's "city" is "the kingdom of God." But this political characterization of the eschaton is throughout the theological tradition paired with a characterization that is at first thought quite different: the fulfillment of human existence as "deification" or the "vision of God" (the first term is, of course, dominant in the East, the second in the West). Also, this notion is scripturally supported, since "eternal" life, "perfect" righteousness, "infinite" love and the like – all biblical evocations of the eschaton – can in fact only be *God's* life, righteousness, love, and so forth. If we are to have *eternal* life this can only be if we are to share God's life, for God not only is eternal but is eternity, according to the rule that God is identical with his attributes.

But if both eschatologies are true, then somehow entry into the kingdom of God must be entry into the triune life of God, and vice versa. That is, entry into the kingdom of God must somehow be entry into a polity that God himself is in himself. And that is indeed what is to happen, for classic doctrine of the triune

God displays precisely a perfect polity. The following hardly describes what most religion thinks of as God, but it is indeed the way the doctrine of Trinity identifies the specific *deus christianorum*, the strange God of the Gospel and the church.

There is in the triune God a plurality of *social personae*: Father, Son, and Spirit each genuinely have a different role, both in God himself – the Father begets and is not begotten, the Son is begotten and does not beget, the Spirit frees and is not freed – and in God's works, in the doing of which "All action . . . begins with the Father and is actual through the Son and is perfected in the Holy Spirit" (Gregory Nyssenus 1958: 125). The three are nevertheless not three gods, precisely in that their communal *virtue* or *righteousness* is perfect; for each subsists at all only as complete investment in self-giving to the others. This righteousness is not a silent perfection, but occurs as a *discourse*, for the second identity, in whom God knows what God is, is a *Word*. Moreover, *decision* occurs in this discourse, since God is who and what he is *freely*, and so in his own eternal decision to be who he is (Jenson 1997: 221–3). The divine "nature" that each has with the others so that they are God instead of something else, and which is thus identical with their righteousness, is the *common Good* of the three; for to be God is to be the Good, first of all for God. And finally, in consequence of all the above, the eternal triune life is a space of *moral action*: there are "source, movement, and goal" in God himself and not just as adaptation to his relation with us. God is not eternal because he lacks such poles but because with him "there is no conflict between them" (Barth 1957: 690); because with him they are not steered by the *libido dominandi*.

The created Polity of God can enter this eternal political life of God because Jesus the Son brings the church with him. Drawing one last time on Augustine, it is the risen Jesus *with* his body the church that is the *totus Christus*, the "whole" Christ; there can no more be a person who is "the head" without a body, then there could be a person who was a "body" without a head. Thus as the fact is, whatever might have been, the second person of the Trinity is eschatologically a communal reality that includes a created community. The entry of redeemed humanity into the life of God does not transform God from a Trinity into a multiplicity, because we enter only as those in whom the Son invests himself and with whom he identifies himself. But the investment and identification are real: the Son truly *is not* without his disciples, also not as an identity of God.

How, then, are we to think of the End? We are to think of a human polity whose enabling common good is God, as is now true of the church, but with two differences. Making these differences is the work of the "Last Judgment."

First: The kingdom's members will belong to no other communities; for whatever is to be the final value of the communities of this world will have been gathered into the kingdom. Here we must stop for a fundamental point about eschatology. Eternal life is not resuscitation; the saints do not simply pick up and go on with their lives. With death, "the moving finger" writes indeed a last line; only so does a temporal life make a whole, which can have a meaning. Eternal life is rather the infinite *appropriation* and interpretation of accomplished lives within the discourse of the triune life. Just so, also the accomplished mortal communities of this world, its polities and its families and its civil societies, their glories and their horrors, will be matter for the communal discourse of the kingdom.

Thus citizens of the community of the kingdom will not be divided in their mutual righteousness by membership in other communities. It is of course poesy when Christians speak of longing to check a point of philosophy with Socrates, or to hear the angels play Mozart, but it is a poesy that speaks truth; and the point for our present concern is that the saints will not need to turn to any other intersecting community, to find all created beauty and truth. Continuing with eschatological poesy, to delight in "jasper . . . , sapphire . . . , agate . . . , emerald . . . , onyx, carnelian . . . , chrysolites" and the like, they will not need to look away from one another to a separate community of commerce or art, but simply to "the foundations of the walls" of their own city (Rev. 21: 19–20).

Second: The animation and shaping of the created polity's life by that of the divine polity will be immediate. In this age, the church is the body of Christ only in that Christ is present bodily within it as an other; an other, moreover, that is apparent only to faith. Neither Christ's word as spoken in the church, nor his body and blood as present on the eucharistic table, nor any other of the church's mysteries, look or sound like what they are; the presence of Christ in and to the church. Christ's presence in the church in this age is indeed – to use another piece of Augustine's language – the "sign" of the church's true being, which is Christ's presence for the world. But this sign, Christ's presence in the church, itself requires to be signed by audible and visible signs if it is to be apprehended at all, and is as much hidden by these signs' native visibility as seen in it. In the kingdom enveloped in the triune life, the bread and cup, the water, the audible preaching, and all such mediations will not be needed: we will know ourselves as Christ's body as directly as we now know the signs of bread and cup.

> I saw no temple in the city, for its temple is the Lord God the Almighty and the Lamb. And the city has no need of sun or moon to shine on it, for the glory of God is its light, and its lamp is the Lamb. The nations will walk by its light, and the kings of the earth bring their glory into it. . . . People will bring into it the glory and the honor of the nations. But nothing unclean will enter it. (Rev. 21: 22–7)

Penultimates

Readers concerned for this world's politics may well be rather impatient by now. What has all this metaphysical speculation and poetry to do with anything? It has everything to do with everything, if we just turn it around.

The mere existence of the church in the world relativizes all polities of this age, and must do so in their own eyes. "How many divisions has the Pope?" the tyrant notoriously asked. But he is gone and so is his empire, while the church remains and will remain, until the end.

No polity that now is, except the church, will prevail against the gates of death. Knowing that, however dimly, is the one thing needful for polities of this age if they are to be healthy, even within the limits set by their inherent fragility. The not merely conflicted but murderously insane polities of late modernity are deranged precisely by the supposition that they can be an eschaton: National Socialism plotted a "millennial empire;" Marxism dreamed that when the dictatorship of the proletariat was achieved, no other dominating class could supersede it; and ideologies of globalization reproduce the Marxist delusion in obverse.

Nor is the relativizing of the world's kingdoms by the presence of the church something that only the church's members can perceive. If anything like Augustine's analysis is true, the kingdoms themselves must feel it, however they may try not to. For the loves by which this age's polities are constituted have their true and enabling object in that Good which only the church openly acknowledges and seeks. When this world's polities see the church,[3] they cannot but be unsettled by perception of their own need and failure to be what the church is. Why, after all, have the totalitarian states of modernity devoted such energy to crushing the church, and the church's even more disquieting sibling, Judaism – or, failing that, to co-opting it?

The first political calling of the church, its first way to be a blessing for the polities of this age, is simply to be itself, to be a sign of the eschaton. We may even say that the first political calling of the church is to celebrate the Eucharist (Cavanaugh 1998). The church is a perfectly visible diachronic community within this age, with its own modes of government, its own sort of patriotism, and its own inner culture, that is visibly loyal to the one Good the polities of this world cannot manipulate, and moreover goes about recruiting to that loyalty. The church is gathered by a common Good that its leaders' and factions' worst efforts cannot make uncommon. The church has a hierarchy that, however unwillingly, is compelled by its own establishing documents to acknowledge that it is to serve, not dominate.

The church is a polity visible in this age that visibly offers a gate through which the nations must pass and will not, into the only future there is. The Roman authorities of the church's first centuries were – despite civil strife and perverse emperors – a uniquely able governing elite, and so accurately perceived the challenge. So now, though far less accurately, do the liberal states, which know they must for their own pretensions relegate the church to a "private" realm; the religious totalitarianisms, which persecute it straightforwardly; and post-civilized China, which may be the first of many such nations. The church's first task is always to return.

The church is the gateway to the eschatological polity, and so relativizes all polities of this world. We must, to end this essay, consider that this is not a merely negative effect. To relativize something is to relate it to something else; in this case to relativize the kingdoms of this world is to relate them to the kingdom of God.

There is a deceptively obvious maxim: What will be can be. If a created community of *tranquilitas ordinis*, of righteousness and love, will be at the End, then righteousness and love are not impossible for created communities. In this age, they are always fragile and indeed at some depth perverted, but they can happen. Those who know the kingdom is coming know also of this possibility. A polity perverted by manipulation and competition to possess manipulation's levers can be cured a little, and a relatively just and mutual polity can be made yet more just and even loving. Those who await the kingdom are the very ones who know that this is so.

The very fact that God will by his own absolute and personal act establish his kingdom means that history is not determined by irresistible mere forces, that our human action need not be futile. The evil of abortion on demand, now established in American and some other law, and the at once dim-witted and wicked justifications provided by court decisions, were put in place by human error. Just so, they can be replaced by human truth, by decision and action faithful to the kingdom and so sustained by God's Providence – if, of course, the scourge is not itself a divine judgment aimed at the nations' undoing. Or again, the choice between homogenization and tribalism, seemingly posed by economic globalization, is a choice construed by human thought; with God's blessing, human thought can cast other possibilities.

The approximation for this age of the kingdom's mutuality is the Eucharist. Therefore it provides the true ideal of political striving. The body of Christ that gathers the church is the same reality as the body of mutual love that is the church (1 Cor. 10: 17–34). Thus we see that the good of a polity is not instrumental – to, say, the national product – but is identical with the mutual service of citizens. Of course, since the good around which a polity of this world gathers is not the one God, but some partial good, its mutuality will be given its actual dynamics by the character of that good, and will be infected by the *libido dominandi*. But much can be accomplished by reminding ourselves and others that finally the good to be gotten from being a citizen is the privilege of acting as a citizen – which is, one must quickly observe, something very different from being the obedient servant of a state or other political collective.

All classes and races drink from the one cup and eat the one bread, and so share equally in the good that gathers the church. The cry for "social justice" has sometimes been used as a cover for dubiously faithful purposes, but its origin is deep in the life of the church. Unless a polity is fallen so deeply that its common good is in fact a poison – in which case nothing but revolution and resistance unto death will serve – a chief goal of political striving must always be equal sharing of that good.

The discourse of the Eucharist is paradigmatically common prayer. In this discourse, all speak and all are heard. No doubt merely representative democracies are relatively good polities, but one thing cannot happen within their mechanisms: I do not myself appear in the forum where decision is argued and made, so that my interests cannot be transformed by the discourse there. My representative can do much for me, but he or she cannot repent for me. In polities where it is even conceivable, it should be a goal to create and nurture many empowered forums where the future of the community is debated by all – subpolities, if one will.

Finally, the Eucharist does know a hierarchy, of celebrant and people and of various ministries to both. Since the one God is the Good of this gathering, the hierarchy within it does not impede the mutuality of the discourse, or establish an oligarchy or even a merely representative democracy. The citizens of the eucharistic polity know that differences of gifts, even differences of more and less, are not in themselves evil, and are to be cherished in polities of this world also. And they know that the anarchistic impetus internal to all Western politics since the French Revolution is to be resisted.

Because their faith is eschatological, Christians are uniquely placed in the polities of this world. When everyone is on the hustings or in the streets, they will be there if the cause is in any analogy to what they know in the Eucharist; but they will also be in their own eucharistic and other gatherings, praying. For they know that the polities of this age cannot be perfected, and that even penultimate structures will fall unless the Lord builds the house. And when everyone else has given up and gone home, they will be still working and demanding, because they know that justice and peace are, despite all appearances, possible. They know these things because they know of the eschaton.

Notes

1 I will for the most part relate this story as Israel finally did, indulging in "historical–critical" reconstruction of it only for specific purpose. And I will presume readers' general acquaintance with this story.
2 Augustine's word is *civitas*, which it is of course customary to translate "city." But since Augustine's Latin stands in for the Greek *polis*, and since the entity of this age with which he is concerned is indiscriminately the City of Rome and the Roman Empire, "polity" is surely the far better translation.
3 It will, of course, be obvious that the divisions of the church call all such claims into question. But that is only to say that the divisions of the church call the church's very existence into question. Can there *be* such a thing as a divided church? It is a genuine question, but one that can hardly be answered here (Radner 1998).

References

Augustine (1972). *The City of God*, trans. Henry Bettenson. Harmondsworth: Penguin.
Barth, Karl (1957). *Church Dogmatics* II, 1. Edinburgh: T. & T. Clark.
Cavanaugh, William T. (1998). *Torture and Eucharist: Theology, Politics, and the Body of Christ*. Oxford: Blackwell.
Gregory Nyssenus (1958). *That There Are Not Three Gods*, ed. F. Mueller. Leiden: Brill.
Jenson, Robert W. (1969). *The Knowledge of Things Hoped For*. Oxford: Oxford University Press.
——(1997). *Systematic Theology*, vol. I. Oxford: Oxford University Press.
——(1999). *Systematic Theology*, vol. II. Oxford: Oxford University Press.
Milbank, John (1990). *Theology and Social Theory*. Oxford: Blackwell.

Radner, Ephraim (1998). *The End of the Church*. Grand Rapids, Mich.: Eerdmans.

Schleiermacher, Friedrich (1976). *The Christian Faith*, ed. H. R. Mackintosh and J. S. Stewart. Philadelphia: Fortress.

Wright, N. T. (1998). "Paul's Gospel and Caesar's Empire." *Reflections* 2: 42–65.

PART IV

Structures and Movements

29 State and Civil Society   423

30 Democracy   439

31 Critical Theory   455

32 Postmodernism   471

33 Globalization   486

CHAPTER 29

State and Civil Society

Daniel M. Bell, Jr.

The temptation is to approach the topic of the state and civil society from the vantage point of the various currents of theological thought that since the mid-1960s have been identified as "political theology." The task would then be to examine the ways these theologies have both interpreted those political realities and construed Christianity's relation to them. But, as other essays in this volume suggest, the question of Christian political engagement precedes the birth of the contemporary theological movements collectively known as "political theology." Indeed, as the proponents of several strands of political theology remind us, all theology is always already political. Expanding upon this insight, this essay begins with an understanding of "the political" and "politics" in the broadest sense. Politics and the designation "political" do not in the first instance refer to the machinations and deceits of state and party officials, but to the social arrangement of bodies, the organization of human communities (the root meaning of "polity" or "politics"). Moreover, intrinsic to this organization, to politics, is an act of imagination. Although always concerned with the arrangement of bodies, every politics involves the (re)production of a vision, a *mythos*, of community.

This insight provides our entrée to the theological and, in particular, to political theology. To assert that every theology is always already political is to recognize that every theology embodies, either implicitly or explicitly, a *mythos*, a vision of how human communities ought to be organized. As Carl Schmitt (1888–1985), a rather notorious forerunner of contemporary political theology, recognized early in the twentieth century, theological concepts and images have political correlates. (See chapter 8 by Michael Hollerich in this volume.) Of course, the recognition of the political impact of the theological, and of the Christian *mythos* in particular, has roots that extend much deeper than the early twentieth century. In the history of Christian thought it finds one of its earliest and most profound articulations in Augustine's *City of God*. There the political theology of Rome is subjected to a theological critique, the heart of which is Augustine's claim that such a theology cannot bestow salvation, for salvation is found at the altar of another city, the city of God (See chapter 3 by Jean Bethke Elshtain in this volume.)

Given that all theology is always already political, to address the issue of the state and civil society in political theology beginning with political theology's contemporary manifestations is to commence the story too late. This is the case, however, not because the history of Christian political engagement is much older, for actually the history of Christian engagement with what we recognize as "the state" and "civil society" is not *that* much older than contemporary political theology. Rather, the concern is a theological one. This is to say, if the treatment of these matters is to be particularly theological – that is, governed by norms and modalities of judgment anchored in the Christian *mythos* instead of in the *mythos* of modern social science or political philosophy – then we are compelled to initiate our tale just prior to the advent of "the state" and "civil society." For, as we will see, to begin the conversation once the state and civil society have been ensconced in our imaginations such that they have attained the status of a "given," such that they appear as simply "facts," is to have acquiesced, perhaps unknowingly, in a crucial theological judgment regarding the character of Christianity's political presence in the world.

There are a number of ways one could treat the similarities and differences that characterize the approaches of the sundry forms of contemporary political theology to the state and civil society. The popular imagination might suggest that the truly important differences lie along the axes determined by such categories as liberal and (neo)conservative, greens and laborites, capitalists and socialists, and so forth. As a distinctly theological reading, advanced in the spirit of Augustine, the axis of judgment in this essay is at once soteriological, eschatological, ecclesiological: What are the theological presuppositions that underwrite contemporary political theologies? What do their visions of the state and civil society say about the nature and mission of the church, the nature of God's activity in history, the character of salvation? What is the proper political correlate of the Christian *mythos*?

Such an analysis suggests that the proponents of three prominent strands of political theology – political theology proper, Latin American liberation theology, and public theology – for all of their important differences, nevertheless are in substantial agreement concerning the nature of Christian engagement with such political realities as the state and civil society. I identify these strands as collectively constituting the dominant tradition of Christian political theology today. While no single movement currently exerts hegemonic influence over the field of contemporary theological reflection, nevertheless, taken together these movements embody what is unquestionably the dominant paradigm for conceiving of political theology today. By way of contrast, I then present what may be labeled an "emergent tradition." This emergent tradition may loosely be called "postliberal." In theological parlance, such a designation usually refers to certain methodological moves associated with the likes of Alasdair MacIntyre and George Lindbeck. Here the emphasis is upon the political difference such moves engender in the work of several prominent theologians typically identified as postliberal.

The Advent of the Modern State and Civil Society

As suggested previously, to approach the state and civil society from the vantage point of a present where those realities have attained normative standing is to foreclose consideration of a crucial theological judgment regarding the character of Christianity's political presence and thus to conceal the determinative division in political theology today. Toward the end of illuminating both that judgment and that divide, this section presents a brief genealogy of the modern state and civil society that highlights contrasting interpretations of those realities.

In discussions of Christian political engagement, terms like "the state" are often invoked as if they were static realities that have changed little over time. Thus we speak of the early Christian attitude toward the state, or we read Augustine as purveying a theory of the church and state, or we study the medieval theory of church and state. In each of these cases, even as a certain historical fluidity is attributed to the Christian attitude, "the state" is granted a stability that seemingly defies such development and change. It is taken as self-evident that the state is that ensemble of institutions that exercise public authority, enforced through a monopoly on the legitimate use of violence. Such a habit of mind, however, reflects the ways our imaginations have been so thoroughly shaped by our contemporary experience of the state; the state so defined is of recent historical vintage. It is the distinctly modern nation-state.

Indeed, it is anachronistic to speak of the church and the state as if these were two distinct social entities prior to the advent of modernity (Ladner 1947). On the contrary, medieval Christendom consisted of a single social body, in which the ecclesial and the civil marked not spatial jurisdictions or even modalities of rule, but ends. Ecclesial authorities were concerned with the supernatural end of human community, while civil authorities concerned themselves with the temporal ends of that same community. Society was an organic whole, governed by two parallel and universal powers – the Pope and the Prince. In fact, when "the state" first appears in general use in political discourse in the fourteenth century, it refers neither to the ruling institutions and apparatuses nor to a geographically bounded space over which princely rule is exerted, but rather to the state or condition of the temporal princes themselves.

The wars of religion and civic peace: Two visions of the state's advent

What is today recognized as "the state," namely a centralized power holding a monopoly on violence within a defined territory, appeared in the midst of the bloodshed and turmoil that convulsed western Europe over the course of the sixteenth and seventeenth centuries. The standard account of these events and their relation to the rise of the modern nation-state, which is widely repeated not only by historians and political philosophers but by theologians as well, identifies those conflicts as "wars of religion" and attributes to the modern nation-state a veritable redemptive significance insofar as it is commended for delivering us from the bloodshed and brutality of religious disagreement. In the wake of the Reformation, the standard account goes, Catholics and Protestants were locked in conflict and, as religious passion mixed with political power, a bloodbath ensued. Consequently, horrified by the excesses of armed religious fervor, Europe developed a political order whereby religion would no longer have access to the weapons with which to work its woe. Henceforth, religion was construed as a private matter and the public, political realm was to be watched over by a sovereign and secular state charged with keeping the peace.

This particular way of construing social space, dividing it into a public, political sphere presided over by a sovereign state and a private, religious realm is developed with compelling clarity by the German sociologist Max Weber (1864–1920), whose work has been tremendously influential in setting the terms for the development of contemporary political theology. Weber embraced the distinction between religion and politics, noting that we inhabit various "life-spheres," each of which possesses its own laws and ethical functions. Of course, he noted, to draw this distinction is not to suggest that the realms do not interact. On the contrary, the realms are complementary. In particular, Weber noted that religion was principally about the task of furnishing ideals, whereas politics was a fundamentally about the manipulation of means in order to attain, not the ultimate end or ideal, but what was pragmatically possible. Moreover, and of particular interest to us, politics was defined as statecraft. Politics, Weber wrote, is about "the leadership, or the influencing of the leadership, of a *political* association, hence today, of a *state*" (Weber 1946: 77, emphasis in original). As we shall see, Weber's construal of religion as a private, apolitical sphere that serves as a repository of values or ideals that then must be instantiated in the political realm by means of statecraft largely defines the problematic for the dominant tradition of contemporary political theology.

In recent years, the standard account of the advent of the modern state has been challenged on historical and theological grounds. Historically, it has been suggested that the conflicts of the sixteenth and seventeenth centuries are not accurately described as "wars of religion" and that the modern nation-state did not emerge from the fray wearing the mantle of the benign peacekeeper with which it is so frequently adorned, in retrospect, today. According to this counter-reading, these conflicts were not principally instances of interreligious conflict waged between Catholics and Protestants over confessional differences; on the contrary, in the course of these wars Catholics and Protestants frequently fought on the same sides and just as frequently ended up facing one another across the battle lines (Cavanaugh 1995).

That the battle lines do not simply correlate with confessional identities and differences suggests that the conflicts were about more than religious differences, which brings us to the theological challenge to the standard account. Whereas that account holds that the modern state evolved in the aftermath of these conflicts to secure civic peace and deliver us from the cruelties of religious conflict, the alternative account contends that a more accurate theological appraisal, and one that more closely corresponds to the contours of the historical record, is that the sixteenth- and seventeenth-century conflicts were in fact the birth pangs of the modern state as it struggled to break free of the remnants of the medieval order, as it strove to subsume all other social groupings under its sovereign authority. In particular, these conflicts were about the replacement of a public church, which as the font of the virtue *religio* united medieval society, with a sovereign state. In other words, it is as a result not of ecclesial incivility but of an ecclesial defeat at the hands of an ascendant sovereign state that a Weberian world appears, in which the church is shorn of its public, political presence and politics becomes a matter of statecraft. For the emergent tradition of contemporary political theology, it is this theological shift in how the nature and mission of the church are understood that defines the problematic of Christian political engagement.

The taming of Leviathan: The emergence of civil society

Civil society is a middle term of sorts, a semi-public space, classically understood as referring to a mediating realm between the state and the individual, which is inhabited by a host of voluntary associations. It is frequently associated with organizations like the family, neighborhood groupings, the business corporation, and the various social associations with which people voluntarily affiliate. What distinguishes civil society from the state is precisely the voluntary, noncoercive nature of its government. Whereas the realm of the state is ultimately delimited by the (ideally unspoken but always implicit) threat of state violence, civil society is a space of self-government, a space where people associate and interact that is ordinarily free from the threat of state violence and coercion.

With regard to contemporary political theology there are, broadly speaking, two ways of approaching civil society, two models of civil society. According to the dominant model, civil society is fundamentally a space of freedom. Mirroring the presentation of the state as a space of freedom from the inevitably violent political pretensions of religion, this model envisions civil society as a space of freedom (usually understood in terms of pluralism, democracy, and/or a *laissez-faire* market) meant to protect the individual from the totalitarian proclivities of the state. Civil society stands over against the state, restraining it. One could say that it tames Leviathan. According to this vision, civil society is the source of the state's legitimation. The state draws its authority from civil society insofar as it finds its calling in protecting and preserving civil society and draws from that society moral guidance and direction. Weaker versions of this model suggest that social change is effected when, through the organs of civil society, people influence and guide the state; the state serves as an instrument of the popular will. Stronger, more libertarian versions assert that civil society itself is the locus of social change and that the state's proper function is not to effect change but only to protect civil society and perhaps, in rare circumstances, address certain needs and problems that civil society proves incapable of handing. The church's relationship to civil society varies in this model. Some versions recognize the church as a fully fledged participant in civil society, alongside other voluntary organizations; other versions ignore the church or place it outside the mediating realm of civil society in the realm of the individual.

The alternative reading casts civil society in a decidedly less benign light. Far from establishing a space of freedom, a buffer between the individual and an overweening state, civil society, according to the counter-vision, is understood as essentially a disciplinary space. It is a space where persons are shaped and formed in the state's image, in the image that corresponds to the state's end (which is now increasingly an economic one). Through a vast array of disciplines, learned not at the hands of government officials and bureaucrats, but "voluntarily" through the ministrations of experts, managers, and therapists, people "freely" and gently and, for the most part, willingly find their place in the dominant *mythos*. As such an educative or disciplinary space, civil society is but another species of the power exerted by the state in its victory over the medieval public church. Accordingly, civil society is understood here as a component of Leviathan's taming of society and the church, in particular. This is not to say that civil society is the instantiation of some dark conspiracy led by a monolithic state but rather that civil society, no less than the modern state, is a political correlate of the modern *mythos* about how human communities are organized, a *mythos* that deprives the church of a forthright, concrete political presence. Hence, this model does not embrace civil society as a legitimate space for the church. Stronger versions of this approach tend to cast civil society as intrinsically antithetical to the Christian *mythos*, whereas weaker versions suggest that civil society is not intrinsically but only contingently opposed to the church's proper political presence. That is to say, the weaker version holds out hope that civil society, no less than the modern state, could conceivably coexist peaceably with, and perhaps even serve the mission of, the church.

The Dominant Tradition

As these visions of the state and civil society are incorporated into the various strands of contemporary political theology, they give rise to very different soteriological, ecclesiological, and eschatological convictions regarding the character of Christian political engagement. What I identify as the dominant tradition of contemporary political theology embraces the standard reading of the state and civil society, whereby those institutions are heralded as agents of freedom

while the church is shorn of a concrete political presence in favor of an apolitical or at most only abstractly and generally political presence as a custodian of
values. This is to say, the dominant tradition takes as its starting point the
modern, Weberian *mythos* of how human community is ordered. Consequently,
the fundamental task of political theology becomes the propagation of the
values and ideals deemed necessary to sustain and perfect the freedom that
appeared with the advent of modernity. This is evident when we consider three
of the major strands of contemporary political theology.

Political theology

"Political theology" proper, that movement begun in Germany in the mid-1960s
by Johann Baptist Metz, Jürgen Moltmann, and Dorothee Sölle, arose as a reaction against a bourgeois Christianity that had been so thoroughly privatized that
it left the social and political status quo unchallenged (Metz 1981). According
to these theologians, as a result of its privatization Christianity is rendered effectively irrelevant in a situation where social and political life approaches the brink
of barbarism, as evidenced by Auschwitz, the nuclear arms race, the reality of
global poverty, and, more recently, ecological devastation (Moltmann 1999).
Over against this domesticated Christianity, political theology envisions the
church as an institution of "critical freedom." As such it is not the bearer of
middle-class consolations, but the herald of an eschatological future that always
calls into question the status quo, destabilizing the present in the name of a
peace, justice, and freedom to come.

   At first glance, it may strike one as odd to suggest that political theology
embraces the modern *mythos* of politics as statecraft. After all, one of the hallmarks of political theology is its rejection of the bourgeois privatization of the
church that deprives the church of any political influence. However, when it is
considered how political theology positions itself in relation to the advent of
modernity, it becomes clear that the state and civil society are embraced as the
principal agents of social and political change while the church's political presence is reduced to that of a guardian of abstract values. Opposed to what it calls
a "traditionalist" theology that resists modernity, political theology is forthrightly and enthusiastically a modern movement (Metz and Moltmann 1995).
Indeed, it understands itself to be the theological vision that corresponds to the
advance of freedom in the world that went hand in hand with the emergence of
the modern West. According to political theology, modernity's emancipation
from tradition, the advance of secularization, the Enlightenment, and the rise of
the nation-state are all manifestations of a spirit of freedom that infuses history.
Of course, political theology is not uncritical in its support of modernity. After
all, the freedom that modernity promises has not yet been realized in its fullness
– witness the continued struggles against injustice and oppression. Hence, even
as they embrace modernity as a stage in the advance of freedom, the political
theologians insist that the church function as a permanent critic of any and

every social order in the name of a more just future, in memory of history's victims (Metz 1980).

How the vision of political theology correlates with the modern *mythos* of the state and civil society should be evident. Even as it criticizes the privatized theology of the bourgeois, political theology does not challenge the modern, Weberian vision of how social space is ordered. Politics remains a matter of statecraft and the church, as an institution of permanent critique, is political only in the most general and abstract sense that it announces values that have political consequences, that should inform political engagement in the realm of the state and civil society. Indeed, any attempt to give Christianity a more substantive public or political content – whether by associating Christianity with concrete and specific political programs or suggesting that the church is a public, political formation in its own right that might contest the state's hegemony – is denounced as a pernicious form of "political religion" from which modernity has rightly liberated us (Moltmann 1999). Political theology amounts to the demand, in the name of an eschatological future, that Weber's correlation of religious ideals and political realities be completed. In the writing of political theologians this becomes support for progressive politics, whether associated with social democracy, democratic socialism, or human rights more generally.

Latin American liberation theology

Latin American liberation theology appeared in the late 1960s and gained global attention through the efforts of theologians such as Hugo Assmann, Leonardo Boff, and Gustavo Gutiérrez. Like its northern cousin, Latin American liberation theology arose as a reaction against a Christianity that was too closely wedded to the status quo. In particular, it was a response to a crisis of faith sparked by an irruption of the poor in Latin America, raising their voices against the poverty that inflicted premature death and the programs that inevitably failed to mitigate their plight (Gutiérrez 1988). Against a church that traded in spiritual verities while ignoring the material plight of the masses, the liberationists articulated a vision of the "church of the poor" that proclaimed the good news of God's "preferential option for the poor" by championing the revolutionary cause of justice and the rights of the poor (Sobrino 1984).

Given that the liberationists are often considered to be among the most politicized of theologians, it is counter-intuitive to suggest they embrace the modern vision of politics as statecraft and cordon off the church in the apolitical realm of values and ideals. Nevertheless, that this is the case is evident in several aspects of their work. Even as they urge the church to opt for the poor, the liberationists are adamant that there can be no return to the era of Christendom, when the church directly wielded political power. In this way, the liberationists are as committed to the freedom modernity brought from the ecclesiastic domination of politics as the political theologians. They too recognize the modern desacralization of politics as a victory in the march of freedom through history

(Gutiérrez 1983). The rise of the secular state, and the clear differentiation of the religious dimension of life from the political and economic realms, are achievements rightly celebrated. Yet, as was the case with the political theologians, the liberationists' embrace of modernity is not uncritical (Gutiérrez 1983; Sobrino 1984). They too recognize that modernity's freedom has not yet materialized in its fullness. While political freedoms, such as freedom of speech and thought, have largely borne fruit, social and economic freedoms remain elusive. Hence, modernity's promise is incomplete, and the liberationists prod the church to proclaim justice and support those who struggle for it.

This revolutionary vision, notwithstanding the force of its challenge to the current politico-economic order, is firmly grounded in the modern *mythos* of politics as statecraft. Whether one considers their early hopes that the oppressed would seize the state and establish a just social order (then usually identified with some form of socialism) or their more recent turn to civil society in the hope that the voluntary associations located there might influence the state, the liberationists consistently embrace statecraft and accord the church a public presence that can be characterized as political only in the most general and *indirect* sense that it, in true Weberian fashion, fosters the values and ideals that should motivate and guide engagement in secular politics. Any more substantive and directly political presence for the church is rejected as a return to the misguided "politico-religious messianism" of a bygone era (Gutiérrez 1983, 1988).

Public theology

"Public theology" is a broad movement of predominately North American theologians that attained prominence in the latter half of the twentieth century. Although their political views range widely from progressive to conservative, these theologians share a commitment to resisting the sectarian impulses in Christianity that would acquiesce in the disintegration of the moral consensus that has underwritten Western liberal polities for generations. These theologians derive from Christianity a "public philosophy" or "public theology" capable of underwriting the moral consensus necessary to sustain the health and vitality of Western liberal society.

In its Catholic manifestations, for example in the work of Richard John Neuhaus and Michael and Kenneth Himes, public theology is a conscious attempt to continue the project initiated by John Courtney Murray (1904–67) of articulating a "public philosophy" for society. According to the neoconservative Neuhaus, it is Christianity's eschatological vision that provides such a foundation (Neuhaus 1987). That vision is a paradoxical one that even as it holds out the transcendent promise of the kingdom of God, recognizes that such a promise must remain a promise, the gift of a transcendent future, and as such it stands in critical judgment upon every human political program. Such a transcendent critique of all politics finds its political correlate in the "American experiment in ordered liberty" insofar as a democratic and pluralist polity linked to a free market economy rightly wards off efforts to impose a single social–political vision while nevertheless nurturing what limited good and freedom is realistically attainable now. The Himeses, too, argue that Christianity provides the moral foundation for a pluralist, liberal democratic social order (Himes and Himes 1993). Their version of public theology seeks to deduce the social significance of the central symbols of the Catholic tradition. This is to say, according to their vision of public theology, Christianity provides a worldview or orientation, expressed in such symbols as the Trinity, Incarnation, and Grace, that founds the core values of Western liberalism at its best – desacralized politics, human rights, solidarity, justice and equality, and so forth.

In its Protestant versions, as developed by theologians such as Ronald Thiemann and Max Stackhouse, public theology locates itself in the tradition of Reinhold Niebuhr (1892–1971), whose career exemplifies the public potential of Christianity, and of theology, in particular. The Lutheran Thiemann develops his vision as a contribution to the effort by Christians to regain a public voice and a sense of public responsibility (citizenship) in a pluralistic culture (Thiemann 1996). Beyond merely finding a voice, however, like his Catholic counterparts Thiemann believes that Christianity can actively contribute to the construction of a new public philosophy for American public life. In particular, he sees Christianity as a fount of the moral renewal of liberal democracy, which in its commitment to freedom, equality, and tolerance reflects values that correspond to the basic convictions and principles of the Christian faith. Because the Christian Gospel entails the recognition of God's enduring presence in the public realm, it is a source of the hope that is crucial to sustaining the effort of pluralistic liberal societies to work for a common human good. For Max Stackhouse, a Reformed theologian, Christianity rightly understood provides the moral and spiritual fiber for Western civilization (Stackhouse 1984). More specifically, Christianity set in motion a historical trajectory that, under the impact of the Protestant Reformation, eventually blossomed in modern liberal democracy, with its limited (and secular) state, flourishing civil society, and abiding commitment to the universal moral law summed up in modern human rights. Starting from the biblical notion of covenant, the Hebrew prophets, and the life and teaching of Jesus, Stackhouse argues that the basic values of Christianity entail pluralism, the separation of powers, ordered freedom, and a broad social space free from coercion where voluntary, self-governing associations can flourish.

In this brief sketch of several of its prominent incarnations, the affinity of public theology for the modern, Weberian *mythos* is readily discernible. In each of these conceptions, politics remains a vision of statecraft. The public theologians share an aversion to the medieval vision of an immediately public and concretely political church as a terrible distortion of the faith. Indeed, they insist that Christianity, rightly understood, is essentially a matter of values, worldviews, or basic orientations from which no specific political agenda can be inferred in any direct and unmediated fashion. Hence, what constitutes the public character of public theology is the insistence that the Weberian correlation be completed. More specifically, the "publicness" of public theology takes the form of the call for the recognition that Christianity's value-system or vision is necessary for the enduring viability of modern liberal social orders. And at the pinnacle of those social orders, suitably restrained and guided, as these theologians insist, by a vibrant civil society, rests the sovereign state.

Theological synopsis

Earlier I suggested that the most significant division in contemporary political theology was not that between more politically progressive and conservative visions, but rather was fundamentally theological in nature. Important theological judgments underwrite the approaches of the various political theologies to the state and civil society. Ecclesiologically, the dominant tradition consistently portrays the church as an apolitical (or political only in the most general and abstract sense) space that traffics in values and visions, which leaves politics – the concrete arrangement of bodies – to the state. Likewise, the Christian eschatological vision is interpreted either in terms of an *absence* – named "the future" or "promise" by Neuhaus and the political theologians – that impinges upon the present as a permanent critique or in terms of a *presence* – the liberationists' identification of the Spirit in the revolutionary movement of history or Thiemann's sense of providence in liberal democratic processes – that stimulates political responsibility. Soteriologically, the dominant vision endorses the salvific mission of modern politics (recognizing, of course, that this does not exhaust the fullness of salvation, either temporally or eternally). For at least this time between the times, here and now, salvation takes social and political form in the success of statecraft, whether construed in terms of the universal recognition of human rights, the spread of liberal democracy, the strengthening of the "American experiment," or the establishment of some form of democratic socialism. And the church, as the herald of salvation, is called upon to advance that salvation by fostering the (critical) vision and values that undergird the success of statecraft.

The Emergent Tradition

What I am calling the "emergent tradition" of contemporary political theology,[1] identifiable with certain postliberal theologians such as Stanley Hauerwas, John Milbank, and Oliver O'Donovan, bears an unmistakable affinity for the alternative reading of the state and civil society which recognizes in the standard account an *apologia* for the eclipse of the proper public, political character of the church and, consequently, a distortion of its mission. Accordingly, the emergent tradition rejects politics as statecraft and envisions the church as a concrete public, political space in its own right. The contours of this postliberal political theology are best discerned by considering both what it deems problematic in the dominant tradition as well as the ways it attempts to recover an Augustinian vision of the church as the site of a distinctly theological politics.

The political captivity of political theology

From the perspective of the emergent tradition, the embrace of the modern *mythos*, with its account of politics as statecraft, by the dominant tradition is symptomatic of the political captivity of that tradition. An explanation of this charge begins with the politically reductionist nature of the dominant tradition. To suggest that the dominant tradition is politically reductionist is *not* to claim, as is frequently done, that political theology reduces faith to temporal, political matters and dismisses the transcendent–spiritual dimension of Christianity. Rather, the charge of political reductionism (ironically) pertains precisely to the ways the dominant tradition attempts to distance itself from the charge of reducing faith to politics. Whether it is Neuhaus's eschatological prohibition of sanctifying any political order, Gutiérrez's condemnation of "politico-religious messianism," or Metz's and Moltmann's abhorrence of "political religion," the refusal to grant the Christian *mythos* a political presence more substantive than the "general" or "indirect" role accorded the church as a guardian of values *reduces* Christian political engagement to the options offered by the world, more specifically, by the regnant liberal order. This is to say, the dominant tradition conceives of Christian political engagement on the world's terms (Milbank 1990). Indeed, each strand is quite explicit in its embrace of modernity's cartography of social and political space. At the heart of the dominant forms of political theology is the insistence that Christians, under the influence of Christian values and vision, commit themselves to politics on modernity's terms, whether in its more conservative or progressive modes, and each strand is equally vehement in its denunciation as sectarian or narcissistically ecclesiocentric any effort to articulate Christian political engagement on terms other than those circumscribed by the modern *mythos* of statecraft.

What renders this symptomatic of political captivity is the way in which it reflects a certain forgetfulness on the part of the dominant political theologians. They have forgotten their own lesson, that all theology is always already political. The modern differentiation of life into autonomous spheres, the separation of theology and politics, is a ruse. Every theology embodies a *mythos*, a vision of human community. The political theologians rail against political religion, against the church's identifying with a concrete political program, even as they embrace the political vision of the modern West and insist that Christianity's political task is to nurture that vision. Although they claim that Christianity is not concretely or immediately political, they argue that Christianity is politically correlated with liberalism, statecraft, socialism, "the American experiment." In the end, political theology is but another, albeit modern, instance of the political religion its advocates profess to abhor.

That the dominant tradition is a modern instance of political religion, however, is not what renders that tradition liable to the charge of political captivity. According to the emergent tradition, political religion is not intrinsically problematic. What renders the dominant tradition problematic, and a form of political captivity, is that it sanctions the *wrong* politics. The dominant tradition is an instance of political captivity insofar as it identifies the Christian *mythos* with the wrong political correlates – the modern state and civil society.

The dominant tradition rightly fears the deadly results of bad Christian politics (although it erroneously attributes the sixteenth- and seventeenth-century conflicts to the Church *simpliciter*), but its solution fails. Instead of articulating a true Christian politics, it attempts in vain to distance the church from politics and as a result delivers Christians – body and creed – to the agony of modern politics as statecraft (statecraft has proven at least as bloody as Christendom). The emergent tradition seeks to escape this captivity by recovering a true politics.

Toward a true politics

The emergent tradition's rejection of the modern *mythos* of politics as statecraft is founded on theological judgments concerning the church, salvation, and eschatology that differ from those that underwrite the dominant tradition. Refusing the modern nation-state's claim to the right to organize human community in its own image, the emergent tradition sees in the practices of the church the true politics. This is to say, the emergent tradition finds the political correlate of the Christian *mythos*, not in the secular state and civil society, but in the church (Hauerwas 1991; Milbank 1990). Hence, Christian political engagement takes shape in a distinctly theological politics that is not reducible to a Weberian correlation of abstract values with secular political options. The church is no longer viewed as the apolitical (or only "generally" political) custodian of values or worldviews, and its mission ceases to be the advancement of Western liberalism. Rather, Christian politics takes form in the distinct witness of the church to Christ's redemption of politics as the renewal of the friendship/communion of humanity in God.

It is no mistake that the works of two of the leading voices of this effort to recover a theological politics have been compared to Augustine's *City of God*, for the theologians in the emergent tradition see themselves as working out Augustine's vision of theological politics. Recall that in his *City of God* Augustine leveled the startling charge against Rome that it was not, in the true sense, a republic. He unmasked the Roman order as politically reductive, as less than a genuine politics, because, founded as it was on self-interest and violent *dominion*, it could not enact redemption. The communion it offered was but a simulacrum or parody of genuine human community, the true polity or politics. By way of contrast, Augustine lifts up the Christian community. Its life is truly public and authentically political. This is the case, observes Augustine, because the order of its life is liturgical, which is to say that because it eucharistically participates in Christ's reconciling sacrifice it is able to effect redemption – the renewal of human communion/community. And this is precisely what the true polity, the true politics, is about.

Reclaiming the church as the true politics, however, need not necessarily entail a wholesale rejection of other political formations like modern states and civil society. While these postliberal political theologians insist that a properly theological politics precludes a *theory* of such institutions and their relation to the church (on the grounds that such theories inevitably reify what is properly understood as temporal – meaning, as it originally did in Christian political discourse, "contingent," "passing," "temporary"), some of these theologians, such as O'Donovan and Yoder, have offered ad hoc judgments that amount to modest affirmations of some functions and forms of particular political (or, more accurately, in an Augustinian vein, "sub-political") formations distinct from the church. O'Donovan, for example, has developed a careful and nuanced defense of some forms of early modern liberalism, on the grounds that in some instances early modern liberalism could be construed as a form of statecraft that *serves* the church by maintaining an order that enables the church to carry out its properly public and political mission, which is the proclamation and ingathering of the true human communion/community (O'Donovan 1996; see also Yoder 1997). One should note that this is an instance, not of erecting the church within the parameters of the modern *mythos* as the dominant tradition does, but of positioning the early modern state within the Christian *mythos*, with the result that social and political space is shared by the church and a state for the sake of the church's mission. In other words, O'Donovan's recognition of the early modern state as an (admittedly ambiguous) servant of the church eludes the political captivity of the dominant tradition both by refusing to reduce the church to an apolitical (or only "generally" political) entity and by reversing the direction of authority in the Weberian model, where the church effectively serves the state.

What O'Donovan and Yoder make particularly clear is that the heart of the emergent tradition is not simply the replacement of a sovereign state with a hegemonic church, but a political rendering of the claim that Christ is Lord. For the proponents of the emergent tradition, the claim that the church is the exemplary form of human community is first and foremost a claim that the meaning of all politics and every community flows from participation in Christ. The true form of politics is visible only as every political form is drawn into relation with Christ, the desire of the nations.

Theological synopsis

The emergent tradition's rejection of the modern *mythos* of politics as statecraft in favor of a distinctly theological politics is founded on the conviction that God is active in history now bringing about a new age, the contours of which are discernible not in Western liberalism, democratic socialism, or the *Pax Americana* but in Christ, in the work of Christ's Spirit as it gathers Christ's body, the church. There, in that space where humanity is eucharistically joined once again in communion with one another and with God, we see the true community, the true polity, the true politics – a politics that modern statecraft, embedded as it is in the (dis)order of *dominion* and the endless conflict of self-interested individuals, cannot even dream of, but only mock.

Conclusion

Assessments of the state and civil society in contemporary political theology diverge over the issue of freedom and discipline. Are the state and civil society agents of freedom that Christianity should serve with its values and critical vision? Or are the state and civil society disciplinary formations that have eclipsed the true public and political mission of the church? In the final analysis, the issue is one of theological judgments concerning ecclesiology, eschatology, and soteriology that can be summed up in the question, "What is the proper political correlate of the Christian *mythos*?" Leviathan or the Body of Christ?

Note

1   The designation "emergent" implies no prophecy about the tradition's future status as dominant, incorporated, etc.

References

Cavanaugh, W. (1995). "A Fire Strong Enough to Consume the House: The Wars of Religion and the Rise of the State." *Modern Theology* 11: 397–420.
Gutiérrez, G. (1983). *The Power of the Poor in History*. Maryknoll, NY: Orbis.
Gutiérrez, G. (1988). *A Theology of Liberation*, rev. edn. Maryknoll, NY: Orbis.
Hauerwas, S. (1991). *After Christendom*. Nashville: Abingdon.
Himes, K., and Himes, M. (1993). *The Fullness of Faith*. Mahwah, NJ: Paulist.
Ladner, G. (1947). "Aspects of Medieval Thought on Church and State." *Review of Politics* 9: 403–22.
Metz, J. B. (1980). *Faith in History and Society*. New York: Seabury.
Metz, J. B. (1981). *The Emergent Church*. London: SCM.
Metz, J. B., and Moltmann, J. (1995). *Faith and the Future*. Maryknoll, NY: Orbis.
Milbank, J. (1990). *Theology and Social Theory*. Oxford: Blackwell.
Moltmann, J. (1999). *God for a Secular Society*. Minneapolis: Fortress.
Neuhaus, R. J. (1987). *The Catholic Moment*. San Francisco: Harper & Row.
O'Donovan, O. (1996). *The Desire of the Nations*. New York: Cambridge University Press.
Sobrino, J. (1984). *The True Church and the Poor*. Maryknoll, NY: Orbis.

Stackhouse, M. (1984). *Creeds, Society, and Human Rights*. Grand Rapids, Mich.: Eerdmans.

Thiemann, R. (1996). *Religion in Public Life*. Washington DC: Georgetown.

Weber, M. (1946). "Politics as a Vocation." In *From Max Weber*, ed. H. Gerth and C. Mills. New York: Oxford University Press.

Yoder, J. H. (1997). *For the Nations*. Grand Rapids, Mich.: Eerdmans.

CHAPTER 30
Democracy

John W. de Gruchy

No system of government is perfect, nor can any claim to be Christian. Yet democracy is widely regarded today as the best available political polity, and many church traditions, even those previously wary of democracy, now regard it as a form of governance that resonates well with Christian values. However, despite such consensus not all theologians or social theorists agree on what is meant by democracy. One reason for this is the complex history of the concept; another is the way in which it has been variously formed and understood within different national contexts. Even more problematic is the gap between the rhetoric of democracy and the social realities evident in many countries committed to democratic rule. Democracy can, in fact, be used as a slogan in the interests of political expediency. Yet, despite these problems and shortcomings, the vision of a democratic world order is a compelling one. In what follows I will begin by considering the nature of democracy, commenting on both its origins and the forms or systems of governance in which it has become embodied.

The Nature of Democracy

All democrats agree that democracy implies a form of government elected by and responsible to the people in free and fair elections. They would also agree that democracy requires the rule of law, the protection of civil liberties, the separation of legislative and judicial powers, the freedom of the media, and the upholding of human rights. A major point of disagreement, however, concerns the extent to which personal liberties should be constrained by social responsibilities. This has led to the distinction between liberal and social democracy, and more radical anarchist versions of both. Anarchism is a rejection of any tendency toward statism or totalitarianism. As such it provides an enduring critique of any tendency within democracy which leads away from the voluntary participation and cooperation of people in governing themselves.[1]

While all democrats profess a commitment to the will of the people and the common good, liberal democracy stresses the importance of personal liberties and generally supports a free-market economic system. Such an understanding of democracy is currently dominant in the West, where it is regarded as normative for all societies claiming to be democratic. However, many committed to democracy believe that some form of social democracy is vital to deal not only with the demands of their own contexts but also with those facing global society, especially the growing gap between rich and poor. For social democrats, the equitable distribution of resources and equal opportunities for all are essential ingredients of a genuinely democratic order. The struggle for a global democratic order, then, is not simply a matter of extending liberal Western democracy to places where this does not exist, but of developing a genuinely democratic world órder that is rooted in the particularities of different contexts. Such an order would have the capacity to protect human rights and promote the common good. This would apply equally to countries which have a long tradition of democracy, but where its development has come to a standstill.

The liberal tradition has undoubtedly contributed enormously to the development of democracy, especially through its insistence on protecting individual rights and liberties. But without the more egalitarian vision of social democrats and their concern for social responsibility, democracy easily becomes a means of protecting individual self-interest rather than pursuing the common good. For example, the linking of democracy and the free-market system is often stressed to the advantage of the economically powerful and to the detriment of developing countries. Indeed, the trade policies of the United States of America and other "first world" countries are often protectionist rather than open to others. So finding the balance between the liberal and social democratic traditions is not easy, given the constraints placed upon democratically elected government by political and economic interests. The struggle to enable both individual freedom and social responsibility to flourish amid the realities of particular historical contexts is at the heart of the continuing debate about democracy's ability to provide political stability and achieve its goals of justice and equity.

A further area of disagreement among democrats concerns the way in which "popular power" should be structured and exercised. Such differences have led to distinctions being made between direct, participatory democracy, and representative democracy. Participatory democracy heightens the involvement of the people as a whole in the democratic process, but is often impractical even though desirable. Representative democracy, whereby the people elect others to make decisions and act on their behalf, has become necessary at regional, national, and global levels. This requires parliamentary structures and procedures, as well as the development of political parties and organizations that are able to govern democratically. But representative democracy always runs the danger of becoming detached from grassroots needs and developing an unwieldy and self-perpetuating bureaucracy. Hence the need for a strong civil society that is able to keep a check on the way in which those elected to office exercise their power. This cannot be done simply through an electorate exercising its right to vote every four or five years. Hence, too, the need for political maturity within party political structures and especially the eschewing of any resort to violence in set-tling differences.

Civil society is comprised of a range of institutions and structures (e.g. orga-nized labor, educational bodies, the media, faith communities) which are not controlled by government or political parties. If political society refers to the structures of government or the state, including the civil service, then civil society is that network of nongovernmental organizations that provides the means whereby people can participate in pursuing social goals and protecting particular interests. Civil society is important not only for the sake of critically monitoring the exercise of power; it also provides the framework within which many people can participate in shaping the structures and values of society. A government that begins to oppose the organs of civil society has begun to attack one of the pillars of democracy. It is therefore in danger of undermining both its own legitimacy and the future of democratic rule.

Globalization and contemporary struggles for democracy, along with the theo-retical debates they have evoked – particularly with regard to gender, culture, and economic issues – have made it necessary to go beyond the debate between liberalism and socialism, or participatory and representative government. They have also highlighted the need for democracy to be contextually understood, embodied, and developed. What has become evident is that if democracy is to flourish it has to be constructed and sustained in ways that serve the cause of justice, equality, and freedom today rather than remain trapped in past formu-lations and embodiments. This suggests the need for a further distinction in democratic theory between *system* and *vision*: that is, the recognition that democracy is a *system* of government built on those constitutional principles and procedures, symbols and convictions, which have developed over the centuries in order to embody the unfolding democratic *vision* of what a just and equitable society requires. If we regard democracy simply as a system of governance, we fail to appreciate its character as an open-ended process that is ever seeking to become more inclusive, more just, and more global in response to the needs and hopes of society. This democratic *vision* resonates with fundamental elements within the Christian tradition even though Christianity has not always been sup-portive of democracy as such.

Christianity and Democracy

The roots of democracy in the Western world may be traced back to ancient Athens and Renaissance Italy. But democracy as we now know it developed only after the European Enlightenment and especially the French Revolution. As a result it has become the polity of modernity. The relationship between

Christianity and democracy both before and during the modern period has been full of ambivalence, ambiguity, and even hostility. Christians have by no means always regarded democracy as the best form of government; indeed, the contrary has more often been true, especially in Europe. Moreover, there are contemporary Christian theologians who are decidedly suspicious of linking Christian witness to democracy (Hauerwas 1981). Much depends, of course, on how democracy is understood within particular historical contexts. But the fact remains that fundamental impulses within democracy may be traced to the ancient Hebrew prophets, and Western Christendom has historically provided the womb within which modern democracy gestated (Berman 1983; de Gruchy 1995). In this regard we may point to at least five trajectories within Christian tradition that have made significant contributions to the development of democratic theory and praxis.

The first is the egalitarian communal experience and example of the primitive church itself, and its anticipation of the imminent arrival of the reign of God with its promise of universal justice and peace. In some ways, this was embodied in various radical movements within post-Constantinian Christianity, including the early monastic movement. The second, which emerged within medieval Catholicism, brought Christianity into creative interaction with Aristotelian political philosophy. Key political notions, such as subsidiarity and the common good, were developed on a Christian basis. These ideas have played an important role in shaping social democratic theory, affirming in particular the personalist and organic character of society and the need for human solidarity. The third trajectory, the covenantal, derives from the Reformed or Calvinist tradition. This has stressed human responsibility before God and toward others on the basis of God's covenant in Jesus Christ. In some ways this corresponds with the secular doctrine of the social contract. However, its binding force is not that of social obligation, but a commitment to others within the body politic under the authority of God. This leads to a strong emphasis on accountability both to an electorate and to God. The fourth trajectory, the liberal Christian, which we find expressed variously in the heirs of the radical Reformation, English nonconformity, and liberal Protestantism in North America, affirms the dignity of the individual, human rights, the freedom of conscience, separation of church and state, and religious toleration. The fifth trajectory, that of Christian socialism, insists that there can be no democracy without a just economic order. Key concerns are human solidarity, participation in the democratic process, and economic justice. This resonates strongly with many of the concerns of liberation theology.

Each of these trajectories emerged within specific historical contexts as Christians of different epochs and traditions sought to express their faith within the public arena on the basis of the dominant theological motifs and insights of the time. While they vary in emphasis, each rejects tyrannical and absolutist forms of government, though they have developed different strategies for opposing such; all acknowledge that human sinfulness leads to political corruption, though some are more optimistic about human nature than others; and all eschew selfish individualism in the interests of genuine community. These trajectories, though complementary, are not identical in the way in which they have understood or influenced the development of democracy. Nor is there always a clear causal line between them and the way in which democratic governance has developed. But each in its own way has contributed to democratic theory and practice as each has sought to express the prophetic demand for social justice and equity.

As already intimated, the French Revolution heralded the birth of modern democracy. However, because the Revolution was anticlerical and often anti-Christian, democracy, especially in Europe, was identified with social forces inimical to Christianity. This was less the case in Britain, where nonconformists were generally strong advocates of democratic governance, and in the United States, where Christianity played a formative role in the shaping of the new American republic. Despite these exceptions, for much of the nineteenth century Roman Catholic, Eastern Orthodox, and mainline Protestant Christianity remained either skeptical about or hostile to democracy. Democracy, for them, implied the rejection of Christian faith and of the church's role as the moral guardian for the nation. It was the political expression of secularism and atheism.

A decisive reversal came about during the twentieth century, especially following the demise of Fascist, Nazi, and Stalinist totalitarianism. This does not mean that all ecclesiastical antipathy to democracy has disappeared, but it does appear that ecumenical Christianity is committed, possibly irrevocably, to the retrieval of democracy as essential to its vision of a just world order. Indicative of this new Christian appreciation of the value of democracy is the fact that Catholic social teaching, after centuries of hostility and ambivalence, is now strongly in favor of democracy as the best form of political governance.[2] It is also noteworthy that while previously Anglo-Saxon Protestantism was the home of democratization, the so-called "third democratic transformation" which we have witnessed during the past few decades began in predominantly Roman Catholic countries such as Portugal, Spain, Poland, and Chile. However, this espousal of democracy cannot be taken for granted as there remains within sections of Christianity a strong tendency toward hierarchy and absolutism.

Democratic Transition and Transformation

The Allied victory over Germany, Italy, and Japan in World War II was hailed by the West as a victory for democracy and soon led to the establishment of democratic governments in those countries. Shortly after the war, India and many countries previously under colonial rule, notably in Africa (e.g. Botswana, Ghana, Nigeria, Uganda), gained their independence. All of them adopted democratic constitutions. Other examples of transition from oligarchic or authoritarian control occurred in Spain and Portugal, as well as in several Latin American countries (e.g. Nicaragua, Argentina, and Chile) and some in Asia (e.g.

Malaysia). But perhaps the most dramatic transitions to democracy occurred in the late twentieth century. Notable among these were the democratic revolutions which occurred in former communist-ruled countries of eastern Europe (e.g. Poland, East Germany, Hungary, Czechoslovakia, and the Soviet Union), and in apartheid South Africa. Many more countries across the globe have begun to follow suit.

These transitions to democracy, whether initially imposed from without or achieved from within, have changed the face of global politics. They have demonstrated the potential of democratic rule, but also its fragility and hence the need to implement measures which can help new democracies to reach maturity.

Countries with a long democratic tradition are obviously in a different historical situation from those that have undergone a sudden transition to democracy from colonial or authoritarian rule. In the former, it is unlikely that elections will be disrupted by widespread violence, whereas in the latter holding free and fair elections without violent intimidation is often a problem. Democracy requires the development of an ethos, and accordingly cannot be built overnight. Such an ethos includes political tolerance, a working relationship between opposing political parties and leaders that excludes violence for the sake of the common good, and, of course, the building of a strong civil society. This takes considerable effort. In established democracies the challenge is to keep the democratic spirit alive and not take democracy for granted. Hence the need both for civil society and for a growing appreciation of the democratic vision. In those countries where democracy is a recent introduction there is a need for consolidating what has been achieved, for the development of appropriate institutions, as well as to press on urgently toward the democratic transformation of society. There now exists a growing network of institutions and agencies around the world whose mandate is to facilitate the transition to democracy in countries undergoing such change. At the same time older democracies may well learn a great deal from the newer; for if democracy is to realize its potential and fulfill its promise, it requires constant critique, development, and revitalization.

The transition to democracy, especially after years of authoritarian or totalitarian rule, invariably requires that a nation deal with its past history of injustice and oppression. While the transition may require political compromises, the sustainability of what has been achieved demands the overcoming of legacies that potentially threaten to undermine those gains. The Truth and Reconciliation Commission in South Africa and similar commissions elsewhere provide examples of what can and has been done in this regard. Following up their recommendations has not always proved easy or politically expedient, but without some process of restorative justice being implemented national healing and reconstruction are unlikely to take place. And without the latter, democracy will be constantly under threat.

But the transition to democracy not only requires dealing with the past; it also requires responding to new issues and concerns. This brings us to the question of democratic transformation. If democracy is understood not only as a *system* of government but also as a continuing moral quest, then as soon as one stage is reached in the struggle for justice and equity, other issues emerge that need to be addressed and embodied in democratic practice. The extension of the franchise to freed slaves or women in many countries came about long after those countries – the United States and Switzerland are good examples – had embarked upon the path of democracy. So, today, the rights of homosexuals, of unborn children, of refugees and foreigners more generally are matters of considerable concern in the shaping of contemporary democratic legislation. Some would also argue that democracy should encompass animal rights as well.

Throughout this essay I have emphasized the importance of civil society in the consolidation and protection of democracy. In many countries the transition to democracy has come about *because of* pressure from civil society; in no country is democratic transformation possible *without* such participation. A strong civil society is indispensable if democratic transition from authoritarian rule is to be sustained, reversals resisted, and democratic transformation pursued. This brings us to the contemporary role of the Christian church, along with other faith communities, in democratization.

Faith Communities and Civil Society

From a theological perspective, the church can never be regarded as simply another NGO within civil society. Nonetheless, the church – along with other faith communities – is a significant institution within civil society. Especially in twentieth-century democratic transitions, the church has played a key role in a variety of contexts, whether in eastern Europe (Poland and the former East Germany), or Latin America (Nicaragua is a good example), or South Africa. In South Africa the ecumenical church was deeply involved both in the struggle against apartheid and in the processes which led to the transition to democracy. This happened in a variety of ways, both at the national level and in many local contexts. For example, the ecumenical peace monitoring task force established by the South African Council of Churches with the help of overseas ecumenical partners was of considerable importance in enabling free and fair elections to take place in 1994. Indeed, the church had its own unique and specific contribution to make because of its direct connection to grassroots communities and their leadership. Likewise, as in the civil rights struggle in the United States, where voter registration was such a key issue, the church has often played a vital role in voter education.

At a local level, the role of the churches has to do with the building of communities in which participatory democracy is practiced. Of course, churches are often very hierarchical, patriarchal, and undemocratic, a matter to which we will shortly return. But there are many examples of congregations in which community lay leadership is encouraged, along with the development of the necessary values and skills. Many of the leaders in political organizations, labor unions, NGOs, civic associations, and the like have had their initial training in local churches. This was certainly true in Britain in the nineteenth century and it has been true more recently in South Africa and elsewhere.

Just as the church is often undemocratic, so it is often ethnically captive. But there are also many instances where the church, at both a wider and a local level, represents a diversity of culture and political ideology. As such, it has the potential to build that new ethos of understanding and tolerance among people of different ethnic communities without which democracy is impossible. Again South Africa serves as an example: apartheid in the church was widely practiced, but it is also true that many people of different racial backgrounds had more meaningful contact with each other through the churches than was generally the case elsewhere.

This raises a further issue of fundamental importance, namely the need for Christians to cooperate with people of other faiths in building a democratic culture. In the struggle against apartheid people of different faiths discovered not only that they could work together for justice, but also that they shared similar values and concerns in doing so. Even though believers disagree on many things of importance, all the great religious traditions affirm the dignity of human beings, the need for justice, equity, and compassion in society. These values (and there are others) are of considerable importance in shaping a truly democratic and civil society. In fact, such a society cannot come into being or exist without them.

Most religious traditions, for example, stress the importance of the individual and of the community, and seek to maintain the value of both without allowing the former to degenerate into a selfish individualism, or the latter into a depersonalized collectivism. For this reason, some religious traditions are critical of the way in which liberal democracy too often exalts human freedom above social responsibility, especially in the economic sphere; or the way in which totalitarian communism has denied human freedom in the interests of maintaining central control over all aspects of life. Many of the major religious traditions stress the need for community-building in which individual needs and rights are inseparable from a commitment to the common good. While this may be contested by many advocates of liberal democracy, from a Christian theological perspective it is the essence of democracy (Barth 1960; Niebuhr 1960; Maritain 1986; Dorrien 1990).

It is not surprising that political and religious radicalism and fundamentalism flourish in situations of political uncertainty and transition. But a major test of a truly free and democratic society is the extent to which it permits and protects religious freedom – not just the freedom of worship, but also the freedom of witness and social critique. Religious commitment often leads to intolerance toward others, reinforcing social and political divisions, and providing what believers regard as divine sanction for conflicting positions, as is the case in Northern Ireland, the Middle East, India, and elsewhere. Religious conflict in South Africa has been largely among Christians, who have been radically divided with regard to apartheid and the political role of the church. Fortunately there has been very little conflict between the adherents of different faith communities, though the potential for such conflict is undoubtedly there.

Disagreement among people of different faiths and even of the same tradition is inevitable, as is political disagreement within a nation; it is also healthy if a society is to develop and change for the better. Indeed, the interaction of conflicting views is of the essence of democracy, which is why some religious traditions that stress the importance of conscientious dissent have played an important historical role in shaping democratic societies. But all of this requires the development of a culture of tolerance, respect, and mutual understanding within the churches and other faith communities. In adopting such a stance, religious believers will not only learn how to relate to one another, they will also be making a major contribution to the development of a democratic culture.

This broadening of ecumenical vision does not mean a lack of concern for the truth claims of the Christian Gospel, nor does dialogue imply an end to witness. Tolerance does not indicate a lack of concern for the truth, but an ability to speak the truth in such a way that it helps to build rather than break down community. It encourages a very different attitude and approach toward other religions, and a sharing together with them in ensuring justice in society, in dealing with the environmental crisis, and in enabling humane values to flourish. Churches and other religious communities can help their adherents to change their own attitudes and perspectives, learn how to forgive those who have wronged them, and help those who are guilty of oppressing others to see the need to make restitution and reparation. Churches should enable people to handle difference and change, to live through crises, and to participate more fully and creatively in the processes of social transformation. In many places, churches have the potential to create and sustain a vast network of people who do care, who do have a sense of justice, and who, through the resources of their faith and mutual support, can cope with social transformation. Moreover, many churches, especially those which stress lay participation and responsibility, provide a training ground for developing interpersonal skills that are of vital importance in community-building and, where necessary, in helping to resolve conflict in a creative way.

A democratic order implies that there will be a genuine separation of "church and state." In many countries in Europe, this is complicated by the existence of established churches, part of the legacy of Christendom. For some of them disestablishment might not be a realistic option, nor would it necessarily make them more effective in serving the common good. But even so, a democracy requires that all faith communities should be respected and treated fairly by those in authority. This has important implications for issues such as religious education in schools, as well as for the broader role which religion might play in public life more generally. Certainly, the separation of "church and state" need not mean that prayer is excluded from public events, or that a national anthem does not refer to God (after all, "Nkosi Sikele' iAfrika," the South African national anthem, was originally composed as a hymn). But it does mean that people of all faiths, as well as people who are secular in outlook, should be able to identify with the symbols of the nation and regard them as their own.

The separation of church and state also means that religious communities should have the necessary freedom to worship and live out their faith in daily life. Part of what this means is that religious communities have a responsibility to the broader public. Religion is not simply something of the private sphere. Hence religious freedom is necessary not only for the purpose of worship, but also in order to exercise the prophetic task to which I have referred. From a theological perspective, the freedom of the church is not contingent upon democracy; it is rather a freedom that is derived from faithfulness to the witness of the church. And it is through exercising this freedom, and especially its prophetic witness to justice and equity, that the church best serves the democratic vision.

Critical Theology and Prophetic Witness

The democratic *vision* of justice and equity has its origins in the messianic hope for a society in which the reign of God's *shalom* will become a reality. Of course, the custodians of this vision, whether Jewish or Christian, have often failed to witness faithfully to its demands. As a result, the vision has been secularized in various ways, some of them revolutionary, as in Marxism. These too have generally failed to fulfill their promise of a new and just world order. But the vision has endured, and it re-emerges through history out of the longing for or the experience of liberation from oppression, the struggle to affirm human equality and achieve social justice. Furthermore, it continually reminds us that the touchstone of a truly democratic society is the way in which it cares for the disadvantaged, and thus seeks to develop structures in which all share equitably in a nation's or global resources. Utopian as it may appear, this prophetic impulse has been the driving force behind the struggle for democratic transformation in many parts of the world, even if its religious roots are often unacknowledged. The establishment of a new democratic social order in formerly oppressive contexts will not bring in Utopia or the kingdom of God, but without such expectation and hope, the struggle for democratic transformation will not be engaged.

Critical theological reflection on democracy must continually return to this prophetic source of Christian faith. In doing so, we need to remember that the struggle for democracy has often in the past been a struggle against a reactionary church which has done everything in its power to prevent social change. Within the Old Testament canon itself there is tension between the royal trajectory, with its tendency toward absolutism, and the egalitarian trajectory of the eighth-century BCE prophets. This tension has continued through Christian history. But the prophetic tradition provides the basis upon which Christianity must reject all absolutist political claims as idolatrous because they invariably oppress and dehumanize. It also keeps the church aware of the danger of giving uncritical theological legitimation to any particular expression of democracy, for that too can easily lead to its corruption.

The prophetic tradition also provides the church with the basis for dealing with issues such as national sovereignty in relationship to global needs, for example, in the development of environmental policies and practices. Many of the problems facing the future of humanity, not least those concerning the world economic order, social development, health, and the environment, are not and cannot be confined within national boundaries. International cooperation and political will are essential if they are to be dealt with satisfactorily. Just as the tension between individual and community interests is dealt with through the democratic process, so there is no other way for the future of just and peaceful world politics than through dealing with the tension between national and international interests in the same way. A democratic world order does not mean imposing the Western model on all nations, but developing a genuinely global democratic order through which matters of global concern can be addressed.

Even as Christians rightly and necessarily seek to engage in nation-building, they must be wary of the dangers of nationalism. The relationship between genuine national aspirations, as in building a nation out of the ruins of apartheid, and a nationalism that leads to xenophobia and even war against neighboring states, is a critical issue facing democracies and the churches. The collapse of communism in eastern Europe resulted not only in the attempt to create democratic societies, but also in the resurgence of historic nationalisms that have threatened the stability of the region and led to ethnic cleansing. The church as an ecumenical community has a key role to play in countering any form of nationalism and patriotism that is uncritical, jingoistic, and unjust. National sovereignty has legitimacy, but not in any absolute sense.

In the church struggle against apartheid, critical theology had the clear task of countering the idolatry of racism; today, within a secular democratic society committed to multicultural and religious tolerance, the challenge is to ensure that both Christian faith and theology remain publicly engaged and prophetic. It is not easy for prophets who have supported the cause of liberation to exercise their critical craft against former comrades who have finally achieved power. In South Africa, for example, there is still the need to speak out against corruption, the abuse of power, racial and gender discrimination, economic injustice, the destruction of the environment, and whatever else may destroy the well-being of society. In this regard, key questions need to be addressed. This critical task is essential for the future well-being of democratic society not just in the new democracies but also in those that are historically well-established. For example, how does the church affirm democratic values and goals without selling out to a secular ideology in which Christian faith inevitably becomes privatized? What contribution can and should Christian theologians make to contemporary democratic theory and praxis?

If the prophetic vision provides the necessary utopian and iconoclastic basis for critical theological reflection and ecclesial praxis, reflection on the doctrine of the Trinity provides us with the insights necessary to overcome the way in which democracy has become a casualty of the contradictions of modernity. Indeed, by bringing the prophetic (critical) and the trinitarian (sociality) dimensions of Christian theological reflection and tradition together we have a theological basis for both contributing to the debate about democracy and enabling the church to discern its role within the democratic process.

The triune God, in whom Christians believe, is not a homogeneous collectivity in which the uniqueness of each person is subsumed within the whole, but a community within which the distinctness of each person is affirmed and therefore within which the other remains a significant other. At the same time, God is one, but not the monolithic, patriarchal sovereign of the universe remote from human history, relationships, struggles, and sufferings. By analogy, a trinitarian theology cannot support an understanding of society that promotes individual self-interest at the expense of the common good, even under the guise of personal freedoms. But equally, a trinitarian theology cannot support an understanding of society in which personal identity and freedom are trampled on by a collective. It is not easy to avoid these two tendencies under certain historical circumstances. But a truly democratic order, from a trinitarian perspective, requires constant effort to discern ways of transcending this split between individualism and collectivism, which has bedeviled the debate between liberalism and socialism, and to develop an understanding of human sociality in which both individual rights and the common good are complementary rather than conflictual.

The Church as Democratic Model

From the beginning of the Christian movement the role of the church in society has been not only to proclaim the message of the reign of God but to seek to be a sign of that reign within its own ecclesial life and structures. Hence, in the course of Christian history, canon law and the polity of the *ekklesia* have had a considerable influence on the shaping of Western constitutional law (Berman 1983). Furthermore, in many situations, such as the Third Reich, the structure of the church became a matter of considerable theological and political importance. As the Barmen Declaration of 1934 indicates, ideological critique of Nazism on its own was insufficient; there was also the need for an ecclesiology of human sociality and solidarity.

As mentioned previously, from a theological perspective the church is not simply another NGO, though it is part of civil society. NGOs are essentially voluntary organizations called into being to serve a particular role at a given time in society, and generally composed of like-minded people. Once their purpose has been served, and sometimes once their founder or leader is no longer involved, NGOs tend to dissolve or are disbanded. The church, on the other hand, is a community of very diverse people who have been baptized "into Christ," that is, they participate in an organic life that exists beyond themselves or their own choice, and for a purpose that derives from God's purpose for the world. The church, then, is not a democracy, that is, a community that is governed by the people and for the people, for Christ is the head of the body that exists to serve the purposes of God. This understanding of the church is, as already emphasized, a theological one, but it is essential for the church's own self-understanding, that is, in order for the church to understand its particular and peculiar role in society. The church exists both as a means to an end that has to do with God's justice and *shalom*, and as an end in itself, that is, as a community in which human divisions are transcended in the "unity of the Spirit."

The issues regarding the relationship between the church and democracy are complex, not least because of the various church polities that now characterize the different denominations and confessions. For some traditions hierarchy is of the essence of the church, whereas for others the goal is an egalitarian community; and there is a range of options between these ends of the spectrum. But all church traditions would insist that the final authority for the church is not the will of the majority but the will of God as revealed in Jesus Christ "according to the scriptures." This allows for the possibility of the prophet who is seldom in the majority but often the authentic voice of revelation. Indeed, for the church to be a prophetic witness in society it has to be careful not to become the mouthpiece of any majority will which might well contradict the Gospel. Take, for example, the way in which the Reich church in Nazi Germany became captive to the national will and the Nazi persecution of the Jews.

But if the church exists to serve God's purposes of justice and peace in the world, and if democracy is the best polity for approximating that goal, then there is a clear connection between the church's life and witness, and the struggle for a just democracy. If democracy should promote human fulfillment and flourishing within the body politic, how much more should the life of the church enable its members to discover an even deeper fulfillment and freedom in Christ? If the church is a key institution within civil society, and in some ways the handmaiden of democracy, is it not important that the church itself should emulate democratic values? After all, the participation of the "whole people of God" in the life of the church, not least though not always in the governing structures, is an important element in most forms of church government. This is symbolized by the sacrament of baptism, which declares that all those who are baptized, irrespective of gender, social class, or ethnicity, are united as equals within one body and share together in the mission of the church in the world.

The debate about the democratization of the church is really about the implications of baptism. From this perspective, the holders of hierarchical offices should be regarded as those who serve the people of God rather than dominate or rule over them. This was certainly the understanding of the Second Vatican Council, which Latin American liberation theologians began to express in their "base community" ecclesiologies. A similar development took place within feminist/womanist theologies, whose critique of the dominant paternalistic structures of the churches led to an alternative ecclesiology related to the wider democratic transformation of society. Some African indigenous churches have also found ways to combine hierarchy and participation that have potential for developing the relationship between traditional culture and democratic transition in Africa.

It is difficult to determine precisely to what extent such ecclesiologies have, in fact, contributed to the democratization of societies at large, but at least they have given embodiment to the democratic vision and raised issues that are of considerable importance for both church and society. Among these is the question of the relationship between equality and difference, an issue that has become critical both for democracy and for the public witness of the Christian faith today. The recognition of gender difference in the life of the church, and how this impacts on the ordination of women, is clearly of fundamental importance in raising questions about the relationship between patriarchy and hierarchy. Should women allow themselves to be co-opted into the hierarchical structures of the church rather than bring about the transformation of the church as a whole in ways which express human solidarity, enable equal participation, overcome patriarchal domination, and promote justice within society? From this perspective, ecclesial vision is directly related to the heart of the democratization process: that is, to the sharing of power within the life of the church and society.

A further issue of ecclesiological significance is the globalization of democracy. This has now become essential because a "global interconnectedness" has created "chains of interlocking political decisions and outcomes among states and their citizens, altering the nature and dynamics of national political systems themselves" (Held 1993: 39). Thus, while the focus of democratization in the past shifted from the city-state to the nation, so its future focus must be the ecumene as such. Ecumenism is not primarily about the church, but about a just world order; the search for the unity of the church, and its mission within the world, are bound up with a vision of the world characterized by justice, peace, and the integrity of creation.

The Future of Democracy

Democracy by its very nature is a fragile form of government, and the transition from an authoritarian to a democratic order is beset with enormous problems. In many countries the process is exacerbated by large-scale inequalities, a lack of resources, including money and time, and an inadequate education and preparation for democratic participation. In countries such as South Africa, this has been made worse by a legacy of racist oppression in which people have been systematically deprived of resources. To assume, then, that a new democratic order of world justice and peace is around the corner and that all that is required of us is some mopping-up operation, would be theoretically foolish, politically fatal, and theologically unsound. However cogent democratic theories might be, they are not self-fulfilling.

Yet the fact remains that we have entered a new historical epoch, for good or ill. We cannot ignore the risks, the current disorder, and the promise of more to come; but all is by no means dark for those who live and work in anticipation that the present democratic transformation will fulfill its promise. The transition to democracy, whether on a national or international scale, will inevitably involve a long and difficult march. But there is no alternative to pressing on in the struggle for a new democratic order in the modern world. What needs constant affirmation, however, is that democracy requires the commitment and participation of all citizens if it is to work properly. This may be an ideal, but it is an ideal that is worth striving for. Perhaps that is why some writers insist that democracy is ultimately dependent upon the development of a spirituality in which human freedom, genuine community, and a willingness to share undergird political programs and action.

Notes

1 On anarchism and other issues related to democracy see the articles in the *Dictionary of Ethics, Theology and Society*, edited by Paul Barry Clarke and Andrew Linzey (London: Routledge, 1996).
2 The development of Catholic social teaching on this and related matters can best be seen in terms of the papal encyclicals *Rerum Novarum* (1891) and *Centesimus Annus* (1991). See *Catholic Social Thought: The Documentary Heritage*, edited by David O'Brien and Thomas A. Shannon (Maryknoll, NY: Orbis, 1992).

References

Barth, Karl (1960). *Community, State and Church*. New York: Doubleday.
Bellah, Robert, et. al. (1991). *The Good Society*. New York: Knopf.
Berman, Harold J. (1983). *Law and Revolution: The Formation of the Western Legal Tradition*. Cambridge, Mass.: Harvard University Press.
de Gruchy, John W. (1995). *Christianity and Democracy*. Cambridge: Cambridge University Press.
Dorrien, Gary J. (1990). *Reconstructing the Common Good: Theology and the Social Order*. Maryknoll, NY: Orbis.
Dunn, John, ed. (1992). *Democracy: The Unfinished Journey, 508 BC to AD 1993*. Oxford: Oxford University Press.
Gifford, Paul, ed. (1995). *The Christian Churches and Africa's Democratisation*. Leiden: E. J. Brill.
Hauerwas, Stanley (1981). *A Community of Character: Toward a Constructive Christian Social Ethic*. Notre Dame, Ind.: University of Notre Dame Press.
Held, David, ed. (1993). *Prospects for Democracy*. Cambridge: Polity.

Maritain, Jacques (1986). *Christianity and Democracy*. San Francisco: Ignatius.

Niebuhr, Reinhold (1960). *The Children of Light and the Children of Darkness*. New York: Charles Scribner's Sons.

Provost, James, and Walf, Knut (1992). *The Tabu of Democracy within the Church*. London: SCM.

Witte, John, ed. (1993). *Christianity and Democracy in Global Context*. Boulder, Col.: Westview.

CHAPTER 31
Critical Theory

Marsha Aileen Hewitt

> *Marxism is the consummation . . . of the most progressive thoughts of humanity.*
>
> Ernst Bloch

The term "political theology" is by its nature ambiguous and potentially misleading, for at least two main reasons. The first rests on the assumption that there is something distinctive or uniquely different about a theology that is "political," as if some or most theology were not in any case "political." The idea that theology is apolitical is blind to the inner contradiction between the repressive and emancipatory impulses within theology that become visible through critical self-reflection. It ignores the fact that theology, like all cultural forms and theories, is mediated through human action and experience, generating its own forms of social organization and power hierarchies, and is thus inevitably political. Rosemary Radford Ruether's remark about the role of experience in feminist theology comes to mind as precisely relevant to the question of the political nature of theology. She observed that the concept of experience is not unique to feminist theology, since all the "objective sources" of theology "are themselves codified collective human experience" (1983: 12). Especially since the ideology critique of Karl Marx and its subsequent development in the critical social theory of the Frankfurt School, it is no longer possible to overlook the ideological and political dimensions of all theology.

One of the key questions that must be asked in order to evaluate the political meaning of theology and its role in shaping and directing human action is: Whose interest do specific theological doctrines and ideas serve? In her critique of Rudolf Bultmann's assertion that historical meaning is located in the present, Dorothee Sölle writes, "In the face of such a statement, we have no right to disregard the interests that produced it, which means concretely that we must raise the questions originally posed by Karl Marx. Whose interest is served by perceiving the meaning of history always in the present? *To which class* do those persons belong who talk that way?" (1974: 49, emphasis added). The interest here does not involve an assessment of Sölle's critique of Bultmann, but rather concerns her critical *method*: *Whose material interest* is being served with particular theories and how openly is it acknowledged? A theology that disregards this question accommodates itself, consciously or not, to the social conditions in which it is contextualized. It is a theology devoid of a sense of "social obligation" (Moltmann, 1967: 316) that, if confined merely to the realm of "constant metaphysical reflection" is little more than "romanticist escapism" (p. 315). The question *Whose interest?* locates the political nature of theology and includes any theory of human experience. All the critical theologies of liberation that have emerged in the wake of the more liberal theological climate generated by the Second Vatican Council – liberation theology, feminist theology, black theology, Minjung theology, and so on – implicitly or explicitly raise this question in order to promote the liberation of those people in whose interest their theory and practice operates. An important feature of a liberationist theological method is that it not only sides with specific oppressed groups but also is critical of the implicit and disavowed political interests of mainstream theology that contribute to oppression. Thus, these theologies are explicitly political in two ways: one, in their advocacy for the emancipation of oppressed groups, and two, in their recognition that theological traditions are "defined by contemporary questions . . . and conditioned by contemporary political interests and structures of domination" (Schüssler Fiorenza 1984: xvii). This point is central to political theology.

The second ambiguous element associated with the term "political theology" concerns what specifically is meant by the term "political." A common, historically prevalent meaning of "political" theology refers to the theological justification of the hegemony of a particular political order and its supporting ideology. Christianity is still invoked as justification for certain political policies and state actions, placing them above reproach. The Latin American theologian José Comblin illustrates this usage of political theology in his comments on the ideological role of Christianity for former Latin American military governments in support of their "national security" ideologies, which often resulted in the brutal persecution of those suspected of being dangerous to the "national security" of the state. He writes that many Latin American governments

> praise democracy and Christianity with the most lyrical enthusiasm. According to their own declarations, the only purpose of their entire politics is the salvation of democracy and Christianity. They all want to create a new society based on Christian principles. Reading the Declaration of Principles of the Chilean junta, one has to weep tears of joy and wonder – surely no government in the modern world has ever had such a Christian purpose. (Comblin 1979: 77)

Comblin's bitter observation raises an important question about the *kind* of politics we are talking about when we refer to "political" theology.

Closely related to this is the issue of theological method: that is, how is the relationship between theology and politics conceived of and deployed? The political theology that underlay the former brutal military juntas of Latin America imposed extensive dictatorships whose rationale was to protect and promote a Christian society. The juntas combined an authoritarian conservative politics with a rigidly hierarchical power structure enforced through terror and violence, justified in part by the "need" to preserve Christian values. However, these dictatorships could be understood from another and equally "Christian" point of view as negating Christian values. Thus the questions of what kind of politics is meant by current usage of "political" theology, and how theology and politics connect, are crucial both in understanding the term and in differentiating it from its more prevalent historical usage. Contemporary political theology understands itself quite differently.

The concept as it is currently used was first introduced by Johannes Baptist Metz in 1966 (Davis 1980: 13). For Metz, theology must be reconceived as practical and oriented to action in the world. The "'spirit' of Christianity is permanently embedded in the 'flesh' of world history and must maintain and prove itself in the irreversible course of the latter" (Metz 1969: 16). Since Christianity is itself a "secularization of the world" (p. 39), it must move theology out of the private realm that focuses on one's personal relationship to God and salvation into the public realm of social action. Political theology involves a "critical correction" (Metz 1970: 35) of the prevailing tendency to separate private faith from the public realm of social action. The result is that religion and society enter a new relationship, in which theology fully embraces and participates in world history without sacralizing politics or identifying with any specific state or party structure. He writes: "Political theology claims to be a basic element in the whole structure of critical theological thinking, motivated by a new notion of the relation between theory and practice, according to which all theology must be of itself 'practical,' oriented to action" (p. 35). Jürgen Moltmann pushes this idea further when he writes that "[t]hose who hope in Christ can no longer put up with reality as it is, but begin to suffer under it, to contradict it. Peace with God means conflict with the world, for the goad of the promised future stabs inexorably into the flesh of every unfulfilled present" (1967: 21).

Both Metz and Moltmann remain *necessarily* vague about what *form* the theory–action relationship, oriented to social justice and a transformed reality, would take. To do otherwise would risk political theology's aligning itself with a particular political ideology or group, which could compromise its critical force, irrespective of such group's latent or explicit values espousing peace and democracy. One of political theology's main concerns was not to identify itself with any particular political ideology or group. Rather, its effort was motivated by the desire to *formulate a methodology* for a new understanding of the relationship among theology, society, and action that would render theology an effective force for historical change without falling into ideology. Political theology affirms that "the central promises of the reign of God in the [New Testament] – freedom, peace, justice, reconciliation – cannot be made radically private affairs. *They cannot be entirely interiorized and spiritualized as corresponding to the individual's longing for freedom and peace*" (Metz 1970: 36, emphasis added). This concept of political theology contests judgments such as Theodor Adorno's that theology and metaphysics are "condemned . . . to serve as ideological passports for conformism," while embracing his further insight that the "metaphysical interests of men would require that their material ones be fully looked after" (Adorno 1973: 398). Like Adorno and his colleagues Max Horkheimer and Herbert Marcuse, Metz also includes concrete human experience and the material conditions that produce it among the necessary and worthy objects of theological reflection and action. This is one of the central features political theology shares with critical theory.

Resonances with Critical Theory and Marx

In his essay "Philosophy and Critical Theory," Marcuse rejects a philosophy whose interest in reconciliation resides in the realm of ideas rather than in concrete reality. By recasting metaphysical philosophy as social theory with a practical, emancipatory intent, the interest in reconciliation is directed toward concrete human happiness (Marcuse 1968: 142). The material conditions that render human happiness possible are themselves the object of theoretical interest. "The philosophical ideals of a better world and of true Being are incorporated into the practical aim of struggling mankind, where they take on a human form" (p. 142). Critical theory confronts the "bad facticity" of an unjust and therefore irrational world with the "better potentialities" inherent in history and social forms. A distinguishing feature of a "rational" society is one where the economy serves human needs and where freedom and happiness are pursued as ends in themselves rather than being accidental by-products of success in a competitive, aggressive, and acquisitive world (1968: 144). Critical theory reverses the "flight toward the eternal" (Horkheimer 1978: 45) that is a central feature of metaphysics and theology, recasting the hope of the future as not in "the afterlife of individual existence in a Beyond but [in] the solidarity with men who will come after us" (p. 102).

Marcuse understood that in so far as philosophy accommodates or ignores the role of economic and political structures in determining the human condition it colludes with injustice (Marcuse 1968: 153). Critical theory refuses to depict a future world or ally itself with any particular politics or social organization, preferring to dwell with the negative from which hope emerges. Critical theory's focus on the negative means that it must account for the negativity of human experience and the reasons for unnecessary human suffering. Thought must achieve a "felt contact with its objects," meaning it must be mediated by the particular (Adorno 1974: 247). In this respect, critical theory engages in the kind of "critical correction" of philosophy that Metz proposed for theology. "Political theology," he writes, "is now also the effort to formulate the eschatological message of Christianity in the conditions of present-day society" (Metz 1970: 35). From this perspective Christian concepts such as salvation are reformulated to express eschatological hope as the struggle for justice, "the *humanizing* of man, the *socializing* of humanity, *peace* for all creation" (Moltmann 1967: 329, emphasis in original). These statements by Metz and Moltmann illustrate the strong impact of critical theory on the development of critical, political theology (Fierro 1977: 108).

Political theology and, to an only slightly different extent, the liberation theologies that emerge along with it unfold within, on the one hand, the parentheses of Jas. 2: 17 – "faith, by itself, if it has no works, is dead" – and, on the other, Marx's eleventh thesis on Feuerbach – "the philosophers have only *interpreted* the world . . . the point is to *change* it" (Marx and Engels 1976: 5). The critical relationship between theory and practice elaborated by political theology has its source in Marxian social theory, which in some respects resonates with the social justice themes of the Hebrew and Christian scriptures that emphasize the connection between love of God and humanity and the praxis of "doing justice" (Gutiérrez 1973: 194–6). Here thought is a practical activity. The Marxist philosopher Ernst Bloch, another important intellectual source for political theology, describes Marx's second thesis on Feuerbach as proposing an idea of truth that is not "a theory relationship alone, but a definite theory–practice relationship" (Bloch 1995: 268). Marx writes that the question of "objective truth" is not "a question of theory but is a *practical* question. Man must prove the truth, i.e., the reality and power, the this-worldliness of his thinking in practice" (Marx and Engels 1976: 3, emphasis in original). Thought for Marx is "an activity, a critical, insistent, revealing activity" (Bloch 1995: 268), and is concrete and dynamic only when mediated in political action (Davis 1980: 17).

Davis agrees with Marx's rejection of the traditional division between theory and practice where theory is reduced to contemplation of "stable object[s]." Davis writes that, for political theology, theory becomes "the consciousness of practice, the reflective element of social activity and, as distinct from ideology, inseparable from the concrete historical effort to overcome the contradictions of existing society" (1980: 117). Jürgen Moltmann seems to have something similar in mind with his own "Thesis 4," which states that "The new criterion of theology and of faith is to be found in praxis," which means among other things that Christianity must "bring the hoped-for future into practical contact with the misery of the present" (Moltmann 1969: 139). Like philosophy which has hitherto been content with interpreting the world, Christianity has too long speculated about an "eternity beyond time," with the effect that it has inevitably supported the status quo of domination. Political theology seeks to address the contradictions within religion in order to uncover its inner dialectic of emancipatory and regressive inclinations that helps clarify the contribution of theology to injustice. In this way political theology aspires to be in itself a force of social change. This idea is taken up by Gutiérrez as well when he describes liberation theology as "part of the process through which the world is transformed" (1973). Quoting Schillebeeckx, he writes: "The hermeneutics of the Kingdom of God consists especially in making the world a better place" (p. 18).

The Marxian idea that thought is itself a practical activity with emancipatory potential is a central concept of early critical theory. Horkheimer's famous 1937 essay "Traditional and Critical Theory" emphasizes this point as a key difference from "traditional" theory. Critical theory does not merely present "societal contradictions" as an "expression of the concrete historical situation," but also acts itself as a "force" within history "to stimulate change" (Horkheimer 1972: 215). The object of inquiry – history, society, and human experience – cannot be treated separately from theory, as is the case with traditional theory as well as theological and philosophical metaphysics. "Every part of the theory presupposes the critique of the existing order and the struggle against it along lines determined by the theory itself" (p. 229). For Horkheimer and for political theology, critical thought generates transformative action. The role of the theoretician engaged in such analysis is to form "a dynamic unity with the oppressed class" (p. 215). In a statement that strongly resonates with Schillebeeckx, in the passage quoted above, Horkheimer writes that the "Marxist categories of class, exploitation, surplus value, profit, pauperization, and breakdown are elements in a conceptual whole, and the meaning of this whole is to be sought not in the preservation of contemporary society but in its transformation into *the right kind of society*" (p. 218, emphasis in original). For both critical theory and political theology, the task of the theorist/theologian is to organize his/her thought in terms of what is needed to bring into being "the right kind of society," or make the world "a better place."

Political theology shares with critical theory a method of recasting the relationship between theory and practice with an emphasis on negative critique. As has been stated, neither critical theory nor political theology advocates a particular form of politics or social organization, although they certainly may be understood to imply it. For Metz, the eschatological message of Christianity has a critically negative function which helps prevent it from falling under the spell of any particular ideology, since it advocates a sustained critical negation of all particularity, of the concrete existent. From the point of view of critical theory, the kind of sustained negativity advocated by Metz becomes somewhat blunted by the theological symbolism of the Incarnation and the Crucifixion, in that the Incarnation represents God's embracing of the world in its full secularity while the Crucifixion stands not only as the sign of the negation of the existing world, but also as the guarantee that it is not the last word. Unlike critical theory, which deliberately refuses any such consolation, political theology turns to the eternal realm as guarantor that there is meaning in human suffering, which will one day be vindicated. The famous controversy between Horkheimer and Walter Benjamin some sixty years ago illustrates critical theory's rejection of any such consolation, on the grounds that inherent in such consolations is a tacit acceptance of the conditions that produced the need for it in the first place. For Benjamin the case was somewhat different. For him, the historical past had to be open so that people living in the present could forge an anamnestic solidarity with the dead of past generations. He hoped that in this way their suffering and death would not be meaningless. Horkheimer thoroughly rejected this idea:

The thought is monstrous that the prayers of the persecuted in their hour of great-est need, that the innocent who must die without explanation of their situation, that the last hopes of a supernatural court of appeals, fall on deaf ears and that the night unilluminated by any human light is also not penetrated by any divine one. The eternal truth without God has as little ground and footing as infinite love; indeed, it becomes an unthinkable concept. But is the monstrousness of an idea any more a cogent argument against the assertion or denial of a state of affairs than does logic contain a law which says that a judgment is simply false that has despair as its consequence? (Horkheimer, cited in Peukert 1986: 209–10).

Political theology preserves a religious consolation that critical theory rejects because, from the latter's point of view, religious consolations inevitably support the status quo. In the end suffering will be overcome and justice established not in history, but in a future beyond history. For critical theory, this means that political theology ultimately loses its critical social and practical function. For Horkheimer, "good," or perhaps authentic religion maintains its focus on the immediate, real conditions of human beings so that the desire for change is constantly nurtured. Such religion must "sustain, not let reality stifle, the impulse for change, the desire that the spell be broken, that things take the right turn. We have religion where life down to its every gesture is marked by this resolve" (1978: 163). From its own point of view, political theology intends exactly that.

New Constellations: Political Theology and Critical Theory

When brought together in a kind of dialogue or "constellation," as Benjamin and Adorno would express it, political theology and critical theory can be seen to intersect at key theoretical points. Both critical theory and political theology focus on a method that relocates theory in terms of practical activity while refus-ing to endorse any specific form of life. Yet this is not entirely true, since politi-cal theology is rooted in a specific religious worldview whose values and beliefs it ultimately does not contest. Horkheimer explains that, in analogous fashion with the prohibition of visual representations of God in Judaism, critical theory too prohibits identifications of what is the good life (1978: 236). The freedom, justice, and reconciliation hoped for in critical theory and political theology have never been concretely experienced in any epoch known to humanity. Conceptu-alizations of the good life can only be fashioned out of existing possibilities, which is why critical theory and perhaps political theology refuse to engage in programmatic constructions for a just society. It must be sufficient that the concept of negativity contains the positive what-might-be-hoped-for, as its oppo-site (p. 236). Charles Davis comments that the only religious identity implied by a political theology is that of an "active participation in the present shaping of a universality to be realized in the future," rather than allegiance to a particular religious tradition. As critical theory attempts to rend the veil that distorts the real relations between human beings and the conditions that structure them, political theology insists on being a critical theology that is mediated by the public sphere, which in turn demands political action in the world. Politics in this sense refers not to a struggle for power and its distribution but rather to a "collective shaping of norms and values" (Davis 1980: 178).

In the sense that both critical theory and political theology focus on a method of elaborating the relationship between theory and practice and refuse, in their further focus on the negativity of "bad facticity," to outline or promote a better way of life and strategic political action, they remain for many deeply unsatisfying. One of political theology's inheritors, liberation theology, defines itself against political theology by aligning itself with specific groups of people and with a specific form of political activity, although it adopts a methodology similar to that of political theology and is also deeply influenced by a Marxian social theory that is mediated by critical theory as opposed to an older, Soviet-style "scientific socialism." One of the methodological points emphasized by liberation theology has its source in Marx's notion of the "protest" nature of religious longing. "*Religious* distress is . . . the *expression* of real distress and also the *protest* against real distress. Religion is the sigh of the oppressed creature, the heart of a heartless world, just as it is the spirit of spiritless conditions" (Marx and Engels 1975: 175, emphasis in original). The protest character of religious activity is affirmed by the Brazilian liberation theologian Leonardo Boff when he identifies "ethical outrage" as a way of working out faith in the practice of liberation (1989: 409). Gutiérrez openly acknowledges the influence of Marx's critique of religious alienation on liberation theology's effort to cast a critical light on the alienating effects of theology as a necessary part of theology's transformation into a practical, emancipatory force. "[I]t is to a large extent due to Marxism's influence that theological thought, searching for its own sources, has begun to reflect on the meaning of the transformation of this world and the action of man in history." One of the most important ideas that liberation theology appropriated from Marx is contained in his thesis eleven, that human action in history is the "point of departure for all reflection" (Gutiérrez 1973: 9). However, Gutiérrez significantly altered this position with the "revised" edition of *A Theology of Liberation* (1988). Nonetheless, many Latin American liberation theologians openly acknowledged the importance of Marx in shifting their method of thinking about the structural reasons for suffering and injustice. In similar fashion to Marx's critique of philosophy, they heralded the need for a "revolution" in theology where theology would become itself a critical theory, following as a reflective "second step" to action (Gutiérrez 1973: 11).

The commitment to a new theological method, where theology becomes an emancipatory force with the explicit goal of changing the world, is common to both political and liberation theologies. Moltmann went so far as to speculate upon the "latent revolutionary potential" of a transformed Christianity (1969: 133). Leonardo and Clodovis Boff's location of the "reality of social misery" and the "liberation of the oppressed" as the only starting point and goal for theology

(1984: 24) applies to political theology as well. The difference between political theology and liberation theology lies in the latter's sometimes explicit commitment to a socialist politics. Leonardo Boff writes that "Christian thinking is more nearly congruent with socialist ideals than capital[ist] ones. It is not a matter of creating a Christian socialism. It is a matter, rather, of being allowed to say that the concept of socialism – provided that it is really fulfilled and realized – makes it possible for the Christian to live the humanitarian and divine ideal of his or her faith more completely" (1989: 422). Juan Luis Segundo refers to a statement by third world bishops calling for a "system that is juster and more suited to the needs of the day . . . 'authentic' socialism is Christianity lived to the full" (1976: 72). He also asserts that religious faith is "dead as a doornail" unless mediated by political ideology: "faith, when properly understood, can never dissociate itself from the ideologies in which it is embodied" (p. 181). The issue for Segundo concerns *which* ideology is more likely to bring about liberation – for that is the ideology to be embraced. Like the political theologians, he also focuses on the importance of theological method over substantive content in the struggle for liberation. Yet he is critical of the political theologians because of the "stress on the eschatological element, to the detriment of the historical element" in their thinking. In his view, this emphasis on eschatology detracts from the focus on history (p. 144).

Gutiérrez criticizes political theology as too vague in its theoretical focus on recasting the theory–practice relationship and its inadequacy in analyzing the contemporary political situation. One major reason for this shortcoming, in Gutiérrez' view, is political theology's emergence in the European context, meaning it cannot "penetrate the situation of dependency, injustice, and exploitation in which most of mankind finds itself" (1973: 224). This criticism is not quite fair, given that it is based on the brute fact that the political theologians live and write in the affluent countries; the implication seems to be that, since they lack the experience of people in poor countries, they are somehow incapable of adequately theorizing political struggle against exploitation. Gutiérrez assumes somewhat dismissively that they cannot know the "experience of the aspiration to liberation which emerges from the heart." This is one of the assumptions Gutiérrez makes as accounting for the abstract nature of political theology. He also says that political theology would be more robust and relevant if it had taken "certain aspects" of Marx's thought more seriously (1973: 224). However, as argued above, Marx is one of political theology's most important intellectual sources (Fierro 1977: 16). Gregory Baum criticizes political theology's focus on negative critique, preferring a "positive commitment to action" and "positive recommendations for a strategy of social change." In his view, the negative critique of political theology and its refusal to promote positive alternatives places the "political mission" of the church at a "prophetic distance" (1975: 288). Baum accuses political theology of not choosing "the side of the exploited and . . . [its] countervailing movement," meaning that it remains "identified with the interests of the ruling class" (p. 289). Baum doesn't appear aware that for political theology the case is quite the reverse. For Baum and other liberation theologians, critique of the status quo cannot be effectively made without a political identification with the specific revolutionary movements.

This kind of criticism misses the point that political theology's goal of emancipation is clearly directed toward alleviating the unnecessary misery of the oppressed. Further, it does not necessarily follow that meaningful negative critique requires political allegiance to a specific revolutionary subject or ideology in order to retain its emancipatory force. Strategic politics are constructed on ideological scaffoldings that do not easily tolerate too much critical self-reflection, which is understandable from a *strategic* point of view. Ideologies and their adherents tend to demand and enforce conformity, marginalizing or obliterating dissent for the sake of preserving their goals. The logical and inherent tendency of ideology is to curb critique rather than cultivate it, with the result that its underlying premises and values cannot be subject to serious critical scrutiny from within or without. Ideology is not universal, but rather is a set of ideas that corresponds to a particular set of social relationships and cultural forms. In this sense, ideology regulates not only human action, but also *what can be thought*. The critical theorists knew this, which is another reason why they refused to align themselves with social programs or political movements. The exception to this was Marcuse, who in his later life participated in the student protest movements of the late 1960s.

Nonetheless, the critical theorists did not wish to compromise the independence of critical thought by risking premature reconciliations that would inevitably coincide with existent social conditions. "The only philosophy which can be reasonably practised in the face of despair," Adorno wrote, "is the attempt to contemplate all things as they would present themselves from the standpoint of redemption . . . Perspectives must be fashioned that displace and estrange the world, reveal it to be, with its rifts and crevices, as indigent and distorted as it will appear one day in the messianic light" (1974: 247). Political theology is closer to critical theory on this point than to liberation theology, and, unsatisfying as such a position may be, especially in the face of urgent social injustice and widespread suffering, it must preserve a "prophetic distance" in order to be attentive to the ideological elements inherent in all human thought and action. The fact that the political theologians, like the critical theorists, reside and work in the northern hemisphere does not of itself narrowly determine the critical quality of their thought, or its usefulness. Many of the early Latin American liberation theologians were either foreign born and/or European educated, which actually contributed to their ability to mount a Marxian social analysis of oppression that was also able to cast a critical and revelatory light on the ways in which the Christian churches and theology contribute to social injustice. In many respects, like the political theologians, the liberation theologians spoke *on behalf of* the poor; they did not themselves generally belong to the category of the oppressed non-person however much in solidarity they were with them. José Comblin's point is well taken that theologians "are conditioned by their economic and social context . . . their background, *curriculum vitae*, their social position, and their income will . . . have some connection with theological convictions they hold" (cited in Fierro 1977: 384). This, however, does not render them incapable of critical thought or any less in solidarity with those less fortunate.

Political theology resists being completely absorbed by ideology in so far as it remains aware that all theory is conditioned by social, historical, and economic factors which it tries to reflect upon and make explicit. Although political theology develops "under the sign of Marx, just as truly as scholasticism was a theology operating under the sign of Aristotle and liberal Protestant theology was one operating under the sign of Kant" (Fierro 1977: 80), this does not mean it is a *Marxist* theology. Nor does political theology align itself with a specific social movement, despite the fact that it emerges in the social context of revolutionary activity in Latin America, Africa, the American civil rights movement, the student protest movements in North America and Europe, and May '68 in France (p. 81). All that political theology attempts is to create a new concept of theological justification that is thoroughly historical and social. Despite the fact that liberation theology consciously espouses a general socialist political practice, like political theology it generally does not sacralize a particular politics, nor any party or state. Moreover, neither political nor liberation theologies accept that any form of society, no matter how advanced or democratic, can be "fixed and finished once and for all" (p. 25). This feature is primarily what distinguishes these theologies from the political theology of Christendom and the Latin American juntas. Political and liberation theologies are less interested in Christian politics defined and enforced by nominal Christian elites and power groups than in *Christians in politics*, how they conduct themselves, how they promote Christian ethics and values, and on whose behalf.

Is Public Theology Regressive with Respect to Political Theology?

A more recent variant of political theology has emerged in the form of contemporary "public theology," which is quite different from political and liberation theologies. A brief discussion of public theology is important here, since it might be seen as an "inheritor" of political theology, which it is not. Public theologians assume the role of "religious critics" whose task is to formulate and develop the "ultimate meanings" and "spiritual culture" of society (Dean 1994: xiv) in order to rescue modernity from anomie and spiritual breakdown through a revitalization and updating of Christian values. This represents a shift from the focus on historical change and political action to a more spiritual renewal of societal values along Christian lines. From this perspective, the political relevance of Christian beliefs and values contributes to a more authentic understanding of human nature and society in modernity (Schüssler Fiorenza 1992: 3). David Tracy advocates revising Christianity by "correlating" it with "a common human experience" (1978: 43) that is resistant to modernity's banishment of religion to the purely inward, personal realm of spiritual faith and individual salvation. Christianity, or the "*Christian fact*," as Tracy puts it (p. 43), corresponds to a universal human experience that can be elaborated through rational public dialogue. According to Matthew Lamb, "Christian theologies for the public realms communicate a universality through the solidarity of the reign of God" (1992: 113). Public theology is "faith seeking to understand the relation between Christian convictions" and the larger social, cultural context (Thiemann 1991: 21). The question is: What is a "universal" human experience and who and what defines it? How can there be a "universal" human experience in the modern, pluralistic, and diverse societies to which Christian theology speaks?

Many of the public theologians have long been interested in the theory of communicative rationality developed by Jürgen Habermas, seeing in his expanded concept of reason a way to rehabilitate Christian values over against instrumental concepts of reason that have colonized most areas of human experience in modernity. The public theologians lament the fact that Habermas does not take a serious interest in the role of religion in society and individual life (Schüssler Fiorenza 1992: 3). They contend that Habermas' theory can be used to show that religion (by which they mean Christianity) provides a rationally defensible meaning for reality and the human experience of it that is compatible with the insights of modernity. Aided by Habermas' critique of the ambiguities of modernity, they posit that an updated theology that takes seriously the accepted cognitive insights of modernity and revises itself accordingly would be able to demonstrate its own truth, normative appropriateness, and sincerity within a pluralistic world. Religion then is demonstrated to have its own internal rationality that coincides with modern culture, so that a "public correlational theology" becomes a "fully modern critical discipline" in its own right (Tracy 1992: 35–6).

It is not difficult to understand the appeal of Habermas' theory of communicative action, along with his critique of the hegemony of instrumental reason in modern societies, for contemporary theologians interested in promoting a critically reflective and socially relevant Christianity. Their position is that Christianity offers unique and superior ethical and spiritual resources for the public sphere. They even follow the spirit of Habermas in agreeing that a public, political theology must be "willing to submit its religious claims and their political implications to the challenge of public discourse" (Schüssler Fiorenza 1992: 6). A statement such as this is disingenuous at best, since however "correlative" or updated any theology strives to be, it inevitably rests upon certain axiomatic assumptions that are inherently non-negotiable. This is inevitably the case with a theology that claims to account for universal human experience.

In Habermas' view, any theory that aspires to account for all of human experience by appealing to the universal validity of a totalizing view of reality is self-contradictory and premodern. Habermas' critique of metaphysical philosophies applies to theology as well: "Philosophy can no longer refer to the whole of the

world, of nature, of history, of society, in the sense of a totalizing knowledge
. . . All attempts at discovering ultimate foundations, in which the intentions of
First Philosophy live on, have broken down." His theory of communicative rationality regards "determinate theological affirmations" as "meaningless" (1985:
12). Habermas makes this point quite clear in his reply to the public theologians
that the "premodern certainty" (1992: 240) provided by religions has no place
in modern, complex, and diverse societies where religious traditions and metaphysical worldviews have collapsed (1990b: 72). Since theology is embedded in
a specific religious tradition that has its own language and symbol system, it can
have no *universalizable* claims to truth beyond its own borders of belief. Yet the
public theologians continue to assert the universal validity of Christian values
and truth claims in their efforts to privilege Christian sensibility and political
values in public, political life. This is a very different approach from that of political theology. Consider Davis's view that "there is no specifically religious
language," and that "the indirect nature of all religious meaning makes it
impossible to ground a political claim upon it in confrontation with other competing claims" (1994: 115). For Davis, an argument for privileging a specific
religious tradition over all others lies beyond "what can reasonably be urged" (p.
204). To do otherwise is to abandon a critical theology that engages in an emancipatory critique of all traditions, including its own, and to risk losing sight of
its own participation in the structures of social domination.

Public theology has fallen behind the intent of the former political theology,
whose critical method, however limited, rejected attempts to Christianize the
world. Public theology intends to substitute Christian theology for history and
society as the locus of meaning in the quest for social justice, resulting in a
theology that is merely applied to politics and society. The dialectical nature of
the theory–practice relationship sustained by political theology collapses into
an identification of political practice with Christian values and goals. Public
theology reverses political theology's acceptance of the "secularized," "religiously emancipated society" (Metz 1970: 37) in an attempt to restore itself
implicitly to cultural and political hegemony. Whereas political theology asserted
"its essentially universal categories . . . as a negative critique" (p. 37) in its effort
to mount and sustain an ideology critique of society and of itself, public theology prefers to forge the "universal categories" of Christianity into a political ideology. To achieve this in modern pluralistic societies can only result in the
marginalization of difference to the peripheries of political action.

Toward the end of his life Max Horkheimer declared that "a politics which,
even when highly unreflected, does not preserve a theological moment in itself
is, no matter how skilful, in the last analysis, mere business" (1975: 60). By "theological moment," Horkheimer was not expressing allegiance to any particular
religion or political ideology. The "theological moment" rather refers to the
longing for "perfect justice," what might be for Marx "the heart of a heartless
world." In Horkheimer's view, the idea of God functions as a repository for the
hope that justice is not a mere illusion and that the misery of this world is not

without alternatives. "Dissatisfaction with earthly destiny is the strongest motive for acceptance of a transcendental being" (1972: 129), he maintained.

Critical theory and political theology, in their different ways, attempt to shift the hope for justice from an eternal beyond to the historical present by transforming the longing for a humane world into social action with an emancipatory goal. In Horkheimer's view, this utopian move cannot be adequately supported or advanced by religion *as theology*: "Mankind loses religion as it moves through history, but the loss leaves its mark behind. Part of the drives and desires which religious belief preserved and kept alive are detached from the inhibiting religious form and *become productive forces* in social practice" (1972: 131, emphasis added). Although critical theory argues that religion and its attendant theology have reached their historical threshold with the transition to modernity, their contents have not disappeared, but rather enter new forms that are more commensurate with those forms of action whose conscious intent is the emancipation of human beings from all manner of alienation. Horkheimer's argument for preserving a "concept of infinity" that is conscious of "the finality of human life and of the inalterable aloneness of men" is that "theological moment" that is transformed in critical theory into a utopian ideal rooted in historical possibility and solidarity with living, finite human beings. Unlike political theology, critical theory will offer neither guarantees nor consolations, thus maintaining its negative critique while political theology ultimately reverses its negativity into the positivity of divine promise. This is perhaps one of the reasons why political theology and liberation theologies could not sustain or develop their critical impact, especially in complex pluralistic, modern societies. The question of the future of religion in modernity requires further exploration.

References

Adorno, Theodor W. (1973). *Negative Dialectics*, trans. E. B. Ashton. New York: Continuum.
——(1974). *Minima Moralia: Reflections from Damaged Life*, trans. E. N. F. Jephcott. London: Verso.
Baum, Gregory (1975). *Religion and Alienation: A Theological Reading of Sociology*. New York: Paulist Press.
Bloch, Ernst (1995). *The Principle of Hope*, vol. I, trans. Neville Plaice, Stephen Plaice and Paul Knight. Cambridge: MIT Press.
Boff, Leonardo (1989). "The Contribution of Liberation Theology to a New Paradigm." In Hans Küng and David Tracy (eds.), *Paradigm Change in Theology*, trans. Margaret Kohl. New York: Crossroad.
Boff, Leonardo, and Boff, Clodovis (1984). *Salvation and Liberation*, trans. Robert R. Barr. Maryknoll, NY: Orbis.
Browning, Don S., and Schüssler Fiorenza, Francis, eds. (1992). *Habermas, Modernity, and Public Theology*. New York: Crossroad.
Comblin, José (1979). *The Church and the National Security State*. Maryknoll, NY: Orbis.
Davis, Charles (1980). *Theology and Political Society*. Cambridge: Cambridge University Press.

——(1994). *Religion and the Making of Society: Essays in Social Theology*. Cambridge: Cambridge University Press.

Dean, William (1994). *The Religious Critic in American Culture*. New York: State University of New York Press.

Fierro, Alfredo (1977). *The Militant Gospel: A Critical Introduction to Political Theologies*, trans. John Drury. Maryknoll, NY: Orbis.

Gutiérrez, Gustavo (1973). *A Theology of Liberation: History, Politics and Salvation*, trans. Sister Caridad Inda and John Eagleson. Maryknoll, NY: Orbis. Rev. edn. 1988.

Habermas, Jürgen (1979). *Communication and the Evolution of Society*, trans. Thomas McCarthy. Boston: Beacon.

——(1985). *Philosophical–Political Profiles*, trans. Frederick G. Lawrence. Cambridge, Mass.: MIT Press.

——(1990a). *Moral Consciousness and Communicative Action*, trans. Christian Lenhardt and Shierry Weber Nicholsen. Cambridge, Mass.: MIT Press.

——(1990b). *The Philosophical Discourse of Modernity*, trans. Frederick G. Lawrence. Cambridge, Mass.: MIT Press.

——(1992). "Transcendence from Within, Transcendence in this World." In Don S. Browning and Francis Schüssler Fiorenza (eds.), *Habermas, Modernity, and Public Theology*. New York: Crossroad.

Horkheimer, Max (1972). *Critical Theory: Selected Essays*, trans. Matthew J. O'Connell et al. New York: Continuum.

——(1975). *Die Sehnsucht nach dem ganz Anderen: Ein Interview mit Kommentar von Helmut Gumnior*. Hamburg: Furche.

——(1978). *Dawn and Decline: Notes 1926–1931 and 1950–1969*, trans. Michael Shaw. New York: Seabury.

Lamb, Matthew (1992). "Communicative Praxis and Theology: Beyond Modern Nihilism and Dogmatism." In Don S. Browning and Francis Schüssler Fiorenza (eds.), *Habermas, Modernity, and Public Theology*. New York: Crossroad.

Marcuse, Herbert (1968). *Negations: Essays in Critical Theory*, trans. Jeremy J. Shapiro. Boston: Beacon.

Marx, Karl, and Engels, Frederick (1975). *Collected Works*, volume III. New York: International.

——(1976). *Collected Works*, vol. V. New York: International.

Metz, Johannes Baptist (1969). *Theology of the World*, trans. William Glen-Doepel. New York: Herder & Herder.

——(1970). "Political Theology." In *Sacramentum Mundi: An Encyclopedia of Theology*, volume V. London: Burns Oates.

Moltmann, Jürgen (1967). *Theology of Hope*, trans. James W. Leitch. New York: Harper & Row.

——(1969). *Religion, Revolution and the Future*. New York: Charles Scribner's Sons.

Peukert, Helmut (1986). *Science, Action, and Fundamental Theology*, trans. James Bohman. Cambridge, Mass.: MIT Press.

Ruether, Rosemary Radford (1983). *Sexism and God-Talk: Toward a Feminist Theology*. Boston: Beacon.

Schüssler Fiorenza, Elisabeth (1984). *In Memory of Her*. New York: Crossroad.

Schüssler Fiorenza, Francis (1992). "Introduction: A Critical Reception for a Practical Public Theology." In Don S. Browning and Francis Schüssler Fiorenza (eds.), *Habermas, Modernity, and Public Theology*. New York: Crossroad.

Segundo, Juan Luis (1976). *The Liberation of Theology*, trans. John Drury. Maryknoll, NY: Orbis.

Sölle, Dorothee (1974). *Political Theology*, trans. John Shelley. Philadelphia: Fortress.

Thiemann, Ronald F. (1991). *Constructing a Public Theology: The Church in a Pluralistic Culture*. Lousiville, Ky.: John Knox.

Tracy, David (1978). *Blessed Rage for Order*. New York: Seabury.

——(1992). "Theology, Critical Social Theory, and the Public Realm." In Don S. Browning and Francis Schüssler Fiorenza (eds.), *Habermas, Modernity, and Public Theology*. New York: Crossroad.

CHAPTER 32
Postmodernism

Catherine Pickstock

The Question of Epochs

Have we entered a "postmodern" phase of history? And if so, is this to be celebrated or regretted? If the modern phase is progressive, then is the postmodern inevitably reactionary at heart, for all its clever disguises? In what follows, I will examine the relation of the postmodern to the modern through a double perspective. In the theoretical sphere, I will focus on the conjoined philosophical legacy of univocity and representation which can be taken as the ultimate presupposition of modern thought. In the practical sphere, I will focus on the category of "civil society" which is normally regarded as the core of a secular public space in modern times.

In his book *We Have Never Been Modern* the French philosopher of science Bruno Latour exposes the falsity of the myth that there are absolutely irreversible breaks in cultures through time (Latour 1993). This observation bears strongly upon the theme of the present essay, for in tracing certain theoretical and practical transformations from the later Middle Ages to the early modern period, one can see that certain aspects of late medieval theological thought in fact underpin later characteristically "modern" ideas, even though much in the Enlightenment may also be seen as a qualified reaction against these changes. It has of course been common to account for the origins of modernity in terms of the vague edifice of "the Enlightenment," and to see modernity as coextensive with the rise of the secular modern state needed to quell the wars of religion, together with the rise of systematic organization of medical, educational, and penal institutions. But given that attempts to improve society in a secular way via the state and market have so visibly failed, perhaps this revised genealogy, which stresses the legacy of a distorted religious theory and practice, could also point us indirectly toward a more serious alternative future polity than the liberal and postmodern critiques.

But one can even go further than this. Against the one-dimensional "modern" vision of progress, postmodern philosophers and cultural theorists have protested in the name of the diverse, the more than human, the incommensurable. In doing so, some of them (in particular Gilles Deleuze, Alain Badiou, and Jacques Derrida) have explicitly appealed back to the thirteenth-century figure of Duns Scotus for their alternative vision. They regard his leveling of the infinite and the finite to a univocal being, his unleashing of the virtual and unmediably discontinuous, as permitting a radical break with a totalizing rationalism. But it has recently been argued that all these Scotist innovations themselves lie at the inception of modernity (Alliez 1996; Cunningham 2002). How can they provide the key to a break with modernity? Surely they betoken a radicalization of, and a return to, the very origins of modernity?

Duns Scotus' flattening out of actual necessity to pure virtuality, and of being to the bare fact of existence, which are modern "rationalist" moves (and which undergird the primacy of epistemology over ontology), do indeed suggest a radicalization of the modern in a more anarchic direction. All possibilities acquire a limitless and equalized range, and all existence is rendered merely phenomenal and ephemeral, lacking altogether in depth or any symbolic pointing beyond itself toward either eternal truth or abiding "human" values.

This suggests that one way to understand the postmodern is as the "late modern," or the intensification of certain trends established within modernity. The invocation of Duns Scotus and the later Middle Ages by Deleuze, Badiou, and Derrida (and many others) is a crucial part of what is best understood as a revised understanding of the nature of modernity itself.

The Grammar of Being

In the philosophical sphere, modernity used to be characterized by the turn to the subject, the dominance of epistemology, and the guaranteeing of secure knowledge by the following of a reliable method. Today, following tendencies beginning early in the twentieth century with the work of Etienne Gilson, and climaxing in the rigorous scholarship of Marion, Courtine, and Boulnois, we have become aware of the way in which both the Cartesian and the Kantian moves depended upon shifts within Latin scholasticism, to such an extent that one can now validly say that both thinkers remained to a degree "scholastics" (Boulnois 1995; Burrell 1986; Courtine 1990; Gilson 1952; Marion 1982).

In particular, it can be seen that Descartes and Kant did not simply transfer allegiance for objectively critical reasons from an unwarranted claim to know being as it really is to an attempt to define true knowledge and even being in terms of the unequivocally graspable and internally consistent. Rather, a prior change in the understanding of being, a prior reorientation of ontology, was necessary in order to make possible the move from ontology to epistemology. As long as the Greco-Arab and then Western Catholic synthesis of Aristotle with neo-Platonism remained in place, a turn toward epistemology could have possessed no critical obviousness. Within this synthesis, every abstraction of properties – such as "being" or "truth" or "good" or "entity" – from the real, was still concerned with their instance *as* universal elements within the real (as opposed to logical abstractions), while even the act of abstraction was regarded as an elevation toward that greater actuality and perfection which characterized a more purely spiritual apprehension. The working assumption was that the finite occurrence of being (as of truth, goodness, substance, etc.) restricts infinite being in which it participates. Hence when knowledge grasps finitude in its relatively universal aspects, it does not simply mirror finitude, but rather fulfills its nature in achieving an elevation of its reality (Boulnois 1990: 308–14).

To conceive, by contrast, of knowledge as a mirroring, or as "representation," requires that one think of the abstraction that is clearly involved in all understanding in an entirely different fashion. To abstract must involve not an elevation, but rather a kind of mimetic doubling. It is now regarded as a demand of rigor that one keep a "transcendental" universality strictly distinct from "transcendent" height and spirituality, and logical abstraction from spiritual ascesis. This is what Duns Scotus achieves by reading Pseudo-Dionysius and Augustine in his own fashion. For Scotus, Being and other transcendental terms now imply no freight of perfective elevation. Instead, finite creatures, like the infinite Creator, scarcely "are," as opposed to "not being" in a punctilear fashion – they are "the same" *in quid* as regards existing which belongs to them as an essential property, just as substance and accident, genus, species, and individuality all exist in the same fashion, *in quid*. Only *in quale*, as regards specific differences of a qualitative kind, including the difference between finite and infinite, and the differences between the transcendentals (*Ordinatio*, I d 8 q 3 nn 112–15), is there no univocity, but rather, it seems, something like pure equivocity. This provides a very complex and notoriously subtle picture, but put briefly: as regards the pure logical essence of *esse*, there is univocity between all its instances; as regards ultimate differentiating qualitative properties there is equivocal diversity; thus although *esse* is univocal *in quid*, in the fully determined quiddative instance there is always something existentially present that is over and above pure univocity, and appears indeed to be entirely "different." Nevertheless, because differences are instantiated only in things that are, Scotus declares that uncreated being and the ten genera of finitude are all included "essentially" within being as univocal and as a quasi-genus. Moreover, even the specific differences of finitude, the property of infinitude, and the *passiones* or transcendentals are "virtually" included within being as univocal.

The Relation of Analogy

When Scotus speaks of analogy, as Boulnois concludes, this seems to reduce either to the equivocal, or to degrees of "intensity" upon a quantitative model

(Boulnois 1999b: 290–1). Though, indeed, Scotus allows that an infinite degree transcends the quantitative, this excess is once again conceived in an equivocal fashion, while the model of intensive ascent itself remains quantitative in its paradigm, as is shown by Scotus' insistence that the idea of "more good" does not – *contra* Augustine – affect our grasp of the meaning of "good" (*Ordinatio* I d 3 358–60).

The position of the analogical, as a third position or medium between identity and difference, whereby something can be like something else in its very unlikeness according to an ineffable co-belonging, is rejected by Scotus because it does not seem to be rationally thinkable (Duns Scotus, *In Elench.* q 15 para [8] (22a–23a); *In Praed.* q 4 para [5] (446b–447a) and para [6]; 447a; Boulnois 1999a, 1999b: 246–7). What remains is a semantic world sundered between the univocal and the equivocal.

Since finite being is now regarded as possessing in essence "being" in its own right (even though it still requires an infinite cause), when the mind abstracts being from finitude, it undergoes no elevation, but only isolates something formally empty, something that is already a transcendentally a priori category and no longer transcendental in the usual medieval sense of a metaphysically universal category which applies to all beings as such, with or without material instantiation. For this reason, it now represents something that is simply "there," without overtones of valuation, although it also represents something that must be invoked in any act of representation, and is in this new sense "transcendental." Scotus here echoes the Avicennian view that the subject of metaphysics is being and not the first principle (as Averroës held), for "Being" can now be regarded as transcendentally prior to and also as "common to" both God and creatures (Boulnois 1999b: 327–405, 457–93). In one sense, this inaugurates onto-theology, and so is "modern" and not "postmodern." But in another sense, Scotus opens up the possibility of considering being without God, and as more fundamental (supposedly) than the alternative of finite versus infinite, or temporal versus eternal. And this space is as much occupied by Heidegger, Derrida, and Deleuze as it was by Hegel. Here, Scotus' proto-modernity involves also the "post-modern."

Something similar applies to the Scotist impact upon theology. As a "proto-modern" thinker, Scotus' contributions had implications for the alliance between theology and the "metaphysical" (in the broad sense, not meaning onto-theology). For within the former discourse of participated-in perfections, there was a ready continuity between reason and revelation: reason itself was drawn upwards by divine light, while, inversely, revelation involved the conjunction of radiant being and further illuminated mind. Here, as we have seen, to rise to the Good, before as well as within faith, was to rise to God. But once the perceived relationship between the transcendentals has undergone the shift described above, to abstract to the Good tells us nothing concerning the divine nature. To know the latter, we wait far more upon a positive revelation of something that has for us the impact of a contingent fact rather than a metaphysical necessity.

One can interpret the latter outcome as modern misfortune: the loss of an integrally conceptual and mystical path. Already before Scotus the business of "naming God" was beginning to change; it was gradually losing the accompanying element of existential transformation of the one naming. With Scotus, the mystical dimension is lost, and it is declared that the way of denial, or *via negativa*, only removes finite imperfections from a positively known quality, and does not introduce us to a mysterious yet palpable darkness (Duns Scotus, *Ordinatio*, I d 8 q 3 n 49, and nn 70–86). This shift in the mystical component then delivers theology over to the ineffable authority of the church hierarchy, and, later, alternatively, to that of scripture (Tavard 1959). Yet one can also read Duns Scotus as offering a theological anticipation of postmodernity: by foreclosing the scope of theological speculation, he demoted intellect in general and opened up theology as the pure discourse of charity. Thus, we receive the loving will of God, and respond to this with our answering will (Duns Scotus, *Ordinatio* I dist 8 pars I Q 4; Boulnois 1999b).

In the end, though, it becomes illogical to uphold the "postmodern" Scotus while denouncing the "modern" Scotus, and this applies both in philosophy and theology. If one cannot countenance Scotist onto-theology, one must also question a "pure" philosophy concerned with a nondivine being, since this is ultimately grounded in univocity and the refusal of analogy in any sense consistent with the Dionysian naming of God. In this way, Heidegger comes into question. Likewise, if one is wary of the Scotist separation of abstraction from elevation, or, rather, his particular refusal of the mystical, one must be wary also of his semivoluntarism. For the very same sundering, applied by Duns Scotus to Augustine's discourse on the Trinity, ensures that one must interpret the divine intellect and divine will as univocally similar in character to the human intellect and will. Will is regarded as a movement of pure spontaneity outside the heteronomy of the laws of motion (a movement is always from another, according to Aristotle) and independent of the recognitions of the intellect (Boulnois 1999b:107–14; Scotus/Wolter 1975: 5 a 3). If the intellect now simply "represents" a neutral being, without evaluation, then, concomitantly, "will" begins its career of the pure positing of values without foundation. This is the co-inauguration of pure piety and pure irresponsibility.

The issue, then, should not be anything to do with a contrast between the modern and the postmodern. It is rather that both represent "a certain Middle Ages" (with roots which reach back before Duns Scotus to his Franciscan forebears and Avicenna) within which our culture still mostly lies, and whose assumptions we might at least wish to re-examine.

Modernity and the "Representation" of Subjects

So, can one sustain any notion that postmodernity is a more fundamental matter than modernity? Is the enthronement of univocity in postmodernity not just a

more advanced stage of "modern" representation? Somewhat parallel considerations apply in the cultural domain. One might focus upon such things as
individual rights, bureaucratic formality, and abstract economic equivalence
as characterizing "the modern." By contrast, one might take an emphasis upon
style and the subtle conformity of fashion as denoting "the postmodern."
However, from the outset modernity concerned the rise of civility as a substitute
for "liturgy." All that is occurring in our own epoch is the increasing slide of fixed
manners into temporarily fashionable idioms of behavior. But in many ways
this augments the formal lack of underlying rationale and shows an equally
increased need for surface reliability, rendering what goes on behind the surface
not so much irrelevant as nonexistent.

From the outset of modernity, moreover, civility undergirded rights etc. just
as univocity undergirded representation. The "representation" of subjects as
formal bearers of equal rights was possible only once their humanity had been
abstracted out from their creaturehood without any concomitant advance
toward deification: a movement strictly in parallel with the Franciscan shift
toward an immanent leveling of perfection terms. Whereas, in the Middle Ages,
deification involved, among other things, a cultivation of the virtue of "cleanness," which for both monks and knights encompassed spiritual purity and
physical integrity with bodily hygiene, from the Renaissance through to the
eighteenth century the "human being" became increasingly a literally dirty
bearer of an abstract, nominal, spiritual essence of detached reason and indeterminate freedom. Included within the continuing medieval "Platonic" practice
of preventive medicine was the continued devotion to the Roman practice of
bathing, sometimes indeed within old Roman baths. In the later Middle Ages and
the Renaissance, by contrast, public bathing started to be viewed as a threat to
morals and water as itself possibly contaminated. For the generalized "baptism"
of lustration was now substituted the frequent change of clothes and resort to
cosmetic concealment: a bodily equivalent of the art of dissembling which the
new civility was specifically recognized as concealing and which is culturally
equivalent to the perspective of ontological anarchy opened up by the formal
distinction.

The medieval "clean," universal humanity, just as it reached down into the
body, also reached up into transcendence. With St. Paul, after Christ, there was
now a universal humanity and no longer just Greek and Jew, male and female,
slave and free, because all human beings were no longer merely human, since
God had entered humanity. Therefore, human beings became human beings
only by elevation beyond humanity, just as to recognize the good (prior to
Bonaventure and Scotus) was to advance toward God in one's substantive being.
But, by contrast, within modernity, human beings could be human beings
without transformation: as simply thinking (representing) or willing (positing
values). This new mode of formal recognition implied a shift in social ontology.
No longer was society seen in terms of the liturgical body of Christ (Lubac
1949). Initially, it had been only by this *mythos* of divine descent ("the glory of
God is humanity fully alive") and theurgic ascent ("the life of a human being is

the vision of God," to complete Irenaeus' couplet) (Williams 2002: 21) that general human interrecognition was first established. But now, with the advent of civility as liturgy, a general humanity was given merely in the uniform practice of empty formal codes. So, to sum up: once upon a time there was only generality beyond locality via universal myth and ritual. Later there was only generality where all styles were measured in conformity and equivalence with one another and in the same ever-dictated and appropriate circumstances. And today? Today there is a general humanity where all wear the same back-to-front unmediable styles in the same spans of time.

Postmodern "Cleanness"

This general legal and "democratic" representation (the abstraction of the general will so that it can constitute supposedly a single mirroring mind of government) presupposes civility, just as cognitive representation presupposes univocity. But here also, there is a reciprocal foundation (Alliez 1996). Civility also presupposes formal representation. For, even if there must be orderly behavior and handshakes between rivals if there is to be an election or a court trial, nevertheless the hidden presupposition of civility is abstract equality and formal negative freedom. All may use forks (a Renaissance innovation) and wear their conforming or alternative styles, or be dirty or externally clean (now without any symbolic resonance) in manifold conventional or subversive fashions (Bossy 1985: 121–2); it denotes nothing and therefore nothing (or everything) is affirmed or subverted in the fullest conformity. If all are to be free and to aim for anything, then, paradoxically, behavior must be made more and more predictable; but, inversely, an essentially contentless behavior always proclaims freedom, and the sublime gesture. "Postmodern" civility and "modern" representation therefore continuously spring up together. And they both conform to "a certain Middle Ages": a Middle Ages tending to privatize devotion and separate clerical from lay power – thereby immanentizing the latter.

Civility and rights coalesce around the idea of a normative formalism. Rights allow an appearance of peace through regularity that disguises the *agon* of the marketplace and competing state bureaucracies. Civility prevails in the space of "civil society" or of free cultural intercourse that is supposedly aside from state mechanisms and not wholly subordinated to the pursuit of abstract wealth. Any radical analysis of contemporary society has to expose these twin formalisms as disguising the operations of concrete if self-deluded interests. Do postmodern discourses attain to such radicalism?

Here it is possible to isolate three tendencies that one can associate with the names of Lévinas (and to a large extent Derrida), Deleuze, and Badiou respectively.

First of all, a Lévinasian perspective tends to merge together the perspective of rights with the perspective of civility. A Kantian formalism regarding the generalized other is supposedly exceeded at the point where a legal acknowledgment of freedom passes over into the nonlegislatable style of regarding the other's specificity. This is a matter of cultivating a manner, rather than simply following a rule. And apparently this is a liturgical idiom, because respect for the other is described by Lévinas in terms of the worshipful acknowledgment of the absolute Other, in his irreducible absence (Lévinas 1969). At this point, Alain Badiou objects to Lévinas that such a religious perspective mystifies and obscures human relationships. If every human being presents to us the absolute distance of God, then we are always asked to respect the ineffable in mortals, and nothing is said regarding how we are to respect the actual appearing attributes of mortals, save vacuously, insofar as they contain a "trace" of the unsoundable (Badiou 2002). Here the merging of rights with the protocols of sublime civility toward others in fact removes one even further from a characterization of those others, whose noumenality now exceeds even the rationality and freedom of the Kantian bearer of rights. It is not clear that this sort of respect for the other rules out any act of violence that one might commit against appearing bodily subjects, since nothing that appears is here regarded as a token of what warrants absolute respect, and furthermore the realm of appearing is for Lévinas always necessarily – beyond the whit of politics – contaminated by totalizing oppression. Because of this latter perspective, Lévinas does not seem to deny that a certain instrumentalization of human life and human bodies is unavoidable in the world of human labor and striving; but he then has no means of teleological discrimination between acceptable and unacceptable instrumentalizations. In consequence, the most diabolical instrumentalization could still present itself as compatible with respect for the nonappearing other. With reason, Badiou avers that this is just what the West tends to do with the discourses of rights and pluralism: when respect for the other harmonizes with the power of a capital-owning minority, liberalism is affirmed; when this particular mode of arbitrary power is threatened by relatively noncapitalist forces, liberalism is suspended and all sorts of terroristic acts and torturings are legitimated (Badiou 2002: 18–40).

Ultimately, the hopeless formalism of Lévinas's ethics is determined by its reactive character. The ethical impulse is for Lévinas born with our "persecution" by the sufferings of others. That is to say, his ethic assumes death and violence as the fundamental facts of ethical relevance; such a perspective is perfectly compatible with nihilism and in some ways Lévinas appears to offer an ethic for nihilists. This negativity means that for Levinas the only shared attribute of human beings beyond ineffability is the fact that we are all going to die. Against this perspective, Badiou suggests, in some ways in keeping with Augustine, that the good has primacy over evil, and that the good for human beings arises in those acts of imagination whereby we conceive of noble projects that transcend our mere animality and mortality. Evil is therefore more or less privative and not the radical positive force which wields the instrument of death in the name of totalization as for so many of the followers of Lévinas, Derrida and even Žižek (Badiou 2002: 40–90).

One might say that for Lévinas the best one can do is to exercise a kind of metaphysical politeness in the face of death. However, Badiou surely oversimplifies the problem in saying that Lévinas illustrates the danger of letting ethics be contaminated by religion. One could argue that Lévinas also commits just the opposite error: transcendence is reduced to the essentially immanent distance of the subjective other, who occupies just the same univocal space as ourselves.

If Lévinas can be construed as *the* contemporary philosopher of rights and civility, this is in no way obviously true of Gilles Deleuze. To the contrary, a Deleuzian perspective would fully recognize that notions of civil society tend to conceal from view the playing out of power disputes. It is not an abstract respect for rights which is promoted by Deleuze, but rather a Spinozistic wider and wider combining of active forces in order to permit mutual flourishing (Deleuze 1968).

For Deleuze, such forces manifest no basic drives or possibilities, but are themselves always the play of surface simulacra which conceal no real original essences. A certain Nietzschean distance from pure Marxist orthodoxy is indicated by what is in effect a refusal to read the late capitalist "society of the spectacle" (Debord 2001) purely in terms of an augmentation of the role of the spell of the fetishized commodity as an element in sustaining conformity. For Deleuze, as for most of the post-1960s generation marked by Nietzsche, there can be in a sense only fetishes, and the specifically capitalist illusion concerns the confinement of the play of substitution and divergence by abstract fundamental norms, rather than the older substantive norms of transcendence. This is the holding back of complete "deterritorialization" (Deleuze and Guattari 1987).

Nevertheless, the modern, capitalist order still represents for Deleuze an important, and even it would seem fated, stage of deterritorialization within the historical process. Where Deleuze's position appears truly incompatible with Marxism is at the point where it would seem that pure deterritorialization can never arrive, any more than Derrida's pure gift, or pure difference and deferral uncontaminated by presence can arrive. For "territory" in Deleuze's philosophy is constituted within the space of epistemological representation. Beyond this space, and always governing it and undoing it, resides the virtual, which does not represent but constitutes new regimes of the event, and is not mere "possibility" because of its anarchic unpredictability. However, just as for Heidegger the history of Being ensures that there must be ontic illusion which is "folded back" into Being, so also for Deleuze, there must be the realm of representation and of temporary territorial illusion which is "folded back" into the virtual (Badiou 2000: 82–91).

It follows that one can say that, whereas Aquinas questions the instance of the Avicennian (and later Scotist) regime of representation, Deleuze affirms its sway within a certain realm of the real. Again, as with Heidegger's Being, this is because for him the virtual has no real ontological content. Just because this absolute is *not* God, it is paradoxically parasitical upon the very set of temporary orders which it institutes and ceaselessly undoes. The absolute speed of positive difference is too fast for being and understanding; their secondary illusion arrives always too late, but just for this reason belatedness is inescapable, and all that remains is the conformity of the vacuum of empty belatedness.

Part of Badiou's quarrel with Deleuze is a political one: Isn't all this Scotist apparatus of univocity, virtuality, and formal distinction (whereby anything can get composed with anything else and anything equally can get unraveled) only likely to issue in a nonrevolutionary politics of relative speeds where the theorist is simply the spectator of fated conflicts between territorial presidents and deter-ritorializing terrorists and mavericks which only obscurely allow some mode of ingress for a vision of justice and freedom? Deleuze's metaphysics does not allow any place for clean breaks – or even for any discontinuous ruptures whatsoever. At best it would seem to allow, after all, only for the development of civil proto-cols of temporary balance between restraint and emergence – while one would always have the suspicion that the real manners pertaining between emperors and nomads occurred according to a predetermined and impersonal code.

So what is Badiou's third alternative to Lévinas and Deleuze? And does this offer a postmodern escape from the coils of civility?

In one sense it does. Badiou's manners are much more those of revolution-ary rupture. He celebrates the pure event or arrival of innovation in the spheres of politics, cosmology, art, and eros (Badiou 1989). Compared with Deleuze, this event of arrival is granted no ontological underpinning – not even the contra-dictory one of emergence from a virtuality which it simultaneously cancels or contradicts. At the same time, however, the event in Badiou's philosophy ceases to have the sense of plural fragment that still clings around Deleuzian and Derridean difference. To the contrary, Badiou insists that the revolutionary event in any sphere is henceforward universally compelling for all humanity, and he combines this with a traditionalist Marxist (or Maoist) impatience at the politics of ethnic, racial, and sexual difference (Badiou 2002: 18–30).

In this fashion, for Badiou, the universal emerges from a singularity, not from a hidden background of neo-Platonic unity. Though he shares Deleuze's affir-mation of univocity, he declares that if he were forced to choose between the univocal and the multiple, he would choose the multiple. And for Badiou events occur not against a background of the henological virtual which generates an agonistic play between movement and stasis, but rather against a background of meaningless multiplicity. Here he develops a fundamental ontology on the basis of the Cantorian theory of infinites (Badiou 1988b).

All that there is is an infinite set of multiples that themselves endlessly break down into infinite sets and subsets. All these monadic universes, one could say, enshrine the mirror-play that allows the illusion of representation; but in con-trast to Deleuze, these universes are originally there, and therefore the possibil-ity of representation is more primary and it lies in a noncontradictory relation to fundamental ontology. What stands in contrast to representation now arises not before but after it, in the field of the pure event, which is a kind of surface counter-current to ontology, governed by the Platonic priority of the Good over Being; but with the Good now defined in terms of the radical imagination of new possibilities.

The pure event is held to break with the static given "situation" that embodies some set or other of the multiple. Here Badiou appears much closer to the situationists and their surrealist legacy than Deleuze, because the break with the spectacular universe of the commodity is seen as absolute, and the pure event performed with integrity as a genuine origination uncontaminated by secondariness or mimesis. There is no longer any need for a civil or well-mannered social governance of an unavoidable ontological *agon*, between what totalizes and what breaches and innovates. Thus politically Badiou advocates militant industrial disturbances plus removal from parliamentary processes, and yet, at the same time, pressure on the state to force it to make destabilizing concessions. He claims, against Deleuze, that nothing in his ontology renders impossible the realization of the socialist hopes which drive such stances (Badiou 2002: 95–145).

This political approach has its parallel in Badiou's deployment of religious analogues. We have already seen that he is critical of Lévinas for his religiosity, and he is a far more militant atheist than Derrida – and perhaps even than Deleuze or Nietzsche, since in place of the Spinozistic substantive void, or the Dionysiac will to power (the "will of a god" perhaps literally for Nietzsche), we have instead the pure Mallarméan random throw of the cosmic dice (Badiou 2000: 74–5).

And yet it is possible to claim that this purer atheism is less obviously nihilism; less obviously the worship of a dark Lord. For in Badiou's philosophy, the random and agonistic are in no way subtly affirmed and fated by a more primary virtuality or Being into which they are "folded back." As with Mallarmé, the hope here persists that a single throw or series of throws of the dice may yet somehow defeat the desert of chance itself (Mallarmé 1999: 122).

On one level this would appear to be a humanist hope; and there is far more residue of Sartrean humanism in Badiou than in other of the *soixante-huitards*, however he might protest this. Yet this is not entirely accurate: Badiou retains the tincture of transcendence in the Mallarméan hope. It would seem indeed that he must do so, if he is to explain how the singular event can have the lure of the universal: how, for example, the French Revolution or Cubist painting or Cantorian mathematics or the cult of romantic love should rightly elicit the admiration of *all* humanity, and yet be entirely self-founded, appealing to no pregiven ontological or epistemological circumstances.

It is here that Badiou proclaims himself still Platonist, offering a "Platonism of the multiple" that expresses the radical thrust of the later Platonic dialogues. And yet Badiou (too hastily perhaps) rejects the continuing role of the Forms in the later Plato, together with his account of *methexis*. He ascribes without warrant to Plato a recognition of the univocity of being. This leaves a flattened-out ontology of the multiple, in myriad combinations. In this cosmos the absoluteness of human practices is not guaranteed by participation in the forms, in Being, in the One, or in God. But how, then, can something with a singular beginning represent more than the arbitrary sway of power? In asking this question, Badiou remains in effect postmodern, yet appears to break with postmodern nihilism and the enthronement of the *agon* of difference.

Events of Grace

The only possible answer is that the event is the event of grace. This is exactly what Badiou declares, and he is forced to see the event of the advent of Christianity as one crucial paradigm of the event as such; this is set out in his book on St. Paul (Badiou 1997).

Yet of course this is grace without God; an event of grace which delivers its own grace and yet only arrives by a grace that seems to exceed its merely empirical or mathematical instance as a member of a pregiven set or situation. One may well find such a conception contradictory, since if an event in order to be a universal event must bear an excess over itself, the notion of an "elsewhere" seems inescapable. In line with such a consideration would be a further question: Does Badiou ignore the fact that the event of the Incarnation was not just a supreme instance of an event, but rather the first event of the arrival of the field of events (singularities that inaugurate a new universal) per se?

If Badiou commendably escapes from the infinite/finite dialectics of "folding," and refreshingly points out that Heidegger's Being/beings and Deleuze's virtuality/representation *schemata* are simply variants of traditional metaphysical dualisms and monisms, and not "post" anything whatsoever, then all the same he seems to offer instead a stark neo-Cartesian and Sartrean dualism without mediation. If we may applaud the refusal of that postmodern despair which sees every rupture as doomed to retotalize, we may nonetheless stand aghast before the adolescence of a perspective which thinks there is a neat distinction to be made between politically repressive "situations," on the one hand, and liberating "events" supposedly without any antecedents, on the other. If, indeed, Badiou genuinely lacks civility, he merely offers us an unredeemed rudeness, which at times aspires to a kind of liturgy but does not fully envisage it. All too readily one surmises that followers of acclaimed "events" would demand absolute universal submission to the implications of those events of which they would regard themselves as the privileged *avant-garde* interpreters.

Indeed, the pluralist criterion to prevent a slippage into evil only opens again the postmodern prospect of potentially unmediable difference, this time between possibly rival universals. While clearly Badiou will view the event of Incarnation as a falsely self-absolutized event, could not this be to fail to ask whether it is just the event which seeks to be open to all events in audaciously offering to them, not the perspective that subsumes them, but rather the impossible idiom of their co-belonging? Without such an event of events, it would seem that Badiou's laudable desire to restore universality in the face of lamentable fixation upon diversity cannot possibly be accomplished.

Badiou's insights into the possibilities of a liberal totalitarianism should therefore not blind us to the stark opening to an old-fashioned illiberal totalitarianism in his own philosophy, whose reverse face is itself a continuing postmodern liberalism.

We have seen that postmodern politics offers variants of modern civility, if sometimes in the negative mode of incivility. Can there be a more substantive mode of civil blending that goes beyond the formal distance of polite respect?

In accepting the postmodern sense that all is simulacrum, we still need to be able to distinguish a fake from a true copy and in this way to locate Badiou's event of universal import. The way to do so is to suppose that there may be non-identical repetition without rupture, and thus at times some instance of a positive relation between the virtual and that which the virtual provides. In this way there would be no folding back of the event into the virtual that would entail its cancellation. But by the same token one would not countenance Badiou's absolute contrast of event and situation: every creative event would rather be seen as developing the hidden and repressed seeds of a largely diabolical past, just as the New Testament is taken by Christianity as fulfilling in an unexpected way the fragments of antiquity.

To say this is not at all to deny that often, or even most of the time, Deleuze's and Badiou's diverse pictures do not correspond to historical reality. For the most part, history, including the history of the church, is indeed the violent interplay between stasis and movement, or the alternation between fixed situations and revolutionary breaks (though Badiou's picture is the less realistic one). The point, rather, is whether this historical reality reflects the ultimate ontological situation, and whether, if it does not, there can at times, if fleetingly and fragmentarily, be historical processes which disclose other, nonagonistic possibilities. It may be that such rare sequences of events are, for all their paucity, more "compelling" than the overwhelming weight of terror, in rather the way that Badiou intimates.

If they are so compelling, and if true events are not in total discontinuity with situations, then this requires an ontological grounding. If general situation and singular event can occur in harmony, it must be the case that there is a higher ground for both these aspects of higher reality. This higher ground cannot be the neo-Platonic One, nor the merely virtual, realized in what it cancels, but rather a plenitudinous, infinitely actual Being that is expressed in a certain measure in the finite being that it provides or lets be.

This notion of participation in the source of all situations and events which is an infinite unified multiple implies that what truly emerges as event is a gift since it is good in its harmony, and as good expresses toward us a good will – since how can we detach the notion of goodness from the notion of an intention of beneficial providing as coming toward us? For this reason, participation requires that the event be the event of grace. At the same time, however, it also requires that the mystery of the source be preserved, since in seeing that the event is a gift from a higher source we recognize that source only in its self-manifestation as inexhaustible by us and infinitely reserved. Participation is always of what cannot be participated in; grace declares to us the unknown god.

By comparison, postmodern thought is unable to hold together grace with the *via negativa*. Characteristically, it seems to search for secular equivalents to theological themes. Thus Lévinas and Derrida present us with a secular negative theology; Badiou with a secular account of grace. Yet, as we have seen, the former delivers a formalism of civility that is more formalistic than the Kantian formalism of rights, and can equally serve as a mask for terror. Inversely, the latter subscribes to a mystique of *avant-garde* self-grounding that renders grace a mask for pure human affirmation without possibility of redress, or analogical mediation or appeal to a higher authority.

Could one not say that one requires both grace and negative theology? Then political ethics could cease to be reactive and we could accord primacy to the projects of the human imagination that combine appearing bodies and do not just futilely acknowledge invisible subjects. But equally we could retain suspicion of these projects as only partially and inadequately displaying what we can never fully command, while also acknowledging that that mystery was somewhat present in human beings never reducible to players in civic processes. The secular equivalent of both grace and the *via negativa* would in this way think beyond either the idolatry of the humanly instituted, or the more subtly idolatrous hypostasization of the unknown "beyond being." It would rather conceive the appearance of the withheld or the withholding within appearance. This thought also requires the liturgical practice of searching to receive as a mystery from an unknown source that grace which binds human beings together in harmony.

But to think such a thing is to think theologically; the "secular equivalent" fades into the thinking of incarnation and deification, and the search for a liturgical practice that would allow for the continuous arrival of the divine glory to humanity. It transpires that the postmodern secular theologies were never anything so grand. They were partial theologies after all.

Acknowledgments

I would like to thank the following for their criticisms and comments on this essay: David Burrell, Hans Ulrich Gumbrecht, Fergus Kerr, John Milbank, Robert Sokolowski, and Thomas Harrison.

References

Alliez, Eric (1996). *Capital Times: Tales from the Conquest of Time*, trans. Georges van den Abbeele. Minneapolis: University of Minnesota Press.
Badiou, Alain (1988a). *L'Etre et L'Evènement*. Paris: Seuil.
——(1988b). *Court Traité d'Ontologie Transitoire*. Paris: Seuil.
——(1989). *Manifesto for Philosophy*, trans. Norman Madarasz. Albany: State University of New York Press.
——(1997). *Saint Paul: La Formation de l'universalisme*. Paris: Presses Universitaires de France.
——(2000). *Deleuze: The Clamor of Being*, trans. Louise Burchill. Minneapolis: University of Minnesota Press.

—— (2002). *Ethics: An Essay on the Understanding of Evil*, trans. Peter Hallward. London and New York: Verso.

Bossy, John (1985). *Christianity in the West: 1400–1700*. Oxford: Oxford University Press.

Boulnois, Olivier (1990). *Duns Scot: sur la connaissance de Dieu et l'univocité de l'etant*. Paris: Presses Universitaires de France.

—— (1995). "Quand commence l'ontothéologie? Aristote, Thomas d'Aquin et Duns Scot." *Revue Thomiste* 1 (Jan.–March), 84–108.

—— (1999a). "Duns Scotus: Jean." In J.-Y. Lacoste (ed.), *Dictionnaire Critique de Theologie*. Paris: Presses Universitaires de France.

—— (1999b). *Etre et représentation: Une généalogie de la métaphysique moderne à l'époque de Duns Scot*. Paris: Presses Universitaires de France.

Burrell, David B. (1986). *Knowing the Unknowable God: Ibn-Sina, Maimonides, Aquinas*. Notre Dame, Ind.: University of Notre Dame Press.

Courtine, J.-F. (1990). *Suarez et le système de la metaphysique*. Paris: Presses Universitaires de France.

Cunningham, Conor (2002). *A Genealogy of Nihilism*. London: Routledge.

Debord, Guy (2001). *The Society of the Spectacle*, trans. Donald Nicholson-Smith. London: Verso.

Deleuze, Gilles (1968). *Différence et répetition*. Paris: Presses Universitaires de France.

Deleuze, Gilles, with Guattari, Felix (1987). *A Thousand Plateaus*, trans. Brian Massumi. London: Athlone.

Duns Scotus (1969). *Opera Omnia*. Hildesheim: G. Olms.

—— (1975). *God and Creatures: The Quodlibetal Questions*, trans. Felix Alluntis OFM and Allan B. Wolter OFM. Washington DC: Catholic University of America Press.

Gilson, Étienne (1952). *Jean Duns Scot: introduction à ses positions fondamentales*. Paris: Vrin.

Latour, Bruno (1993). *We Have Never Been Modern*, trans. Catherine Porter. New York and London: Harvester Wheatsheaf.

Lévinas, Emmanuel (1969). *Totality and Infinity; An Essay on Exteriority*, trans. Alphonso Lingis. Pittsburgh: Duquesne University Press.

Lubac, Henri de (1949). *Corpus Mysticum: l'eucharistie et l'eglise au moyen-age*. Paris: Aubier-Montaigne.

Mallarmé, Stephan (1999). *To Purify the Words of the Tribe*, trans. Daisy Alden. Huntington Woods, Mich.: Sky Blue Press.

Marion, Jean-Luc (1982). "Une époque de métaphysique." In *Jean Duns Scot ou la révolution subtile*, pp. 62–72. Paris: Editions Radio-France.

Tavard, George (1959). *Holy Writ and Holy Church*. New York: Harper & Row.

Williams, Rowan (2002). "The Converging Worlds of Rowan Williams: Living the Questions." *Christian Century*, April–May, 21.

CHAPTER 33
Globalization

Peter Sedgwick

I shall argue that there are two challenges for Christianity from globalization. First, theology has long engaged with political thought in the West, especially in terms of Luther's "two kingdoms" theory. There is also the relationship of Christianity to the great nineteenth-century ideologies of socialism and neo-liberalism. However, the impact of globalization is such that there is little certainty any more about the future of politics (Lloyd 2001a). Once there were political theories of justice, which were rationalist, utilitarian, and dependent on classical theories of the citizen in the nation-state. In their place today comes a much greater reliance on ad hoc theories, which are pragmatic in a fast-changing world. For example, Martha Nussbaum and Amartya Sen speak of "multiple identities" as a basis for a theory of justice which can enable a response to poverty. Even if globalization as a phenomenon has been overinterpreted (Hay and Marsh 2000), such a philosophical shift is of great significance, and has led many political scientists to rethink much of their analysis of political life.

The second challenge is the practice of mission. Local churches in large cities are the future for much of Christianity across the world. As these become less and less Western in their understanding of authority, tradition, and beliefs, the practice of Christianity will become more diffuse and harder to fit within a conventional doctrinal framework. The issue of mission is central to the global future of Christianity. There has been a great deal of writing in contemporary theology on the future of mission, arising from the idea of "the church as counterculture" (Budde and Brimlow 2000). David Bosch, Murray Demster, and others have all highlighted the importance of urban mission, as have Laurie Green and Andrew Davey. Their writing is important because it mediates the praxis of non-Western, yet urban, Christianity into England. The challenge is to contextualize the practice of mission in a way that is sensitive to the local culture.

What is interesting is how the discussion of justice and multiple identities combines with reflection on mission. The theories of justice found in Nussbaum and Sen are important because they generate in communities a vision of what is possible. Such a vision in turn has the power to create social change, and to prevent catastrophic poverty and famine. The agents in developing countries are local – often faith – communities. In the case of the churches, it is clear that the local Christian communities which Sen and Nussbaum see as fundamental are both engaging with theories of justice in a way very different from traditional political theories, and also seeking to practice new forms of mission. The tension is very creative: in the expanding global cities the crucial factor is to hold together both a mission strategy and a justice strategy. The fascinating question is whether the alliance of Christians with secular bodies against poverty is affected by the growth of local forms of Christianity: whether, in fact, the question of justice and identity is related to the issue of mission. In my view, the question of the understanding of mission and justice by local churches across the globe will introduce a new factor into the debate about the future of Christianity.

In other words, I think that the future of non-Western Christianity will be on the one hand a struggle, in alliance with secular bodies and environmental and feminist movements, against poverty and violence. On the other, it will be about the mission of local Christian groups ("churches") in predominantly urban areas. The alliance with secular bodies raises the complex philosophical issue of which theory of justice unites Christian groups with these bodies. The issue of mission and inculturation raises a different question: that of the identity of Christianity in the movement of the Spirit.

What is Meant by Speaking of Globalization?

It is no longer the view of international theorists that globalization is a single process. Rather, several changes have taken place. First, there is a return to the pre-1914 situation of global trade, capital mobility, and immigration. It is not exactly the same, but the trends point to a rough similarity. In particular the mobility of capital is now very great, as it was before 1914, but on a much vaster scale. Second, there is a series of processes, including flows of information, capital, etc., which exacerbate many local political, social, cultural, and economic tendencies to breaking point. These flows do not amount to a "global process" – globalization is not a demonic external force – but they do produce a crisis for political life in many regions of the world. Putting it another way, what has happened is that political forces in many societies have devalued the legitimacy of the modern state. Globalization has helped that, but the process was underway in any case. Much of the political legitimacy built up between 1945 and 1980 in non-Western nations that had gained political independence during these years was very fragile at best, and in Western democracies in this period the power of the state overreached itself. The secular ideologies of socialism were very strong in the period 1945–60: Ben Gurion in Israel built a secular,

Israeli state, with kibbutzim as the great vision of the future; there were similar commitments in India with Nehru, Nasser in Egypt, and Nyerere in Tanzania. Most of these saw little relevance in religion except as a private matter (Nyerere was an exception here). These political movements were overambitious and by 1990 were shattered, both economically and in terms of ideology. Third, there is an awareness that cultural patterns and flows now reach across the globe, even if again it is a mistake to speak of global culture. This spread is combined with enormous and desperate poverty for some people who live in the growing sprawl of cities across the developing world. However, here again there has been to my mind persuasive criticism by Hay and Marsh (2000) of the unwarranted determinism of a neo-Marxist reading of what is in fact contingent, local culture, even if it is affected by patterns which are replicated across the globe. There is no determinism in the development of nations, nor of their citizens.

Forms of Discourse about Globalization

Globalization has been discussed at length in the last decade, within academic, political, and business circles. It is hardly surprising that theologians, church members, and church leaders have also commented on it (Stackhouse and Paris 2000; Selby 1997). The churches are seen as the defenders of local culture, welfare states, and sustainable economics against the imperialism of global forces, harsh multinationals, and the trivializing of culture. However, within the secular debate there are distinct discourses, which have particular forms of dialogue.

Economists discuss the extent to which the market approximates to perfect competition, as in neoclassical theory, by the perfect, global mobility of goods, labor, and capital. Capital in turn can be created by both financial and social, or institutional, investment. A global market has been created by deregulation, financial liberalization, and the changes created by information and telecommunications technology. It is sometimes called a "technological revolution," although it should be noted that the time between a technological advance and its full implementation in business and society may be considerable.

In a similar, related, but nevertheless distinct area, political economists debate whether these economic processes contribute to the diminution of the power of the state. In one way it is clearly true. In my own quite short lifetime, the British government has ceased to ration mortgages through indirect controls on lending by financial companies, withdrawn to a large extent from its management of the export of capital, and ceded the setting of interest rates to the national Bank of England. Capital mobility and the power of the markets may weaken the authority of national governments in fiscal and monetary policy.

Sociologists have also argued about whether there is a global civil society, especially in the growing number of nongovernmental organizations (NGOs). A similar debate occurs about the increased urbanization of our world, and how

far such cities share common features. Finally, cultural theorists, and urban theorists, seek to explain how vast (essentially trivializing) cultural forces may overwhelm tradition and local communities. Even before any theological reflection
on these realities begins, it is worth noticing that this literature analyses flows
of people and information. These flows might be of capital, people, culture, technology, or images. Such dynamic realities have different textures and shapes, and
changing identities. Any response, including that of theology, must be complex
and multidisciplinary. However, even this caution is not enough. An interdisci-
plinary approach might suggest either that there is one process of globalization,
or that globalization is itself a discrete, identifiable process. Political scientists
since the late 1990s have come to be critical of this way of describing globalization, as though it were a thing, or an irresistible force. Instead, it is better to
envisage multiple global processes, interacting in contingent ways, which are
unevenly developed in different places and times.

The reason for caution lies in the way in which, again and again, history gives
examples of economic transformation coming to a stop and instead turning into
a slow, inexorable process of decline, for a variety of cultural and political
reasons (Landes 1998). The first example comes from the fact that the European
economy, and especially that of Russia, went into reverse after 1914, initiating
a series of protectionist economic policies, civil wars, and ultimately a total
breakdown of economic relations, which finally created the global catastrophe
of World War II. It took many years to recover from the catastrophe, so that only
since the 1990s have politicians and academics begun to use the language of
world trade and international relations common before 1914. A second example
is that of fifteenth-century China, where the state controlled technical progress.
The Ming dynasty (1368–1644) prohibited overseas trade for over a century.
The country's lead, built up over several centuries, in the skills of ironmaking,
printing, and other industries declined. Existing knowledge fell into disuse. Since
there was no private enterprise to challenge the state, as happened in medieval
Europe where the guilds supplanted the power of the monarchy and feudal aristocracy by means of civic political representation, China regressed for centuries
in technology, economics, and eventually national and international political
power (Coyle 2000). These examples show cogently, if proof were needed, that
there is nothing inevitable about economic progress or cultural change.

The Myth of Economic Globalization

There has been a powerful academic debate about how to describe globalization.
The debate began in the late 1980s, and has moved through two stages in a short
time. The first began when politicians, and the media, discovered the reality of
globalization. It was seen as a vast all-conquering monster, which would swallow
up civil society, the welfare state, and the nation-state. Capital, culture, and communications would erase what had been accepted for decades, if not centuries,

and the "false dawn" (Gray 1998) of globalization would herald the destruction of much of our civilization. The response by many academics has been that this literature is crude and uncritical and generates a powerful mythology. They argue that the mythology of business globalization is not to be accepted at face value. From 1995 to 2000, a second wave of academic debate debunking globalization developed, which spelled out these reservations about the use of the term as a world-conquering fact of our times.

The economic arguments are complex, but can be summarized. First, it has been argued that high levels of social expenditure on the welfare state correlate positively (in regions such as Scandinavia) with competitive advantage in the world economy, so it is not true that globalization means the end of the welfare state. There is no reason to expect deeply rooted domestic institutions to be radically altered because they adversely affect the profitability of firms. This is particularly true of the welfare state, which remains extremely popular among most citizens of the OECD. Second, productive capital and foreign direct investment (FDI) are not as mobile as had been thought. Such movement occurs in certain cities and industries, primarily in the great trading blocs, although here too national boundaries remain important. Domestic producers, especially in the United States and Asia, still largely satisfy domestic demand. Indeed, FDI flows as a percentage of gross domestic product in many advanced industrial countries are no greater now than they were during the period 1900–14. Thus European financiers and industrialists, or their American and Asian counterparts, have done no more than return to the sort of economy common before World War I, with foreign imports, exports, and capital investments again becoming a central part of the economy. The two differences are the much smaller role that migration plays now, compared with the beginning of the twentieth century, and the far greater role of international financial speculation today. The final factor is that productive capital continues to be highly aware of national economic regulation, as it always has been, even given the withdrawal of the state from many areas of economic life.

The counter-argument spells out the falsity of the first-wave argument in the economic debate about globalization. Indeed, many commentators point to the patterns of trade before 1914 as a much more integrated global system, where labor was free to move around the globe, bringing millions through Ellis Island off New York as immigrants to the New World. Keynes, in a well-known passage, reflects on the ease of travel and investment of capital, and the speed of communications, in the period 1900–14. While globalization is a reality, it is also far less of a new phenomenon than we might think.

The Fallacy of Urban Globalization

Similar cautions exist in the field of urban theory. For example, Smith (2001) claims that neo-Marxism always reduces culture to "deeper political-economic determinism." Martha Nussbaum and Amartya Sen make the same criticism. Universalism is conflated with progressive rationality. The general public is assumed to be passive in the face of "the sea change in cultural production ushered in by aesthetic and cultural elites" (Smith 2001: 46). The vibrancy of migrant social networks is not recognized by Marxism, since it argues that capital has commodified culture. Cultural and religious movements, not based on class, are dismissed as local, partial, and ineffective. Smith lays emphasis rather on local, social movements, which hold to a politics based on ethnicity, religion, sexuality, environmental issues, and gender. These are "the myriad transnational practices of politics and culture that now criss-cross the landscape of transnational cities throughout the world, inexorably irrigating their politics and social life" (p. 188). Such cultural forces have been well charted by Castells (1997), Bauman (1998), and Sassen (2000). They are also the context for urban mission. We shall return to this point in the next section.

Mission as the Dialogue of Theology and Globalization

The relevance of such a theoretical discussion of globalization to theology is that there are new, and increasing, challenges to the accepted place of the existing churches and faith communities within society and to existing cultures, social traditions, and values. Theology's task is to discern what the implications of these changes are for the identity of the Gospel wherever these challenges arise, and what it means to be the church.

Pentecostalism makes an interesting case-study. The response of pentecostalism to the changes brought about by the experience of globalization in East Asia and Latin America illustrates how much it has been forced into a re-examination of its beliefs by the economic and social changes occurring in these continents. Much pentecostalism has emerged from contexts of economic poverty and social marginalization

> The pentecostal churches' experience of the Gospel in the midst of economic poverty is a key gift to the global church. It has empowered individuals and families who address their economic poverty through the transformation of their personal and family life. It needs to develop a spirituality that is capable of equipping people to address larger cultural and socio-political issues. (Samuel 1999)

There are signs that this is beginning to happen. Ronald Bueno (1999) says that the shifting landscape of persons which he studies as an anthropologist and as a pentecostalist is made up of "immigrants, refugees, exiles, guest-workers and other moving groups and persons." He suggests that the experience of unequal power shapes pentecostalism deeply. Pentecostalism illustrates one Christian response to the challenge posed by globalization to existing societies and their values.

Others are very critical of the silence of pentecostalism in East Asia in the face of huge economic problems. The explosive growth of pentecostalist churches has been achieved at the expense of tackling social and economic oppression. Yet even here there are now programs for drug addicts and alienated urban youth in pentecostalist Korean and Philippine churches (Jungja Ma 1999). Whichever view is correct, it is evident that mission and ecclesial identity are deeply affected by the rapidity of social and cultural change.

One of the critical issues is the ecclesial identity of mission-oriented churches, whether pentecostalist or not. The new ecclesiology of the poor in Latin America "reflects the culture, daily life and deep-seated longing for justice" (Cadorette 2000). Cadorette argues that justice is not a vision which the institutional church has often pursued. He claims that the institutional nature of Roman Catholicism is in sharp contrast to the nature of popular Christianity in Latin America. There is above all the issue of leadership and authority. The community, not the clergy, is the primary bearer of mission. The old distinction between the teaching and the learning church will take a long time to be expunged, but nevertheless the clergy are only one part of the life of the community. What is needed is a theology of the laity, who are active in the local community (Bosch 1996).

The previous paragraphs have described the engagement of pentecostalism with mission. Another response to globalization has been the commitment of the churches in the affluent West to reform the international economy. To this response I now turn.

The Struggle for Justice

There is a close link between violence and poverty. It is striking that in a survey of armed conflicts across the globe in 2001, the (London) *Financial Times* argued that 25 of the 27 wars currently taking place were civil wars. Civil war does not automatically correlate with religious or ethnic division, or with economic inequality within a country, but with severe deprivation. Warlords in intensely poor African countries are able to finance their civil wars by the export of, for instance, diamonds or oil. Asian and South American insurgents export the raw materials for drugs and finance insurrections with the wealth from these exports. Western churches have begun to initiate a dialogue with their own governments on this issue, at the same time as churches, and other faith communities, have fought to end the burden of debt repayment, especially through the Jubilee 2000 campaign. Rightly, churches have seen the burden of debt as a great moral evil which stunts human life, and which must be removed as soon as possible. There has been a greater reluctance for some local churches to address the problem of civil wars, and corrupt governments or warlords (for a positive view see Shriver 2000).

Churches played a major role in the struggle against apartheid in South Africa, and in Central America against right-wing dictatorships in the 1970s and 1980s. However, the local church has not found it easy to take a stand in the present violence in Zimbabwe and Zaire. The fact that some Anglican bishops in Zimbabwe support President Mugabe illustrates the problem. Much of the violence centers on poverty (e.g. the control of minerals in Zaire) and the abuse of power. The control of raw materials confers power, and access to wealth, in a situation of deprivation and poverty, and enables exploitation and violence to take place.

Churches have increasingly wrestled with the issues of fair trade and global debt. Governing the world economy has become one of the central issues for both campaigners and policy-makers. "The world economy cannot be milked for the benefit of a tiny minority for long without generating unsustainable crisis and conflict" (Coyle 2000). Markets require strong regulation within an institutional and legal framework. Financial instability can overwhelm small, open economies, such as are often found in Asia or South America. There is an incompatibility, perhaps even an "unholy trinity" in developing nations of currency stability, capital mobility, and national monetary autonomy. However, it is not simply market instability that is the problem. There is also the issue of the monopoly power of large corporations, which can control access to new technology by governments of poor nations, and apply lower standards of corporate responsibility in poorer countries.

Free markets can be defended as a way of opening up the interests of the majority of the population against elites wishing to protect their inherited values and interests. The example of the Ming dynasty is a powerful one at this point (Sen 1999b). It is also the case that free markets diffuse their benefits widely, whereas the benefits of restrictions are often concentrated in vested interests. What free markets create is not disorder, but a new form of social order. Jubilee 2000 shows that long-term changes can be won by an effective coalition, however hard the campaign may be. There is a great need to allow the balance of trade to shift to the advantage of the developing countries. Equally important is the need to continue to expose exploitative practices in the third world by means of the world media, consumer campaigns, and eventual international cooperation to raise the incomes of those who work in the industries of developing nations. There are certainly encouraging signs of progress, which is not always the picture that is presented. For example, "the adult literacy rate for the developing countries rose from 43% in 1970 to 64% in 1994" (Hicks 2000). Life expectancy has also risen over the last few decades. If economic change could be achieved by the reduction of the debt owed by many nations, much energy might be released. Poverty and debt act as severe constraints on the ability to bring about the slow transformation of a society to fulfill all the capabilities of its citizens.

Philosophical Considerations

So far we have examined mission and the struggle for justice. It is time to relate these concerns to philosophical considerations about justice. The American philosopher Martha Nussbaum asks how religion relates to justice. What happens when there is a conflict between religion and liberty, as has happened in India and other non-Western nations? There arises a dilemma for the liberal state. Interfering with the freedom of religious expression is a damaging attack on one of the basic capabilities of humanity. Yet such religious practice may coerce some people, especially women. Child marriage, harsh divorce settlements, and other practices may infringe human capabilities. Secular feminists do not see the problem, since for them the values of women's equality and dignity outweigh all religious claims. Religion may be seen in Marxist terms, and therefore as patriarchal. Others portray it in liberal terms, and therefore believe that its content can be translated into moral values. A third, feminist, position reverses the valuation: core, traditional values of a community oppose the acids of modernity; being a traditional Muslim, Christian, or Hindu is on this view an affirmation of human dignity. Some such arguments stem from cultural relativism, where it is held that crosscultural moral norms are by definition impossible of justification. Others, especially in the Christian evangelical movement, think local values and tradition are a better way to lead one's life, since they spring from an organic understanding of what it means to be a person in that place and time. The conflict between religion and liberalism arises from a lack of agreement as to how the changes brought by globalization are to be met.

One way of resolving the argument between religion and liberalism is from the notion of capabilities. In *Women and Human Development* (2000), Nussbaum argues on the basis of a concept of the capabilities of human beings, which can command a broad cultural consensus. Consequently, this is a notion which can be endorsed for political purposes. It serves as the moral basis for constitutional guarantees endorsed by people who do not agree on what a complete good life for a human being would be. These central capabilities have value in themselves, and are not just instrumental in making possible further actions. Nussbaum argues for ten such "central human functional capabilities": life; bodily health; bodily integrity, including absence of domestic violence, absence of sexual abuse, and choice in reproduction; sense, imagination, and thought, which covers religious practice, freedom of expression, and the use of literacy and numeracy; emotions, which refers to not having one's emotions blunted by trauma, fear, or anxiety; liberty of conscience and the ability to form a conception of the good life by practical reason; affiliation, social interaction, and having the social basis of self-respect and nonhumiliation, which entails the absence of discrimination on the basis of race, religion, sexual orientation, caste, or place of origin; expressing concern for other species, and the world of nature; play and laughter; and control over one's environment, both political and material.

Such a list, argues Nussbaum, is how we come to conceive of what justice might be. Some of her list is made up of "natural goods," where the vagaries of life and the sheer presence of luck play a part. Health and emotional balance are at least in part based on natural attributes, but governments can aim to deliver the social basis of these capabilities. Nussbaum argues, for instance, that a government cannot determine the emotional health of a woman, but governments can implement laws on violence, rape, and family relationships. They can also determine whether a nation is at peace internally, by preventing civil wars.

Why should one opt for capabilities and not functioning? Capabilities allow for human choice, so a person who chooses to fast may do so, and a person who wishes to be celibate may be so. There is no one global world, or global process, but a myriad of local cultures, traditions, and values. It is important that choices are respected. Such a view means that human rights become "capability rights." If a person in theory has freedom of political participation, but in practice has none, then there must be doubts about its meaningfulness. "Women in many nations have a nominal right of political participation without having this right in the sense of capability; for example, they may be threatened with violence should they leave the home. In short, thinking in terms of capability gives us a benchmark as we think about what it is to secure a right to someone" (Nussbaum 2000: 98).

The dilemma between religion and human rights is made sharper because of a decline in political power, one of the ways in which in many countries global-ization has impinged on the nation-state. This is a difficult problem, since reli-gion can play a role in promoting moral conduct, though Nussbaum repeats that she is not adopting a liberal understanding of religion, which reduces religion to rational accounts of moral choice. The resolution of the issue by Nussbaum is not my concern here. What matters is that she recognizes that it is a dilemma, in which religion can have a central role to play.

Amartya Sen puts the issue in a different way. He is concerned with the rela-tionship of justice and political institutions. He argues that when Rawls's *A Theory of Justice* postulates an account of justice as fairness this leads him to a difficulty. If universal justice, drawing on classical utilitarianism and Kantian rationality, is to be related to political institutions, where are such universal insti-tutions, capable of implementing these rules of justice? They manifestly do not exist. Rawls therefore opts to set his theory within individual political societies, in which institutions can develop and so bear the weight of implementing his theory. However, he cannot let go of a universal vision and in the 1996 revision of *A Theory of Justice* he speaks of nation-states and other collectivities having relations based on justice. Is not Rawls restricting his theory of justice too much? Rawls postulates two places where justice can be found: within the nation-state, and between states and societies. This move brings him into potential conflict with an alternative view of solidarities based on transnational collectivities. Sen's essay was written before the publication of Nussbaum's appeal to feminist solidarity across the world, but it is clear that Sen has this option in mind, along with professional obligations arising from membership of a profession, or worker's solidarity. Sen argues, in a way similar to Nussbaum, that the future of justice in a global world demands the consideration of "multiple identities." Indi-viduals may have different identities (female, Christian, citizen, member of an NGO, etc.).

He sums up his argument as follows: "The exercise of assessing the relative strength of divergent demands arising from competing affiliations is not trivial, but to deny our multiple identities and affiliations just to avoid having to face this problem is neither intellectually satisfactory nor adequate for practical policy (Sen 1999b)." Sen refuses to let the concept of person as citizen be the trump card in much the same way as Nussbaum rejects the subordination of religion to secular values. Global public goods include codes of business ethics which keep corruption in check, generate rules of conduct, and foster healthy relationships with customers and other businesses. The implication for churches is that they need to be aware of the power of multiple identities.

Multiple identities raise the question of ecclesial identity, and so we are once again faced with the issue of mission. A local church will see its identity as to do with faithfulness to the Gospel, holding on to its apostolicity. "When the Church seeks to be truly apostolic it must drive forward . . . we are moulded by and carry the story which we seek to make fresh in every generation" (Green 2001). Urban mission means simultaneously acknowledging the identities of individuals as immigrants, only a few years in their new country, and yet also enabling them to feel empowered by the presence of the Spirit. How mission is contextualized becomes important.

Theological Conclusion

In the global reality of social and political change the secular, left-wing ideologies of the post-1945 era have withered and died in virtually every nation that received its independence from European empires in those years. In their place have come a series of cultural and social changes, sometimes described as flows. The modern city is not a secular, planned, and socialist settlement but a chaotic growth of ethnic, religious, and cultural migrants. Davey is critical of Castells for failing to give due weight to the vibrancy of religion in the modern city (Davey 2001). Many migrants in pentecostal and other churches have a deep commitment to mission. At the same time there is an exploration of new patterns of worship, authority, and dialogue with other faiths. It is not always a comfortable agenda for Western Christians, and the emphasis on the supernatural can be disturbing. However, there is also a constant struggle for economic and social justice, with the need to build alliances between churches and secular bodies.

At the same time the reformulation of political theory into a more pragmatic approach requires an account which can justify alliances between churches and governments. The key issue here is how NGOs and faith communities can listen to one another without each losing its integrity. Liberation theology in Latin America can be reformulated into a capability approach, deeply indebted to Sen. Such socioeconomic factors provide minimum requirements for personhood. Thus, while one should not overlook other spheres of life, there is justification for particular attention to socioeconomic goods in discussion of an equality of basic capability (Hicks 2000). If one moves back to England, then it is clear that churches will survive in urban areas only if they create partnerships with secular agencies, thus raising again Sen's account of multiple identities and persons belonging to different agencies, all concerned with justice (Atherton 2000). How Christian communities can contribute to the formulation and enforcement of democratic contracts by alliance with secular bodies and NGOs is a constant refrain in this argument. Nussbaum shows, as does South African Joyce Seroke (2000), that religion cannot be regarded simply as a hindrance in achieving a secular, democratic society. What is needed is an alliance between religious bodies, political groups, and NGOs to develop human capabilities in a way that removes obstacles to their expression. In particular, Nussbaum's combination of classical philosophy and an attention to the needs of women is an innovating approach that allows local religious traditions to contribute to the enhancement of human capabilities. Sen equally argues that a theory of justice, which responds to poverty, cannot simply be universalist in the utilitarian or Kantian traditions, but must be fashioned out of local identities.

The global world of the twenty-first century is beginning to take shape. The most appropriate political theology is local, contextual, and found in the cities of the developing world. It will be made up of the interaction of theological and philosophical discourses. Christian communities are caught up in the massive changes created by technology and capitalism. They need to link their commitment to mission to awareness that oppression can be challenged. There are signs that this is beginning to happen. At the same time the philosophical approach pioneered by Sen and Nussbaum needs to be taken further. Churches are as much involved with the nurturing of human capabilities as any other agency.

The solidarities which support justice-making in the global cities of the future draw on ecclesiologies of complex, multiple identities. That is the most important point to make at the end of this essay. Many writers have overemphasized globalization as a force, and the reality is far more subtle and complex than is often allowed for. Nevertheless, the search for such identities will be the crucial task of this century. Churches can often be too accepting of the cultural and national relations in which they are set. They become too easily prisoners of their own culture (Williams 2000). The task which faces churches in many of the new, dynamic cities of the globe allows no such easy resolution of the issue.

There are two challenges for Christianity. One is the change in political thought, which is a shift to pragmatic, ad hoc theories of "what works," allowing no room for theories of human nature, but only appeals to the skills of technical experts in a particular area. This can isolate Christianity as, in the view of its critics, a religion which is insufficiently pragmatic, and too bound up with theories of justice which are dependent on past understandings of the relationship of citizen and nation-state. The second challenge is about the redefinition of mission, in terms of its contextualization. This article has resisted strongly the idea that globalization is a single, unitary process. Instead, there are a series of changes interacting with these challenges to Christianity. There is rapid urbanization across the globe alongside a decline in the power of nation-states to plan in the manner espoused by Western socialists after 1945. In these chaotic, fast-growing cities churches and other faith groups seek to evangelize, but they are repeatedly challenged as to their identity as the cultural identity of their city itself changes. They are also caught up in the struggle for justice. I have suggested that Nussbaum and Sen offer a way through this confused situation with their two key ideas. One is that of capabilities, whereby the struggle for justice allows for capabilities to be developed, without prescribing how these capabilities will be used. This means that there does not have to be a tight definition of what it means to be a person, but rather only an agreement as to what is necessary if one is to achieve one's personal identity, whatever that might be. In this way pluralism is built into the debate. The second idea is that of multiple identities, which again means that a theory of justice can be many sided. Both these ideas relate to the complex reality of the struggle to survive, and be a person, in the modern city.

Finally, global capitalism needs to be reformed. Hicks (2000) puts the point well: If the debt of many nations could be written off, much good would be achieved. The complexity of globalization stems from its reality as a series of local flows of information, capital, and human beings, which place many local cultures under a pressure to change that leads to breaking point. Only 50 years ago political theorists thought of the power of the state as being harnessed to produce a new society: planned economies interconnecting with social development. This was a worthy vision, but it is now dead. In its place is the energy of the global market, which churches struggle to contain so that it does not create yet more victims in its path. At the same time this energy is a challenge to the churches to find again the dynamic of the Gospel, which can speak through the challenges of globalization.

References

Atherton, J. (2000). *Public Theology in Changing Times*. London: SPCK.

Ballard, P., and Couture, P. (1999). *Globalization and Difference: Practical Theology in a Global Context*. Cardiff: Cardiff Academic Press.

Barnet, R. J., and Cavanagh, J. (1994). *Global Dreams: Imperial Corporations and the New World Order*. New York: Simon & Schuster.

Bauman, Z. (1998). *Globalization*. Cambridge: Polity.

Bosch, D. J. (1996). *Transforming Mission*. Maryknoll, NY: Orbis.

Budde, M. and Brimlow, M., eds. (2000), *The Church as Counterculture*. Albany: State University of New York Press.

Bueno, R. N. (1999). "Listening to the Margins". In M. W. Demster, B. D. Klaus, and D. Petersen (eds.), *The Globalization of Pentecostalism*. Oxford: Regnum.

Cadorette, C. (2000). "Legion and the Believing Community". In M. Budde and M. Brimlow (eds.), *The Church as Counterculture*. Albany: State University of New York Press.

Castells M. (1997). *The Information Age*, 3 vols. Oxford: Blackwell.

Cohen, B. (2000). "Money in a Globalized World". In N. Woods (ed.), *The Political Economy of Globalization*. London: Macmillan.

Coyle, D. (2000). *Governing the World Economy*. Cambridge: Polity.

Davey, A. (2001). *Urban Christianity and Global Order*. London: SPCK.

Garrett, G. (2000). "Globalization and National Autonomy". In N. Woods (ed.), *The Political Economy of Globalization*. London: Macmillan.

Gascoigne R. (2001). *The Public Forum and Christian Ethics*. Cambridge: Cambridge University Press.

Gorringe, T. (1999). *Fair Shares: Ethics and the Global Economy*. London: Thames & Hudson.

Goverde, H. (2000). *Global and European Polity?* Aldershot: Ashgate.

Gray, J. (1998). *False Dawn*. London: Granta.

Green, L. (2001). *The Impact of the Global: An Urban Theology*. Sheffield: New City.

Gunnell, B., and Timms, D. (2000). *After Seattle: Globalization and its Discontents*. London: Catalyst.

Hay, C., and Marsh, D. (2000). *Demystifying Globalization*. London: Macmillan.

Hicks, D. (2000). *Inequality and Christian Ethics*. Cambridge: Cambridge University Press.

Jungja Ma (1999). "Pentecostal Challenges in East and Southeast Asia". In M. W. Demster, B. D. Klaus, and D. Petersen (eds.), *The Globalization of Pentecostalism*. Oxford: Regnum.

Kaul, I., Grunberg, I., and Stern, M. (1999). *Global Public Goods: International Co-operation in the Twenty-First Century*. Oxford: Oxford University Press/United Nations Development Programme.

Landes, D. (1998). *The Wealth and Poverty of Nations*. New York: Little Brown.

Lloyd, J. (2001a). "Blessed Are the Pure in Heart". *New Statesman*, 23 April, 8–10.

Lloyd, J. (2001b). "How New Labour Wrestled with a World it Never Made". *New Statesman*, 30 April, 9–11.

Madeley, J. (2000). *Hungry for Trade*. London: Zed.

Micklethwaite, J., and Wooldridge, A. (2000). *Future Perfect: The Challenge and Hidden Promise of Globalization*. London: Heinemann.

Nussbaum, M. C. (2000). *Women and Human Development*. Cambridge: Cambridge University Press.

Ohmae, K. (1990). *The Borderless World: Power and Strategy in the Interlinked Economy*. London: Collins.

Reich, R. (1992). *The Work of Nations*. New York: Vintage.

Rugman, A. (2000). *The End of Globalization*. London: Random House.

Samuel, V. (1999). "Pentecostalism as a Global Culture". In M. W. Demster, B. D. Klaus, and D. Petersen (eds.), *The Globalization of Pentecostalism*. Oxford: Regnum.

Sassen, S. (2000). *Cities in a World Economy*. London: Sage.

Schaeffer, R. (1997). *Understanding Globalization*. London: Rowman & Littlefield.

Sedgwick, P. (1995). *God in the City*. London: Mowbray.

——(1999). *The Market Economy and Christian Ethics*. Cambridge: Cambridge University Press.

Selby, P. (1997). *Grace and Mortgage*. London: Darton, Longman & Todd.

Sen, A. (1999a). *Development as Freedom*. Oxford: Oxford University Press.

——(1999b). "Global Justice". In Kaul et al. (1999).

Seroke, J. (2000). "The Church – Advocate of Democracy". In L. S. Mudge and T. Wieser (eds.), *Democratic Contracts for Sustainable and Caring Societies: What Can Churches and Christian Communities Do?* Geneva: World Council of Churches.

Shriver, D. W. (2000). "The Taming of Mars: Can Humans of the Twenty-First Century Contain their Propensity for Violence?" In Stackhouse and Paris (2000).

Smith, M. P. (2001). *Transnational Urbanism*. Oxford: Blackwell.

Stackhouse, M. L., Dearborn, T. and Paeth, S. (2000). *The Local Church in a Global Era*. Grand Rapids, Mich.: Eerdmans.

Stackhouse, M. L. and Paris, P. J., eds. (2000). *God and Globalization*, vol. I: *Religion and the Powers of the Common Life*. Harrisburg: Trinity.

van Leeuwen, M. S. (2000). "Faith, Feminism and the Family in the Age of Globalization". In Stackhouse and Paris (2000).

Williams, R. (2000). *On Christian Theology*. Oxford: Blackwell.

Woods, N. (2000). *The Political Economy of Globalization*. London: Macmillan.

PART V

Perspectives

34   The Islamic Quest for Sociopolitical Justice   503
35   Abrahamic Theo-politics: A Jewish View   519

CHAPTER 34

The Islamic Quest for Sociopolitical Justice

Bustami Mohamed Khir

The impact of Islam on politics in today's world attracts wide interest and has led to a flood of writings on so-called "political Islam," a term apparently newly coined (Beinin and Stork 1997). "Political Islam" is defined as "the doctrine and/or movement, which contends that Islam possesses a theory of politics and the State" (Ayubi 1991). The phenomenon is viewed to be at odds with modernity, and so Muslim political activism is customarily equated merely with terrorism and extremism. Many overlook the continuing movement within the Muslim world to relate Islam to contemporary social concerns.

The aim of this essay is to examine briefly the emergence of modern Islamic ideas of sociopolitical justice and how different Muslim groups are attempting to realize these in today's Muslim world. Since an understanding of the present Muslim situation necessitates a familiarity with the past, the essay begins with a short introductory history of the major changes that have affected the development of Islamic political thought and its sources. This is followed by an overview of the impact of Western imperialism on modern Muslims, and the revolts and reforms that have occurred in response to it. Modern views of Muslims on justice have developed in a context of encounters with Western modernity, and among the major issues raised are liberation, equality, alleviation of poverty, and protest against oppression. These will be briefly examined, taking into consideration the views of a few influential modern Muslim thinkers.

The discussion presented below reveals a number of corollaries and differences between Islamic political ethics and political theology. However, the term "political theology," with its specific origin and connotations, may not be directly applicable to Islam, and so it has seldom been used (Obermann 1935). It may always be problematic to describe other cultures in Western terms and notions, except only in approximation. Consequently, the style used here is to let Islam speak for itself and present its ideas in its own terminology. As the famous French orientalist Louis Massignon suggested, it is essential that such a study be "from the inside," concentrating on "the categories of thought imagined by the Muslims, in order to appreciate their original interdependence, their intimate structure and their historical growth" (cited in Kerr 1966: 12).

Relevance of History

The Prophet of Islam, Muhammad, commenced his message around 610 CE in his native city, Mecca, which was an important religious, economic, and cultural center of Arabia at that time. His political maneuvers in that early era secured a growing band of followers. In the beginning he established an underground movement and led a peaceful and passive resistance in the face of the severe opposition and persecution with which he and his followers were met. Islam gained momentum due to several factors, including its being a liberating force for the weak and poor from the injustices of Meccan society. That epoch ended when the Prophet secretly migrated to a nearby city, Medina, in 622 while the native Meccans were plotting to assassinate him. His migration, *hijra*, was a significant axial turn and was taken by Muslims as a starting date for their calendar. The experience of the Prophet Muhammad and his followers in their *hijra* from oppression set an example that has continued to influence Muslim tactics throughout the centuries and up to the present time.

The new home of Muslims, Medina, became an Islamic polity under the leadership of Muhammad after a covenant was agreed among its inhabitants, forming an alliance with the Muslims (Bashier 1990: 99–119); some writers call this the "constitution of Medina" (Watt 1968). The Jews of the city were among those who signed the covenant, and that participation laid the foundation of the relationship with covenanted non-Muslims, later called *dhimis*, who lived within the Islamic territory. The Prophet became the effective ruler of Medina, wielding political and religious authority and enacting various laws to regulate that society. The emerging Muslim polity fought several victorious wars against neighboring tribes, including those of Mecca. Military struggle, *jihad*, thus became an important instrument of Islam for defense, survival, and dominance, and the cry for it remains loud even today.

The death of the Prophet in 623 created a problem of succession that was quickly resolved, thus giving birth to the first system of the caliphate. For about 30 years the caliphate was consolidated while the territory under Muslim control expanded swiftly to include vast areas in Asia and North Africa. The legal precedents that shaped the government of the first four caliphs, described as *al-rāshidūn* (the rightly guided), initiated early developments in Sunnite theories. The practices of *al-rāshidūn* were viewed as an authority by later generations in the belief that they were supported by *ijmā'*, consensus of opinion (Maududi 1980: 203). The most important principle derived from this line of argument is that the caliphate system was an elective office based on consultation and consent. The Sunnites authenticated this in their report that the first caliph, Abu

Bakr, was duly elected at a meeting of the notables of Medina after the death of the Prophet. 'Umar, the second caliph, was quoted as having commented on the incident in a public speech in Medina when he said: "If any one swears allegiance to a man without taking counsel with the Muslims he is not to be obeyed." However, there appears to have been no agreed precise way of conducting the procedures of election, and elections of the second, third, and fourth caliphs followed variant methods (Khir 1996: 85–6). Nonetheless, modern thinkers use the principle as a basis of democratic rule.

The model of the *rāshidūn* caliphate did not last long: after about 30 years a civil war broke out. In the aftermath of the conflict a major change took place in the form of rule. The caliphate, which was in origin an elective authority based on consent, was transformed into a monarchy, *mulk*, founded on force (Ibn Khaldun 1958: 598–608). Muslims adopted the type of rule that was common in ancient empires and power was passed on through hereditary succession. The first family to seize control was the Umayyad dynasty, and their imperial, despotic type of rule continued throughout Muslim history up to the time of the Ottomans, whose rule ended at the beginning of the twentieth century. One of the results of this development is that Muslim society began to take an effective role in administering its affairs independently of the government. Nongovernmental autonomous establishments carried out many of the functions of social justice that were no longer performed by the rulers. The services that enjoyed a sphere of autonomy free from governmental intrusion comprised, among others, education, health, transport, mosques, and mystic orders. A huge enterprise system of endowments, *awqāf*, generated income to run the services and facilitated their independence. "These institutions played roles analogous to those institutions we today identify with civil society" (Hashmi 2002: 61).

Sources of Political Thought

The origins of acceptable political principles are found in the sacred book of Islam, the Qur'an. Muslims viewed the practices and traditions of the Prophet as explanations and practical exemplifications of Qur'anic political values. The traditions, called Ḥadīth or Sunna, are collected in a number of books and authenticated by applying different methods of criticism. These prophetic traditions contain a number of principles that have served as directives for political activity throughout Muslim history. In addition to the Qur'an and the Hadith, there have been many and diverse theorizers on politics. Among others, they included jurists, theologians, philosophers, ethicists, and historians. The complexity of the nature of politics and its intertwined links with many disciplines necessitated varied approaches from different backgrounds. Politics, however, did not develop as a discipline in its own right. Jurisprudence (*fiqh*) was viewed to be the most proper place for discussing questions of governance (Rosenthal 1958: 38). The branches of *fiqh* that concerned themselves with political matters can be expressed in modern terms as constitutional, administrative, and international law.

In theology, different schools of thought emerged, two of which were most significant: the Sunnites and the Shiites. The Shiites regarded the doctrine of leadership (*imamate*) as one of the main principles of faith and it was, therefore, mainly included in Shiite theology rather than in jurisprudence. In philosophy, there had also been some progress. Translations into Arabic of Greek political philosophy included Plato's works, the *Republic* and the *Laws*, but not Aristotle's *Politics*. As a result, Platonic themes and approaches dominated the Muslim mind (Butterworth 1992). Three features characterized Muslim political philosophy. First, by and large, it was imitative rather than creative, except in trying to bring about a synthesis between revelation and hellenism. Second, it was idealistic and had barely any practical influence. Third, its close affinity with Shiism, particularly extreme forms, alienated it from mainstream Islam.

The Impact of the West

Modern Islamic history is commonly defined as beginning "with the impact of the West, or more specifically of European imperialism – its first arrival, its spread and the process of transformation which it initiated" (Lewis 1996: 273). This impact has been dated either from the defeat of the Ottomans by Russia in 1792 or from the arrival of Napoleon in Egypt in 1798, and it gained momentum in the nineteenth century. For different natural and historical reasons, Turkey, Egypt, and India became the first regions to encounter the conflict between Islam and the West. The transformation of Turkey serves as a standard example of the process of Westernization in Muslim lands. The first "dose" of Westernization was "injected" into the traditional Ottoman system in the era of Selim III (1789–1807), in the form of borrowed Western technologies of war. But this initial step caused a strong pressure towards the imitation of the West in all aspects. A few decades later, new reforms, called the *Tanzimat*, were introduced that split society into two competing systems. "In politics, in administration, in education, in intellectual life, two sets of institutions, two sets of ideas, two loyalties – one to the old and the other to the new – stood side by side" (Berkes 1959: 17). The impetus of Western modernization succeeded in the promulgation of an Ottoman constitution modeled on Western charters in 1867 and the formation of a parliament. However, the constitution and parliament did not last for long. The traditional regime was able to resist until its total collapse was brought about after the defeat of the Ottomans in World War I in 1918. On March 3, 1924 the caliphate was abolished and the last Ottoman sultan was expelled from the country (Black 2001: 311–14).

With the fall of the Ottoman caliphate and the spread of Western secularism over all regions of the Muslim world, Islam was removed from state power. The new phenomenon of "powerless" Islam is a key to the understanding of most of the current Muslim political ideas and trends, from liberation movements to fundamentalism. The introduction of Western modernity into Muslim lands through imperialism in all its forms, political, economic, and cultural, resulted in major dislocations. The effects were both destructive and constructive. Evidently, imperialism had dismantled Muslim culture and replaced it with Western modes of thought and action. But it may be argued that modernization was beneficial to the Muslims. The balance sheet of imperialism was undoubtedly difficult to evaluate (Fieldhouse 1976: 42). Muslims, however, generally believed that the evils exceeded the benefits. Even after the decolonization that followed World War II, many still attributed their political and economic underdevelopment to the continuing dominance of the West, whether by neocolonialism or globalization. The present reality in Muslim countries is best described in the following remark:

> In the last decades of the twentieth century, the Middle East faces two major crises. One of them is economic and social: the difficulties arising from economic deprivation and, still more, economic dislocation, and their social consequences. The other is political and social – the breakdown of consensus, of the generally accepted set of rules and principles by which a polity works and without which a society cannot function, even under autocratic government. (Lewis 1996: 485)

Islamic Revolts and Reforms

The Algerian thinker Bennabi argued that the chaos of the modern Muslim world was attributable not only to colonization but also to the weakness and decline of Muslim societies, which put them in a state that he called "colonizibility." But, in his view, colonization would in the end negate this status of weakness and act as a stimulus for reform. He explained (Bennabi 1987: 53): "one would then ascertain that colonisation introduced itself in the life of a colonised people as a contradictory factor that helps it to surmount its colonisibility. By the intermediary of colonisation, colonisibility thus becomes its own negation in the consciousness of the colonised; the latter then forces himself to become non-colonisable."

Bennabi's remark that "Europe unknowingly played the role of the dynamite that explodes in a camp of silence and contemplation" (1987: 23) is borne out by the revolts and reform movements that surfaced in the Muslim world during and after the period of colonization. Most of the revolts, particularly in early colonialism, occurred chiefly in resistance to European imperial conquests. Muslims resisted the Dutch in Southeast Asia, the British in India, the Russians in the Caucasus, the French in Algeria, and the Italians in Libya (Keddie 1994; Peters 1979). There were also bitter liberation wars fought to gain independence in the years following World War II. The most significant one was the Algerian War of Independence, which lasted for more than seven years and cost the lives of many thousands of Muslim and French soldiers and civilians. The creation of Israel in 1948 sparked a movement of resistance lasting right up to the present time.

At the intellectual level, reform movements attempted to address the decline and stagnation of Muslim thought. Revivalism is deep rooted in Islamic tradition, and Muslims believe that there is a continuous cycle of updating and revision of thought and practice. Throughout Islamic history, there have been a number of thinkers to whom the role of revival was ascribed (Esposito 1984: ch. 2). The reform movements that emerged in modern times have attracted great interest, and there is a vast literature on them. Historically, it is possible to identify several phases (Keddie 1994). The first wave of movements, in the eighteenth and nineteenth centuries, had largely advocated purity of doctrine and practice and used armed struggle, *jihad*, particularly to encounter European imperialism. The movements of the late nineteenth century and the beginning of the twentieth century were mainly concerned with intellectual reformism as a means of liberation from Western cultural and political dominance. The next phase of reform appeared before World War II with a vision of establishing Islamic sociopolitical systems that would replace secular Western systems. Reform groups in the second half of the twentieth century became more diversified both in their visions and in the methods of achieving them. The success of the Iranian revolution in 1979 was an impetus that intensified Islamic political activism and made it more visible.

Ideas of Sociopolitical Justice

Modern Islamic intellectual reform had developed in a context of close encounter with Western modernity. But it would be a simplistic view to consider it influenced solely by Western modes of thought and ideas. It is noticeable that "movements of thought and artistic creation which responded to the new power and ideas of Europe did not, in the work of most thinkers and writers, represent a complete break with the past, but rather a more or less responsible attempt to adapt traditional categories of thought to the needs of changing societies in a new world" (Hourani 1991: 128–9). In light of the above remark, it is important to view the development of modern ideas on sociopolitical justice in Islam in its duality: as both a response to external influences and an internal evolution from within. Basically, the thinkers have attempted to use traditional ideas and present them in modern language.

The quest for sociopolitical justice comprised both theorization and activism, and contributors to it represented a wide spectrum of campaigners. But the writings of the following thinkers are most influential. A pioneer work was *The Socialism of Islam* by Mustafa al-Siba'i (1914–64), a leader of the Muslim Brothers movement in Syria (Enayat 1982: 144–9). The writings of Sayyid Qutb (1906–66), a famous Egyptian exponent of Islamism in modern times, had a great impact on many activists, particularly his book *Social Justice in Islam* (Shepard 1996). Equally important is the political thought of the Pakistani thinker Sayyid Abul A'la Al-Mawdudui (1903–79), and that of Muhammad Husayn Fadlallah (b. 1936), the Shiite thinker of Hizbullah (Party of God) in Lebanon. It is not possible to examine the work of each of these figures separately, but it will suffice to present a few selected ideas, concentrating especially on the writings of Qutb, in order to portray the general trend of modern Islamic thought on social justice.

The Meaning of Liberation

In Qutb's view, the cornerstone of Islamic social justice is the complete liberation of the human soul from all that dominates its true nature. This liberation stems from the relationship that Islam sets up between humans and God (Shepard 1996: 41–56). God is the essence of religious experience, and in the confession of Islamic faith, the *shahāda*, Muslims witness that there is no God but God. The name of God, Allah, simply means "The God." This statement in its brevity is at once an affirmation and a negation. It affirms the presence of God, who should occupy a central position in a human being's conscience, thought, and action. It negates the servitude of humans to anything other than God (Al-Faruqi 1992). This negation, Qutb argues, is the liberation of humans from all forms of submission and domination. Servitude to God alone frees the soul from being a slave to itself or to other human beings, from its desires and fears, and from external considerations and social pressures. Qutb asserts:

> Islam, thus, seeks to rouse the greatest desires and the highest powers in human nature and through them to push for the clear and complete liberation of the soul, since without liberation it cannot resist the factors making for weakness, submissiveness and servility and will not demand its share in social justice. Nor will it endure the burdens of justice when justice is given to it. (Shepard 1996: 56)

Qutb maintains the view that there should be no intermediary between God and humans in any form, neither priesthood nor sacred hierarchy. Qutb's theological arguments about the freedom of human spirit appear utopian, particularly in the face of abuse of religion by the powerful who use it as a tool to justify their oppression. Muslim religious scholars, the *'ulamā'*, have exploited religion for their worldly interests and helped the exploitation of the poor by the wealthy and powerful throughout history and in modern Muslim countries. Though Qutb admitted that such exploitation occurred, he condemned the attitudes of scholars because "the true spirit of this religion rejects such behaviour." He added that there had also existed another type of religious scholar who encouraged the underprivileged to demand their rights and criticized the oppressive rulers and the persecutors for their injustices (Shepard 1996: 15). He asserted that the "spiritual" liberation does not stand on its own but must be a foundation for political, legal, and economic justice, because Islam "recognises both the practical side of life and the power of the soul" (p. 56). In other words, liberation must be both spiritual and material.

Equality

Qutb's second foundation for social justice is equality, which he elaborates quoting the primary sources of the Qur'an and the Sunna, as well as referring to juristic formulations and historical precedents (Shepard 1996: 56–68, 182–276). The theory of Islamic equality rests on the belief that humans were all created from the same origin. The Qur'anic text proclaims that all people descended from the same pair and asserts that humans are constituted into tribes and nations in order that they may mutually cooperate and enrich each other (Qur'an 49: 13). Any claims for distinction or superiority on the basis of race are thus eliminated. A tradition of the Prophet is commonly quoted in which he said: "O People, indeed your Lord is one and your father Adam is one; indeed there is no superiority of an Arab over a non-Arab, nor for a red person over a black person." Consequently, moral values and legal injunctions are one for all, and cannot be restricted to any segment of humanity. Humans are equal in rights and duties before the law and before God, in this world and in the next (Shepard 1996: 56–7; Al-Faruqi 1992: 96; El-Awa 1980:110–13).

On the basis of the principle of equality, it is argued, Islam has formulated basic individual rights, which may be equated with modern human rights. The debate over the issue is intense, and there are many areas of disagreement. On the one hand, there is the view that Islamic political culture is not conducive to the protection of human rights. This is supported by examples of the present poor record on human rights in many Muslim countries, particularly those with Islamic political orientations. The position of religious minorities – Christians or Jews, traditionally called the *dhimis* – is also used as evidence of discrimination and nonequality (Price 1999: 157–76). Objections are also raised about gender inequality and the inferior status attributed to women. A number of Muslim women have turned to feminism in order to defend their rights in contemporary Muslim societies (Price 1999: 161). However, many writers have mentioned that Islam has firmly embodied various individual rights in its established laws and has granted them to all humans on an equal basis (Moussali 2001; Osman 2001; Mawdudi 1976).

The roots of human rights in Islam are found, it is claimed, in classical jurisprudence under different terminology, and that is one of the reasons for contemporary misunderstanding. Islamic law has spoken about what it calls *huqūq al-'ibād* (individual rights), and jurists mention five necessities that must be protected: life, religion, property, intellect, and honor. Building on these foundations, modern Islamic thinkers have listed a number of basic rights that every individual must enjoy. A few of them will be briefly discussed below. Mawdudi (1976) mentions first the right to life, where protection of the sanctity of the human soul is made an important obligation. The Qur'anic verse which says, "do not kill a soul which God has made sacred except through the due process of Law," is cited to support the right to life. Only a court is entitled to pass a sentence of capital punishment. The word "soul" in the verse is general and comprises all people without any distinction or particularization based on race, nationality, or religion. Therefore, human life is sacred and must be safeguarded in all circumstances. If a person is in danger of death from any cause, such as starvation and disease, Muslims have a duty, individually or collectively, to provide the means to prevent any ensuing loss of life (Mawdudi 1976). Feeding the needy and the hungry is incumbent on the rich because, in the words of Qutb, "nothing is a greater cause for humiliation than need and an empty stomach knows no lofty ideals" (Shepard 1996: 55).

The protection of honor is another important right in Mawdudi's view. He quotes the Qur'an, which says: "You who believe, do not let any group of people make fun of another group, do not defame one another, do not insult each other by using nicknames, and do not backbite or speak ill of one another" (49: 11, 12). These directives are not only moral values but have been incorporated within the Islamic law, with corresponding punishment. Defamation is an offense that is liable to be penalized according to the type and seriousness of the offense (Mawdudi 1976: 26). Religious beliefs and sentiments should be respected and honored, and "nothing should be said or done which may encroach upon this right" (Mawdudi 1976: 33).

The question of gender equality and the place of women in society attracts much attention and can only be referred to briefly here. Al-Faruqi (1982: 133–4) asserts: "men and women are made equal in their religious, ethical and civil rights, duties and responsibilities." However, there are a "few exceptions and these pertain to their functions as fathers and mothers." Numerous verses of the Qur'an have established the equality of the sexes (3: 195; 9: 71–2; 16: 97). Men and women are given different but complementary roles. It is argued that the functions of motherhood, looking after children, and home-care, and those of fatherhood, home protection, livelihood earning, and overall responsibility "call for different physical, psychic and emotional constituents in men and women." The differentiation in roles does not imply discrimination or segregation, as both roles are protected by ethical norms and require talent, energy, and self-exertion. These areas of activities of the sexes can cross normally accepted boundaries where natural aptitude or necessity makes this desirable.

The rights of religious minorities in a Muslim society, and the attitude of Islam toward other faiths, have prompted special explanation. Al-Faruqi (1998: 281–301) argues that Islam has acknowledged that all humans possess a tendency to be religious and to develop what he calls natural religion. On another level, Islam affirms that God has given every nation a revealed knowledge but that, through the passage of time, divinely inspired religion becomes transformed into historical religion. Dialogue between faiths is, therefore, encouraged by Islam in order to discover the divine origins of each religion, including Islam, and to differentiate between these and their historical forms. As for Christianity and Judaism, Islam has identified itself with many of their beliefs and the Qur'an itself establishes many bridges between them and the Muslims. Muslim jurists extended these privileges to include other religious groups that encountered Islam such as Zoroastrians, Hindus, and Buddhists. Al-Faruqi (1998) goes on to mention a number of rights of entitlement for non-Muslims: the right to observe their faith, to express it publicly, to educate their children in accordance with it, and to actualize all the cultural and social norms pertaining to their own value systems.

Alleviation of Poverty

Qutb (Shepard 1996) discusses the problem of poverty and regards it as one of the greatest evils that result from social inequalities. The alleviation of poverty, therefore, is an important foundation in the scheme of Islamic social justice. Qutb and other Islamic writers tend not to use terms such as distributive or economic justice. Rather, they coined the term "social solidarity" (*al-takāful al-ijtimā'ī*). After the early writings of Qutb, al-Siba'i and Mawdudi, there came a massive literature on what has come to be known as "Islamic economics" (Siddiqi 1981). Justice in the economic system is claimed to be an important aim of Islam and enshrines its view of wealth. One of the basic principles is the right of private ownership, because "it achieves a just balance between effort and reward and accords with human nature" (Shepard 1996: 126). In order to strike a balance between the interests of the individual and those of society, Islam affirms that the real owner of everything is God. In practical terms, the society, on behalf of God, is the original owner of property and the individual owns property only as a trustee. There are moral and legal controls on private ownership, and if those are not met then society has the right to claim back private property. The right of intervention is given to courts and to the government in circumstances of great need. Society has the right to acquire public resources, such as water, and no individual has a right to own these. The acquisition of wealth is regulated through different means, the most important of which is that it should be achieved as a result of work. On this basis, Islam is against monopoly, usury, and deceitful commercial practices. The ethical principles of production include just wages, just pricing, and just profit, though these are not defined in a restrictive way but left to the social order to determine in any given circumstances. Consumption is also controlled through moral and legal rules. Islam realizes that spending is important in fulfilling the function of wealth. However, consumption must be undertaken only to satisfy basic needs and in moderation. Islam hates luxury, and the Qur'an (17: 16) describes it as one of the causes of corruption and a sign of decline of morality in the community. It eventually leads to the complete destruction of the basis of civilization (Shepard 1996: 128–61).

The Qur'an speaks of the circulation and distribution of wealth, and bases this on the principle that it should not be left to accumulate in the hands of the few (59: 7). Therefore, several means are designed in order to ensure a wider and more just distribution of wealth. One of these means is a wealth sharing tax called *zakāt*, which is an annual levy payable to the duly constituted authority of the community. This is levied at an approximate rate of 2.5 per cent on types of wealth that exceed a prescribed minimum. The recipients of this fund are strictly defined and include the poor and the needy. Another means of distributive justice is charity and, although it is made a moral and not a legal obligation, the Qur'an gives it the strongest recommendation and describes it as atonement meritorious of great reward. Throughout history, Muslim endowments have established several institutions for the service of the community independently from the government and have played a role similar in many ways to modern civic society. Islamic rules of inheritance are another tool that secures the distribution of the wealth of a person after death among his or her close relatives (Shepard 1996: 142, 162; Al-Faruqi 1992: 181). The application of those rules is mandatory and not dependent on personal wishes, although a person is allowed, if a will is made, to include others than heirs within the limits of a third of the person's wealth. There may also be an obligation on wealth in addition to the *zakāt* whenever there is compelling necessity, for example in times of famine. Using the general objectives of the comprehensive code of law called the Shari'a, Qutb allows taxation in order to care for the general welfare of society (Shepard 1996: 165). Al-Sibai uses the same principles to support nationalization "of any source and material which, if allowed to remain in private hands, might lead to monopolised exploitation of public need" (Enayat 1982: 146).

Islamic writings on economic justice tend to be idealistic, and they have not been seriously put to the test of practicality. Even so, they have been met by strong criticisms. "The apologetic exaggeration in these assertions cannot be denied," argues Mintjes (1977). In addition, they have been charged with contradictions and inconsistencies. Kuran (1989) says:

> Despite their ambitious claims, Islamic economists have not established that the injustices they find in existing social orders would be absent from an Islamic order. They have shown neither that the distribution of wealth would be relatively more equal in an Islamic order, nor that an Islamic order would be fairer, even by their own standards of fairness. The injunctions they propose are riddled with inconsistencies.

Protest against Oppression

In the theories of classical and modern writers, the ideal Islamic social order should be based on justice; one of the features of this model is the establishment of an elective authority that comes to power by the choice (*ikhtiyār*) of the ruled and governs through collective consultation (*shūra*). Modern interpretations are inclined to claim that there are democratic elements in Islamic rule, or at least that Islam does not hinder democracy or facilitate harsh, authoritarian rule (Price 1999: 137). However, since very early in Islamic history political realities have witnessed sharp departures from what Muslims have perceived as the ideal, and authoritative rulers have been more or less the norm right up to the present time. Thus, the question of the nature and extent of permissible protest against oppressive regimes arose very early on and remains at the core of modern Muslim political thought.

In the early centuries of Islam there were many revolts against unjust rulers, carried out mainly by sectarian minorities: the Shiites and the Kharijites and a very few Sunnite groups. The Kharijites, in particular, advocated the use of violence in order to redress injustices, and many find affinities with their thought in modern Muslim terrorist groups (Enayat 1982: 7). However, the Sunnites and the Shiites have gradually adopted a form of more quiet and peaceful protest. Leading Muslim Sunni scholars have argued strongly against armed revolt (*khurūj*). They considered it unfruitful and worse than an unjust ruler because of the destruction caused in the confrontation. The Shiites have also developed an increasing tendency toward passive noncompliance with the established order. These two views, espousing respectively violent and passive resistance, are more or less characteristic of Islamic reform groups in modern times. It is worth discussing in more detail specific modern trends of thought, namely those of Qutb and Fadlallah, in relation to responses to oppression.

Qutb considers Islam a revolutionary process against all systems that do not recognize the absolute sovereignty of God. In his view, there is no liberty and respect in a society that gives some men the right to legislate and compels others to become submissive and obedient to them. Any society in which such a condition prevails is to be considered reactionary and backward, or, in the Islamic terminology, as polytheistic and part of *jāhiliyya* (ignorance). *Jāhiliyya* is a characteristic and not a historical period that prevailed before Islam. Today, it prevails in many societies that give sovereignty to human beings rather than to God alone. These include Muslim countries where Islamic law is replaced with secular law (Khir 1996: 142–3).

The views of Qutb have far-reaching consequences. They call for a continuous struggle to change regimes in order that they may acknowledge the sovereignty of God. He himself advocated this contest when he said, "those who consider themselves Muslims, but do not struggle against different kinds of oppression, or defend the rights of the oppressed, or cry out in the face of dictators are either wrong, or hypocritical, or ignorant of the precepts of Islam" (Abu-Rabi' 1996: 130). The major form of oppression, according to Qutb, is the rejection of Islamic law as a supreme legislation. It is worthy of note that Qutb was writing at a time when the Egyptian regime of Nasir confronted Islamic movements and persecuted and oppressed their followers. Qutb himself was executed for his views on the basis that they induced violence. Although Qutb was radical in describing Muslim societies as being non-Islamic in that they were submissive to secular rulers, there is no evidence that he advocated violent change. On the contrary, it seems that he emphasized a step-by-step establishment of the Islamic order in place of secular systems (Abu-Rabi' 1996: 183). Nonetheless, his ideas have been interpreted as endorsing violent struggle and are used by many current Islamic groups for that purpose. Islamic groups in Algeria, Syria, and Egypt are representative of this radical trend.

Many moderate Islamic groups advocate nonviolence in their campaign to bring about an Islamic political order. Al-Ghannoushi, the leader of an Islamic party in Tunisia, writes claiming that "today, most Islamic parties have rejected the use of force to achieve political ends, and instead, initiated a search for opportunities that would enable them to effect changes through peaceful means" (Al-Ghannouchi 2001: 115).

In contrast, Fadlallah, the leader of the Shiite party in Lebanon, the Party of God (Hizbullah), justifies the use of power to change the critical conditions of the oppressed. Abu-Rabi' (1966: 220–47) describes him as developing a liberation theology out of the Shiite tradition and detects some Marxist influences in it. Fadlallah argues that the rich minority have used power to exploit and oppress the poor and weak in society. It is, therefore, the responsibility of the Muslim elite to alert the silent and oppressed majority to their plight and to the doctrinal and ethical Islamic attitude opposed to such a state of affairs. The oppressed are justified, in Fadlallah's view, in using power in order to ward off their inner defeat and apathy, to realize Islam in its true form, and to fight neocolonialism. Fadlallah, it should be noted, was writing at a time when Lebanon was disintegrating due to an internal civil war and an external invasion by Israel and Syria. In his vision, the armed struggle of the Party of God, Hizbullah, is the spearhead to the materialization of justice, first in Lebanon and then in other parts of the Muslim world.

Comparisons

Dorraj (1999) attempts to identify certain features that constitute a basis for comparison between modern Islamic movements and political theology. "Unlike Orthodox Christianity, liberation theologians negated the avowed separation of state and church . . . and cited the example of Jesus who suffered and fought against the social injustice of his day" (Roelofs 1988, cited in Dorraj 1999: 230). By defining the essence of their message as political, liberation theologians agree with Islam, which from its emergence regarded the social and political order as an integral element of the sacred. Islamic reform movements and liberation theology also agree in their challenge to the official religious establishments and secular authorities. Additionally, Christian liberationists conceive two forms of liberation: freedom from and freedom for. Freedom from is understood to mean the acceptance of the limitless love of God, which "is existence in freedom from literally everything else" (Ogden 1979, cited in Dorraj 1999: 232). Without overlooking the differences in the nature of God, the Christian notion of liberation can be compared with Qutb's view of spiritual and material liberation. By spiritual liberation the inward soul frees itself from all forms of submission and domination to anything other than God, which is a prerequisite for material liberation.

Both Christian and Islamic liberationists address the underprivileged (an "option for the poor") and present themselves as "the voice of the oppressed." Both have established alternative sources and means that can help in alleviating poverty. Many established Christian-based associations function as self-help centers that provide pastoral care for the poor and deliver special services such as literacy and health care. The counterparts of these organizations among Muslims are mosques, Islamic banks, Islamic schools, and health centers. All operate as centers of power and create a state within the state (Dorraj 1999: 232).

However, there are undoubtedly major differences between Islamic movements and liberation theology in intellectual origins and scope of proposed reforms. While Islam is conceived as a total system of life and is strictly defined in the Shari'a, liberation theology is less directive and holistic. Christian liberationists are more open to secular ideological influences such as liberalism and socialism (Dorraj 1999), whereas Islam tends to preserve continuity of its tradition and allows little room for change. Feminist theology, on the other hand, finds Islamic attitudes toward gender issues totally unacceptable. Controversies over these and related issues continue and are unlikely to be resolved soon.

Conclusion

A number of conclusions emerge from this study. The cry for justice is loud within the current Islamic reform movements and has its roots in Islamic tradition and history. Most of these groups believe in Islam as a total system of life, and it is this vision that makes them struggle for its realization. The ideas of justice formulated within these groups contain some elements of inconsistency, and there seem to be a number of ambiguities and unresolved issues. But this does not negate the meaning and value of justice as a driving force for modern Muslims.

Many factors have contributed to the rise of revival movements, including

> a widespread feeling among Muslims that they are not yet in control of their own destiny, a strong desire for independence and autonomy, and a widespread belief that today's ruling elites in Muslim countries are dominated by foreign powers and ideologies and thus have become alien to their own countries and cultures. But it is also important to note that this quest for autonomy, including cultural autonomy or authenticity, is not limited to Muslim societies or to Islamic groups in these

societies. Indeed, this quest is widespread throughout the Third World, where traditional cultures feel threatened by the spread of foreign cultures, often as a result of political domination. (Hunter 1988: 282)

References

Abu-Rabi', Ibrahim (1996). *Intellectual Origins of Islamic Resurgence in the Modern Arab World*. Albany: State University of New York Press.

Al-Faruqi, Ismail (1982). *Al-Tawhid: Its Implications for Thought and Life*. Herndon: Islamic Institute of Islamic Thought.

——(1998). *Islam and Other Faiths*. Leicester: Islamic Foundation.

Al-Ghannoushi, Rashid (2001). "On the Dilemma of the Islamic Movement: A Political Party or a Reformist Organisation?" In A. El-Effendi (ed.), *Rethinking Islam and Modernity*. Leicester: Islamic Foundation.

Ayubi, Nzia N. (1991). *Political Islam: Politics and Religion in the Arab World*. London: Routledge.

Bashier, Zakeria (1990). *Sunshine at Madinah*. Leicester: Islamic Foundation.

Beinin, Joe, and Stork, Joe, eds. (1997). *Political Islam: A Reader*. London: I. B. Tauris.

Bennabi, Malek (1987). *Islam in History and Society*, trans. Asma Rashid. Kuala Lumpur: Berrita.

Berkes, Niyazi (1959). *Turkish Nationalism and Western Civilization*. London: Allen & Unwin.

Black, Antony (2001). *The History of Islamic Political Thought*. Edinburgh: Edinburgh University Press.

Butterworth, Charles, ed. (1992). *The Political Aspects of Islamic Philosophy*. Cambridge, Mass.: Harvard University Press.

Dorraj, Manochehr (1999). "The Crisis of Modernity and Religious Revivalism: A Comparative Study of Islamic Fundamentalism, Jewish fundamentalism and Liberation Theology." *Social Compass* 46: 2, 225–40.

El-Awa, Muhammad (1980). *On the Political System of the Islamic State*. Indianapolis: American Publication Trust.

Enayat, Hamid (1982). *Modern Islamic Political Thought*. London: Macmillan.

Esposito, John (1984). *Islam and Politics*. Syracuse, NY: Syracuse University Press.

Fieldhouse, D. K. (1976). *Colonialism 1870–1945*. London: Macmillan.

Hashmi, Sohail, ed. (2002). *Islamic Political Ethics*. Princeton: Princeton University Press.

Hourani, Albert (1991). "How Should We Write the History of the Middle East?" *International Journal of Middle Eastern Studies* 23: 2, 125–36.

Hunter, Shireen (1988). *The Politics of Islamic Revivalism*. Washington DC: Centre for Strategic and International Studies.

Ibn Khaldun, Abd al-Rahman (1958). *The Introduction (al-Muqaddimah)*, trans. Franz Rosenthal (1958). London: Routledge & Kegan Paul.

Keddie, Nikki (1994). "The Revolts of Islam, 1700 to 1993." *Comparative Studies in History and Society* 36: 3, 463–87.

Kerr, Malcom H. (1966). *Islamic Reform: The Political and Legal Theories of Muhammad 'Abdu and Rashid Rida*. Berkeley: University of California Press.

Khir, Bustami Mohamed (1996). *The Concept of Sovereignty in Modern Islamic Political Thought*. Leeds: Leeds Institute for Middle Eastern Studies.

Kuran, Timur (1989). "On the Notion of Economic Justice in Contemporary Islamic Thought." *International Journal of Middle Eastern Studies* 21: 2, 171–91.

Lewis, Bernard (1996). *The Middle East*. London: Phoenix.

Maududi, Abul A'la (1980). *The Islamic Law and Constitution*. Lahore: Islamic Publications.

Mawdudi, Abu 'Ala (1976). *Human Rights in Islam*. Leicester: Islamic Foundation.

Mintjes, H. (1977). *Social Justice in Islam*. Amsterdam: Institute for the Study of Religion.

Moussalli, Ahmad (2001). *The Islamic Quest for Democracy, Pluralism, and Human Rights*. Gainesville: University Press of Florida.

Obermann, Julian (1935). *Political Theology in Early Islam*. Philadelphia: American Oriental Society.

Ogden, Schubert M. (1979). *Faith and Freedom: Toward a Theology of Liberation*. Nashville: Abingdon.

Osman, Fathi (2001). "Islam and Human Rights: The Challenge to the Muslims and to the World." In A. El-Effendi (ed.), *Rethinking Islam and Modernity*. Leicester: Islamic Foundation.

Peters, Rudolph (1979). *Islam and Colonialism: The Doctrine of Jihad in Modern History*.The Hague: Mouton.

Price, Daniel (1999). *Islamic Political Culture, Democracy and Human Rights*. Westport, Conn.: Praeger.

Roelofs, Mark H. (1988) "Liberation Theology: The Recovery of Biblical Radicalism." *American Political Science Review* 2: 2, 549–66.

Rosenthal, Franz (1958). *Political Thought in Medieval Islam*. Cambridge: Cambridge University Press.

Shepard, William (1996). *Sayyid Qutb and Islamic Activism: A Translation and Critical Analysis of Social Justice in Islam*. Leiden: E. J. Brill.

Siddiqi, Muhammad Nejatullah (1981). *Muslim Economic Thinking: A Survey of Contemporary Literature*. Leicester: Islamic Foundation.

Watt, Montgomery (1968). *Islamic Political Thought*. Edinburgh: Edinburgh University Press.

CHAPTER 35

Abrahamic Theo-politics:
A Jewish View

Peter Ochs

Abraham's Tent

Hashem ["The Name," the Holy One] appeared to him by the oaks of Mamre, as he sat at the entrance of his tent in the heat of the day. Looking up, he saw three men standing near him. As soon as he saw them, he ran from the entrance of the tent to greet them, and, bowing to the ground, he said, "My lord, if it please you, do not pass by your servant. Let a little water be brought, wash your feet, and rest under the tree. Let me bring a little bread, that you may refresh yourselves and after that you may pass on – since you have come your servant's way." They replied, "Do as you have said." Abraham hastened into the tent to Sarah, and said, "Quick, three *selahs* of choice flour! Knead them and make cakes!" Then Abraham ran to the herd, and took a calf, tender and choice, and gave it to the servant-boy, who hastened to prepare it. He took curds and milk and the calf that he had prepared and set these before them; and he waited on them under the tree while they ate. (Gen. 18: 1–8)[1]

This Tent of Abraham is not the usual model for Jewish political theory, but we live in an age that should prompt reconsideration of the usual. We have completed an epoch of several hundred years that imposed, on both secular and religious policy-makers, a series of dichotomous choices: argue either on behalf of a given nation-state or against it; argue either for identifying or separating church and state; and, if you argue for religion, argue only for one denomination or another (Reform or Orthodox; Jewish or Christian or Muslim). Over the past century we have, however, received enough signs that the epoch of the "great dyads" has passed. Colonialism, world wars, and Holocaust should have been sufficient warning that the great "isms" of modernity had exhausted their positive contributions to human betterment; and September 11 is only a more recent sign. It was the epoch of great "isms," after all, that made the dyad a civilizational flag: the law of excluded middle, true vs. false, universal vs. particular, individual vs. tribe, reason vs. unreason, white vs. black, progressive vs. old, autonomous vs. law-bound, the public realm of politics vs. the private realm of religion.

Abraham's tent is a meeting place for religious thinkers of the age after dyads.

Abraham's Call Restated

> Hashem said to Abraham, "Go forth from your native land and from your father's house to the land that I will show you." (Gen. 12: 1)

My assumption is that even recent discussion of theo-politics tends to reflect two of the dichotomous features of the modern epoch. These are the assumptions that political theory is *either secular or religious*; and, that, if religious, it is either liberal (accomodationist and universalist in the manner of secular thought) or orthodox (antimodernist and strictly particularist or unidenominational in its traditionalism).

My unsurprising thesis is that September 11 is an index of our already having, for some time now, entered into an epoch other than the modern one, for which these dichotomies are now obsolete. The current epoch offers a time for a theo-politics that is at once secular and religious, at once tradition-bound (alias orthodox) and attentive to immediate social conditions (alias liberal, in this sense).

My more unconventional thesis is that there is a nonliberal, Abrahamic theo-politics, yet to be articulated but already practiced, that subverts the dichotomous logics of modernity. Certain Muslim, Christian, and Jewish scholars/religious leaders will proclaim this theo-politics as the tripartite work of God in response to the dominant political crisis of the contemporary West.

The main features of this crisis are: (1) the inadequacy of the nation-state as a privileged context for theo-political inquiry and work; (2) the inadequacy of late modern alternatives to the nation-state, which alternatives are still dominated by the universalist economic contraries of anticapitalist socialism or global capitalism; (3) the inadequacy of value-neutral models of nation-state democracy; (4) the inadequacy of late modern alternatives to these models, which alternatives are still dominated by the primarily secular contraries of societal communitarianism and individual-rights liberalism; (5) the inadequacy of both antimodern religious orthodoxies and antireligious secular universalisms as sources of norms for responding to this crisis.

While no single response is adequate to this crisis, I will, with limited space, focus on the one serious response that has received the least attention: a call for Abrahamic theo-politics. This is a call for Muslim, Jewish, and Christian leaders and scholars to draw aspects of our three scriptural traditions into *shared* theo-political work. Appropriate to a new epoch in Western religious history, this work should provide an alternative to the sharp dichotomies that defined the previous epoch: secularity vs. religiosity, and each form of religiosity vs. any other. Abrahamic theo-politics is a call to articulate the axioms of a new epoch:

- that all three are Abrahamic traditions that have, appropriately and sufficiently, already devoted more than an epoch to defining our irreducibly different missions in the world;
- that, since each of our missions represents a living covenant with the living God of Abraham, we now recognize that, not only our separate missions, but also our overlapping areas of work belong to God's plan for the redemption of this world;
- that all aspects of our lives should be devoted to this work: from personal and familial conduct to local communal life (including our participation in local schools and civic government), to regions of intercommunal, national, and international relations;
- that there is therefore no "value neutral" space of social life for us, but that the different aspects and geographic regions of our social lives should be guided by different degrees of cooperative interaction among our separate and our overlapping covenants with God.

Arising from this last point, we may envision three prototypical degrees of covenantal interaction, appropriate to three degrees of social interaction:

First, *nearly homogeneous spheres of religious practice.* Our personal prayer and public worship spaces, for example, tend to be guided by single covenantal traditions and, typically, by single denominations within each tradition. The sphere of worship is only "nearly" separate, however, because we can no longer ignore the intercommunal consequences of even private prayers that treat the other covenants, or human life outside the covenants, with malevolence. Family life tends to be guided by separate covenants, but, again, it is only nearly separate for the reason just given and also because our sphere of intercommunal social engagement cannot be wholly independent of our intrafamilial practices. Within each Western democracy, and across various nations outside of Europe and the Americas, Muslims, Jews, and Christians sometimes live in small regions or entire states guided by religious laws or traditions. We must also begin, however, to consider such regions and states as only "nearly" separate, again for the reasons just given and also because members of other denominations or traditions may also find themselves living in them.

Second, *purportedly "religion-neutral" spheres.* This is the most innovative dimension of Abrahamic theo-politics, inserting intercovenantal religiosity into regions of public policy and public life that Western democracies tend to define as value-neutral or, at least, religiously naked. Among these regions are public school boards; nonsectarian universities and colleges; all areas of policy and decision-making that serve local, regional (state, in the USA), and national governments; and all areas of policy- and decision-making that serve regional and global economic, societal, and political institutions – from businesses to the World Bank to United Nations programs and bodies. According to this new Call of Abraham, all regions of public life should now be defined as regions affected by Abrahamic theo-politics. This does not mean that all these regions should be *governed* by Abrahamic bodies, but that Abrahamic (Muslim/Jewish/Christian) bodies should lobby for influence in all these regions, asserting both their right to offer shared guidelines for decision-making in these regions and the wisdom of whatever specific judgments they recommend. To illustrate concretely: an Abrahamic group should lobby the school board in Albemarle County, Virginia, to ensure that history classes no longer avoid teaching about the major religious groups and religious events in each period of world history; an Abrahamic group should lobby the US Congress on every policy decision it makes, from stem-cell research to US plans for a war against Iraq; Abrahamic groups of shareholders should attend and offer briefs at shareholders' meetings of every international corporation.

Third, *religiously heterogeneous spheres*. A less radical dimension of Abrahamic theo-politics is to re-enter areas of interreligious dialogue that have already been opened in the late modern period, but now from the perspective of this new epoch. Until recently, interreligious dialogue had been an activity of liberal religionists: defined, that is, by concepts deemed to be universal to the three Abrahamic religions, or to all religions, rather than by covenantal, scriptural, and doctrinal directives that are made visible only within each tradition in its particularity. Liberal interreligious dialogue has therefore been driven by claims that could also be made outside the traditions: for example, about the importance of dialogue, peace, human rights, love, justice, or even of God, but understood as the referent of faith rather than as the source of unexpected disclosures and demands. Proper to this epoch, however, Abrahamic dialogue begins with the unpredictable phenomenon that some groups of observant Muslims, Jews, and Christians have been called, at once, to gather separately to serve the God of Israel or Allah or Christ in their distinct ways *and* to gather on occasion together to declare their overlapping loves of the one God of Abraham. To declare love of God is also to act on that declaration, so that this overlapping declaration also accompanies overlapping forms of religious behavior. This behavior begins with acts of speaking the love of God, of studying scripture as the most intimate access to God's word, of discussing together each tradition's readings and interpretations of scripture, and of uncovering through that discussion a sense of how God's spirit can sweep at times from one reading to the next, from one Abrahamic discourse to the next, and from a time of shared reading to a time of shared action. To act in this sense means nothing other than to have read out of God's word a shared directive to act.

One Illustration of Abrahamic Theo-political Action

"Everything that Hashem has said we will do and we will comprehend [*naaseh v'nishmah*]" (Exod. 24: 7). "*naaseh v'nishmah*": The Israelites committed to doing before hearing [practice precedes theory] (*Babylonian Talmud Shabbat* 88a).

Abrahamic theo-politics should count as both an academic and a practical discipline, but, to theorize about it, one must come to terms with its irreducibly existential – or, we should say, pneumatological – features. This theo-politics is possible only if, *in fact*, there are learned and observant Muslim, Jewish, and Christian scholar–leaders who sit down together to ponder their scriptures and receive from them overlapping directives to act. The spirit that moves such study groups will, alone, be the direct source of Abrahamic theo-political action. Any arguments for the possibility of an Abrahamic theo-politics therefore follow from, rather than precede, the action. For the purposes of this brief essay, I hope that one illustration of the action will suffice to open readers' minds to the possibility of more.

For the past four years, a group of 20 Jewish, Muslim, and Christian scholars of scripture, philosophy, and religious politics have met together for periods of intensive study of each other's scriptural traditions. Their work has been inspired by the primary hypothesis that, contrary to the persistent assumptions of most researchers and leaders in international policy, the Abrahamic scriptural traditions are untapped resources for conflict resolution. Confirming their first hypothesis, these initial meetings have been surprisingly successful, generating joyous camaraderie and deep friendship as well as intellectual productivity. Participants have discovered that the three traditions share as many interpretive rules and strategies as they do not share, and that the closer their readings come to intimate belief in God, the more closely they seem to understand each other and the more deeply they are moved by similar passions and hopes. These discoveries have led the group to a second hypothesis: that Jewish, Muslim, and Christian clergy could also join together for successful meetings of this kind, and that such clergy could come from any part of the world. A year's successes in bringing clergy into the group's meetings has led to a third hypothesis, which defines the group's current work agenda. The hypothesis is that clerical leaders of this kind could also engage at least some of their congregants in successful sessions of Abrahamic study. A concluding, speculative hypothesis is that such sessions may generate innovative models for efforts of peacemaking that emerge from out of the indigenous religious traditions of Muslim, Jewish, and Christian peoples who are currently, or potentially, engaged in various forms of political conflict.

Now self-named the Children of Abraham Institute (CHAI), the group is currently setting up a variety of study groups – in South Africa, Singapore, the UK, and in several cities in the United States – that may test out corollaries of these hypotheses.[2] They want to ask, for example, if diplomatic efforts are more lasting when they emerge from out of, or at least reinforce, practices of inquiry and of interpersonal relations that are warranted by the combatants' (or disputants') own sacred traditions. They will ask, furthermore, if, despite their differences, various Abrahamic orthodoxies display overlapping patterns of conflict resolution that are visible *only* when the discussants are enacting aspects of their orthodoxies rather than when, as is more typical in diplomatic efforts, they are asked to "leave their more intimate practices at the door." Assuming that significant political and social leaders are, in fact, congregants in traditional houses of worship, they will ask, finally, if, when brought by clerical leaders into extended sessions of Abrahamic study, such political and social leaders may be moved to levels of shared understanding that they could not achieve outside such sessions.

Arguing for Abrahamic Theo-politics: From Practice to Scriptural Reading

A theory for Abrahamic theo-politics moves from the fact of some practice to scriptural readings and interpretation that might cast light on that practice. More conceptual work would follow, generating plans for more practice. The brevity of this essay leaves space only to illustrate the move from practice to scriptural reading. In this case, the readings are to provide some basis for assuming that Muslims, Jews, and Christians have overlapping as well as separate, political missions.

Sabbath as the telos of human creation

> And God created Adam/Humanity in His image . . . On the seventh day God finished the work that He had been doing . . . God blessed the Sabbath day and declared it holy. (Gen. 1: 27, 2: 1)

We are finite creatures on this earth, dependent on our Creator and yet touched by and in ways sharing in the Creator's image. Eschewing Maimonidean intellectualism, shall we gloss "image" as the capacity to act beyond the bounds and limits of our given, creaturely, finitude, but only in direct relation to God? And shall we locate the telos of this action in the holiness of Shabbat?

Human failing

> Cursed be the ground because of you; by toil shall you eat of it all the days of your life . . . The Lord God . . . drove Adam out. (Gen. 3: 17, 24)

We fail to enact the divine image in ways appropriate to its infinity and holiness. Our actions therefore go off the mark, embodying our illusions about who we are and upsetting the finite/infinite order in which we find ourselves. Failing in this way to win life in Shabbat, we must lead lives of work, that is, lives devoted to repairing, *l'taken*, what our errors have made wrong in this world.

Our temptation is jealousy

> Hashem paid heed to Abel and his offering. Cain was much distressed and his face
> fell. And Hashem said to Cain, "Why are you distressed . . . Surely if you do right,
> there is uplift; But if you do not do right, Sin crouches at the door; its urge is toward
> you, yet you can be its master." (Gen. 4: 4–7)

Our sins of action follow from jealousy, rather than from any error of judgment or action, and it is jealousy of another's religion: that is, of another's
apparently greater success in seeking God's favor. Seeking God's favor directly,
we might imagine, is one way to cut short a lifetime of work. If so, to be jealous
is to wish the other did not receive such favor: perhaps so as not to be reminded
that our own work is not yet done? If so, to be jealous also means failing to recognize that both our work and the other's is infinite, which means that it cannot
be completed without God's direct involvement *and* that we cannot predict the
time and manner of that involvement. We cannot learn from one offering,
cannot predict the future by induction. Just like our parents, we act out of our
illusions, misunderstanding both our finitude and infinitude: as if the other's
absence would guarantee God's favor in the future. As if the church could do
away with the Jews and thereby curry God's favor? As if the mosque could do
away with the church and the Jews and win this favor? As if the Jews could re-
win God's favor by boasting of their privileged relation? As if offerings of the past
guarantee those of the future? As if there were any such short cut out of work?
But we need not act on our jealousy. We *do* have the power to overcome it – if
not the jealousy, then at least the impulse to act on it.

Our ultimate failing is violence

> Cain said to his brother Abel . . . (Gen. 4: 8)

We do not overcome the consequences of jealousy. To act out those consequences is to bring violence into the world: violence understood as our confused
effort to re-remove the other and thereby, magically, without work and merit, to
become God's only, and thus God's favorite, and thus the one whom God would
free from the toil of redemptive labor. Christian, Muslim, and Jew: who is God's
favorite? It seems we cannot resist the tendency to act out our jealousies of one
another.

Violence becomes second nature to us

> The earth became corrupt before God; the earth was filled with violence. (Gen. 6: 11)

Although not inborn in us like our tendency to err, the tendency to act out the consequences of jealousy becomes so strong a habit that it appears as if part of our nature, a "second nature." The Creator considers: Shall I do away with this tendency by doing away with all creatures who have acquired it as second nature? What age of violence prompts the divine flood? The expulsion of 135–6? The crusades? Europe's religious wars? The world wars and Shoah? Mideast conflicts? The conflicts symbolized by September 11? The salvation history of Israel should no longer be ignored by the church and the mosque: enslavement in Egypt, destruction of the first temple (586 BCE), destruction of the second temple (70 CE), expulsion from Jerusalem (135–6 CE), expulsion from Spain (1492 CE), Chmielnicki pogroms, Russian pogroms, Soviet pogroms, Shoah ... Do you suppose floods are only Old Testament stories? Do you suppose floods are merely "universal," and not also universal to particular covenants at particular times? Do you suppose these pertain only to the "old" dispensation, or, otherwise put, do you suppose you have necessarily left that dispensation? Does your doctrine say one thing and the material history of your covenants reveal another? Are there no cycles to your salvation histories as well? If you no longer belong to the land that can spew you out, is the whole earth not your land? Do you have an account to offer of the violence and destruction that visits you, too, periodically? Are you not also the child of the Mosaic covenant? Does the Deuteronomic theodicy truly never apply to your people: "Hear, O heavens, and give ear O earth, For Hashem has spoken: I reared children and brought them up – And they have rebelled against Me!" (Isa. 1: 2)? Or the theodicy of the Suffering Servant (Isa. 41ff.)? Is the Servant only an Other, or also you, O Israel,[3] and do you not suffer for their violence, and theirs and theirs ... ? Have you truly escaped the throes of earthly salvation history, the birth pangs still of Messiah even if of another coming?

But we cannot escape it in this world

> Never again will I doom the earth because of Adam/humanity, since the devisings of Adam's/humanity's mind are evil from youth. (Gen. 8: 21)

If that second nature is indeed our earthly nature, there is nothing to be gained from punishing the earth for what we have become. But the experiment of flood was not fruitless: the covenant of Noah is no longer the covenant of Adam, since humanity's redemptive work will no longer succeed unless it is led by God's redemptive word. The imago is not enough; God must send his spoken Word, without which humanity cannot redeem its sins. The spoken Word begins with the worded covenant of Noah, articulated in rabbinic tradition as the Noahide laws disclosed in Gen. 9: set up courts of justice, no idolatry, no blasphemy, no sexual immorality, no murder, no robbery, no tearing flesh from living animals (*Tosefta Avodah Zarah* 8. 4). Humanity and God are thereby partners in the work of redemption: the divine word and the human work (*avodah*). This work is divine service as well as service to the world, what we tend to call "religion."

Recognizing that we remain jealous of another's divine service, we seek to resolve the jealousy on our own, through our own construction

> Let us build us a city, and a tower with its top in the sky, to make a name for ourselves; else we be scattered all over the world. (Gen 11: 4)

Shall we all be Christians, or all Muslims? If by God's hand, then, indeed, for in the end of days, in the Garden of Eden, in the world to come, in Shabbat, we shall all be Christians, all be Muslims, all be Jews, all be children of Abraham. Indeed, we are one, already, in Shabbat, in the divine presence, which is the world to come now. But we are also many, in this world, these six days of work, which are not yet redeemed, and who are we to choose of our own will, according to our creaturely nature, when and how we shall all be one in this world? Is it for us to say when this world is the world to come? Or is this not what we mean by violence in the world after Noah: the willful effort to do away with the difference between ourselves? Is this not, indeed, the mark of political violence after Noah: the effort to do away with Abel by incorporating him into our own construction, which is our own religious construction, since it is the means through which we seek to complete our labor of redemption, once and for all?

But have we not already inherited two epochs of failed attempts to resolve matters this way: the epoch of religious empire and the epoch of secular empire? Have these not brought on the flood?

Children of Abraham

> Go forth from your father's house to a land I will show you. (Gen. 12: 1)

For Abrahamic theo-politics, the broken Tower of Babel serves as a mark of two failed epochs of efforts to force unity on the world through human will, alone. One marks efforts to force a single Abrahamic religion on the world. The other marks efforts to force a single political regime or single socioeconomic system or single philosophic system on the world. These are two epochs of political violence, because they are defined by efforts to do away with the otherness of Abel and, thereby, to evade the hard, slow labor of transforming one's second nature into divine service and, then, undertaking that service as the very long

work of redeeming the world from the effects of human sin. Neo-orthodox practitioners may protest that this is precisely the work of converting the world to
Abraham's covenant. Our response is to read such Abraham's covenant as the
point of departure from such neo-orthodoxy as well as from its secularizing
doppelgänger.

Go forth from your father's house. If Noah's covenant represents a point of
departure from Adam's covenant of creation toward the Noahide covenant of
spoken Word, then Abraham's covenant departs from a Word spoken to all
humanity toward a Word spoken to a particular language-family. This spoken
Word emerges neither within Abraham's creature-heart nor without that heart,
in the structures of his creature-communities and creature-polities. The Word is
"nigh unto him" (Deut. 30: 14), neither in the heavens nor in his flesh, but
alongside him, with him, in the name of the God *ehyeh imach*, "who will be with
you" (Exod. 3). This is a third place, neither here nor there, not *of* this world, but
with it, which is *of the other world* that knows neither place, here nor there, but
only relation with. It is in this sense a Word of language, but not of the natural
language we often suppose. Noah already had that; even in his drunkenness, he
soaked up the language of creaturely socialization. This Word is *with* natural
language, not of it; with Hebrew, not of it, even if the Word is introduced alongside it; it is therefore also with Arabic and with Greek.

Separated from his father's house, Abraham is separated from the house that
became a tower. Christian towers and Muslim towers are still towers, as for that
matter are the towers of a nation-state, even a Jewish one, or even a Muslim
Palestinian or a Christian Palestinian one. Small nation-state towers are more
modest towers, indeed, but within their scale they are still built in the memory
of Babel's nation-state. And towers do not belong to the epoch of Abrahamic
theo-politics.

Tents are another matter.

> Hashem appeared to Abraham by the oaks of Mamre, as he sat at the entrance of
> his tent in the heat of the day. He looked up and saw three men standing near him.
> When he saw them, he ran from the tent entrance to meet them, and bowed down
> to the ground. He said, ". . . Let me bring a little bread, that you may refresh your-
> selves, and after that you may pass on – since you have come to your servant."
> (Gen. 18).

Scholars and religious leaders of the Children of Abraham Institute meet
together under a tent they call both the "Tent of Meeting" and "Abraham's Tent."
It is an imaginary tent, built of images, at once, of Jacob's ladder (Gen. 18:
10–22), of Peter's sleep (Luke 9: 28–36), of Abraham's "House of Worship"
(Qur'an, Sura Bakarah 2: 125–34), of Abraham's Tent (Gen. 18), of the place
where Moses meets the divine presence (Exod. 40). All participants in CHAI are
also members of what they call "houses" – that is, denomination-specific houses
of worship, or synagogues, mosques, and churches. Like ancient Israel's
Jerusalem, set up outside the precinct of any single tribe, the tent is raised outside

any particular house. In this, literal sense, CHAI participants leave their houses in order to enter the tent; but, unlike Abraham, they in no way leave the religion of their houses: they retain full allegiance to their houses, within which they worship and acquire their primary relations to God and congregation. CHAI offers its participants a source of secondary relations. Under their imagined tent, Muslim, Jewish, and Christian participants teach their scriptures to one another, inviting one another to ponder and discuss their traditions' readings, both singly and in relation to readings from the other traditions. In this way, each participant and each tradition offers hospitality to the others, which includes the hospitality of both listening and active response. All of them are children of Abraham; the participants recognize one another as servants of the same God of Abraham, and they encounter one another as one would a messenger of that God.

> The men set out from there and looked down toward Sodom . . . Now Hashem had said, "Shall I hide from Abraham what I am about to do?" (Gen. 18: 16–17)

CHAI participants recognize, however, that they are not brought together merely to enjoy each other's hospitality. There is the matter of Sodom: not Sodom, per se, but the fact that violence remains one of the most conspicuous features of inter-Abrahamic relations. CHAI participants remember that they are children also of Adam, whose labor in this world is to redeem the consequences of Adam's failings; and that they are children of Cain, of the generation of the flood, and of the generation of the tower. They acknowledge that, both singly and together, they are children of Abraham, whose task it is to help redeem the world, now, according to specific missions disclosed through their several scriptural traditions. They acknowledge that their missions are different and that, in some significant ways, they remain competing missions. But, "looking down toward Sodom," they also say now to one another, "come, let us not now hide from one another what we think we are now called to do; there are, indeed, members of all our houses in the valley of Sodom, some sinners, some innocent; their social spaces and their lives are mostly intermingled, so that there is no way we can now take action toward one group without affecting all the others; without losing our three separate missions, let us now, in this moment, also adopt a fourth, additional mission: to work, together, to redeem the social space that our fellow congregants share."

All CHAI participants offer allegiance to this shared mission, in addition to (and within the laws of) their traditions' separate missions. Their shared mission is theo-political by definition, since it is to work, from out of shared study of the Abrahamic scriptural traditions, to remove violence as a condition of relationship among Abrahamic peoples. It is therefore a mission to remove inter-Abrahamic jealousy as a motive of action among Abrahamic communities. It is thus a mission to undo these communities' efforts to curry God's favor by removing one another as objects of God's favor. This means it is, furthermore, a mission to undo these communities' efforts to shorten the labor of world repair (*tikkun olam*) through mere, religious self-expansion or self-aggrandizement. It is a mission of Muslims, Christians, and Jews to help each other redirect their sepa-rate, tradition-specific missions to the aboriginal goal of laboring for the redemp-tion of Cain and for repair of the earth he has polluted.

There are many ways that Muslim, Jewish, and Christian communities could work together under the "Tent of Abraham." The efforts of CHAI's scholars and religious leaders represent one modest example. In their case, the first stage of work has been to gather religious and academic scholars to share a practice of scriptural study and, from out of their experience of this practice, to compose models of an inter-Abrahamic "hermeneutics of peace." A second stage has been to invite religious leaders into this tent and to ask these leaders how they would extend CHAI's hermeneutic to members of their congregations. Accord-ing to CHAI's plans, the next stage is to help groups of Abrahamic religious leaders, in various regions of the world, to draw select members of their con-gregations into CHAI study groups: in particular, members who also hold posi-tions of social, political, or economic leadership in their regions. A goal of this stage of work is to nurture such groups into nongovernmental bodies that could offer an Abrahamic voice, or serve as a source of Abrahamic policy-statements, in response to social, political, and economic crises in their specific regions of the world.

Christian Theological Arguments Supportive of an Abrahamic Theo-politics

There is insufficient space here to show how these scriptural readings may under-write a broader, Jewish theological argument on behalf of Abrahamic theo-politics. In the context of this *Companion to Political Theology*, however, it seems fitting to close by sampling the contributions some of the book's previous chap-ters could make to *Christian* theological arguments on behalf of this theo-poli-tics.[4] While these chapters are all devoted to Christian-specific theo-politics, and to theo-politics articulated once-and-for-all-times, I will suggest that some of their claims may, nonetheless, also contribute to an Abrahamic theo-politics *within the specific context of this third epoch of salvation history*. In order to offer this sugges-tion, I adopt the axiom that a Christian-specific eschatology does not necessarily contradict Jewish- and Muslim-specific eschatologies, nor a more generally Abra-hamic eschatology. To be sure, within the logic of the first two epochs of Muslim, Jewish, and Christian theological history, I could assume, to the contrary, that all these eschatologies contradict *and* compete and that this competition supersedes any overlapping, Abrahamic vision. But, since this vision is situated only in this third epoch, and since there is no reason to assume that eschatologies are leveled by some universal law of excluded middle, I see no compelling reason to adopt the latter axiom, and I will stick with the former. In these terms, Abrahamic theo-politics shares these (among other) features of Christian theo-politics.

A Bible-based and, in this sense, a story-based, narrative theology

In Robert Jenson's words, Christian theo-politics belongs to "a dramatic story [that] can truly be told about reality as a whole" (Jenson, ch. 28, p. 1). For Stanley Hauerwas, Christian reality is thus "narratively constructed" (Reno, ch. 21, p. 7).

Life led according to this story is always theological and always political.
Theo-politics is labor offered to redeem humanity

In Jenson's words, "the Scriptures' eschatology . . . are directly and almost exclusively a discourse about politics" (p. 1). For Bonhoeffer, in Hauerwas' reading, Christian theology is always political: "sanctification . . . is the church's politics" (ch. 10, p. 5), since "it is essential to the revelation of God in Jesus Christ that it occupies space within the world" (p. 8). We have already noted that, for Abrahamic theo-politics, religion becomes the theo-political labor of redeeming Cain and repairing the world he has polluted. In Hauerwas' terms, the scriptural story nurtures Christian virtue, and virtue, as I understand Reno and Hauerwas, is our capacity to engage in this labor (Reno, ch. 21, 5ff.) In Walter Bruggemann's terms, "Israel is attentive to social pain as a datum of the politics that is evoked in the public process of power" (ch. 1, p. 6). This means, as I read it, that Israel's prophetic religion is to remove the source of this pain, which is ultimately the violence of Cain.

This redemptive labor is always eschatological. And the Kingdom of God for
which we labor is also always already present among us as the immediate
motive, end, and guide for our labors

In Jenson's words, "Christians and Jews are working for the end, or eschaton of all history (ch. 28, p. 1). The "kingdom of Heaven" is the end of Abrahamic as well as of Christian theo-politics. Abrahamic theo-politics is, indeed, an eschatological vision of the unified kingdom of Heaven, operating here and now as the rule and condition of our redemptive labor. This kingdom is *here* in Shabbat, in prayer, in blessing, in communion, in the life of church and synagogue and mosque, and only because it is here can we be led by it to perform our reparative work. God pushes us by way of the present kingdom and pulls by way of the future kingdom. The Tent of Abraham is erected to serve as one meantime instrument of the kingdom. In Brueggemann's words, the eschaton was (and is) present here and now in the political imagination through which Israel creates and labors for "an alternative world of justice, mercy, peace, hope, and fidelity" (ch. 1, p. 13).

Abraham's call is for all time and on behalf of redeeming the entire world

For Jenson, the call to Abraham "was not to found a new cult . . . , but to perform an historical act with political significance . . . : the creation of a new nation with a specific relation to other nations, that she would be their 'blessing'" (ch. 28, p. 2). In terms we used earlier, Abrahamic religion is no longer an effort to perfect Cain's offerings, but an effort to redeem his being on earth. In Brueggemann's words, it is illustrated in Israel's efforts, under Nehemiah, to "stop this taking of interest, [to] restore . . . their fields, their vineyards" (ch. 1, p. 11).

Augustine's distinction of a city of God and city of the world does not reflect a dyadic theo-politics; it responds to a dyadic secular politics. In these terms, his distinction serves the eschatology and practice of Abrahamic as well as Christian theo-politics

As interpreted by Jenson and by Jean Elshtain, Augustine's doctrine of the two cities is surprisingly pertinent to Abrahamic theo-politics. The division of the two cities appears dyadic only from the perspective of worldly politics, for which both the earthly and heavenly cities are crafted by humans: political leaders on the one hand, priests on the other. From the perspective of the city of God, however, which is the present kingdom of heaven, no law of excluded middle can separate earth and heaven, but only the recalcitrant human will. The earthly city is not contrary to the heavenly city by definition, but only if its citizens refuse to give God a place in their hearts and institutions. In Jenson's words, "God intends a *res publica* . . . , with sovereignty and citizenship and mutual duties: . . . [one that] must co-exist with creation." It is only Rome's choice to pursue a politics that is as much at odds with creation as with the divine legislator, so that is therefore "destabilized" by its own "inner contradiction" (ch. 28, pp. 5, 6). In Elshtain's words, Augustine's city "creates barriers to the absolutizing and sacralizing of any political arrangement" (ch. 3, p. 11), condemning the "lust for dominion that distorts the human personality" (p. 13). Like "God's city," Abrahamic theo-politics also comes to resist and subvert the violence of Rome's politics: that is, of the totalizing politics of any tower-nation or tower-empire.

Hauerwas notes that, for Bonhoeffer, "the Creator does not turn from the fallen world but rather God deals with humankind in a distinctive way: 'He made them cloaks.'" For Abrahamic theo-politics, these cloaks become the words of the Noahide covenant, through which humanity is to repair its own troubled creatureliness. Bonhoeffer has a term for the distinction: the words represent the "orders of preservation" (or, later, "the mandates"), through which humanity is to be led away from the "distorted passions" and violent politics of the "orders of creation" (ch. 10, p. 9).

The point, I take it, for both Augustine and Bonhoeffer, is that God alone redeems humanity from its errant creatureliness: "I and not an angel" (as God speaks in the Passover Haggadah; and Brueggemann, ch. 1, p. 8). That is why God's presence must itself join CHAI participants together under Abraham's Tent.

In their empirical life in this world, both Israel and the church display inner tensions and divisions that reflect the dyadic divisions of the secular city. Both Abrahamic and Christian theo-politics labor against tendencies of any of the houses of God to succumb to the temptations of Cain

In Brueggemann's words, ancient Israel's theo-politics was marked by deep tensions between "centralized political authority" and "local authority," between "haves" and "have nots," between autonomous polities and imperial regimes, and generally between "covenantalism" and "totalism" or accommodation to it (ch. 1, pp. 1, 2, 9). This, he suggests, is not a creative tension, but an inner battle between the direct influence of God's word – displayed through Israel's redemptive imagination – and submission to the temptations of Cain. For Hauerwas, this tension is reflected within the church, in the opposition of Jesus' story to the power of Constantinianism (Reno, ch. 21, p. 8). For Abrahamic theo-politics, this is the tension between the twin temptations of totalizing secularism/totalizing orthodoxy and the redeeming work of Abraham's covenant, what Bonhoeffer calls sanctified politics – provided, that is, that this "covenant" or this "sanctified politics" refers to the divine presence in our theo-politics, and not to our own conceptualizations of it or desires for it, no matter how well intentioned these may be.

Afterword

Yes, indeed, I say to fellow Jews, look what they have done to us. But we have suffered more than a loss of flesh and place. It was a loss of time, an end of a time. And such a loss brings us, sadly but with eyes forward now, to another time, if we are prepared to enter it. If not, I fear that the terms of a previous drama can only be replayed, one way or another. That very time is dead; I, at least, will not ask my daughters to re-enter it. Will there be another time? Such questions are answered in the doing, which means with faith, and ours has always been a faith born of corporate call, Hear O Israel, the "hearing" of which has always entailed "knowing" as well. Doing, trusting, hearing, belonging, knowing: these activities have never passed away from us. To the contrary, we have always rediscovered their power just after we have died, I mean just after our time itself passed away, and in the rediscovery we felt the light of another time coming to us, the light in which we see light and a new day. No final day (we know darkness is still with us), just another day, another renewal, with its own newness. This time, the newness – always strange in first appearance – appears this way: that the call to Israel is also a call to Abraham: Hear, O Abraham! Some of us hear it this way. We do not yet know what it means, except that, without limiting or interrupting the call to Israel, it suggests an additional, expanded belonging as well. More are called: not in place of, but with Israel. If so, I suspect they will not be the same, in this time, nor will we.

Notes

1   Throughout the essay, the biblical translations are my own, with some inspiration from *TANAKH, The Holy Scriptures* (Philadelphia and Jerusalem: Jewish Publication Society, 1985).
2   A website for CHAI is available at www.childrenofabrahaminstitute.org. CHAI's sponsoring organization is the Society for Scriptural Reasoning, whose website and journals are available at http://etext.lib.virginia.edu/journals/ssr/ and http://www.depts.drew.edu/ssr/nationalssr/. Among the founders of these groups are David Ford, Daniel Hardy, and Peter Ochs.
3   See George Lindbeck's non-supersessionist theology of the Church as Israel, illustrated, for example, in "The Church," in James Buckley (ed.), *The Church in a Postliberal Age* (London: SCM, 2002), 145–65, and "What of the Future? A Christian Response," in Frymer-Kensky et al., *Christianity in Jewish Terms* (Boulder, Col.: Westview, 2000), 357–66.
4   This is a mere sampling from chapters I have had the opportunity to read prior to publication; it is not intended to be necessarily representative of the collection as a whole, nor to carry the endorsement of the authors of these chapters. I offer the sampling only to suggest how Christian theologians could conceivably endorse Abrahamic theo-politics within the bounds of a specifically Christian theological mission.

Index of Names and Subjects

Note: Page references in **bold** type indicate main discussions of major topics.

Abelard, Peter   372, 375 n. 3
Abraham
  and history of Israel   409, 410
  Tent   519–20, 528–9, 531, 533
  and theo-politics   **520–34**
  see also Judaism
absolutism   442–3
  and Calvin   74
  in Israel   9–11, 15–16, 18–19, 448
  and Temple   169, 171
Abu-Rabi', Ibrahim   515
accommodationism
  in ancient Israel   17–18, 28
  and the church   21, 23, 30, 32–3, 403
  and culture   203
  and Temple   177
Ackermann, Denise   283
action, transformative   217, 460
Adorno, Theodor   231–2, 243–4, 457–8,
    461, 464
Afanasiev, Nicolas   95, 98
Africa
  and feminist theology   196, 197–9,
    201–2, 206
  indigenous churches   452
  and spirits and mediums   377, 378,
    384, 388
agape, in Niebuhr   185
agency, political
  in feminist theology   218–19, 222, 223

  in Gutiérrez   293
  in Hauerwas   305
  in Niebuhr   180–1
Aldred, Joe   276
Al-Faruqi, Ismail   511–12
Al-Ghannoushi, Rashid   515
Al-Mawdudi, Sayyid Abul A'la   509, 511,
    512
Al-Siba'i, Mustafa   508, 512, 513
alienation: in Augustine   39
  in critical theory   462, 468
  and the cross   371, 374
Althaus, Paul   115
Althaus-Reid, Marcella   197
Ambrose of Milan   83
Amos (prophet)   16, 27
Anabaptist movement   21, 69–71,
    368
analogy
  in Barth   131–3
  in Scotus   473–5
anarchism
  and democracy   186–7, 439–40
  and revolt   113
Anastasios, Archbishop of Tirana   104
Anderson, Victor   277
androcentrism   197–8, 204, 210,
    214–16, 217–18, 222, 343
Anglicanism, and political theology   165,
    177

Anselm of Canterbury, and atonement
    366, 369–70
anthropology, theological
    of Augustine   36–8, 46, 47, 183
    in feminist theology   211, 215
    of Gutiérrez   292
    of Niebuhr   183, 188, 189, 401
    of Schmitt   113–15
anticipation, in Moltmann   229–30, 232,
    238
antisemitism   108–9, 128, 396
anxiety, in Niebuhr   183–4, 188
apartheid
    in black theology   274–5
    and the churches   445, 446, 492
    in feminist theology   196
    and ordering of creation   335
apocalypticism, in Metz   251–2
Aquinas, Thomas   **48–60**
    contemporary relevance   48, 58–60
    and logic and metaphysics   48, 49–51
    and natural law   48, 54–8, 155, 340
    and representation   479
    and scripture   49, 51–2
    and society   55–6, 398
    Summa Theologiae   49, 54–5
    and tradition   49
    and truth   48, 49–54, 58–9
Arendt, Hannah   44, 78
Arguedas, José María   289
aristocracy
    in Aquinas   56
    in Calvin   73
Aristotle   78, 170, 398, 442
    and Aquinas   49, 55–6
Arjakovsky, Antoine   96
Arnold, Thomas   165
asceticism, in early church   23–4
Asian political theologies   **256–69**
    Dalit theology   265–7
    and feminist theology   196, 198–9,
        200, 203–4, 205, 267–9
    and liberation theology   256–63
    Minjung theology   177, 263–5
    and poverty   257–8, 260–3, 268–9
    and religiousness   258–60, 261, 267
Asian Theological Consultation   258
Assmann, Hugo   236, 430
associations, intermediate, in Temple   172
Assyrian Empire   8, 16, 395
Atlantic, and radicalism   384, 386–7, 389

atonement   205, **363–75**
    in Barth   366, 367, 371, 372
    exemplary theory   372–3
    see also forgiveness; justification;
        reconciliation; redemption; sacrifice;
        solidarity
Augustine of Hippo, St.   32, **35–47**
    and the church   312, 412–13, 415,
        416, 435–6
    The City of God   36, 42–3, 65, 82–3,
        408, 423–4, 435–6
    Confessions   35, 37, 307
    De Trinitate   382
    on eschatology   408, 412–13, 414, 415
    on the Eucharist   81, 413, 436
    on human nature   36–7, 182
    and "ontology of peace"   368
    on predestination   71
    on the self   36–8, 47
    on social life   38–41, 46
    on the Trinity   325, 475
    on the two cities   36, 41, 42–4, 65,
        82–3, 87, 120, 397–8, 414, 532
    on war and peace   36, 44–6
Aulen, Gustav   366
Auschwitz
    and Metz   244–5, 248
    and Moltmann   373
authority
    in Augustine   39–40, 397–8
    in Calvin   72–4
    of the church   62–4, 167, 358–9,
        397–9, 404, 492
    local v. central   8, 9, 18, 533
    in Luther   62–4
    in monotheism   321, 323
    in northern feminist theology   217
    in Schmitt   112, 113
    of the state   133, 145, 169, 186,
        397–9, 427–8, 488

Babylonian Empire   8, 395, 411
Badiou, Alain   472, 478–81, 482–4
Bainton, Roland   62
Banner, Michael   177
baptism
    and Anabaptist movement   70
    in early church   23, 24, 148 n. 2,
        396
    and egalitarianism   88, 191, 451
    in Hauerwas   303, 312

Barmen Declaration (1934)   128–30, 131, 132, 235, 450
Barrett, Leonard E.   276
Barth, Karl   32, **123–34**
  and atonement   366, 367, 371, 372
  and Barmen Declaration   127–30, 131, 132
  and Bonhoeffer   142
  "The Christian Community and the Civil Community"   130–1
  The Christian Life   127, 132, 133
  Christology   351
  and the church   87, 128–30, 131–3
  Church Dogmatics   125, 132, 323, 366
  Church and State   133
  context of his work   123–4
  and covenant and creation   339
  Epistle to the Romans   124, 127, 131, 371
  and ethics   305
  and freedom of God   126, 127
  and God and humanity   126–7
  and human freedom   125, 180
  The Humanity of God   132
  and justification   367
  and male–female relations   323
  politics as parable of kingdom of God   131–4
  and revelation and reason   176–7
  theology and politics   124–6, 143
  and Trinity   415
base communities   257, 263, 269, 451
Basil the Great   93–4, 97, 100, 101
Baum, Gregory   463–4
Bauman, Z.   491
Beauvoir, Simone de   215
Beckford, Robert   271, 276, 278, 282, 284, 390
Bellarmine, Robert   116, 118, 154
Bendersky, Joseph   108
Benjamin, Walter   109, 231, 243–4, 460, 461
Bennabi, Malek   507
Berdiaev, Nicolas   98, 104
Berkes, Niyazi   506
Bernard of Clairvaux, St.   23
Bethge, Eberhard   136, 138, 143, 145
Bible
  in Anglican tradition   165
  and anti-imperialism   382–4
  and Aquinas   49, 51–2

  in black political theologies   278, 280–1
  and ecojustice   205
  and eschatology   407–8
  and formation of Christian character   306
  in Korea   264–5
  in Moltmann   233
  in Northern feminist theology   218, 269
  and ordering of creation   341–2
  in Southern feminist theology   196, 202, 205, 269
  as tool of oppression   196, 271
  see also New Testament; Old Testament
Biko, Steve   275, 284
Bingemer, María Clare   199–200
black political theologies   **271–84**, 389
  and body and sexuality   279–80
  in Caribbean and Britain   271, 275–6, 278–9, 281, 282, 283–4
  and Christology   282
  contemporary   276–82
  and feminism   280
  and hermeneutics   271, 280–1
  and new responsibilities   282–4
  origins and development   273–6
  in South Africa   274–5, 277–8, 280–1, 283–4
  and subjectivity   277–9
  in United States   273–4, 277, 279, 282–4, 299
Blake, William   21
Bloch, Ernst
  and Marxism   455, 459
  and Metz   243–4, 250
  and Moltmann   228, 229–30, 231–2
Blok, Alexander   100
Blumenberg, Hans   114
body
  and creation   44, 333–4
  and subjectivity   37, 279–80
Boesak, Allan A.   275
Boesak, Willa   271, 277
Boff, Clodovis   462–3
Boff, Leonardo   430, 462–3
Bonhoeffer, Dietrich   **136–48**
  Act and Being   136, 143
  and Barth   142
  Christ the Center   144
  and Christology   125, 137, 141–3, 144–5, 342
  Creation and Fall   144

[Bonhoeffer, Dietrich] *cont'd*
　Discipleship　137, 138, 140, 142
　Ethics　137, 139, 140, 145–7
　Letters and Papers from Prison　137, 139,
　　142–3, 147
　Life Together　138, 142
　life and work　136–9
　and ordering of creation　144, 145,
　　341–2, 532
　and plot against Hitler　136, 137–9
　political ethic　143–8, 531, 533
　Sanctorum Communio　136, 137, 138,
　　140–1, 143, 144, 147
　A Testament to Freedom　136
　True Patriotism　148 n. 2
　and visibility of the church　139–43,
　　144–5, 147–8
Bonino　236
Børrenson, Kari Elisabeth　212
Bosch, David J.　273, 486
Boulnois, Olivier　472, 473–4
Bradstock, Andrew　389
Breck, John　95
Briggs, Sheila　216
Britain
　and black political theology　271, 275,
　　278, 282, 283
　and democracy　443
Brown, Peter　36–7, 46
Brueggemann, Walter　395, 531
Brunner, Emil　132, 166
Buber, M.　14
Buddhism, and cosmic religion　259, 264
Bueno, Ronald N.　491
Bulgakov, Sergius　94–8, 103
Bultmann, Rudolf　305, 414, 455
Burke, Edmund　170
Buthelezi, Manas　275
Butler, Judith　222

Cabasilas, Nicolas　99
Cadorette, C.　492
Caird, Edward　166
caliphate　504–5, 506
Calvin, John
　and church and state　71–5
　Institutes of the Christian Religion　71
　and predestination　71
Canaris, Wilhelm　137–8
Cannon, Katie　219
capabilities, human　494–5, 496–8

capital punishment　73, 369, 511
capitalism
　and black political theologies　276,
　　277–8, 283
　in Deleuze　479
　and development　196
　global　498
　in Hauerwas　302–3
　and liberation theologies　257, 259
　in Metz　243–4
　in Moltmann　232
　in Schmitt　112–13
Caribbean, and black political theology
　　275–6, 278–9, 281, 283–4
caritas, in Augustine　40–1, 47
caste system　196, 265–6
Castells, M.　491, 496
Castillo, Otto René　272
Catholic Action　289
centralization, in ancient Israel　8, 9, 15,
　　17, 18, 27
Chaguaramas project　281
change
　in Aquinas　50–1
　and civil society　427–8, 429
　and the Holy Spirit　377, 378, 384–8
character, in Hauerwas　305–7
Chikane, Frank　275
Children of Abraham Institute (CHAI)
　　523–4, 528–30, 532
Chopp, Rebecca S.　220
Christendom
　in Bonhoeffer　143, 147
　and the church　62, 393, 396–9, 403
　and liberation theology　430, 465
　"New"　400
　in Temple　167–8
　see also establishment
Christendom Group (Anglo-Catholic)
　　166–7
Christianity
　and colonialism　196, 197–200, 256,
　　258, 261, 280–1
　contextualized　194, 201
　as counter-cultural　22–4, 32, 368,
　　486
　and democracy　441–3
　Eastern Orthodox　93–105
　as emancipatory　198–9, 462
　Minjung　263–4
　pre-Constantinian　22–4

[Christianity] *cont'd*
  and syncretism 203–4, 263
  as way of living 319–20
Christology **348–61**
  in Aquinas 57
  in Asian theology 260–3, 269
  in black political theologies 282
  in Bonhoeffer 125, 137, 141–3,
    144–5, 342
  Chalcedonian 260–1
  colonial 198–9, 205
  Dalit 267
  and dramatic theology 348–53
  in Metz 253
  in Moltmann 230–4, 351
  in Niebuhr 184–5
  in Northern feminist theology 217–18
  and ordering of creation 342
  and sacrifice 348, 349, 355, 356–8
Chung Hyun Kyung 203–4, 205
church **393–405**
  and authority 62–4, 167, 358–9,
    397–9
  in Barth 125–6, 128–9
  and basic communities 257, 263, 269,
    451
  as body of Christ 97, 309, 379, 415,
    451
  in Bonhoeffer 137, 139–43
  and Christendom 393, 396–9
  and Constantinianism 21, 70, 139,
    147–8, 310–12, 314, 396–7
  as "contrast society" 10, 19, 86–7,
    257, 261, 372, 404
  and democracy 445–8, 450–2
  in dramatic theology 353–4, 356, 361
  and eschatology 118, 312, 412–13,
    415, 416–17, 429, 433
  and evangelism 99, 236
  and feasting 236–7
  freedom 153–4, 156, 159, 429
  in Gutiérrez 402
  in Hauerwas 87, 177, 306–12, 314,
    404–5
  and indirect power 116, 118, 154,
    399–402
  in liberation theology 195, 353, 451
  in Luther 64
  in Metz 401–2
  in Moltmann 234–40
  as new Israel 350, 352, 393–6

  and nonviolence 353
  as political household 77–8
  as polity 76, 86–8, 89, 100, 403–4
  and sanctification 140, 168
  in Schmitt 118, 119
  and sectarianism 404–5, 431
  and society 98–100, 104, 130, 393,
    400, 428–30, 433–7, 445–8
  visibility 139–43, 144–5, 147–8,
    310–11, 416, 417
  and women 217, 451–2
  see also establishment; privatization of
    religion; witness
church and state 393–405, 425
  in Anabaptist movement 21, 70
  in Barth 87, 129–30, 131–3
  in Bonhoeffer 139–47, 342
  in Calvin 71–5
  and democracy 447–8
  in Hauerwas 310–12, 404
  and liturgy 82–4, 86–8, 165
  in Luther 63–6, 67, 70, 72, 139, 232
  in Metz 401–2
  in Moltmann 232–3, 341
  in Müntzer 66–9
  in Murray 150–5, 400
  in Orthodox thought 93, 95, 97–8, 99
  and Roman Empire 22–4, 358–9,
    396–7
  in Schmitt 113
  in South Africa 275, 445
  in Temple 167–70
  in Yoder 191–2
Cicero, Marcus Tullius, and the state 36,
    40, 120, 412
circumcision, female 196, 202
citizenship
  and the church 24, 396, 418–19
  and kingdom of God 411, 416
  in Temple 169–70, 172, 175–6
  and worship 78, 84, 85
civil rights, USA 191, 445
civil society *see* society
civility
  in postmodernity 476–7, 480–1,
    482–4
  and representation 477, 480
  and rights 476, 477–9
Cleage, Albert 273–4
cleanness, and postmodernity 476
Clément, Olivier 98

Cohn, Norman   374
colonialism
    and black political theology   276–7
    and exploitation of resources   204,
        280–1
    and sexual theology   197
    in Southern feminist theology   196,
        197–200
    and theology of domination   256, 258,
        261, 264, 266, 280
Comblin, José   456, 464–5
commonwealth, in Augustine   36, 40
communicatio idiomatum   85
communism *see* Marxism; socialism
communitarianism
    in Anabaptist movement   70
    in Müntzer   69
communities, Christian   23–4, 29–30, 32,
        178
    and the Holy Spirit   379–84
    and the individual   321
    intercontinental and intercultural
        389–90
    and order   334–6
    and trinitarianism   320–2, 325, 326,
        330
compassion
    in ancient Israel   11
    in Augustine   41
    in Barth   132
    in black political theology   272
    in Bulgakov   96
    in Evdokimov   95
    in Metz   253
    in New Testament   27, 28
    in Orthodox thought   95, 96, 105
Cone, James   218, 271, 273–4, 277, 283
Conference on Christian Politics, Economics
        and Citizenship (COPEC)   166
conflict
    in Barth   133–4
    in Niebuhr   186, 189
Connell, Francis   157–8
consciousness, black   273, 275
consequentialism, and Niebuhr   189
conservativism
    and Hauerwas   312, 313–14, 341
    and natural law   340–1
Constantinianism   21, 70, 396–7
    in Bonhoeffer   139, 147–8
    in Hauerwas   310–12, 314, 533

constitutionalism, Western   154, 159–60,
        162–3
contract theory
    and covenant   442
    in Milton   24
    and Murray   160
    and Temple   170–1
Courtine, J. F.   472
covenant
    and Abrahamic religions   521, 526–8,
        532
    and Asian Christology   260–3
    and democracy   442
    and doctrine of creation   337–9
    in Israel   11–12, 14, 15–17, 337–9,
        395, 410–11, 526
Coyle, D.   493
creation   **333–45**
    as contingent   336–7
    and ecology   336, 342–4, 345
    and eschatology   334, 345 n. 1
    ex nihilo   336–7, 338, 339, 345
    as good   44, 336, 339, 342, 344–5
    and history and covenant   336–9
    and nature   339–42
    orders   143–4, 333, 334–6, 341–2,
        344–5
    and political theology   344–5
    and redemption   333–4, 338
    restoration   96
    and Sabbath   524, 527
creativity, human, in Niebuhr   183
critical theory   **455–68**
    and history   373
    and Marx   458–61
    and political theology   461–5
    and public theology   465–8
Cromwell, Oliver   75
Crook, Margaret Brackenbury   212
cross
    in Aquinas   54, 60
    in Bonhoeffer   140, 143
    in dramatic theology   350–1
    and forgiveness   372–3
    and justification   367–8
    in liberation theology   260–1, 272, 292
    in Moltmann   230–3
    in Niebuhr   185
    as political symbol   365, 374–5
    and reconciliation   370, 371–2, 374
    and redemption   366

[cross] *cont'd*
  as structure of feeling   364
  see also atonement
Crucifixion *see* atonement; cross
culture, in feminist theology   200–4
Cyprian   23

Dalit theology   265–7
Daly, Mary   212
Davey, Andrew   486, 496
David, king of Israel   27, 410
Davis, Charles   459, 461–2, 467
Davis, Kortright   276, 282
debt
  cancellation   27, 100, 370, 492–3, 498
  consequences   196
decisionism, and Schmitt   110–11, 116,
    117–18
defiance *see* resistance
Deleuze, Gilles   472, 474, 479–81, 482–3
Demant, V. A.   167, 173
democracy   **439–53**
  in Aquinas   56
  in Augustine   413
  in Barth   124, 128
  in black theologies   283
  in Bonhoeffer   146
  and Catholicism   150–63
  and Christianity   441–3
  church as democratic model   450–2
  and critical theology   448–50
  faith communities and civil society
    445–8
  future prospects   452–3
  global   440, 449, 452
  in Hauerwas   303
  and individual conscience   63, 174, 439
  and Islam   514
  liberal   128, 189, 432, 433, 439–40,
    446
  and Luther   63
  and minorities   174
  in Moltmann   233
  and nationalism   174, 449
  nature of   439–41
  in Niebuhr   181, 186–7, 189–90,
    191–2, 401
  participatory   413, 440, 445
  and public theology   431–2
  representative   440–1
  in Schmitt   108, 113

social   128, 439–40, 442
  in Temple   173–5
  and transformation   444–5, 448, 453
  transition to   443–4, 452–3
Demster, Murray   486
dependency theory, and liberation theology
    298
Derrida, Jacques   472, 474, 477, 478,
    479, 481, 483–4
Descartes, René   273
development
  and Asian theology   257
  and feminist theology   194, 195
dialogue, interreligious   522
difference
  and equality   88, 452
  and gender   221
  in Paul   78
  in postmodernism   480–1, 483, 484
  and race   233
  and the Trinity   321, 322, 325, 331
Diggers   377, 384, 385–6, 389
Dignitatis Humanae   152
dignity, human   25, 159, 160, 172, 253,
    290, 360, 446, 494
discipleship
  and forgiveness   372
  in Hauerwas   314
  in Metz   245, 250–1
  in New Testament   29–30, 32
dissent
  in ancient Israel   16–17, 19
  and democracy   160, 211, 447
distribution of resources, in ancient Israel
    8
Dix, Dom Gregory   79, 80–1
doctrine
  in Hauerwas   307–8
  see also atonement; Christology; church;
    creation; eschatology; Holy Spirit;
    Trinity
Dohnanyi, Hans von   137–8
domination, male, in feminist theology
    197–8, 268, 342
domination system, and atonement   366
domination theology, and colonialism
    256, 258, 261, 264, 266, 280
dominion
  in Augustine   36, 39–41, 42, 43, 45,
    412–13, 435, 532
  in Niebuhr   186–7, 190

Donoso Cortés, Juan   111, 114, 401
Dorraj, Manochehr   515
Dostoevsky, Fyodor   94, 99, 114
Douglas, Kelly Brown   279
Doupanloup, Felix   156
dramatic theology   348–53
    and the church   353–4, 356, 361
    and history   358–61
    and sacrifice   356–8
    and salvation drama   348–53
    and social sciences   354–6, 359
"dread" in black theology   282, 390
Dube, Musa   198, 202, 271, 280–1
Duns Scotus   472, 473–5

Eastern Orthodox Christianity   **93–105**
EATWOT see Ecumenical Association of
    Third World Theologians
ecclesiology see church
ecofeminism   204
    and creation   342
    and Jesus Christ   205–6
ecojustice   204–6
ecology
    and creation   336, 342–4, 345
    and natural law   340
economy
    covenantal   12, 16–17, 19
    and globalization   489–90, 493
    in Islam   512–13
    and the state   488
    and subordination of politics   272
economy, political, of ancient Israel
    11–12, 18
ecospirituality, in cosmic religions   258–9
Ecumenical Association of Third World
    Theologians (EATWOT)   257–8, 267
ecumenism
    and democracy   445–7
    and Moltmann   236
    and Murray   157–8
    and Temple   168
egalitarianism
    baptismal   88, 191, 451
    in the church   442, 451
    eucharistic   81–2, 191
    and the Trinity   321, 322
ekklesia, church as   79, 395–6, 405, 450
Eluard, Paul   100
emotion, in Augustine   37
Enayat, Hamid   513

enclosure, and Levellers and Diggers
    385–6
Enlightenment
    and democracy   441
    in Metz   249–50, 253
    and modernity   471
    and sacrifice   348, 356
    and secularization   393, 401
environment
    in feminist theology   268
    in Moltmann   233
    and national sovereignty   449
    in Old Testament   11
epistemology see knowledge
equality
    and difference   88, 452
    in Islam   510–12
    in Niebuhr   185–7, 189
Erskine, Noel   276
eschatology   **407–19**
    Abrahamic   530, 531
    in Augustine   408, 412–13, 414, 415
    and the church   118, 312, 412–13,
        415, 416–17, 429, 433
    and creation   334, 345 n. 1
    and history of Israel   27, 408, 409–11,
        531
    in Metz   244, 250–1, 402, 458, 460
    and modernity   413–14
    in Moltmann   228–30, 231, 458
    in New Testament   22
    in O'Donovan   403–4
    in Orthodox thought   94
    and politics   407–11, 433, 463
    and polity of God   408, 414–16
    see also future; kingdom of God
Eschweiler, Karl   117
establishment   168, 236, 311, 447
Eternal League of God   68–9
ethicists, and Hauerwas   302–3, 305
ethics
    in Aquinas   55, 58
    in Augustine   39, 43
    in Bonhoeffer   144–7
    and creation   339–41
    decision-based   304–5
    in Hauerwas   302–3, 304–6, 307,
        308–9, 341
    Kantian   305
    in Lévinas   477–9
    in Luther   64–5

[ethics] *cont'd*
  and moral consensus   431–2
  in Niebuhr   181, 182–8, 189, 192, 214
  in Northern feminist theology   214, 219
  quandary ethics   304
  situation ethics   137, 305
  see also law, natural
Eucharist
  in Augustine   81, 413, 436
  in dramatic theology   353–4, 357–8
  in early church   79, 80–2, 396
  and Hauerwas   303, 309
  and Luther   84–6
  as sign of mutuality   417–19, 437
  and Temple   168
  and Yoder   86, 87–8, 191
Eusebius of Caesarea   120, 322
evangelism
  in Moltmann   236
  in Niebuhr   192
Evans, James H.   279
Evdokimov, Paul   95, 98–100, 103
evil
  in Augustine   44
  in Hauerwas   309–10
  in Northern feminist theology   214
  in Temple   166
Exodus
  and creation   337
  and creation of Israel   10–11, 12–14, 409
  historicity   10
  in liberation theologies   257, 261, 266, 274
  and redemption   365
experience
  black   280
  in critical theory   460
  and liberation theology   288
  and public theology   466
  and theology   177, 455–6
  of women   201, 211, 213–14, 216, 221–2, 223, 455
expiation, and atonement   367
Eze, Emmanuel Chukwudi   277

Fabella, Virginia, and Oduyoye, M. A.   207
Fadlallah, Muhammad Husayn   509, 515
Fanon, Franz   271

fascism
  and doctrine of creation   335
  and Temple   167, 173, 175
  see also National Socialism
feasting, in Moltmann   236–7
feminist theology, Northern   198, **210–23**
  as critique and reconstruction   216–21
  future prospects   221–2
  historical overview   211–13
  and natural law   340, 341
  and salvation   366–7
  and Southern cultural practices   202
  as theology of liberation   213–14, 289
  and tradition   214–16, 218–20, 223
feminist theology, Southern   **194–207**
  African   196, 197–9, 201–2, 206
  Asian   196, 198–9, 200, 203–4, 205, 267–9
  and Christian symbolism   198–200
  and colonialism and Christianity   196, 197–200
  and cosmic religions   268
  and cultural politics and theology   200–4
  and ecojustice   204–6, 268
  Latin American   195, 197, 199, 201, 204–5
  and Northern feminism   202, 269
  and race   201, 271
  sociopolitical contexts   195–7
Fenton, Joseph   157–8
Fierro, Alfredo   465
Finnis, John   340
Fiorenza, E. S.   210, 215, 216–18, 342, 367, 456, 466
Fletcher, Joseph   137
forgiveness
  and atonement   372–3
  in Augustine   37
  in Barth   129
  in Bonhoeffer   141
  as costly   368, 370
  in dramatic theology   349–50, 352
  and sacrifice   370
  in Yoder   191
Foucault, Michel   220, 271
Francis of Assisi, St.   23
Francis Xavier, St.   266
Frankfurt School *see* critical theory
free will, in Augustine   44

freedom
  in Barth   125, 180
  of belief and worship   152, 154, 446,
    448, 494
  in Bonhoeffer   146
  and the church   429
  and civil society   427–8, 437
  and democracy   439–40, 446
  of God see God
  in Hauerwas   304–5
  in Metz   401
  in Moltmann   236–7
  in Murray   153–4
  in Niebuhr   181, 183–4, 187, 189,
    192–3
  in Orthodox thought   104
  in Temple   172
Frei, Hans   181, 192
Freire, Paulo   373
French Revolution
  and democracy   146, 441, 443
  and popular sovereignty   173
  and separation of church and state
    156, 159
Fretheim, T. E.   11
Freud, Sigmund, and the self   47
Friedan, Betty   212
friendship
  in Augustine   39
  in Gutiérrez   295
  in Metz   252
  in Moltmann   237–8
Fukuyama, Francis   1
fundamentalism
  and Minjung theology   265
  and role of women   200
future
  and critical theory   458, 460–1
  in Metz   244, 250–2
  in Moltmann   228–9, 231
  see also eschatology
Fyodorov, Nicolas   94

Gadamer, Hans-Georg   229–30, 231
Gandhi, Mahatma   265–6, 373
Garaudy, Roger   243–4
Garvey, Marcus   389
Gebara, Ivone   194, 199–200, 204–5
Gelasius I, Pope   83, 153–4, 155
gender
  and class   267–8, 299
  critical theories   221, 340, 452

  and Islam   510, 511, 516
  and monotheism   197–8, 204
  sin as gendered   214
  theological tradition as gendered   218
  and trinitarianism   323
  see also feminist theology, northern;
    feminist theology, southern; patriarchy;
    womanism
generosity, of YHWH   11–12
George, Susan, The Lugano Report   368
German Christians   128, 132, 341
Gillet, Lev   98, 101
Gilson, Etienne   472
Girard, René   354–6, 357, 359, 368–70
Gladden, Washington   182
globalization   486–98
  definition   487–8
  and democracy   440, 449, 452
  and doctrine of creation   335
  economic   489–90, 493
  and eschatology   417, 418
  and feminist theology   196, 204, 206,
    207
  forms of discourse   488–9
  and justice   486–7, 492–3
  and liberative theologies   177
  and mission   486–7, 491–2
  philosophical considerations   493–6
  and theology   496–8
  urban   490–1
Gnanadason, Aruna   203, 206
God
  freedom   9, 126–7, 153, 336–7, 415
  humanity of   98, 103, 104
  and humankind   126–7
  as immanent   204, 343–4, 382
  as nonviolent   351–3, 366
God and Caesar
  and Exodus story   10–11, 12–13, 19
  in Milton   24–7
  in New Testament   27–30, 32–3
  in pre-Constantinian church   22–4
Gogarten, Friedrich   116
good, common
  in Aquinas   56, 57, 58
  in Augustine   412
  in black political theology   272
  in Calvin   74
  and democracy   440, 442, 450
  in faith communities   446
  and liturgy   76
  in Murray   400–1

[good, common] *cont'd*
  in Niebuhr   401
  supernaturalist view   157, 159
  in Temple   172
  in Yoder   190
Gordon, Lewis Ricardo   277
Gospels, and kingdom of God   22, 27–30, 408
Gossman, Elisabeth   212
governance
  in Aquinas   56, 155
  in Calvin   72–3
  divine   192, 409–10
  and doctrine of creation   333
  global   186–7
  in Islam   505–6
  in Luther   63–6
  in Niebuhr   186–7
  see also democracy; socialism
grace
  in Aquinas   57
  events of   482–4
  in Gutiérrez   293, 402
  in Hauerwas   305, 306, 313
  in Luther   62–3, 65, 139
  in Rahner   246–7
Grant, Jacquelyn   218
Green, Laurie   486, 496
Green, T. H.   170
Gregory VII, Pope   83
Gregory XVI, Pope   157
Gregory of Nazianzus   378
Gregory of Nyssa   96, 415
Grisez, Germain   340
guilt
  in Niebuhr   184, 185
  and scapegoating   369, 370
Gundlach, Gustav   117
Gunton, Colin   369
Gurian, Vigen   95
Gurian, Waldemar   109, 119
Gutiérrez, Gustavo   236, **288–300**, 430, 434
  and the church   402
  critique and dialogue   298–300
  on the Holy Spirit   382
  La Casas: In Search of the Poor of Jesus Christ   295–6
  and liberation   292–3, 459, 462–3
  and Medellín   289–90
  On Job   294, 295
  and political theology   462–3
  and preferential option for the poor   288, 290–2, 294–7, 299–300, 430
  and spirituality   293–8
  A Theology of Liberation   257, 288, 290, 297, 298, 462
  The Truth Shall Make You Free   299
  We Drink from Our Own Wells   294

Habermas, Jürgen   348, 356, 466–7
Ḥadīth   505
Halévy, Elié   363
Halkes, Catharina   212
Hall, Stuart   279
han, in Minjung theology   264
Harakas, Stanley   95
Haraway, Donna   222
Harnack, Adolf von   153
Haroutunian, Joseph   381
Hartsock, Nancy   221
Hartt, Julian   162
Hashmi, Sohail   505
Hauerwas, Stanley   **302–14**, 433, 532
  Character and the Christian Life   304–6, 311
  and the church   87, 177, 306–12, 314, 404–5
  and command   304–5
  and conservatism   312, 313–14, 341
  and Constantinianism   310–12, 314, 533
  and ethics   302–3, 304–6, 307, 308–9, 341
  and liberalism   307–8, 311, 312–14
  and Niebuhr   181, 188–90, 191
  With the Grain of the Universe   310
Hay, C., and Marsh, D.   488
Healy, Nicholas   405
Hefner, Philip J.   333
Hegelianism
  and Moltmann   231
  and Temple   165, 170, 176
Heidegger, Martin   474–5, 479, 482
  and Metz   249, 251
  and Moltmann   229, 231
  and Rahner   248
Held, David   452
Hengel, M.   365, 369, 373
Henry, Paget   279
Henson, Herbert Hensley   176
hermeneutics
  in black political theologies   271, 280–1
  in feminist theology   216–20

[hermeneutics] *cont'd*
  and hermeneutical circle   290, 359
  of suspicion   216–17, 278
Herwegen, Ildefons   116
Hicks, D.   498
hierarchy
  and anti-imperialism   383–4
  in the church   63, 80, 207, 210, 417,
    443, 451–2
  and creation   338, 367
  and trinitarianism   322–3
Hilary of Poitiers, St., and the Trinity
    324–5
Himes, Michael and Kenneth   431–2
Hinga, Teresa M.   198–9
Hinkelammert, Franz   370
Hirsch, Emmanuel   116, 127
historicity
  and Metz   244–5
  and Old Testament   7, 10
history
  in black political theologies   272
  and creation   336, 337–8
  in dramatic theology   353–4, 358–61
  "end" of   1
  in Hauerwas   309–10
  in Islam   504–5
  in liberation theology   195, 245, 290,
    293, 294, 373–4
  in Metz   247, 250–2
  in Moltmann   229–30, 373
  in Niebuhr   184–5, 187–8, 192–3
  in Temple   176
  see also eschatology
Hitler, Adolf
  and Barth   124–5, 127, 128–9, 132,
    143
  and Bonhoeffer   136, 137–9, 143
  and ordering of creation   335, 341
  and Schmitt   108, 115
HIV/AIDS   196, 279, 283
Hobbes, Thomas
  and Augustine   35
  and Schmitt   111, 116, 118–19
  and Temple   171
holism, in Gutiérrez   292–3
Holy Spirit   **377–90**
  in Aquinas   57
  and atonement   372
  in the Bible   378–80
  and the church   97, 405

as comforter   379–80
  in dramatic theology   352–3
  in early Jesus movement   382–4
  as empowerer   379, 496
  in feminist theology   382
  as interreligious   390
  and liberating change   377, 378, 384–8
  in liberation theology   382, 388–9, 390,
    433
  and mystical politics of liberation
    378–84, 388–90
  as person or power   380–2
  and revolts and resistance   377–8,
    384–8
hooks, bel   277
hope
  in Augustine   47
  in critical theory   458, 467–8
  in Metz   244–5, 248–9, 252–3
  in Moltmann   227, 229–30, 231, 373,
    457
Horkheimer, Max   231, 243, 375 n. 12,
    458, 459–61, 467–8
Hosea (prophet)   28
Hourani, Albert   508
household, political   77–8
Hromadka, J.   126
Huber, Ernst   108
Huber, Wolfgang   148 n. 4
human nature
  in Aquinas   55–8, 398
  in Augustine   36–7, 182
  in Barth   126–7, 132
  in Bonhoeffer   147
  in Bulgakov   97
  and *imago dei*   38, 174, 334, 340, 343,
    360, 524
  in medieval thought   476
  in modernity   476–7
  and natural law   340–2
  and nature   343–4
  in Niebuhr   180, 183, 185, 188
  and participation in the divine purpose
    304, 305, 338, 360
  and political responsibility   180–1, 183,
    187, 188–93
  as sinful   525–6
  in Temple   170–1, 172
  unity and diversity   335
  see also dignity; freedom; perfectibility;
    relationships

human rights
  in Barth   124
  in black theology   283
  in Bonhoeffer   146–7
  and capabilities   495
  and civility   476, 477–9
  and democracy   433, 440
  and duties   174
  in Islam   510–11, 512
  in Niebuhr   189
  in Temple   174
humanism
  and Barth   132
  and Hauerwas   313
  and postmodernism   481
  and Temple   169
Humphreys, Lee   18
Hunter, Shireen   516–17
Hurston, Zora Neale   219
Hutterites   69–71

idealism
  Hegelian   165, 170, 176
  and Niebuhr   180, 187
identity
  cultural   200–4
  multiple   486, 495–6, 497–8
  political   78
ideology, and theology   297, 371–2,
    455–7, 460, 463–5, 467
Ignatius of Antioch   79
imagination, in Moltmann   231
imago dei   38, 174, 334, 340, 343, 360,
    524
imitation see mimesis
imperialism
  and anti-imperialism of Jesus movement
    382–4
  and Augustine   36, 38, 44–5
  Christian   198–9, 271, 280–1, 283
  and Islam   506–7
  and Israel   8, 9, 10, 17–18
  and Niebuhr   187
  see also colonialism
Incarnation
  in Badiou   482
  in Bonhoeffer   142–3
  and creation   337, 343
  in liberation theology   260–1
  in Metz   243, 460
  in Moltmann   328

  in Murray   153–5
  in Orthodox thought   94–5, 96, 98,
    103, 104
  and Temple   166, 176
inculturation   487
  and Asian theology   260, 266
India see Dalit theology
indifferentism   157–8
indigenization   260, 266
individualism
  and democracy   443, 446, 450
  and Henson   176
  and Reformation   63, 167
  and Social Gospel   182
  and the Trinity   330
inequality, in ancient Israel   8
Institute for Contextual Theology (ICT)
    275
Irigaray, Luce   221
Isasi-Diaz, Ada-Maria   213, 219
Isidore of Seville   46
Islam   **503–17**
  and equality   510–12
  history   504–5
  and impact of the West   506–7
  and liberation   509–10
  "political"   503
  and political theology   503–4, 515–16
  and poverty   512–13, 516
  and protest   513–15
  and revolts and reforms   507–8, 515
  and sociopolitical justice   503–17
  sources of political thought   505–6
Israel, ancient
  as "chosen"   10, 128, 307, 394–5
  and church as new Israel   350, 352,
    393–6
  as "contrast society"   10
  and covenant   11–12, 14, 15–17,
    337–9, 395, 410–11, 526
  and eschatology   408, 409–11
  and monarchy   8, 15, 27, 395,
    409–10
  as political community   7–8, 13,
    410–11, 533
  and theological community   9–10, 531

Jantzen, Grace   218
Jayawardena, Kumari   195
jealousy, interreligious   525–7, 529
Jeremiah (prophet)   16–17, 27, 29, 351

Jesus Christ
    in black political theology   272
    in colonial imagery   198
    and covenant   337
    as Dalit   266–7
    in ecofeminist theology   205–6
    as empowerer   198–9, 313
    as friend   237–8
    in Hauerwas   307–8
    humanity   148, 217, 333
    and identification with the suffering
        217–18
    as a Jew   396
    in liberation theology   260–3, 269, 293
    message of judgment   350
    and proclamation of kingdom of God
        22, 27–30, 349–50, 351–2, 353, 411
    as prophet   28–9, 199
    and the state   31
    see also Christology; Incarnation;
        Resurrection; Trinity
John the Baptist   28, 29, 377
John Chrysostom   93–4, 97, 100
John of Patmos   29
John Paul II, Pope   100
Jones, E. Stanley   373
Jones, L. Gregory   372
Jones, S.   216
Jones, William R.   274
Josephus, Flavius   28
Jubilee   27, 278, 284, 389
Juche philosophers   265
Judaism   519–33
    and eschatology   407, 417
    and political theology   244–5, 530–3
    and theo-political action   520–30
judgment, in message of Jesus   350
just war theory
    and Augustine   36, 44–6
    and Calvin   74
    and Niebuhr   189
    and Schmitt   118
    and Temple   175
justice
    in ancient Israel   27–8
    in Aquinas   56–8
    in black political theology   272, 277
    comparative   46
    distributive   512–13
    and globalization   486–7, 492–3
    Islamic perspective   503–17

    in Moltmann   233–4, 458
    in Niebuhr   169, 184–8, 189
    in Northern feminist theology   220, 299
    in Orthodox thought   93, 100, 104
    philosophical considerations   493–6
    restorative   277, 368, 444
    in Temple   169, 174
    and worship   295
    see also ecojustice
justification
    and atonement   367–8, 370
    by faith   62, 65, 186, 367
    in Hauerwas   304
Justin Martyr   23

Kaas, Ludwig   108
Kairos Document   26, 275
Kant, Immanuel   305, 320
    and epistemology and ontology   472,
        484
    and Metz   243, 248, 250
Kanyoyo, Musimbi R. A.   201–2
Kaufman, Gordon   217, 343
kenosis
    in liberation theology   292
    in Orthodox thought   95
Kern, Kiprian   101
Keynes, John Maynard   490
Kierkegaard, Søren   114, 183
Kim Yong-Bock   177
King, Ursula   218
kingdom of God
    as Abrahamic   531
    in Barth   131–4
    in Bonhoeffer   145
    in dramatic theology   349–50, 351–2,
        353, 356, 358
    and eschatology   407–8, 411, 414–16,
        418, 431
    in liberation theology   195, 348,
        353
    in Metz   249
    in Moltmann   229, 235, 236
    in Müntzer   69
    in Niebuhr   183
    in Orthodox thought   94
    in proclamation of Jesus   22, 27–30,
        33, 349–50, 351–2, 353, 411
    and salvation   370
    and Social Gospel   182
    in Temple   168

Kirk-Duggan, Cheryl   284
Klepinine, Dimitri   101, 102–3
knowledge
   in Augustine   38
   in feminist theology   215–16,
      218–20
   and modernity   472–3, 479
   and salvation   259
   subjugated   271
Knox, John   74
Kodalle, Klaus-Michael   148 n. 4
Koenen, Andreas   108
Kojève, Alexander   109
Korea *see* Minjung theology
Koyama, Kosuke   371–2
Kunnie, Julian   278
Kuran, Timur   514

Lamb, Matthew   466
Lampe, G. W.   379
language
   in Augustine   37–8, 39, 40
   gendered   330
   in Northern feminist theology   215,
      217, 223
Las Casas, Bartolomé de   296
Latin America
   and feminist theology   195, 197, 199,
      201, 204–5
   see also liberation theology
Latino/Latina theology   211, 213,
      299–300
Latour, Bruno   471
Lauermann, Manfred   109
law
   canon   65, 112
   and covenant   339
   divine   55–7
   Islamic   513, 514, 516
   in Schmitt   112
law, natural
   in Aquinas   48, 54–8, 155, 340
   in Barth   131
   as conservative   340–1
   and creation   334, 339–42, 345
   in Murray   151, 154–5, 157–8, 160,
      161–3, 400
   "new"   340
   and Schmitt   116, 117–18
   in Temple   167, 173, 176, 178
Lawrence, Stephen   284

legitimation
   in Bonhoeffer   145
   by civil society   427, 441
   and globalization   487
   by Israelite temple   8, 15, 27–8
   in Schmitt   112–13
Leo XIII, Pope   154, 157, 159
Levellers   211, 377, 384, 385, 386–8,
      389
Lévinas, Emmanuel   477–9, 481, 483–4
Lewis, Bernard   506–7
liberalism, political
   and Bonhoeffer   145–6
   and Calvin   75
   and the church   393, 432
   and Hauerwas   312–14
   and Murray   159–60, 162
   and Niebuhr   176, 189, 400
   and O'Donovan   436
   postmodern   482
   purposiveness of society   336
   and Schmitt   108, 113–15, 117
   and Temple   167
   and theology   1, 213, 486, 494
   and truth and power   59–60
liberalism, religious   116
   and Bonhoeffer   140–2, 145
   and democracy   442
   and feminism   213
   and Hauerwas   307–8, 311, 314
   and sacrifice   357
liberation, in Islam   509–10, 516
liberation theology   177
   and Asian Christianity   256–63
   and black theology   274, 389
   and Christology   260–3, 348
   and the church   195, 353, 451
   critiques   298–300, 402
   and the Holy Spirit   382, 388–9, 390,
      433
   and Islam   515–16
   and kingdom of God   195, 348, 353
   method   288, 299–300, 456, 462–3
   and Metz   245
   and Moltmann   236
   and natural law   340
   and Northern feminism   207, 213–14,
      216, 219–21, 299, 389
   origins   289
   and political theology   463–4
   and praxis   290, 294–8, 462

[liberation theology] *cont'd*
  and secularization   402
  and socialism   257, 289, 340, 442,
    462–3, 465, 516
  and solidarity   373
  and Southern feminism   195, 200, 201,
    203–4
  and state and civil society   430–1
  see also Gutiérrez, Gustavo
liberative theology *see* liberation theology
Libertatis Conscientia   298
Libertatis Nuntius   298
life, eternal   414–16
Lilburne, John   24
Lindbeck, George   425
Linebaugh, Peter, and Rediker, Marcus
    384, 385–6, 387–8
liturgy   **76–89**, 165
  and civil religion   82–4
  in dramatic theology   353–4
  as enactment of memory   9, 10, 14
  in Gutiérrez   295–6
  and household polis   77–8
  and loss of the offertory   80–2
  in Moltmann   235
  Orthodox   93
  as political   76, 77–80, 84–8, 89, 395
  as public   78–80
  and service   102
  see also Eucharist
Lohfink, Gerhard   394
Lonergan, Bernard   271
love
  in Augustine   41, 43–4, 45–6
  in Evdokimov   95, 99
  in Hauerwas   307
  in liberation theologies   261–2, 294,
    295, 297–8
  in metacosmic religions   259
  in Niebuhr   181, 184–8, 189
  and ordering of creation   341
  in Schmitt   177
  in Skobtsova   95, 101–3
  and Social Gospel   182
  in Temple   169
Lowe-Ching, Theresa   280
Löwith   231
loyalty to state   108, 199
  in Hauerwas   314
  and Murray   163
  in New Testament   32–3

  and Niebuhr   184, 189, 192
  and Temple   170
Loyola, St. Ignatius   373
Ludlow, J. M.   166
Luther, Martin   32, 62–6
  *Against the Murderous and Thieving Hordes
    of Peasants*   66
  and church and state   62–6, 67, 70, 72,
    139, 232
  and the cross   371–2
  and Eucharist   84–6
  and justification by faith   62, 65,
    367–8
  and rebellion   65–6
  and three estates   84–6
  Von weltlicher Oberkeit   63–4
Lutheranism
  and power of God   306
  and two-kingdom tradition   64–5,
    143–5, 169, 486

McFague, Sallie   217, 220, 343, 382
McGrath, Alister E.   64–5
Machiavelli, Niccolò   35, 109, 167–8
MacIntyre, Alasdair   177–8, 424–5
MacKinnon, Donald   167, 176
Madison, James   384, 387
Maimela, Simon   275
Mallarmé, Stéphane   481
Mananzan, Mary John   195, 197, 199
mandates, in Bonhoeffer   145, 342,
    532
Marcuse, Herbert   458, 464
marginalization
  in ancient Israel   8
  in black political theologies   271
  of the church   150, 393
  and liberative theologies   177, 300
  in Moltmann   233
  in Southern feminist theology   194,
    198–9, 201
Mariátegui, José Carlos   289
Marion, Jean-Luc   472
Maritain, Jacques   399–400, 401
Markus, Robert   42
Marley, Bob   271, 276, 377–8
Marsilius of Padua   83
martyrdom
  in early church   23, 24, 31, 32, 374
  and justification   368
  sacrifice as   358

Marx, Karl
  and the church   97
  and critical theory   455, 458–61,
    463–4
  and history   336
Marxism
  and black theologies   280, 282
  and Bloch   455, 459
  and Deleuze   479
  and eschatology   417, 448
  and Juche philosophers   265
  and liberation theology   195, 201, 266,
    298, 340, 462–3
  and Metz   243
  and Moltmann   228
  in Orthodox thought   94, 95–6
  and Schmitt   113
Mary, Blessed Virgin
  in colonial imagery   198, 199–200
  in feminist theology   268
  in New Testament   29
  as Our Lady of Guadalupe   200
Massignon, Louis   503–4
Maurice, F. D.   166
Maurras, Charles   119
Medellín conference of bishops   289–90
Meier, Heinrich   109, 110, 113–14, 118
memory
  and cult of saints   374
  in Hauerwas   308
  and liturgy   9, 10, 14
  in Metz   244–5, 248, 252
  in Moltmann   227, 229–30, 231
Men, Alexander   104
Methodism, and atonement   363–4
Metz, Johann Baptist   **241–53**
  and the church   401, 429, 457
  critiques   253
  and eschatology   244, 250–1, 402,
    458, 460
  and fundamental theology   242, 243,
    245–53
  and Moltmann   227, 232, 236
  and political religion   434
  and productive noncontemporaneity
    242–3
  and Rahner   242, 246–9, 253
  and theodicy   249–50, 253
Meyendorff, John   95
Micah (prophet)   16
Michel, Ernst   119

Milbank, John   87, 177, 372, 433
Milton, John, *Tenure of Kings and Magistrates*
    22, 24–7, 31
mimesis   481
  and violence   45, 354–6, 360, 368–70
Minjung theology   177, 263–5
Mintjes, H.   513
mission
  and globalization   486–7, 491–2
  shared   529
  urban   491, 496, 497–8
missionary movement, and colonialism
    197–8, 256, 258, 261
Moberly, R. C.   372
modernity
  and black political theology   272, 273
  and democracy   441, 450
  and dichotomies   204, 519–21
  and epistemology   472–3, 479
  and eschatology   413–14
  and Islam   503
  and liberation theology   431
  and Metz   243–53
  and ontology   472–3, 474, 479–81,
    483
  and political theology   429–30, 434,
    468
  and public theology   465–6
  and Rahner   242
  and representation   471, 473, 475–7,
    479–80
  and secularization   471
modernization
  and Islam   506–7
  and Metz   242
  and role of women   200
Moltmann, Jürgen   **227–40**, 429, 457
  and atonement   372, 373
  Christology   230–4, 351
  The Church in the Power of the Spirit
    234–5
  The Coming of God   230, 237
  The Crucified God   230–1, 237, 373
  ecclesiology   234–40
  eschatology   228–30, 231, 458
  and the ideal and the concrete   227
  on memory and hope   227, 229–30,
    231, 373, 457
  and order   234, 341
  and political religion   434
  and praxis   459

[Moltmann, Jürgen] cont'd
  and revolutionary potential of
    Christianity   462
  Theology of Hope   227, 228, 230–1,
    234, 238
  and the Trinity   323–4, 328, 372
monarchy
  in ancient Israel   8, 15, 27, 395,
    409–10
  in Aquinas   56
  in Calvin   73
  and episcopate   80
  of God   320
  and Milton   24–7
  in preaching of Jesus   28
  and revolution   156
monasticism
  as counter-cultural   23, 97, 373
  and egalitarianism   442
  and practical service   101
monotheism
  and authoritarianism   321, 323
  and gender asymmetry   197–8, 204
Montesquieu, Charles de Secondat   170
morality see ethics
Mosala, Itumeleng   280–1
Moses, as prophet   410
Muhammad, Prophet of Islam   504, 505
Müntzer, Thomas, and rebellion   66–9, 70,
    389
Murdoch, Iris   313
Murray, John Courtney   **150–63**, 400
  and Catholic supernaturalists   150–1,
    155–9, 163
  compatibility thesis   150–5, 161–3
  and intercredal cooperation   157–8
  and public philosophy   160–1, 162, 431
  and secular separationists   150–1,
    159–61
  and thesis/hypothesis distinction
    156–7, 158–9
  We Hold These Truths   150–1, 152,
    161–3
Murrell, Nathaniel   281
mutuality
  in Augustine   41, 43, 408
  in early church   24
  and eschatology   407
  in the Eucharist   417–19
  in Niebuhr   185, 188
  in the Trinity   326, 345

mysticism: in Metz   252–3
  private and personal   218
myth, in Bultmann   414

narrative
  and dramatic theology   348–53, 530–1
  in Hauerwas   306–8, 313, 531
National Socialism
  and Barth   125, 128, 132
  and Bonhoeffer   137–9, 143
  and the church   450, 451
  and eschatology   417
  and ordering of creation   335, 341, 345
  and sacrifice   348
  and Schmitt   108–9, 115–17
  and Temple   166, 169, 173
nationalism
  black cultural   273
  and democracy   128, 174, 189, 449
  and feminism   195, 200
nature
  in cosmic religions   258–9, 268
  and creation   339–42
  and humanity   343–4
  and stewardship   206, 334, 343–4
Naumann, Friedrich   132
Nehemiah   17, 18
neo-Marxism   490–1
neocolonialism
  and black theology   282, 283
  and feminist theology   194, 195, 200,
    204
  and Islam   515
Neuhaus, Richard John   431, 433, 434
New Testament   **21–33**
  and Holy Spirit   378–80
  and humanity of God   98, 103, 104
  interpretation   21–2
  see also Gospels; Revelation
Ngugi Wa Thiong'o   271
Niebuhr, H. Richard   181, 192, 315 n. 6
Niebuhr, Reinhold   **180–93**
  critiques   181–2, 188–93
  and feminist theology   214
  and justification by faith   186
  and love and justice   169, 184–8,
    189
  and political responsibility   180–1, 182,
    183, 187, 188–93, 400–1
  and public theology   432
  and Temple   166, 167, 169, 174, 176

Nietzsche, Friedrich
  and Deleuze   479, 481
  and Pilate   58–9
  and sacrifice   356–7
  and the self   47
  and slave morality   365
nihilism
  and Bonhoeffer   146
  and Lévinas   478, 481
Noack, Paul   108
Nobili, Roberto de   266
nonconformity
  and democracy   442, 443
  and feminism   211
  and Milton   24–7
  in pre-Constantinian church   22–4
Nussbaum, Martha   486–7, 491, 494–5,
    496, 497–8

obedience
  in Calvin   72, 74
  in Hauerwas   313–14
  in Müntzer   67–8
  in New Testament   22, 330
  in Schmitt   118
O'Donovan, Oliver   43, 177, 397, 403–5,
    433, 436
O'Donovan, Oliver, and O'Donovan, Joan
    Lockwood   62
Oduyoye, Mercy Amba   194, 197, 201–2
offertory, and lay participation   80–2
Ogden, Schubert M.   515
Old Testament   **7–19**
  and politics   7–8, 448
  and salvation history   14, 393–5
  and theology   9–10
Omri dynasty   15–16
ontology
  and Heidegger   248, 249
  and modernity   472–3, 474, 479–81,
    483
  and Scotus   473–5
oppression
  in ancient Israel   27
  in black political theologies   278, 280,
    299
  in feminist theology   194–6, 197, 201,
    216–17, 222, 299
  and Islam   504
  in liberation theologies   291, 456,
    462–3

"option for the poor"
  and feminist theology   195, 213
  and liberation theology   280, 288,
    290–2, 294–7, 299–300, 430
  in Luke's Gospel   29–30
order
  in Aquinas   56–8, 60
  in Augustine   39–41
  and doctrine of creation   143–4, 333,
    334–6, 341–2, 344–5, 532
  ecological   336
  in Luther   64, 65, 341
  in Moltmann   234, 341
  in Niebuhr   186–7
  of preservation   144, 145, 342, 532
  and social structures   117, 336, 354
Origen   96, 99
Ortega, Ofelia   280, 281
Orthodoxy see Eastern Orthodox
    Christianity
Our Lady of Guadalupe   200

pacifism
  and Bonhoeffer   137
  and Calvin   74
  and Hauerwas   302
  and Hutterites   70, 71
  and Niebuhr   187–8, 191
  and Temple   175–6
pain, social, in ancient Israel   13
panentheism   343
papacy
  and indirect power   399
  and Reformation   62, 65, 259
  and Temple   167
participation
  in the church   78, 210
  in creation   338, 360
  in Hauerwas   304, 305
Pascal, Blaise   183
Paton, William, The Church and the New
    World Order   146–7
patriarchy
  and Augustine   39–40
  and hierarchy   452
  and Northern feminist theology
    215–16, 220, 366–7
  and sacrifice   348
  and salvation   366–7
  and Southern feminist theology   194,
    196, 197, 199, 202, 204, 268, 281

Pattel-Gray, Anne   206
Paul, St.
   and the church   396
   and the cross   365–70
   and the Holy Spirit   379
   and justification   367
   and new political culture   24, 31
   and predestination   71
   and reconciliation   371–2
   and sacrifice   368–70
   and the state   26–7, 31, 32, 89, 171
Paul VI, Pope, *Progressio populorum*   100
peace
   in Augustine   38, 39, 40–1, 43, 44–6
   hermeneutics   530
   ontology of   368, 372
Pentecost   97, 352–3, 356, 372
pentecostalism   390, 491–2, 496
perfectibility   46–7, 180, 185
perichoresis   322, 324, 327–8, 330–1
Persaud, Winston   282
Persian Empire   9, 17–18
personalism, in Orthodox thought   94,
   103, 114
personality, in Temple   166, 169, 172,
   174
Peterson, Erik   111, 118, 120
Pharaoh
   and Solomon   15
   and YHWH   10–11, 12–13, 19
Philips, Dirk   71
Pickstock, Catherine   398
Pieper, Joseph   229
pietism
   in Bonhoeffer   142
   in Hauerwas   305
piety, subversive   283
Pilenko, Elisabeth *see* Skobtsova, Maria
Pius IX, Pope, *Syllabus of Errors*   156
Pius XI, Pope, *Quas Primas*   157
Plaskow, Judith   215, 218
Plato   43, 49, 170, 176
Platonism, of Badiou   481
Plekhanov, Georgi Valentinovich   96
pluralism   349, 482, 498
Pohier, Jacques   337
politics
   in ancient Israel   7–19
   in black political theology   272
   and church as counter-cultural   22–4
   definitions   1, 423, 426

   and economics   272
   and eschatology   407–11, 463
   and friend–enemy distinction   113–15,
     117, 355
   and historicity   7, 10
   interruptive   12–13
   mystical   378, 382–8, 390
   in Northern feminist theology   217
   and order *see* order
   as parable of kingdom of God   131–4
   progressive   323–4, 330, 430
   as rhetorical   19
   as salvific   433
   in Southern feminist theology   194
   as statecraft   426–7, 429–31, 432, 433,
     434–5, 436–7
   theological   9, 10
   as vocation   64, 84–5
Polycarp of Smyrna, St.   33
polygamy   196, 197, 202
Porter, Jean   340
postfeminism   222
postliberalism   424–5, 433–7
postmodernism   37, **471–84**
   and events of grace   482–4
   and representation   475–6, 479–80,
     482
   and Scotus   473–5
   and univocity   471, 472–6, 477,
     479–81
   see also pluralism; virtuality
poststructuralism, and feminist theology
   220, 221, 222
poverty
   in Asian theology   257, 258, 260–3,
     268–9
   and globalization   488
   in Islam   512–13, 516
   in liberation theology   195, 280, 288,
     290–9, 430
   in Moltmann   238–40
   as protest   292
   spiritual   291–2
   and violence   492–3
power
   in Aquinas   52–4, 56, 59–60
   in Augustine   41, 42, 44
   black   273–4, 276
   in black political theologies   272, 273–4
   Christian   303–4, 305, 310, 398–9
   in Hauerwas   302–4, 305, 306, 310

[power] *cont'd*
  in Moltmann 232
  in Niebuhr 183–4, 186–7, 189
  in Northern feminist theology 217
  in Revelation 30–1, 33
  in Schmitt 117–18
  see also sovereignty
power politics, in ancient Israel 8, 10–12, 15
praxis and theology
  in Asian political theology 261–3
  in black political theology 272, 273, 275, 278
  and critical theory 458–60, 461–2, 467
  in feminist theology 220–1
  in liberation theology 195, 290, 294–8, 462–3
  in Metz 251, 457, 467
  in Moltmann 459
  see also liturgy
prayer
  and action 294–5
  and forgiveness 372
  and friendship 238
  and kingdom of God 133
predestination, in Calvin 71
Prenter, Regin 335, 341
preservation, orders of 144, 145, 342, 532
Preston, Ronald H. 177
pride
  in Niebuhr 184, 401
  sin as 214
privatization of religion 457, 488
  and black political theology 272
  and the church 393, 399, 401–2, 417
  and feminism 218
  and Gutiérrez 402
  and Metz 244, 247, 249–50, 401
  and Murray 160
  and the state 426, 429–30, 449
  and Temple 173
promise
  to Israel 410
  in Moltmann 228, 231, 238
prophets
  and democracy 442, 448–9
  and divine governance 409–10
  and divine righteousness 27–9, 410–11
  and eschatology 413
  and the excluded 8

protest, nonviolent 191
Puebla conference of bishops 290

queer theory 221
quietism, and Luther 66
Qur'an 505, 510–13
Qutb, Sayyid 508–11, 512, 514–15, 516

race
  in feminist theologies 201, 271, 299
  in Moltmann 233
racism
  and black political theologies 276, 277, 279, 299
  and fascism 109, 335
  and feminist theologies 195
  and liberation theology 299
radicalism
  of Evdokimov 100
  of Israelite prophets 28
  of Milton 24–7
  and mystical politics 378, 384–8, 390
  of Paul 32
  of Skobtsova 95, 101–3
Rahner, Karl, and Metz 242, 246–9, 253
rahtid (wrath) 271, 278
Ramsey, Paul 189
Rashdall, Hastings 372
Rasmussen, Arne 315 n. 2
Rasmussen, Larry 147, 148 n. 1
Rastafarianism 276, 378
Ratzinger, Joseph, Cardinal 298
Rauschenbusch, Walter, and Social Gospel 182, 307
Rawls, John 495
realism, Christian
  and Augustine 35, 45, 47
  and Barth 124–5, 132
  and Niebuhr 187, 189–90
  and Temple 171–2
reality
  and eschatology 407
  in Hauerwas 305, 531
  in Moltmann 231
reason
  in Aquinas 50–1
  instrumental 112, 349, 466
  and natural law 340
  in Niebuhr 181
  in Temple 165–6, 173, 174–5, 176–8

rebellion
  in Luther   65–6
  and Müntzer   66–9
reconciliation
  and atonement   132, 370, 371–2, 374
  and critical theory   458, 461
  and kingdom of God   349
redemption
  and atonement   365–7
  and the church   435–6
  and doctrine of creation   333–4,
    338
  in liberation theology   195, 200
  and redemptive personhood   367
  in Temple   166
  and victimhood   374
reductionism
  in liberation theology   298–9
  political   434
  in Protestant liberalism   307, 308
Reformation   **62–75**
  and church and state   311, 359
  and individualism   63, 167
  and liturgy   84
  and orders of creation   341
  and person/office distinction   145
  and wars of religion   426
  see also Anabaptist movement; Calvin,
    John; Luther, Martin; Müntzer,
    Thomas
relationships, human
  in ancient Israel   12
  in Augustine   38–41
  and Holy Spirit   381–2
  and nature   342–4
  and trinitarianism   319–21, 323,
    324–31
religion
  as law   371
  political   430, 434–5
  see also privatization
religions
  Abrahamic   **519–33**
  cosmic   258–9, 268
  metacosmic   259–60, 264, 267–8
religiousness, in Asian theology   258–60,
  261, 267
representation, in postmodernity   471,
  473–7, 479–80, 482
res publica, in Augustine   40, 82, 412,
  532

resistance
  in ancient Israel   13, 14, 15–16, 19
  in black political theologies   273,
    274–5, 282
  and Calvin   72, 74–5
  in Hauerwas   309
  and the Holy Spirit   377, 384–90
  in Islam   513–15
  and Müntzer   67–9
  and Niebuhr   186, 187, 190–1
  in Northern feminist theology   220, 222
  and poverty as protest   292
  see also violence
responsibility, political
  and democracy   147, 439–40, 446
  in dramatic theology   359
  and ecology   344
  in Metz   251, 252–3
  in Niebuhr   180–1, 182, 183, 187,
    188–93, 432
  in Northern feminist theology   217
Resurrection
  in Bonhoeffer   142–3
  in dramatic theology   351–2
  in Moltmann   228–9
  as vindication of creation   334
revelation
  and reason   176–7, 245–6, 474
  and rejection of state power   30–1,
    33
rhetoric
  in ancient Israel   19
  rediscovery   47
Ridderbos, Herman   379
righteousness
  in Hauerwas   307, 309
  in Israel   27–9, 410–11
  and justification   367
  and the Trinity   415–16
  through works   304–5, 368
ritual, and structures of feeling   364
Roberts, J. Deotis   271, 273–4
Robinson, J. A. T.   82
Robinson, Marilynne   136–7
Roman Catholicism
  and democracy   150–63, 443
  and liberation theology   289, 298–9,
    492
  and Metz   242, 243, 245–6
  and Schmitt   107–8, 109, 110–11,
    112–14, 115–20

[Roman Catholicism] *cont'd*
  and Southern feminist theology   197,
    199–200
  and supernaturalists   150–1, 155–9
  and thesis/hypothesis distinction
    156–7, 158–9
  see also law, natural; Second Vatican
    Council
Romero, Oscar   358
Roncalli, Angelo (later John XXIII)   120
Rosenzweig, Franz   231
Roubl, William   70
Ruether, Rosemary Radford
  and creation   338, 342
  and experience of women   216, 219,
    455
  and liberation theology   212, 213,
    299
  and salvation   218, 366–7
Runciman, Steven   364
Russell, Lettie   213
Ryan, John   157

sacramentalism
  and Temple   168, 169, 175
  and Yoder   86
sacraments, in Aquinas   57
  church as sacrament   309
sacrifice
  and atonement   368–70, 374
  death of Jesus as   323, 348, 355,
    356–8, 369, 374
  and scapegoat   351, 355, 368–70
saeculum (earthly realm), in Augustine   41,
    42–4
Saiving, Valerie   212, 214
salvation
  and the church   393–4, 396, 403–5,
    413
  and dramatic theology   349–53,
    361
  in feminist theology   366–7
  and kingdom of God   370
  and knowledge   259
  and liberation   293, 458
  in Luther   62–3
  in Moltmann   328
  and politics   433
salvation history   14, 393–8, 399, 401,
    403, 404–5, 526
Samuel, V.   491

sanctification
  in Bonhoeffer   140, 531, 533
  in Temple   168
Sassen, S.   491
Sattler, Michael   70
scapegoat   351, 355, 368–70
Schillebeeckx, E.   459, 460
Schleicher, Kurt von   108
Schleiermacher, F. E. D.   320, 382, 413
Schleitheim Confession of Faith   70
Schmemann, Alexander   95
Schmidt, K. L.   133
Schmitt, Carl   **107–20**, 401
  and antisemitism   108–9
  The Concept of the Political   114–15,
    116–17, 118, 119
  Glossarium   110, 119
  and Hobbes   111, 116, 118–19
  and National Socialism   108–9,
    115–17
  Political Theology   110, 112, 116
  and political theology   355, 423:
    Catholic reception   115–20, 207; and
    legitimation   112–13; as neutral
    diagnostic tool   111–12; and political
    as the total   116–17; and question of
    priority   113–15; writings   110–11
  and Roman Catholicism   107–8, 109,
    110–11, 112–14, 115–20
  Roman Catholicism and Political Form
    110, 112
  Staat, Bewegung, Volk   117
scholasticism, and modernity   472
Scipio   36, 40, 412
scriptures, and Abrahamic theo-politics
    523, 524–30
Second Vatican Council
  and baptism   451
  and feminism   212
  and Gutiérrez   289–90
  and Murray   152
  and Schmitt   119
sectarianism   404–5, 431
secularization   393
  and Barth   126
  and Bonhoeffer   141, 142
  and Gutiérrez   402
  and Metz   243, 401–2, 457
  and modernity   471
  and Schmitt   116, 118
  and Temple   167

Segundo, Juan Luis   463
self *see* subjectivity
self-love, in Augustine   412, 413
self-sacrifice   323, 348, 357–8
self-transcendence, in Niebuhr   183,
    184–5, 188
Sen, Amartya   486–7, 491, 495–6, 497–8
Sens, Council (1141)   375 n. 3
separatism
    and Anabaptist movement   70–1
    and black political theology   271
    and Lutheranism   143–5, 169
    and Murray   150–2, 155–9
    and the New Testament   21
    secular   150–1, 159–61
Seroke, Joyce   497
Servetus, Michael   73
sexism, and liberation theology   267, 299
sexuality
    in black political theology   279–80
    and queer theory   221
    in Southern feminist theology   197, 202
Shabbat, as telos of creation   524, 527,
    531
Shi'a Islam   506, 514, 515
Simeon the New Theologian   100
Simons, Menno   71
sin
    in Abrahamic theo-politics   524, 525
    in Aquinas   57, 58
    and atonement   363–75
    in Augustine   37, 38, 40, 43, 44
    in Gutiérrez   293
    in Niebuhr   183–4, 185–8, 191–2, 401
    in Northern feminist theology   214
    in Schmitt   115
    in Temple   171–2, 175
Skobtsova, Maria   95, 100–3
slavery
    abolition movements   377, 378, 388
    in Augustine   36, 39
    and redemption   365–6, 373
Smith, M. P.   490–1
Smith-Christopher, Daniel   18
Sobrino, Jon, and Christology   253
Social Gospel
    and Hauerwas   307
    and Niebuhr   182, 188
    and Temple   171
social sciences, and theology   354–6,
    359

socialism
    and Barth   124, 132
    and Christianity   486
    and liberation theology   257, 289, 431,
        462–3, 465, 516
    and secularization   487–8
    and Temple   167, 173, 174–5
    see also Marxism
socialism, Christian
    and democracy   442
    eucharistic   88
    and Evdokimov   100
    and Moltmann   232, 233
    and Temple   166, 176
sociality
    in Augustine   38–41, 43, 46
    and democracy   450
society
    ancient Israelite   8
    in Aquinas   55–6, 398
    in Augustine   38–41, 43
    and church   98–100, 104, 130, 393,
        400, 428, 445–8
    "contrast"   10, 19, 86–7, 257, 261,
        404
    and democracy   440–1, 444–5
    emergence   427–8
    and faith communities   445–8
    global   488–9
    in Müntzer   69
    "natural"   341
    and ordering of creation   341–2
    and postmodernism   477–9
    as purposive   336
    and sacrifice   356–8
    and state *see* state and society
    supernaturalist view   157
    in Temple   170, 178
solidarity   245, 485
    and atonement   365, 373–5
    in black political theology   272
    and democracy   442, 450, 452
    in feminist theologies   203, 207
    in Islam   512
    in Israel   17, 410
    in liberation theology   290, 292, 293–7
Sölle, Dorothee   213, 217, 429, 455
Solomon, king of Israel   8, 15, 27, 410
Soloviev, Vladimir   96
soteriology, metacosmic   258, 259–60,
    261

South Africa
  and black political theology 271,
    274–5, 277–8, 280–1, 283–4
  and transition to democracy 444, 445,
    446, 449, 452
  see also apartheid
Southern Agrarians 313
sovereignty
  divine 157, 250
  national 449
  popular 24, 171, 173, 440
Spellman, Francis, Cardinal 152
Spencer, Stephen 176
spiritism, in the Bible 378–9
spirituality
  ecospirituality 258–9
  in Evdokimov 99
  in Gutiérrez 293–8
Stackhouse, Max 432
state
  alternatives to 520
  in ancient Israel 8, 395
  in Augustine 39–40
  in Barth 124
  in Bonhoeffer 342
  in emergent tradition 433–7
  and globalization 487, 495
  inadequacy 520
  and international relations 175–6
  loyalty to 32–3
  as natural growth 170
  and orders of creation 341
  and Paul 26–7, 31, 32, 89
  in Revelation 30–1
  small 8, 9
  "total" 116–17
  and violence 310
  see also church and state; contract
    theory
state and society 400, **423–37**
  and Christian *mythos* 423–4, 428,
    434–5, 437
  and the church 433–4, 435–7
  in dominant tradition 428–33
  and emergence of society 427–8
  and emergence of the state 425–8, 431
  and liberation theology 430–1
  and political captivity of dominant
    tradition 434–5
  and political *mythos* 423, 428–31, 432,
    434–6

in Schmitt 117, 423
  and wars of religion 425–7, 471
stewardship of nature 206, 334, 343–4
story see narrative
Stout, Jeffrey 178
Stuttgart Declaration (1945) 129
Styapel, Wilhelm 116
subjectivity
  in Augustine 36–8, 47
  black political 277–9
  as embodied 37, 279–80
  in feminist theology 221–2
  in Gutiérrez 293
  in Hauerwas 304–6
  in Metz 241, 246, 249, 251, 253
  in Temple 166, 169, 171–2, 174
suffering
  and atonement 368, 373–4
  in black political theology 272
  and colonial Christianity 199
  in critical theory 460–1
  in Gutiérrez 288
  in Metz 244–5, 252–3, 460
  in Moltmann 231–2, 237, 351
  and nonviolence of God 351–3, 366
Sunni Islam 506, 514
supernaturalism, and the state 150–1,
    155–9, 163
symbolism
  "center" 371–2
  and colonialism 198–200
  and feminist theology 215, 223, 268
syncretism 203–4, 263, 390

Tamez, Elsa 201, 367, 370
Tanner, Kathryn 220
Taubes, Jacob 110, 114, 120
Taylor, Mark Lewis 283
technology
  in Asian theology 258–9
  in black political theology 272
  and progress 46
Temple, Frederick 165
Temple, William **165–78**
  background and life 165–7
  Christ in His Church 166, 174
  Christian Democracy 166, 174–5
  and Christianity and politics 170–6
  Christianity and Social Order 167,
    171–2
  Christianity and the State 166

[Temple, William] *cont'd*
  Christus Veritas   166
  Church and Nation   166
  and church and state   87, 167–70
  Citizen and Churchman   167, 169
  Essays in Christian Politics   173–4
  and establishment   168
  evaluation   176–8
  and international relations   175–6
  Mens Creatrix   166
  Nature, Man and God   166, 172
  and Social Gospel   171
  "What Christians Stand for in the Secular
    World"   167
Tertullian   99
theodicy
  in Augustine   44
  in Metz   249–50, 253
Theodosius I, Emperor   83
theology
  contextual   194–5, 201, 206–7, 344,
    389–90, 455, 497
  definition   1
  feminist *see* feminist theology, northern;
    feminist theology, southern
  fundamental   243, 245–53
  liberation *see* liberation theology
  natural   188
  philosophical   217
  public   431–3, 465–8
  social   177
  and social sciences   354–6, 359
  womanist   211, 213, 214–15, 219,
    221, 276, 279, 284
  see also dramatic theology; praxis
theology, political
  Abrahamic   **520–33**
  and Christianity   1–2
  constructive *see* atonement; Christology;
    church; creation; eschatology; Holy
    Spirit; Trinity
  definition   1
  dominant tradition   428–33, 434–5
  emergent tradition   433–7
  Islamic perspective   503–17
  leading figures *see* Barth, Karl;
    Bonhoeffer, Dietrich; Gutiérrez,
    Gustavo; Hauerwas, Stanley;
    Moltmann, Jürgen; Murray, John
    Courtney; Niebuhr, Reinhold; Schmitt,
    Carl; Temple, William
  and legitimation   112–13
  and modern dichotomies   204,
    520–1
  as neutral diagnostic tool   111–12
  political captivity   434–5
  and question of priority   113–15
  sources *see* Aquinas, Thomas; Augustine
    of Hippo, St.; liturgy; New Testament;
    Old Testament; Reformation
  structures and movements *see* critical
    theory; democracy; globalization;
    postmodernism; society; state
  task of   2
  types *see* Asian political theologies; black
    political theologies; Eastern Orthodox
    Christianity; feminist theology,
    Northern; feminist theology, Southern;
    liberation theology
Thiemann, Ronald   432, 433
third world, and theologies of liberation
    256–63
Thompson, E. P.   363, 374
Tillich, Paul   381–2
time, in Metz   251–2
Tolstoy, Leo   367–8
Tommissen, Piet   108
totalism
  and Exodus narrative   10–12
  in Israel   15–16, 18–19, 533
  and Metz   243–4
  resistance to   13, 16, 532
totalitarianism
  and Barth   132
  and the church   417, 443, 446
  and Eastern Orthodoxy   98, 103
  liberal   482
  and Temple   166–7, 169
  and "total state"   116
Tracy, David   217, 221, 465–6
tradition
  in Hauerwas   308, 313–14
  in Moltmann   235
  in Northern feminist theology   214–16,
    218–20, 223
Trent, Council   71
Trinity   **319–31**
  and creation   337, 340, 345
  and democracy   449–50
  difference in   321, 322, 325, 331
  economic   234, 322–3, 327–31
  human participation in   328–31

[Trinity] *cont'd*
  and human relationships   320–1, 323,
    324–31
  immanent   322, 323, 325–7, 330–1
  inflated claims for   321–4
  in Moltmann   323–4, 328, 372
  in Northern feminist theology   217
  as polity   414–16
  relationships within   322, 323–4, 325,
    328
  see also Holy Spirit; Jesus Christ
Troeltsch, Ernst   140–1, 142
truth
  in Aquinas   48, 49–54, 58–9
  in Hauerwas   303–4, 306, 308–9, 310,
    312, 404
  in Nietzsche   58–9
Truth and Reconciliation Commission (TRC;
    South Africa)   277–8, 444
Tutu, Desmond   277
two-kingdom tradition
  and Augustine   36, 41, 42–4, 65, 82–3,
    87, 120
  and Bonhoeffer   143–5
  see also church and state
tyranny
  in Aquinas   56, 60
  in Calvin   73, 74, 75
  in Luther   66
  in Niebuhr   186

United States of America
  and black political theology   271,
    273–4, 277, 279, 282–4, 299, 389
  and Catholicism   150–63
  and civil rights   191, 445
  and consensus   154–5, 159–63
  and democracy   443, 445
  and feminist theology   209–10
  and Hauerwas   310–11
  and individualism   182
  and Latino theology   299–300
  and Niebuhr   181, 182, 187, 188, 189,
    191–2
  and pentecostalism   390
Universal Declaration of Human Rights
    123–4, 233
universalism   132, 394, 497
univocity, and postmodernism   471,
    472–6, 477, 479–81
Urban II, Pope   364

urbanization   488–9, 497–8
Ure, Andrew   363, 370
US Constitution, First Amendment   151,
    154
utilitarianism   305
  and Niebuhr   189
  and Temple   172, 176

Vallejo, Cesar   289
Valliere, Paul   96
Vico, Giovanni Battista   170
violence
  in ancient Israel   13, 531
  in Barth   133–4
  in black political theology   283, 284
  and caste system   266
  and democracy   444
  in dramatic theology   351–3, 357–8,
    359, 368–9
  in Hauerwas   310, 341
  and interreligious relations   526–7, 529
  in Müntzer   68
  in Niebuhr   189, 191
  and nonviolence of God   351–3, 366
  and poverty   492–3
  and resistance   514–15
  and the state   425, 427
  against women   195, 196, 199
  in Yoder   190–1
virtuality, and postmodernity   472,
    479–80, 482–3
virtue
  in Aquinas   48
  in Hauerwas   305–6, 531
vocation, to politics   64, 84–5
Volf, Miroslav   323
voluntarism
  and Murray   160
  and Schmitt   117
von Balthasar, Hans Urs   358
von Weizsäcker, C. F.   359

Walker, Alice   219
war
  in Augustine   36, 44–6
  in Murray   162
  in Niebuhr   188–9
  in Yoder   191
wealth
  in Islam   512–13
  in liberation theology   262, 291–2

Weber, Max
  and asceticism   93
  and Calvinism   71
  and capitalism   196
  and politics   1, 393–4
  and power   82
  and public and private spheres   426,
    429–30
Wedderburn, Robert   388
Welker, Michael   339
Westernization, and Islam   506–7
Westhelle, Vitor   336, 338
"will-to-power"   214, 481
William of Ockham   65
Williams, Delores S.   219, 271
Williams, Lewin   276, 283
Williams, Raymond   333, 338, 364
Williams, Rowan   40–1, 337
Wilmore, Gayraud   283
Wink, Walter   133, 366
Winstanley, Gerard   24, 385–6, 388, 389
Wisdom tradition, in feminist theology
    205–6
witness of the church   19, 29, 435
  in Barth   128, 130
  in Bulgakov   98
  and democracy   448–50, 451
  in Hauerwas   309–10

  in Niebuhr   189–90
  in Yoder   190–1
womanism   211, 213, 214–15, 219, 221,
    276, 279, 284
  and the church   451–2
women see feminist theology, Northern;
    feminist theology, Southern; gender
World Council of Churches   213
worship see liturgy
Wright, N. T.   396

"Year of Release"   11
YHWH
  as generous   11–12
  as holy   13–14, 18–19
  as political agent   9, 10–14, 15
Yoder, John Howard   137
  and the church   86, 87–8, 139, 190–1,
    436
  and history   192

Zehr, Howard   368
Žižek, S.   478
Zizioulas, John   95
Zwingli, Ulrich   70

*Index compiled by Meg Davies (Registered
Indexer, Society of Indexers)*

Index of Biblical References

Old Testament

Genesis
  1: 26 344
  1: 27 524
  1: 28 344
  2: 1 524
  3: 17 524
  3: 24 524
  4: 4–7 525
  4: 8 525
  5: 3 360
  6: 11 526
  8: 21 526
  9 527
  11: 4 527
  12: 1 520, 527
  12: 3 394
  18 528
  18: 1–8 519
  18: 16–17 529
  28: 10–22 528
  37–50 18
  41: 14–57 11
  47: 13–26 11

Exodus
  1: 13–14 13
  1: 17, 19 13
  2: 11–15 13
  2: 23–5 13
  2: 23 13

  3 528
  3–14 379
  3: 4 14
  3: 7–9 14
  3: 11–4: 17 14
  3: 10 14
  5: 1 14
  7–11 14
  14 14
  14: 13–14 14
  15: 1–18 10
  15: 20–1 14
  16: 17–18 11
  19: 5 410
  20 410
  24: 7 522
  35: 31–2 379
  40 528

Leviticus
  16 368
  25 27

Deuteronomy
  6: 10–12 11
  8: 7–20 11
  9: 10 395
  10: 4 395
  10: 19 11
  15 27
  15: 1–18 8, 11
  15: 15 11
  17 27

17: 14ff.   27
18: 16   395
23: 19–20   17
24: 17–22   11
24: 22   11
26: 5–12   266
26: 5   409
30: 14   528
30: 15–18   12
34: 5–12   410

1 Samuel
7–15   8
8   27, 397
8: 7–20   409

2 Samuel
23: 1–2   410

1 Kings
3–11   15
3: 1   15
4: 20–8   8
6–8   15
7: 8   15
7: 14–22   8
7: 48–51   8
9: 16   15
9: 24   15
11–12   15
11: 1–8   15
11: 10   15
11: 26–40   15
12: 1–19   8, 15
16–II Kings 10   15
18   15, 28
21   15–16

2 Kings
9–10   16
16: 1–20   8
18: 14–16   8

2 Chronicles
26: 16–21   16

Nehemiah
5: 10–11   17

Psalms
89   27
132   27

Proverbs
8: 22–31   97

Isaiah
1: 2   526
5: 8–10   8
20   28
25: 7   411
40–55   337
41ff.   526
43: 18–19   411
53   369
53: 2ff.   266
53: 11   367
61: 1–4   8

Jeremiah
1: 10   29
5: 27–9   8
15: 5   351
18: 18–32   351
26: 11   16
26: 16–19   8
26: 16   16
29   83
29: 7   405

Ezekiel
28: 3   19

Daniel
2   68
3: 16–18   19
4: 27   8
7: 27   67, 69

Hosea
2: 14   28

Amos
3: 13–15   16
4: 1–3   16
6: 1–7   16
7: 10–17   16
7: 16–17   16
8: 4–6   16

Micah
2: 1–4   8
3: 12   16–17
4: 3   411

Deutero-Canonical Books

3 Esdras
3: 12   51
3: 19   51

4: 10   51
4: 30   52
4: 35   52
4: 39   52
4: 40   52
4: 43–6   52

Sirach (Ecclesiasticus)
34: 18–22   296

New Testament

Matthew
2: 2   28
2: 16ff.   28
3: 10–11   377
5: 3–12   28, 291
5: 17–18   396
5: 21ff.   371
5: 23   79
7: 12   261, 339
7: 21ff.   28
9: 36   28
10: 42f.   28
11: 2ff.   27
11: 13   28
13: 35   369
14: 14   28
15: 32   28
16: 17f.   28
17: 24–7   25
18: 2   28
19: 14   28
19: 16   322
20: 25–7   25
20: 31   28
21: 5   28
22: 15–22   22
22: 16–21   25
22: 40   261
23   371
23: 26ff.   28
25: 31ff.   3, 28, 239, 371
25: 31–46   239
25: 40   239
27: 54   292

Mark
1: 15   28, 396, 411
8: 29   356

8: 33   356
8: 34   272
10: 18   322
10: 21–7   411
10: 42   27
10: 43   372
12: 1–10   352
12: 10–11   352, 354
12: 13–17   31
13: 9ff.   29
13: 22   322
14: 3ff.   29
14: 29   356
14: 31   356
14: 66–72   356

Luke
1: 76   28
4: 14   383
4: 16   27
4: 18   383
6: 20–3   291
6: 31   339
7: 34   237–8
9: 28–36   528
10: 29–37   261
16   30
18: 18   322
20: 20   25, 31
22: 24–30   190
22: 25   25
23: 2   31
23: 12   355
23: 34   351, 370

John
1: 1–18   337
3: 10ff.   29
4: 16   29
7: 36ff.   29
8: 2f.   29
10: 25ff.   29
11: 49   28
12: 37   355
12: 42   355
12: 43   355
13: 10   29
14: 28   322
15: 1ff.   29
15: 14   237–8
15: 15   238
15: 16   238

17: 11   29
18: 33–19: 22   52–4
18: 36   396
23: 27   29
23: 49   29
23: 55   29

Acts
2   383
2: 7   383
4: 27   356
4: 32   78
5: 29   22
10   30
17: 6   23

Romans
1: 4   353
5   132
5: 18–19   367
5: 20   361
7: 14–25   353
8   386
8: 19ff.   234
12–14   371
12   24
13   26, 31, 64, 67, 73, 76, 139
13: 1–10   22, 25
13: 1–7   275
13: 1   67
13: 3   67
13: 4   73, 89
13: 6   89
15: 25   24

1 Corinthians
2: 8   236
6: 1–7   79
6: 20   365
10: 17–34   418
10: 23   389
11: 17–34   396
11: 22   80
14   70
14: 26   78
15: 25   31

2 Corinthians
8–9   24

Galatians
3: 13   371
3: 26ff.   78

3: 28   23, 266, 269
4: 7   63
6: 14   365, 405

Ephesians
1: 7   366
2: 13–16   371
2: 19   76, 77, 396
4: 13   77
6: 12   366

Philippians
1: 27   77
2   24
2: 5ff.   365, 373
2: 6–7   292
2: 7–8   373
3: 20   396

Colossians
2: 14   31
2: 20   366

1 Thessalonians
5: 3   114

Hebrews
9: 14   353
13: 14   408

James
2: 17   459

1 Peter
1: 1f.   26
2: 13–15   26
2: 16   26
2: 23   366

2 Peter
3: 13   394

1 John
4: 20   99, 380

Revelation
10: 11   29
11: 7   29
13: 1–18   360
13: 15   360
18: 13   29
19: 16   24
21: 1   394
21: 19–20   416
21: 22–7   416
22: 17   97